**8** Moving coil instruments may be arranged to measure alternating current or voltage by incorporating a rectifier, usually of the bridge type.

## 14 Electromagnets

**1** A limitation to the amount of power generated in permanent magnet dynamos and other electrical equipment is due to the relatively weak magnetic field strength of the permanent magnet. The solution lies in the use of the electromagnet, which consists of an iron core over which a coil is wound.

**2** Passing direct current through the coil will induce a magnetic field in the iron, which may then bear a strong resemblance to an ordinary permanent magnet with the differences that:

(a) *the strength of the magnetic field can be controlled (within limits) by varying the current in the coil*

(b) *the magnetic field virtually disappears when the current is switched off*

**3** The arrangement of the electromagnet is shown in Fig. 1.11, together with a graph showing the way in which field strength varies with coil current. Note that beyond a certain current the magnetic flux density flattens off – the iron is said to be saturated.

**4** The electromagnet finds many uses in electrical equipment for cars; instead of a permanent magnet in a dynamo or alternator it is possible to use electromagnets, with the advantage that the electrical output can be regulated by varying the current in the electromagnet windings. In motor and generator practice, the electromagnets producing magnetic flux are called field poles and the coils are field windings.

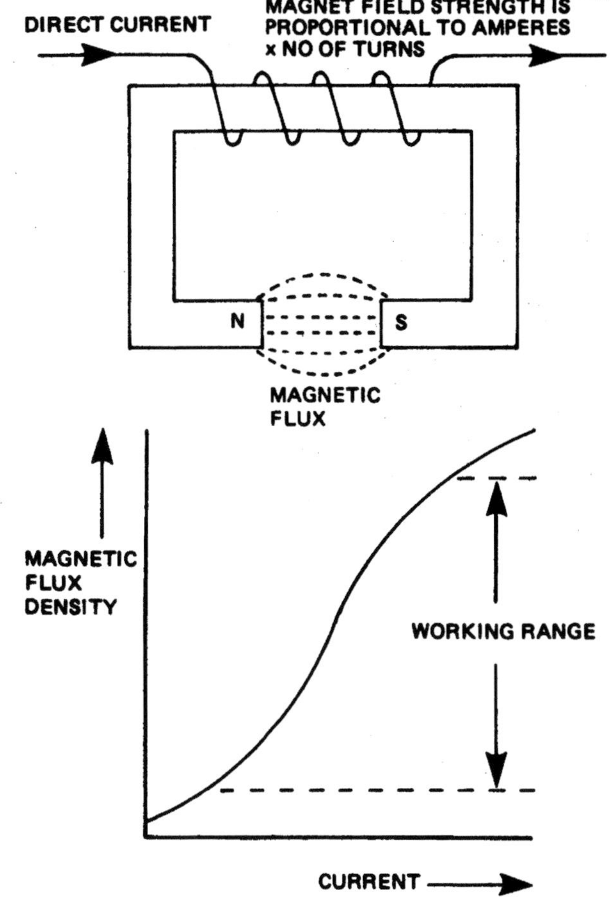


*Fig. 1.11 The electromagnet*

## 15 Electromagnetic relays and solenoids

**1** The relay is used to switch heavy current on, or off, by means of a much smaller control current (Fig. 1.12). A typical example is the starter motor, where the current rises to several hundred amperes. In this particular instance, the heavy cable needed to carry this current from the battery must be short to avoid voltage loss, and could not conveniently be brought to a dashboard switch anyway because of the cable stiffness and bulk. The relay overcomes this problem since it is located in the short path between battery and starter and only a thin control cable need go to the dashboard.

**2** It is well known that magnetic poles will exert a pull on nearby iron or steel. This effect is used in the relay in which a strip of iron is pulled by the magnetic field created when

*Fig. 1.12 Principle of the relay*

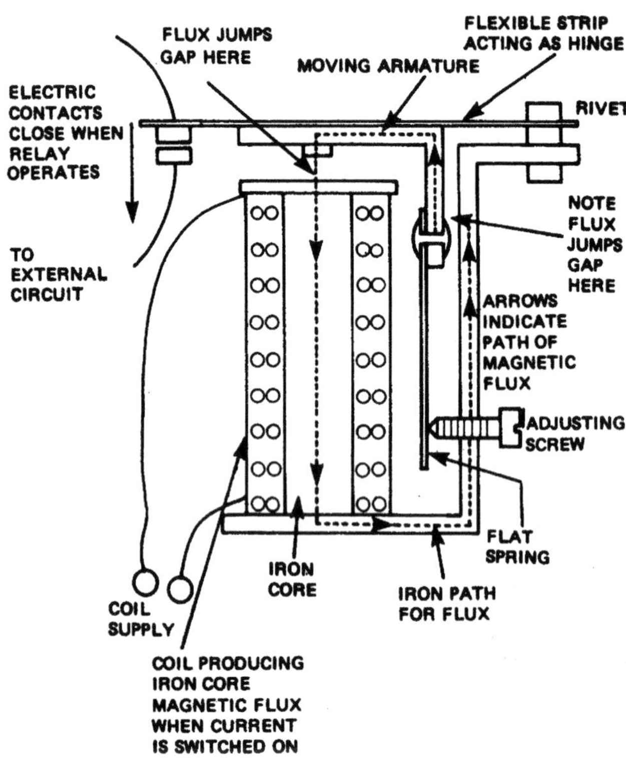


*Fig. 1.13 Magnetic relay*

current is switched on. The movement of the iron strip or **armature** can be made to open or close electrical contacts, which may act as a switch for a variety of uses, some of which will be described later in this book.

**3** A simple relay is shown in Fig. 1.13 in which the armature is held in one position by the flat spring until the coil current is switched on. Then the magnetic flux set up by the coil causes the armature to be attracted to the central iron core and so closes the contacts. When the current is switched off the magnetic field disappears and the armature returns to the rest position, the contacts opening. This type of relay is widely used in automotive engineering.

**4** A different type of actuating device is the solenoid, often used on starter motors. This relies on the fact that an iron core is attracted towards the mid point of a coil carrying current (Fig. 1.14). The pull exerted on the iron armature can be so great that its movement may be powerful enough to engage the starter pinion gear into a flywheel gear ring and also switch on the heavy current of the starter motor.

## 16 Magnetic field strength

**1** It is found that the magnetic field in an iron circuit depends upon several factors over which the designer has control:

*(a) the number of turns of wire on the coil*
*(b) the current flowing (amperes)*
*(c) the iron path details*

**2** In general, magnetic flux will pass more readily through iron than air and so if a strong field is required, then an iron path of large cross-sectional area is necessary, together with a coil designed to make the product of amperes x turns as large as possible (Fig. 1.15).

## 17 Motors and generators

**1** Millions of motors, dynamos and alternators are in use in motor vehicles and probably represent the greatest use of electrical machines in any branch of industry. It is a credit to designers that relatively few failures occur, for these machines are subject to heavy utilisation, need very little maintenance and work in a hostile environment, having to cope with wide temperature ranges, dust, damp and, in the case of generators, speed variations from a few hundred to thousands of revolutions per minute with high acceleration forces.

**2** The motor and generator (included here are dynamos and alternators) are not really separate for it is only a question of

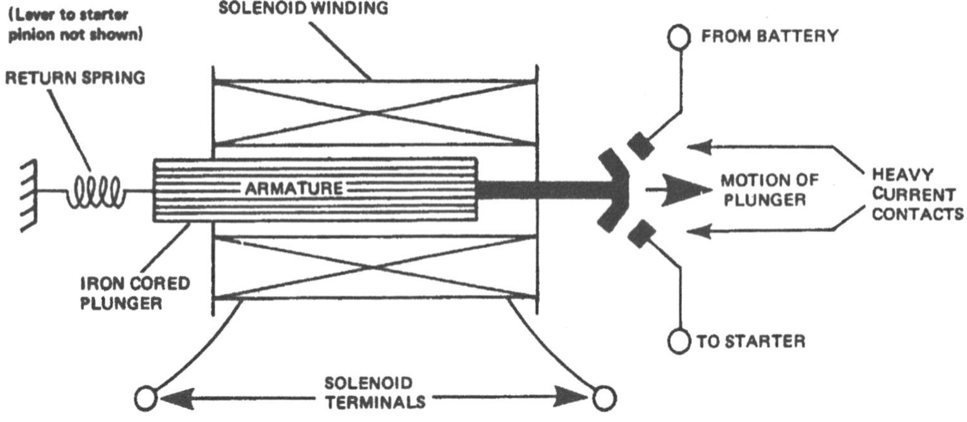


*Fig. 1.14 Diagrammatic representation of a starter solenoid*

# AUTOMOBILE ELECTRICAL & ELECTRONIC SYSTEMS

by Martynn Randall

The Haynes Manual for understanding and troubleshooting automotive electrical and electronic systems

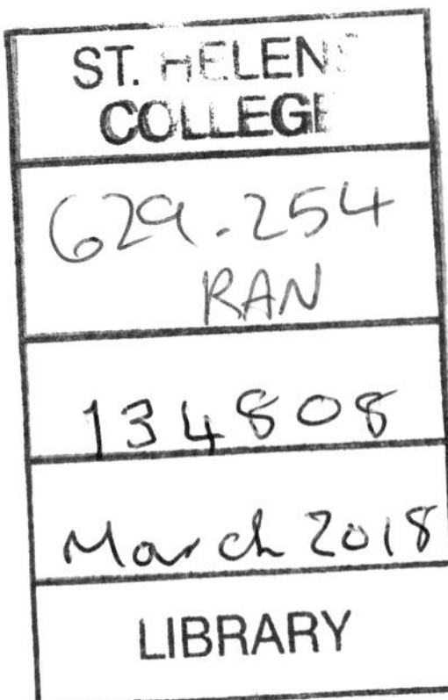


Haynes Publishing
Sparkford, Nr Yeovil, Somerset BA22 7JJ England

Haynes North America, Inc
861 Lawrence Drive, Newbury Park, California 91320 USA

**Acknowledgements**
Thanks are due to the staff engineers who generously gave time and information for the preparation of this book. Acknowledgements and thanks for permission to reproduce technical information are given to FKI Crypton Ltd and Robert Bosch Ltd.

This manual is not a direct reproduction of vehicle manufacturers' data, and its publication should not be taken as implying any technical approval by the vehicle manufacturers or importers.

**While every attempt is made to ensure that the information in this manual is correct, no liability can be accepted by the authors or publishers for loss, damage or injury caused by any errors in, or omissions from, the information given.**



A book in the Haynes Service and Repair Manual Series

Printed in the UK



**ISBN 978 1 78521 371 7**

**British Library Cataloguing in Publication Data**
A catalogue record for this book is available from the British Library

*(4251-288)*

# Contents

# Preface

This book has been written for those requiring an understanding of electrical and electronic equipment in the modern automobile.

No prior electrical knowledge has been assumed and relevant fundamentals are covered in the first chapter.

All explanations are based on first principles for which there is no substitute; with a firm mental picture of electrical and electronic principles the reader may progress to the chapters on present day advanced technical equipment.

Specific details of any particular type of vehicle are given only by way of illustration and example.

While it is hoped that up-to-date practice is adequately described, older equipment is also dealt with, being found in millions of vehicles still on the road.

A. Tranter
Guildford 1990

# Electrical and electronic essentials

# 1



## 1 Introduction

**1** If the reader is well experienced in electrical matters he may skip this chapter, but if he has never followed a course of instruction, or his knowledge is rusty, then time spent in reading will be an investment.

**2** To read manufacturers' manuals, it is essential to have a clear understanding not only of electrical principles but also of the correct use of terminology; this is the reader's mental toolbox and is in every way as important as his practical toolkit.

## 2 The Atom – the source of electricity

**1** All material consists of atoms which are, in turn, made up of protons, electrons and neutrons. The atom has a centre (or nucleus) which consists of protons and neutrons. Around the nucleus, electrons orbit at definite distances from the

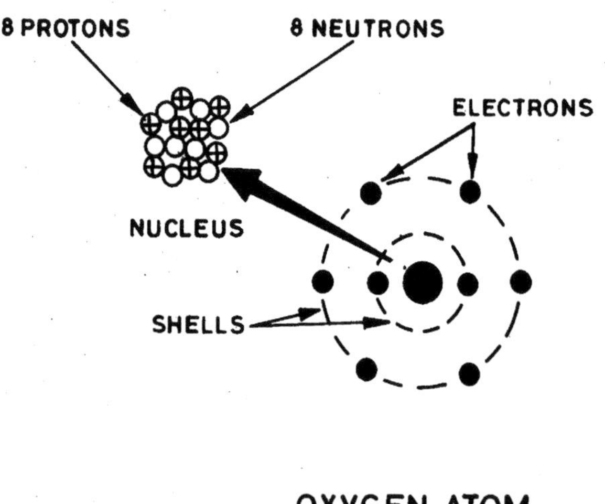


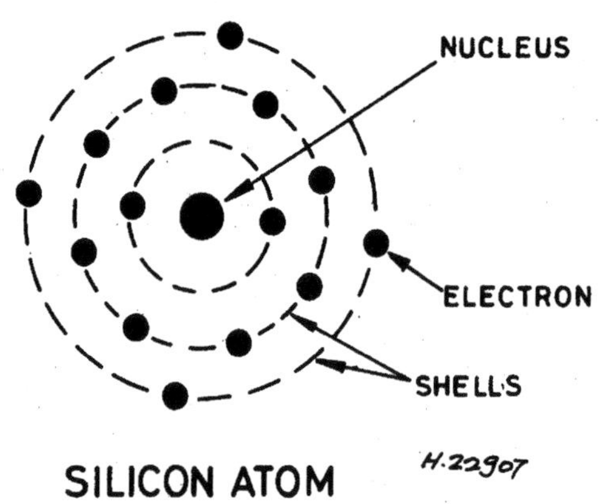


*Fig. 1.1 Simple atomic systems*

centre and are grouped into orbits (called shells) each at a different radius. Fig. 1.1. shows two simple atoms both of which will figure later in this book.

**2** The proton carries a positive electrical charge, the electron a negative charge and the neutron has no charge. Normally an atom is electrically neutral overall, meaning that the number of (positive) protons in the nucleus is matched by the number of (negative) electrons rotating in the orbital shells. In the table below note that in each case the numbers of protons and electrons are equal.

| Atom | Protons | Neutrons | Electrons |
|---|---|---|---|
| Hydrogen | 1 | 0 | 1 |
| Oxygen | 8 | 8 | 8 |
| Copper | 29 | 34 | 29 |
| Silicon | 14 | 14 | 14 |

Neutrons and protons are strongly attracted when close together in the atomic nucleus and when they are split apart huge amounts of energy are released, a phenomenon which is exploited in the nuclear reactor and the atomic bomb.

**3** Because of the relatively large mass of the nucleus it may be regarded as fixed in place in solid materials. Electrons are held less firmly in the atom and in some circumstances may leave the parent atom. It is this feature which is the basis of electronics.

**4** The atom is small, requiring millions to cover the width of a hairline, yet the internal dimensions are even more remarkable. To give some idea, if the nucleus were an apple then the overall size of the atom could be thought of as that of a concert hall and the electrons as flies buzzing around!

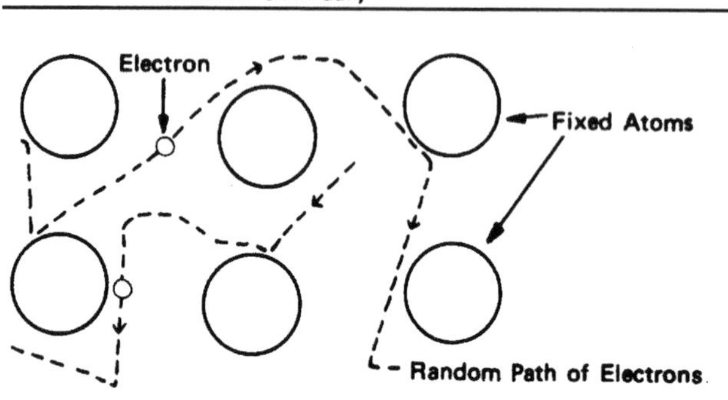


*Fig. 1.2 Free electron drift*

## 3 Free electrons (conduction)

**1** An atom is, in practice, a complicated structure; the outermost orbital electrons are sometimes held very loosely to the nucleus like a distant planet may be to the sun. Collisions may occur, which result in some electrons being driven from their normal path and drifting through the material lattice (Fig. 1.2). These are called **free electrons**. Some materials are rich in them, and others have few, or none at all. A material with many free electrons is a **conductor** and without free electrons is an **insulator**.

**2** Imagine a copper wire as a mass of heavy copper atoms with swarms of free electrons in the spaces between them. These electrons are so small that there is plenty of room for them to fly about in all directions, but on the whole they do not progress very far in any one direction; their motion is random.

## 4 Electron flow = current

**1** If a cell or a battery (a battery is merely a collection of cells) is connected to the ends of a copper wire, the free electrons drift along it, all in the same direction, just as when a pump is started, sending a current of liquid along the pipes to which it is connected.

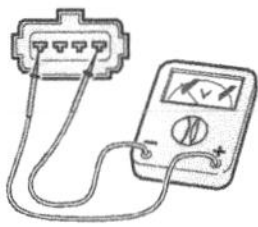



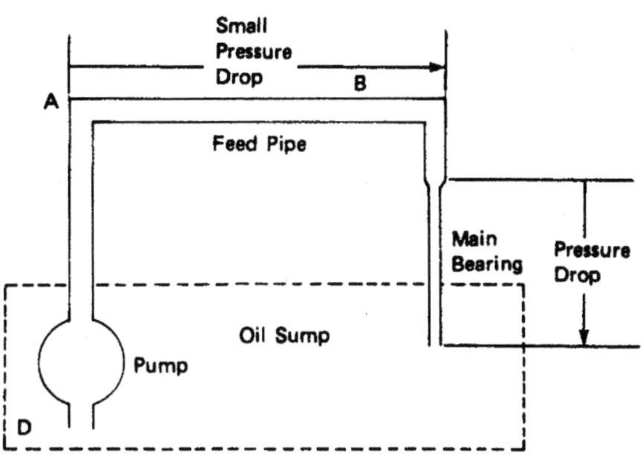


*Fig. 1.3 Oil pump and feed*

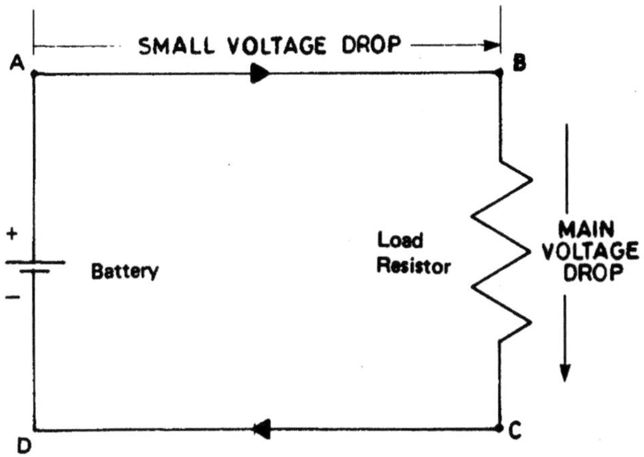


*Fig. 1.4a Battery and load*

**2** It is important to understand that a battery does not make the electricity any more than a pump makes a liquid. The battery and the pump are merely agencies to set in motion something which already exists.

**3** Carrying the analogy further, it might be said that it is not the pump which moves the fluid, but the pressure difference which the pump creates that causes the motion. This is a valuable idea because without stating the method used, it is the pressure difference alone which causes fluid flow. This also applies to electricity. Any device (eg battery, dynamo, alternator) which will set up a **potential difference** in an electric circuit can give rise to electric current flow.

**4** As a pump produces a certain pressure, so a battery or dynamo produces an electromotive force **(emf)** measured in **VOLTS.**

**5** The idea of electron flow being the basis of electric current came long after a general convention that current flowed from the positive battery terminal, through the circuit back to the negative terminal. Electrons, in fact, flow in the opposite direction and so care must be taken over which convention is used.

Conventional current flow (+ to –) is nearly always used except where stated otherwise.

## 5 The complete circuit

**1** A circuit, as the name implies, is a complete uninterrupted path round which current may flow.

**2** The battery or generator which pumps electrons round the circuit is similar in many ways to an oil pump working in a car. The oil flows continuously round the oil circuit and is primarily used for lubricating bearings.

**3** It is helpful to compare the electrical and oil systems of Figs. 1.3 and 1.4a.

**4** The oil pump produces a pressure difference between points A and D and this causes oil to flow through the feed pipe B to the main bearing where a large pressure drop occurs. This is because of the constriction between journal and bearing and most of the pump energy is expended in forcing oil flow. Ideally, no energy is lost in the feed pipe.

**5** Coming to the equivalent electric circuit, the battery produces potential difference (pd) between points A and D and this causes current to flow along the wire B to the load

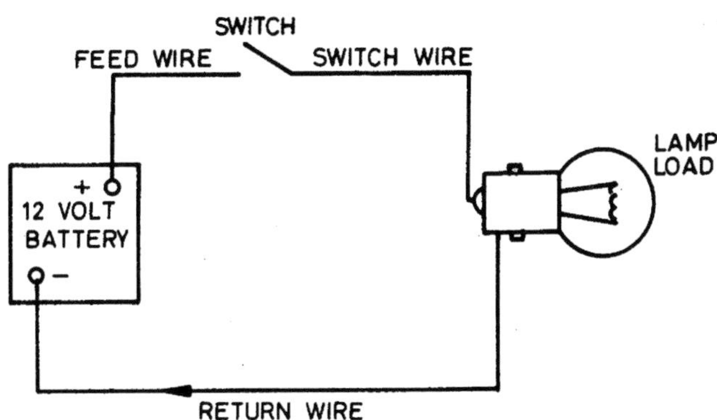


*Fig. 1.4b Simple practical circuit with insulated return*

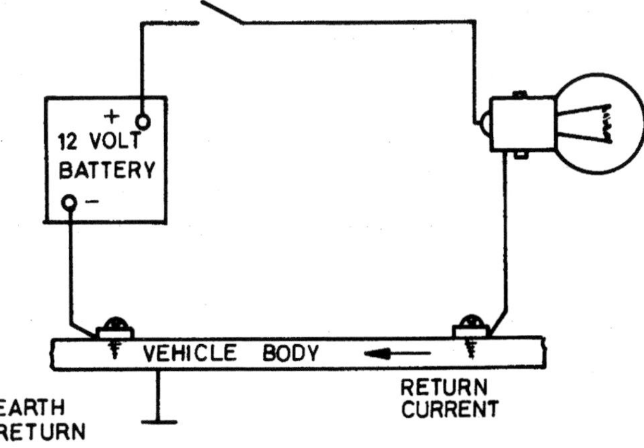


*Fig. 1.4c Use of vehicle body as earth return*

resistor where a large voltage drop occurs. This is because the resistor is made of high resistance wire and most of the battery energy is expended in forcing current flow. Ideally no energy is lost in the connecting wires but in practice a small loss will occur.

## 6 Fundamental quantities

**1** The number of electrons set in motion by a battery is astronomically large, so a convenient number (how many does not matter to us!) are lumped together and called a **COULOMB.**

**2** Again we are not often interested in the amount of electricity, but the speed of flow round a circuit. The number of coulombs flowing past a point each second is the **rate** of flow and 1 coulomb per second is called an **AMPERE.**

| | Liquid system units | Electrical system units |
|---|---|---|
| Quantity | gallon | coulomb |
| Pressure and pressure drop | pounds per sq. inch | volt |
| Rate of flow | gallons per second | coulomb per second or ampere |

## 7 Ohm's law

**1** The load resistor is where the electricity will produce the desired effects. For example, an electric fire element consists of a spiral of wire with a resistance much higher than that of the connecting leads.

**2** The well known effect is that heat is produced, a phenomenon which will be considered later. Equally, the headlamp bulb of a car is a load resistor and the main effect of current flow will be so much local heat in the filament that white light is produced. Resistance is measured in **OHMS,** the name deriving from the German experimenter Georg Simon Ohm.

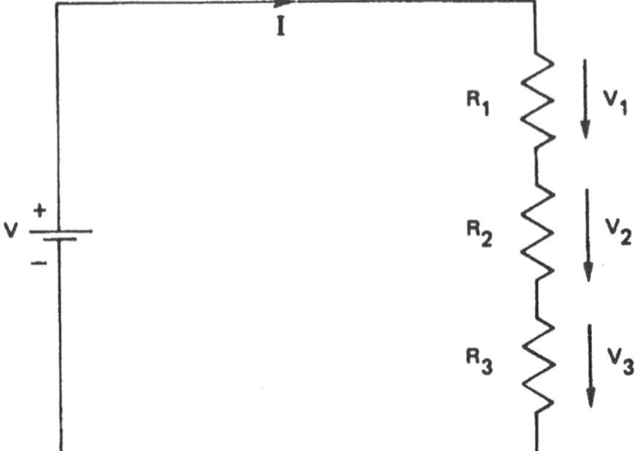


***Fig. 1.6 Voltage drop***
*Voltage drops around a circuit add up to the supply voltage*

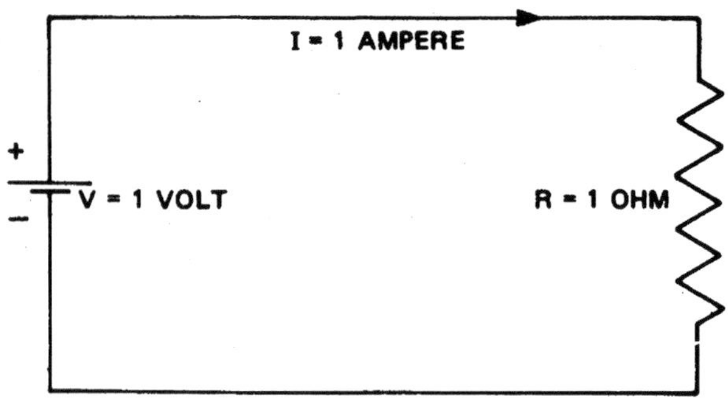


***Fig. 1.5 The relationship between volts, amperes and ohms***

It is easy to visualise the value of 1 ohm, for it is such that a voltage of 1 volt would cause 1 ampere of current to flow (Fig. 1.5).

Georg Ohm is famous for his conclusion that the current increases in direct proportion to the voltage applied.

or $V = I \times R$
ie Voltage = current x resistance

Today this seems elementary but its statement in 1826 cost Ohm his job because it did not fit the theory of the day.

**Example**

**3** A headlamp bulb working off a 12 volt battery takes a current of 3 amperes. What is the resistance of the bulb filament?

$V = I \times R$
or $12 = 3 \times R$
so $R = 4$ ohms

**4** It pays to learn the proper abbreviations for electrical quantities which are written thus:

12 volts as 12 V
3 amperes as 3 A
4 ohms as 4 Ω

## 8 Series and parallel circuits

**1** It is rare that a circuit consists of simply a battery connected to a load resistor. Often two or more resistors are involved and if they are end to end as in Fig. 1.6 they are said to be in **series** and, if as in Fig. 1.7 in **parallel**.

## 9 Series connection

**1** If for Fig. 1.6 Ohm's Law is rewritten it becomes

$V = I \times (R_1 + R_2 + R_3)$

**Note:** The resistances add, and the volt-drops $V_1$, $V_2$, $V_3$ always add up to the total supply voltage V, a point to remember when fault tracing.

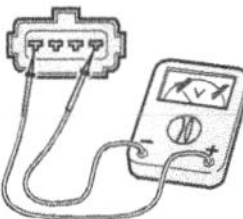

**2 Example**

To see how this equation might be used in practice, suppose $R_1 = 3\Omega$, $R_2 = 4\Omega$, and $R_3 = 5\Omega$.
What current would be drawn from the battery if V = 12 volts?

$12 = I \times (3 + 4 + 5)$
or $12 = I \times 12$
so $I = 1$ ampere

**3** In practice, the internal resistance of the battery may be significant (especially if it is wearing out) and there may be unwanted resistance in the cables and connections. These undesired resistances would have to be taken into account for some purpose by using Ohm's Law as above. See the example given later.

## 10 Parallel connection

**1** Referring to Fig. 1.7 it is clear that the battery must supply the current to all three branches and that the total current is the sum of the branch currents: that is, $I = I_1 + I_2 + I_3$

**2** Each branch has the full voltage V applied to it, so in this case the separate currents may be calculated and added.

**3** Note that this is the most frequent arrangement to be met in a car electrical system – for instance $R_1$ could be the lighting load, $R_2$ the horn, $R_3$ the ignition, and the current demand on the battery would be the sum of the separate currents.

**4 Example**

Suppose again the supply voltage was 12 volts and the load resistors were $R_1 = 6\ \Omega$, $R_2 = 3\ \Omega$, and $R_3 = 4\ \Omega$, as in Fig. 1.8.

$$I_1 = \frac{V}{R_1} = \frac{12}{6} = 2\ A$$

$$I_2 = \frac{V}{R_2} = \frac{12}{3} = 4\ A$$

$$I_3 = \frac{V}{R_3} = \frac{12}{4} = 3\ A$$

The total current drain from the battery is therefore I = 9A. By using Ohm's Law again, it will be seen that if the equivalent resistance of the 3 branches in parallel, $R_T$, is worked out, it is given by

$$V = I \times R_T$$

$$12 = 9 \times R_T$$

$$R_T = \frac{12}{9} = 1\tfrac{1}{3}\ \Omega$$

**5** The practical case fitting the parallel connection is, in fact, all the components connected to a car battery.
For example, if the head and rear lamps take 5A and 0.5A respectively and the ignition coil 1.5A, then if they are all on together the total current drain is:

$$I = 5 + 0.5 + 1.5 = 7\ A$$

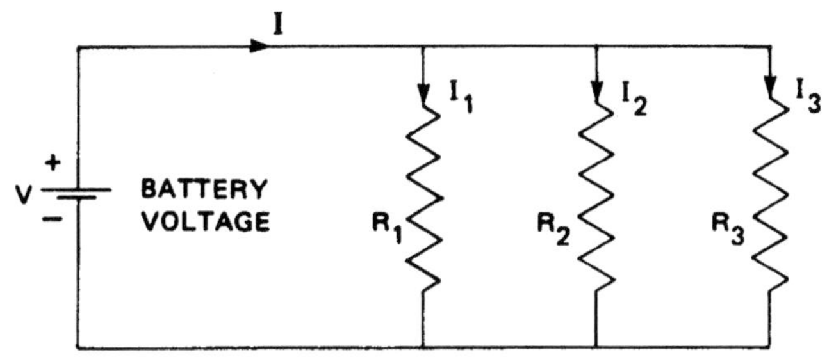


*Fig. 1.7 Resistors in parallel*

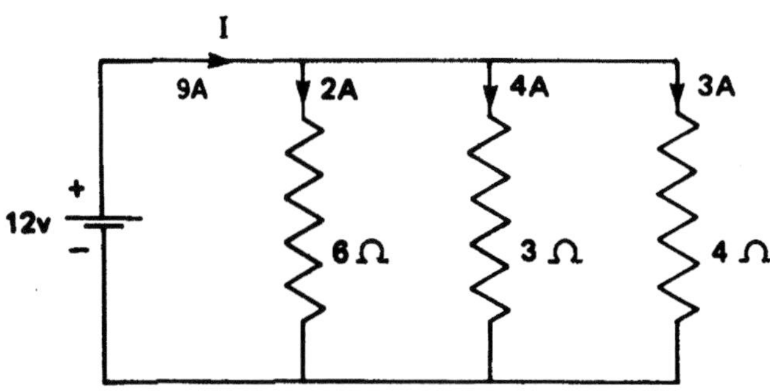


*Fig. 1.8 An example of current drain by resistors in parallel*

## 11 Energy and power

**1 Energy** (or work, as it is sometimes called) is measured in **JOULES** where 1 joule is the energy expended when a pressure of 1 volt drives a current of 1 ampere through a load for 1 second.

So joules = volts x amperes x seconds
or, in symbols $J = VIt$

**Example**

If a 12 volt battery delivers 3 amperes of current to a headlight bulb for 20 minutes, how much energy is used?

Energy $= V \times I \times t$
$= 12 \times 3 \times 20 \times 60$
$= 43{,}200$ joules

The joule is not used very much in routine electrical work, but it is of interest to note that it is also the unit of energy in mechanical engineering if SI (metric) units are used.

**2 Power** is closely related to energy, for it is simply the rate of utilising energy. The unit of power is the **WATT.**

$$\text{Watts} = \text{joules per second ie } \frac{\text{joules}}{\text{seconds}}$$

Remembering that joules = volts x amperes x seconds we have

$$\text{watts} = \frac{\text{joules}}{\text{seconds}} = \text{volts x amperes}$$

so Watts = volts x amperes for a direct current circuit

In the example described, the battery delivering 3 A at 12 V is giving a power of $W = V \times I = 12 \times 3 = 36$ watts

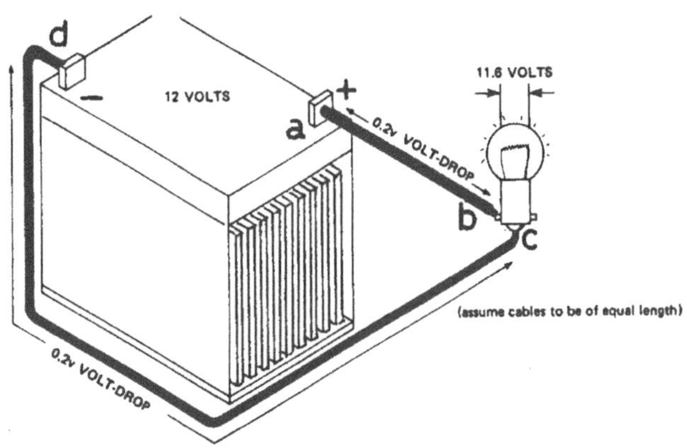


*Fig. 1.9 Volt-drop in connecting cables*

## 12 Wiring volt-drop

**1** Examination of the wiring loom of a car will show that the wires and cables are of different thicknesses, and that often the wire is not one solid strand, but made up of many strands or filaments twisted together.

The designer chooses a cable so that the current flowing from the source to the load does not produce an undue waste of energy in the wires carrying it.

It is important to remember that although the wires are made of copper, which is a good conductor, nevertheless there is some finite resistance in which heating loss and volt-drop will occur. This means less power to the load, and inefficiency.

The battery shown connected to the bulb in Fig. 1.9 has a terminal pressure of 12 volts and ideally all this voltage should appear across the bulb; however, here the connecting wires have a resistance which gives a loss of 0.2 volt for both go and return, leaving only 11.6 volts to light the bulb filament.

**2** The result in this case is poor illumination due to the waste of power in the wires. Better results would be obtained by using thicker cables, but the limits to increasing diameter are determined by the cost of copper and undesirable stiffness of thick wires.

## 13 Ammeters and voltmeters

**1** There is no need to know much about the internal workings of electrical instruments in order to use them, and the basic rules are simple. An ammeter measures the current flowing **through** a circuit; it is connected so that this current flows through the instrument, ie in **series** with the load, as shown in Fig. 1.10.

**2** The instrument designer keeps the internal resistance of the ammeter as low as possible; if by accident the ammeter were connected **across** the load, instead of in **series** with it, this would be disastrous. Because of the low ammeter resistance a heavy current would flow, destroying the instrument and possibly melting the connecting wire insulation.

**3** Fortunately the voltmeter is not so vulnerable because it is designed to have a high resistance and is less likely to be burnt out.

The voltmeter measures electrical **pressure** and should be connected **across** parts of a circuit. For instance, in Fig. 1.9, if connected across a and d the voltmeter would measure the battery voltage; across b and c the bulb voltage, and from d to c, or a to b the volt drop in the cables.

**4** Sometimes instruments have a switch to give different ranges. Clearly the user will choose the range so that the pointer needle gives a reading well up the scale, for there is a considerable risk of reading error at low readings where the thickness of the pointer may be comparable with the amount of deflection.

**5** Instruments should never be regarded as wholly accurate, and very cheap equipment can be a poor investment in terms of reliability of readings.

**6** Multi-purpose instruments are useful for workshop testing, but care is even more important – make sure that the right range is selected and alter the range switch with the leads disconnected. The reason for this is that a rotary range switch may pass through current ranges – amperes – before reaching the desired voltage position. If connected to a supply this can spell the rapid end to an expensive instrument.

**7** Most test instruments have a moving-coil movement; this type responds to direct current (dc) only.

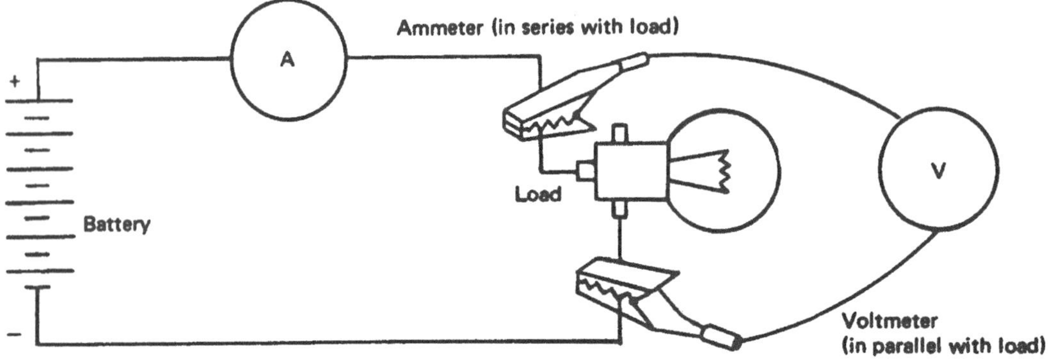


*Fig. 1.10 Connections for ammeter and voltmeter*

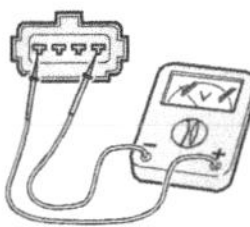

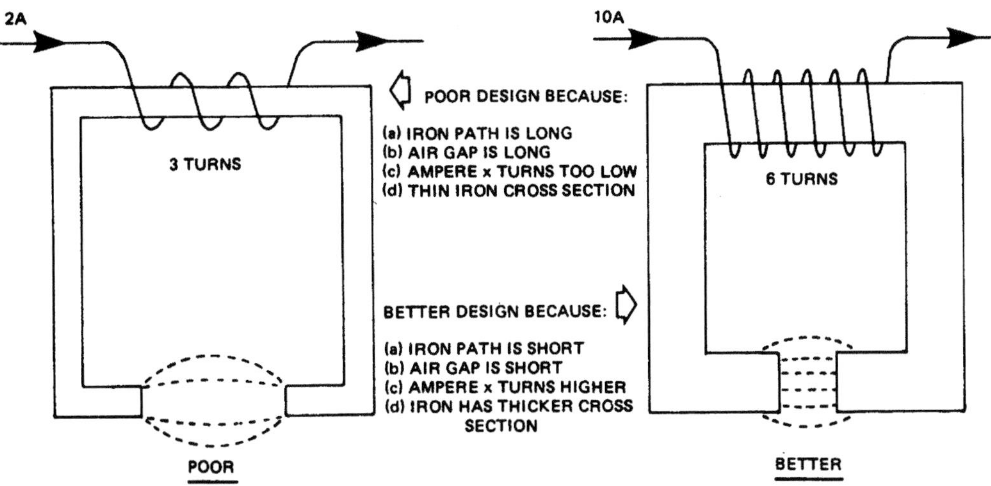


*Fig. 1.15 Design factors for iron circuits*

energy flow. Thus in the case of the direct-current motor, electrical energy is put in and mechanical energy emerges at the shaft. The same machine could be driven by an external prime mover and electrical energy would be available at the terminals. The dc motor and the dc generator are, then, essentially the same device. A similar picture may be stated for the alternator which could be driven as a motor by connecting it correctly to an alternating current supply. The relationship between the dc motor and generator is particularly important here.

**3** Most electrical pointer instruments are really a highly specialised form of direct-current electric motor operating over a limited angular range of 90° to 120° only. Designers use the same form of calculations in designing both instruments and dc motors.

**4** The details of dc generators, alternators and motors will be dealt with in the later chapters of this book. Here the two important principles of motor and generator action are stated, and armed with this information, the way in which machines and instruments work will be readily understood.

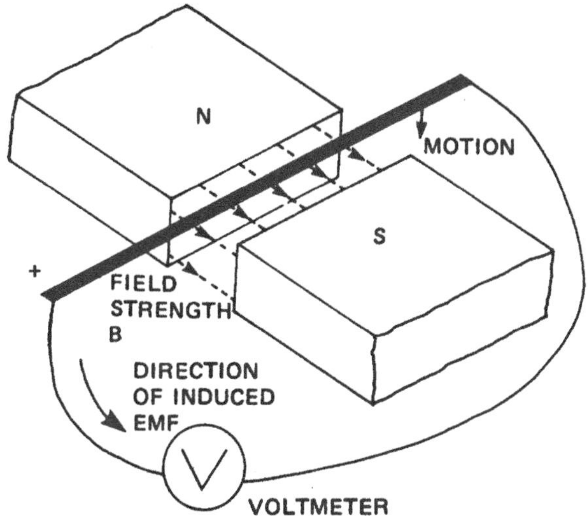


*Fig. 1.16 Induced EMF in moving conductor*

## 18 The generator rule

**1** If a wire moves across a magnetic field it is found that a voltage is generated in it for so long as there is motion (see Fig. 1.16). The voltage obtained is found to depend upon:

(a) *the length of wire in the magnetic field*
(b) *the velocity of the wire at right angles to the magnetic field*
(c) *the strength of the magnetic field*

The actual value in volts is:

$$E = Bl\,V \text{ volts}$$

where: B = strength of magnetic field measured in webers per square metre (or Tesla)
$l$ = length of wire (metres)
V = velocity of wire at right angles to the magnetic field (metres per second)

No need to be concerned about any calculations to read further: all that is important is to remember the factors which fix the size of the generated voltage.

**2** In order to make a generator, the wire is formed into a rectangular coil and spun round inside the magnetic field. All the rest is detail, but upon this basic rule depends the operation of the dynamo and the alternator. This theme occurs in the book several times – it is well worth remembering.

## 19 The motor rule

**1** This is the converse of the generator situation. Electric current passed down a wire located in a magnetic field will experience a force at right angles to both current and field directions.

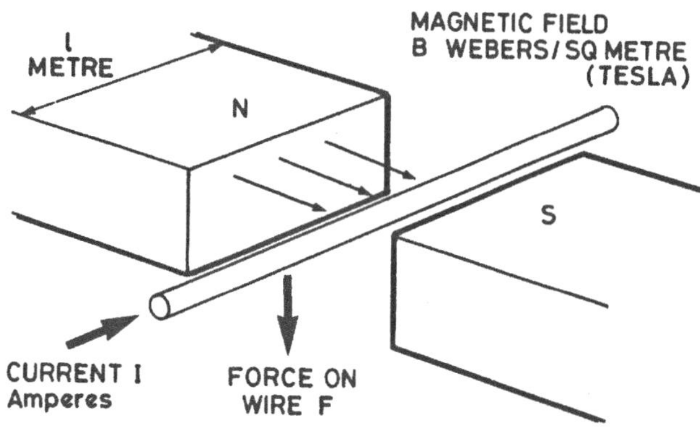


*Fig. 1.17 Force on a wire carrying a current*

**2** Fig. 1.17 shows a wire carrying a current. The wire is situated in a magnetic field, the direction of which is conventionally agreed to be from N to S in the air path. The wire will create a magnetic field of its own and this field will interact with that of the motor field giving rise to a force acting downwards. The numerical value of the force will depend upon:

(a) *the strength of the magnetic field,* B *webers per sq. metre (Tesla)*
(b) *the amount of current flowing in the wire,* I *amperes*
(c) *the length of wire inside the magnetic field,* $l$ *metres*

The force is:

F = BI$l$Newtons

**3** If now the wire is bent into a rectangular shape and located within the magnetic field again, the direction of current in the two sides is opposite and so will be the forces acting on them. It now remains only to pivot the rectangular coil on bearings for it to become a simple electric motor, for the two forces will give rise to rotation, Fig. 1.18.

This idea of motor operation will be particularly useful when reading the Chapter on Starters, where the subject will be developed further.

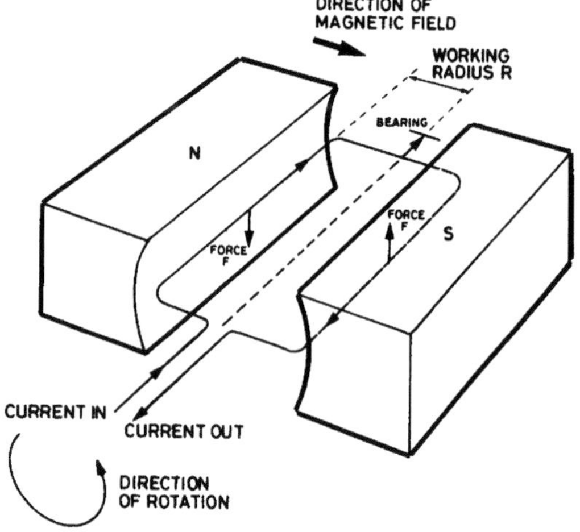


*Fig. 1.18 Basic electric motor*

**4** Torque is an important concept in engineering. In Fig. 1.19 torque is applied to a nut by means of a spanner and is a measure of turning capability. It is simply the force and distance multiplied, but on the condition that the direction of force is at right angles to the direction to the nut centre.

**5** Looking again at the simple motor of Fig. 1.18, the coil radius is R, and there are two operating sides each giving a force F, so:

Motor torque = 2 x F x R Newton-metres
(or pounds-feet in Imperial units)

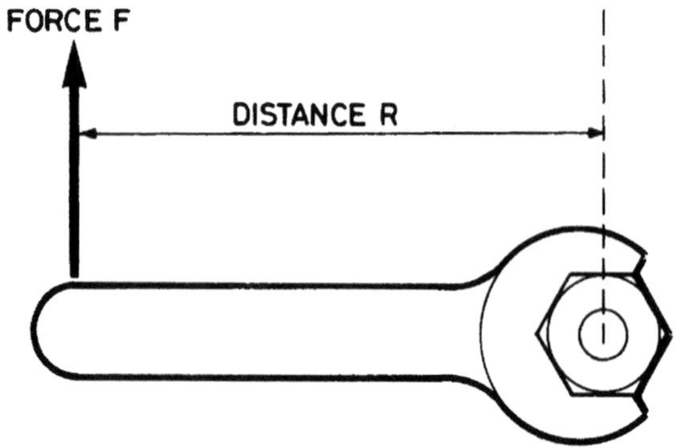


***Fig. 1.19 Illustration of torque***
*Torque = F x R*
*In the Metric system torque is measured in Newton-metres (Nm), or, less correctly, kilogramme-metres (kgf m). In the Imperial system torque is measured in pounds-feet (lbf ft)*

## 20 Resistance

**1** The resistance R of a wire depends upon three factors:

*(a)* the length L (metres)
*(b)* the cross-sectional area A (square metres)
*(c)* the resistivity $\rho$ (ohm-metres)

$R = \frac{\rho L}{A}$ ohms

## 21 Temperature coefficient of resistance

**1** Most metals increase in resistance with a rise of temperature, and semiconductors decrease in resistance with rise in temperature.

**2** The temperature coefficient is the change of resistance per ohm per degree Celsius.

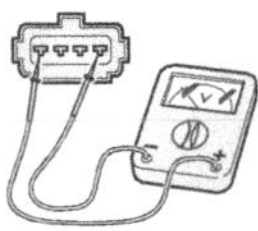

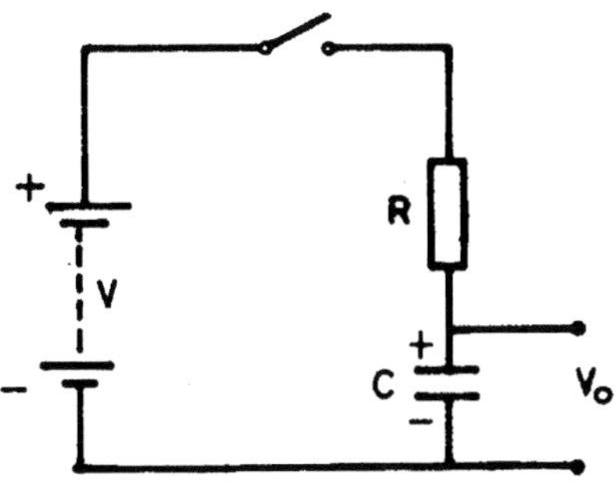


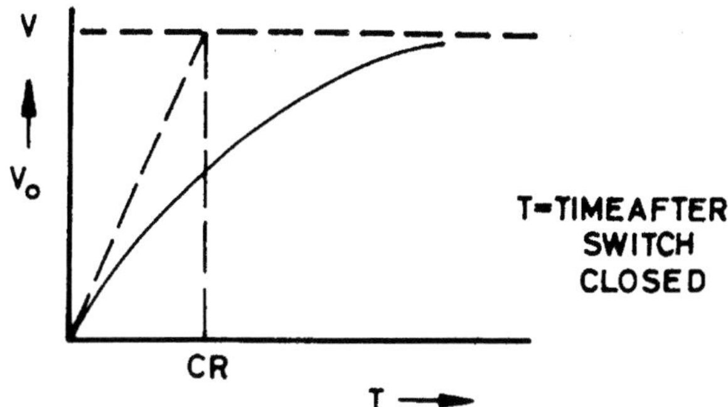


***Fig. 1.20 Charging capacitor C through resistance R***
*Voltage across C reaches 63% of V in CR seconds CR = Time constant*

## 22 Capacitance

**1** The capacitor consists of two large-area conducting surfaces separated by a thin insulator. Usually the surfaces (or plates) are two long rectangular aluminium foils separated by a slightly wider strip of impregnated paper and rolled up like a swiss roll. Wires are attached to the two foils and the whole is encapsulated in some form of plastic material.
**2** Capacitors are components that can store electric charge q which increases with the voltage between the plates.

In fact, the ratio $\frac{q}{V} = C$

The capacitance C is measured in farads, the microfarad (μF) and picofarad (pF) being used in practice. Here q is the charge on the plates expressed in coulombs.
The microfarad is one millionth of a farad and the picofarad is one millionth of a microfarad.
See Chapter 6 for more detail and application of the capacitor.

## 23 Inductors

**1** If a coil of wire carries a current, a surrounding magnetic field is set up. If the current is changed, say reduced, the collapsing magnetic lines of force cut the coils and induce a voltage in the coil so as to try to oppose the change of current (Lenz' law).
It is the RATE of change of current which determines the induced voltage, together with a factor called inductance L.

Induced voltage = rate of change of current x L

L is measured in henrys

Cutting off current to an inductor suddenly will induce a spike-shaped voltage which can damage other components.
An inductor behaves much like a flywheel; this opposes any change in speed.

## 24 CR charge and discharge

**1** If a capacitor C is connected to a supply voltage V through a resistor R ( Fig. 1.20) the voltage rise $V_o$ across the capacitor follows a curve.
The time taken for the voltage to rise to 63% of the supply voltage V is the **time constant** of the circuit and equals CR seconds.
**2** Similarly the time taken to discharge a capacitor C through resistance R is CR seconds where by discharge is meant that the voltage falls to 37% of the initial voltage (Fig. 1.21).
Both CR charge and discharge are widely used in electronic timing circuits.

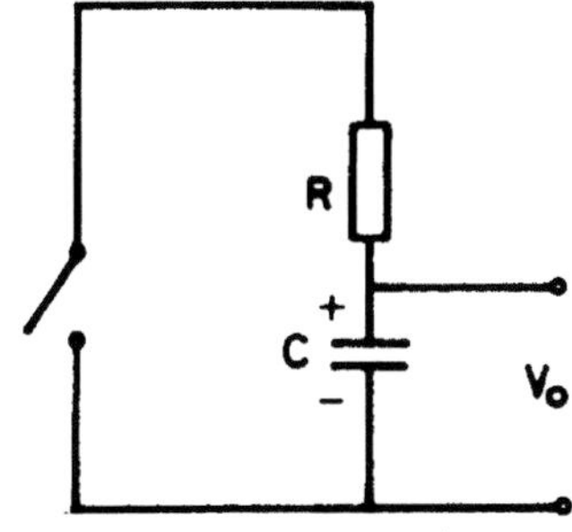


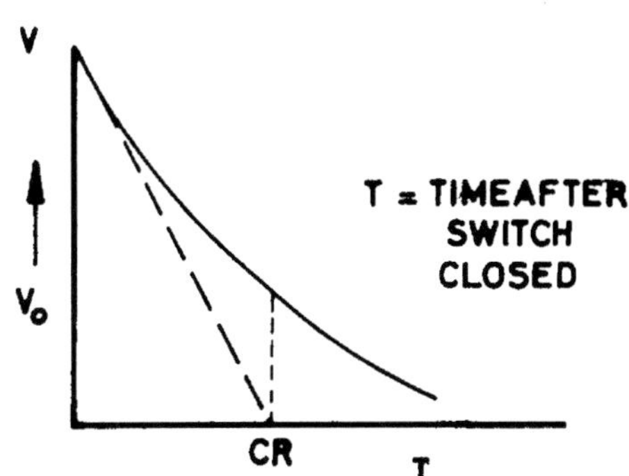


***Fig. 1.21 Time of discharge of CR circuit***
*Capacitor C initially charged to V volts Voltage across C falls to 37% of V in CR seconds CR = Time constant*

## 25 The p-n junction diode

**1** If a silicon crystal has impurities added, ie it is doped, such that one region is p-type and the other n-type, then where the diffusion layers meet is a p-n junction. P and n-types both mean silicon with impurities added, one of which gives an excess of electrons in the material and the other a deficiency of electrons, known as holes.

**2** The effect at the meeting layer is that of a barrier potential rather as though a battery had been connected across the junction (Fig. 1.22). External current may flow across the junction in one direction but not in the other. In other words, the p-n junction is a rectifier or diode (Fig. 1.23).

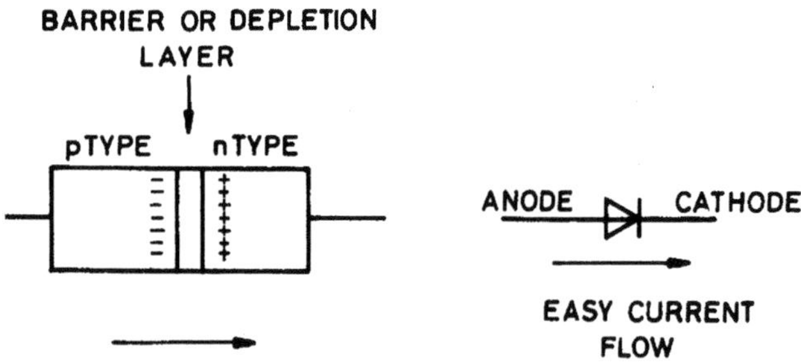


***Fig. 1.22 A p-n junction diode***
*Current flows easily if external polarity is + to p type*

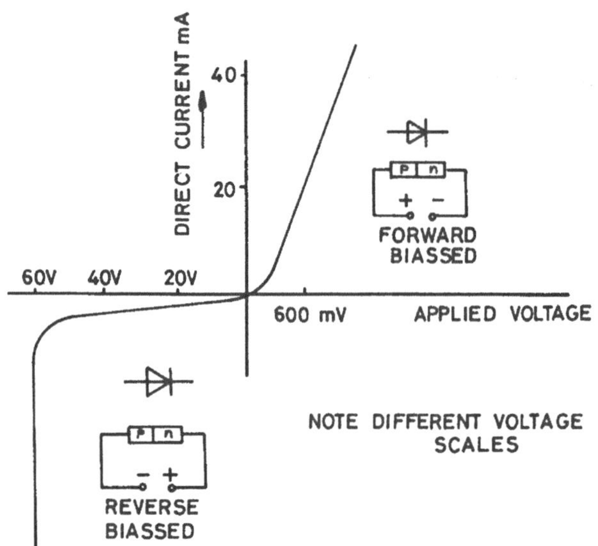


***Fig. 1.23 Rectifying action of junction diode***

## 26 The transistor

**1** The junction transistor is a sandwich or p-n-p or n-p-n material, rather like two diodes back to back.

If a current can be made to flow between the middle section of the sandwich and one outer layer, then a much greater current would be able to flow straight through between the outer layers.

Fig. 1.24 shows the action. Current into the base $I_b$ will permit a current flow between collector and emitter. The current flow from collector is much larger than the base current and is controlled by it. Switching $I_b$ on or off simultaneously switches on or off the main collector current flow.

Regarded this way the transistor is a **switch.**

**2** If on the other hand the base current $I_b$ is varied, say, in a sine wave fashion, the collector current will also vary in a sine wave shape but with about (typically) 50 times the amplitude.

Used this way the transistor is a **current amplifier**.

**3** To obtain voltage amplification (or gain) a load resistor $R_L$ in the collector circuit may be used. Current variations through $R_L$ produce voltage variation across it (Fig. 1.25). Bias is obtained by resistors $R_1$ and $R_2$ to avoid the use of a bias battery. $R_3$ compensates for temperature effects; as

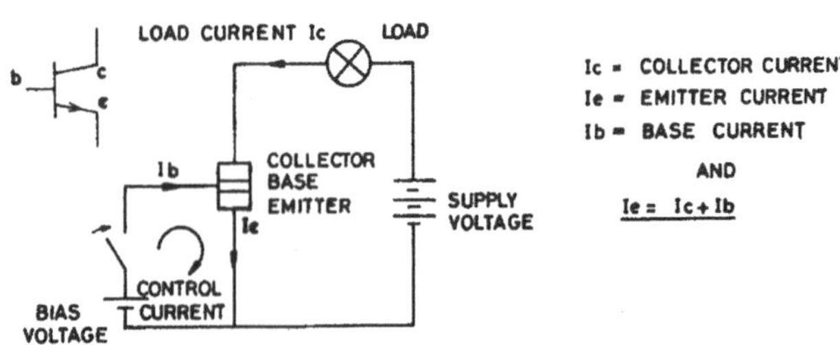


***Fig. 1.24 Transistor action***
*The base-emitter junction must be forward biased to allow current into base. About 650 mV is needed to forward bias a silicon transistor. Base current is typically only 1/50th of the collector current. The transistor may be regarded as a switch – this is how it is most often used in automobile electronics. If Ib is varied, rather than switched on and off, the collector current Ic will also vary, but about 50 times as much. The transistor is acting as a current amplifier*

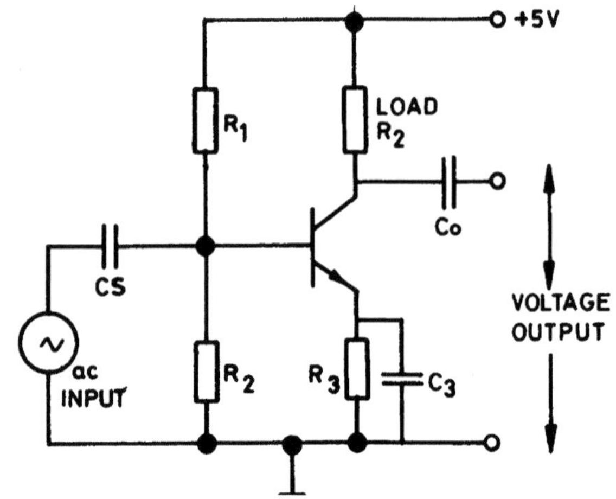


***Fig. 1.25 Single stage common-emitter amplifier***
*Co and Cs block dc $R_1$ and $R_2$ provide forward bias*
*$R_3$ acts as temperature compensator*

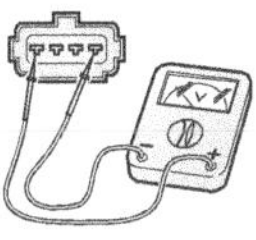

| | MODE | CURRENT GAIN | VOLTAGE GAIN | INPUT RESISTANCE |
|---|---|---|---|---|
| (circuit: + , Vo) | COMMON EMITTER | LARGE 50-500 | HIGH | MEDIUM ABOUT 2kΩ |
| (circuit: + , Vo) | COMMON BASE | LESS THAN 1.0 ABOUT 0·99 | HIGH | LOW ABOUT 50 Ω |
| (circuit: + , Vo) | COMMON COLLECTOR | LARGE | LESS THAN 1.0 | VERY HIGH ABOUT 1 MΩ |

***Fig. 1.26 Transistor operation modes***
*Biasing not shown*

temperature rises the emitter current will rise, but the extra volt-drop this causes in passing through $R_3$ is sensed by the base as a bias tending to reduce emitter current. Capacitor $C_3$ passes an alternating component to earth preventing ac feedback to the base.

**4** The junction transistor can be operated in three different ways which are named according to which terminal is common to both the input and output. They are common-emitter (CE), common-base (CB), and common-collector (CC). Their characteristics are shown in Fig. 1.26.

## 27 The field-effect transistor (FET)

**1** While the junction transistor is essentially a current operated device, the field-effect transistor has a much higher input resistance and is voltage-controlled.

**2** The junction field-effect transistor JFET is shown in Fig. 1.27. A p-type region (the gate) is let into two sides of an n-type silicon base, forming a channel. Current will flow from one side of the n-silicon to the other, ie from source to drain, and is controlled by the voltage applied between the gate and source. Eventually the gate field effect pinches off the source-drain current. P channel devices work the same way but with supply polarities reversed.

**3** An even higher input resistance (greater than $10^{12}$ ohm) has been achieved by a further FET development, the metal-oxide field-effect transistor MOS, in which the gate is electrically insulated from the n or p channel.

## 28 Power MOS devices

**1** Power MOS FETs are increasingly replacing conventional bipolar transistors in vehicle application. This technology extends to integrated circuits (IC) and it is estimated by Nippondenso engineers that power MOS FET and power MOS IC units will comprise nearly one half of the general market power transistors in the 1990 decade.

**2** Because the power MOS FET is a voltage driven device,

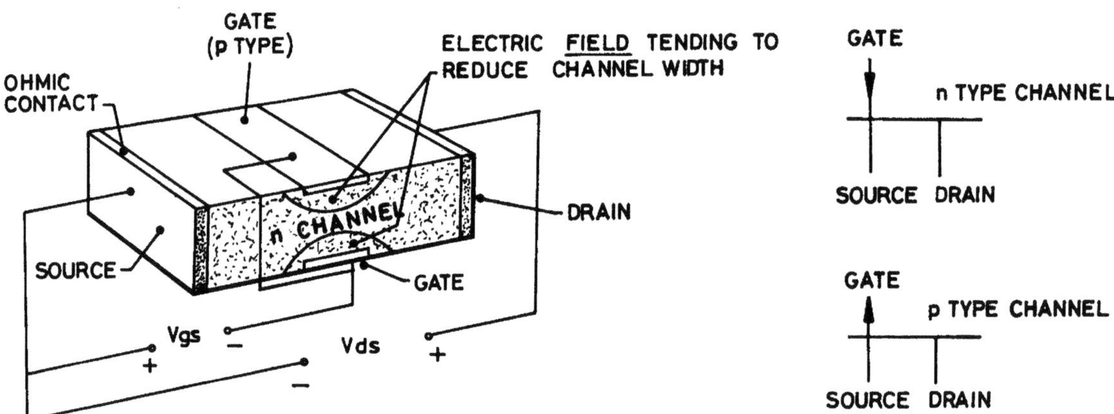


*Fig. 1.27 Junction Field Effect Transistor (JFET)*

heat generation will be reduced to about one tenth of the heat generated in bipolar transistors. This leads to the possible integration of the power stage with the ECU (Electronic Control Unit) giving numerous advantages, including reduced circuit size.

## 29 Smart Power

**1** A development of MOS techniques is that of the Smart Power device for use in automobile electronic technology. This represents the interface between the electronic management systems and the equipment to be driven.

The electro-mechanical solution is presently a range of solenoid and motor based actuators using relays. By semiconductor standards, a relay has relatively low reliability and cannot be interrogated about its own or the load condition.

**2** The ideal device required for automotive work will have low drain-source resistance $R_{DS}$ MOS-based compatible with logic circuits, fully protected against overloads and able to give status information. Finally, the switch should be in the positive supply not the return.

**3** One solution, based on what is becoming known as PIC (Power Integrated Circuit), is the PROFET. Overvoltage protection against inductive load switch-off is by means of a Zener diode, while over-temperature protection is achieved by an on-chip temperature sensor which causes immediate switch off when 150°C is reached. Short circuit protection is incorporated by monitoring the output voltage. Instant turn-off is not required, since automotive loads often require high start-up currents. A short circuit, therefore, results in a current limit of 25A being imposed for 40 microseconds, then the device shuts itself off.

Open load detection is also featured and so is undervoltage shut down, and compatibility with the associated logic circuits.

Not all these facilities are always required and a simpler over-temperature device, the TEMPFET, is available.

**4** The TEMPFET, using MOS technology, has two chips, a conventional p or n-channel MOS chip and a temperature-sensitive MOS thyristor chip.

The thyristor chip, in thermal but not electrical contact, is made so that its temperature trigger point is slightly below the maximum rated temperature of the power MOS device (Fig. 1.28).

On over-temperature the thyristor will trigger, shorting the gate to source. This discharges the MOS input capacitance and turns off the component.

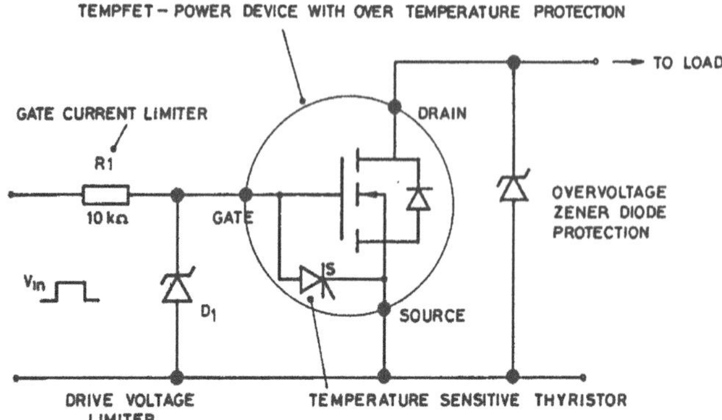


*Fig. 1.28 Smart power device – the TEMPFET*

## 30 Zener diode

**1** This diode is used as a voltage limiter, applications being in voltage stabilisers or peak voltage clipping.

Below its operating voltage the Zener diode behaves (almost) as an open circuit, but when a certain voltage is reached reverse current flows, the voltage across the Zener remaining almost constant (Fig. 1.29).

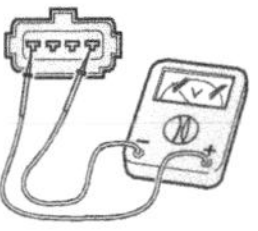

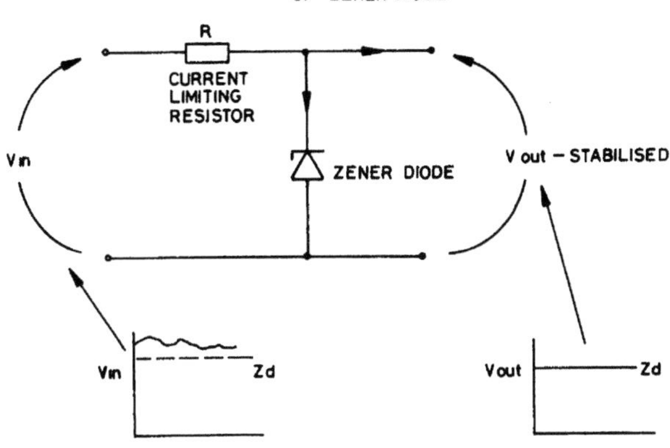


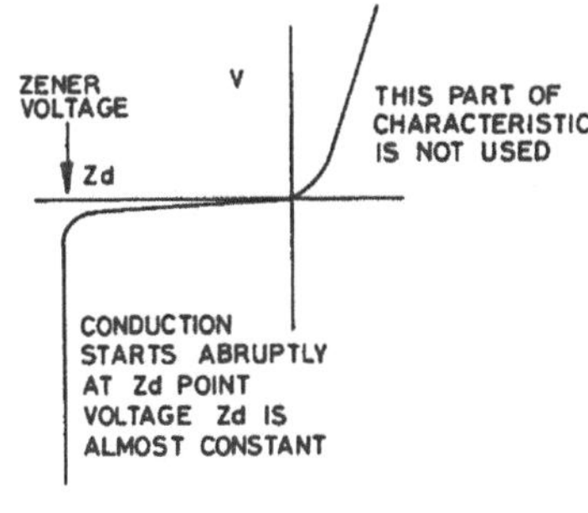


***Fig. 1.29 Zener diode – characteristic and one application***
*The Zener diode conducts by reverse current*

## 31 The thyristor

**1** This is a 4 layer pnpn device which has the property of rapid current switching. Like a mechanical switch, it is either fully on or fully off but has no moving parts and is switched from the OFF to the ON state by a small current fed into the gate terminal.

**2** When the gate current triggers the thyristor, current flows from anode to cathode and from this point the gate has no further effect. Only by reducing the anode-cathode voltage to (near) zero can the device be switched off. This characteristic is ideally suited for capacitor discharge ignition (CDI) – see Chapter 6 – and also for several other automobile electronic applications.

**3** Referring to Fig. 1.30, if the anode is positive relative to the cathode, a triggering pulse of current at the gate switches on the device in a few microseconds.

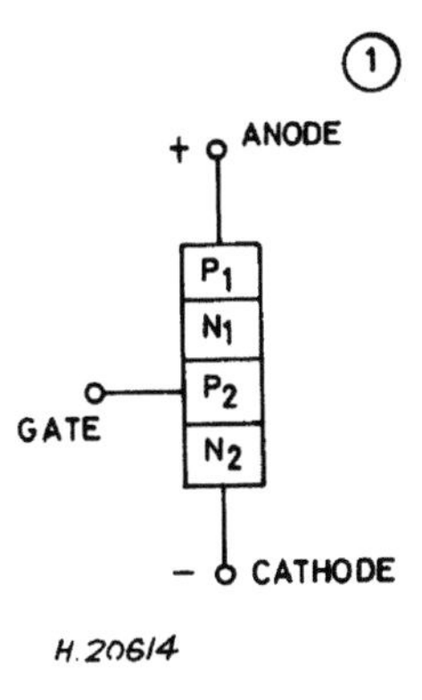


**1** The thyristor is an electronic switch and consists of 4 layers of p type and n type silicon.
As shown here the junctions $P_1 N_1$ and $P_2 N_2$ are forward biassed and separately would allow current flow, but junction $N_1 P_2$ is reverse-biassed so current cannot flow from anode to cathode.

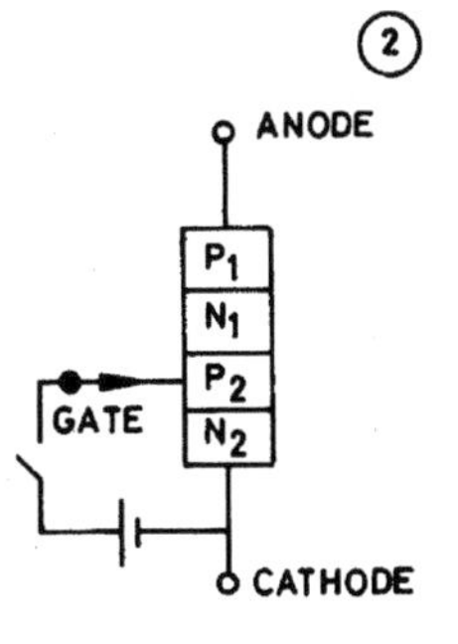


**2** If now a pulse of current is fed into the gate, this allows avalanche breakdown of the barrier at the reverse biassed junction $N_1 P_2$ so current flows through the thyristor between anode and cathode.
The thyristor is a very efficient switch with rapid action and no mechanical contacts to wear out – typically 60 mA of gate current is sufficient to switch on 10A of anode-cathode current.

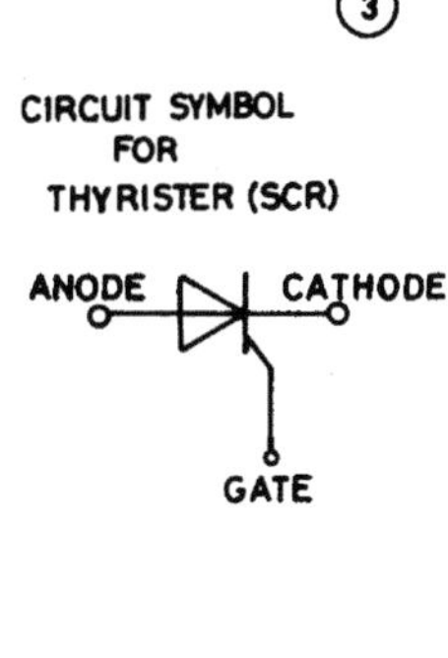


**3** It is inconvenient to draw 4 layers so a symbol is used as shown. The thyristor is sometimes known as a silicon controlled rectifier (SCR).

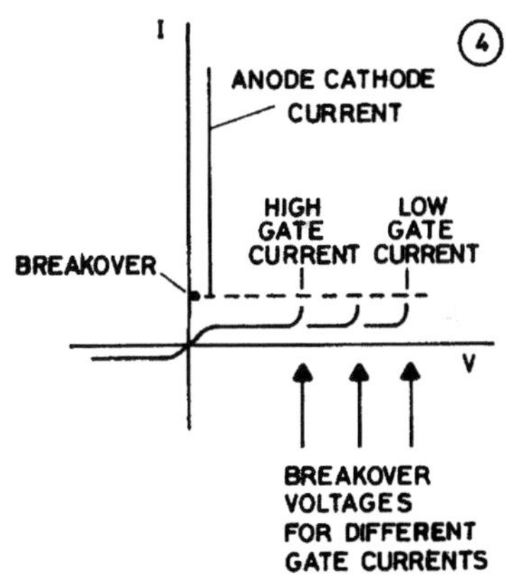


**4** Once switched on, the gate has no further control over the anode-cathode current. With a low gate current a high anode-cathode voltage to cause breakover (ie current flow) is required; a higher gate current requires a lower anode-cathode voltage for breakover. On the graph, V is anode-cathode voltage and the anode-cathode current.

***Fig. 1.30 The Thyristor***

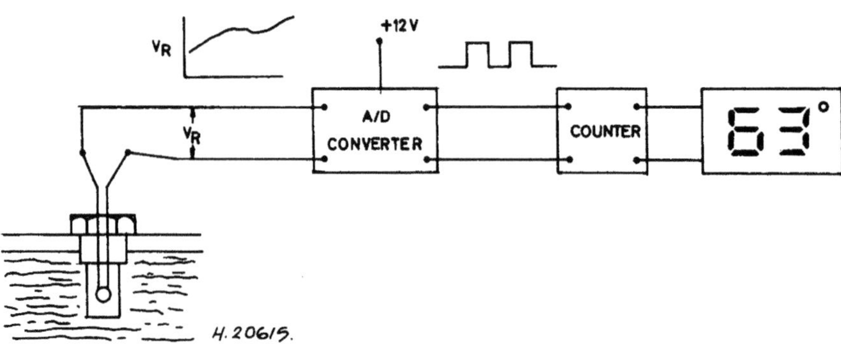


***Fig. 1.31 Analogue to digital conversion requirement***

It will then have an almost constant voltage drop of about 1 volt independent of the amount of current flowing from anode to cathode.

A thyristor switching a 10 A current might typically require a gate triggering current of 60 mA at 3 volts.

The thyristor is alternatively known as a silicon controlled rectifier (SCR).

## 32 Analogue and digital signals

**1** Analogue quantities are those which are continuously present, the most common example being the indication of a pointer on an instrument. Calculations in vehicle on-board electronics could be carried out in analogue form, but these methods have been superseded by digital methods.

**2** Digital quantities are expressed in numbers, and, moreover, only two numbers (0 and 1) are used in calculations.

Any number in the conventional denary scale (ie to base 10) can be converted into digital binary form (ie to base 2), and *vice versa.*

Examples where conversion from analogue to digital is required are found frequently in this book, particularly on ignition and fuelling systems. Temperature, as measured by a temperature dependent resistor will be an analogue quantity, and before it is usable in the computer, the signal must be converted into digital form (Fig. 1.31).

**3** The principle of A-D conversion is to convert the analogue voltage at any instant into a ramp waveform. As the voltage rises, a square wave pulse generator (the clock) operates and the number of pulses is counted. This is a digital measure of the analogue quantity.

## 33 Sensors and actuating devices

**1** Measurements of quantities such as speed, temperature, pressure, airflow, etc is by a range of SENSOR devices.

When the sensors have passed signals for processing, the desired result is often some form of movement. This is performed by **actuators.**

Sensors and actuators are described in the text as they occur.

## 34 Further reading

**1** Only a simple survey of electrical engineering principles has been possible here, but all are directly relevant to the automobile.

Those wanting to have a deeper understanding should consult the many good textbooks.

# Instruments and dashboard displays

## 1 Instrument panels

**1** Driver information on the operating condition of his vehicle is displayed on an instrument panel (or dashboard panel). Rapid developments in measurement and display systems have led to the all-electronic instrument panel with easy-read displays and information not previously utilised.

**2** The basic requirements remain the same, however, in that the driver will need to know:

(a) *vehicle speed and distance travelled*
(b) *contents of the fuel tank – and to be advised by at least a warning lamp of low fuel level*
(c) *engine temperature*
(d) *oil pressure*
(e) *headlamp main/dip beam*
(f) *handbrake on/off*
(g) *ignition on/off*
(h) *flashing turn and hazard indicators*
(i) *generator charging*

**3** Additional information may be displayed showing engine speed, brake pad wear limit, low brake fluid, bulb failure, low coolant and window washer levels, low oil level, air temperature, rear window heater on/off, etc.

A **trip computer** may be used to read:

(a) *instantaneous fuel consumption rate*
(b) *average speed*
(c) *estimated time of arrival*
(d) *fuel used*
(e) *fuel cost per mile or kilometre*

**4** Recent developments include the fitment of satellite navigation systems, service interval displays, and even television.

**5** In addition to the above, all new petrol engined models sold after 01/01/2000, all existing models with petrol engines from 01/01/2001, and all diesel engined models sold after 2005 in Europe, must be equipped with European On-Board Diagnostics (EOBD). A central theme of EOBD is that the driver must be notified where any emission related engine operating faults occur by illuminating the MIL (Malfunction Indicator Light) in the instrument cluster. When the MIL illuminates, the fault (and the distance travelled since the fault occurred) is be

# Chapter 2

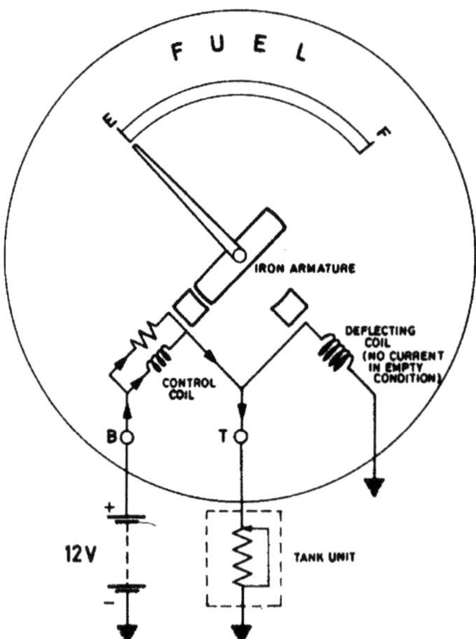


*Fig. 2.1a Moving-iron fuel gauge – empty*

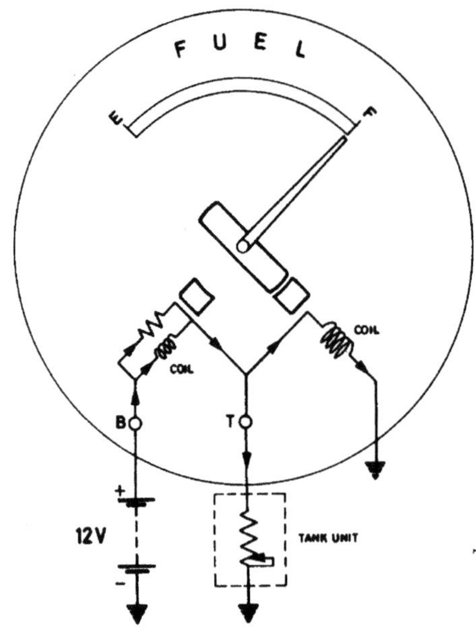


*Fig. 2.1b Moving-iron fuel gauge – full*

recorded by the on-board ECM (Electronic Control Module) for later retrieval by a fault code reader via the standardised diagnostic connector. For further information on this subject, refer *Haynes Fault Code Manual* by Martynn Randall.

## 2 Analogue instruments

**1** An electronic display is not available in all new car designs, and traditional analogue (pointer) instruments remain in wide use.

Electrical instruments found in such vehicles are:

*(a) moving-iron type – used for many years and now less popular. Pointer moves quickly*

*(b) bi-metal type – sluggish pointer movement which requires a stabilised supply voltage*

*(c) moving coil type – instant response, used for battery voltage indicators. Higher cost than bi-metal type*

## 3 Moving-iron instruments

**1** These depend upon the relative magnetic pulls of two coils upon a small pivoted iron armature to which the dial pointer is attached (Fig. 2.1).

The control coil and deflecting coil both attract the magnet when carrying current, and the position of the magnet and its pointer are a measure of the fuel tank contents.

The variable-resistance fuel level transmitter has low resistance when the tank is empty, and high resistance when full. As the fuel level rises there is increasing resistance to current passing through the fuel level transmitter. Instead, the current passes through the deflecting coil which then attracts the magnet on the indicator needle.

**2** There are two disadvantages of this instrument system:

*(a) the system is undamped and the pointer moves quickly to follow petrol waves and disturbances*

*(b) the difficulty of measuring tank content when nearly empty just when accuracy is sometimes most needed*

**3** The instrument has advantages of cheapness and the readings are independent of supply voltage.

## 4 Bi-metal instruments

**1** This instrument is used with several vehicle measuring devices, but as a fuel gauge it employs a variable resistance unit and float in the tank together with a bi-metal current indicator (Fig. 2.2).

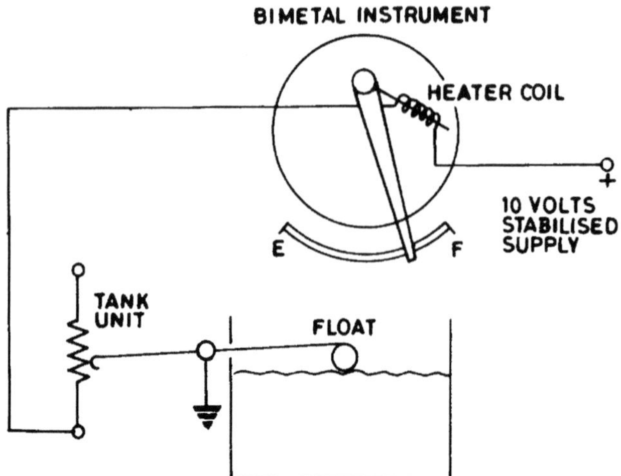


*Fig. 2.2 Bi-metal fuel gauge*

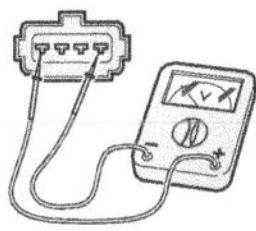

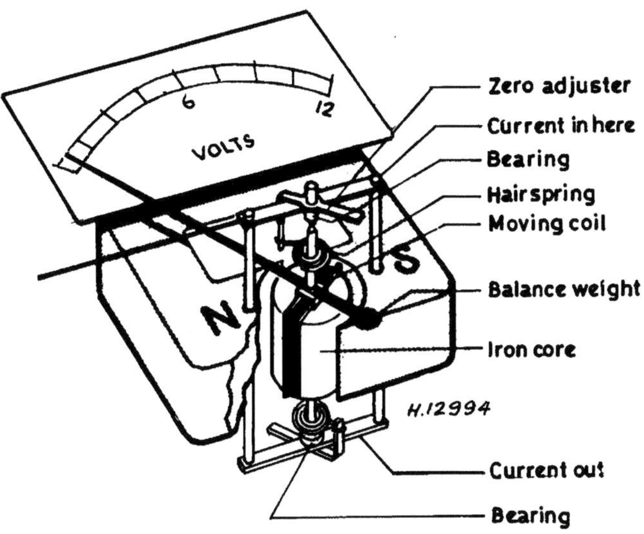


*Fig. 2.3 Moving coil instrument*

**2** The instrument consists of a bi-metal strip in the form of a 'U' with a heater coil wound on one leg. As the strip bends due to the unequal expansion of the two different metals used, a pointer moves across the scale to indicate fuel level. The U-shape, as a whole, compensates for any ambient temperature changes – so the instrument always zeros correctly.

**3** Sometimes the float is arranged so that its loading weight, and therefore its depth of submersion, varies with fuel level.

**4** At the empty end the float has least submersion and is most sensitive to change. This is further aided by the winding of the tank resistor being graded to give the required scale form on the indicator.

**5** Due to the thermal lag, this instrument responds slowly and is not sensitive to fuel surges when braking or cornering.

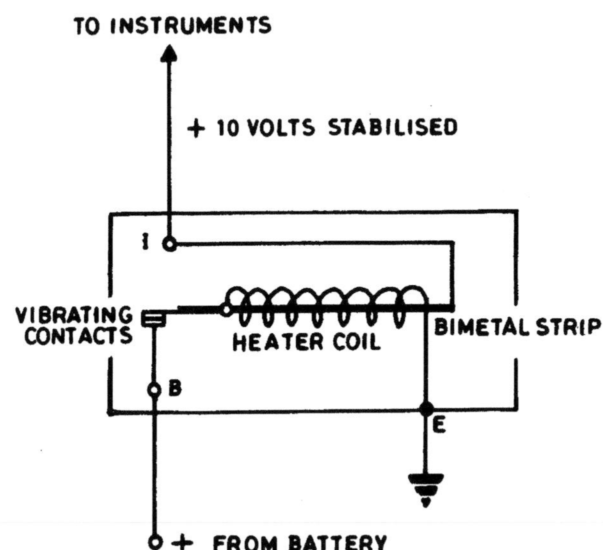


*Fig. 2.4 Bi-metal stabiliser*

## 5 Moving coil instruments

**1** This works on the same principle as a direct current electric motor except that the armature has a limited arc of movement (about 90°) and acts against spiral springs (Fig. 2.3).

The rectangular coil is wound on a light aluminium former and is located in a strong magnetic field provided by the permanent magnet; to concentrate the magnetic field an inner core of iron is used. The coil moves through the gap between the inner core and the permanent magnet, while the aluminium former serves to damp down oscillations since any tendency of the coil to swing would generate current in the aluminium.

This eddy current creates a power loss which can only come from the moving energy of the coil which will therefore quickly come to rest.

**2** Coiled hairsprings at either end of the shaft serve to oppose the torque produced by current flow in the coil. When the torque of the current coil equals the opposing torque of the hairsprings, the pointer comes to rest and indicates on the instrument scale the current being measured. The hairsprings are wound in opposite directions so that any deformations due to temperature change cancel out; additionally, current to the moving coil is through the springs.

**3** This type of instrument reads dc only but can read ac if a rectifier is used. With a high value series resistor it works as a voltmeter, and with a low value shunt resistor across its terminals it works as an ammeter. Because of its inherent accuracy, low power consumption and versatility it is the standard movement for analogue test meters.

**4** The moving coil instrument can be made to give a full scale reading for currents as low as 50 microamperes and as such can be a precision instrument. For automobile use the movement is made less sensitive and more robust.

## 6 Instrument voltage stabiliser (IVS)

**1** This is another example of bi-metal strip application. Instead of moving a pointer, the stabiliser uses the bi-metal heated strip to open contacts which cut off the supply to its own heater and also to other loads connected to it.

**2** The strip cools down, the contacts reclose and the cycle continues at a relatively slow rate, depending upon the voltage of battery or generator/alternator. The average voltage is 10 volts for most stabilisers and, since it is designed to supply equally sluggish instruments, the switching on and off has no adverse effect (Fig. 2.4).

**3** Stabilisers can become faulty, giving rise to erratic readings on instruments. Care must be taken to mount the stabiliser according to manufacturer's instructions, since the attitude is important.

**4** The method of testing a stabiliser is to connect a good quality dc voltmeter to the I terminal and earth. The voltage should pulse with a mean value of 10 volts (NB *Some stabilisers work at 7 volts*).

## 7 Temperature transmitters and indicators

**1** In earlier vehicles, temperature was measured by a liquid capsule connected by a thin pipe to a Bourdon gauge mounted on the dashboard. These were difficult to fit and have now given way to either a thermistor (semiconductor) or the thermal (bi-metal) type.

**2** Thermal temperature units (Fig. 2.5) use bi-metal elements at both the temperature measuring end and in the indicator. The transmitter is in the form of a voltage stabiliser in which the contacts open and close at a rate which depends upon the temperature. For higher temperatures the tension between contacts is lower and they will therefore be closed for a shorter period. It follows that less average current will flow through the indicator.

Most current will flow when the temperature is lowest and so the indicator zeros at the hot end of the scale; the effect of the making and breaking of contacts will not be noticed on the indicator due to the long thermal time constant.

This type of unit is now becoming obsolete but is still in service on older vehicles.

**3** Thermistor (semiconductor) units are based on resistors made from semiconductor material which exhibit a marked negative temperature-coefficient of resistance. That is, unlike most metals, the resistance goes down with a rise in temperature.

**4** The transmitter is a brass capsule containing a pellet of semiconductor material in close contact with a brass heat sink to dissipate the heat generated by the indicator current. The temperature of the liquid surrounding the capsule determines the resistance of the thermistor – at high temperatures the resistance is low, current and scale indication is therefore high.

**5** From Fig. 2.6 it will be seen that these transmitters can be used with moving iron or bi-metal indicators; in the latter case a stabiliser unit is required.

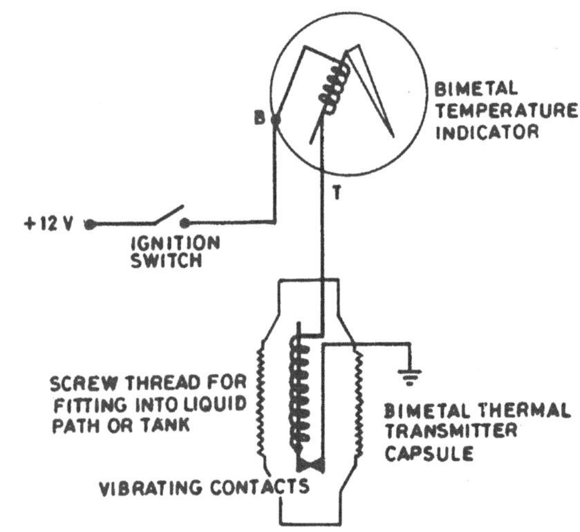


*Fig. 2.5 Thermal temperature measurement units*

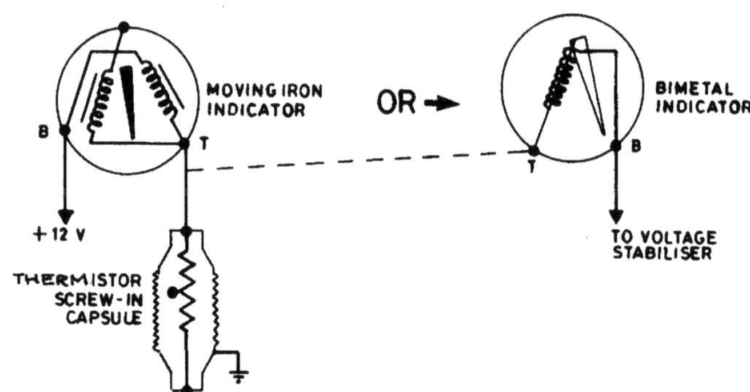


*Fig. 2.6 Thermistor (semiconductor) transmitter used with a moving-iron or bi-metal indicator*

## 8 Pressure indicators

**1** Oil pressure dashboard instruments are fitted only on luxury or sports cars, or as an after-sales kit. Most cars have only a warning light which will light continuously or flash if oil pressure falls below a minimum.

**2** An oil pressure switch in common use is the diaphragm and spring type shown in Fig. 2.7. The oil pressure switch is screwed into an oilway in the engine block. At low pressure

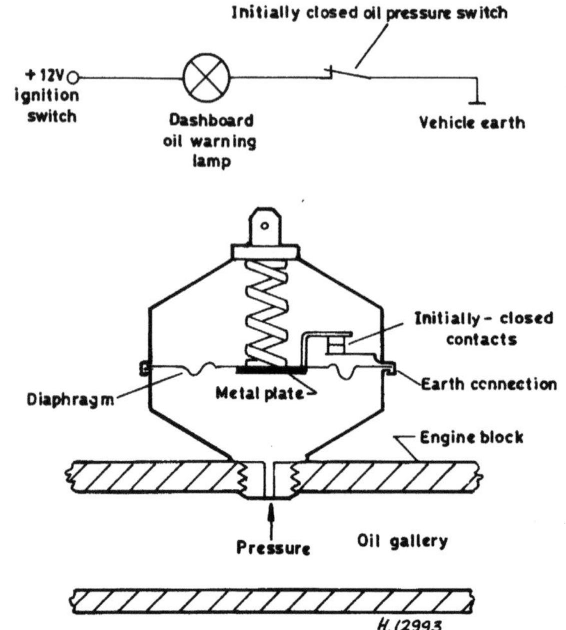


*Fig. 2.7 Oil pressure switch*

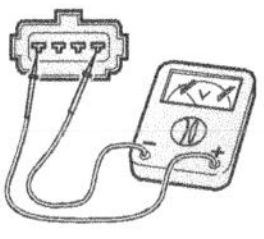

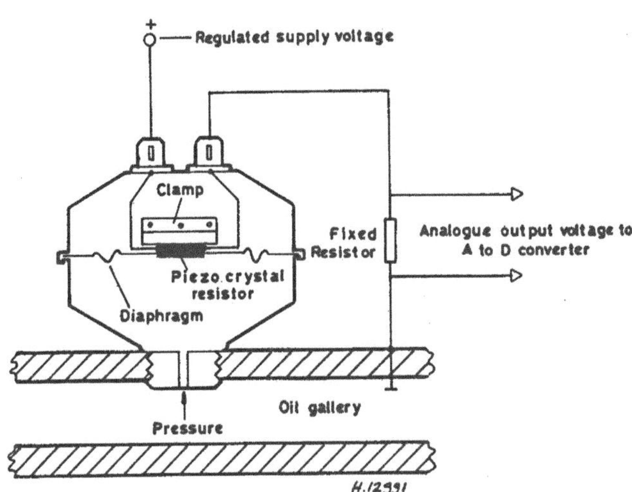


*Fig. 2.8 Oil pressure sensor*

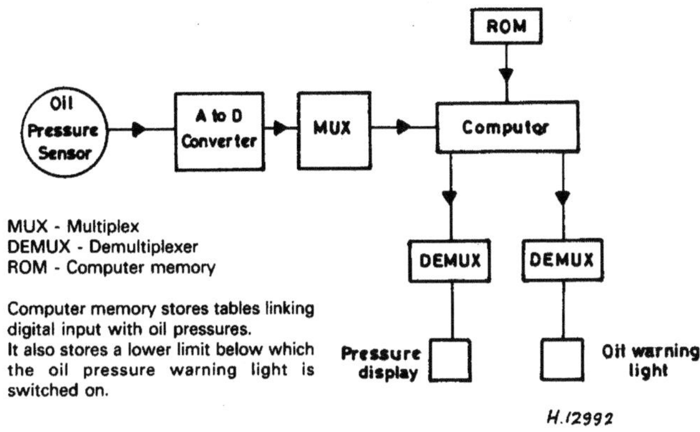


*Fig. 2.9 Electronic oil pressure measurements*

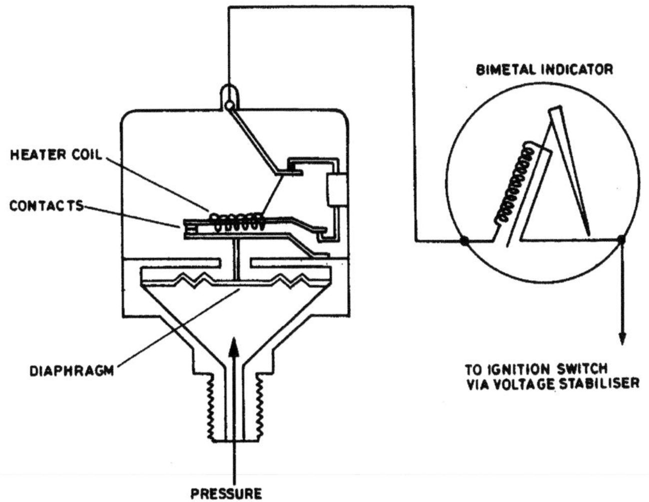


*Fig. 2.10 Thermal pressure transmitter and indicator*

the switch is closed but opens when the oil pressure overcomes the spring pressure. A low wattage warning light in the dashboard alerts the driver to the low pressure condition.

**3** A similar diaphragm operated device is the piezo sensor (Fig. 2.8). A semiconductor piezo crystal in the form of a thin block has the property that a change of pressure on a pair of opposite faces will be accompanied by a change of resistance between the other two opposite faces. The piezo crystal is connected in series with a fixed value resistor across a regulated dc supply. When the oil pressure acts on the diaphragm the piezo resistance change causes a voltage variation across the fixed resistor which is proportional to the oil pressure. This type of circuit is often part of an electronic dashboard display (Fig. 2.9). The output voltage will be first converted to a digital pulse code and then presented to a computer in which the fixed-memory (ROM) has in store a table of digital voltage values which correspond to oil pressures, again in coded form. The computer, having identified the oil pressure code, produces an output signal to drive the dashboard display.

Note in the circuit diagram the use of the multiplexer (MUX).

This is effectively a sequential switch which allocates time to the oil pressure sensor to be connected through to the computer. The same procedure is happening with other circuits needing the use of the computer – the alternative would mean the provision of a computer for each circuit!

Output will be signals indicating 'oil warning' and/or 'oil pressure' and will arrive at the display indicators after the computer output has passed through a de-multiplexer (DEMUX). This unit is synchronised with the MUX electronically.

**4** An analogue system using a thermal pressure sensor and a bi-metal pointer instrument is shown in Fig. 2.10. The diaphragm will flex when subjected to pressure and will affect the force between two contacts of a bi-metal vibrator.

This vibrator works on the same principle as the voltage stabiliser IVS (Fig. 2.4); heater coil current will bend the bi-metal strip over which it is wound, opening the contacts and cutting off the heater current. The contacts now close again.

The rate at which this occurs depends upon the oil pressure diaphragm force on the lower contact. Average current flow is shown by the indicator which may be calibrated in pressure units.

## 9 Speedometers

### Analogue speedometer

**1** The first automotive instrument was a speedometer, based on the centrifugal governor principle, fitted in 1899. Various designs followed, and for many years up to the present day, the drag cup magnetic induction speedometer was the

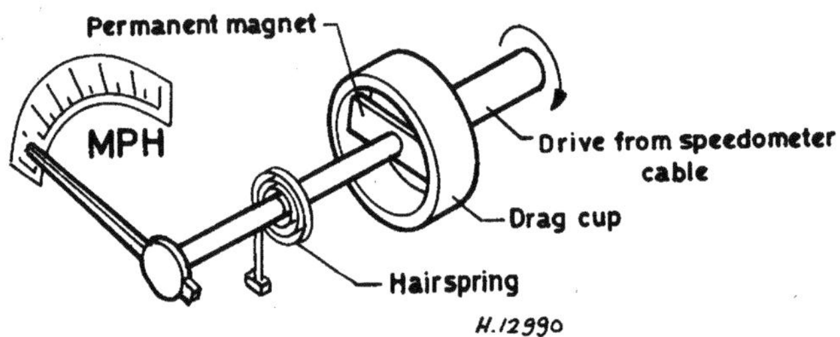


Fig. 2.11 Magnetic induction speedometer

classical design (Fig. 2.11). The drag cup is a light aluminium pressing and, as it rotates in the magnetic field of the permanent magnet, currents are induced in it. Local magnetic fields are set up by these currents resulting in the magnet being dragged after the cup.

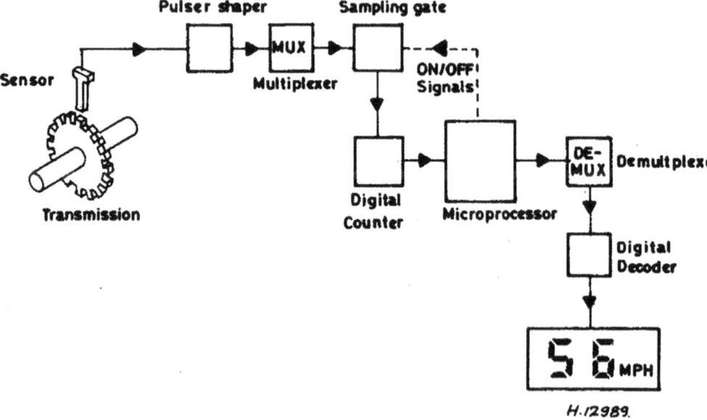


***Fig. 2.12a* Principle of the digital speedometer**

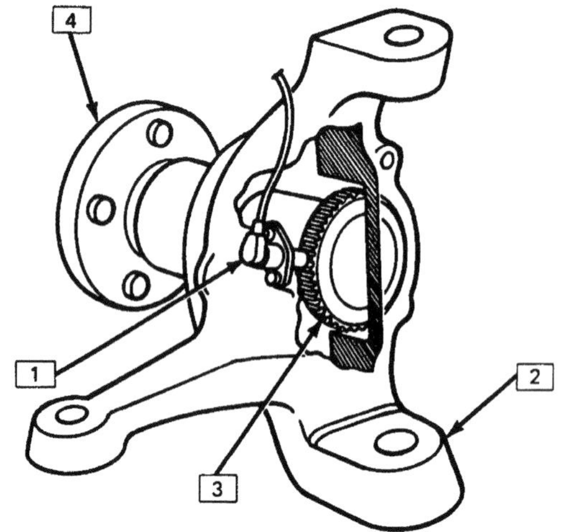


***Fig. 2.12b* Typical wheel speed sensor**

*1 Front wheel speed sensor*
*2 Hub carrier*
*3 Toothed signal rotor*
*4 Front hub and bearing assembly*

**2** The speedometer driven shaft also activates a trip and total distance odometer recorder, this being a mechanism on the principle of the bicycle cyclometer. With the disadvantage of bringing a speedometer cable to the dashboard, however, designers are changing rapidly to more convenient methods.

### Digital speedometer

**3** Speed indication is by a sensor mounted in the transmission, the sensor being of the magnetic induction, Hall generator, or photocell type (Fig. 2.12a). Output pulse frequency is proportional to the vehicle speed and after passing to a pulse shaper (Schmitt trigger; see Chapter 6, Fig. 6.71), the now square topped pulses pass to a multiplexer.

The multiplexer works on the same principle as described in Section 8, paragraph 3. The multiplexer sends the pulse train to a sampling gate which accepts the pulses for a set period, the ON and OFF points being operated by the microprocessor. During the sampling time, the number of received pulses measured by the digital counter is proportional to the vehicle speed. After each count the counter returns to zero ready to receive the next batch of pulses through the gate. The microprocessor, being the arithmetic operator, sends out signals to a digital display unit via a de-multiplexer. Numbers from 0 to 9 are made up of seven illuminated bars and, to write a number, a digital decoder is required.

**4** On recent models equipped with ABS, it's common for the signal used by the speedometer to be taken from the wheel speed sensors used by the ABS computer to monitor wheel slip (Fig. 2.12b). Here the ABS ECM (Electronic Control Module) is networked with other ECM's (engine management, transmission, etc.). Thus the signal from the wheel speed sensors, is used to monitor and regulate not only the ABS but traction control, and electronic stability programmes (ESP). The wheel speed signal is also used by trip computers, navigation systems, and crash/fault data recorders.

## 10 Tachometers

**1** The tachometer measures engine speed. It is now fitted as original equipment on medium-priced cars but formerly was available only on sports and luxury vehicles.

**2** In principle, the tachometer works the same way as the speedometer in that pulses are repeatedly counted over a fixed period and then displayed as a digital or analogue read-out. The ignition system provides a ready means of sensing engine speed; the voltage pulses at the coil negative terminal (ie the contact breaker or trigger terminal) are taken to a Schmitt-trigger pulse shaper and the remainder of the circuit is similar to that of Fig. 2.12a for digital types. For analogue readings the pulses are converted to a direct current and applied to a moving coil instrument calibrated in rev/min.

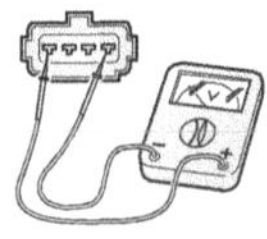

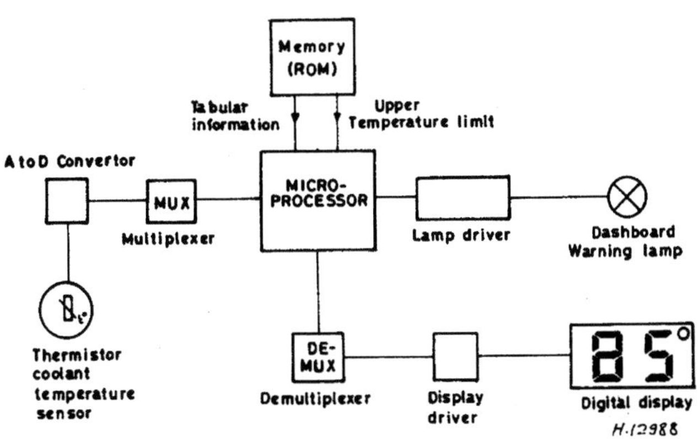


*Fig. 2.13 Coolant temperature display and warning circuit*

## 11 Coolant temperature measurement (digital)

**1** In Section 7 bi-metal and thermistor devices have been described for obtaining an analogue instrument dashboard reading. However, electronic displays require the use of the microprocessor and the thermistor sensor gives a suitable signal for incorporation into such a system.

**2** The thermistor is enclosed in a screwed capsule and fitted in the engine block close to the thermostat. It will be surrounded by coolant and the temperature will determine the thermistor resistance, there being a negative temperature coefficient of resistance.

**3** The thermistor is connected in series with a fixed resistor across the supply and the voltage taken off the fixed resistor. This is analogue in form and is converted into pulses by the A to D converter (Fig. 2.13). A multiplexer gains access to the microprocessor which has stored in memory a table of values linking the incoming digital signals to a corresponding temperature. The microprocessor uses the memory figure to operate the numerical display; should the temperature exceed a set limit stored in memory, the warning lamp is switched on.

## 12 Fuel metering (digital)

**1** Accessing the microprocessor through a multiplexer, a float-operated resistive potentiometer will provide an analogue voltage. After conversion to digital pulses, the microprocessor will look up in memory the fuel quantity corresponding to the incoming pulse signal. When the fuel level falls below a set level a low-fuel warning lamp is activated.

**2** To allow for fuel waves in the tank, the microprocessor stores incoming readings over a period of seconds and calculates the average value which is then looked up in the stored tables in ROM to determine the fuel quantity.

## 13 Trip computers

**1** These have been available for some time as after market accessories and, with the falling cost of microprocessors, are now appearing as original equipment (Fig. 2.14).

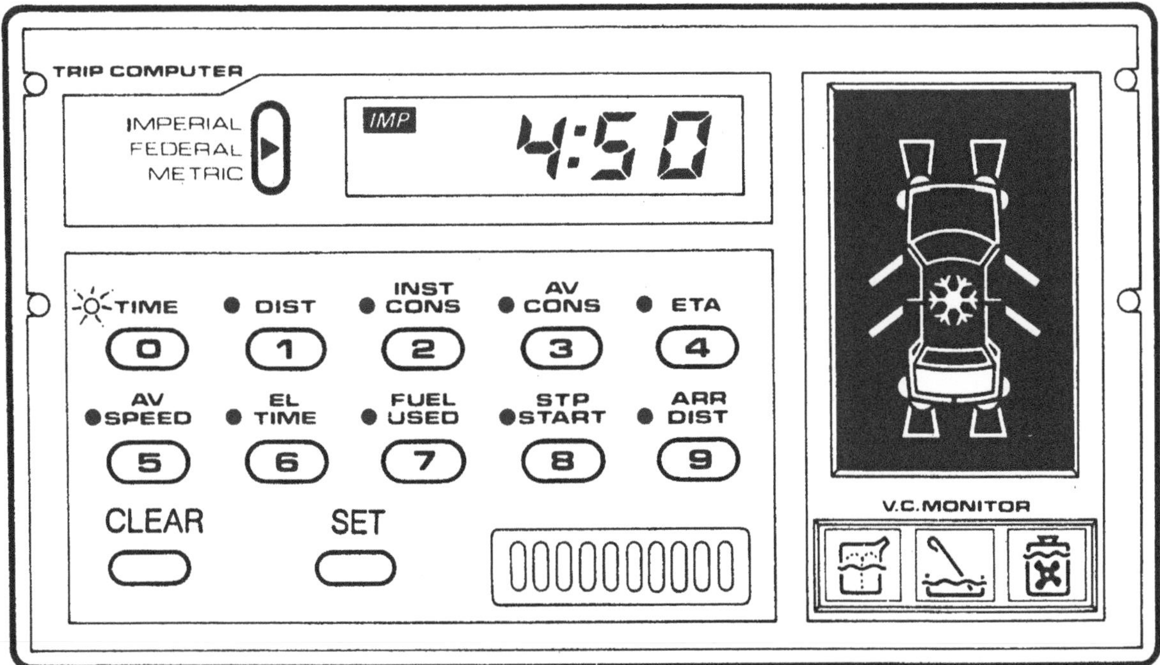


*Fig. 2.14 Combined trip computer and vehicle monitor display*

2 Using the principles outlined so far in this chapter the systems available will read typically the following:

*Date and time*
*Rate of fuel consumption*
*Average fuel consumption*
*Cost of fuel per mile*
*Estimated time of arrival*
*Distance travelled before running out of fuel*
*Fuel used*
*Outside air temperature*
*Distance covered*

3 Certain of these computations require input from the driver and, once basic journey starting information is keyed in, the computer will then be able to read the above quantities at the touch of the selector button. With a built-in quartz clock, operations are timed with great accuracy. Most of the input quantities are measured by sensors already described; fuel flow rate being the exception. This can be in the form of a rotating vane wheel located in the fuel supply line. As the wheel rotates due to fuel flow the vanes interrupt light from a light emitting diode (LED) to a phototransistor. A train of rectangular pulses results, the frequency of pulses being a measure of fuel flow rate.

## 14 Vehicle condition monitoring (VCM)

1 The purpose of dashboard information display to the driver is to monitor and warn of abnormal conditions, so to this extent VCM is not new but rather an extension of existing provision. Now that service intervals are up to 12 000 miles for some vehicles there is greater chance of blown bulbs, low oil or brake fluid, etc and so extra monitoring is provided.

2 Displays or warning lights are normally clustered together within easy view of the driver and on a separate panel.

An example is the Lucas combined Trip Computer/Vehicle Monitor fitted to the Rover 800 Vitesse (Fig. 2.14). Map displays show a diagram of the car and will show by the lighting of bulbs:

*Doors or boot open*
*Main and dip beam*
*Sidelights*
*Turn indicators*
*Brake lamps*
*Rear foglamps*
*Rear number plate lamp*

The lights will glow if the lamp or circuit is working correctly, but if faulty, the segment concerned will not light. An extra light or buzzer will come on to alert the driver of a fault.

3 The display technology available can use filament bulbs, vacuum fluorescent display (VFD), liquid crystal display (LCD), light emitting diodes (LED), DC electroluminescence (DCEL).

Display style can be alphanumeric, dot matrix, bar graph or by use of symbols – these terms being explained later.

Most systems use a microprocessor for multichannel units handling several sensors, while single channels may use an integrated circuit chip.

4 All vehicles monitor charging, fuel tank content, lights, flashers, oil pressure and coolant temperature. Extra monitoring can now, in a mid-cost system, cover the following:

*Defective lights*
*Liquid levels, eg brake fluid, engine oil, washer bottle, coolant*
*Brake pad wear*

## 15 VCM operation

1 Most sensors used for monitoring will be switches to signify that a preset limit has been exceeded. If a switch opens as part of the operation the effect would be the same as an open circuit fault. To overcome this, the switch opens across a fixed resistor so that a circuit, albeit resistive, is still made (Fig. 2.15). Reed switches with coils, and reed switches with magnet and float are used for low fluid level sensing, while the hot wire resistance sensor is used for oil level monitoring.

2 When the ignition is switched on, all the warning lamps at the dashboard panel will light for 5 seconds as a check on filaments and circuits. After 5 seconds the lights will extinguish unless the quantity being measured is out of limits. If a circuit fault is present the monitoring electronics will cause the lamp of the circuit concerned to flash for a period of 40 seconds with then a pause and repeat.

### Lighting faults

3 A reed switch is used to check that lamp current is

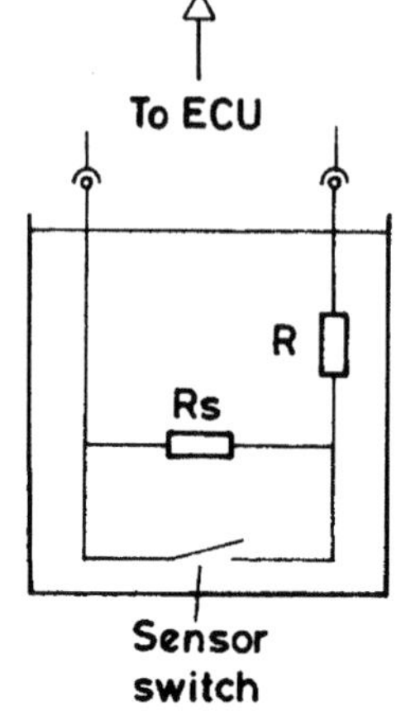


Rather than use a simple ON-OFF switch, two levels of resistance are preferred. This avoids false readings due to a wiring open-circuit fault.
This idea is seen in several sensor circuits described in this Chapter.

**Open gives high resistance Rs + R**
**Closed gives lower resistance R**

*Fig. 2.15 Sensor switch*

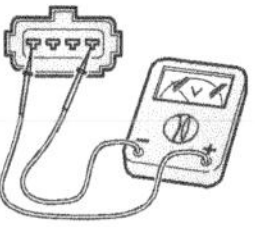

present. Fig. 2.16 shows a reed switch of the type using a surrounding coil. When lamp current flows the magnetic field created closes the contacts and switches on a monitoring lamp. A variation on this theme is the use of two coils wound round the reed switch. Two identical lamps, eg two sidelamps, are fed from the two coils and since the coils are wound in opposite directions, the switch stays open until one lamp fails, when the magnetic imbalance causes the switch to close and the warning light to come on.

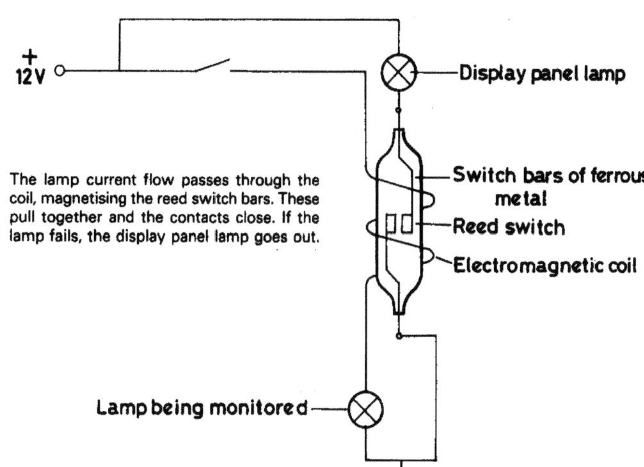


*Fig. 2.16 Reed switch monitor circuit to indicate lamp failure*

## Brake pad wear

**4** This circuit has a number of variations, one of which is shown in Fig. 2.17. To sense the end of the brake pad useful life, a loop of wire is embedded in the brake pad at a depth that when the pad thickness is down to 2 mm the wire is ground away and finally cut by the brake disc. As this happens, the 1200 ohm resistor is put in series with the 180 ohm resistor in the wire going to the warning control circuit. The raising of circuit resistance from 180 ohm to 1380 ohm signals the control circuit to switch on the warning light.

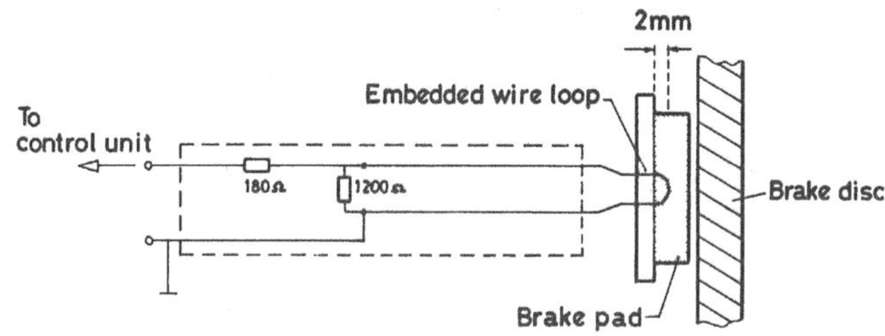


*Fig. 2.17 Brake pad wear sensor*

## Fluid level sensors – float switch

**5** Float switches are the cheapest of a range of sensors suitable for fluid level monitoring. Fig. 2.18 shows a float which has a small permanent magnet attached to the arm. A reed switch mounted on an overhead cantilever is closed by the magnet when near. As the float sinks, there will come a point where the magnetic field is insufficient to hold the reed contacts together. As they open, a signal voltage will be generated by the sudden increase of circuit resistance – this is passed to the control unit for processing and results in the controller lighting a dashboard warning lamp.

## Fluid level sensors – AC impedance type

**6** An insulated boss screwed into the coolant reservoir has two flat metallic rods which dip into the fluid. The metallic rods are supplied with a high frequency alternating current at very low voltage; the conductance of the liquid will be high but when the liquid level falls so that the rods are not immersed, the conductance is very low. The increase of alternating voltage is registered by the electronic controller and a warning light operated.

## Fluid level sensors – hot wire dipstick

**7** The dipstick houses a resistance wire of about 7 to 8 ohms, located inside an insulator moulding beneath the engine oil level. External markings show 'min' and 'max' levels as with a normal dipstick (Fig. 2.19). Two wires from the top of the dipstick are taken to an electronic control unit which measures the resistance value which will vary with temperature. When ignition is switched on, the ECU sends a current of about 0.25 ampere through the wire for a short period, say 2 seconds. If the resistor is below the oil surface the heat generated is carried away by the oil, but if the oil level falls more than 3 mm below the minimum mark then, with no surrounding oil,

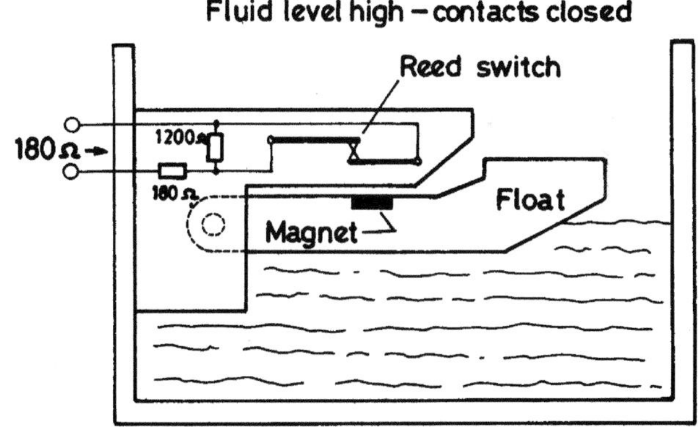


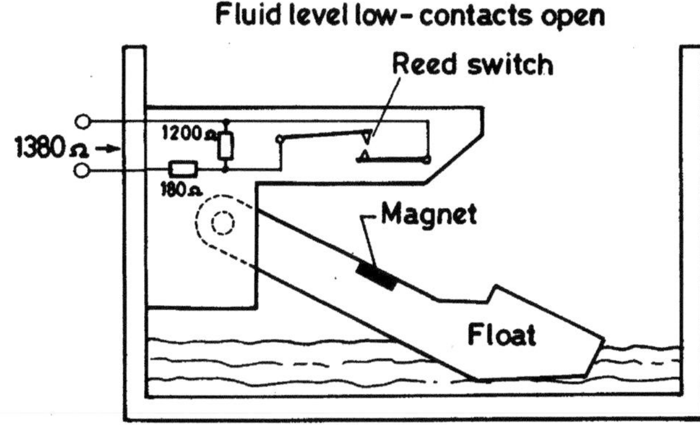


*Fig. 2.18 Fluid level sensor*

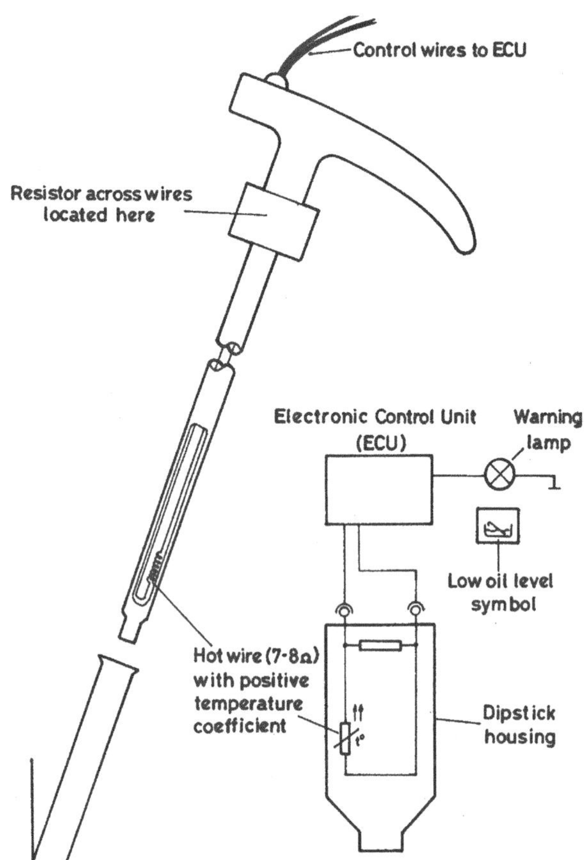


*Fig. 2.19 Hot wire dipstick*

the hot wire will reach a higher temperature during the period of current flow. The resistance will rise due to the positive temperature coefficient of resistance of the hot wire; the ECU compares the resistance values when immersed and when not immersed. Given that the difference exceeds a predetermined limit, the ECU switches on a dashboard warning lamp. The success of this sensor depends upon good connections of plugs and sockets. When looking for a fault, pins should be checked for cleanliness.

## 16 Electronic display technology

**1** Although the analogue dashboard instrument is still holding its place, the solid-state instrument panel is now established. The advantages are lack of moving parts, fast operation, good clarity, greater freedom in locating the panel and finally a choice in the use of display devices. Four types of display units are in common use, sometimes in combination; their main properties will be briefly reviewed as follows:

### LED – light-emitting diode

**2** A forward-biased p-n junction diode will emit light when carrying current, the colour depending upon the proportions of phosphorus and arsenic in the alloy used for the semiconductor (Fig. 2.20). Colours may be red, yellow or

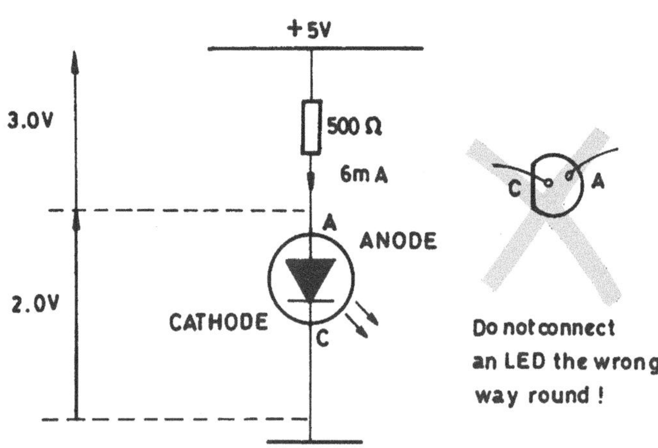


*Fig. 2.20 LED and typical operation conditions*

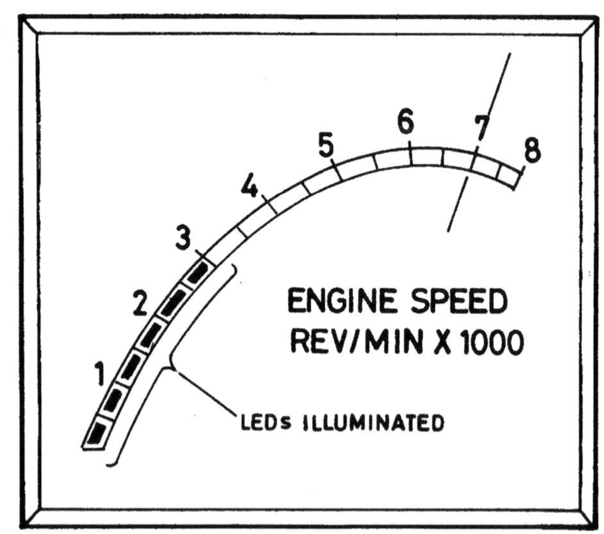


*Fig. 2.21 LED array as a tachometer*

*LEDs are set in separate compartments on a printed circuit board (PCB)*
*Each LED has a silvered reflector on the curved compartment wall*

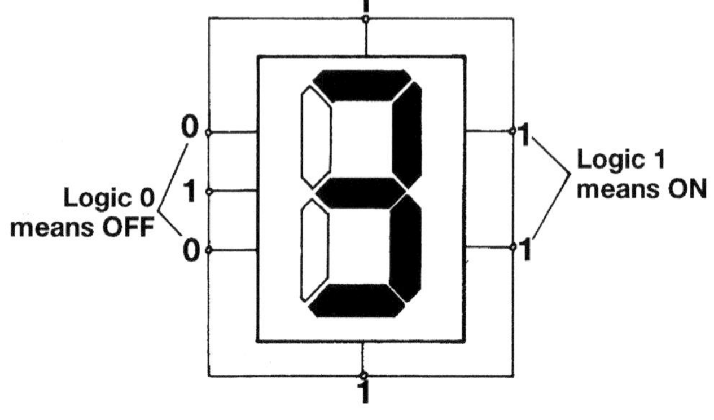


*Fig. 2.22 Number display using 7 LEDs*

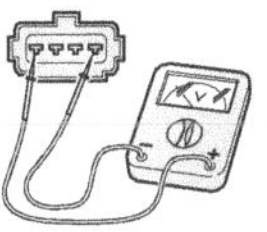

green but maximum optical efficiency is obtained using red light. A current limiting resistor must be used to set the current within the range 2 mA to 25 mA, the voltage drop across red diodes being 2.0 V. LED life is very long; it is rugged and consumes very low power. Bar charts are formed by using a series of LEDs or an alpha-numerical display may be utilised (Figs. 2.21 and 2.22). (Alpha-numerical means letters and numbers.)

## LCD – liquid crystal display

**3** This does not emit light but uses reflected light, so in dark conditions back lighting is necessary to render the display visible. Low cost, and low power consumption, together with a sharp image and different colours using filters, have made this device popular with designers. Liquid crystals with randomly orientated groups of cigar-shaped molecules are located between two glass plates spaced by 10 micrometres with a perimeter seal to form a capsule. The inside surface of the glass plates has a transparent conducting film sputtered on it, together with two polarised filters with a 90° angle between the filter axes (Fig. 2.23). With no voltage applied, incoming light (1) has the horizontal light component removed by the filter (2), is then rotated 90° by the crystals (3), and may pass to the lower glass plate where it is reflected back (4), as a bright image identical to the background. Now, if a voltage of the order of 5 volts is applied to the two conducting films, the electric field acting on the crystals prevents the normal 90° twist of polarisation. The light cannot reach the reflector because of the horizontally polarised filter so a black image is formed. LCD segments each with their individual voltages can be used to form letters and figures or as elements in a bar graph. Temperature range for satisfactory operation is –30°C to +85°C with a current demand of 8 microamperes per numeral.

## Vacuum fluorescent display (VFD)

**4** This is an active display device (ie it emits light) based on the principle of the triode valve. Segments which make up a number or a letter are coated with a powder which will fluoresce when electrons strike the surface in much the same way as fluorescent powders are excited to give off light in a fluorescent tube. Electrons are given off from a hot filament

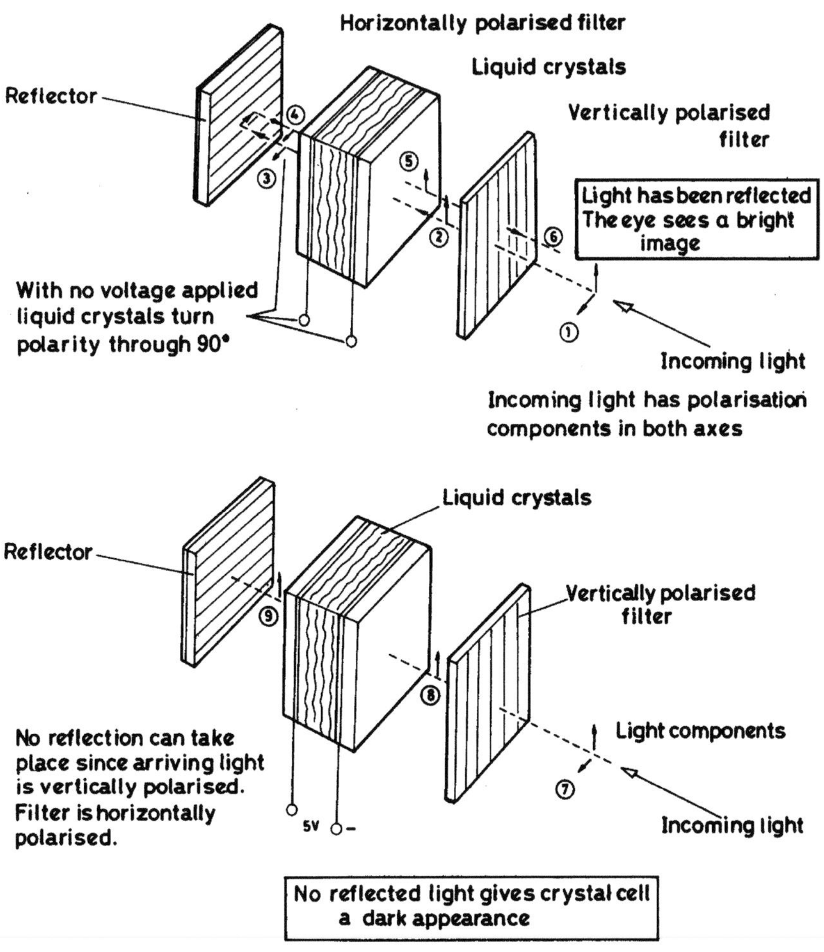


*Fig. 2.23 Operation of liquid-crystal display*

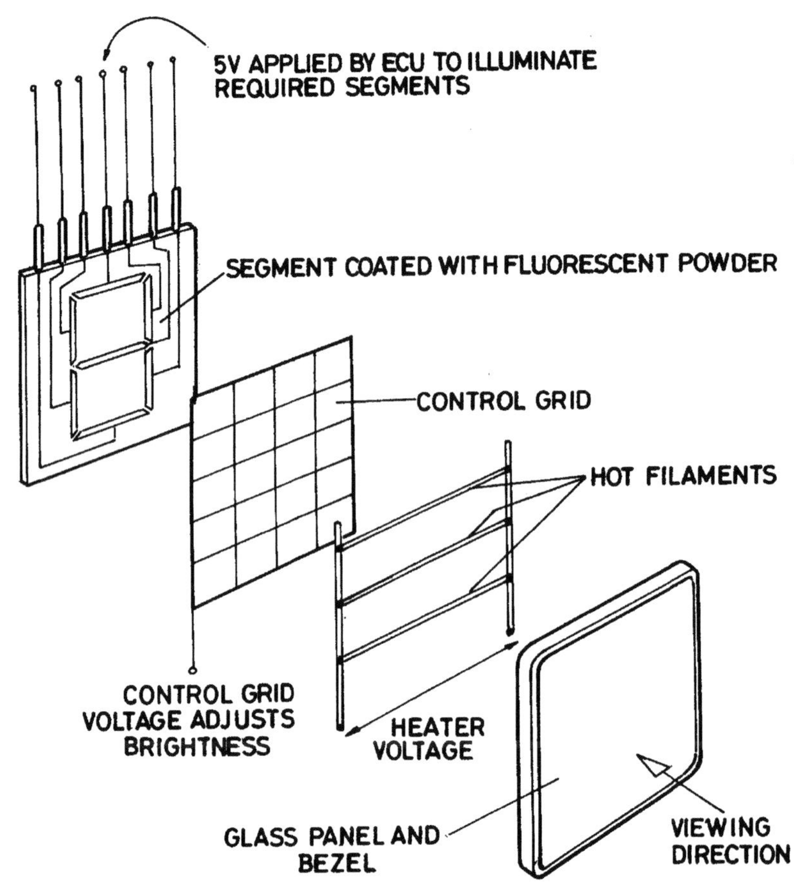


*Fig. 2.24 Vacuum fluorescent display (VFD)*

and surround the filament in an electron cloud. When a segment is made positive with respect to the filament, electrons will stream across the gap and, upon striking the segment (anode), will excite the surface powder to give off light.

Interposed between the filament and the segment anode is a control grid which is held at a potential (voltage) such that no emitted electrons will reach the segments until a signal of about 5 volts is applied to a particular segment. Electrons then pass through the grid striking the segment anode, causing it to fluoresce. Variations of the grid voltage will then give brightness control (Fig. 2.24). The common colour is a green-yellow, but according to the chemical composition of the fluorescent powders, may give a range of colours of which the light blue is attractive and eye-catching on the instrument panel.

### DC electroluminescence (DCEL)

**5** This is a variant of the liquid crystal display in which the liquid crystals are replaced by a compound of zinc sulphide.

The glow emitted can be used as a display in its own right or can be backlighting for another display. Current absorption is negligible and there is rapid response; a variety of colours is available.

## 17 Satellite Navigation Systems

**1** In-car navigation systems are increasingly becoming standard fitment in modern vehicles. There are many different systems, but nearly all rely upon the exact position of the vehicle being pin-pointed by three or more orbiting satellites. With the vehicles exact position established, the on-board systems computer references a map of the area, normally stored on a CD or DVD, to work out the best route to the desired address. This information is shown on a screen on the vehicles dashboard, and/or given by vocal instructions, with the driver being prompted to manoeuvre at the appropriate moment when approaching junctions, roundabouts etc.

**2** On more sophisticated systems, the address or postcode of the destination is entered via in-car phone or display screen. This information is relayed to a call centre which establishes your position. The call centre computer calculates the quickest route, (allowing for traffic conditions), and the navigation instructions are verbally or visually given to the driver at the appropriate time. The information can be constantly updated should traffic conditions change, enabling traffic congestion to be avoided, and alternative routes found.

# Charging systems

## Part A: Alternators



## Part B: Dynamos



## PART A: ALTERNATORS

### 1 Introduction to alternators

The electrical demand for power for ignition, starting, signalling, lighting and other functions requires a generator. Whilst the battery is a power storage device it has only a limited capacity for this purpose and quickly runs down, so some form of recharging is necessary on the vehicle (Fig. 3.1).

The entire current requirement of the vehicle, including that of battery charging, is provided by a generator driven via a belt by the engine, so the ultimate energy source is the fuel.

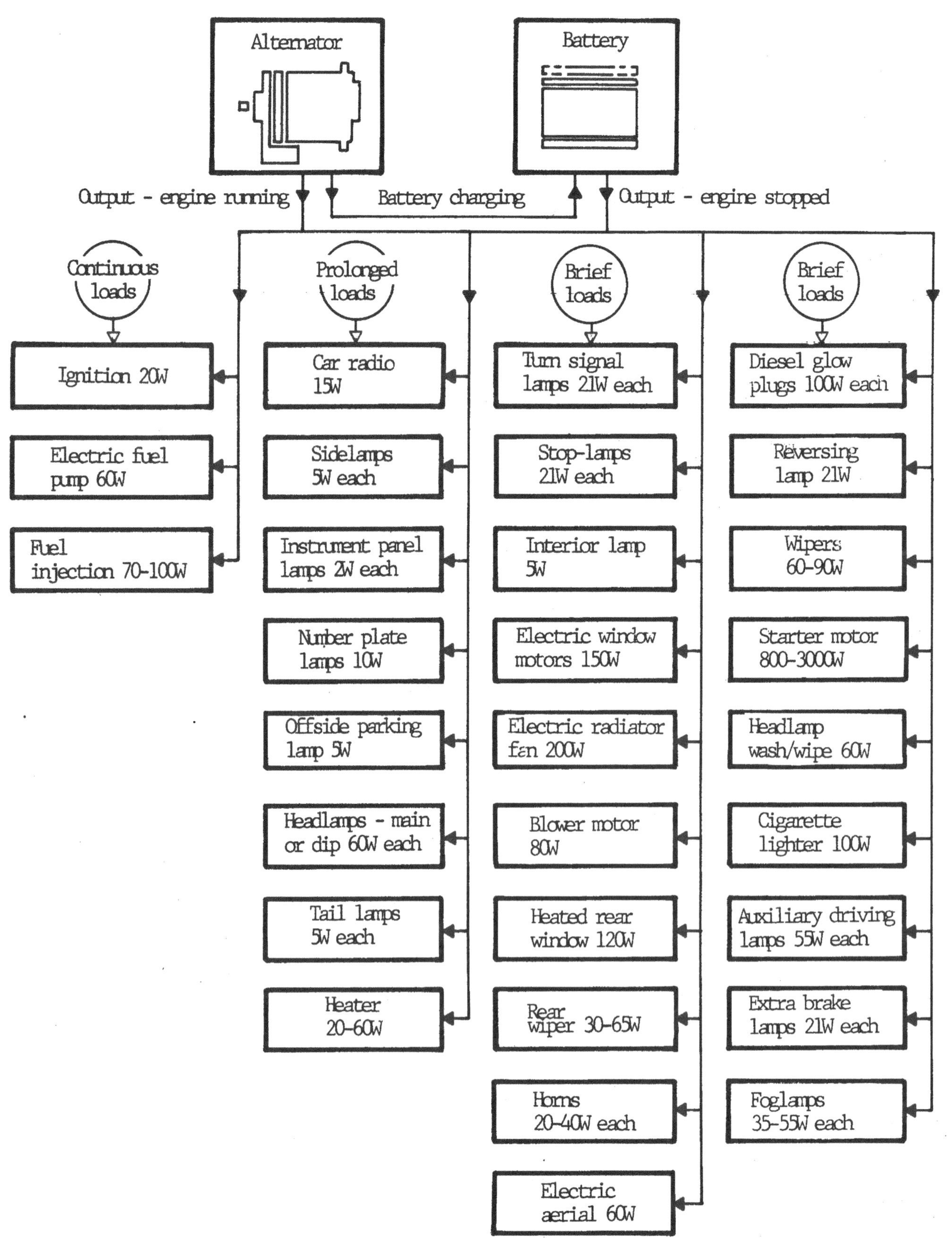


*Fig. 3.1 Typical electrical load for passenger car in late 1980s*

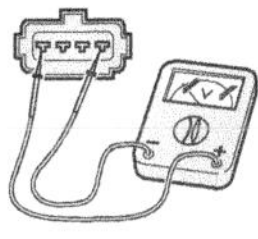

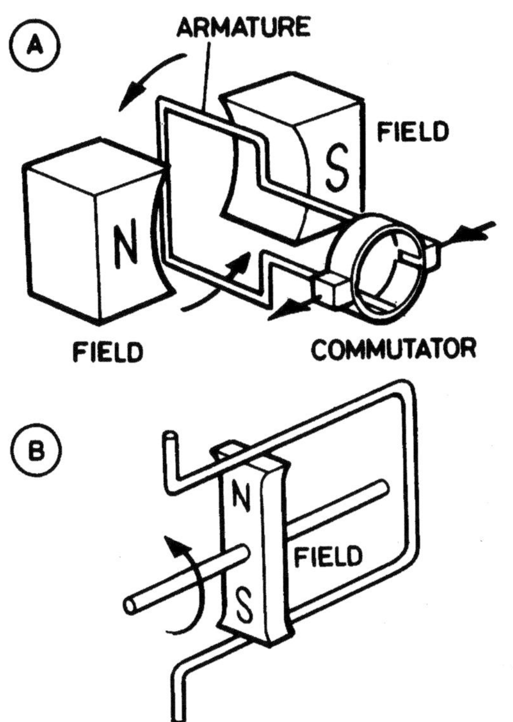


***Fig. 3.2 Essentials of the dynamo and alternator***
*A Dynamo (stationary field) B Alternator (rotating field)*

Large variations of engine speed mean that the generator requires some form of regulator so that the output voltage is as near as possible constant over the working range of speed.

Battery charging requires direct current, so the generator must either be of the dc dynamo type (now obsolete) or an ac alternator with a rectifier.

## 2 Advantages of the alternator

**1** It is estimated that city buses spend up to 40% of their peak traffic time standing still, and similar poor operating conditions can apply to the car.

**2** The direct current generator does not charge its battery at tickover speed, so traffic congestion, coupled with the ever increasing demand of electrical accessories, meant that this form of generator had reached its limit by the 1960s. Other limitations were concerned with the difficulty in taking off the electrical power through carbon brushes and commutator and armature speed limitations. The main current was produced in the rotating armature, the field windings being stationary.

**3** Just the opposite occurs in the alternator, in that the main current windings are stationary and the field coils rotate (Fig. 3.2). The field coils are light and can be made to rotate at much higher speeds than can a dc dynamo, so by using a suitable pulley the alternator is already running fast enough to charge the battery even at tickover speeds. Fig. 3.3 shows a comparison of outputs from a dc dynamo and an alternator with approximately the same maximum power rating.

**4** Finally, the alternator is lighter in weight than the dynamo, requires less maintenance, requires no charging current cut-out, and has a longer service life. The electronic regulator controls output more precisely than did the dynamo regulator and permits the use of maintenance-free batteries.

## 3 Principle of operation of the alternator

**1** When an electric conductor and a magnetic field move relative to each other a voltage (more properly called an electromotive force – emf) is generated. Note that the size of the voltage depends upon:

*(a) the velocity (V) of the wire relative to the magnetic field*
*(b) the length of the wire (l) cutting the magnetic field*
*(c) the strength of the magnetic field (B) thus, generated voltage $E = BlV$ volts*

This principle, discovered by Michael Faraday in 1834, underlies the operation of both the alternator and the dynamo.

**2** In order to increase the length of wire, coils are used; a group of coils is known as a winding. The magnetic flux density is, in practice, always enhanced by using an iron frame on which the field is wound, and this frame is usually constructed of thin laminations stacked to the required thickness. This prevents current being generated within the iron, which would cause wasteful heating and power loss.

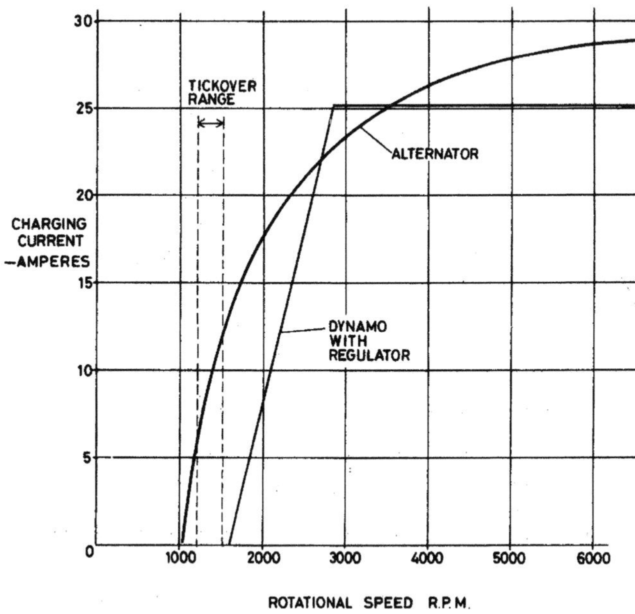


***Fig. 3.3 Generator output comparison between dynamo and alternator***

**3** Imagine now (Fig. 3.2B) the simple coil of the alternator which is cut by the magnetic field of the North and South poles of the rotating magnet. The voltage or electromotive force (emf) generated in the coil sides will change direction as the poles pass close by in cyclic rotation: N – S – N – S etc. Thus if the coil is connected to a complete circuit externally the current flowing will change direction at the same rate, or frequency, at which the poles rotate, hence the name alternating current.

**4** The number of revolutions per second of the magnet will also correspond to the number of repetitions, or cycles, per second of the current wave flowing back and forth through the coil.

**5** This number was defined originally in cycles per second, but is now called Hertz (Hz); thus 50 revolutions per second of the magnet will give a voltage or current frequency of 50 Hertz. A graph or waveform of the way in which the electric waves change with time is shown in Fig. 3.4 and is known as a sine wave.

## 4 Single-phase and three-phase generation

**1** An alternator which uses a simple pair of coils will produce a single sine wave of current. For small power requirements this is an adequate arrangement and so, for example, cycle dynamos and older types of motorcycle alternators produced a single-phase output, requiring two wires only. In the automobile, only a few types of small European cars have used single-phase alternators.

**2** It can be easily imagined that if, instead of two sets of coils 180° apart, the alternator had several sets spread around the iron frame, then the rotating magnet would be able to generate more electricity. This is in fact the case, and it is common to use three pairs of coils to form the stationary winding (hence the name stator), but there has to be a special way of connecting them to bring out the power.

**3** If a rotating magnet sweeps past the three sets of coils, then each will produce a sine wave of induced voltage but in sequence. Since a complete revolution of the magnet corresponds to 360° rotation, then each sine wave of voltage will be 120° apart from the other two (Fig. 3.5). Each coil will have the same voltage generated within it by the rotating magnetic field, but there is a time difference corresponding to the time it takes the magnet to travel from one coil to the next, from 1 to 2, 2 to 3, 3 to 1, etc.

**4** It is possible to avoid using six output wires by connecting the coils together in either a 'star' or a 'delta' configuration. Fig. 3.6 shows these connections, both of which are possible for vehicle alternators, although the star is more usual.

**5** The star connection will result in a higher voltage between any pair of output terminals than is generated by one coil alone, but will not be twice one coil voltage because of the time phase difference between any pair. In fact the voltage between lines (as the output leads are called) is 1.732 x coil voltage. In the delta connection the output voltage will be that of any coil in value, but the currents generated in each coil will add to give a line current of 1.732 x one coil current. Where heavy current is required the stator windings are connected in delta.

## 5 Rectification – converting ac to dc

**1** The vehicle battery acts as a storage unit for electrical energy and is a direct current device. Current flowing out from it is direct current as is the current flowing into it when being charged.

**2** It is necessary to convert the alternating current from the alternator into a form of direct current before it is useful in a vehicle. Referring to Fig. 3.4, the sine wave shows that alternating current flows first one way round a circuit and then in the opposite direction. If the lower half of the sine wave could be eliminated then current would flow in pulses, but always in the same direction. For battery charging this pulsation of current does not matter, and an ammeter would register the average value of current.

**3** A device which will prevent current flowing in one direction, but allow it to flow in the opposite direction, is called a rectifier. Modern rectifiers are usually made of semiconductor materials and are highly efficient. Fig. 3.7 shows a simple circuit consisting of an alternator

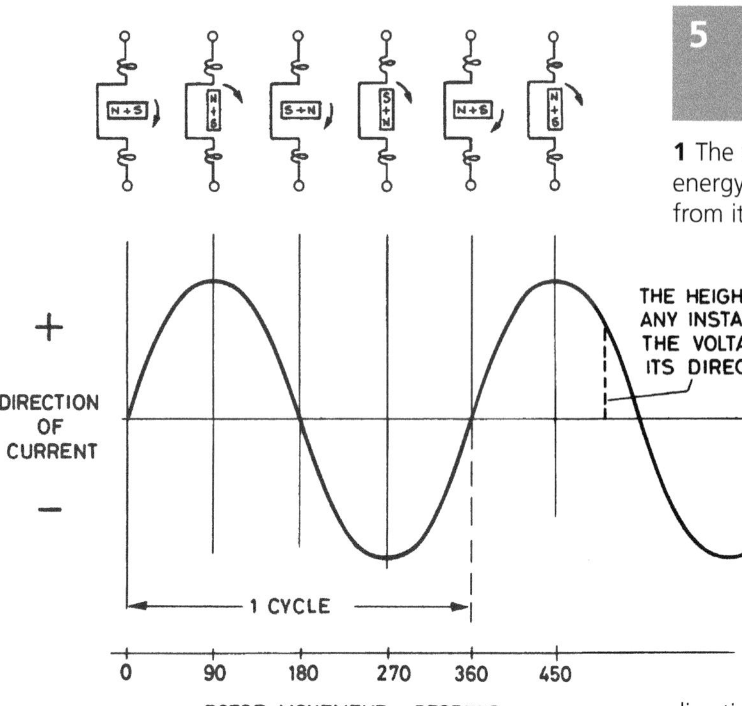


*Fig. 3.4 Curve of alternator voltage*

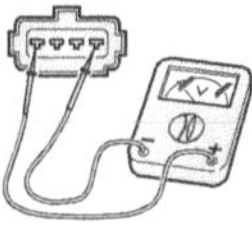

connected to a resistive load, via a rectifier. The lower half of the current wave is stopped by the rectifier, allowing pulses to flow through the resistor, but always in the same direction – that is, direct current. For obvious reasons this is known as half-wave rectification: it is inefficient because the lower half of the current wave is wasted.

**4** A better method of conversion is to use full-wave rectification. As the name implies the whole of the alternating sine wave is used, and to accomplish this, four rectifiers are used, as in Fig. 3.8. The alternator will produce an output voltage which changes polarity so that it is, in effect, like a battery which rapidly reverses its leads.

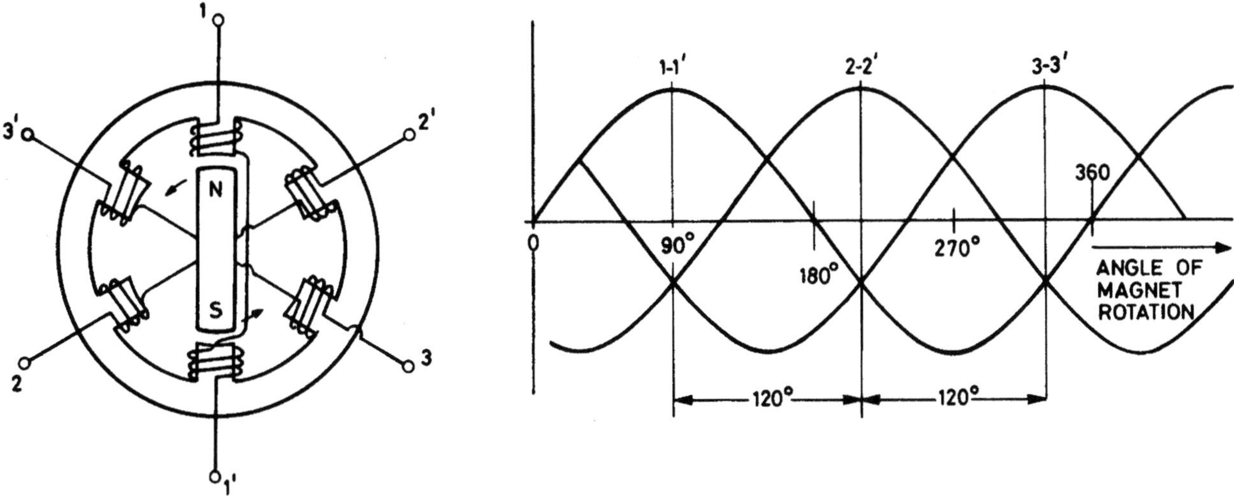


*Fig. 3.5 Three-phase alternator and its waveform*

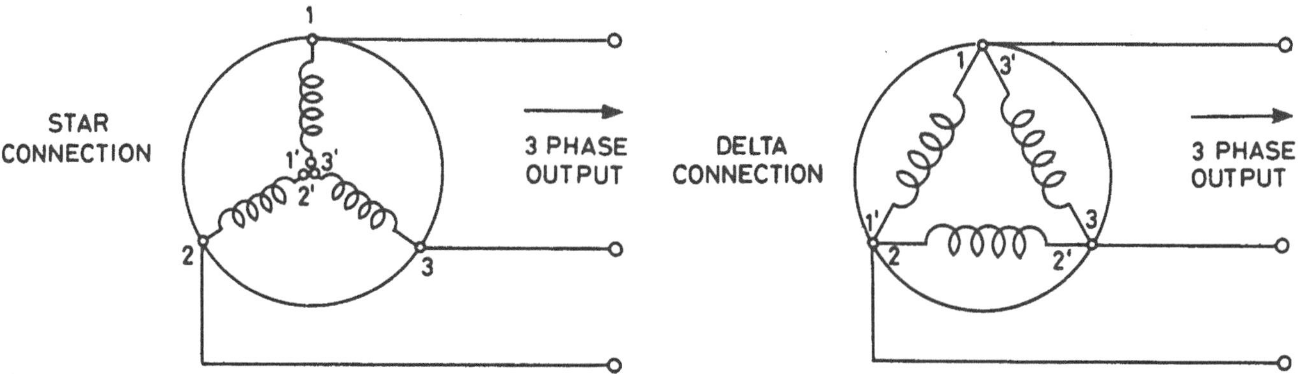


*Fig. 3.6 Star and delta connections*

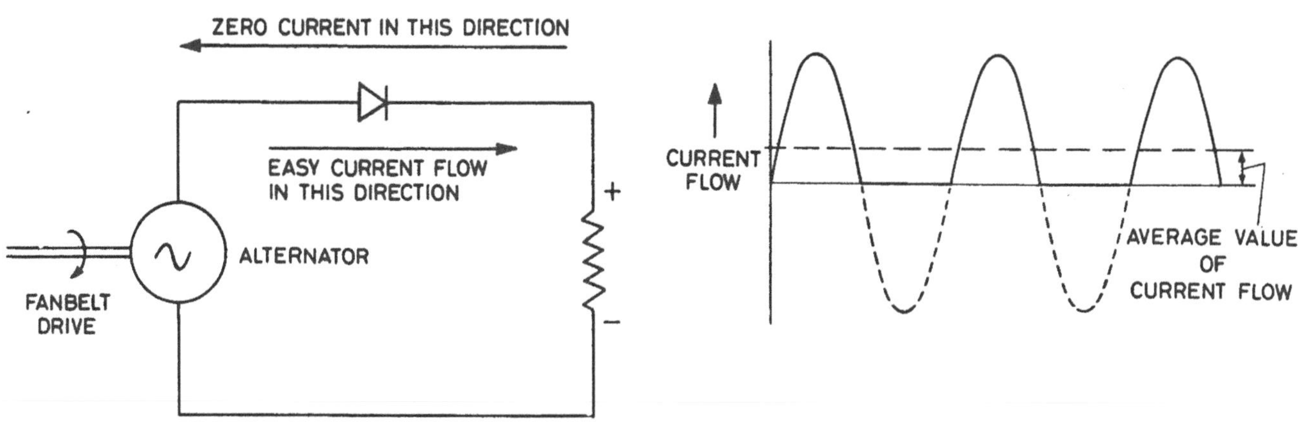


*Fig. 3.7 Half-wave rectification*

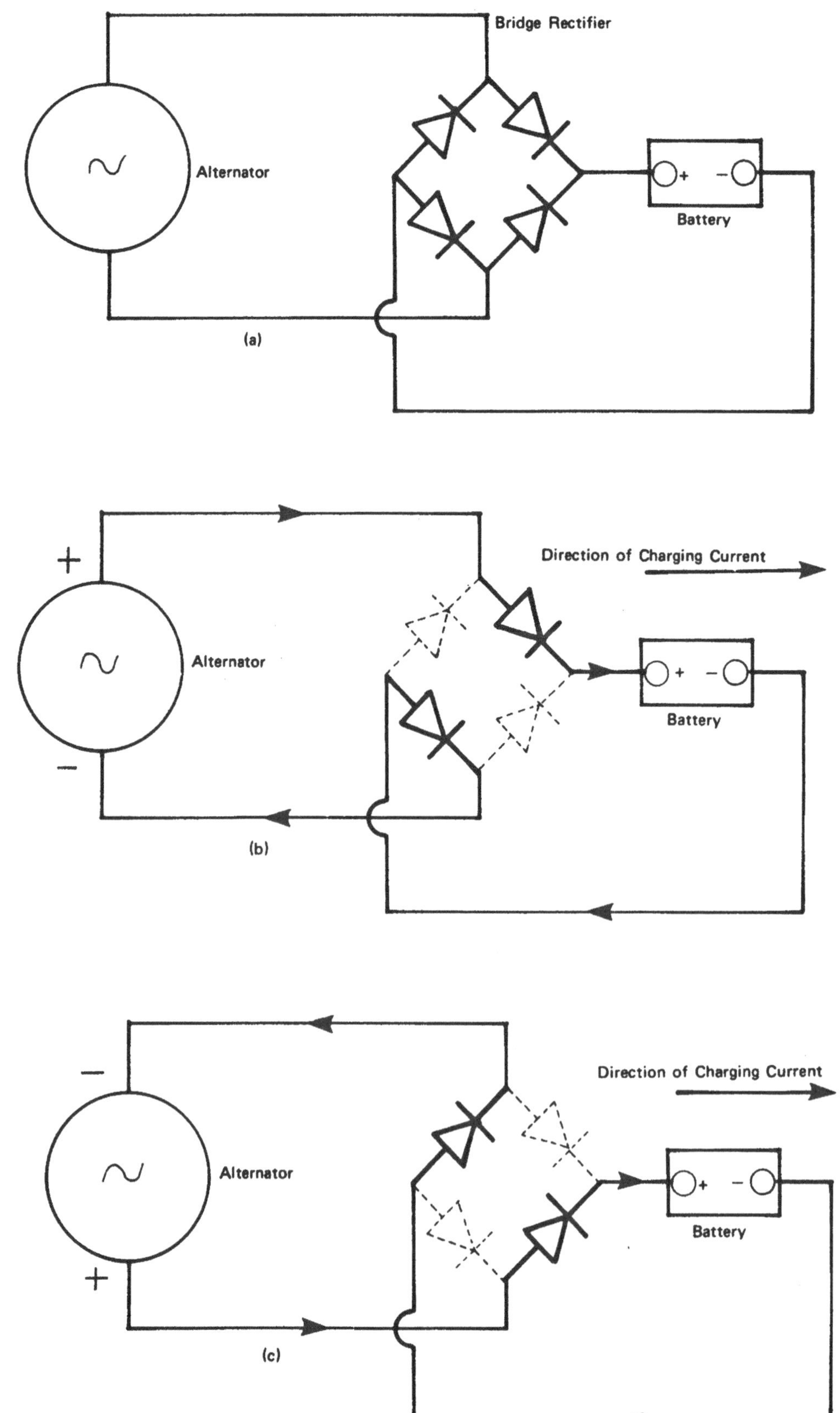


*Fig. 3.8 Action of the full-wave rectifier*

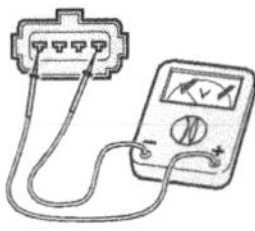

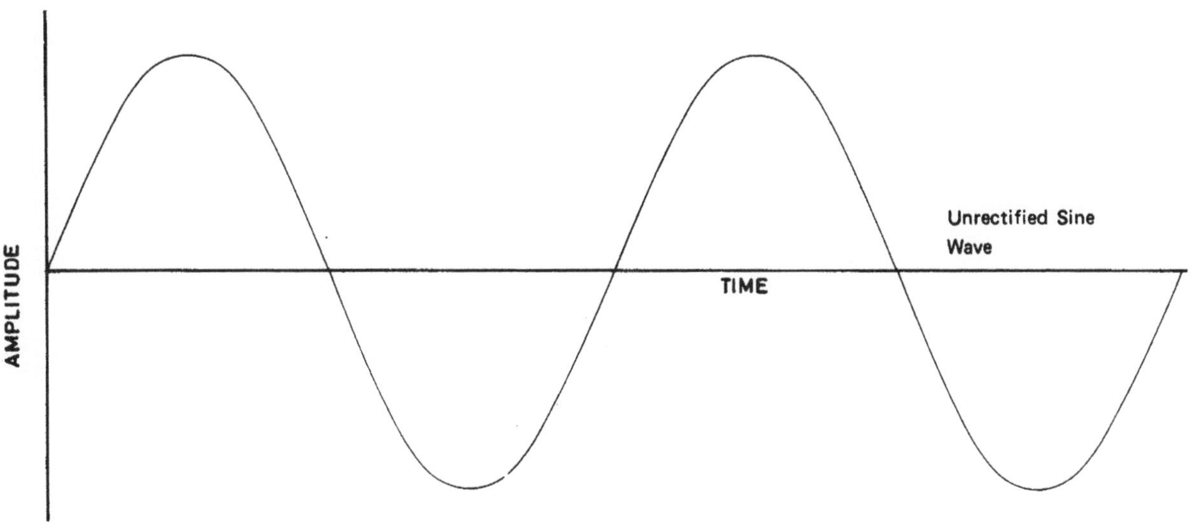


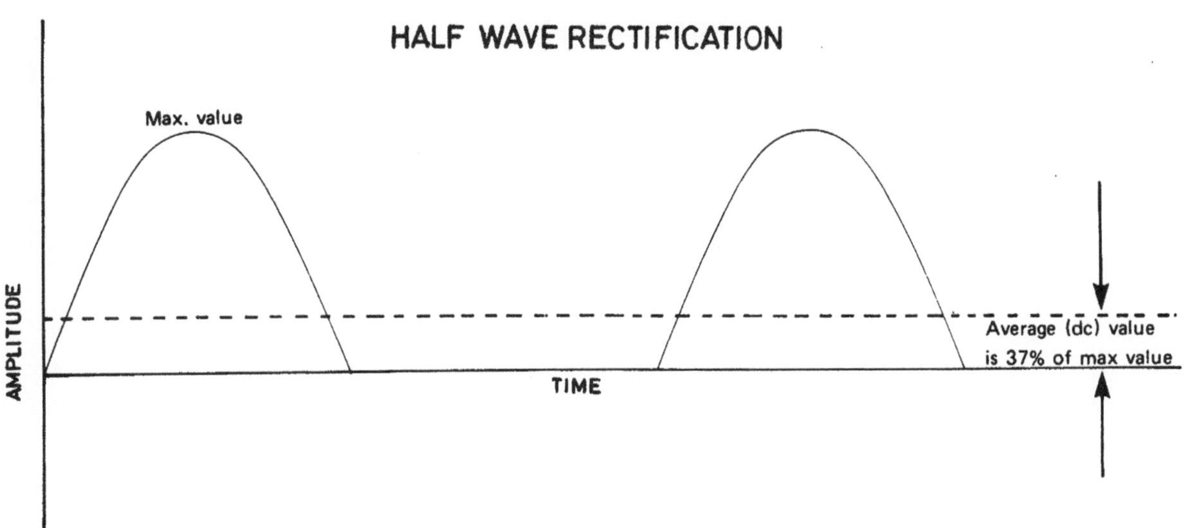

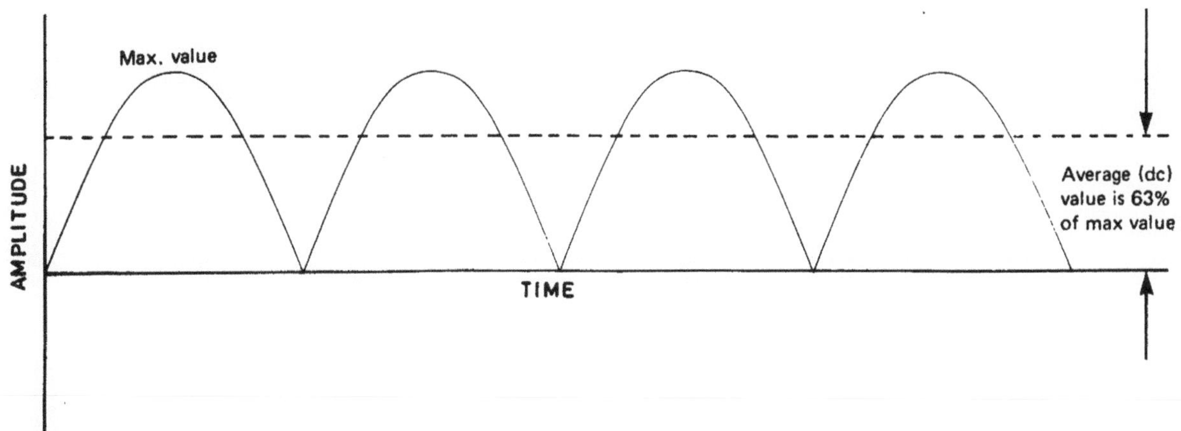


*Fig. 3.9 Alternating current and rectified waveforms*

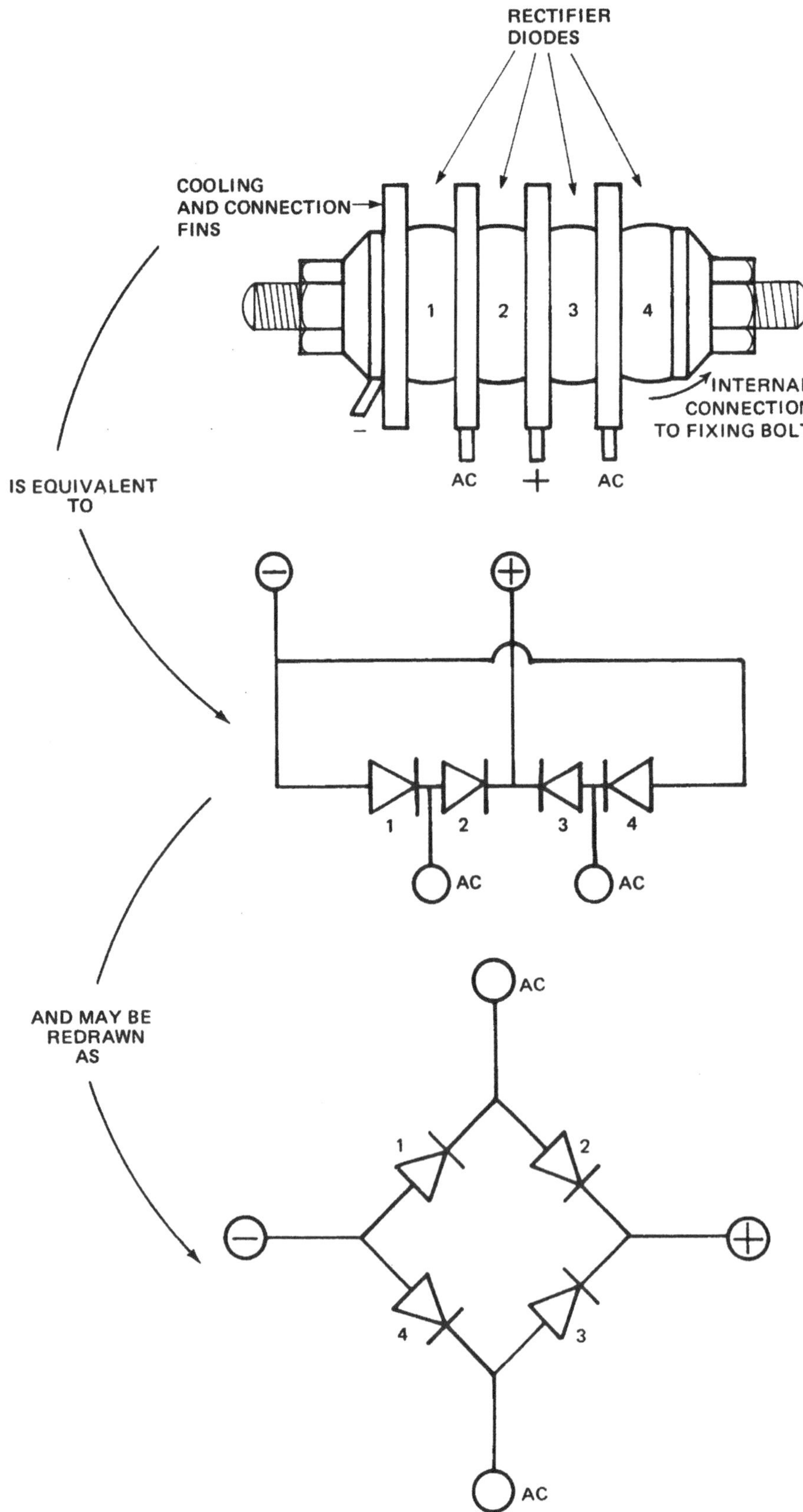


*Fig. 3.10 Layout of a full-wave rectifier*

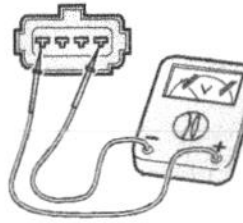

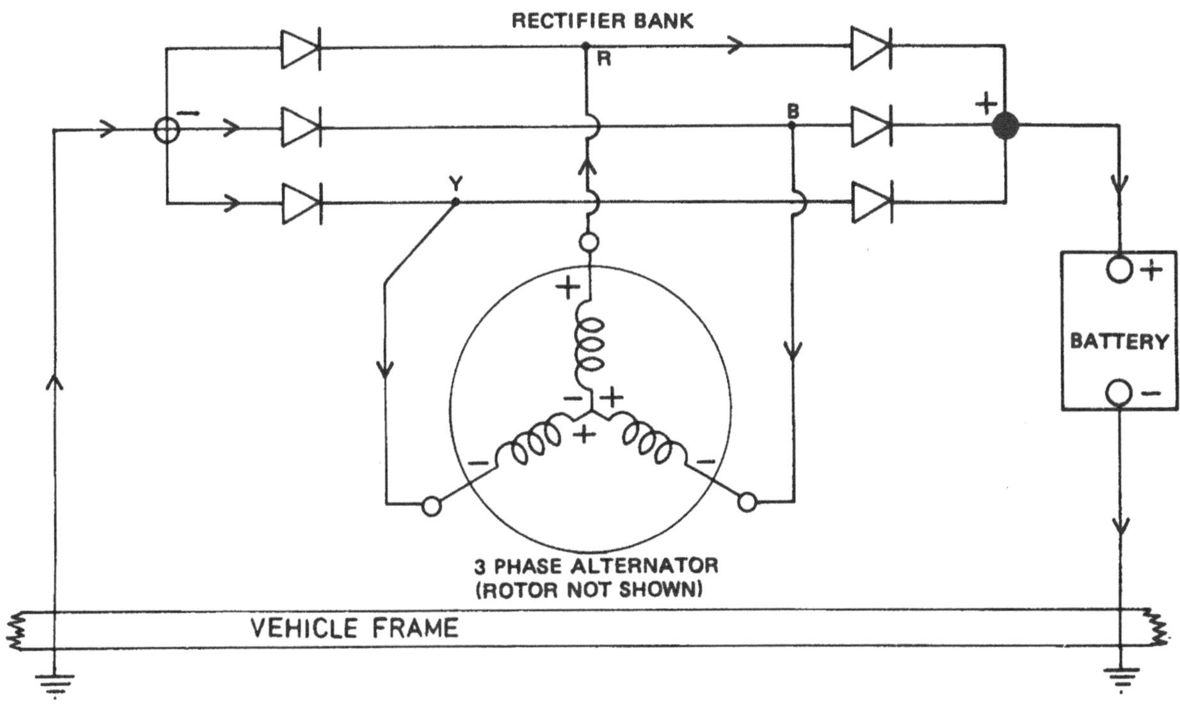


*Fig. 3.11 Three-phase rectification. Current flow is at instant of R phase at maximum voltage*

**5** Current will flow through a rectifier in the direction of the arrow, but not against it, so if the + ve wire at the alternator is traced through, current will flow through the battery and two rectifiers. When the polarity reverses, current flows through the opposite pair of rectifiers, but always in the same direction through the battery. Thus the whole of the ac wave has been caused to pass to the battery. Fig. 3.9 shows the waveforms for both half- and full-wave rectifiers. The physical layout of one type of full-wave rectifier is shown in Fig. 3.10. The individual rectifier elements are often known as diodes, or sometimes as diode rectifiers.

**6** Three-phase rectification is along the same lines as the full-wave rectifier shown (often called a bridge rectifier). Fig. 3.11 shows a three-phase alternator connected to a three-phase full-wave rectifier. The effect of reversing each negative half cycle is to give an output voltage or current which has a high average value and a much lower ripple than for the single-phase case. In fact there will be six 'half-waves' per 360° on the diagram shown (Fig. 3.12) and the average value of direction current or voltage is not much short of the peak value.

Note that this is not a diagram of a complete charging circuit since some form of regulating the alternator output is needed.

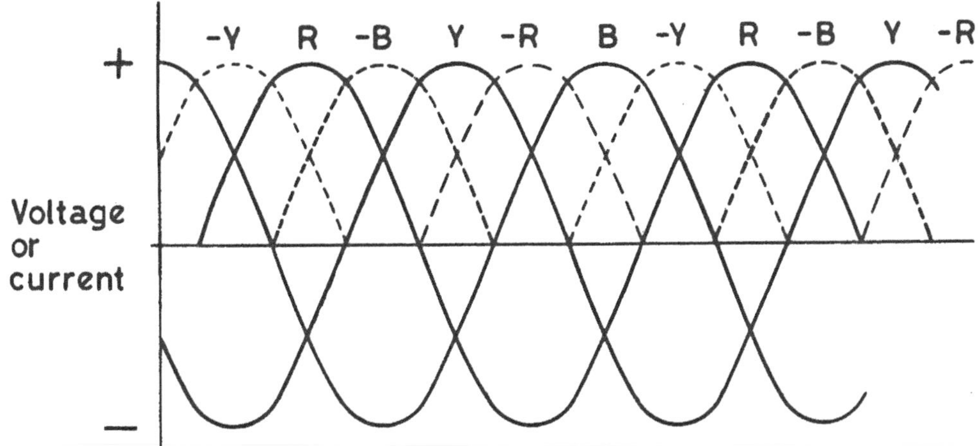


*Fig. 3.12 Waveforms of the full-wave three-phase rectifier*

**7** The three-phase alternator is made with this number of phases on the grounds of efficiency, so that most of the stator is used up with windings, thus giving high output. Any one of the three windings generates a single sine wave, ie a single-phase output.

**8** Some French manufacturers use a single-phase alternator in vehicles where the higher wattage output of a three-phase machine is not essential. This single-phase alternator is cheaper to produce and the rectifier stack will be of the simple single-phase full-wave type. The control principles remain the same, in that the alternator output voltage (or battery voltage) determines the direct current feed to the rotating field winding, as explained in the following Section.

## 6 Field excitation

**1** Excitation is a term used by electrical engineers to mean the provision of a magnetic field. The simple magnet shown so far in this chapter will produce alternating current and voltage in the stationary (stator) windings of an alternator but, in general, permanent magnets are anything but permanent when subjected to vibrations and heat.

**2** It is usual to make the rotor in the form of an electromagnet, that is, of soft steel or iron in which magnetism is induced by a coil of wire carrying direct current, the coil being wound round the steel/iron. The magnetism will vary in strength according to the coil current and there is the additional advantage of being able to control the magnetic field strength, and hence the value of alternating voltage generated, in the stator winding.

**3** If the rotor coil were wound on an iron frame as shown in Fig. 3.13a, then a pair of magnetic poles, North (N) and South (S), would be produced. Because of the long air path the magnetic field lines would be feeble. Imagine now the ends of the iron stretched out to give two annuli facing each other with a small air gap (Fig. 3.13b). Finally, if the iron ends were shaped to interlock, but without touching like two sets of claws, then the magnetic field lines would pass from N to S, there being considerable 'leakage' externally, and it is this leakage which, when cutting the surrounding stator winding, generates the required electrical output (Fig. 3.14).

**4** Note that the rotor must be supplied with dc through brushes and slip rings in order to produce the unvarying North and South poles; two methods of feeding the direct current are in use, self excitation and battery excitation.

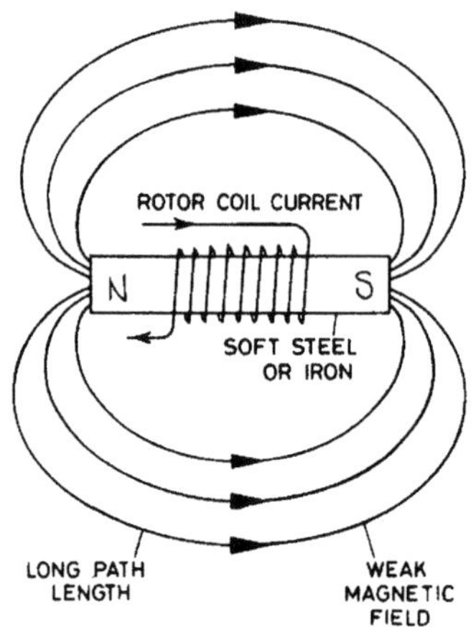


*Fig. 3.13a Simple electromagnet*

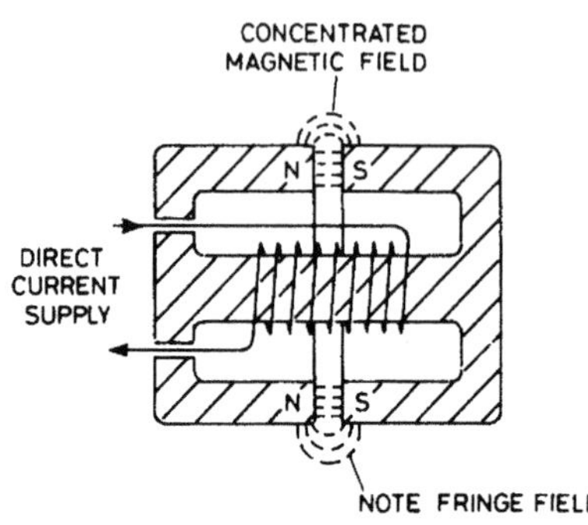


***Fig. 3.13b Ends of an electromagnet folded over to concentrate magnetic field***

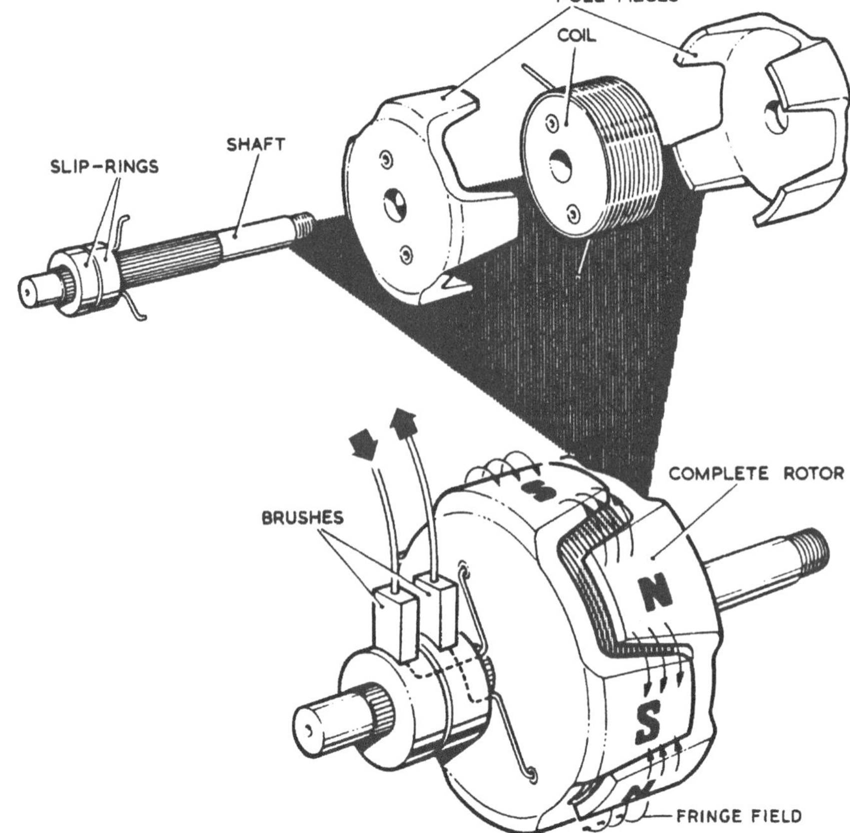


***Fig. 3.14 Claw-pole alternator rotor***

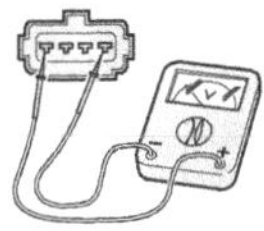

## 7 Self excitation

**1** The iron core of the rotor will possess some residual magnetism but not enough to guarantee that the alternator will start to generate when rotated. The 2.2 watt charge warning lamp connected from the battery to the rotor via the ignition switch gives sufficient rotor current to set up a magnetic field strong enough to give generation.

**2** This bulb also serves as a no-charge warning lamp and will glow when the ignition is switched on but, when the engine drives the alternator, the field diodes produce a supply to the rotor and the lamp is extinguished, since there will be no voltage difference across it. It follows from this that the rotor is supplied with a voltage approximately equal to that of the battery.

**3** In practice, the bulb also has a resistor connected across it, so the alternator will start even in the event of bulb failure. Fig. 3.15 shows the basic arrangement of the self-excited alternator and is distinguished from the battery-excited alternator by the use of nine diodes.

**4** When running, the alternator stator provides all the excitation current – hence the name 'self excitation'. The battery serves only to start up the generation.

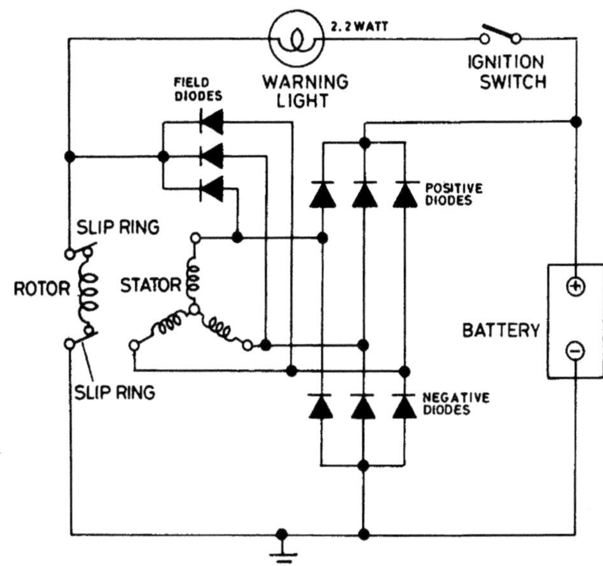


*Fig. 3.15 Self-excited alternator*

## 8 Battery excitation

**1** The vehicle battery supplies the rotor in this method, the means of connection being via a pair of slip rings and brushes. Some means must be provided to disconnect the battery from the rotor (field) when the alternator stops, otherwise the battery would run flat, and this is achieved by a cut-out, or field isolating relay.

**2** Fig. 3.16 shows a simplified arrangement of a battery-excited alternator connected to a battery. When the ignition switch is closed, battery current flows through the coil of the relay, pulling the hinged armature down and closing the contacts (Fig. 3.17). Closure of the contacts connects the battery straight on to the field winding of the rotor. The flow of direct current creates the necessary magnetic field to generate ac power in the stator windings.

**3** The terminal AL is used to operate a dashboard warning light which will glow at engine standstill with the ignition on, but extinguish when the alternator begins to charge. With battery excitation alternators it is necessary to use a thermal (or similar) control device in conjunction with the warning light, the Lucas system being given as an example in the next Section.

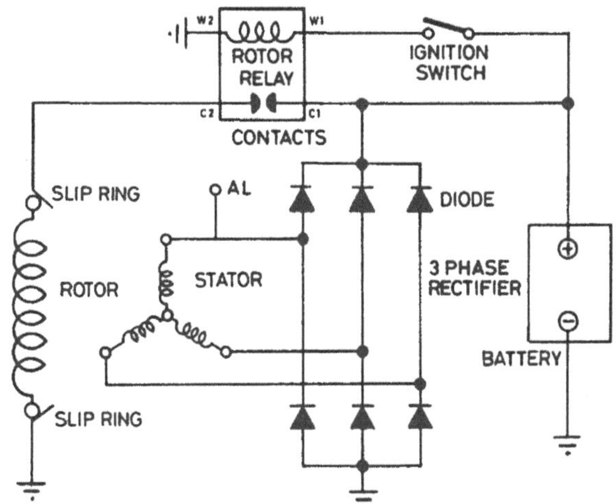


*Fig. 3.16 Battery-excited alternator*

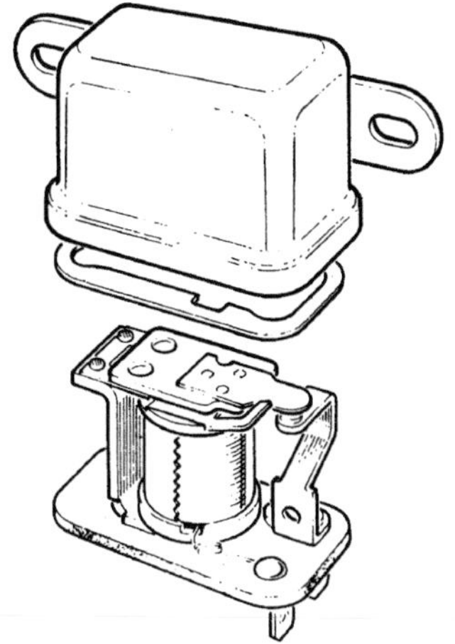

*Fig. 3.17 6RA field isolating relay*

## 9 Warning light control

**1** The Lucas 3AW warning light control has three terminals:

- AL – to the alternator AL terminal
- E – connected to a good earth (ground) point on the vehicle
- WL – connected to the warning light bulb and, through the ignition switch, to the battery

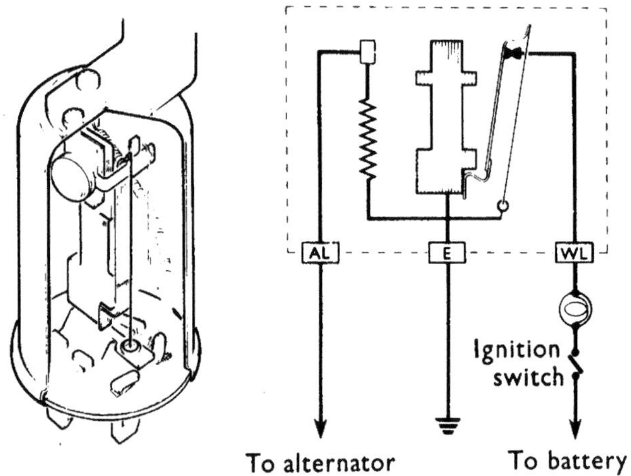


*Fig. 3.18 3AW warning light control*

**2** Fig. 3.18 shows a thin, stretched resistance wire, one end of which goes to earth terminal E and the other via a resistor to terminal AL. Note the contacts are closed at engine standstill by the tension of the wire. Thus, with the ignition on, the warning light will glow. When the alternator output builds up, the current from AL heats up the stretched wire which expands; it has less tension, the spring action of the earth connector strip snaps open the contacts and the warning light goes out.

**3** Battery excitation is now obsolete, but is included here since many vehicles with it are still on the road.

## 10 Regulators

**1** The alternator, being driven by the vehicle engine, is a variable speed machine. As speed rises, the generated voltage rises and, run without a load, could reach 140 volts. Clearly, some control is needed and is well provided by the modern electronic regulator.

**2** The regulator maintains a constant average current in the rotor field winding by switching the current on and off, and the result is an alternator output voltage of about 14.2 volts. Early regulators were of the vibrating-contact type, not unlike those used with direct current dynamos, but present day practice is to use semiconductor circuits. The vibrating-contact regulator is described later in this chapter.

**3** The operating principle of the semiconductor regulator may be explained using a simplified Bosch circuit of their regulator EE14V3 (Fig. 3.19), which has had a period of well-proven reliability: The regulator uses a power stage of two transistors T2 and T3 connected as a Darlington pair to drive current through the field winding of the alternator rotor. Transistors in this configuration give a large power gain and are found in alternator control and in ignition circuits.

The power stage is controlled by transistor T1 and its associated components.

When the alternator output is below the desired regulation voltage of 14.2 volts, the Zener diode ZD does not conduct and so no current flows into the base of transistor T1. Also $R_6$

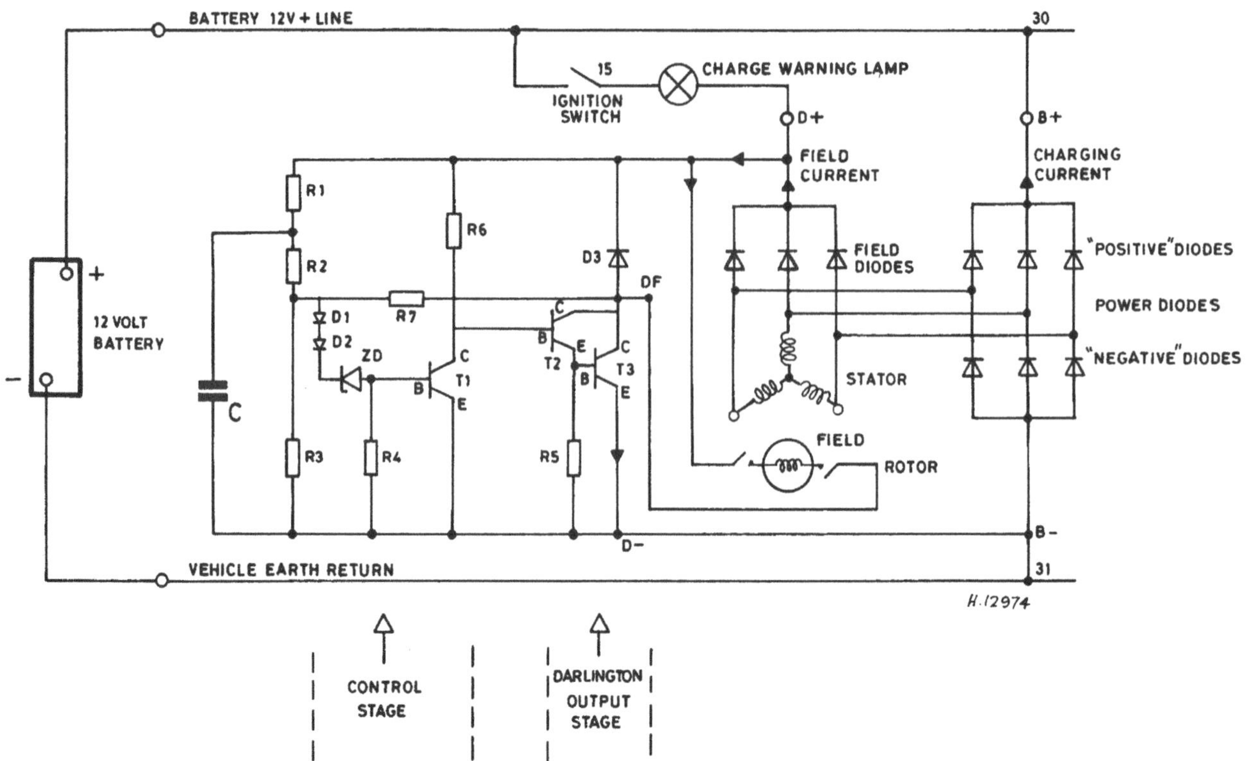


*Fig. 3.19 Electronic voltage regulator*

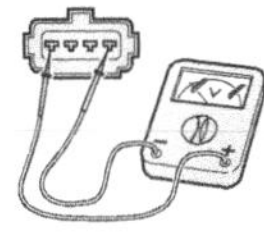

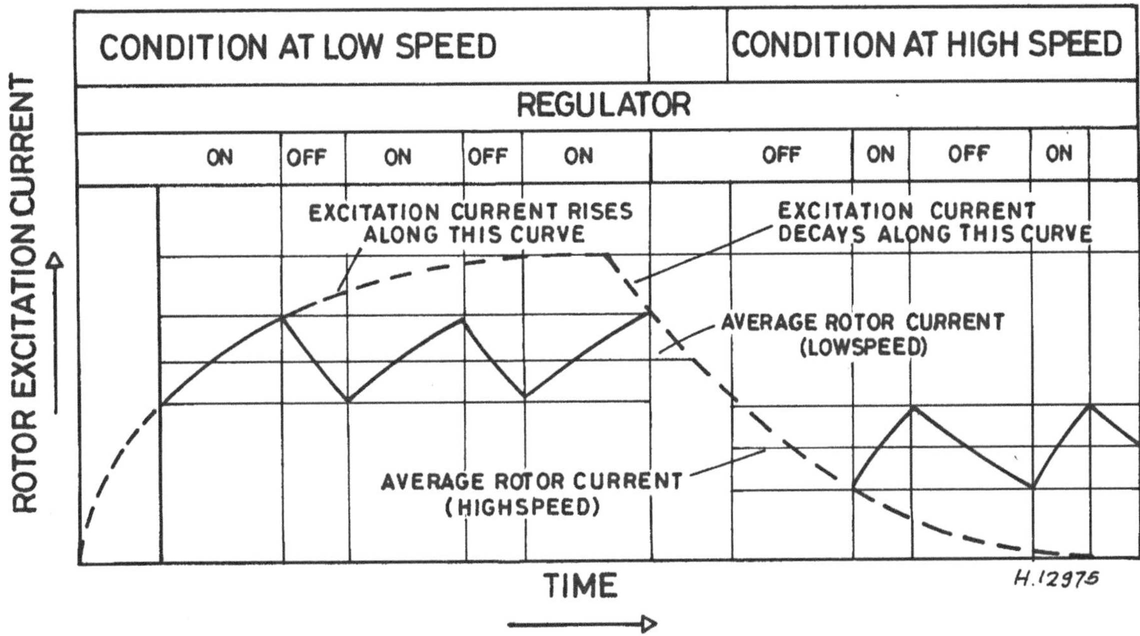


*Fig. 3.20 Rotor current switching*

will allow base current flow into T2 which is therefore ON (ie current flows between collector and emitter). With a Darlington pair, if the first transistor T2 is ON, so is the power transistor T3 since the emitter current of T2 provides base current for T3 by direct connection. Current flows through the rotor field winding causing the alternator to generate a rising voltage.

As the alternator rises to the 14.2 volt level, the voltage across the divider circuit $R_1R_2R_3$ will rise also. When the voltage at the junction of $R_2R_3$ reaches the breakdown voltage of the Zener diode ZD, this conducts and passes current into the base of transistor T1, causing a volt drop across $R_6$ sufficient to switch T2 OFF.

This switches off T3 simultaneously and so

The rotor current is switched off with a consequent fall in generated voltage by the alternator.

The generated voltage now falls until the Zener diode ZD switches off, cutting T1 OFF and again allowing base current to flow into T2, thus switching the rotor current on again. The output voltage rises and falls about the mean level of 14.2 volts, and so regulation of the alternator voltage has occurred.

## Circuit details

**4** At the instant when the transistor T3 cuts off current to the rotor, a high induced voltage will appear across the rotor due to its inductance (see Lenz' Law – Chapter 1, Section 23). D3 is a protection diode (sometimes called a free-wheeling diode) and will absorb this voltage surge acting as a (near) short circuit path across the rotor. Because of the rotor inductance also, when T3 conducts again, the rotor current does not rise instantly but exponentially as shown in Fig. 3.20. The rise and fall of rotor current will average out to the required regulated voltage; note that the average rotor current will be lower at high speed because the stator windings will be cut at a higher rate by the rotor field. $R_1$ and C form a filter to smooth out the ripple in the supply voltage. D1 and D2 are diodes which have a volt-drop when conducting which varies with temperature. They act as temperature compensators such that the output voltage is temperature stabilised, but will cause the output voltage to rise slightly in winter conditions to compensate for heavier lighting and other winter loads (Fig. 3.21). $R_7$ acts as a feedback resistor, picking up voltage changes at the T3 collector and sending them back to the input stage. The result of this is to speed up the ON–OFF transitions and make them more precise.

**5** Hybrid regulators involve the use of circuit components such as resistors and capacitors in association with film techniques having transistors and integrated circuits on a ceramic substrate. The advantages are still further reduction

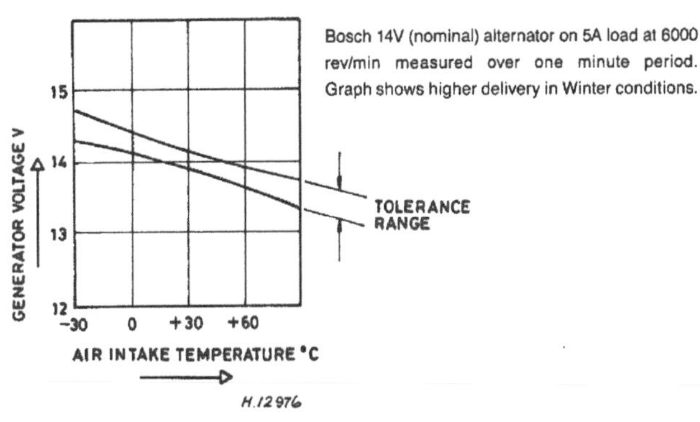


*Fig. 3.21 Regulator characteristics*

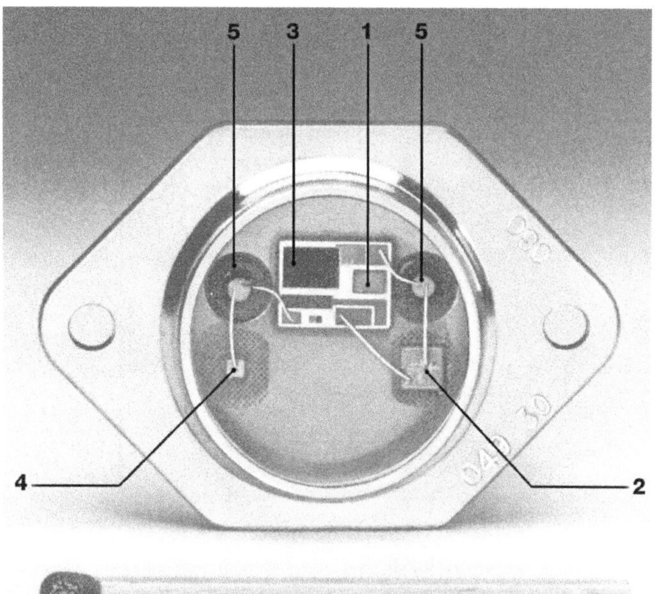


*Fig. 3.22 Hybrid regulator for alternator*

*1 Integrated circuit control stage*
*2 Power stage*
*3 Series resistors*
*4 Protection diode*
*5 Connection leads*

in size with fewer components and connections (Fig. 3.22). Basic principles of operation remain the same and the trend is towards adoption of hybrid regulators as a standard item

## Engine Management controlled systems

**6** On some late model vehicles, the output of the alternator is controlled by the engine management ECM (Electronic Control Module). At certain times (cold starts etc.) the load of driving the alternator can effect the level of emissions from the exhaust system. To lower the emissions levels at these time, the ECM prevent any output from the alternator until the engine has warmed up sufficiently for the emissions level to have dropped, and the catalytic converter has begun functioning.

On some vehicles, the ECM prevents alternator output, when high levels of engine load are demanded by the driver. A modern vehicle electrical system demands a high output alternator, which, when under load, takes a significant amount of power from the engine to drive it. Consequently, if the alternator output is cut, more engine power is available to propel the vehicle. As soon as the engine load demand drops, the alternator output is restored.

# 11 Vibrating contact regulator

**1** Though largely superseded by electronic regulators, the vibrating contact type is still worthy of study, for many vehicles in service still have them. They come in two types, namely the single-contact and the double-contact regulator.

**2** In the former type, the rotor winding is connected directly to the alternator output via a single pair of contacts. When the contacts open, a resistor is connected in circuit, thus reducing the rotor current (and so the alternator voltage) until the lower limit is reached when the contacts close again under spring pressure and short out the resistor (Fig. 3.23).

**3** Whichever method is used, a vital factor is the self-inductance of the rotor winding. Inductance is a property of coils in that current in them cannot change instantaneously, but rises or falls at a rate fixed by circuit parameters. Coils wound on iron frames have a much higher inductance than if air-cored and, indeed, inductance is defined in terms of the

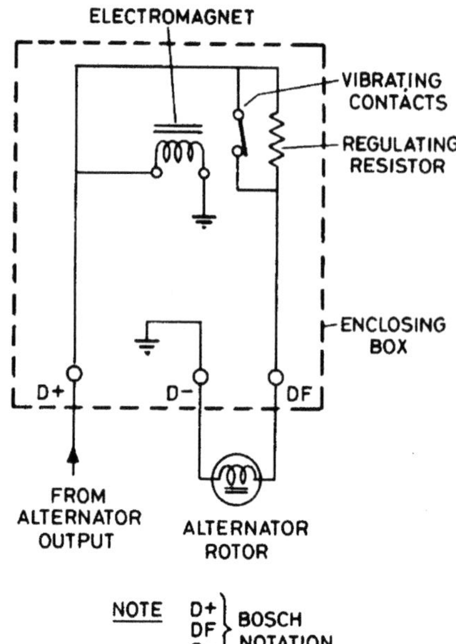


*Fig. 3.23 Single contact regulator*

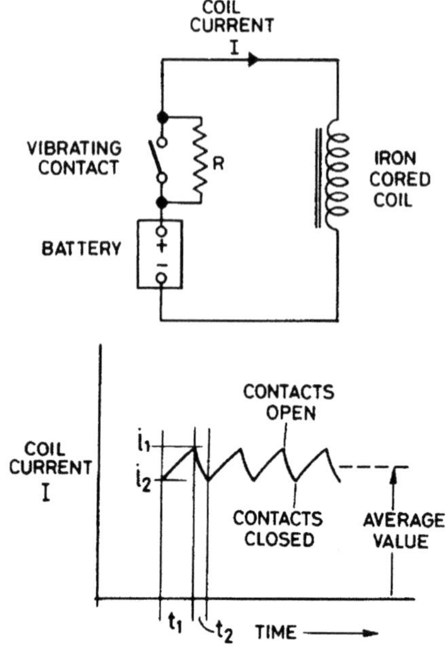


*Fig. 3.24 Vibrating contact control of coil current*

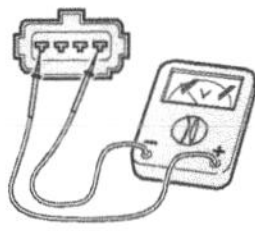

magnetic field produced by an ampere of current through the coil concerned. The greater the inductance, the slower will be the rate of current change.

**4** Fig. 3.24 shows an iron-cored coil connected to a battery via a pair of contacts which are arranged to open when the current reaches a certain value, $i_1$, and to close when the current falls to $i_2$. Note that when the contacts open, current falls because the resistor R is now in series with the coil. The important feature is the time lag for current fall, $t_1$, and for current rise, $t_2$. If the contacts can be operated at a fast rate the actual current flow will vary within a small range, and correspond closely to a steady average value.

**5** The double-contact regulator has a number of advantages over the single-contact type. For best performance of regulators the resistor should be kept to a low value so that the vibrating contacts handle a small change of current and hence have a longer life. However, at high rotor speeds a high resistance is required to reduce the rotor current quickly when the contacts open. Meeting both requirements is difficult, so a second contact was introduced which earths (grounds) the rotor at the upper end of the alternator voltage range.

**6** The advantages are that the voltage falls quickly, and also that a lower value of regulating resistance may be used. A direct consequence is that the contacts can now handle a larger rotor current, a desirable feature in alternator design.

**7** Fig. 3.25 shows a double-contact regulator. At low speeds the operation is the same as for a single-contact type. When the speed is higher the contacts change over so that the moving centre contact now connects to the earthed contact, thus shorting out the rotor, giving a rapid fall in magnetisation and alternator voltage. As with the single-contact type, spring pressure returns the moving contact to connect with the D terminal, ie alternator output line, and so the voltage rises again.

**8** When the contacts open, an inductive voltage will be generated in the rotor winding. In the case of single-contact regulators, a diode may be incorporated across the rotor to absorb transients. Double-contact regulators may use a resistor permanently connected across the rotor, the purpose in both cases being to absorb contact sparks and so prolong contact life.

## 12 Temperature compensation

**1** The voltage regulator bobbin has a shunt coil which has many turns of fine copper wire. Copper wire increases in resistance with temperature at a rate of 0.004 ohms, per ohm of resistance, per degree Celsius (a 0.4% increase for every degree rise in temperature). This means that the voltage applied (ie the alternator charging voltage) will have to be higher to operate the vibrating contacts, a consequence being that the battery will overcharge.

**2** Two methods are used to minimise this effect (see Fig. 3.26).

(a) *A swamp resistor is connected in series with the shunt coil. This resistor has zero change of resistance with temperature, and is also much higher in resistance than the shunt coil thus swamping out the effects of its resistance change.*

(b) *The leaf spring which holds the contacts closed is made of two strips of different metals (a bi-metal strip). As temperature rises one metal expands faster than the other, causing the strip to bend, thus reducing spring tension. This compensates for the fall-off in coil current which is due to the rise in resistance.*

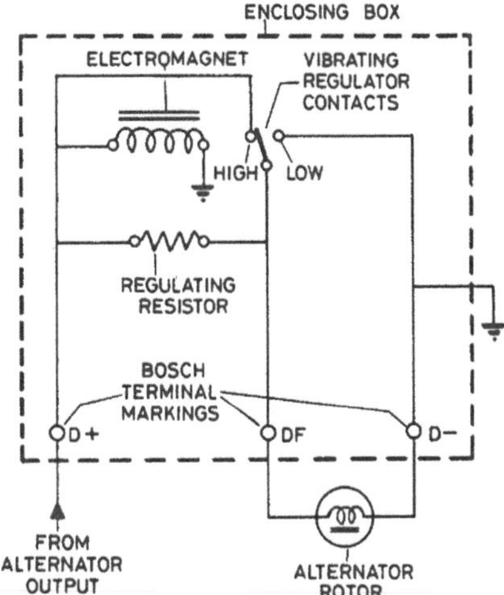


***Fig. 3.25 Double contact regulator outline circuit***

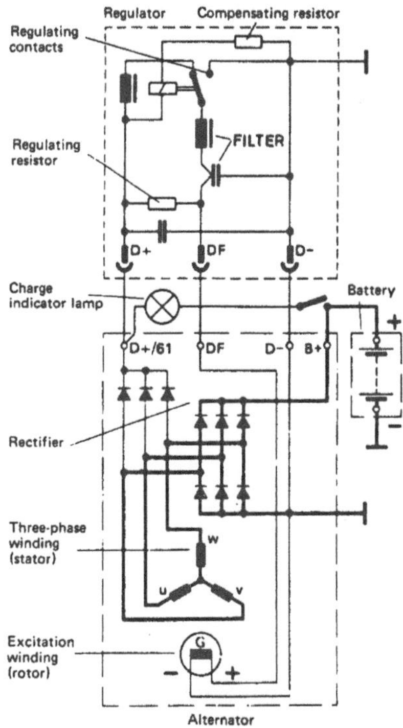


***Fig. 3.26 Double contact regulator with temperature compensation***

## 13 Regulator voltage sensing

**1** The alternator and regulator are usually located some distance from the battery. Due to vehicle electrical loads the dc voltage at the alternator may be different from the battery terminal voltage by the amount of volt-drop in the cable to the point where vehicle loads are taken off.

**2** The battery terminal voltage may be sensed by a separate lead going directly from the + battery or solenoid terminal to the alternator regulator. This is **battery sensing** and connections are made to the B + regulator terminal (Fig. 3.27).

The result of such sensing is to adjust the alternator output to take account of a battery terminal voltage fall under load.

**3** An alternative approach is **machine sensing** in which the B+ regulator wire is connected internally to the + terminal. It is this wire which goes to the Zener diode and hence controls the switching on of the Zener, leading to regulation. The majority of alternators now use machine sensing. In machine sensing, therefore, the alternator is regulated at its design value irrespective of battery loading. Fig. 3.28 shows a Lucas ACR alternator with machine sensing regulation.

The feedback components $R_5$, $R_3$, $C_1$ and $C_2$ cause rapid switching of the Darlington power transistor T3 between the ON and OFF conditions, for it is important from heat considerations that T3 does not remain in the condition of high power dissipation (ie when the transistor is conducting somewhere between ON and OFF).

**4** Figs. 3.28 and 3.30 show a surge protection diode which will limit the alternator output voltage in the event of a battery connection break when the engine is running. The battery normally absorbs system voltage peaks which may be generated on the vehicle mainly from the ignition. If the battery becomes disconnected for any reason, voltage peaks could destroy transistors in the regulator box and the surge protection diode will act as a safeguard. These peaks are in addition to the marked rise in alternator dc output voltage which would occur upon battery disconnection while the engine is running if the surge protection diode were not used.

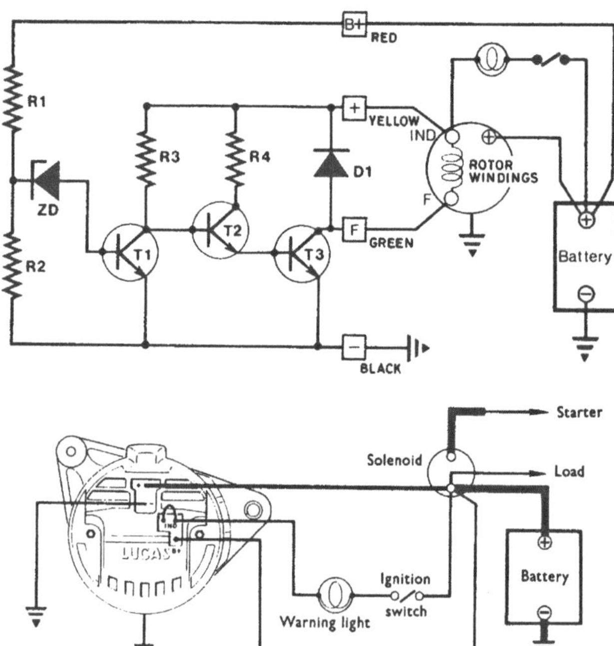


*Fig. 3.27 Battery sensing connections – Lucas system*

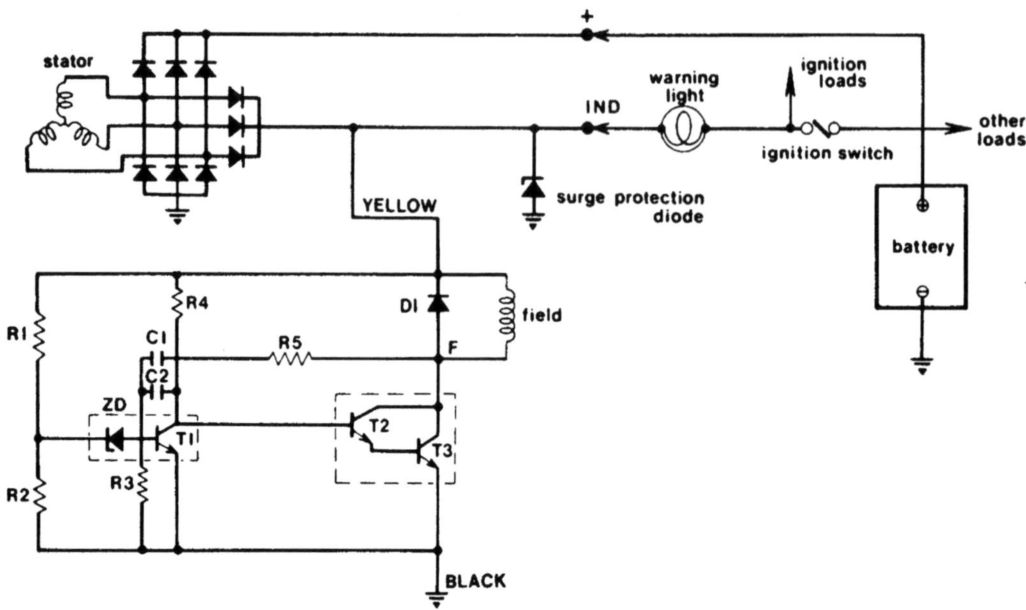


*Fig. 3.28 Lucas ACR alternator with 14TR machine sensing regulator*

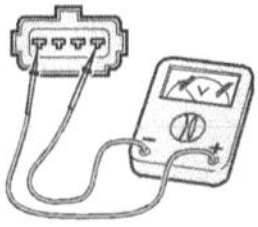

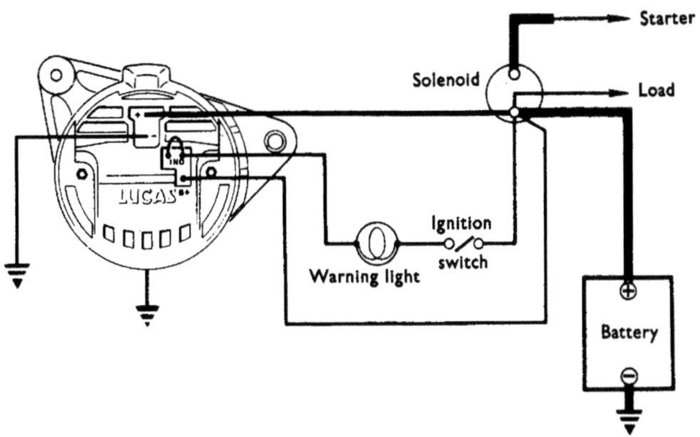


Fig. 3.29a ACR standard terminations – battery sensing

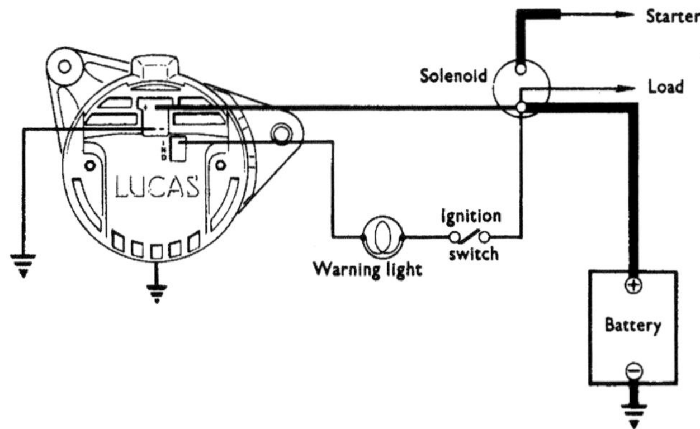


Fig. 3.29b ACR standard terminations – machine sensing

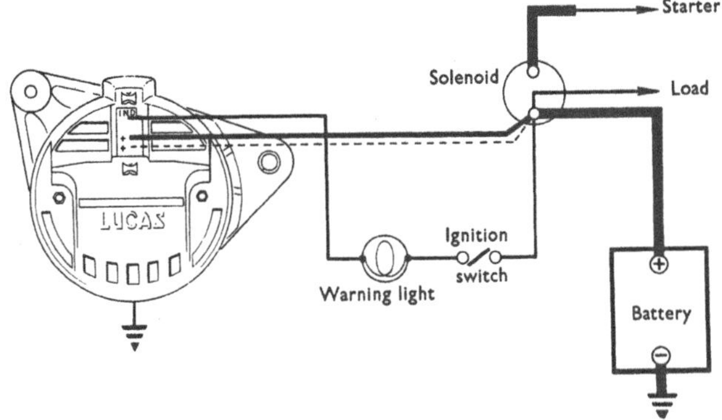


Fig. 3.29c ACR and A115/133 European terminations – machine sensing

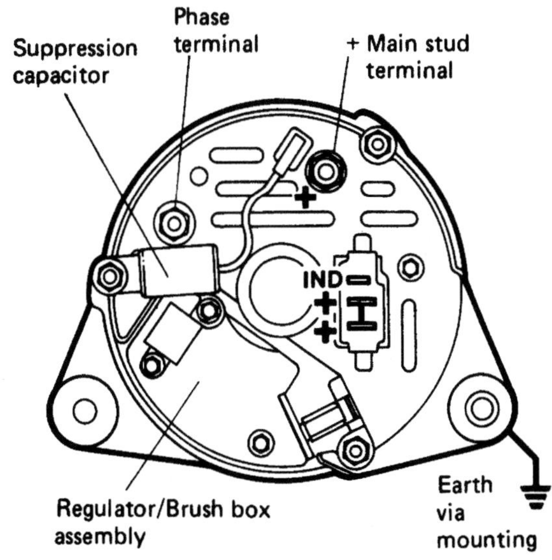


Fig. 3.29d Typical alternator terminals (A127)

## 14 Terminations

**1** Connections vary and some Lucas arrangements are shown in Fig. 3.29.

(a) *ACR battery sensed system*
(b) *ACR machine sensed system*
(c) *ACR and A115/133 European terminations (machine sensed)*
(d) *A127 alternator*

In Figs. 3.29c and 3.29d a double + Lucar blade is mainly to provide a good grip to the socket, but where the machine is rated over 35 A output, two main leads are used.

The A127 alternators from Lucas all have machine sensed regulators and most have Lucar blades (the European termination) and stud terminals for the main output connections. There is also a phase terminal giving 7 to 8 volts output (marked W on Lucas and Bosch machines) which may be used in a choke control application or for a tachometer.

**2** Bosch machines have stud terminals and sometimes blade plugs and sockets and are marked B +, D +, DF and D-, stamped on the end shield (Fig. 3.30). Note the surge protection diode (Bosch notation – uni-directional breakdown diode).

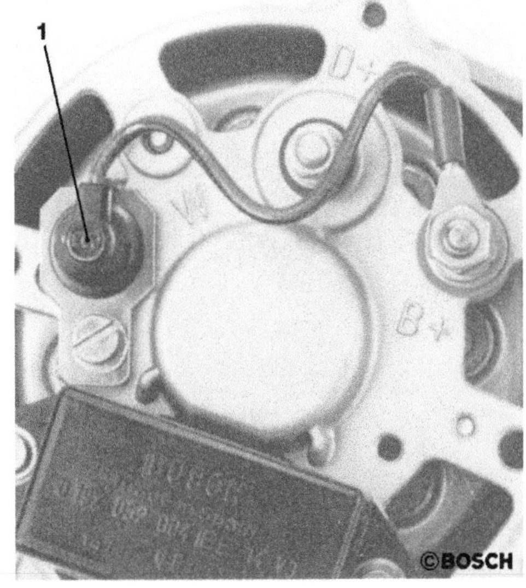


*Fig. 3.30 Bosch stud terminal markings*
*1 Surge protection diode*

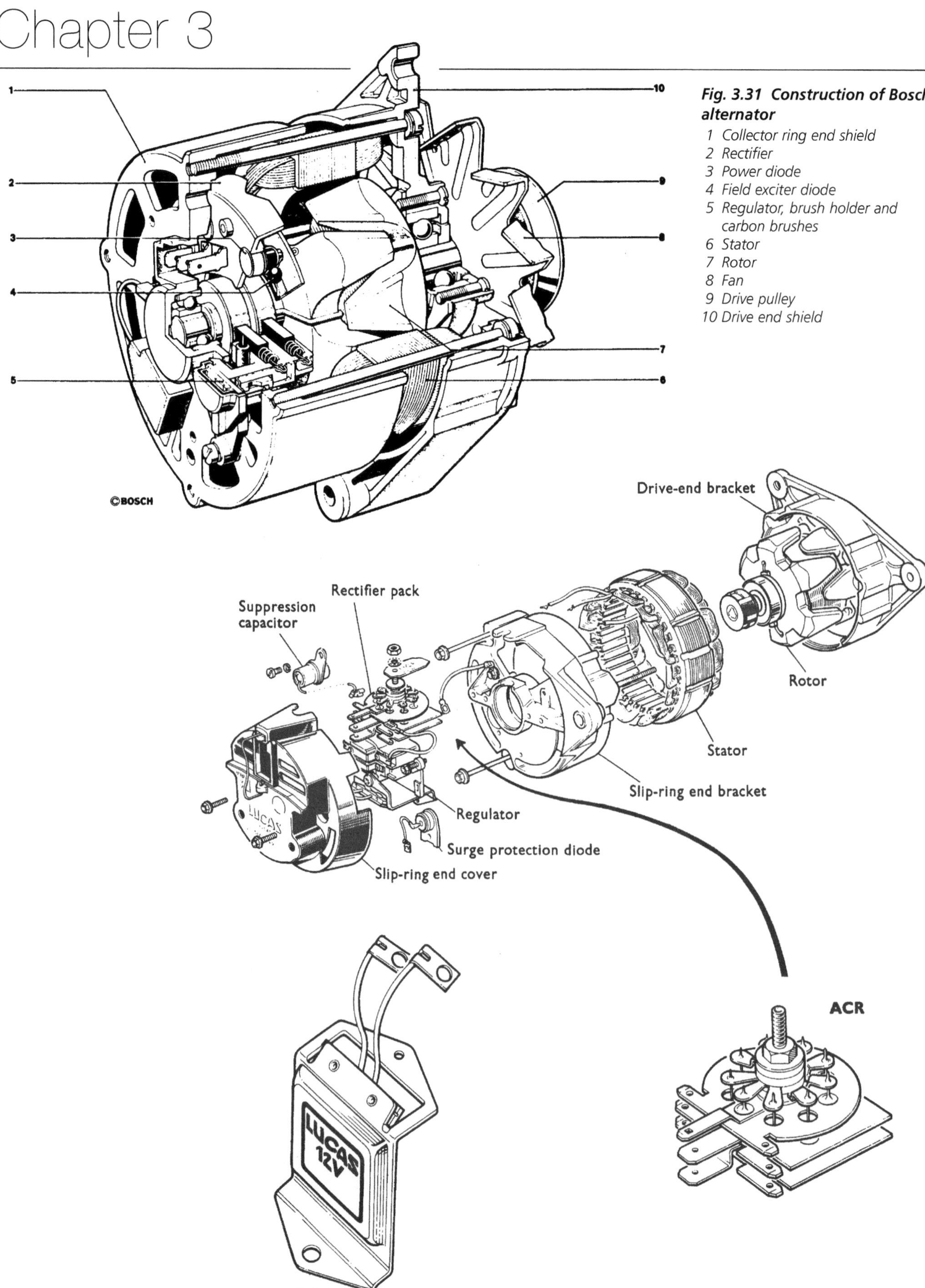


***Fig. 3.31 Construction of Bosch alternator***

*1 Collector ring end shield*
*2 Rectifier*
*3 Power diode*
*4 Field exciter diode*
*5 Regulator, brush holder and carbon brushes*
*6 Stator*
*7 Rotor*
*8 Fan*
*9 Drive pulley*
*10 Drive end shield*

***Fig. 3.32 Lucas ACR series alternator***

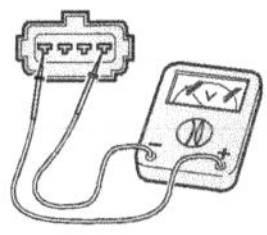

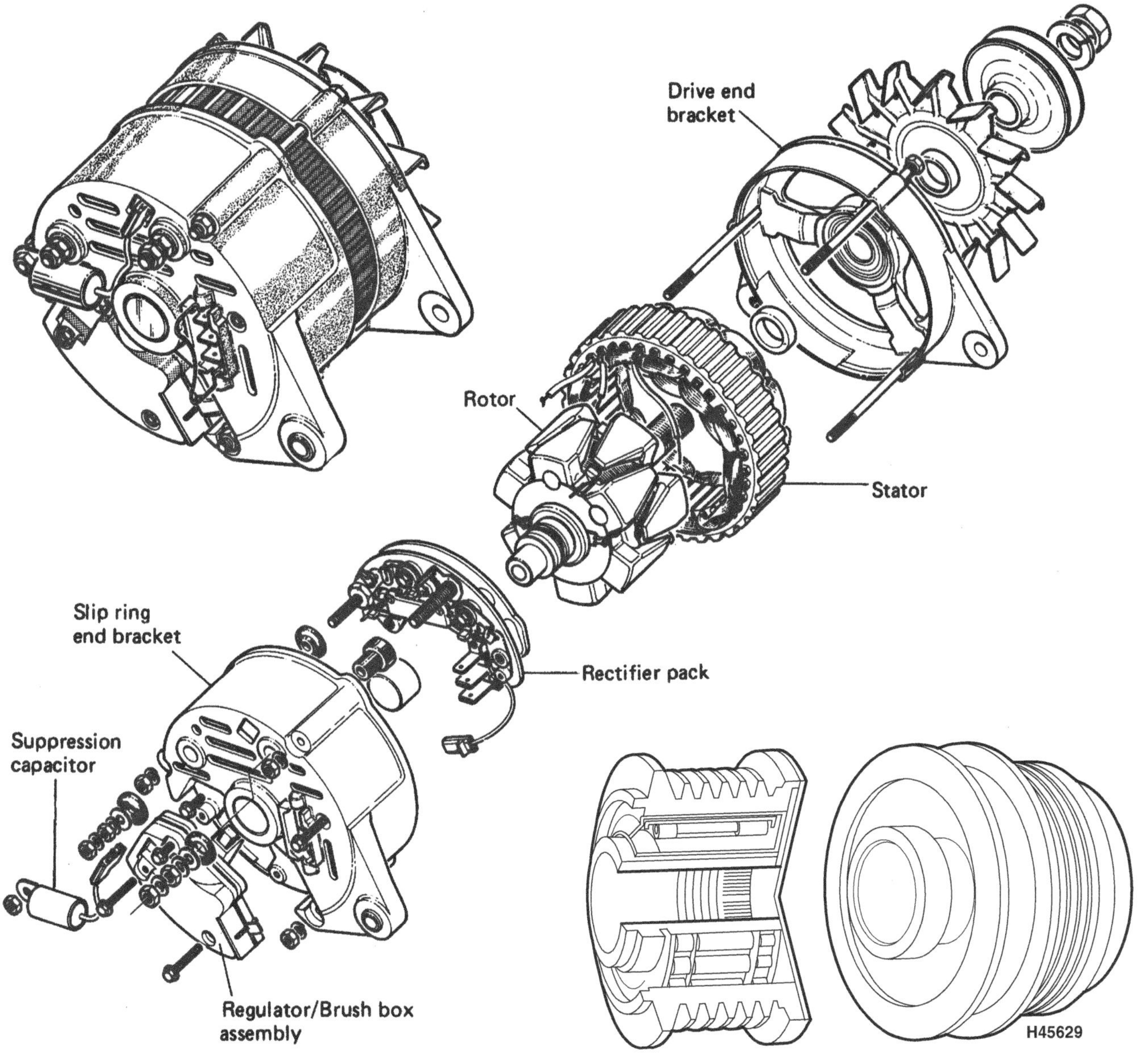

*Fig. 3.33a Lucas A127 alternator*

*Fig. 3.33b Alternator overrun pulley (one-way clutch)*

## 15 Alternator construction

**1** Details vary but typical are the Bosch and Lucas arrangements shown in Figs. 3.31, 3.32 and 3.33a. The ACR range of Lucas alternators has had a long production run and has been superseded by the A range. The later of these, the A127 alternator, is designed for low maintenance and light weight. To achieve high current ratings the stator windings are delta connected. The brush box and regulator are a single assembly attached to the outside of the slip ring end bracket (Fig. 3.33a) giving rapid access for inspection or renewal without dismantling the machine. Surge protection is built into the electronic regulator.

**2** On later vehicles fitted with high-output diesel engines, (normally common-rail), it's becoming common for the alternators to be fitted with an over-running drive pulley. This is due to the sharp crankshaft acceleration and deceleration pulses produced by these engines at low rpm. Theses pulses are transferred to the alternator causing high belt loads, belt slippage, high rates of belt wear and eventually belt failure.

The overrunning pulley is a one-way clutch, which only transfers the acceleration pulses to the alternator (Fig 3.33b), thus greatly reducing the forces transmitted by the belt, which dramatically increases belt life•

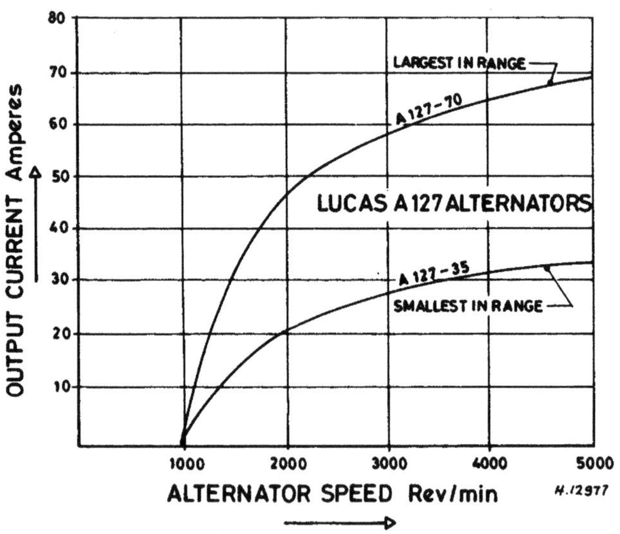


*Fig. 3.34 A127 alternator output curves*

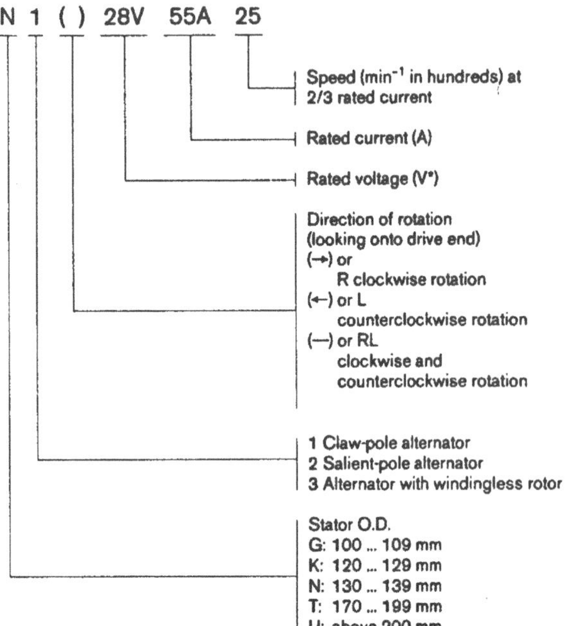


* The rated voltage (14 or 28 V) is a mean value within the permissible tolerance range of the generator voltage. The generator voltage is kept constant by the regulator as the charging voltage for the battery irrespective of speed and loading, but taking into consideration the intake air temperature. The generator voltage must not be confused with the lower rated voltage of the battery (12 or 24 V) for the loads of the vehicle electrical system (e.g. starting motor, electric motors etc.).

*Fig. 3.35 Bosch nameplate coding*

## 16 Output performance

**1** Alternators are made in a range to cover all applications from 28 A full load (Lucas 15ACR) up to 65 A (Lucas 24ACR). The A series go from 28 A to 75 A and the recent A127 alternators from 35 A to 70 A. Charging starts at about 1000 rev/min and levels off as shown in Fig. 3.34. Bosch use a nameplate code which, in addition to the ten digit part number, gives data on size, voltage, maximum current, speed rating and other information as shown in Fig. 3.35.

## 17 Heat dissipation

**1** The alternator works in hostile conditions and a hazard is temperature. The proximity to the engine and exhaust is a principal factor, together with the ambient temperature. Designs are based on the surrounding (ambient) temperature not exceeding 70 to 80°C and for automobile purposes a fan mounted on the drive end behind the pulley provides cooling.

The fan throws air outwards by centrifugal action and in so doing draws air through the body of the alternator (Fig. 3.36).

**2** Semiconductor diodes are particularly prone to high temperatures. Heat generated in them must be dissipated by mounting them on metal plates known as heat sinks. Heat sinks have a large surface area from which to radiate heat and have good conductivity – aluminium often being used. In alternators a dual-heat sink assembly is used and is on the dc side of the three-phase bridge circuit. Three power diodes are mounted with the cathode end on a heat sink which is connected to the battery + terminal, and three power diodes are mounted with anodes to the heat sink which is connected to the battery – terminal. The field diodes which need to dissipate less heat may have a smaller heat sink of their own. One possible arrangement is shown in Fig. 3.37 and should be followed by comparison with the circuit diagram Fig. 3.15.

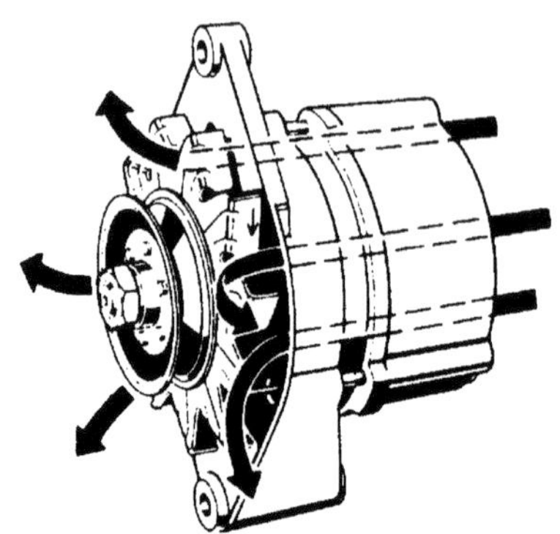

*Fig. 3.36 Alternator cooling fan*

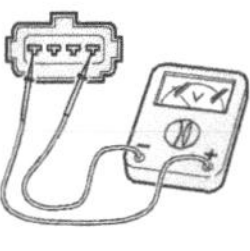

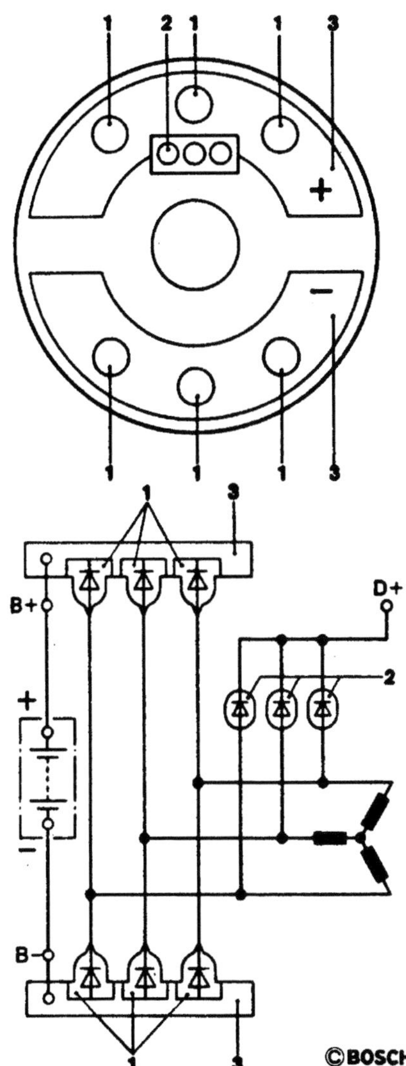


*Fig. 3.37 Dual heat sink to cool alternator diodes*
*1 Power diodes 2 Field exciter diodes 3 Heat sink*

## 18 Alternator problems

**1** Common problems with alternators are:

**Charge warning lamp blown.** The alternator may not start charging.

**Rotor slip ring brushes**. May be sticking in the holders due to dirt or carbon dust. Brushes may be worn down. Slip rings may be greasy or dirty.

**Diode failure.** This may have been caused by corroded or loose battery connection or bad earthing. Even a momentary connection of the battery the wrong way round will result in diode destruction. If the battery or alternator has been accidentally disconnected while the engine was running, failure will probably have occurred. Jump starting with incorrect connection will probably destroy the diodes. Arc welding repair work on the vehicle can cause diodes to fail – always disconnect the alternator first.

**Bearing failure.** Usually caused by the fanbelt being too tight, but can be due to the ingress of grit into the bearings.

**Fan belts.** Check that it is not slipping on load – this is often announced by a squeal. A squeal may also result from a worn belt that has run down the pulley V and is in contact with the V bottom instead of gripping on the sides.

**2** Having seen what the common problems are, it may be necessary to proceed logically to test the charging system. What follows applies to any make of alternator and because many older systems will still be found on vehicles, notes on earlier battery excited machines are included.

## 19 Alternator testing

**1** Little routine maintenance of alternators is required, but periodic checks on the brush length and cleanliness of the slip rings is advisable. Faults in the system can occur in the following:

*(a) Faulty battery*
*(b) Breaks in cables or poor connections at terminals or plugs and sockets*
*(c) Alternator drivebelt loose*
*(d) Failure of the alternator windings or rectifier pack*
*(e) Regulator failure*
*(f) Fault in any auxiliary units, eg field relay, charge warning bulb, warning light control unit*

**2** Before examining the system in detail when a fault is present, a visual inspection is worthwhile to check on belt tension (Fig. 3.38), signs of terminal corrosion, whether a battery cell is gassing unusually when on charge, etc. Assuming nothing is obvious then a logical procedure should be followed.

**3** Test equipment need not be extensive, but the following would be required:

*(a) DC moving coil voltmeter, range 0–20 V (or 40 V if testing 24 V systems)*
*(b) DC moving coil ammeter, range 10–0–100 A*
*(c) Hydrometer*
*(d) An ohmmeter with low and high ranges and desirably*
*(e) Battery heavy-discharge tester*

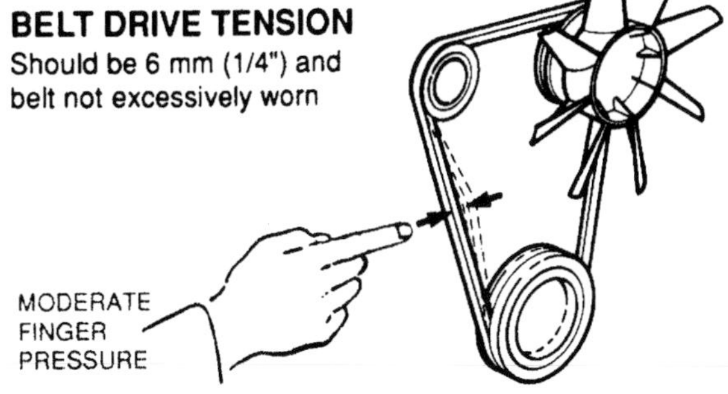


*Fig. 3.38 Drivebelt tension must be correct*

**4** When running an engine, keep hands and clothing away from moving parts. Remember a thermostatically controlled radiator fan may start running even with the ignition off – disconnect it if possible. Switch off ignition before connecting or disconnecting any vehicle cable. Disconnect the battery earth cable when connecting or disconnecting main alternator leads.

**5** The tests show Euro-terminations and equivalents are shown in Fig. 3.39.

## Test procedure

*Test diagrams are reproduced with permission of Lucas Automotive Ltd.*

**State of battery**. Check battery state of charge by switching on headlamp load with the engine off. The voltmeter reading should be 12 volts or above. If below, recharge the battery.

**Cable continuity**. Check the continuity of the cables to the alternator. Take off plug or disconnect stud leads. Check that battery voltage appears at all three wires with ignition on – engine NOT running (Fig. 3.40). If IND reads zero, the warning lamp may have blown.

**Alternator output**. As a simple check on whether the alternator is charging, connect a dc 0 to 20V voltmeter across the battery terminals. Switch on all loads, ie lights, heated rear window, etc (but NOT windscreen wipers – dry screens get scratched!) for 3 to 5 minutes. Then run the engine at a good mid-speed (say 3000 rev/min). Switch off loads and the engine. The battery should reach 13.5 V after the engine has run for a few minutes. If the battery is healthy, suspect the alternator if this voltage is not achieved. An alternative test would be to test the alternator for maximum current output. First disconnect the battery, then make a GOOD connection of an ammeter into the + lead. Remember a bad connection could result in the alternator diodes blowing. A test link with a male blade at one end and a female blade socket at the other will serve to connect to IND (Fig. 3.41). Reconnect the battery, switch on loads as before to partially run down the battery, and then run the engine at about 3000 rev/min. Ammeter should read close to the maximum rated current for the particular alternator. After the test restore connections, not forgetting to disconnect the battery first. If the reading is markedly lower than expected, replace the alternator.

**Circuit volt-drops**. Volt-drop troubles are usually due to dirty terminals or corrosion. With one voltmeter clip (negative) onto the battery + terminal, and the other onto the alternator +, run the engine at charging speed with all vehicle loads on (except wipers). The volt-drop should not exceed 0.5 volt – if it does look for a poor connection. Similarly check for a volt-drop between the battery negative terminal and the alternator frame – again this should not exceed 0.5 volt. Look for poor connections at battery, at the earth-to-body strap and the engine-to-body strap (Fig. 3.42).

**Regulator check**. Run the engine at 3000 rev/min for 3 to 5 mins, and measure the battery voltage over this period.

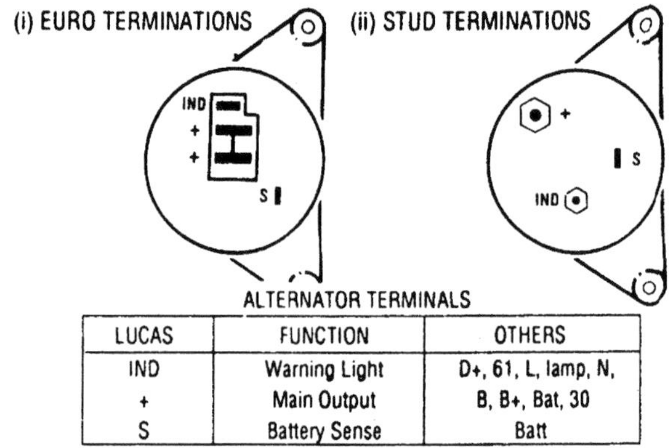


| LUCAS | FUNCTION | OTHERS |
|---|---|---|
| IND | Warning Light | D+, 61, L, lamp, N, |
| + | Main Output | B, B+, Bat, 30 |
| S | Battery Sense | Batt |

*Fig. 3.39 Alternator terminations*

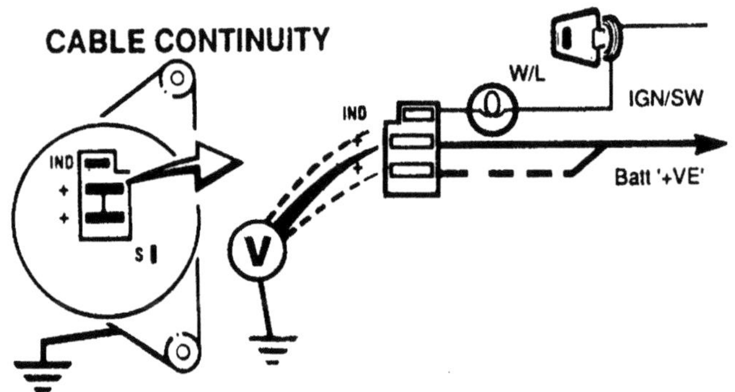


*Fig. 3.40 Checking cables*

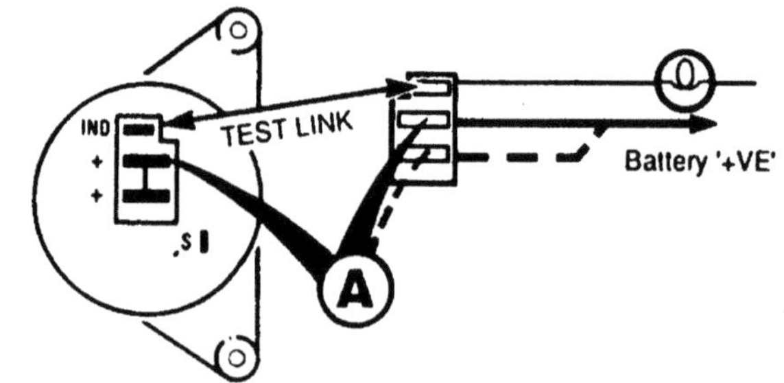


*Fig. 3.41 Full-load testing*

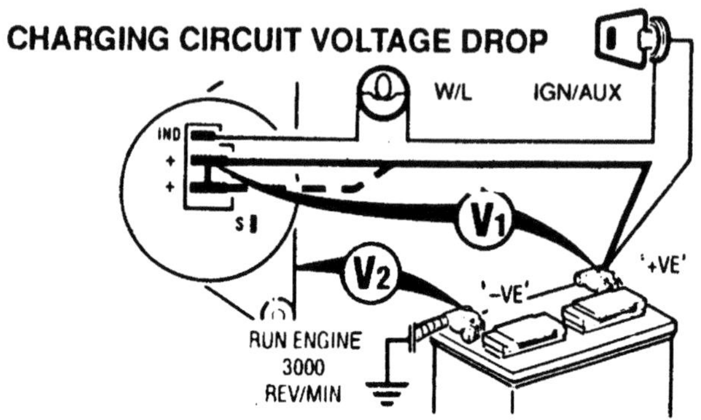


*Fig. 3.42 Volt-drop test*

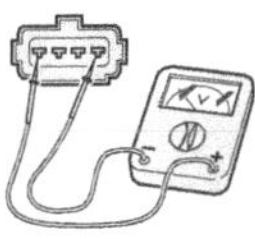

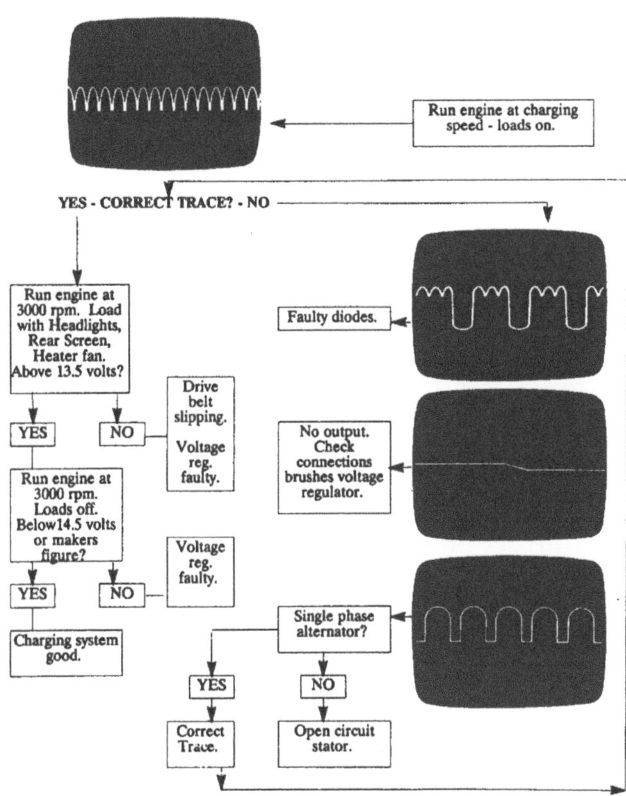


*Fig. 3.43 Alternator testing by waveform traces*

The battery voltage should rise to 13.6 to 14.4V for a Lucas regulator and remain at this voltage. If the voltage is high, low or continually changing, change the regulator. The working voltage range is typical for the many makes and vehicles. For accurate figures refer to the vehicle manufacturer.

**Oscilloscope test.** For those with access to an oscilloscope, the waveform displayed of voltage on the + charging line is revealing. Fig. 3.43 shows waveforms which show correct working and fault conditions.

## 20 Alternator servicing

**1** Four parts may fail in an alternator:

*(a) Power and Field Diode pack*
*(b) Rotor winding*
*(c) Stator winding*
*(d) Bearings*
*(e) Brushes*

**2** Before work is begun it is worth comparing costs of labour and parts against a replacement unit, allowing also for the guarantee that comes with the replacement unit.

**3** Diodes may be tested by first unsoldering from the stator windings, being careful to divert the soldering iron heat away from a diode by clamping the diode lead with a pair of pliers (or heat sink).

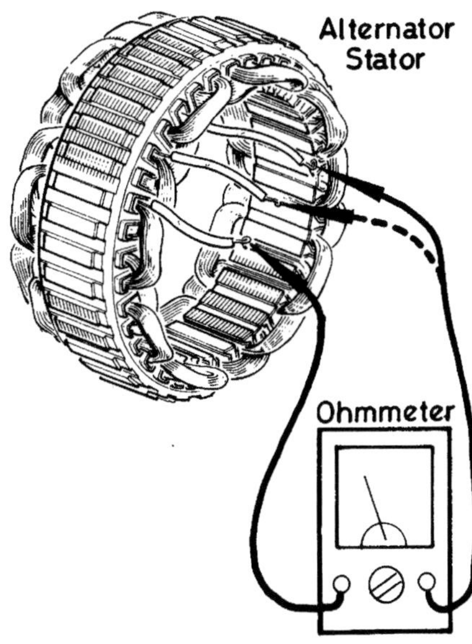


*Fig. 3.44 Stator winding resistance test. Should be identical between leads – expect about 0.1 ohms*

Test each diode by applying 12 volts dc through a 12 V 5 W bulb. The bulb should light up with the supply one way round but not when reversed. Lighting up both ways round indicates that the diode is short circuited.

**4** Stator windings will have three leads whether star or delta wound. The resistance between each pair of leads should be the same: designs vary but expect about 0.1 ohm (Fig. 3.44). Insulation between the windings and the stator iron frame should be high (greater than 1 megohm). If an ohmmeter is not available, use a 25 watt lamp and an ac supply not exceeding 110 volts – the lamp should not light. If it does light or glows, the stator winding has a short circuit to earth (Fig. 3.45).

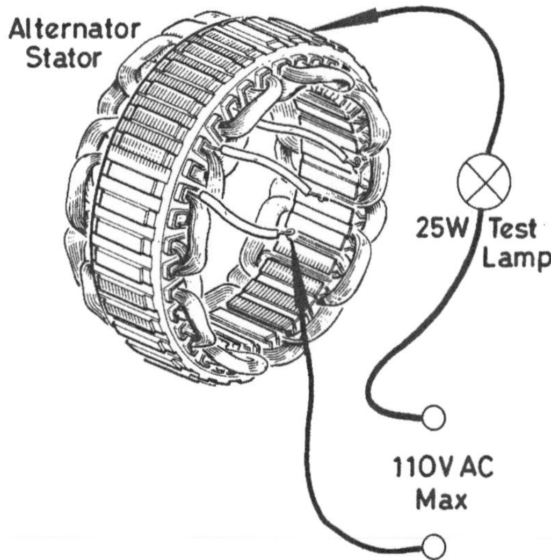


*Fig. 3.45 Stator-to-frame insulation test*

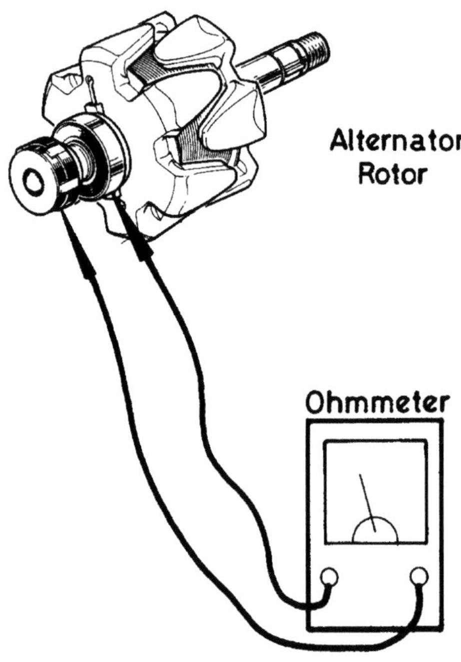


*Fig. 3.46 Rotor winding resistance check*
*3 to 4 ohms is normal*

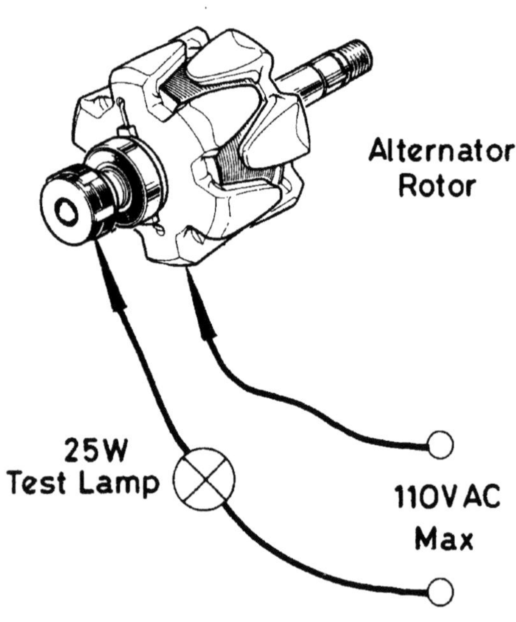


*Fig. 3.47 Rotor-to-frame insulation test*

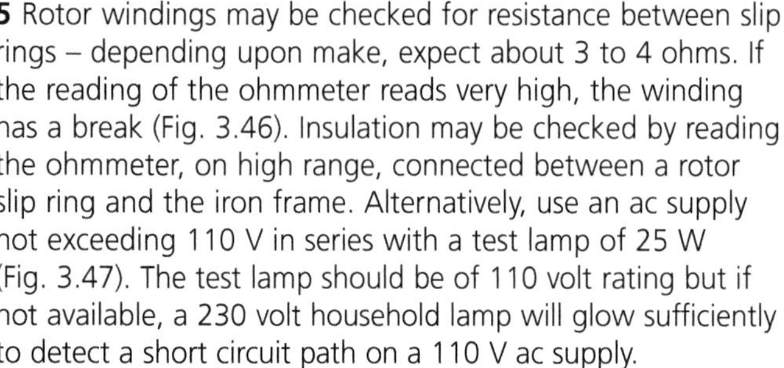
**5** Rotor windings may be checked for resistance between slip rings – depending upon make, expect about 3 to 4 ohms. If the reading of the ohmmeter reads very high, the winding has a break (Fig. 3.46). Insulation may be checked by reading the ohmmeter, on high range, connected between a rotor slip ring and the iron frame. Alternatively, use an ac supply not exceeding 110 V in series with a test lamp of 25 W (Fig. 3.47). The test lamp should be of 110 volt rating but if not available, a 230 volt household lamp will glow sufficiently to detect a short circuit path on a 110 V ac supply.

**6** Brushes should be replaced when worn down to limits (see table). The machines likely to be found on UK vehicles are Lucas A, AC and ACR; Ducellier; Bosch; Paris-Rhône; Femsa; Hitachi; AC Delco; Marelli; Denso; Delco Remy and Mitsubishi. Fitting new brushes is straightforward for most types but Denso, AC Delco, Delco Remy and Mitsubishi alternators need to be stripped right down and it is better to consider a machine exchange or have the job done in an auto-electrical depot. After locating the brushes, check the length and then look at the slip rings. These do not normally get scored, but benefit from cleaning with methylated spirit. If scored, it is best to exchange the alternator for a new one because new brushes would be quickly worn away. Each make has a variation in getting to the brushes, but with certain types it is necessary to unsolder the old brush leads and re-solder the new ones.

| Make | Min. brush length | Special notes |
|---|---|---|
| Lucas AC10,11 | 5 mm | Brushes held by spade terminals. Use small screw-driver to press spade terminal down, then push out |
| Lucas ACR | 5 mm | Remove plastic cover. Note location of wires to brushes. Do not lose leaf spring behind central brush |
| Ducellier | 8 mm | Difficult to clean slip rings – don't bother. Brushes are different – make sure they are correctly located |
| Paris-Rhône | 8 mm | Slim socket needed for brush holder bolts |
| Femsa | 7 mm | Brush box is separate unit at rear of alternator |
| Bosch | 2 mm | Late models – brush box and regulator are single unit. Screws may be tight – do not burr. Lift out unit with care. Soldering iron needed to release old brush leads and attach new ones |
| Hitachi | Brushes have wear-limit marks | Brush holder cover and holder are separate. Withdraw brush holder carefully. Do not disconnect lead marked N |

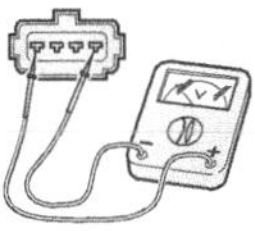



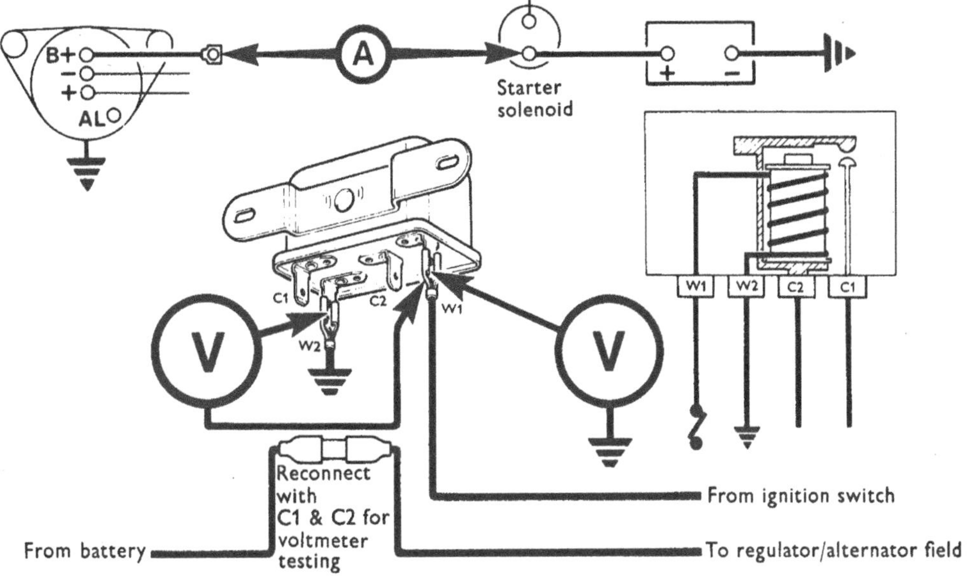


*Fig. 3.48 Checking the field relay*

## Battery-excited alternators (Lucas 10/11 system)

Certain tests will be essentially the same as for the ACR type of alternator, namely, battery state, drivebelt tension and cable continuity. Since the 10AC and 11AC systems have the field fed by the battery, additional tests on the field relay and warning light control are necessary.

### Test 1: Field relay

Referring back to Fig. 3.16 it will be seen that the relay is intended to connect the field winding to the battery through the contacts, terminals $C_1$ and $C_2$ and the ignition switch. Assuming that the fault is that the alternator is not charging, to check the relay connect an ammeter in the alternator main lead as shown in Fig. 3.48, first taking off the battery earth cable. Remove the cable connectors from the contact terminals, $C_1$ and $C_2$, and bridge them with a double spade or a short lead with crocodile clips. Reconnect the battery earth cable and run the engine at about 1500 rpm. If charging now takes place, the fault lies in the relay, or its wiring. A voltmeter connected across $W_1$ and $W_2$ terminals should show battery voltage. If not, then the earth connection at $W_2$, and the supply voltage at $W_1$ should be checked.

### Test 2: Field circuit check

The simplest way to check the field is to pull the connectors off the 4TR regulator and to bridge the leads going to F and – with an ammeter, as in Fig. 3.49. With the ignition switched on, the ammeter should read approximately 3 amperes. If there is no current a break has occurred in the circuit.

### Test 3: Maximum output check

With the connectors again removed from the regulator 4TR, F and – are bridged, as in Fig. 3.50. The ammeter is

*Fig. 3.49 Checking the field circuit*

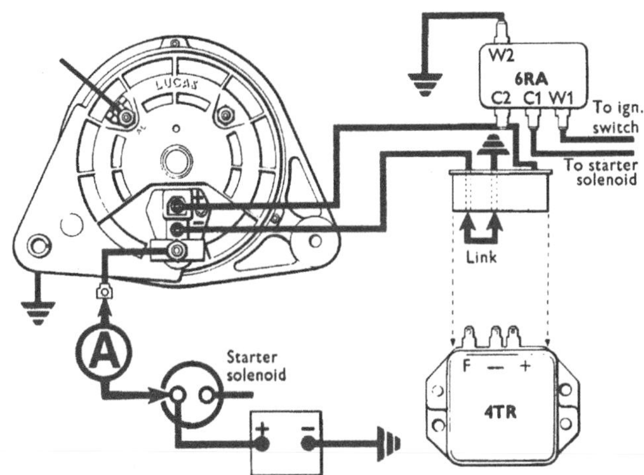


*Fig. 3.50 Checking the alternator maximum output – 10/11AC*

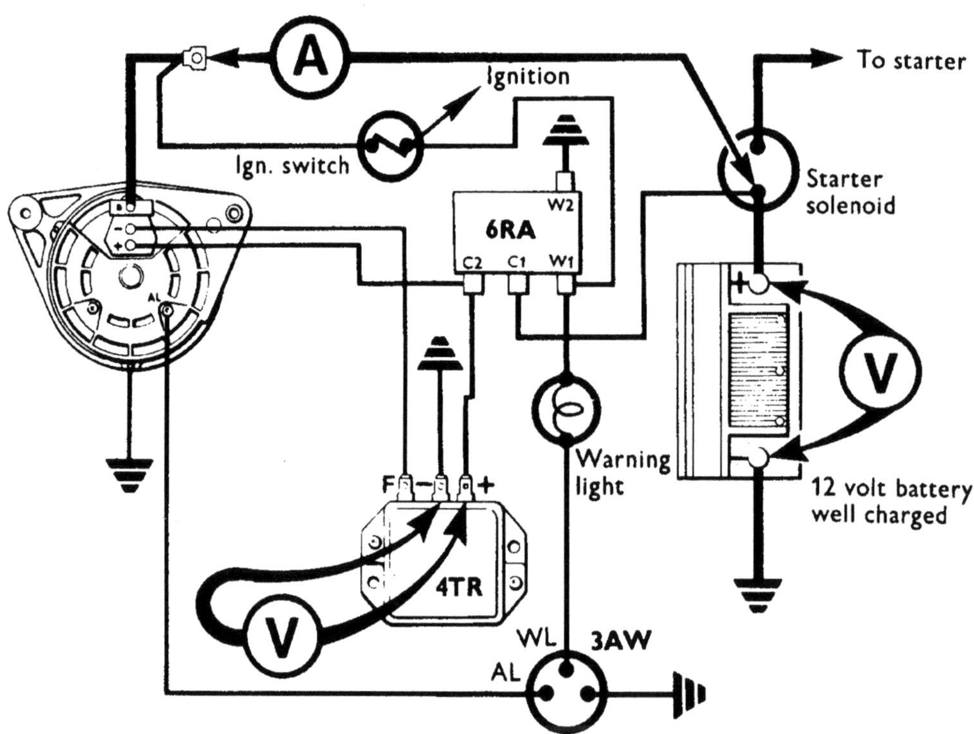


*Fig. 3.51 Checking the 4TR voltage regulator setting*

connected in the main output lead, and with the engine running at about 3000rpm the current should be as follows:

| Alternator | Ammeter reading |
|---|---|
| 10AC | 35 A |
| 11AC | 45 A |
| 11AC (updated model) | 60 A |
| 11AC (24 volt) | 23 A |

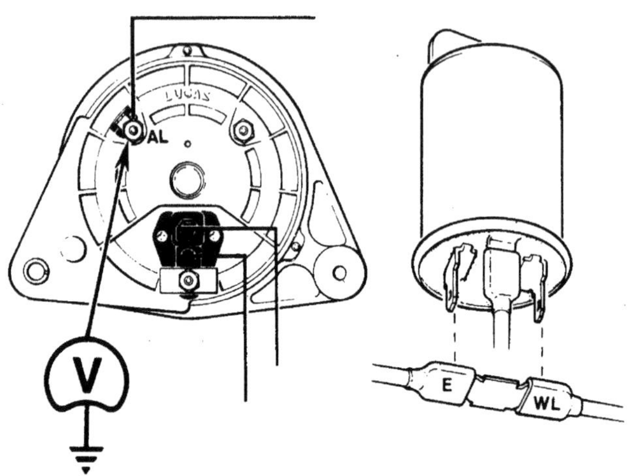


*Fig. 3.52 Checking the 3AW warning light control*

A zero, or low figure, points to a faulty stator, or trouble with the rectifier diodes.

**Test 4: Regulator setting measurement**

The 4TR regulator is tested using a charged battery, and at normal operating temperature. It is necessary to see that the regulator is actually regulating by running the engine until the charge rate has dropped below 10 A and does not change with speed. Load the circuit with side (city) lamps and run the engine at 3000 rpm, connections according to Fig. 3.51. Voltage readings should be within the limits:

| 10/11 AC Alternators | Voltage regulator setting |
|---|---|
| 12 volt system | 13.9 to 14.3 volts |
| 24 volt system | 27.9 to 28.3 volts |

**Test 5: Warning light control 3AW**

If the alternator is charging normally, but the warning light does not work, the first thing to check is the bulb itself. Assuming the bulb is good, check the voltage to earth at the alternator AL terminal. This should be between 6 and 8 volts for a 12 volt system, or 14 to 15 volts for a 24 volt system, with 1500 rpm engine speed. An abnormal AL reading points to a faulty rectifier diode. Next check the 3AW unit by taking off the E and WL terminals and bridging them together (Fig. 3.52). With the ignition on, the warning light bulb should glow. If this is so, then the 3AW unit is faulty.

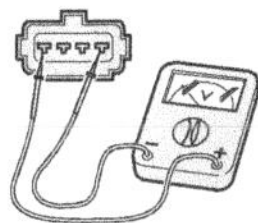

## PART B: DYNAMOS

### 21 Introduction to dynamos

**1** The direct current dynamo has seen motor vehicle service for many years, but has now been superseded by the alternator for good technical reasons, some of which were explained at the beginning of this chapter. There are still many vehicles on the road which have dynamo systems and an understanding of operation and servicing is important.
**2** It is interesting to note that the dynamo armature conductors, in fact, have an alternating voltage generated in them while rotating under the magnetic poles, but the commutator acts as a form of rectifier, so that every time the voltage changes polarity the external leads are connected to the opposite conductors.
**3** A closer look at this process (Fig. 3.53) shows a single loop of wire, the armature, rotating between N and S magnetic poles. It helps to imagine magnetic lines of force crossing from N to S; then with the armature coil being turned as shown the side 'a' is passing down through the magnetic lines (or 'flux' to use the engineering word) while side 'b' is going up through the magnetic flux. The voltages induced will add, so that the combined voltage will come out at the two commutator segments which rotate with the armature. Note the current will flow out through the carbon brush $B_1$ round the external circuit and back in again at carbon brush $B_2$.
**4** When the armature coil has passed through 90° so that sides 'a' and 'b' are at the top and bottom of the magnetic flux field, ie halfway between the poles, then the brushes will just be connecting to the opposite commutator segment. As side 'b' starts to pass downwards under the N pole the generated voltage will now be in the opposite direction from when it was under the S pole; equally the voltage in coil side 'a' has changed. Because the connections to the brushes have changed the voltage appearing at the external load will be a sine wave, but with the negative half above the line, as shown (Fig. 3.53). Thus the voltage and current in the external load do not reverse, but come in the form of pulses which constitute a form of direct current and could be used for battery charging.
**5** A practical direct current dynamo would use a number of coils connected to a commutator with the same number of segments; this way the magnetic field is utilised more effectively and the electrical output is improved. Additionally, the wave form of the resultant output voltage or current is smoother, as shown in Fig. 3.54.
**6** A further substantial improvement comes by embedding the coils in slots of a laminated iron armature core mounted on a steel shaft (Fig. 3.55). This improvement in electrical output arises from the much stronger magnetic field using an iron armature, since the air gap is smaller.
**7** The iron core is made up of thin laminations insulated

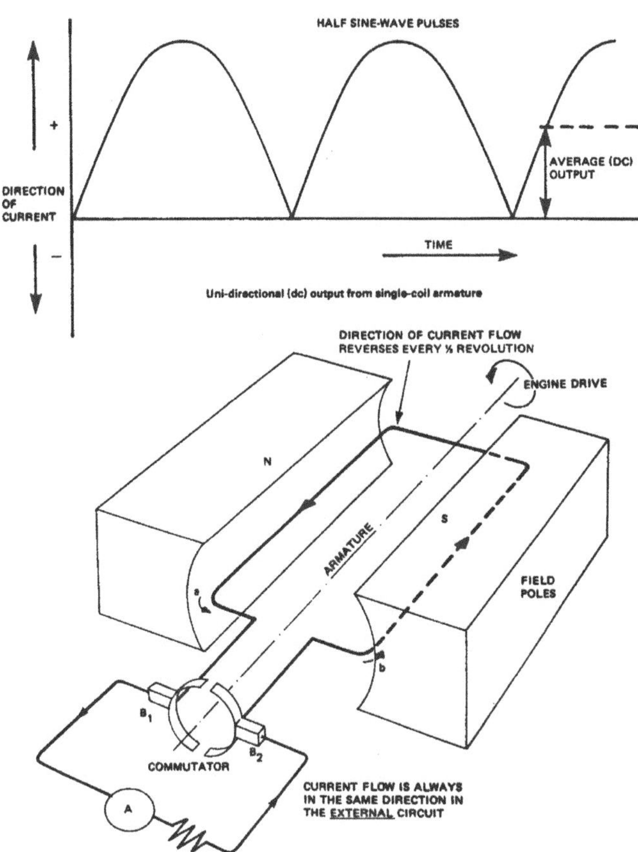


*Fig. 3.53 Rectification by a simple commutator*

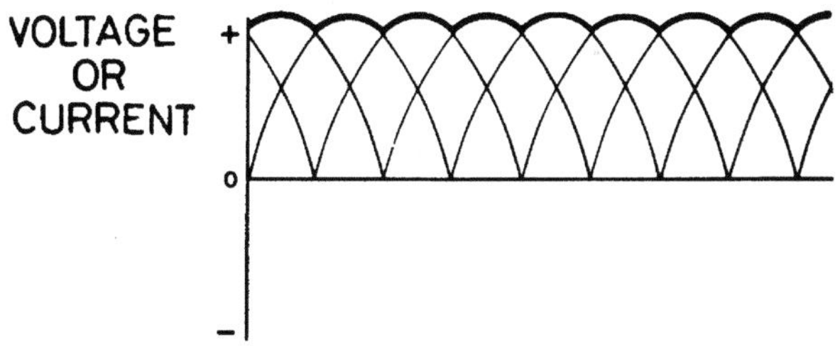


*Fig. 3.54 Multi-coil armature output*

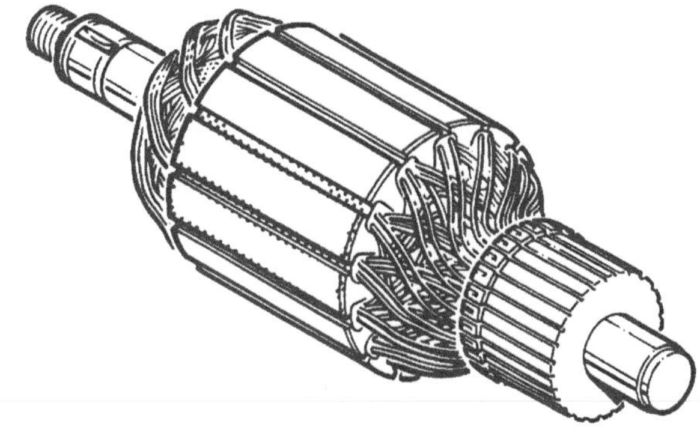

*Fig. 3.55 Typical dynamo armature and commutator*

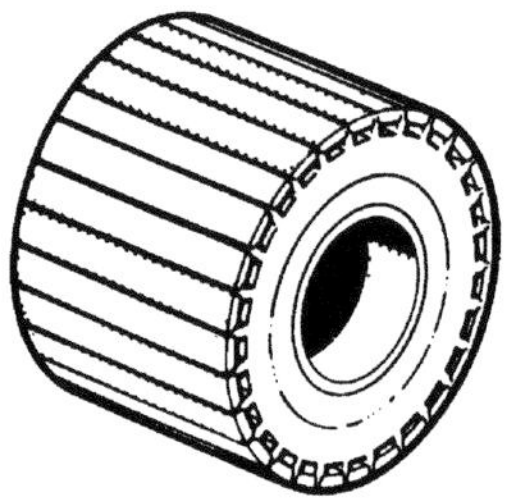

*Fig. 3.56 Practical multi-segment commutator*

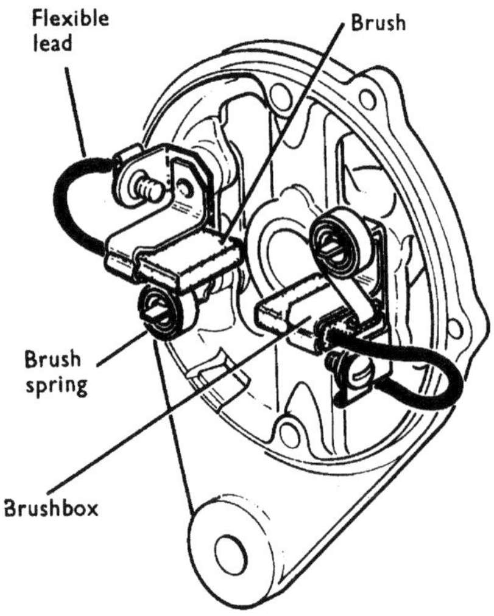


*Fig. 3.57 Brush assembly*

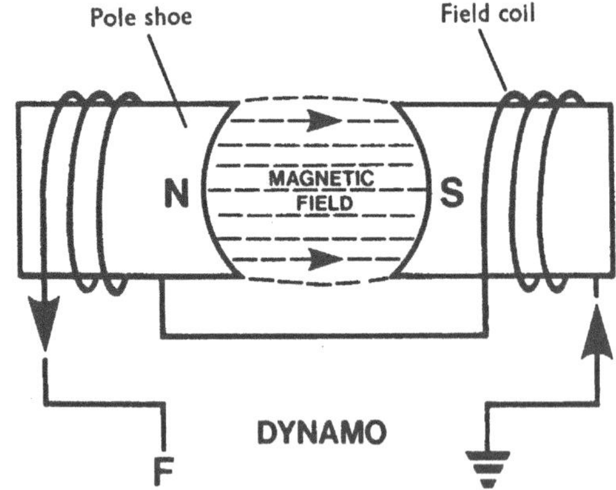


*Fig. 3.58 Schematic diagram of electromagnetic poles*

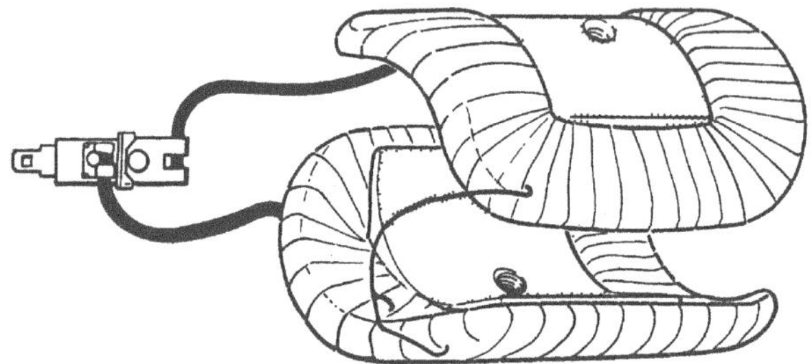

*Fig. 3.59 Actual arrangement of pole shoes and coils*

from each other. If the iron were solid, then it could be imagined as an infinite number of iron wires all short circuited to each other. Rotation in the magnetic field would induce voltages and currents in the iron and the result would be high circulating currents (called eddy currents) which would not only heat the iron considerably, but require high, wasted drive power input.

**8** The practical commutator (Fig. 3.56) consists of a number of copper segments arranged in cylindrical form and accurately machined for good contact with the carbon brushes. Each copper segment is insulated from the next by a material such as micanite, stennite or phenolic resin; since the copper will wear more quickly than the insulating material it is necessary to undercut the insulation (ie below the copper level) during manufacture, and undercutting is sometimes required as a maintenance operation during the life of the dynamo. (See Section 32 of this Chapter).

**9** The commutator assembly is pressed onto the armature shaft, and the armature conductors are soldered to the slots in the commutator segments. The brushes collect the dynamo current and are held in brush boxes, the commutator contact being ensured by pressure on the brushes from coiled springs (Fig. 3.57).

**10** In practice, permanent magnets are not used for vehicle dynamos; instead, electromagnets are employed. A coil of wire carrying direct current and wound round soft iron will produce a magnetic field around the iron similar to that of a permanent magnet, but with the great advantage that the strength of the magnetic field can be controlled by the amount of current flowing through the coil. Such electromagnets are used in dc dynamos, and the supply of the necessary current comes from the dynamo armature itself.

**11** Fig. 3.58 shows a schematic of the pole arrangement. Actually the coils are flattened and fit around the pole shoes as in Fig. 3.59, the latter being screwed tightly to the iron yoke (ie outer frame) of the dynamo.

**12** The field coils consist of a pair of coils connected together in series. Each coil consists of several hundred turns of insulated copper wire which have been factory wound on a rectangular former. The final operation is to insulate the coils by means of cotton tape.

**13** The yoke, pole shoes and armature frame are shown in Fig. 3.60. This shows the path of field magnetic flux; the armature conductors are located in the slots. Note that the steel yoke is part of the magnetic flux path and, observing that air gaps should be as small as possible to keep the flux high, the need for accurately and firmly fixed pole shoes is obvious, as is the need for good play-free armature shaft bearings. Fig. 3.61 shows the location and types of bearings often used in vehicle dc dynamos; some manufacturers employ ball-bearings at both ends.

**14** The armature and field coils are connected in parallel (or shunt) and this type of assembly is known as a dc shunt dynamo. It is fortunate that the soft iron used in the magnetic circuit always retains a small amount of

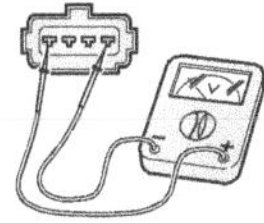

magnetisation even after coil current has ceased for the operation of the dc shunt dynamo depends upon this retention.

**15** Using symbols now, instead of drawing the dynamo in detail, we see in Fig. 3.62 the field and armature connected in parallel. As the armature rotates the conductors cut a weak magnetic field (the residual magnetism of the iron). A small voltage is generated (more correctly termed electromotive force – emf) in the armature and gives rise to a small current output, part of which will flow down through the field coils back to the armature. This strengthens the magnetic field, and so increases the generated emf in the armature; a higher field current flows which, in turn, raises the generated emf. The dynamo thus builds up to its working voltage.

**16** It may occur to the reader that this process could go on indefinitely until the field coils burn out. This probably would happen were it not for the phenomenon of iron magnetic saturation. Iron can sustain only a certain maximum magnetic flux, however large the current in the electromagnet coils, and Fig. 3.63 shows what happens to the generated emf as the field current rises (remembering that the emf varies directly with the magnetic flux). However, the final voltage of a direct current dynamo, left unchecked, would be far too high for charging a battery, and so some form of regulator is required. Incidentally, the shunt generator must always be driven in the correct direction, otherwise it will fail to start, for the initial generated current would tend to eliminate the residual magnetism.

**17** The correct polarisation of the dynamo is thus vital, and when a replacement dynamo is fitted to a car it is necessary to ensure that the residual magnetisation of the iron is correct. To do this the dynamo field F terminal is connected to the battery output lead for a few seconds with D and F leads removed.

**18** Ventilation is important for the dynamo, since some heat will be generated internally. The usual arrangement is

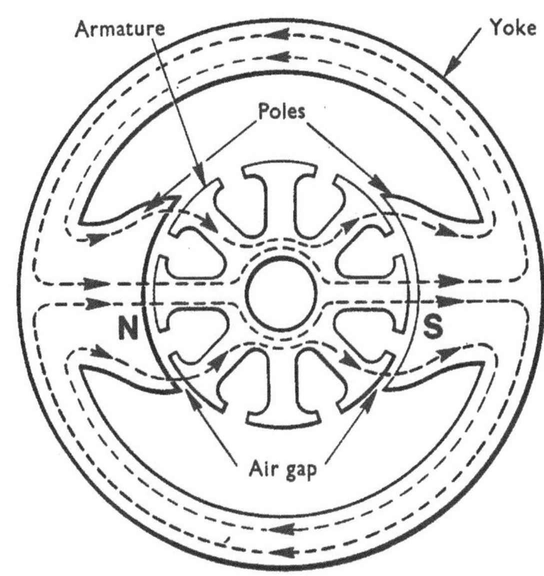


*Fig. 3.60 The yoke forming part of the magnetic circuit*

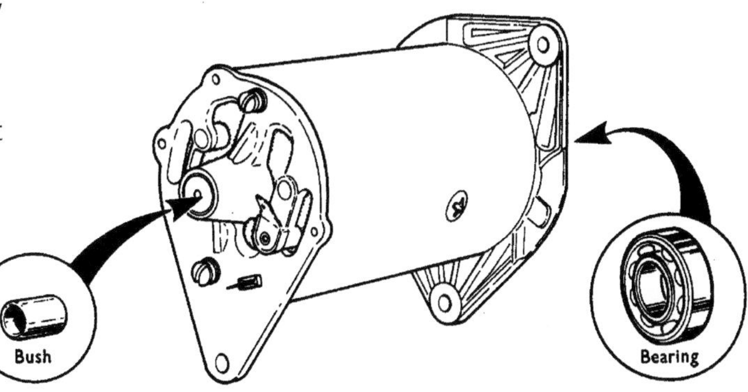


*Fig. 3.61 Bearings for a dc dynamo*

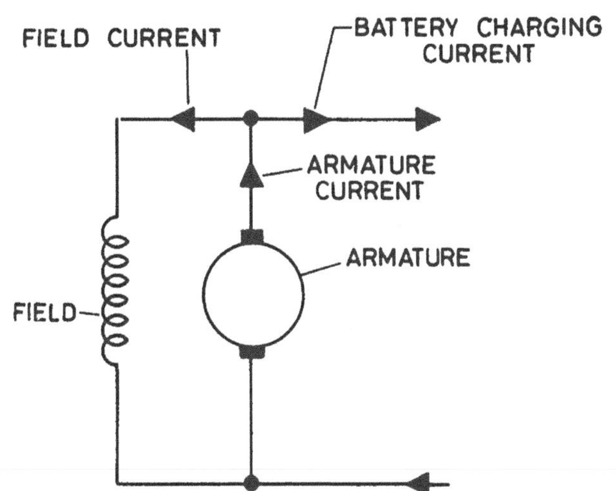


*3.62 Shunt dc dynamo*

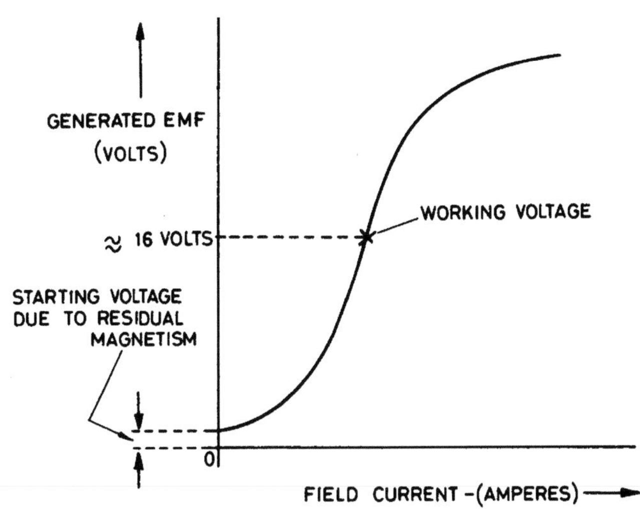


*Fig. 3.63 Shunt dc dynamo characteristic*

that the dynamo endplates will be slotted and a fan is built on to the driving pulley. The fan is of the centrifugal type and draws air through the dynamo (Fig. 3.64). Certain types of dynamos are totally enclosed, but are for special purposes, for example, in agriculture where dust levels can be high. In these machines the electrical power output is reduced to prevent overheating.

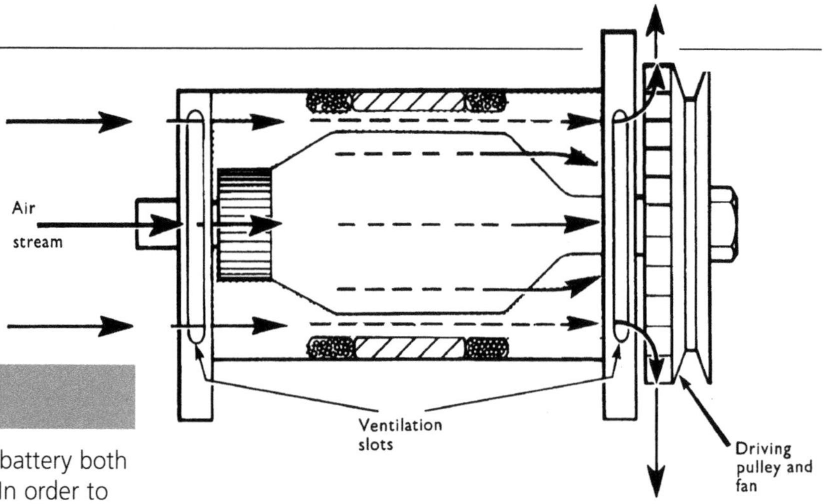

Air stream

Ventilation slots

Driving pulley and fan

*Fig. 3.64 Ventilated dynamo*

## 22 Battery charging

**1** It is important to realise that the dynamo and battery both have terminal voltages in opposition (Fig. 3.65). In order to force current into the battery the dynamo voltage must be higher than that of the battery. This arrangement would be fairly simple to engineer, were it not for the fact that the battery voltage is not constant, but ranges from about 12 volts when low to nearly 16 volts when fully charged.

**2** If the dynamo were regulated to give a constant voltage then the current flowing into a fully discharged battery might burn out the armature. For this reason a regulator used in conjunction with the dynamo is compensated to allow for the load demanded by the battery and auxiliary equipment on the vehicle.

**3** It is worth thinking about what would happen when the dynamo voltage reduces below that of the battery; current would now flow from the battery to the dynamo which, if free, would turn as a motor. Clearly some device is needed to disconnect the dynamo from the battery as required – this device is the cut-out.

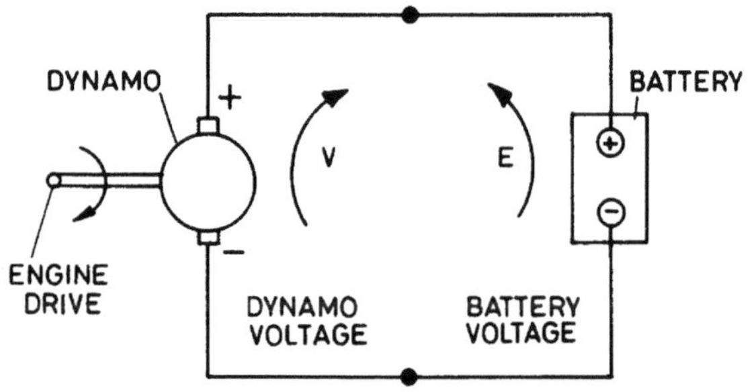

DYNAMO
BATTERY
V
E
ENGINE DRIVE
DYNAMO VOLTAGE
BATTERY VOLTAGE

*Fig. 3.65 Dynamo charging the battery*

## 23 The cut-out

**1** The purpose of the cut-out is to connect the dynamo to the battery when the dynamo voltage rises above the battery voltage, ie at about 13 volts, and to disconnect it at tickover; the cut-out is an electromagnetic relay with a coil connected across the dynamo output terminal and earth. The coil is so designed that it will produce a level of magnetisation in the relay iron path sufficient to pull down a hinged plate (the armature) when the supply voltage to the coil reaches the pull-in voltage (Fig. 3.66). Note that when the engine is stationary and the ignition switch is on, the charge warning light will glow. As the engine runs up to speed, the generated voltage of the dynamo rises to approximately that of the battery, when the warning light will go out. The cut-out contacts close, connecting the dynamo and battery, but also shorting out the warning light.

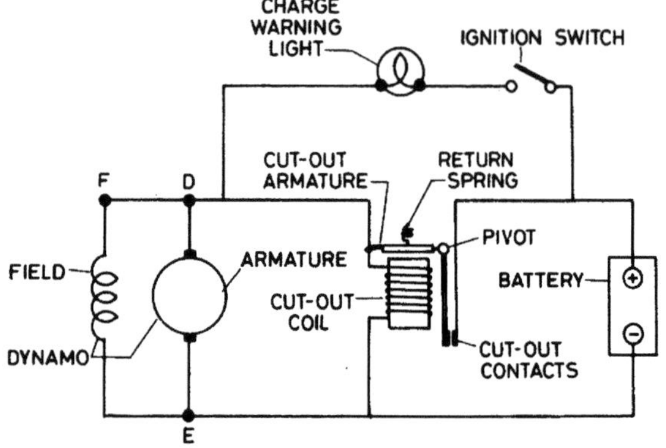


*Fig. 3.66 A simple cut-out*

**2** The armature movement serves to close the cut-out contacts which connect the dynamo main output terminal to the battery. When the engine speed drops the dynamo voltage falls to the point when the magnetic pull on the armature is insufficient to hold the contacts closed and they pull apart under spring pressure. The cut-out is thus a relay, or electromagnetic switch.

**3** In Fig. 3.67, showing a practical cut-out, the bobbin has two windings. The main shunt winding

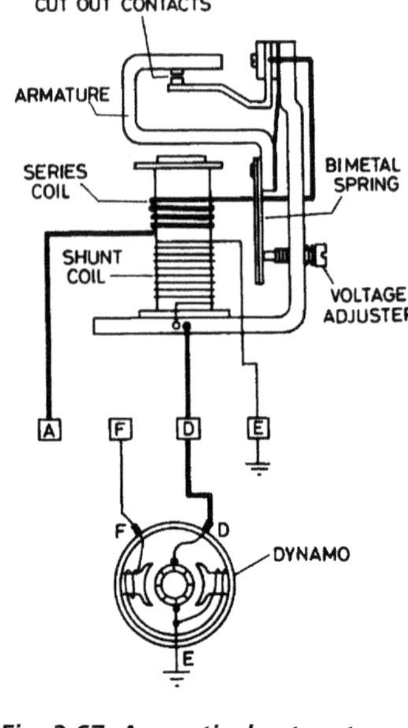


*Fig. 3.67 A practical cut-out*

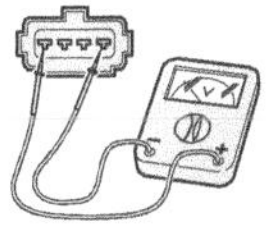

consists of several hundred turns of enamelled copper wire and it is this coil which provides the main magnetic armature pull. A second winding of heavy copper wire, or strip, is in series with the contacts and carries the main charging current. As the contacts close, a heavy initial charging current will produce a magnetisation adding to that of the shunt coil and assists in closing the contacts firmly without chatter. When the dynamo voltage falls below that of the battery, at tickover for example, current flows the other way from the battery to the dynamo. This gives rise to a magnetisation in opposition to that of the main shunt coil and helps to throw open the contacts cleanly.

**4** Note also the leaf spring with an adjusting screw for setting the cut-in voltage of the cut-out. In practice this leaf spring consists of two different metal strips riveted together and having differing expansion rates with heat; with change of temperature the spring will curve. As the temperature goes up, the shunt coil resistance will increase, and so a higher voltage will be required to pull in the armature; in compensation the bi-metal strip will bend away from the adjusting screw so that the spring load is reduced, thus tending to lower the cut-in voltage.

## 24 Regulator

**1** If the dynamo voltage rises too high for battery charging requirements, the regulator unit opens the connection between field and armature and inserts a resistor. This lowers the field current and so reduces the dynamo generated voltage.

**2** Fig. 3.68 shows the regulator, which has an electromagnetic relay like that of the cut-out. The magnetising (shunt) coil is connected between D and E, while the contacts are here shown mounted above the moving armature and are normally closed. When the armature pulls down, the contacts open and D and F are now joined through the resistor. Spring tension is controlled by the adjuster screw and, once again, the leaf spring is bi-metallic to compensate for temperature variation.

**3** This regulator has a drawback in that a battery in a low state of charge will have a low terminal voltage. A heavy charge current would flow and could burn out the armature, so in practice compensation is provided, so that the difference between the regulator voltage and that of the battery is never great enough to cause dynamo damage.

## 25 Compensated regulator

**1** Fig. 3.69 shows an additional coil on the regulator bobbin, consisting of a few turns of thick wire or of flat strip. This series coil carries the load current and produces a magnetic field which aids that of the shunt voltage coil.

**2** When a heavy load current flows the magnetic fields of the two coils add, giving a higher pull on the armature than that due to the shunt coil alone. The regulator contacts open at a lower voltage, and so the dynamo is operated at a variable voltage, according to the current flowing into the battery.

## 26 Load compensation

**1** The idea of a compensated regulator (Sec 25) is extended, so that extra series turns are added which carry currents to various vehicle loads, such as headlights. A battery in a low state of charge will suffer an additional terminal voltage fall when a load is switched on, and if this load current can be made to flow through a load coil such that the dynamo

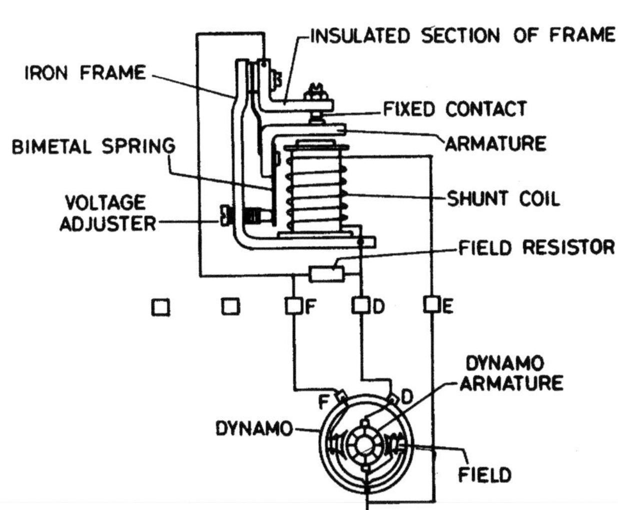


*Fig. 3.68 Voltage regulator*

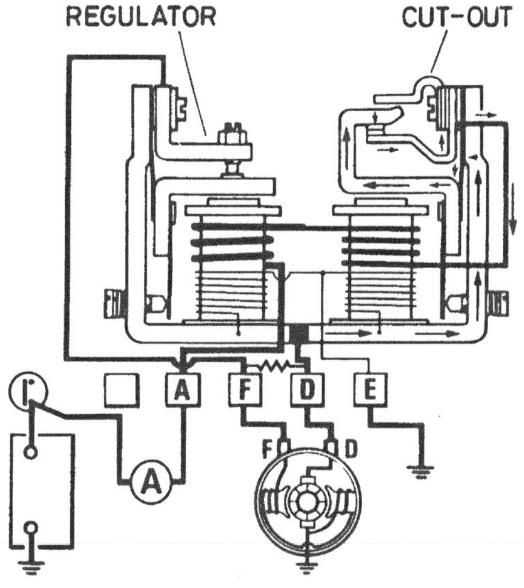


*Fig. 3.69 Compensated voltage control*

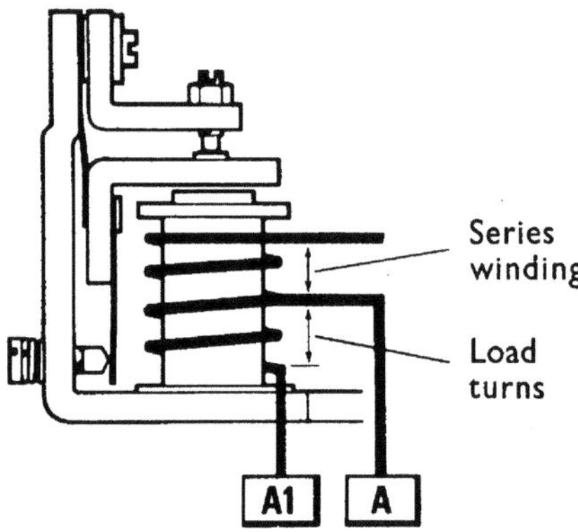


*Fig. 3.70 Load turns*

voltage is lowered with increased current, then additional protection is given (Fig. 3.70).

**2** The number of turns on both the compensation and load coils are made to suit the dynamo and vehicle loads, respectively, so control boxes cannot be interchanged without checking with the manufacturer's recommendations.

## 27 Complete compensated voltage regulator

**1** The compensated voltage control box is shown in Fig. 3.71. Current flows out of dynamo terminal D to the metal frames of the cut-out regulator units. After passing through the cut-out points it goes through the series coils on both bobbins and out to the A terminals for battery and charging, and also out to the A1 terminal for lighting and ignition-switched loads. The circuit is completed, via the vehicle chassis, back to the earth brush of the dynamo.

**2** This form of dynamo regulation has been used extensively for some years. There remains a disadvantage, however, in that the dynamo is not working to its full capacity for a proportion of the battery charging time. What is required is a maximum charge rate until charging is almost complete, thus ensuring the fastest possible battery recovery, and then to taper down gradually to a trickle charge. Such a requirement can be met with only slightly more complication in the current-voltage regulator (Section 28).

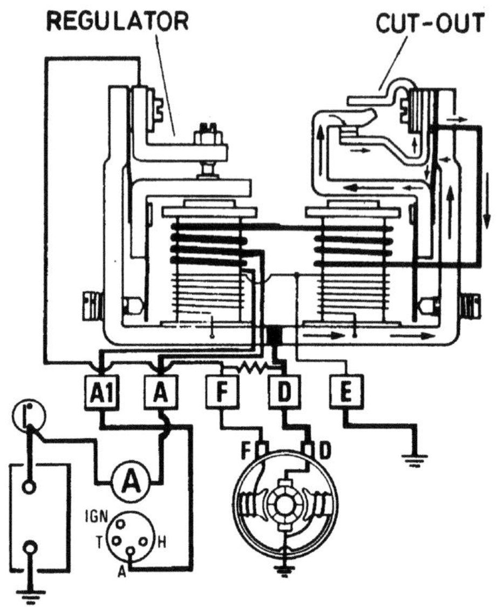


*Fig. 3.71 The complete regulator*

## 28 Current-voltage regulator

**1** Reference to the graph (Fig. 3.72) shows that a compensated voltage regulator starts to charge a discharged battery at a high rate but falls off quickly to a trickle level. Whilst this is happening the battery voltage rises slowly. The current voltage control regulator ensures that the battery is charged at a level rate by the current regulator until the battery voltage rises to a particular value when the voltage regulator takes over and the charge rate drops off to a trickle. The unit consists of three parts:

*(a) The cut-out*

*(b) The current regulator, which allows full dynamo output until the live voltage reaches a set level*

*(c) The voltage regulator, which assumes control of the dynamo for the final phase of charging when the current eventually drops to some 1 or 2 amperes*

**2** Assuming the battery to be discharged initially, the dynamo voltage will rise with dynamo speed up to 12.75 to 13.25 volts when the cut-out contacts close. With further rise in dynamo speed the charging current, flowing through the heavy gauge wire or strip wound round the current regulator bobbin, will cause the contacts (3) to open (see Fig. 3.73). This breaks the link between D and F, and introduces the resistor R, so the dynamo voltage will fall because the field current drops. Note that at this stage the voltage regulator coil contacts are closed. The current to the battery also drops, allowing the contacts (3) to close again.

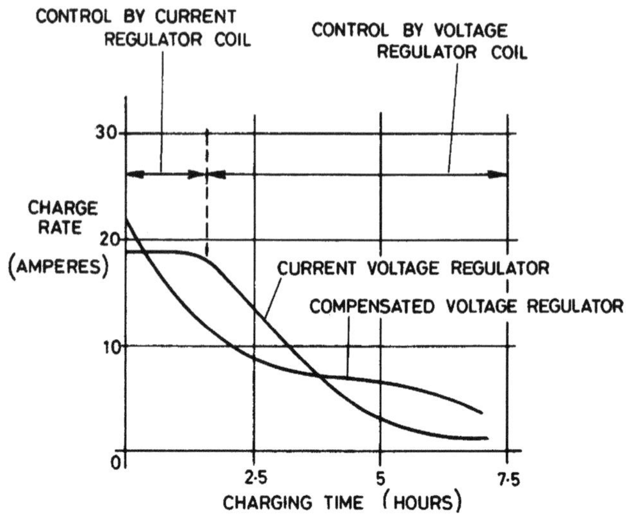


*Fig. 3.72 Comparison of regulator performances*

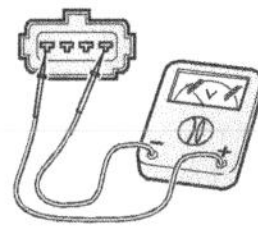

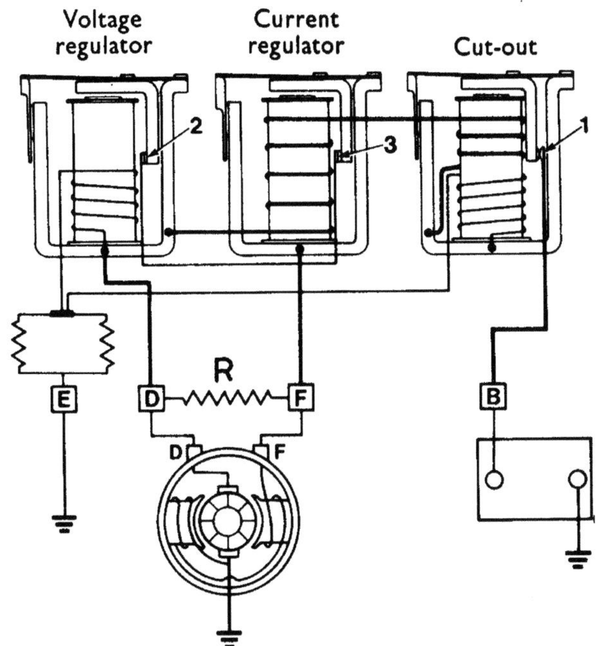


*Fig. 3.73 Current-voltage regulator*

**3** This process continues at a rate somewhere between 60 and 100 times per second, and so the dynamo current is limited to its rated maximum. Eventually, at about one-third full charge, the battery voltage will rise to the point where the voltage regulator armature is pulled in and thence vibrates. From this point it is the system **voltage** which is regulated, and not the current; the current regulator contacts stay closed for the remainder of the charging cycle because the coil current is insufficient to pull in the current regulator armature.

## 29 Bucking coil

Some current voltage regulators have a few turns of thick wire wound over the voltage regulator bobbin to assist the magnetic pull of the shunt coil. The effect is to make the contacts break more rapidly, and also to increase the frequency of the vibration. For this reason it is sometimes called a frequency coil.

## 30 Dynamo system tests

*Assuming that a fault exists in the system, it pays to follow a logical test procedure, unless the area of the fault is obvious.*

**Test 1: Check the battery**

Use a hydrometer and heavy discharge test.

**Test 2: Check belt tension**

In the case of dynamos the belt should deflect about 6.0 to 19.0 mm (1/4 in to 3/4 in) with moderate finger pressure at the centre of the longest span. Note whether the belt is running at the bottom of the pulley V – if so, the belt must be renewed, and possibly the pulley also.

**Test 3: Check for broken connections**

Also check for possible corroded contacts between connectors and fuse carriers.

**Test 4: Armature test**

With the main dynamo output lead D removed from the regulator box, run up the engine to about 1500 rpm (see Fig. 3.74). The voltage from the D lead to earth should be between 1.5 and 3 V, due to the field residual magnetism. If the reading is zero, or much lower than 1.5 V, then either the lead or the dynamo armature circuit is faulty.

**Test 5: Check dynamo field circuit**

Disconnect the D and F leads at the dynamo. Connect an ammeter between D and F terminals of the dynamo, and a voltmeter from D to earth. Run up the engine until the voltmeter reads 12 volts when the field current should be of the order of 2 to 2.5 amperes. Remove the dynamo for field coil repair if the voltage is outside these limits.

**Test 6: Zero load voltage setting**

This checks the regulator voltage setting. For a compensated voltage box such as the Lucas RB106, take off the A and A1 leads and link them together. In the case of the current voltage regulator take off the two B leads and link them (Fig. 3.75). At 3000 rpm engine speed measure the voltage from the D terminal to earth. For Lucas boxes the voltage limits are:

| | | |
|---|---|---|
| Compensated voltage regulators | RB106, RB108 | 16 to 16.5 volts |
| Current voltage regulator | RB340 | 14.5 to 15.5 volts |

Outside these limits, the regulators should be adjusted. Regulator boxes of most manufacturers have similar working

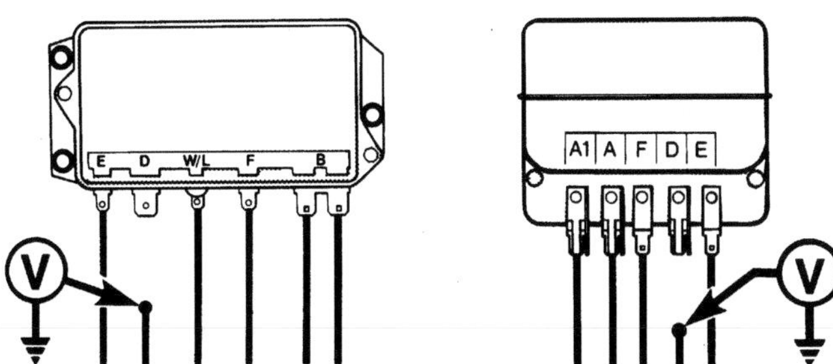


*Fig. 3.74 Checking armature and main lead – Test 4*

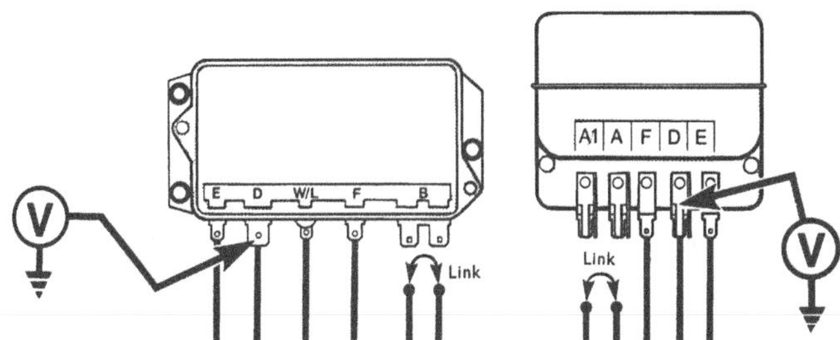


*Fig. 3.75 Zero load voltage setting – Test 6*

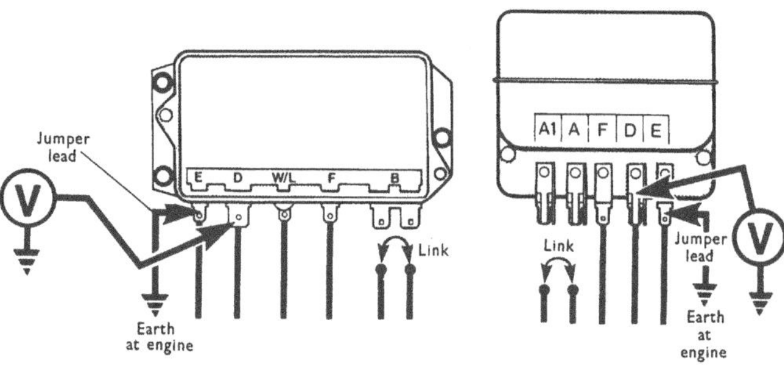


*Fig. 3.76 Control box earthing – Test 7*

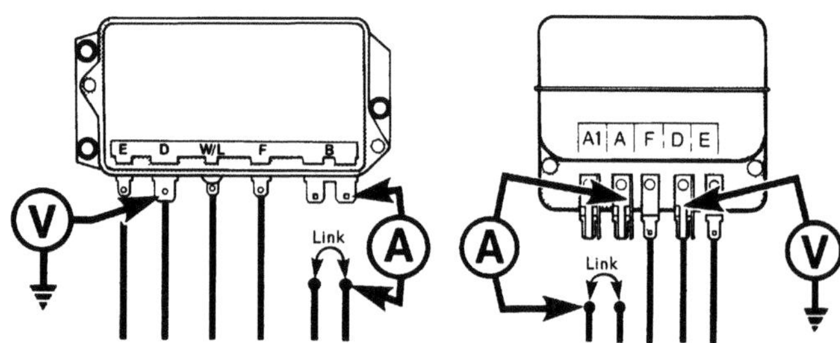


*Fig. 3.77 Cut-in voltage – Test 8*

voltages, and makers' information sheets should be consulted.

**Test 7: Control box earth**

Peculiar results occur if the earthing of the control box is faulty, examples being that the regulator works at the wrong voltage, or is incapable of adjustment. With the A, A1 or B leads bridged, as in Test 6, connect a jumper lead from the box earth terminal to an engine earth point (Fig. 3.76). If the box now regulates correctly, look for a corroded earth point. If the result is negative, renew the control box.

**Test 8: Cut-in voltage**

The box is connected as in Test 6, but with an ammeter between the A or B terminal and the bridged leads; a voltmeter is connected from terminal D to earth (Fig. 3.77). Start the engine, switch on headlights and raise the engine speed slowly. The cut-out contacts should close, indicated by ammeter charge, and the voltmeter should flick back to between 12.7 and 13.3 volts.

**Test 9: Reverse current**

Using the same connections as in Test 8, but with no voltmeter, run the engine up to about 3000 rpm and then slowly decrease the speed until the cut-out points open. At this point the reverse current should be 5A dropping to zero at opening. If reverse current stays present down to tickover or standstill, the contacts are sticking and the control box should be serviced or renewed.

**Test 10: Current regulator setting**

For current voltage regulator boxes only, short out the voltage regulator contacts by bridging them with a suitable clip. Insert an ammeter between B terminal and the linked leads (Fig. 3.78), and run up the engine to 3000 rpm. The ammeter should then show the full rated output current of the dynamo – typically of the order of 22 amperes. Reset the current regulator adjustment screw, if necessary. To check, leave the voltage contacts bridged and raise the engine speed from tickover to 3000 rpm, and recheck the current rating.

## 31 Contacts

**1** Contact cleaning is required occasionally, and it is important to use different methods for the regulator and cut-out contacts.

**2** Regulator contacts are made of tungsten and should be cleaned with either a carborundum stone or silicon carbide paper. Cut-out contacts are silver and hence very soft. These should be cleaned with fine grade glass paper.

**3** All contact dust should be removed with a cloth soaked in methylated spirits.

## 32 Dynamo – servicing notes

**1** After a period of service, wear in moving and sliding parts requires removal of the dynamo for routine maintenance.

**2** The commutator may become scored and grooved and the remedy depends on how badly it is affected. Sometimes all that is required is cleaning with petrol and the segment gaps scraped out. Possibly the commutator might need cleaning with a strip of fine glasspaper, but if it is burned away by arcing, then the armature must be mounted in a lathe and the commutator skimmed true.

**3** With this last treatment, it is necessary to undercut the insulation between segments to a depth of about 1/32 in (1 mm). Often a hacksaw blade with the teeth width reduced

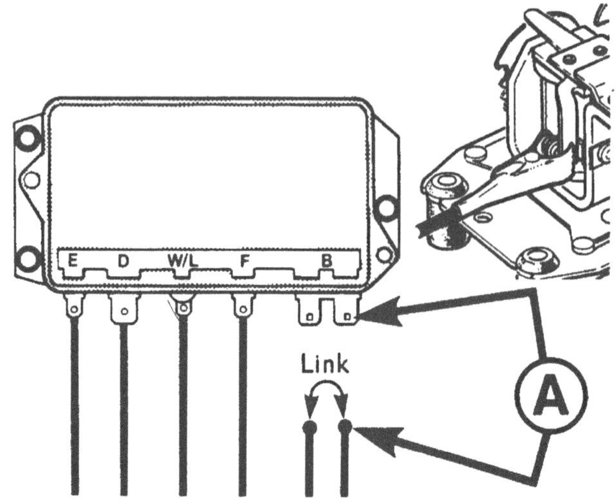


*Fig. 3.78 Current regulator setting – Test 10*

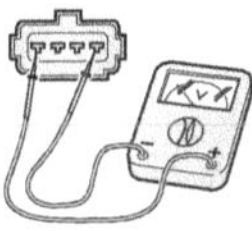

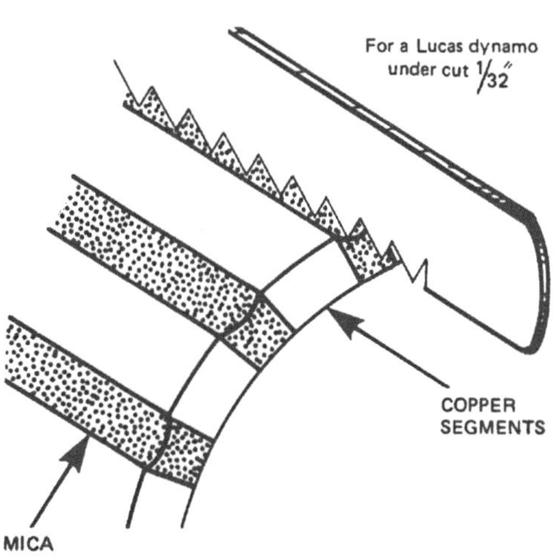


*Fig. 3.79 Undercutting the commutator*

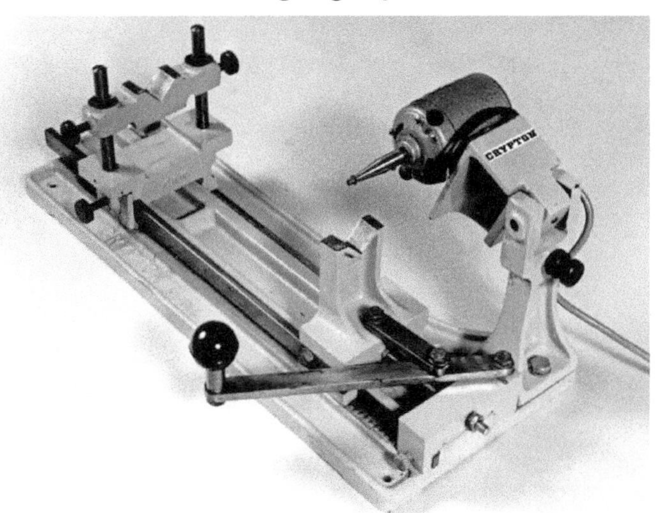


*Fig. 3.80 FKI Crypton commutator undercutting machine*

on a grinding wheel will be used for undercutting (Fig. 3.79). To complete the job care must be taken to remove any burr. FKI Crypton market a machine for commutator undercutting (Fig. 3.80), a valuable piece of equipment for the large scale auto-electrical shop.

**4** Brushes will throw carbon dust everywhere and this may be removed with petrol and a fine brush. It should not need stating that 'no smoking' is the rule, and work should be carried out in a well ventilated room. Brushes should be checked for adequate length and renewed if necessary. If new brushes are fitted, bed them in using a strip of fine glasspaper wrapped halfway round the commutator and rocking it back and forth a few times. This will profile the brush to the correct contour. Finally check for free brush movement in the brush carriers.

**5** Bearing wear gives a rumbling noise and, if bad enough, may cause the armature to rub on the pole shoes, as evidenced by bright areas seen during inspection.

**6** Removal of the bronze bush at the commutator end may be achieved by tapping it out with a suitable drift or, if it is reluctant, by cutting it lengthways and then drifting it out. The replacement bush should be soaked in oil for several hours (it is made of porous phosphor bronze) and then lightly tapped in place with a soft drift, preferably wood, or possibly pressed in ensuring suitable protection against damage. Regular oiling at 6000 mile intervals (Fig. 3.81) will prolong the life of this bearing bush considerably.

**7** The bearing at the drive end lasts longer than the bush at the other end, but if it has to be renewed remove the fan/pulley either by leverage or using a puller, having first removed the shaft nut and washer.

**8** With care the armature shaft can be tapped out from the bearing using a soft drift against the end of the shaft. Protection of the shaft thread is necessary by putting on the end nut; pressing out may be necessary if this method fails. After the bearing has been fitted, repack with high melting point grease.

**9** The presence of solder thrown round the body of the dynamo may mean failure of the armature. It is worth resoldering the joints of the armature conductors and the commutator segments. A large capacity soldering iron will be needed and resin flux, **not spirit flux**, must be used. Indeed, spirit flux must never be used on electrical joints at all.

**10** Failure of a field coil is usually shown by burn marks on the tape binding, and possibly by the coils having different resistance values. Sometimes failure occurs due to shorting down to the metal frame and this again can be checked by a test meter on the ohms range. It is possible to rewind a field coil by counting turns off the old coil and rewinding as a copy. Retaping must be done with care so as not to occupy too much space, yet give protection.

**11** Pole shoes are screwed very tightly to the dynamo yoke

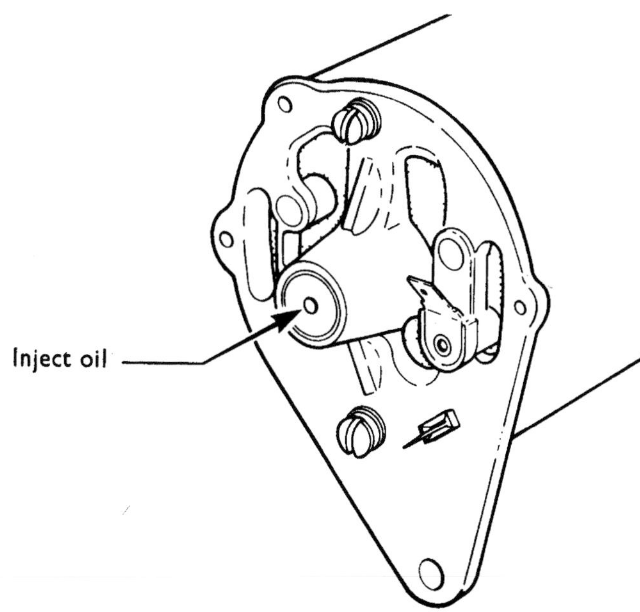


*Fig. 3.81 Oiling the bronze bush in a dynamo*

(body) and often need the use of an impact driver to loosen them. Take care to refit tightly for a pole shoe working loose in service spells total failure of the dynamo. A pole screw machine is available commercially (Fig. 3.82). After reassembly, running the dynamo as a motor (join the field and dynamo terminals) will give a fair indication that everything is in order.

*Fig. 3.82 FKI Crypton pole-screw machine*

## 33 Dynamo to alternator conversion

**1** While the dynamo is designed to power the original equipment of the vehicle, there will be a time when it cannot cope with added accessories. The best solution then is to remove the dynamo and substitute an alternator.

**2** It is simpler to wire in an alternator having an integral electronic regulator, for then only two cables are required. It may be that the mounting and belt tension adjustment bracket will need to be changed or modified, and for some vehicles later models will have alternators fitted as original equipment so that brackets will be available.

**3** Fig. 3.83 shows the changes in wiring. The dynamo control box may be left in place for the convenience of using certain blade terminals. In the example shown two B terminals strapped together internally remain connected to the battery via the live starter solenoid terminal and to the live terminal of the ignition switch.

**4** Next, the charge warning lamp is disconnected from the regulator box (WL terminal in this example) and connected to the cable which has been taken off the regulator box F terminal. This field cable can now be connected at the alternator to the IND terminal. Alternatively a new cable can be used.

**5** Similarly the D cable is disconnected both at the dynamo and the regulator D terminal. It is best not to re-use this, but to make up a fresh cable to connect the alternator main output terminal + direct to the battery or the solenoid live terminal.

**6** Manufacturers will supply an alternator and sometimes it may be possible to buy a conversion outfit with instructions, cables and alternator connectors. It is recommended that any cable joints are soldered to avoid possible trouble from corrosion at crimped joints.

**7** Loading of the alternator will be higher as accessories are used, and so will the torque required at the alternator pulley. Correct tensioning of the drivebelt is important; too loose and slipping will occur, too tight and the alternator bearings will have a short life.

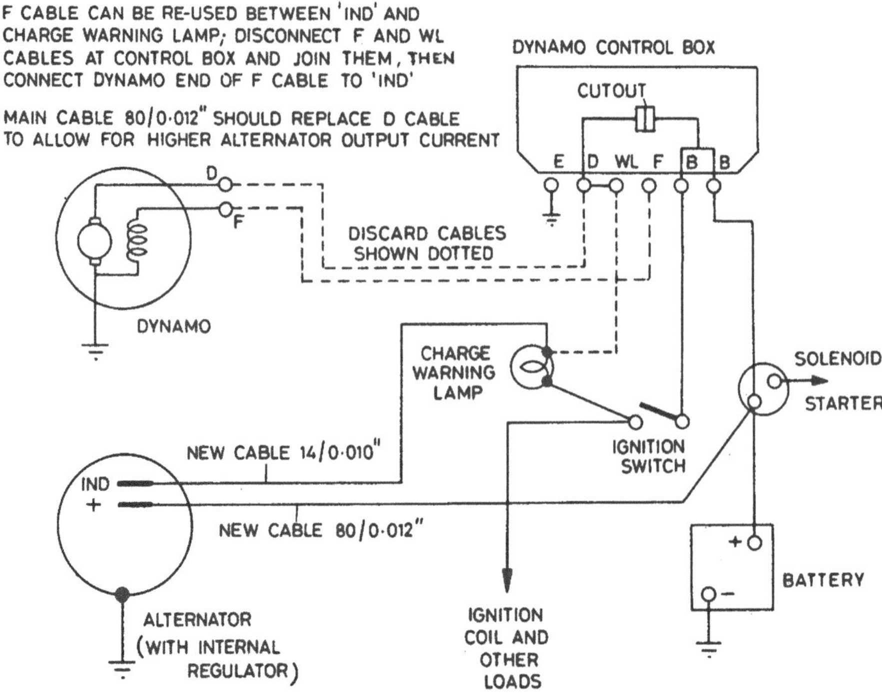


*Fig. 3.83 Conversion from dynamo to alternator*

# Starter motors

## 1 Introduction

**1** Early automobiles relied upon human power to turn over the engine until it fired. Every engine had a crankshaft dog into which a starting handle could be located, but the need for a starter motor soon became important. Engines became more powerful and difficult to swing over by hand and many injuries occurred because of kickback. It was necessary to retard ignition manually, usually by a lever near the steering wheel, before hand starting – if the driver forgot, an engine kickback might result. Cadillac cars were fitted with starter motors in 1912 but it was many years after that before all vehicles were so equipped.

**2** The starter motor takes battery stored energy and converts it into mechanical work needed to turn an engine over until it fires and runs, at which point the starter motor is disconnected mechanically from the engine. Starters for passenger cars generally have a rating of 2 kilowatts upwards and must have sufficient shaft output to run up an engine under cold conditions when lubricants are thick and viscous. Current demand can be as high as 450 amperes under worst conditions and for this reason it is vital that the starter circuit should have a low resistance of not more than

1 milliohm, calling for thick cables, clean terminals and a battery with low internal resistance. In order to start a piston engine, the starter motor should be able to crank it at 100 rev/min and higher for a rotary engine. Such specified speeds are to give sufficient air-intake flow rate to form the air:fuel ratio necessary for combustion.

## 2 Starter motor – basics

**1** The principle of the electric motor is explained in Chapter 1. Motors have a main magnet field which, interacting with the local field surrounding the armature magnetic coils, will produce a force on the armature coils. The simple motor of Fig. 4.1 shows the main field from N to S, an armature loop and a commutator which ensures that the armature current switches so that it always flows in the same direction as it passes under a particular pole. To do this the commutator here is a split ring and current is supplied by two blocks of copper/carbon, known as brushes, which are in sliding contact under a light spring pressure.

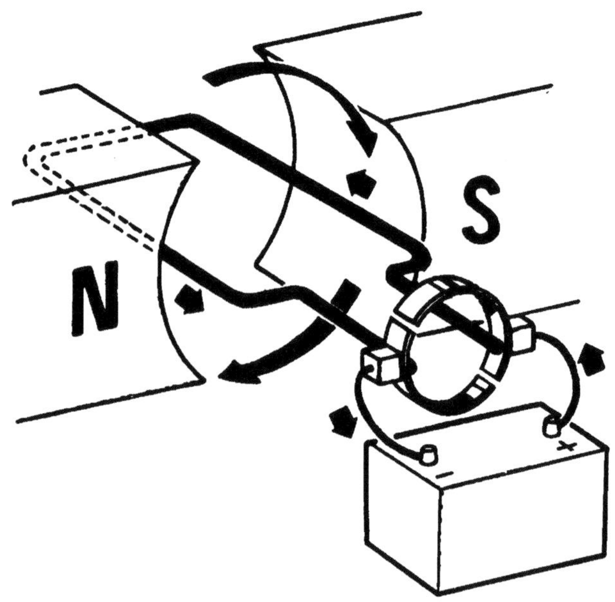


***Fig. 4.1 An elementary dc motor***

**2** The practical armature has a series of coils which are connected to a multi-segment commutator giving a practically uniform torque over a complete armature rotation. Armature coils are carried in slots of the iron frame used to make the iron path for the magnetic flux of the main field (Fig. 4.2). Magnetic flux will pass easily through iron but less easily through air, so air gaps are kept to a minimum. The armature frame is made up of laminations pressed tightly together but insulated one from another, the reason being to prevent the flow of induced eddy currents in the iron, which would cause heating losses.

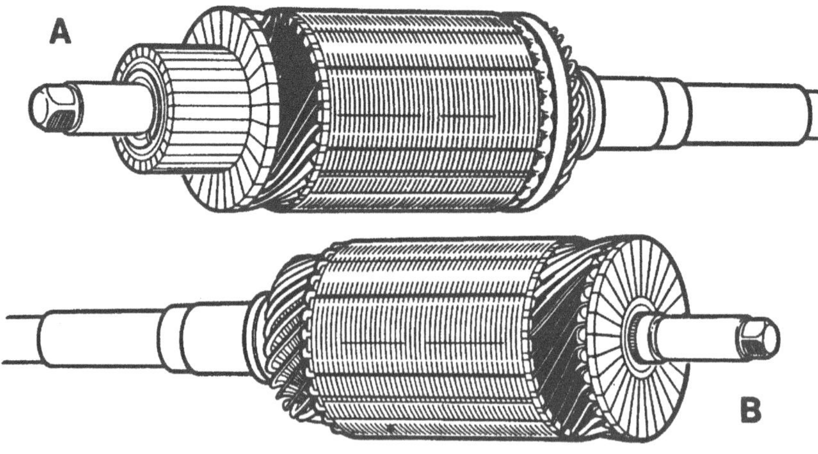


***Fig. 4.2 Typical armatures***

*A Drum commutator*
*B Face commutator*

**3** The main magnetic field may be produced either by permanent magnets or by electromagnets formed by winding excitation coils around the field poles (Fig. 4.3). Permanent magnets are used in certain recent designs of starter motor and have advantages in weight and simplicity over motors which use electromagnetic field excitation.

Important to remember for electromagnetic field poles:

(a) *The force on the armature conductors (hence the motor torque) depends upon the main magnetic field strength, symbol B*

(b) *The main magnetic field strength depends upon the product of:*

Number of field coil turns of wire (N) x Current flowing in them (I)

This factor is referred to as Ampere-Turns.

It follows that in order to produce a given magnetic field strength, the designer may use a high number of turns with low current OR a small number of turns with high current to achieve the same result. The starter motor usually has the

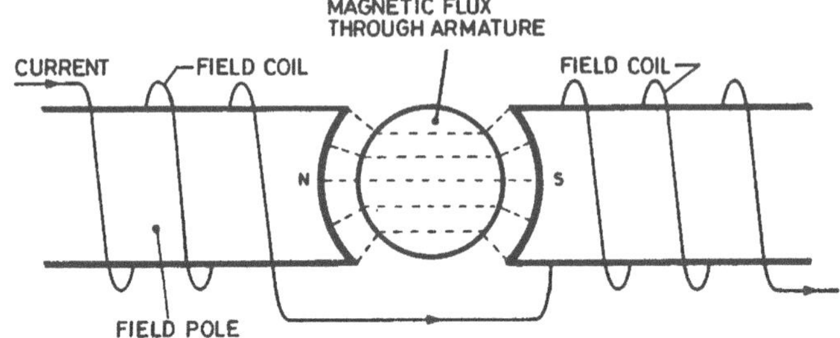


***Fig. 4.3 Magnetic flux depends upon field current and number of field coil turns***

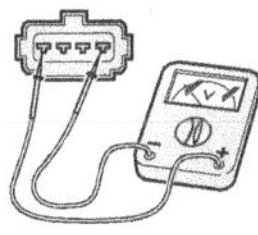

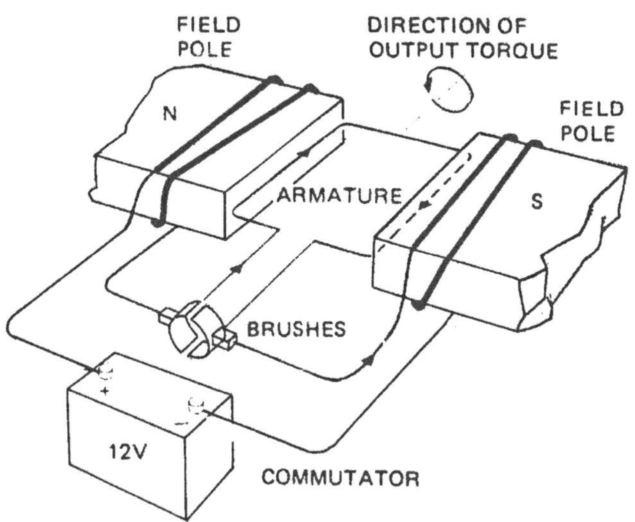


*Fig. 4.4 Direct current series motor*

latter arrangement and the field coils are connected in SERIES with the armature (ie a series motor) (Fig. 4.4).

**4** Finally, the force on the armature conductors (therefore motor torque) depends upon

Magnetic field strength x Armature Current.

## 3 Speed and torque

**1** When an electric motor armature is turning it should be remembered that the conductors of the armature are cutting through the magnetic field and will have a voltage (or back emf) generated in them. This is in no way connected with the fact that the rotation of the armature has been produced by a current supplied by a car battery, for the generated emf would be the same if the armature had been turned by an external mechanical drive.

**2** This back emf, as the name suggests, is always in the opposite direction to an externally supplied voltage, in this case from the car battery, and its value is directly dependent upon the speed of rotation of the armature. Thus, in simple terms, an electric motor when switched on will speed up until the back emf is equal to the supply voltage, less a small amount to allow for the resistance volt-drop in the field, armature and brushes (Fig. 4.5).

**3** Torque depends upon two factors, magnetic flux and armature current, and the series starter motor is ideal for producing a high starting torque for two reasons:

(a) *When the starter key is turned the motor is at standstill. There is thus no back emf to limit the current, only internal resistance voltage drop, and so the starting current is momentarily very high*

(b) *This high current flows through the field coils which are in series with the armature, and so the magnetic flux is also high.*

For these reasons, the series wound dc motor finds favour for starter applications and for vehicle traction work, eg fork lift trucks, because of excellent take-off characteristics.

**4** Another characteristic of the series motor is that it will race up to high speeds off load. Do not leave a starter motor running light, or the armature may be damaged with windings flying out of place due to centrifugal force.

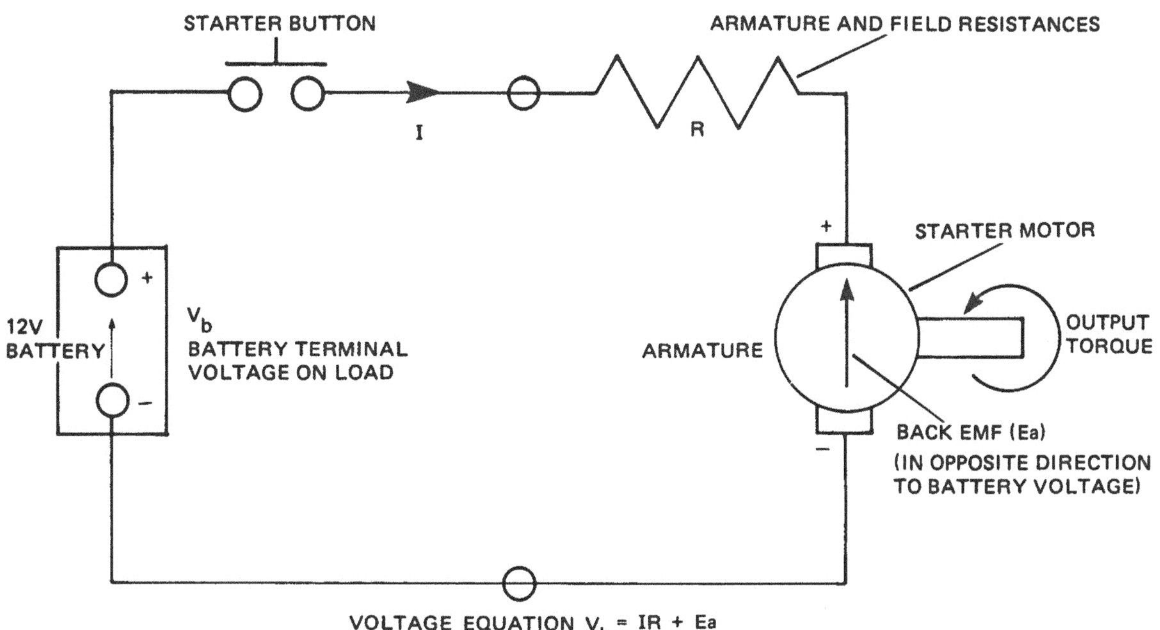


*Fig. 4.5 Starter motor conditions on load*

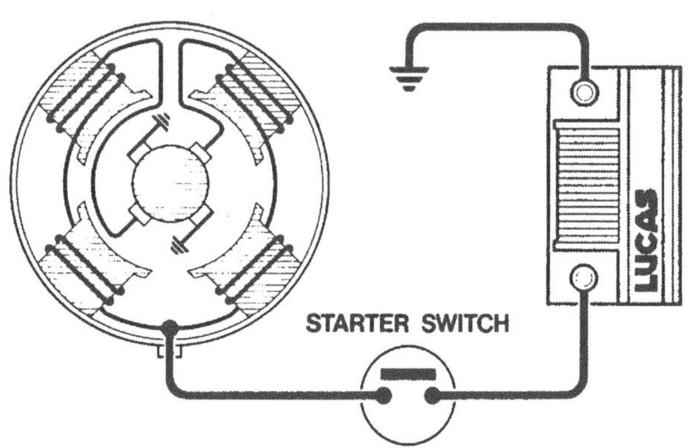


*Fig. 4.6 The starter circuit*

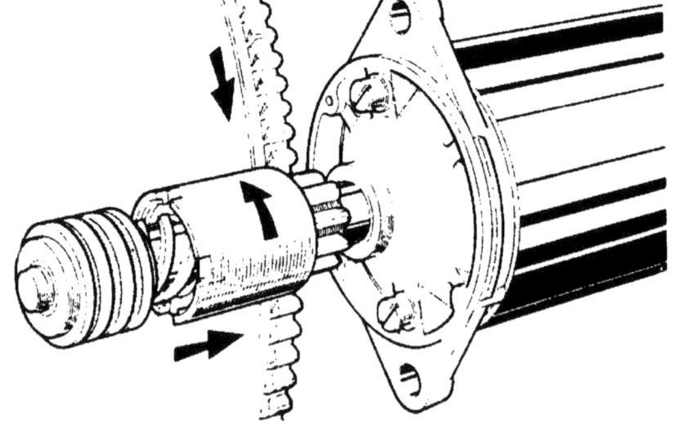

*Fig. 4.7 The simple drive*

## 4 Power transmission

Power transmission takes place in two stages when the starter switch is operated. First there is a power flow from the battery to the starter motor, causing the motor armature to rotate: then there is the power flow from the armature to the vehicle engine, this being accomplished by the engagement of a pinion gear on the armature shaft with a geared ring on the engine flywheel (Figs. 4.6 and 4.7).

## 5 Motor classification

**1** Electric motors are classified by the arrangements for providing the (magnetic) field (Fig. 4.8). Of these, the series field motor (just called a series motor) is probably the most common, but recent development work has resulted in a lightweight permanent-magnet motor. Compound motors are used for heavier duty, the shunt field machine is rarely used for automobile engine starting and will not be considered here.

**SHUNT MOTOR**

*General purpose motor. Not used as starter motor. Field has large number of turns and significant resistance*

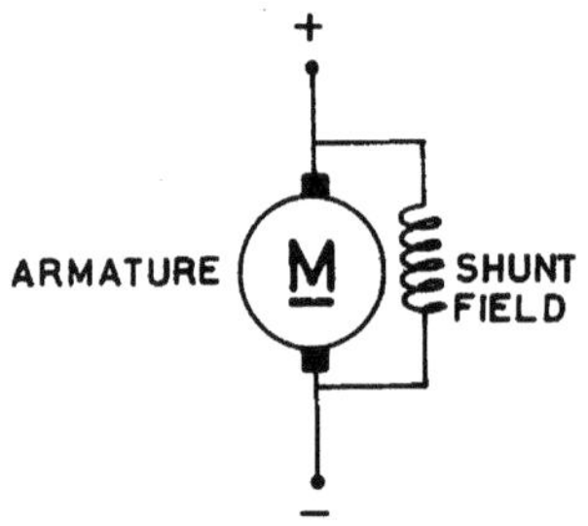

+ ARMATURE M SHUNT FIELD −

**SERIES MOTOR**

*High starting torque, ideal for engine cranking. Field winding is of few turns of heavy gauge wire or strip and is of low resistance*

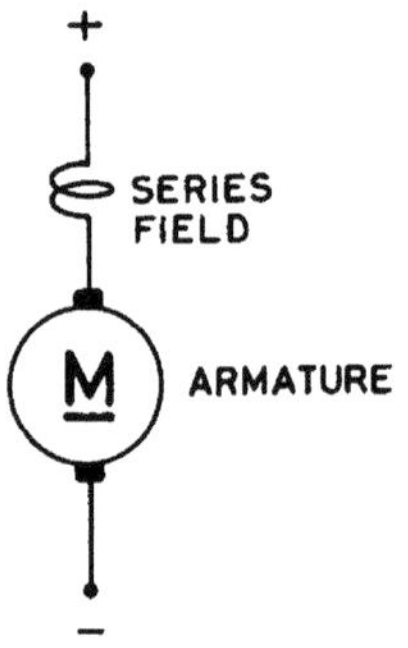

+ SERIES FIELD M ARMATURE −

**COMPOUND MOTOR**

*Sometimes used for larger starter motors. Switched in two stages:*

*1 Shunt winding in series with armature giveing low torque for meshing pinion to armature. Series winding not used*

*2 Switched to connection as shown here - full armature current*

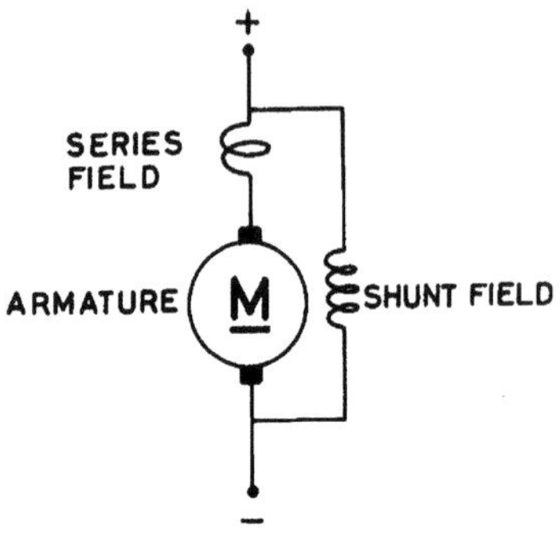

+ SERIES FIELD ARMATURE M SHUNT FIELD −

**PERMANENT MAGNETIC MOTOR**

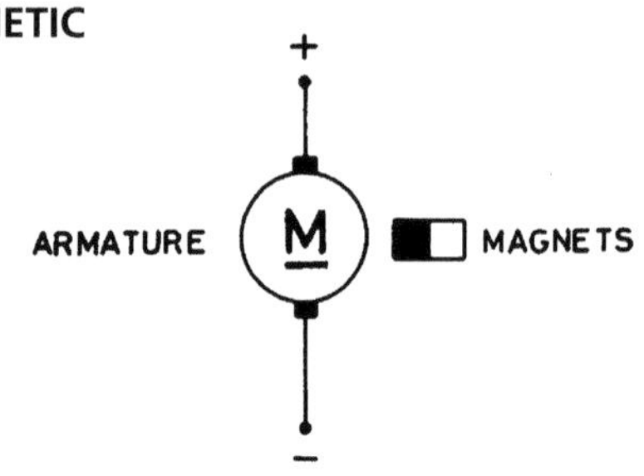

+ ARMATURE M MAGNETS −

*Now used for starter motors due to developments in magnets and othe rmaterials, giving a lightweight geared motor of high efficiency*

*Fig. 4.8 DC motor classification*

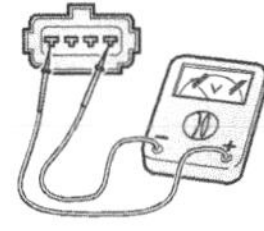

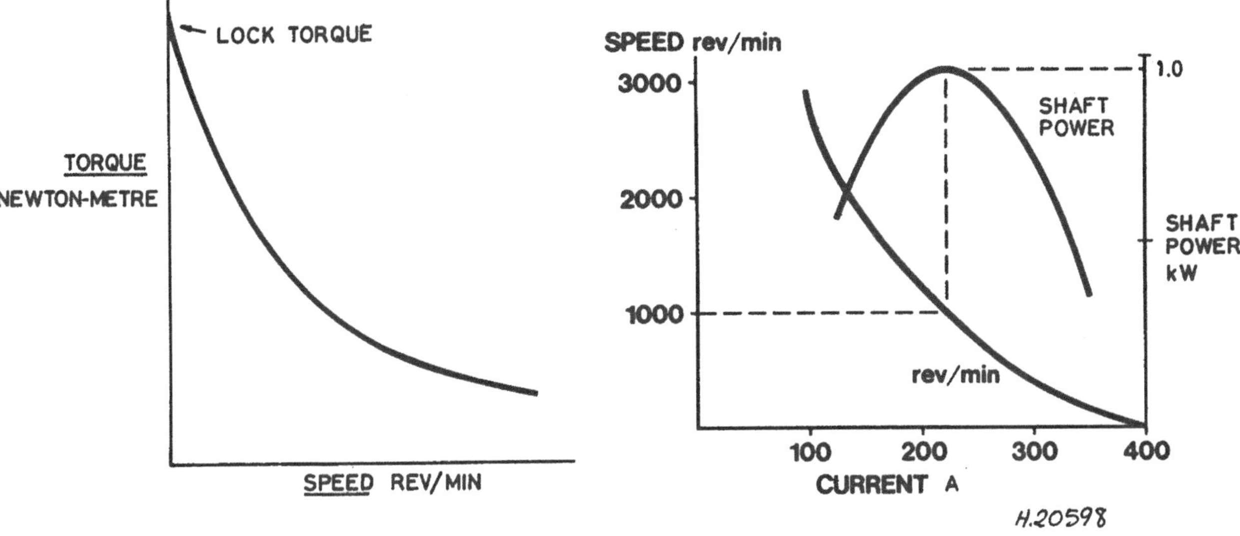


*Fig. 4.9 Characteristics of dc series motor*

**2 The series motor** has the field windings and the armature connected in series; it is the most commonly used type of machine for passenger vehicles. As explained in Section 3 the series motor gives a high starting torque which falls off sharply as speed increases. This characteristic is ideal for overcoming starting resistance or stiction of the engine (Fig. 4.9).

**3 Permanent magnet motors** are small in size and simple in design. Because there is no wound field there is no ohmic volt-drop except internally in the armature. In order to generate maximum power this type of machine may have gearing between the armature and the output shaft.

**4 Compound motors** are used where higher power is needed. This type of motor has both a shunt and a series winding which act in two stages:

(a) *When first activated, the shunt field is connected in series with the armature and acts as a volt-dropping resistor; the current is limited by this and the meshing torque of the armature is low*

(b) *In the second stage, the shunt field winding is connected in parallel with the armature which now has the series field winding in series with it.*

When the pinion is thrown out of mesh after the engine starts, the supply to the starter is switched off and the rotating armature acts as a generator, into the shunt field winding. The energy absorbed by the shunt winding causes the armature to stop quickly – a form of electromagnetic braking.

## 6 Starter pinion/flywheel ratio

**1** Fig. 4.9 shows the performance of a typical starter motor indicating that maximum shaft power occurs at a speed of 1000 rev/min. Allowing that an engine should be turned over at 100 rev/min at starting, the ratio of flywheel-to-pinion teeth will be:

$$\frac{\text{No. of flywheel teeth}}{\text{No. of starter pinion teeth}} = \frac{1000}{100}$$

or 10 : 1

A starter pinion has, say, 9 teeth, therefore the flywheel ring should have 90 teeth in this example. Gearing down is also a method of increasing torque and this is necessary in order to be able to use a physically small electric motor to turn over an engine; Fig. 4.10 illustrates the case of a starter with a torque of say 3 Nm (newton-metres). If the gear ratio is 10:1 then the torque at the crankshaft will be increased by this ratio. This is equivalent to 30 Nm or a force of 30 newtons at a radius of 1 metre. The increase of torque is gained at the expense of crankshaft rev/min which will be 10 times slower than the starter motor.

(For those more familiar with Imperial units:
1 lbf = 4.45 newtons and 1 ft = 0.305 metre)

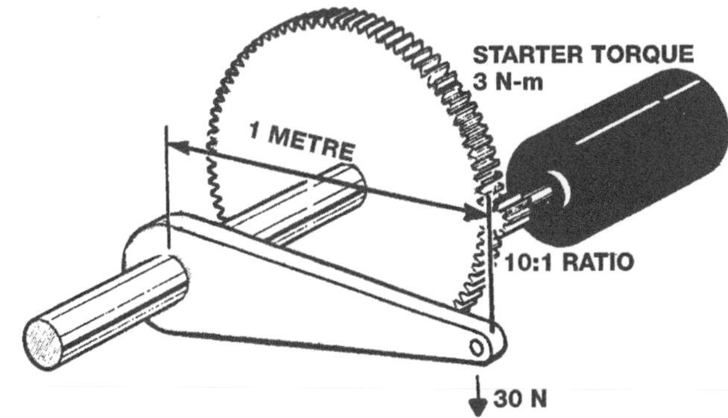


*Fig. 4.10 Torque magnification by gearing*

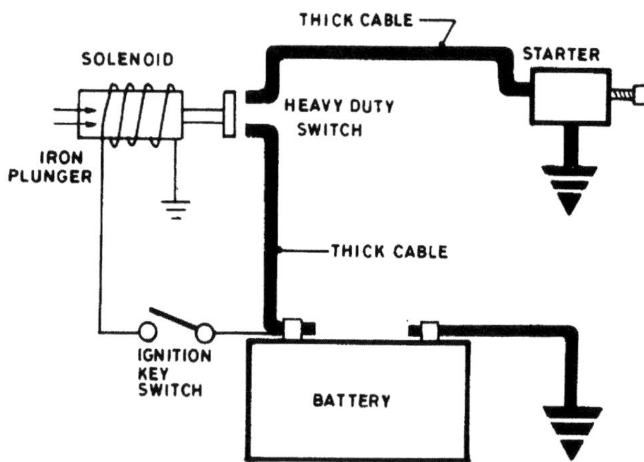


*Fig. 4.11* ***Starter switching circuit***

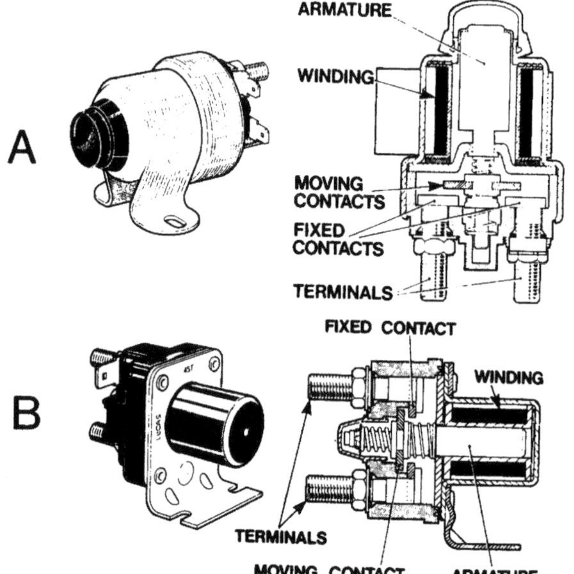


*Fig. 4.12* ***Solenoid switches***

*A Switch with manual button facility*
*B Switch with no manual button facility*

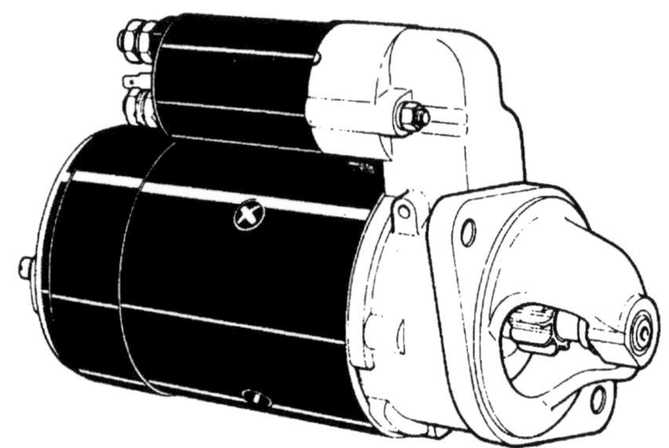

*Fig. 4.13* ***Solenoid mounted on typical pre-engaged starter motor***

## 7 Starter solenoid

**1** Remembering that the starter takes a heavy current on load, it is essential to use thick cables from the battery and the shortest convenient cable route. For these reasons the switch is always remotely operated by a solenoid (or magnetic switch) which is a form of electromagnet. The solenoid coil (Fig. 4.11) takes a low current which is easily handled by the ignition key switch, the solenoid magnetic field pulls the iron plunger to the centre of the solenoid coil, and in so doing closes the heavy duty contacts of the starter switch.

**2** There are two types of solenoid starter switch (Fig. 4.12).

(a) *The separate solenoid which may have a push button for manual operation, and is used with inertia drive mechanisms*

(b) *The integral solenoid which is mounted on the starter body and carries out the functions of first engaging the pinion teeth with the flywheel gearing and then switching on the starter current. This is the pre-engaged starter motor (Fig. 4.13).*

## 8 Solenoid operation

**1** The solenoid has two windings which are connected in parallel (Fig. 4.14). When the ignition key switch is turned on, the heavy gauge winding creates a powerful magnetic field which pulls the iron plunger into the coil centre, closing the heavy duty contacts which connect the starter motor straight onto the battery.

**2** It will be seen that when the contacts are closed, this closing coil is then short-circuited. The second winding acts as a hold-on coil with sufficient magnetic force to prevent the iron plunger from returning to the 'off' position.

**3** When the driver releases the ignition key switch from the

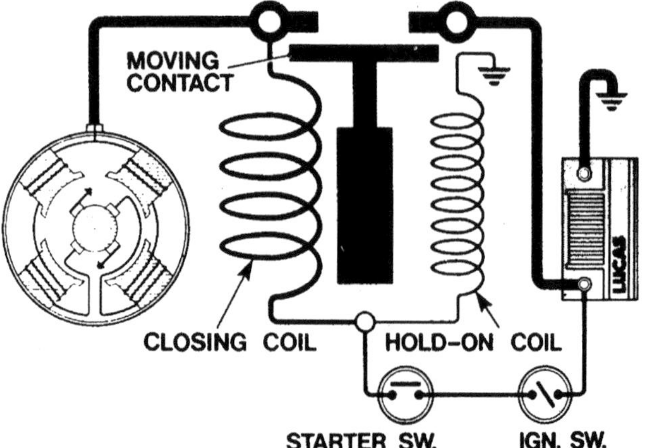


*Fig. 4.14* ***Solenoid operated starter circuit***

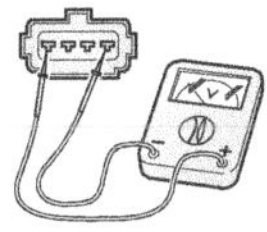

'start' position, the voltage to the hold-on coil disappears and the plunger returns under spring pressure to the 'off' position, simultaneously opening the heavy duty contacts and so disconnecting the battery from the starter. As the plunger returns it withdraws the starter pinion from the flywheel.

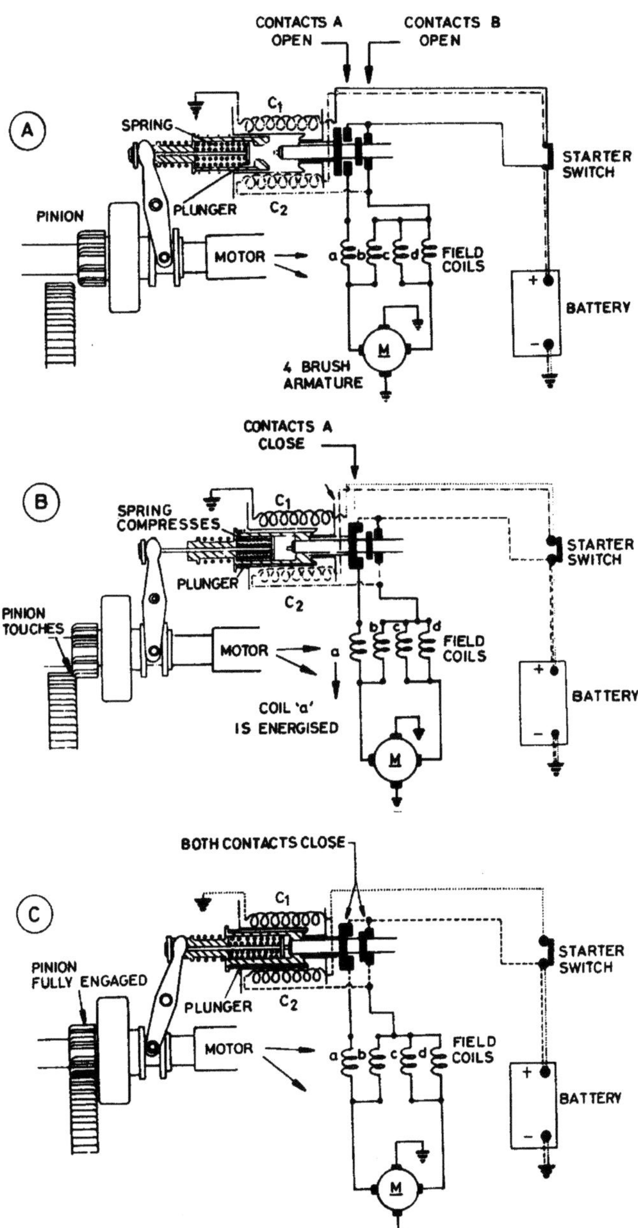


***Fig. 4.15 Low power indexing operation***

*A Pinion moves towards flywheel. Contact A will close before contacts B. No field coils energised so motor does not turn*

*B Pinion touches flywheel in tooth-to-tooth abutment. Contact A closes – motor turns slowly to allow pinion to slide into engagement. Plunger spring compresses forcing pinion into engagement. Coil 'a' only is fully energised*

*C Pinion fully engaged both contacts close. C2 is shorted out, Full power to motor. C1 remains energised to hold in plunger, All field coils a, b, c and d now energised*

**4** A simple version of solenoid is also used with a single winding connected across the supply via the ignition starter switch. In automatic cars, provision is made to prevent starter operation when the car is in gear. This consists of an inhibitor switch which is included in the solenoid switching circuit and will allow starting only in the P (park) or N (neutral) positions of the selector lever.

**5** One variation of solenoid arranges for, initially, limited power to the starter when the pinion teeth come into abutment with the starter ring teeth, prior to meshing in. One of four field windings only is energised. This is known as low power indexing and prevents the severe mechanical jarring that would take place if full power had been applied.

## 9 Inertia drive starters

**1** The action of the inertia (or Bendix) drive is to throw the pinion along a coarse thread and into engagement with the flywheel gear. So long as the starter is driving the engine the pinion gear remains engaged, but when the engine fires and the flywheel rotates faster than the starter pinion, the pinion runs back down the screw thread and disengages (Fig. 4.16). The speed of disengagement is often very high if the engine picks up readily, and so a spring is located at the shaft end to absorb the shock of pinion impact.

**2** A variety of inertia drive mechanisms is in use, depending upon the application. Referring to Fig. 4.17, showing one

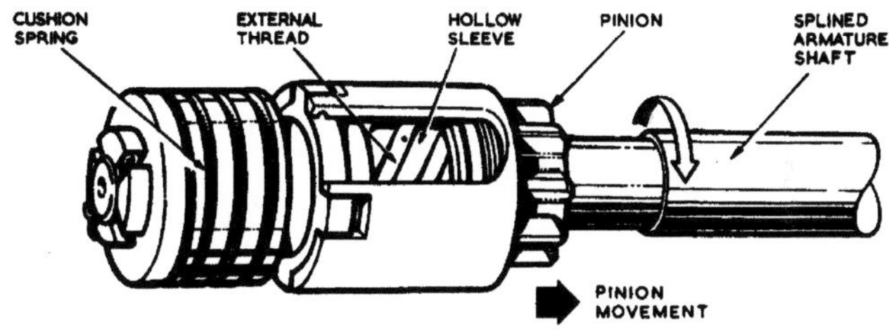


***Fig. 4.16 One type of inertia drive mechanism***

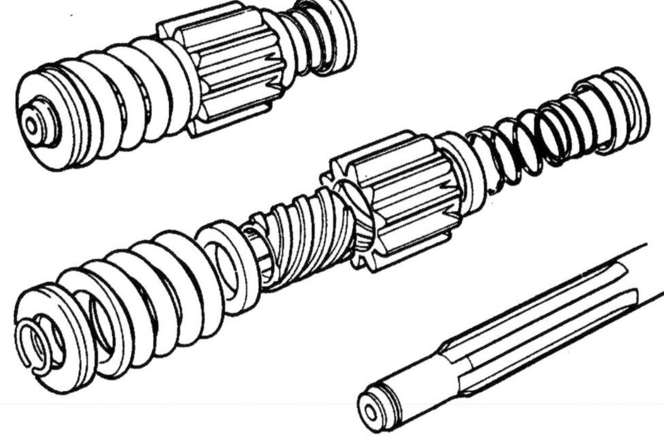

***Fig. 4.17 'S' type drive***

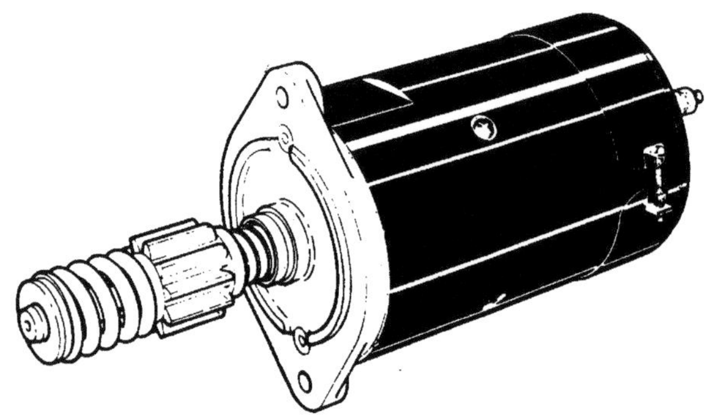

*Fig. 4.18 Lucas M45G inertia drive starter*

*Diameter: 4.5 in (114.3 mm)*
*Application: Large petrol engines*
*Lock torque: 22.5 lb/ft at 460 A*
*Armature: 37 slots*

type, the S drive pinion is mounted on a screwed sleeve, which is carried on the splines of the armature shaft. The sleeve moves along the shaft against a compression spring which reduces the shock at the moment of engagement.

The movement of the pinion in one direction is stopped when the cup washer (or collar) fully compresses the restraining spring and abuts against the shoulder of the fixed sleeve. Movement in the other direction is stopped when the helically screwed sleeve presses the thrust washer against the main spring. The pinion restraining spring is fitted over the armature shaft to prevent the pinion from vibrating into mesh with the flywheel when the engine is running. The Lucas M45G starter shown in Fig. 4.18 uses this type of drive which runs TOWARDS the motor body when engaging the flywheel teeth (known as an inboard starter). Fig. 4.19 illustrates the Lucas Eclipse drive which is similar to the American Bendix drive.

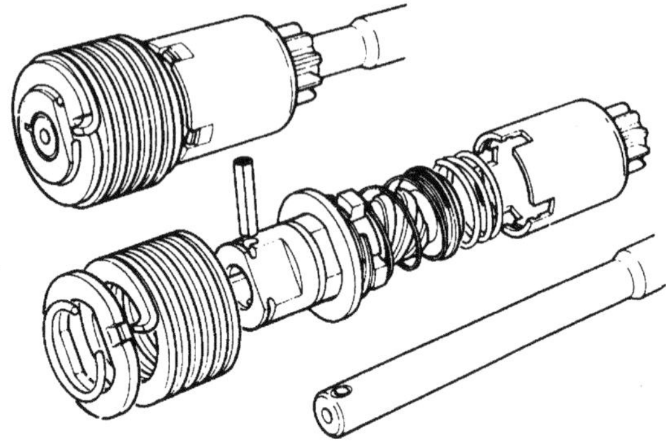

*Fig. 4.19 Eclipse type drive*

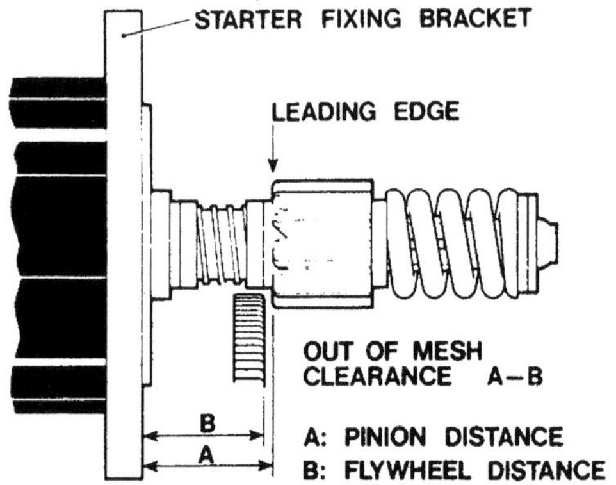


*Fig. 4.20 Out-of-mesh clearance*

## 10 Out-of-mesh clearance

**1** The starter pinion must be set correctly in relation to the starter ring so that it will slide into engagement with the minimum of rotary movement. Out-of-mesh clearance is illustrated by Fig. 4.20 and should be within the limits shown for Lucas starters:

| Drive type | Out-of-mesh clearance |
|---|---|
| All types except Eclipse | 1/8″± 1/32″ |
| Eclipse | 7/32″ nominal |

**2** To check the clearance two measurements must be made:
(a) *From the leading edge of the pinion to the fixing flange of the starter, distance A in the diagram*
(b) *From the leading edge of the flywheel to the starter fixing flange (distance B)*
then: Clearance = A – B

## 11 Pre-engaged starters

**1** In this type of starter, the pinion is slid into engagement with the flywheel teeth before the starter motor turning current is switched on. When the engine starts, the pinion does not eject until the starter switch is released and overcomes the problem of the pinion being flung out of engagement due to a single firing stroke if the engine 'coughs'.

Because of the gentler form of tooth engagement and disengagement, better starting and less flywheel teeth wear is claimed. Once the engine starts, should the driver not release the starter switch immediately, the danger of the engine driving the starter is overcome by an overrunning clutch which disengages drive between the pinion and the armature. Fig. 4.21 shows a cut-away view of a pre-engaged starter motor.

### Operation

**2** The solenoid has two windings, one of which, the closing coil, creates a powerful magnetic field so as to pull the plunger towards the centre of the coil. The second coil is made of finer gauge wire, and is the holding coil which keeps the plunger in position for so long as the starter switch is on. A second function of the solenoid is to close

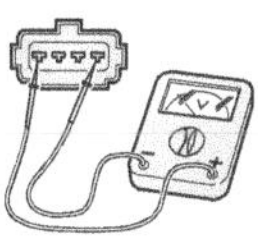

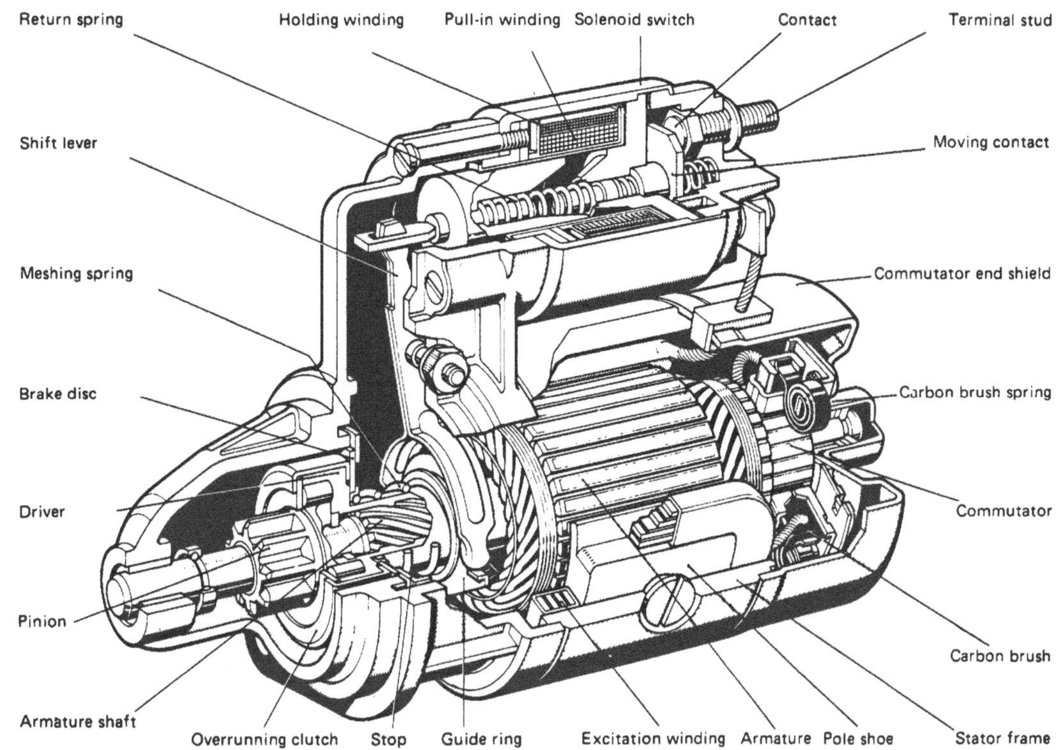


*Fig. 4.21 Cut-away view of a pre-engaged starter motor*

the main contacts between the battery and the starter motor armature.

**3** When the starter switch is closed, current flows from the battery through the closing coil and into the armature (Fig. 4.14). The pinion is drawn into mesh with the flywheel, the solenoid main contacts are closed, short circuiting the closing coil, and full current flows into the armature. The holding coil keeps the plunger in position. Drive is now transmitted from the armature through the uni-directional (overrunning) clutch and the pinion by helical splines on the armature shaft.

**4** Sometimes two teeth of pinion and flywheel come into contact instead of meshing. The plunger continues to travel to the centre of the solenoid, compressing the engagement (or meshing) spring (Fig. 4.21). The main contacts close, the armature begins to rotate and the pinion slips into mesh. The 'lost-motion' spring shown in Fig. 4.22 located around the solenoid plunger assembly ensures that the main contacts open before the pinion has been withdrawn. This avoids the possibility of the motor overspeeding if it had no mechanical load.

**5** When the engine fires, the pinion speed will be greater than that of the armature. The rollers of the overrunning clutch (Fig. 4.23) will disengage drive between the shaft and

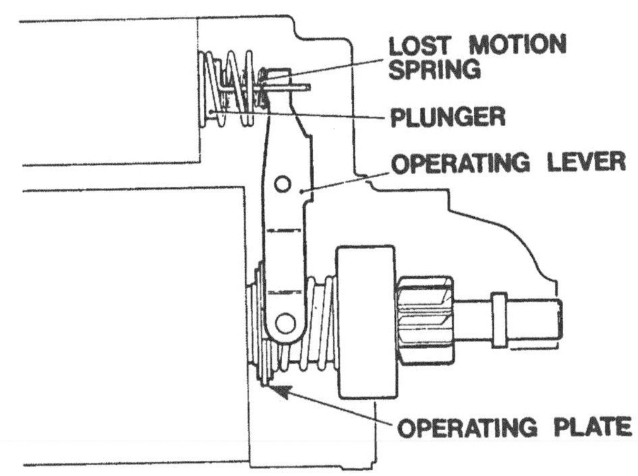


*Fig. 4.22 Drive mechanism linkage*

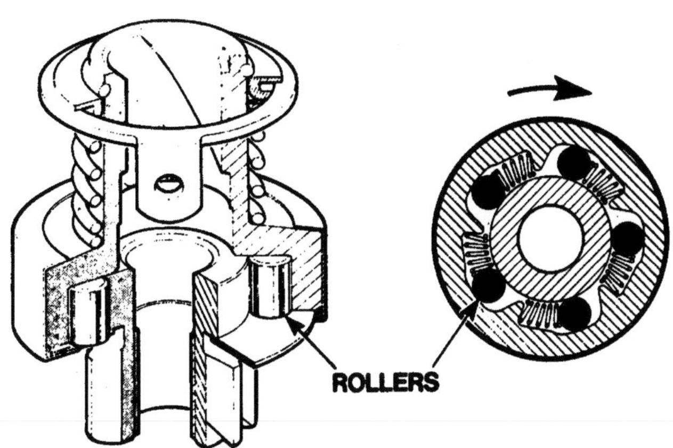


*Fig. 4.23 Roller clutch drive assembly*

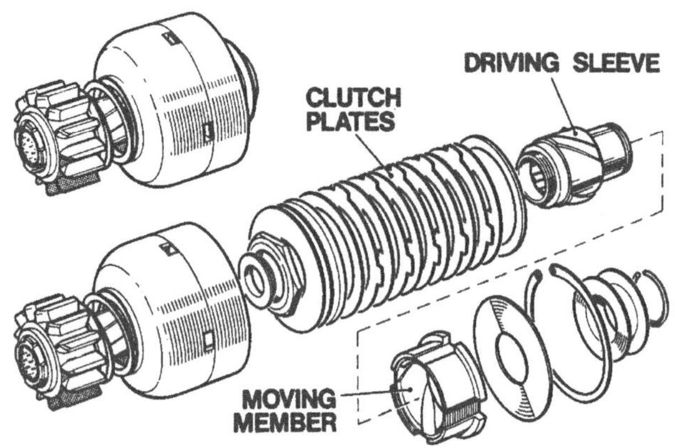


*Fig. 4.24 Plate clutch drive assembly*

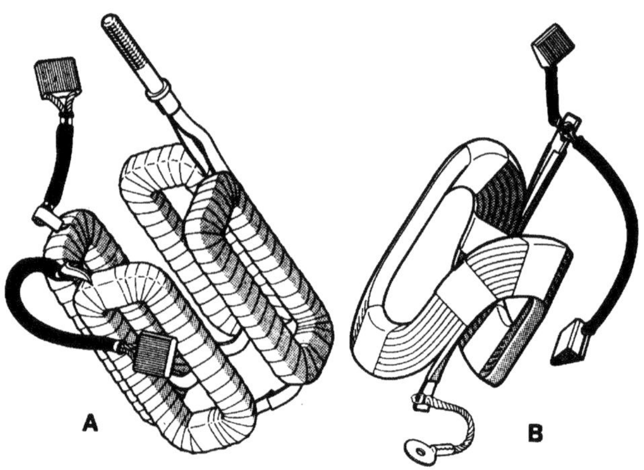


*Fig. 4.25 Conventional field coils (A) and wavewound field coil (B)*

the clutch body and so prevent the engine driving the starter motor. The rollers are spring-loaded and, according to the direction of the drive, they are either free-running or wedge-locked between the driving and driven parts. More rarely, a plate-type clutch is used in starter motors to protect the armature against engine backfiring. This clutch will also slip in the driving direction at two or three times full-load torque (Fig. 4.24).

## 12 Starter motor construction

**1** Earlier, Fig. 4.2 showed armature construction where the two types of commutators should be noted. Field coils are shown in Fig. 4.25. Conventional coils are shown in Part A where they are connected in series-parallel. Part B shows wave-wound coils which are continuously wound with no interconnecting joints. One end of the winding is earthed to the yoke by an eyelet, the other end terminates in a pair of brushes, here shown for use on a face-type commutator.

**2** Brushes are mounted on commutator end brackets. Fig. 4.26 shows:

(A) a 4-brush bracket for use with a drum commutator. Two brushes go to the commutator and two are earthed.

(B) brush gear used with face commutators in which the brushes are mounted in the bakelite moulding. Two brushes go to the supply and two to the field coils.

**3** Fig. 4.27 shows connections for series fields and series-

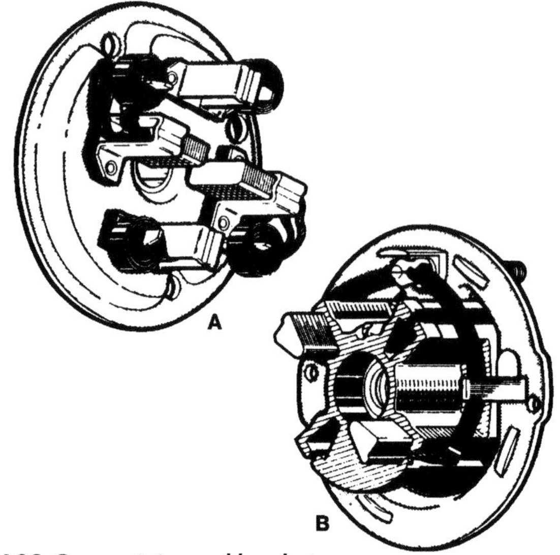


***Fig. 4.26 Commutator end brackets***
*A For drum commutator B For face commutator*

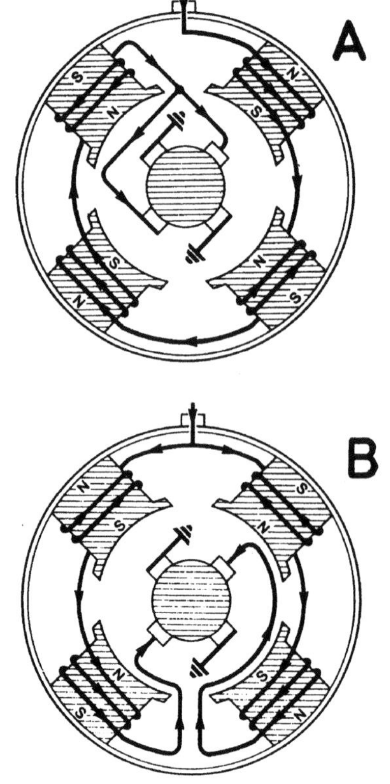


***Fig. 4.27 Starter internal circuit***
*A Series field B Series parallel field*

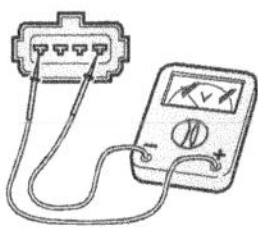

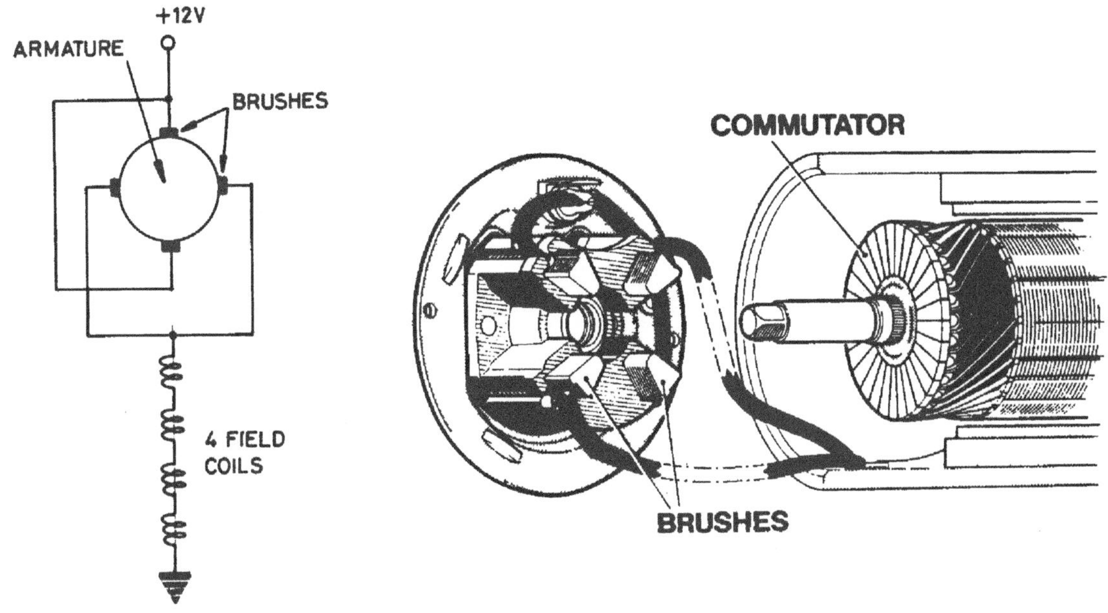


*Fig. 4.28 4-pole starter with wave wound field coils and face commutator*

parallel fields. Note that these descriptions relate to how the field coils are connected to each other. Both motors have the field coil assembly in series with the armature and are still series motors.

**4** The arrangement for a modern design of starter motor with face commutator and wave wound field is shown in Fig. 4.28. Four insulated brushes are used here with the field coils making the earth connection.

## 13 Permanent magnet geared starters

**1** A recent development has seen the emergence of a light weight starter of simple design using permanent magnets for the field and a geared transmission.

**2** Fig. 4.29 shows the armature and gear-drive of a Bosch

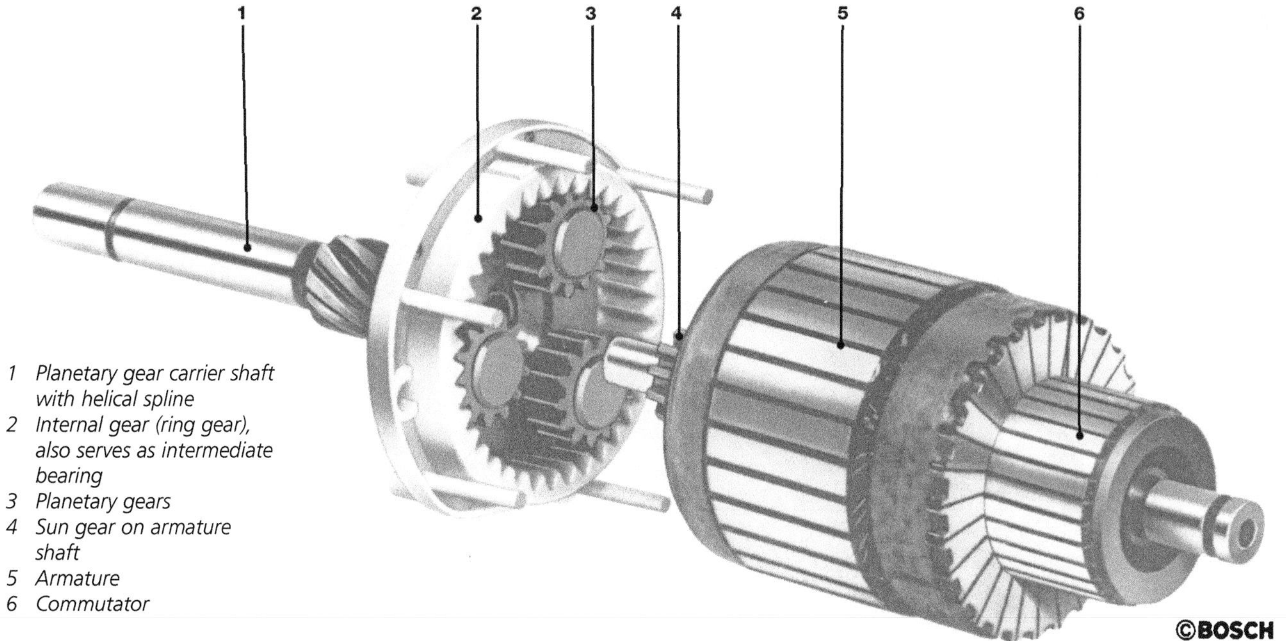


1 *Planetary gear carrier shaft with helical spline*
2 *Internal gear (ring gear), also serves as intermediate bearing*
3 *Planetary gears*
4 *Sun gear on armature shaft*
5 *Armature*
6 *Commutator*

*Fig. 4.29 Pre-engaged, geared starter motor*

*Fig. 4.30a* ***Cut-away view of Bosch DW geared transmission starter with permanent magnet motor***

*1 Drive end shield*
*2 Pinion*
*3 Solenoid switch*
*4 Terminal*
*5 Commutator end shield*
*6 Brush plate with carbon brushes*
*7 Commutator*
*8 Armature*
*9 Permanent magnet*
*10 Field frame*
*11 Planetary gear (intermediate transmission)*
*12 Engaging lever*
*13 Pinion-engaging drive*

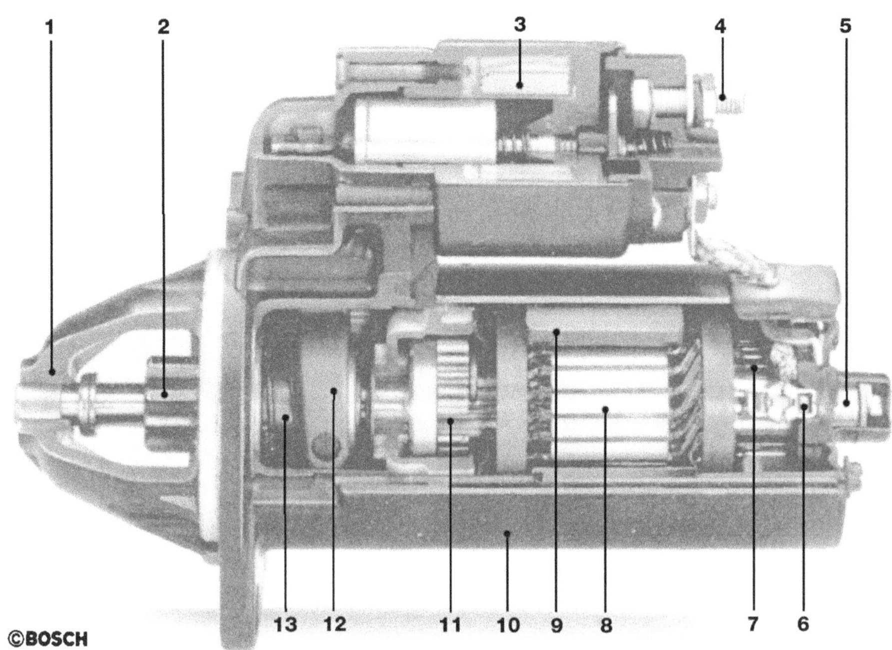


DW starter. The planetary gear drive shows the sun gear (central gear) attached to the armature while the planet gears transfer the drive to the pinion free of any transverse forces. Planet gears are steel and the internal gear is a high grade polyamide compound with mineral additives for good wearing properties. This starter is 40% lighter than a conventional equivalent and is suitable for petrol engines up to 5 litres. Fig. 4.30 shows a cut-away view.

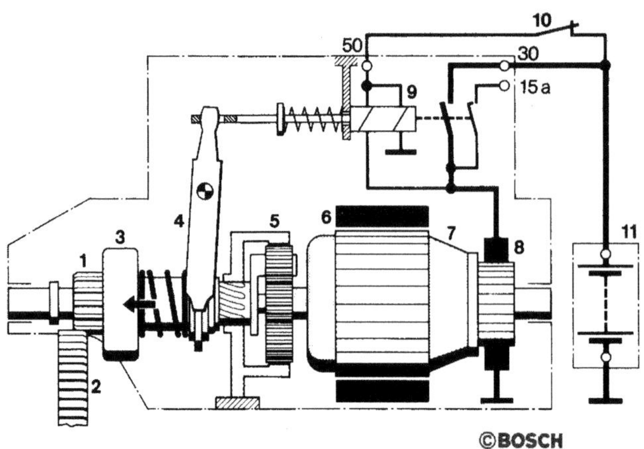


*Fig. 4.30b* ***Outline diagram of Bosch DW geared, permanent magnet starter motor***

*1 Pinion*
*2 Ring gear*
*3 Roller-type over-running clutch*
*4 Engaging lever*
*5 Planetary gear*
*6 Permanent magnet*
*7 Armature*
*8 Commutator with carbon brushes*
*9 Solenoid switch with pull-in and hold-in windings*
*10 Starter switch*
*11 Battery*

## 14 Testing

**1** If the starter is not working correctly, it is worth carrying out a few tests while the starter is still in place.

**2** A battery in a charged state is essential. Check by switching on the headlamps and noting if the brilliance is normal. If necessary test the acid with a hydrometer.

**3** Check that all connectors are tight and there is no white electrolytic growth around a battery terminal. If there is a click and no operation when the starter is switched on by the ignition key, it is often due to a poor battery lug contact. Do not forget to check that the earth strap has a good connection to the body and the engine.

**4** With drive in neutral and the ignition disconnected at the coil feed terminal, crank the engine if possible. Battery voltage should be of the order of 10 volts, and the engine should turn freely under normal temperature conditions. If the operation is sluggish it could be due to a worn out battery with high internal resistance, voltage loss in the cables, connectors or solenoids, or a faulty starter.

**5** If there is no drive, switch on the starter motor with the ignition key and listen for the click of the solenoid operation (inertia type) or, in the case of the pre-engaged type, listen for the motion of the solenoid plunger.

**6** If some starter motor drive exists, in the case of the separate solenoid used with inertia type starters, check the voltage across the main (heavy current) terminals. Before switching, the voltage should be that of the battery, about 12 volts; at the instant of switching the volt-drop should be zero, but in any event not more than 0.25 volt. Any voltage across the terminals points to unwanted resistive volt-drop. Such solenoids are not repairable and should be replaced.

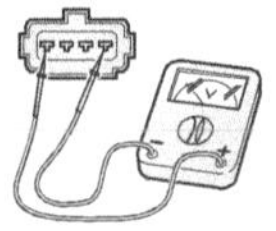

**Note:** *Some types have a manual pushbutton under a large rubber cover, or a smaller plastic button between the main terminals. This facility can be used as a get-home device if the solenoid winding fails, or as a means of starting the engine while undertaking maintenance without having to go into the car.*

**7** If the starter motor fails to turn, the headlamps remain bright and the solenoid operates, then the starter motor is faulty and must be removed (refer to Section 15 for repair procedures).

**8** If the starter motor fails to turn and the headlamps run dim, then the trouble could be a poor condition battery or a jammed motor pinion gear. There is also the possibility of the engine having seized up.

**9** If the starter motor runs, but spins fast without engaging the flywheel, this could be the pinion stuck on the shaft (inertia type) or, in the case of the pre-engaged type, a fault in the solenoid or an overrun clutch failure. Another possibility is low battery voltage which in turn could point to a charging circuit fault.

**10** If the starter motor runs and starts the engine but does not disengage when the engine fires there will be considerable noise from the starter. The fault could be a jammed pinion gear, or a sticking solenoid operating lever in the case of the pre-engaged type.

**11** Should the engine start up correctly but whilst running it is possible to hear a metallic rattling or ringing, this could be a broken Bendix spring (inertia type).

**12** If the engine starts, but upon starter pinion gear disengagement there is a sharp metallic ring or crunch, it is likely that the pinion buffer spring is damaged or possibly there is a damaged driveshaft.

**13** Solenoid plunger chatter is often due to an open circuit hold-in winding in the solenoid. Another possibility is a low battery; since, as it comes on starter cranking load, the voltage drops so low that the solenoid plunger pulls out. This is a cyclic phenomenon.

## 15 Fault finding and repair

### Jammed starter

**1** A starter motor pinion may sometimes stay in mesh with the flywheel, this often being a symptom of gear wear on either or both the pinion and starter ring. When this happens, rocking the car backwards and forwards in 3rd gear (ignition off) will often allow the pinion to return, or alternatively, use a spanner on the square shaft end of the starter.

**Note:** *Recent starters do not have a protruding square end to the shaft. In this case try slackening off the motor through-bolts and pull the armature back. If this does not work take off the starter and examine the pinion and flywheel teeth for wear or damage. The symptom of a jammed starter is that the engine does not turn and lights will be dim. Take care here though, for a dirty battery connection has similar effects.*

### Brushes

**2** When removing a starter motor from a vehicle, first disconnect the battery. Remove the cover over the brushes and raise them from their holders. Check for length and renew if less than 5/16" (8 mm) long

### Drives

**3** The inertia drive should be examined next. Spring strength should be such that it is not possible to turn it on the shaft by hand – if in doubt renew the spring. Dirt on the drive can give rise to sticking, with the result of no or poor meshing between the pinion and flywheel.

**4** Clean drives with petrol or methylated spirit and a brush, and operate the drive by hand until it runs freely. Take care with lubrication – the shaft may be lightly oiled, but the spiral grooves must run dry and clean. Good results have been reported by lightly rubbing the working surfaces with a soft lead pencil. Oil or grease here will attract road dust and result in malfunction. Molykiron (SAE 5) is recommended but if not available leave dry.

### Bearings

**5** Bearing wear can occur, and this is confirmed if there is any sideways movement of the driveshaft. To replace bearings, the armature is removed and the old bearings tapped out with a drift. Graphite and bronze bush bearings can be obtained as replacements, and sometimes need to be soaked in oil before fitting.

### Electrical tests

**6** The armature and field coils are connected in series with current entering at the main terminal, flowing through the field coils, then entering the armature via brushes and out to the frame via earth brushes (Fig. 4.27).

**7** Field coils are of aluminium or copper strip, and should be checked for insulation to the frame. The brushes should be pulled back or removed from their holders, and an ohmmeter check from the main terminal to frame should read infinity, or very high. Alternatively, a battery and bulb may be used, in which case the bulb should not light.

**Note:** *In Lucas face commutator starters, one end of the field winding is earthed; this part of the test procedure would need to be modified with this type, but the principles are the same.*

**8** If a coil breakdown is indicated, the pole shoes complete with surrounding field coils must be removed. Since the retaining screws will be very tight it is usual to employ an impact driver. Locate the fault by visual inspection for charred insulation. With care it may be possible to re-use the faulty coil by taping up the strip, and preferably varnishing with shellac.

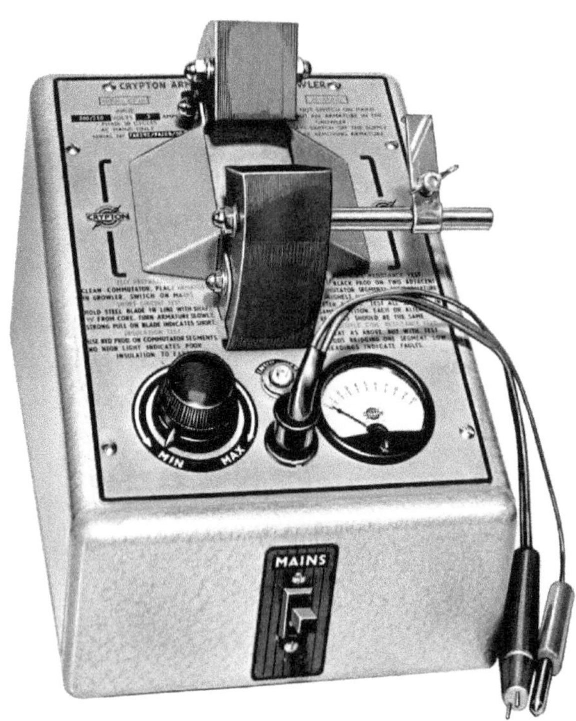


*Fig. 4.31 The Growler*
*Courtesy FKI Crypton*

## Commutator

**9** The commutator segments should be inspected carefully. Thrown solder blobs are an indication of overheating, and with care it is possible to re-solder the armature coils to the commutator, making sure that there is no accidental bridging of two commutator bars.

**10** A commutator of the drum type may be cleaned with fine glasspaper (never emery cloth), but severe wear will require the commutator to be skimmed on a lathe. A face commutator should be cleaned only with methylated spirit, and never with any type of abrasive paper.

## Armature

**11** Sometimes an armature may be found wrecked because of overspeeding, this often occurring through a faulty engagement drive, or by leaving the ignition switch on 'start' too long. In these cases severe failure can occur when the armature conductors fly out of their grooves due to excessive centrifugal force; repairs are difficult, or impossible, and a replacement armature is needed.

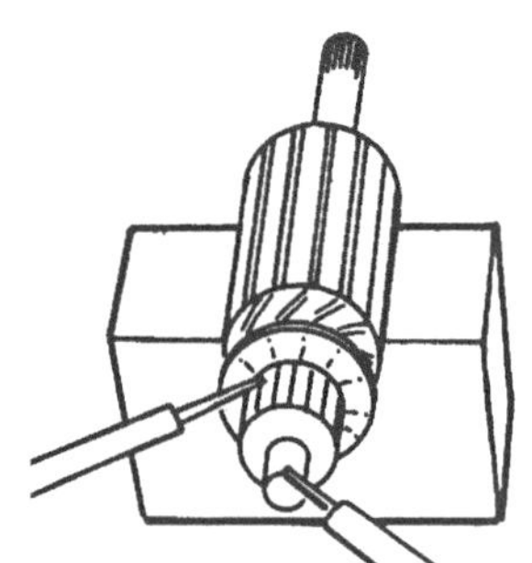

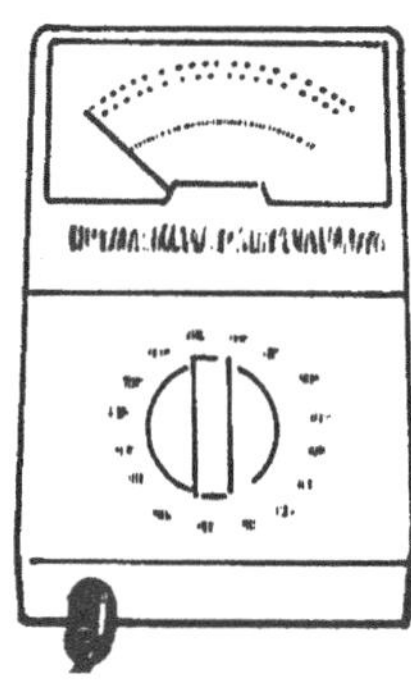

*Fig. 4.32 Insulation test between commutator and shaft*

**12** Similarly, if insulation breaks down between the armature conductors and the steel yoke, then an armature rewind is generally not worth attempting, although not impossible.

**13** Short circuits in an armature winding may be detected by a 'growler' (Fig. 4.31). Placing the armature in the V slot of the growler with its current on will produce alternating magnetic flux in the armature core. A short-circuited coil has heavy current induced in it by transformer action and a steel bar (such as a hacksaw blade) held above the armature will vibrate noisily at the point of short circuit. It is worthwhile cleaning up the commutator bars and the coil ends nearest to the fault, but if no cure is produced, a replacement armature is required.

**14** If no growler is available it is difficult to locate armature winding short circuits by measurement, due to low resistance of the armature wires or strip. Visual evidence of burning is sometimes present, but direct measurement of resistance between commutator segments would require a highly sensitive ohmmeter.

**15** A better check for shorted turns is to pass a current, say 10 amperes, through the armature via the brushes. Then measure the voltage between adjacent commutator segments with a low-range voltmeter using pointed probes. Any variations in volt-drop indicates short-circuited coils connected to the two commutator segments.

**16** Insulation tests between the armature winding and the shaft or between the commutator and the shaft may be carried out using two probe leads in series with a 12 volt battery and a 6 watt bulb, or using the ohm range of a test meter, if available (Fig. 4.32). There should be very high resistance between the armature winding or commutator and the shaft, so the bulb should not light – the ohms reading should be very high in this test.

# Batteries

# 5



## 1 Secondary batteries

**1** The primary battery is an expendable device of the type used in torches and portable radio receivers and is of no importance in motor vehicles. The secondary battery, however, is widely used and differs from the primary type in that it is rechargeable after use.

**2** Nearly all vehicles use a battery of the lead-acid type, but occasionally a steel-alkaline battery is used. This Chapter deals exclusively with the lead-acid battery.

**3** A battery is made up of a number of cells grouped together so that the battery terminal voltage is the sum of the separate cell voltages. A 12 volt battery, for example, has six 2 V cells connected additively in series (Fig. 5.1 overleaf).

**4** In practice, the actual voltage of the battery is not exactly 12 volts, but can reach as high as 14.5 volts soon after being charged, and as low as 10.8 volts in a completely discharged state.

**5** The principal features of a lead-acid battery are as follows:

*(a) It may be recharged after giving up its electrical energy.*

*(b) The internal resistance is low, enabling heavy starter current to be delivered without too great a terminal voltage drop.*

*(c) The liquid electrolyte is dilute sulphuric acid and, being corrosive, should not be allowed to make contact with eyes, skin, clothing or car paintwork. (Apply copious amounts of cold water in case of accidents with acid.)*

*(d) During charge, the electrolyte gives off hydrogen and oxygen. This mixture is explosive and care must be taken to avoid having sparks, cigarettes or naked flames near the battery vents.*

*(e) Water is lost during discharge (except in some maintenance-free batteries see later) and periodic replacement with distilled or de-mineralised water is essential. NB: Tap water is not suitable.*

**6** For chemical storage and release of energy, it is necessary to have two dissimilar conducting materials in close proximity

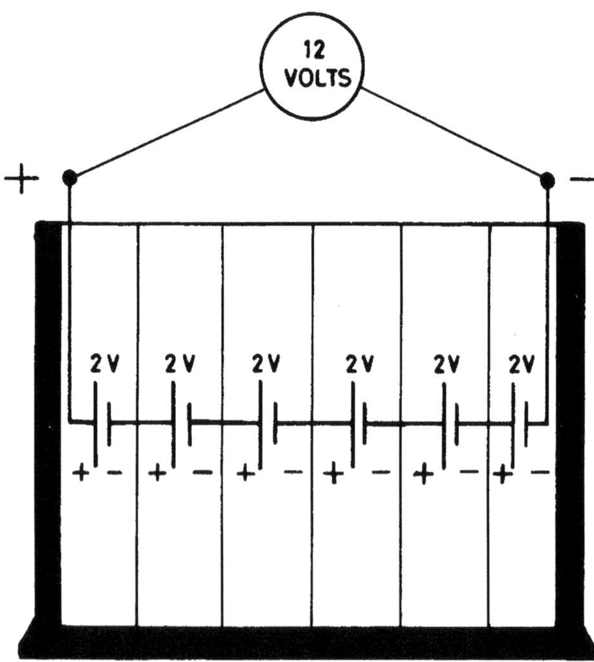


Fig. 5.1 Battery cells in series

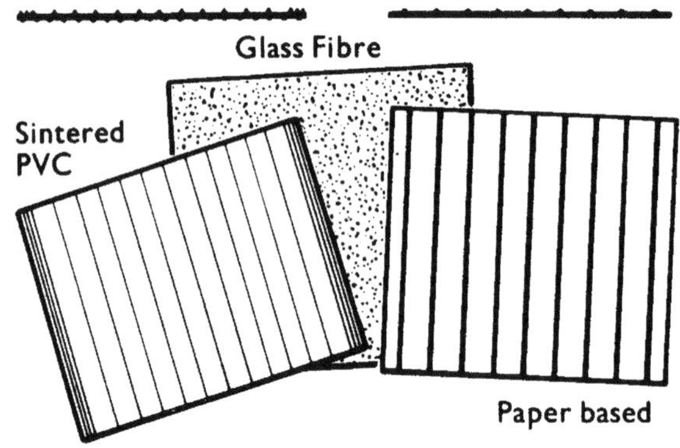


Fig. 5.2 Separators

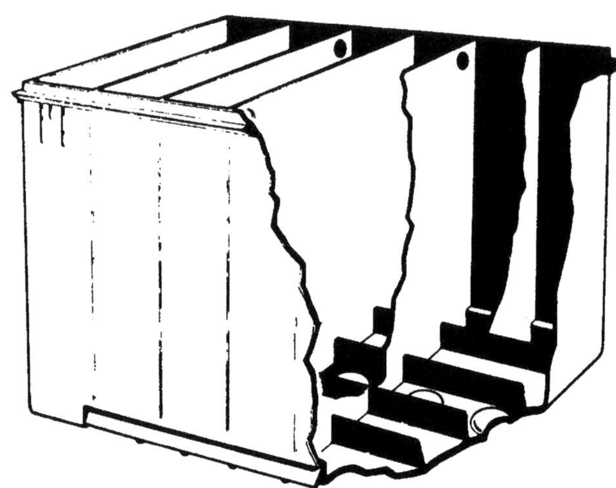

Fig. 5.3 Polypropylene battery case

in a conducting liquid – the electrolyte. The car battery uses a lead-antimony grid of several plates per cell and the grid holes are filled with lead oxide paste. After processing these become lead peroxide for the positive plates (chocolate colour) and spongy lead for the negative plates (grey colour).

**7** When the battery is said to be in a charged state all or most of the grid contents are lead peroxide and spongy lead, ie differing metallic conductors, but as discharge is approached both plates change chemically and become lead sulphate.

**8** Chemically inert separators are used between the plates. Originally they were made of wood or porous rubber, but now use paper-based material and are constructed with non-porous ribs, but for some applications sintered PVC with or without a glass fibre retaining mat is used (Fig. 5.2).

**9** The separators must be strong, for under heavy charge and discharge the plates may swell and distort. Equally they must have a correct pore structure to allow the passage of the electrolyte. Pores which are too small represent an effective internal resistance which would lower the terminal voltage on starter load.

**10** Battery cases were formerly made of pitch and asbestos, but modern batteries use polypropylene (Fig. 5.3) which is translucent; showing battery acid level readily, also having good resilience and low weight.

## 2 Construction

### Wet batteries

**1** Battery grids have two functions:

*(a) To conduct electricity to and from active material inside the battery*

*(b) To support the active material and hold it in place (Fig. 5.4)*

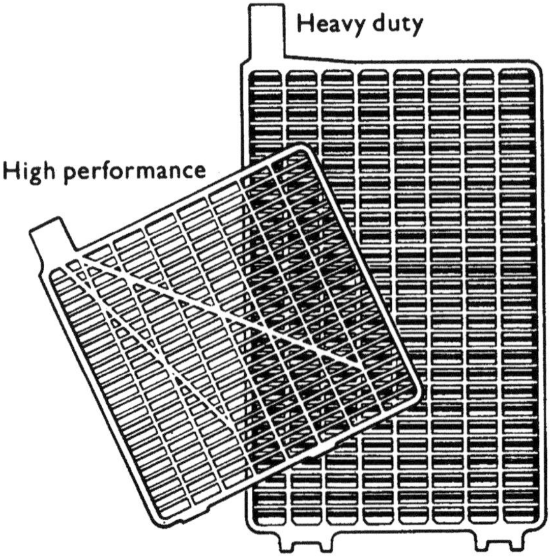


Fig. 5.4 Battery grids (unfilled)

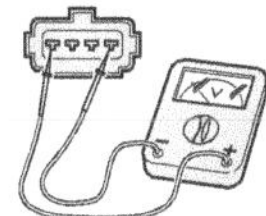

Positive grids are usually thicker than negative grids. A standard car battery has positive grids 0.060 in. (1.52 mm) thick and the negative grid 0.055 in. (1.40 mm) thick for one particular make, while heavy duty batteries might have grids up to 0.25 in. (6.35 mm) thick. It was common practice for batteries to have one more negative plate than positive plates. Modern battery design is now tending to have one more positive plate than negative because a higher current drain for a given battery size is possible. Fig. 5.5 shows plate groups; note this shows one more negative than positive but assembly principle is the same. Grids are made of lead but a hardening agent is added to make the casting process easier. This might be antimony or, for maintenance-free batteries, calcium. Antimony will promote electrolyte gassing and loss of electrolyte, and calcium is being used in its place where minimal gassing is essential. Without the strength given by adding antimony to the lead, grid casting is a precision operation.

**2** The active material is a paste prepared from lead oxide, water and sulphuric acid. The acid reacts with the lead oxide to form lead sulphate which is effectively the cementing material to make the plate firm. The sulphuric acid expands the plate to the maximum size required in service. Both positive and negative plates are made up of the same basic material, but the negative plate also contains additives such as barium sulphate, carbon black or lignin compound.

These improve the low temperature performance of the battery by preventing the spongy lead (which is what the negative plates are converted to at full charge) from hardening, an effect which would reduce the battery capacity.

After the grids are filled with the active paste they are placed in a weak acid solution and a current passed through to 'form' them. Next they are dried and if they come into contact with air in the process a certain amount of charge loss occurs due to oxygen acting upon the plates. Batteries prepared in this way are 'dry uncharged' and will need a further charge before going into service. If the battery is intended to be sold as a 'dry charged' battery, the plates are dried by superheated steam without contact with air.

**3** Plates are next formed in groups + – + – etc with a separator between each pair of plates. The separator ribs are always in contact with the positive plates to give the highest concentration of electrolyte at the positive plate. The number of plates per cell is normally not less than six. Higher quality batteries have the larger number of plates to give lower internal resistance and a higher maximum current together with a greater capacity.

**4** Cells are joined by intercell connectors which pass tightly through the dividing walls. The Bosch cut-away drawing (Fig. 5.6a) shows this clearly.

## Gel batteries

**5** These are very similar in principle to wet batteries, but with the addition of silicic acid, the electrolyte is solidified into a

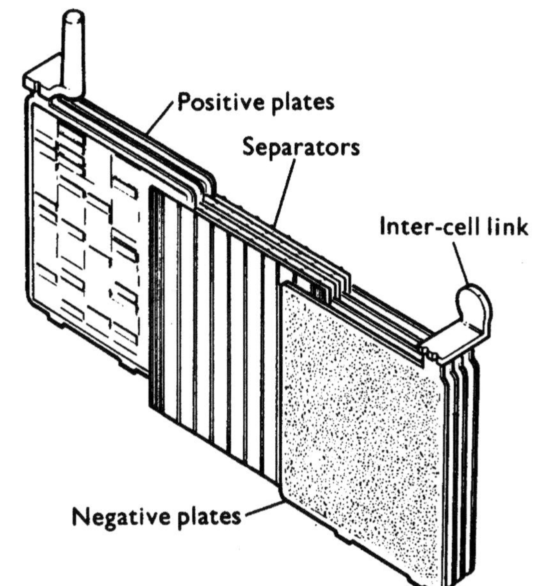


***Fig. 5.5 Plate groups***

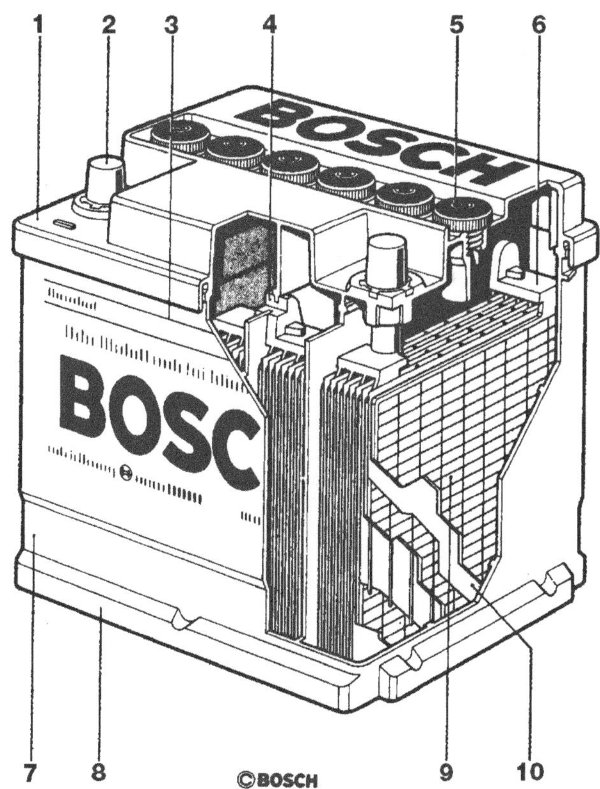


***Fig. 5.6a Design of a Bosch battery***

*1 Cover*
*2 Post*
*3 Electrolyte level mark*
*4 Intercell connector*
*5 Vent plug*
*6 Plate strap*
*7 Battery case*
*8 Bottom rail*
*9 Positive and negative plates*
*10 Plastic separators*

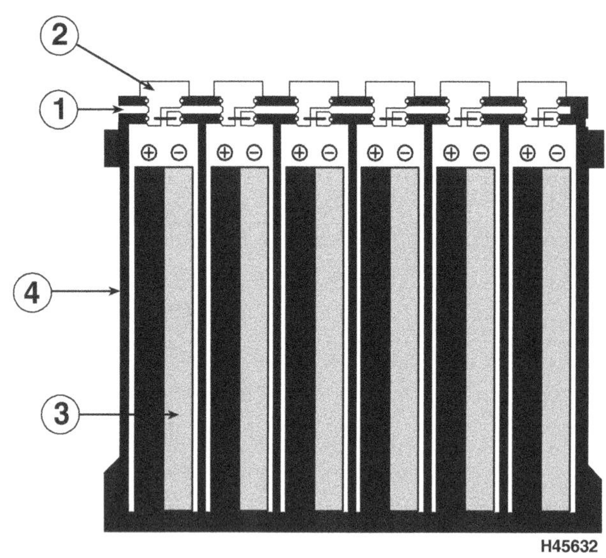


*Fig. 5.6b Gel type battery*

*1 Gas vent channel*
*2 Cover plug*
*3 Solidified electrolyte (Gel)*
*4 Battery casing*

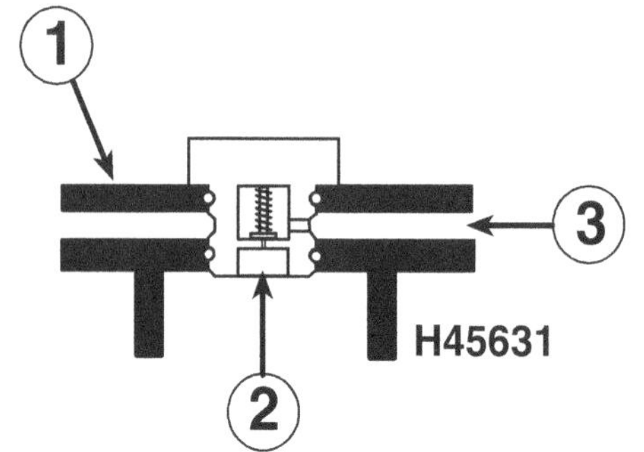


*5.6c Cell sealing plug with a gas vent valve*

*1 Cover 2 Gas vent valve 3 Gas vent channel*

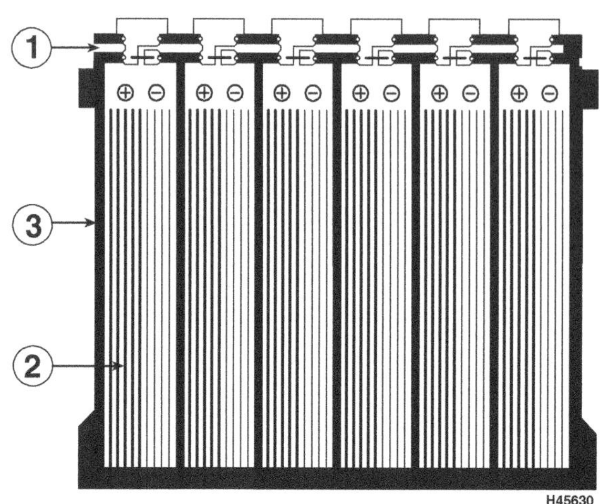


*5.6d AGM (Absorbent Glass Mat) battery*

*1 Gas vent channel 2 Electrolyte absorbed by glass mat 3 Battery case*

gel-like mass (Fig. 5.6b). The advantage of this is a substantial increase in the charge/discharge cycle capacity – offering more favourable conditions for recharging after a deep discharge, which, in turn gives the battery a longer storage life. Other advantages include better protection against leaks, and a low build up of gas. The disadvantages are higher cost, less availability, not compatible with high temperatures (not for engine bay fitment) and poorer cold starting properties.

In contrast to wet batteries, the gel batteries are not vented directly to atmosphere, nor are the cells interconnected for gas discharge. Batteries not vented to atmosphere are classed as VRLA (Valve Regulated Lead Acid Battery). Instead the gasses produced during high loading are converted back into back water in each respective cell. There is however, a safety valve built into each cell to allow surplus gas (produced when over-charging) to escape (Fig. 5.6c). Since there is no provision for replenishing the electrolyte in these batteries, once gas escapes, the life of the battery could be seriously shortened.

## AGM (Absorbent Glass Mat) batteries

**6** Here the electrolyte is solidified by absorbent glass mat (Fig. 5.6d). The glass mat is comprised of very fine interwoven glass fibres, and looks like a fleece. As the glass mat is highly absorbent the full volume of the electrolyte is absorbed, offering good protection against leaks as in the event of the battery casing being damaged, the amount of electrolyte lost is negligible.

Like Gel batteries, AGM batteries are not vented to atmosphere, and are classed as VRLA. They too have a high

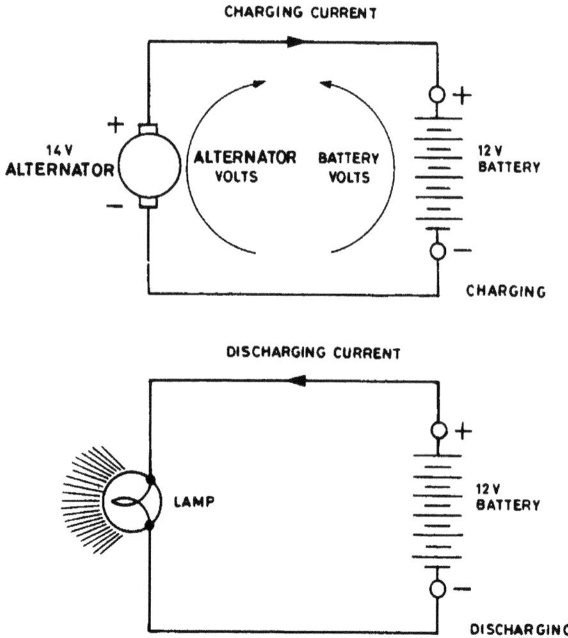


*Fig. 5.7 Charging and discharging action*

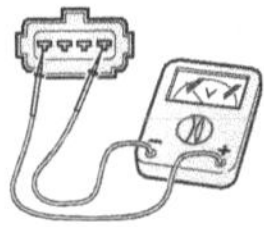

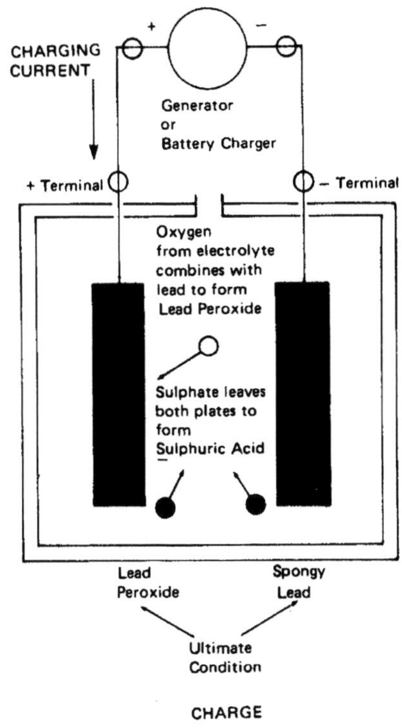


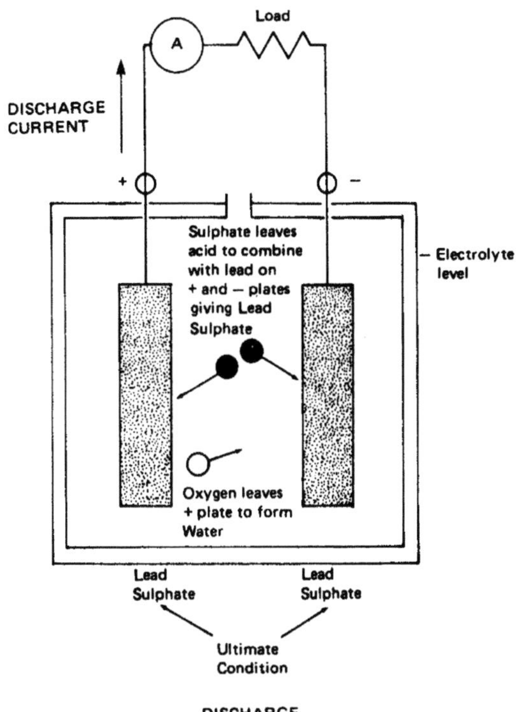


*Fig. 5.8 Charge and discharge actions in a lead-acid battery*

capacity for charge/discharge cycles, but have enhanced cold starting properties. However, the disadvantages are high cost, low availability, and are not compatible with high temperatures so cannot be fitted into the engine bay.

## 3 Charge and discharge

**1** When a battery is charged, current is forced through it in the opposite direction to normal, in much the same way as filling a tank via its outlet tap (Fig. 5.7). The battery gives a direct current (dc) and so it follows that a direct current is required to recharge it. Clearly if the battery has a terminal voltage of, say, 12 volts, then in order to force current into it, it will require a battery charging voltage somewhat in excess of this, say, 14 to 16 volts depending upon the charge rate required and the internal resistance of the battery.

**2** Looking now inside the battery (Fig. 5.8) while under charge conditions we see that the flow of current breaks up the electrolyte and that the electrolyte oxygen moves to combine with the lead of the +ve plate to form lead peroxide. Both plates give sulphate to form sulphuric acid in the electrolyte, and the negative plate turns to spongy lead.

**3** Thus the two plates are altered chemically and the concentration of sulphuric acid increases, ie, the density, or specific gravity, of the electrolyte goes up as charging continues.

**4** When discharging, the flow of current in the cell produces breakdown of the acid such that sulphate leaves it and combines both +ve and –ve plates to form, eventually, lead sulphate, so plates are no longer dissimiliar. In addition, oxygen leaves the +ve plate and returns to the electrolyte to form water. Thus the electrolyte becomes diluted and specific gravity goes down.

**5** The hydrometer is a means of measuring the acid specific gravity and so gives information on the state of charge.

**6** Fig. 5.9 shows a hydrometer which consists of a float inside a suction vessel. The nozzle is inserted into a battery cell and enough acid is withdrawn to read the float. The reading gives a good indication as to the battery charge state, assuming that the correct specific gravity of acid was used for the initial filling.

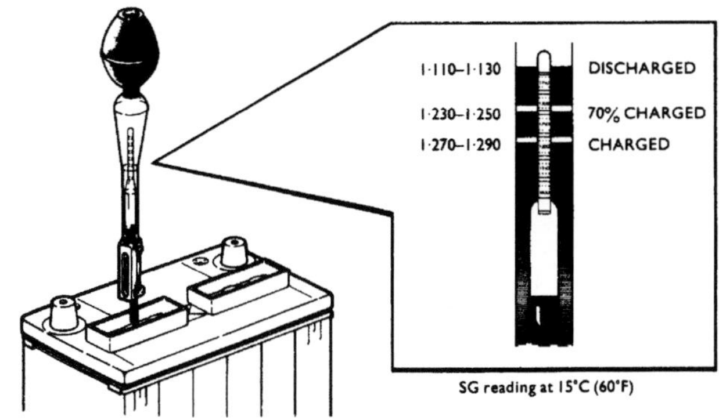


*Fig. 5.9 Using the hydrometer*

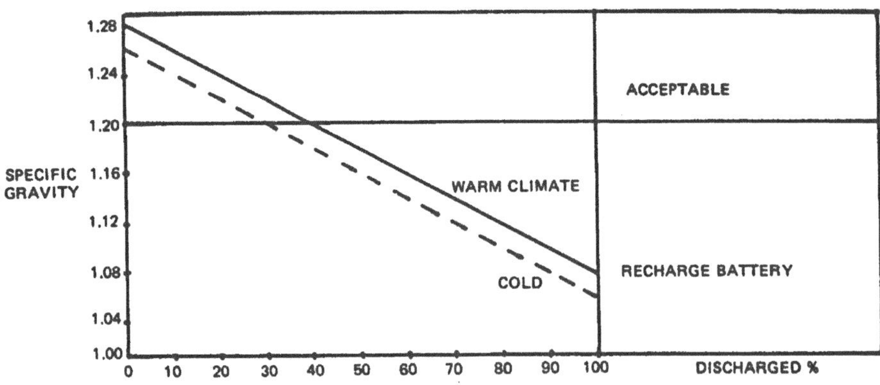


*Fig. 5.10 Specific gravity of battery acid during discharge*

**7** Electrolyte specific gravity temperature correction is necessary because the volume varies with temperature. The volume rises with temperature so the weight per unit volume will decrease, ie the specific gravity will decrease. The standard temperature at which makers' figures are quoted is 15°C (60°F) and so if a hydrometer reading is taken at any other temperature it should be corrected.

A rule of thumb is:

Specific gravity falls by 0.007 per 10°C rise above 15°C

Specific gravity rises by 0.007 per 10°C fall below 15°C

So, for example, if the reading of specific gravity of a battery were taken at 25°C and was measured as 1.22 then:

Specific gravity at 15°C = 1.22 + (1 x 0.007)
= 1.227

**8** For climates normally below 25°C the following are typical figures for a battery in good condition.

| Condition/use | Specific gravity |
|---|---|
| Filling Acid | 1.260 |
| Cell fully charged | 1.270 to 1.290 |
| Cell 70% charged | 1.230 to 1.250 |
| Cell discharged | 1.110 to 1.130 |

A graph giving the relationship over the whole charge range is shown in Fig. 5.10. Again, the assumption is that the battery is in good, near-new condition.

**9** The SI (Systèm Internationale) measures the strength of the electrolyte as density in grams per cubic metre (g/m$^3$) at 25°C.

This can be measured by means of an hydrometer like specific gravity.

Temperature correction is necessary if the readings are taken at other than 25°C.

The correction factor is at the rate of 7 kg/m$^3$ for every 10°C difference from 25°C.

Thus, if the density of the electrolyte is measured at 45°C and the reading is 1250 kg/m$^3$ then at 25°C the electrolyte will be HEAVIER – the corrected reading being:

Density at 25°C = 1250 + (2x7)
= 1264 kg/m$^3$

The table below shows that specific gravity (corrected to 25°C) and density are very nearly the same figures apart from the 1000 factor. It is of interest to see how these figures correspond to the percentage of sulphuric acid ($H_2SO_4$) in the electrolyte.

| Specific gravity (25°C) | Density kg/m$^3$ (25°C) | % Sulphuric acid |
|---|---|---|
| 1.100 | 1099 | 15 |
| 1.137 | 1136 | 20 |
| 1.176 | 1175 | 25 |
| 1.216 | 1215 | 30 |
| 1.257 | 1256 | 35 |
| 1.274 | 1273 | 37 |
| 1.300 | 1299 | 40 |

## Topping up

**10** Near the end of the charging period the chemical reactions give off oxygen from the positive plate and hydrogen plate. Water decomposition takes place and water is slowly lost, needing replacement. (See, however, the section on maintenance-free batteries.) Distilled or de-ionised water is added to the electrolyte in each cell to maintain the correct level. Fig. 5.11 shows that this level is just above the

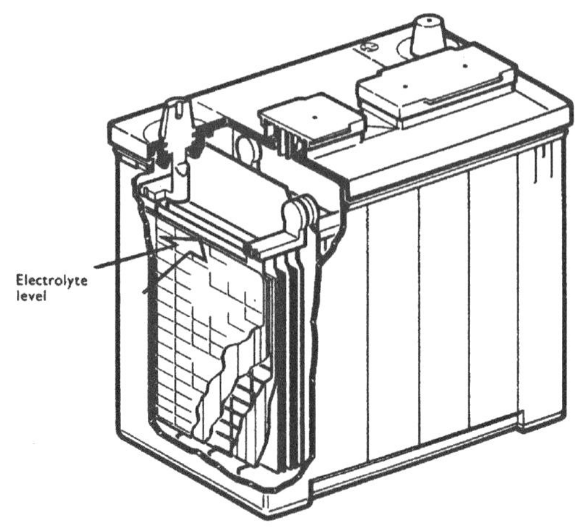


*Fig. 5.11 Maintaining the electrolyte level*

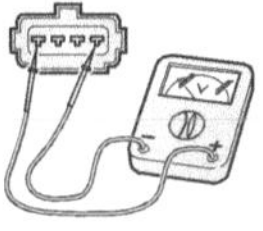

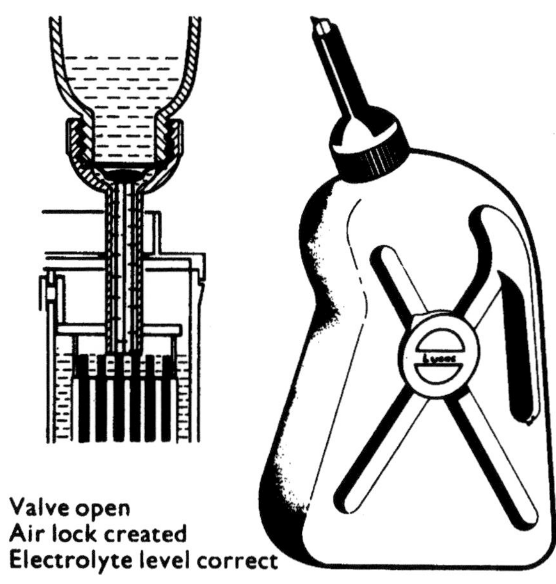


*Fig. 5.12 Lucas battery filler*

active plates. Filler bottles are sometimes used for topping up and it is important not to press down too hard if the nozzle touches the plates or separators. There is often a protection bar built into the battery to prevent filler bottle damage. The Lucas Battery Filler is shown in Fig. 5.12. When filling, the nozzle is pressed down lightly into each cell in turn. A valve opens allowing the de-ionised water to flow into the cell until the correct level is reached at which point the water flow ceases. Removal of the nozzle shuts off the valve so no spillage occurs.

## 4 Battery capacity

**1** The capacity of a battery may be measured in more than one way, but in any event depends upon the construction. Capacity is approximately proportional to the total surface area of the plates and this is why batteries have several thin plates instead of large single + and – plates. Volume of electrolyte is significant and the level should not fall below the top of the active plates. Sulphation develops with age and so reduces the active surface area and the capacity.

**2** How the capacity is defined depends upon what feature is to be shown. For instance, if the information required is how long the battery can sustain a 25 A discharge with the engine off, then the **reserve capacity rating** would be given. However, the main function of a battery used in a car is to provide a high starting current for a short time. The vehicle loads are thereafter supplied by the alternator. In these circumstances, **cold start rating** figures are given. Finally, the **ampere-hour rating** represents the maximum current that a battery will give over a given time.

Looking at these ratings in a little more detail:

**Cold start rating** is the declared current that a battery will give at –18°C for a specified interval of time when the battery voltage falls to an End Voltage. It is unfortunate that three standards are used, namely, BS (British Standards), DIN (German Standards) and SAE (Society of Automobile Engineers).

The Cold Start rating is, then, the current in amperes delivered at –18°C until the battery voltage falls to:

| Standard | Duration | End Voltage |
|---|---|---|
| BS | 60 seconds | 8.4 volts |
| DIN | 30 seconds | 9.0 volts |
| SAE | 30 seconds | 7.2 volts |

SAE ratings will usually appear to be the highest figure so it is important to compare batteries using the **same standard**.

German batteries are stamped with a 5-digit manufacturer's number followed by nominal voltage, nominal ampere-hour capacity and cold start rating, for example:

*00111   12 V   60 Ah   300 A*

**Reserve capacity.** This is defined as the time in minutes for the battery voltage to fall to 10.5 volts with a constant load of 25 A at 25°C.

**Ampere-hour rating.** This indicates the amount of energy, measured in ampere-hours, expected from a fully charged battery until it becomes discharged down to 1.8 volts per cell (or 10.8 volts for a nominal 12 volt battery). The rate at which the discharge is measured was 10 hours or 20 hours, but now only the 20 hour rate is used. For example a 50 Ah battery can be expected to deliver 2.5 amperes for 20 hours before the terminal voltage falls to 10.8 volts. If a higher current were drawn, say 5 amperes, the theoretical time to discharge would be 10 hours (ie 5 A x 10 h = 50 Ah), but in practice would be less than 10 hours, probably nearer 8.6 hours. The Ah rating is used also to estimate how long to charge a battery. The 50 Ah battery in a fully discharged state might be charged at 5 A but because the battery is not 100% efficient an input of, say, 1.3 x Ah rating might be required to give a full charge. A charge of 5 amperes for 13 hours would give a full charge, therefore.

**3** Temperature affects battery capacity, there being a capacity increase with temperature, since the chemical reactions are accelerated and the electrolyte passes through the porous separators more easily.

## 5 Charging rates

**1** On the vehicle the charge rate will be set automatically by the alternator or dynamo regulator. It will depend upon the state of charge of the battery, this in turn being fixed by recent loads and also the age and condition of the battery.

**2** If, however, the charge rate on the bench is to be decided then, provided there is no urgency requiring rapid recharging, a suitable figure is somewhere between 1/10 and 3/10 of the battery capacity.

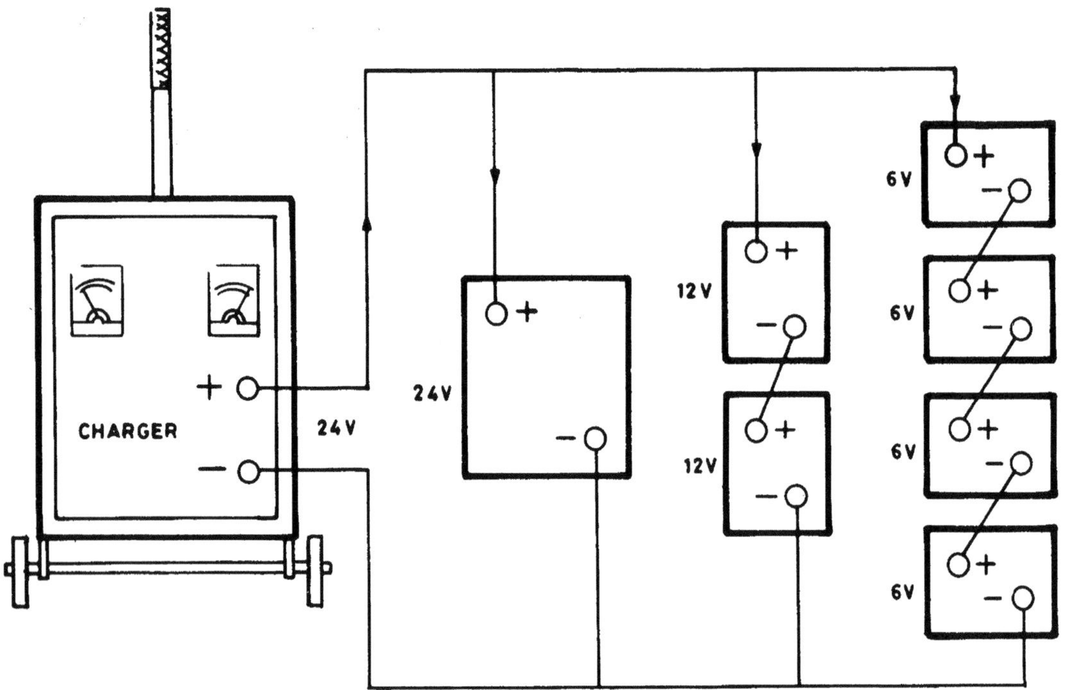


*Fig. 5.13 Series-parallel charging*

**3** For example, if a 36 Ah battery were completely flat, then the ampere-hours of input required would be 46.8 (ie 36x1.3), and at the 1/10th rate:

Charging current = 1/10 x 46.8
= 5 amperes approximately

**4** A high-current charger may be connected so as to charge several batteries simultaneously, an example being shown in Fig. 5.13. Connection or removal of batteries must always be done with the mains switched off to avoid the risk of sparks igniting the gases given off by the charging batteries.

**Note:** In the case shown the battery voltages must add up to 24 V for each path.

## Fast charging (boost)

**5** This should be undertaken with care and employed only in cases of emergency. Batteries can be boost charged to within 70% to 80% of full charge provided the current tapers and does not cause the battery to exceed 43°C (110°F).

Boost charging usually takes 30 to 60 minutes depending upon the initial charge (Fig. 5.14). Correctly carried out, the battery charging should be controlled by a thermostat switch housed in a probe and inserted into either of the two centre cells of a 12 V battery (Fig. 5.15).

*Fig. 5.14 Fast charger*

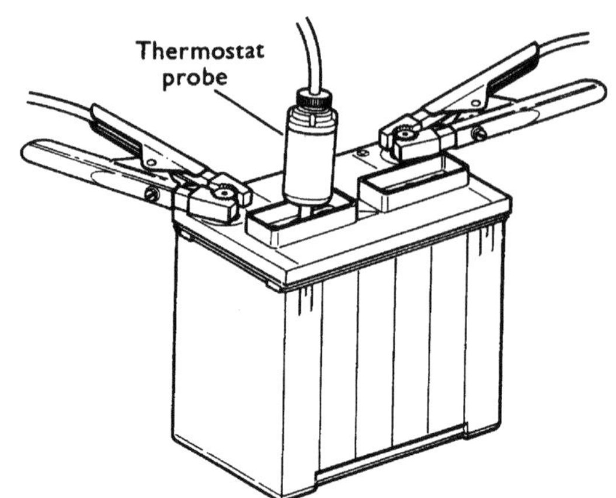


*Fig. 5.15 Thermostat control of fast charging*

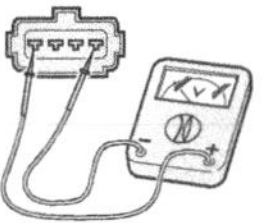

### Charging maintenance-free batteries

**6** This type of battery is more easily damaged by overcharging. If it is necessary to bench charge, the charger should ideally have a 14.4 V constant voltage output. As the charge progresses, the battery voltage will rise, current will fall and charging should be stopped when the current has stabilised.

Important points to remember when charging Maintenance-free batteries:

*(a) Never boost charge*
*(b) Never charge from a supply in excess of 15.8 V*
*(c) Never continue charging after the battery has started to gas*

## 6 Battery filling

**1** There may be an occasion to fill a new, dry battery with acid, in which case it is necessary to dilute concentrated sulphuric acid to the correct specific gravity.

**2** Great care is required and it is recommended that goggles be worn.

**3** To mix the electrolyte, first work out roughly how much distilled water and concentrated acid is required. The table (Fig. 5.16) gives the proportions by volume of distilled water required to 1 part of concentrated sulphuric acid (specific gravity 1.835).

**4 IT IS IMPORTANT TO ADD THE ACID TO THE WATER AND NEVER THE OTHER WAY ROUND.** Considerable heat will be generated, and the acid must be added slowly and stirred until the correct specific gravity is obtained (Fig. 5.17).

## 7 Open circuit voltage

**1** The open circuit terminal voltage is that which would be measured at the battery terminals by a voltmeter, but with no external load.

**2** It is related to the specific gravity, an approximate expression being:

Open circuit voltage = Specific gravity + 0.84 per cell

Thus if the acid specific gravity measured by an hydrometer were 1.25 then:

Cell voltage = 1.25 + 0.84 = 2.09 volts
Battery voltage = 6 x 2.09 = 12.54 volts

since there are 6 cells in series in a 12 volt battery.

The open circuit voltage is, by itself, not particularly useful but is necessary when working out the value of internal resistance and would anyway be measured with a high resistance.

| SPECIFIC GRAVITY REQUIRED | PARTS OF DISTILLED WATER TO 1 OF CONC. SULPHURIC ACID |
|---|---|
| 1.25 | 3.4 |
| 1.26 | 3.2 |
| 1.27 | 3.0 |
| 1.28 | 2.8 |
| 1.29 | 2.7 |
| 1.30 | 2.6 |

***Fig. 5.16 Distilled water/concentrated sulphuric acid ratio by volume***

## 8 Internal resistance

**1** All batteries have an internal resistance, but this is very low in the case of a lead-acid battery in good condition. In fact, it is because of the inherent low internal resistance that this type of battery is favoured for vehicle work where starting current demand can be very high.

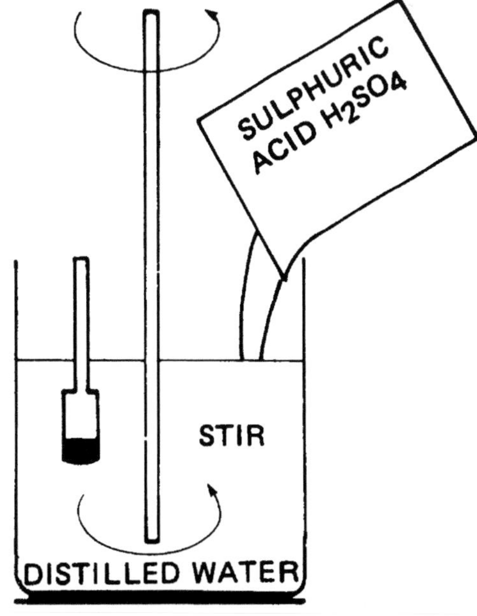


***Fig. 5.17 Mixing acid and distilled water***

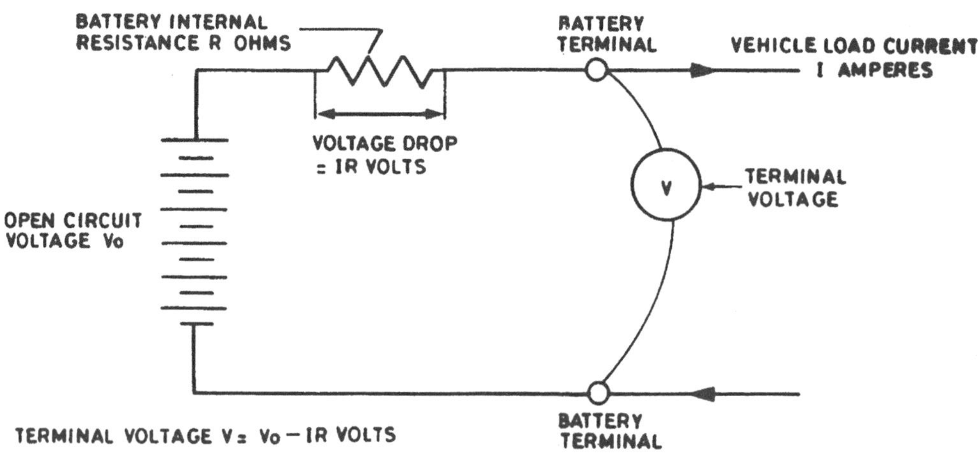


*Fig. 5.18 Internal resistance of a battery*

**2** Fig. 5.18 shows a battery with its equivalent internal resistance. A little arithmetic will show that if, for example, the internal resistance were to be 0.05 ohms and the open circuit voltage 12.0 volts then, with a lighting load of 10 amperes:

Battery terminal voltage = 12 – internal volt drop
= 12 – (10x0.05)
= 11.5 volts

The table shows terminal voltages for this battery under various loads.

| Open circuit voltage | Load current (A) | Internal drop | Terminal voltage |
|---|---|---|---|
| 12 V | 10 amperes | 0.5 volts | 11.5 volts |
| 12 V | 20 amperes | 1.0 volts | 11.0 volts |
| 12 V | 50 amperes | 2.5 volts | 9.5 volts |
| 12 V | 100 amperes | 5.0 volts | 7.0 volts |

**Note:** This example does not represent a good battery in peak condition. A good battery of 12 volt 50 Ah rating should have an internal resistance of about 0.005 ohm at normal temperature.

**3** The internal resistance is made up of various individual resistances, namely between electrodes and the electrolyte, the plate resistances, internal connectors and resistance of the electrolyte to ion flow (ions are particles moving through the electrolyte and carrying a positive or negative charge). Additionally, the internal resistance depends upon the state of discharge and cell temperature, the value being higher as the battery is discharged. The designer controls one factor of the internal resistance by the surface area of the plates. Batteries with a larger number of plates (and therefore ampere-hour capacity) will have a lower internal resistance.

**4** As batteries age, one of the effects is a rise in the internal resistance. Clearly there will come a point where there will be insufficient terminal voltage left to turn the starter motor fast enough for the engine to fire. For a cold morning start, extra torque will be required to free the crankshaft and the minimum engine turnover speed for firing will be about 100 rev/min. It is under these conditions that the end of the battery life is determined.

## 9 Battery selection

**1** Despite all other vehicle loads which may be placed upon the battery it is the starting requirement which determines the size of battery. The cranking speed must be at least 90 to 100 rev/min in temperate climates and the starter system must be capable of operating at temperatures as low as –30°C (in some countries –40°C).

**2** When the starter motor is turning over the engine, the battery terminal voltage will fall due to the internal volt drop, but must not fall below 9 V for satisfactory operation. The minimum voltage at the starter switch should be 8.5 volts, allowing a 0.5 V drop along the battery main lead and battery terminals. Assuming that vehicle batteries are rarely fully charged, an 80% charge is assumed for the specifications above.

**3** Volt/ampere curves similar to Fig. 5.19 are often supplied by the battery company to vehicle designers to assist their selection of a suitable battery.

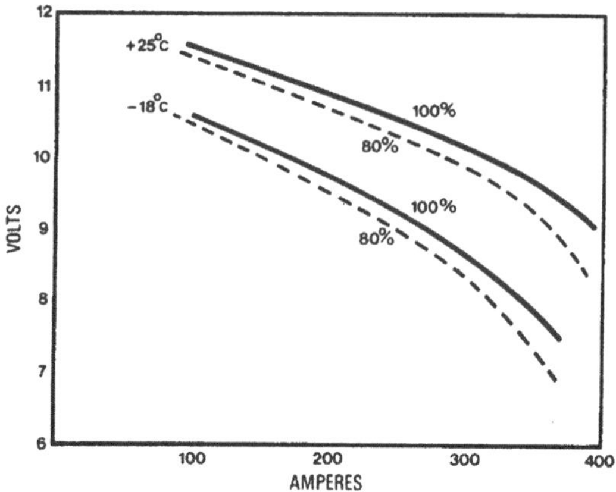


*Fig. 5.19 Volt/ampere curve*

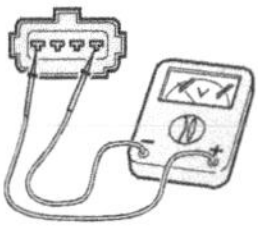

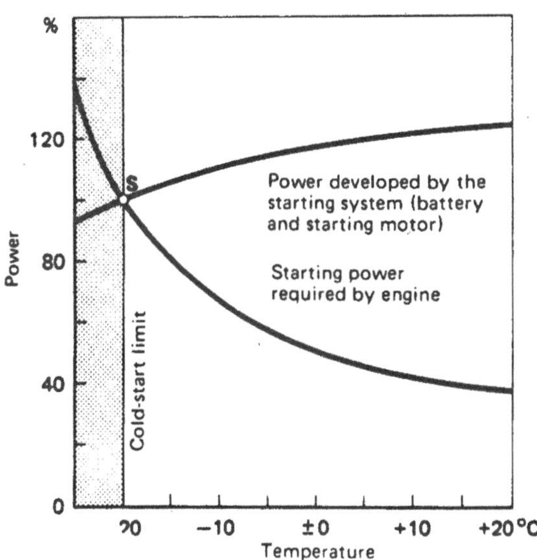


*Fig. 5.20 Supply and demand power curves*

## 10 Temperature effects – frozen batteries

**1** At low temperatures, the electrolyte will be more concentrated and will have a higher specific gravity, but against this, the chemical reactions within the battery are slower and the overall result is a lowering of the battery capacity with temperature.

**2** Fig. 5.20 shows a typical characteristic giving a crossover at –20°C between supply and demand of power for starting a given motor vehicle.

**3** The battery should be protected from freezing, particularly when in a low charge state, because then the proportion of water in the electrolyte is higher, giving a greater tendency to freeze. A good state of charge is a good protection against freezing. The dependence of the freezing threshold on specific gravity of the acid is shown in Fig. 5.21 as is the dependence on charge state.

**4** A frozen battery will give a very small current only, but does not normally suffer permanent damage, although cracking of cases is not unknown. This is because frozen acid electrolyte does not expand appreciably and remains in a gelatine-like state.

**5** It should be noted that recharging in the frozen state is difficult since only a small current can be passed through. Topping up should not be carried out if the outside conditions are below the freezing point of water.

**6** On no account attempt to charge, boost charge, or jump start where it is suspected that the battery electrolyte may be frozen. If in doubt, thaw out the battery first.

## 11 Batteries with a probe

**1** Some batteries have an electrical probe extending to the top surface of the electrolyte, and this is used as an electrolyte level monitor. So long as the probe dips into the acid, then the warning circuit is complete, but as the level drops the probe is no longer in contact and a dashboard warning light is switched on.

## 12 Dry-charged batteries

**1** More correctly, the description should be 'unfilled, charged batteries'. The battery plates are first formed by the manufacturer and then given a full charge. At the factory the acid is drained off and the plates dried out, the negative

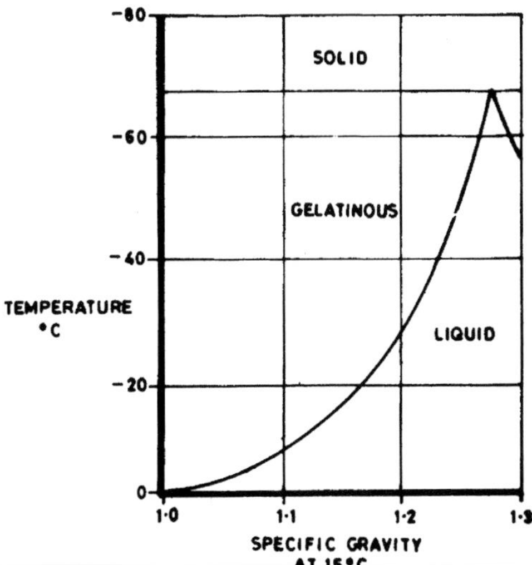


*Fig. 5.21a Dependence of the electrolyte freezing point on specific gravity*

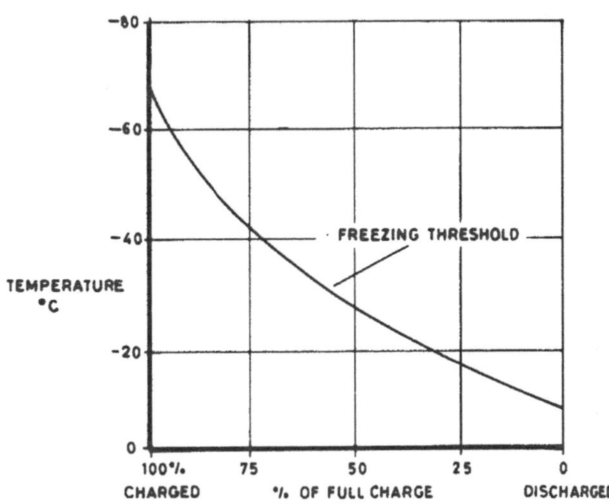


*Fig. 5.21b Dependence of the electrolyte freezing point on % battery charge*

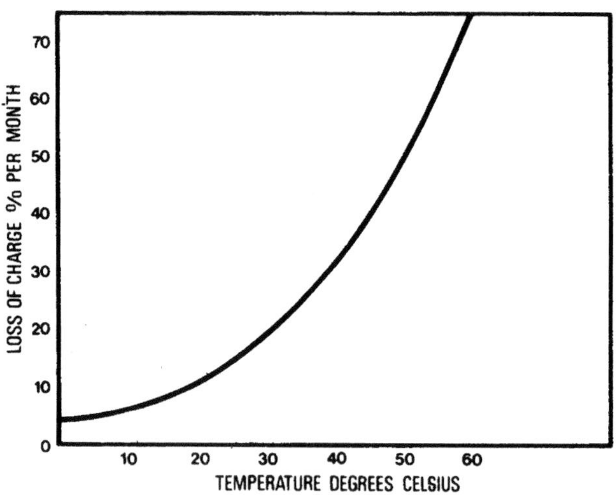


*Fig. 5.22 Self discharge curve*

plates being given a chemical preservation treatment. The battery can then be stored without harm for a long period before being brought into service. When needed, the battery is filled with acid of specific gravity 1.28 (corresponding to full-charge acid gravity) and after about 20 minutes soaking time the battery is then ready for use. Should it not be required at this stage, a recharge after four weeks standing is advised. Note that at a first filling some heat may be generated in the battery and sometimes they are filled in two stages with a delay of 6 to 12 hours between stages.

## 13 Self discharge

**1** Over a period, a battery which is not used will gradually lose its charge due to several factors including the following:

**2 Internal chemical processes:** Batteries which have been in service for some time suffer from the effect of antimony deposits on the negative plates. These set up miniature batteries, in effect, which are short circuited upon themselves and use up the charge of the negative plate. In addition, impurities in added water, particularly traces of iron, will result in the self discharge of both positive and negative plates.

**3 Leakage currents:** Dirt and the effects of acid fumes on the top surface of the battery can result in conducting film paths between the +ve and –ve battery lugs. This trouble can be minimised by periodic cleaning of the battery top (throw the rag away afterwards). Sediment paths at the bottom of the battery case can also lead to leakage paths.

**4** Self discharge takes place at the rate of 0.2% to 1% of the battery ampere-hour capacity per day, depending on the age of the battery. The rate of discharge goes up with temperature and also with the specific gravity value. Batteries of quality use lead of highest purity in the active plate area with the antimony proportion kept small (Fig. 5.22).

**5** The remedy for self discharge is, of course, to charge the battery periodically or to maintain a trickle charge approximately equal to the self discharge rate, this being found by trial and error, or by a rule of thumb which gives the trickle charge rate as:

1/1000 x ampere-hour rating

For example, a 50 Ah battery might be trickle charged at:

50/1000 = 0.005 ampere

**6** If a simple battery charger with no rate control is used for this purpose, a good way of reducing the charge rate is to run the battery on charge with a car light bulb in series. Again the bulb is chosen by trial and error with an ammeter in circuit to check the charge rate.

## 14 Sulphation

**1** Under normal discharging, fine crystals of lead sulphate are formed on the plates and, by recharging, these are convertible. If the battery is left discharged for a long period, however, these crystals turn into coarse lead sulphate crystals which are not easily convertible back to the fine state and may ruin the battery.

**2** The effects of sulphation are (a) a reduction in the battery Ah capacity and (b) to impede the charging process causing the battery to become very hot.

**3** In minor sulphation cases, extended periods of charging at low currents will improve the situation, but in serious cases the battery becomes unusable because of the internal short circuits which result.

**4** When a sulphated battery is first put on charge the terminal voltage rises rapidly, whereas that of a healthy battery rises slowly. As the sulphation breaks down, the battery voltage falls and slowly rises again as normal chemical changes associated with charging take place.

## 15 Battery lugs

**1** Lugs come into three main categories (Fig. 5.23a):

*(a) The die-cast screw-on helmet type*
*(b) The SMMT clamp type*
*(c) The flat type*

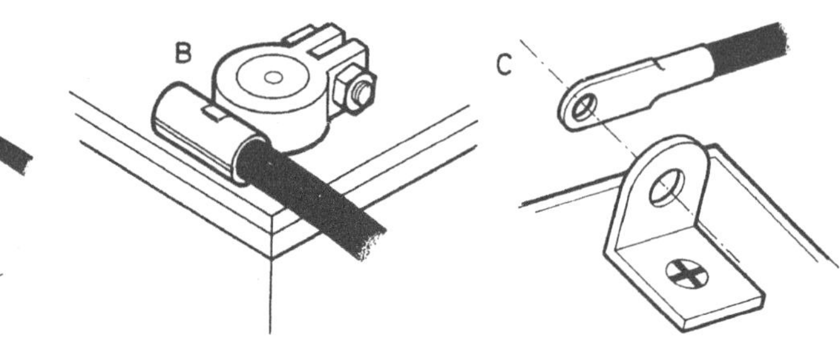


***Fig. 5.23a Types of battery lug***
*A Die-cast helmet B SMMT C Flat type*

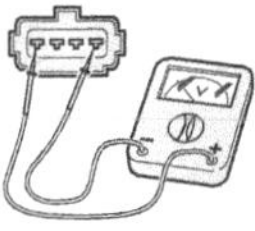

*Fig. 5.23b As the nut is tightened, the wedge on the underside forces the two halves of the clamp together, securing it to the battery post*

**2** Die-cast helmet lugs are still in use but the SMMT clamp lug is found in most modern vehicles. Flat type lugs were in use for many years on Ford vehicles, although later vehicles may have a variation on the SMMT clamp (Fig. 5.23b). Should a helmet lug require replacement, cut off the lug and replace with an SMMT clamp lug of good quality. Lightweight types of unknown composition invariably give rise to white 'fungus growth' corrosion. A better job is obtained by soldering the cleaned cable into a clamp lug rather than using the screw connection type – resin flux ONLY must be used for this (and any) electrical joint, never acid flux or severe corrosion will be the result.

**3** Acid corrosion can cause high resistance contact between the battery posts and the lug. This can reduce the voltage available to the starter and accessories, and can give rise to the phenomenon of an open circuit occurring when the starter is operated. This is signified by a click from the starter solenoid and the dashboard lights going dim. This trouble points to bad contact at the battery or somewhere along the starter cable path – including the earth strap to car body.

**4** If the battery lug has bad contact, or if it has developed a white 'fungus', thorough cleaning is necessary and good electrical contact restored by use of emery paper. A light application of petroleum jelly or a proprietary anti-corrosion grease will keep trouble away.

**5** Fitting lugs to, or removing lugs from, battery posts should not involve force, especially leverage at the battery, otherwise a small gap will develop and acid will find its way out. If a lug is tight, try soaking a cloth in hot water and applying it to the lug; alternatively a puller could be used if available.

## 16 Battery testing

**1** Use of the hydrometer has already been described, and readings may be useful when examining a suspect battery. If one cell has a specific gravity reading markedly different from the rest it points to failure.

**2** Gassing on charge should be even in all the cells, but look for uneven gassing as a guide to a failed cell. A short circuited cell will not gas like the remainder.

**3** The most significant test of a battery is to put it on a heavy-current load while simultaneously measuring the terminal voltage. The heavy-current discharge tester (Figs. 5.24a and 5.24b) is marketed by several manufacturers and consists of a resistor mounted between variable spaced prongs to fit the spacing of lugs on different batteries. Built in is a voltmeter which registers the voltage on load. A battery with sulphation troubles or cell internal short-circuit will be immediately shown up as faulty, not only by the low voltage shown on the meter but a faulty cell may also bubble vigorously while under rapid discharge.

**4** Individual cell testing may be carried out with a cadmium

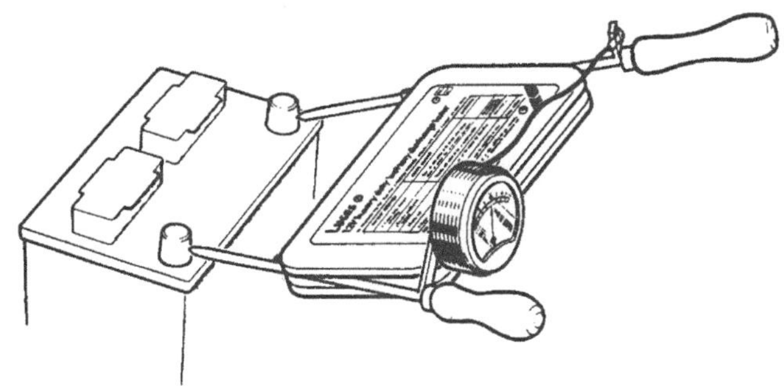

*Fig. 5.24a Lucas heavy duty battery discharge tester*

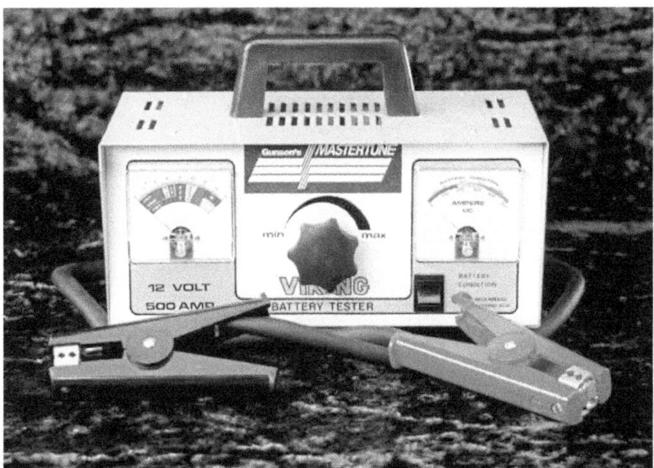


*Fig. 5.24b Viking 500 A battery discharge tester*

tester (Fig. 5.25). Two cadmium probes are inserted into the electrolyte of adjacent cells and the instrument is read, indicating cell condition, ie 'recharge' or 'serviceable'.

**5** The device reads the voltage between the electrolyte and positive plate of one cell and the electrolyte and negative plate of its neighbouring cell. The cadmium probes are electrically neutral and so make no contribution directly to the reading and act as pick-up probes only.

## 17 Maintenance of batteries

**1** Recently major changes in battery design have brought about new terms to describe the level of attention needed. They are:

*(a) Low maintenance*
*(b) Maintenance-free*

to which might be added the traditional battery description:

*(c) regular maintenance*

**2** In the above context the names given to these battery groups refer to the topping up (or freedom from topping up) of the electrolyte, but all batteries require attention to other factors, such as:

*(a) Cleanliness, tightness of lugs and connectors*
*(b) Cleanliness of lid and case, particularly to remove any corrosive acid film*
*(c) Correct clamping of the battery to its position in the vehicle*

**3** Metallurgical developments, together with new construction techniques, have led to ranges of batteries in which topping up has been eliminated, or at least required only after a long interval. Water loss is due to gassing when a battery is charged and much of this gassing is due to the antimony used, with lead, in the grid. Antimony has been replaced by calcium and lead-calcium alloy does not give gassing with the consequent reduction of electrolyte water loss. Lower gassing is also dependent on correct charging. The electronic regulator is precise in maintaining a charging voltage (14.4 V is normal) and the development of the 'maintenance-free' battery has been possible only because of this precision.

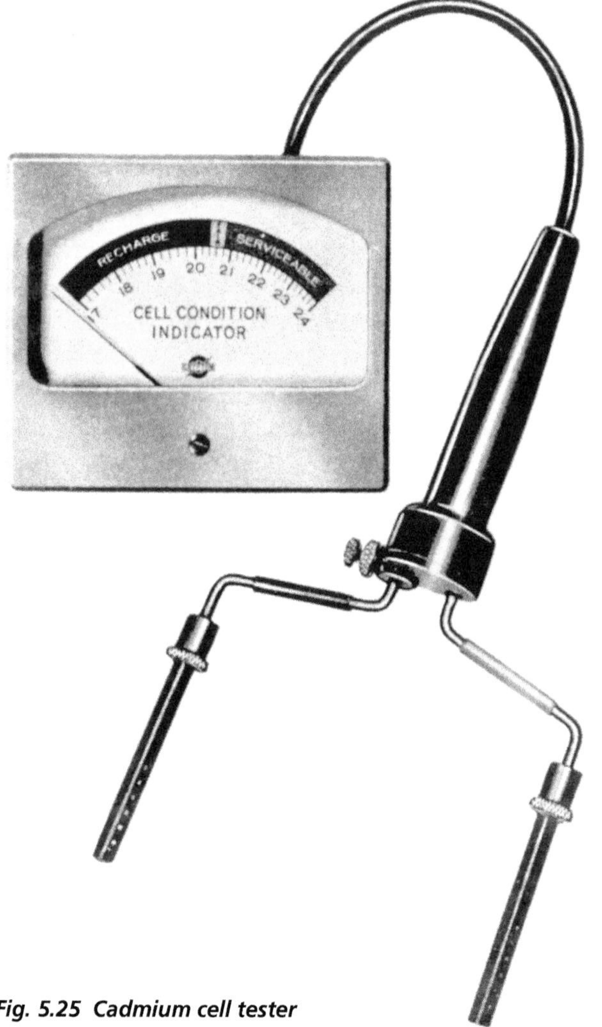

***Fig. 5.25 Cadmium cell tester***

## 18 Low maintenance batteries

**1** The design is similar to that of the traditional battery, save for the lead-calcium grid alloy. Such batteries retain the topping up vent-plugs (or other system) but checking the electrolyte level is necessary once per year or at 50 000 mile intervals. When an older design battery has to be replaced, a low maintenance unit may be used.

## 19 Maintenance-free batteries

**1** The name 'Maintenance-free' has come to mean that no topping up of the electrolyte is required during the battery life. This has largely been brought about by metallurgical advances referred to above, but it is important that the alternator voltage regulator is set accurately at 14.4 volts. If over-voltage occurs then gassing will occur and will result in water loss in vapour form.

**2** All batteries in this class have some form of vent to allow gas escape. Some designs have a fully sealed top so that no topping up is possible, others retain plugs through which topping up is possible in the event of accidental overcharge.

**3** The Fulmen Durastart maintenance-free batteries have a top cover which may be removed to top up in emergency, but given accurate charging voltage there is no need for electrolyte replenishment (Fig. 5.26). One of the principal causes of battery failure is the short circuiting at the bottom of the grids by paste falling to the base of the battery. Fulmen have overcome this by the use of separator envelopes of porous polyethylene, the bottoms of which are sealed.

When paste becomes dislodged from the grids it rests at the bottom of the envelope and short circuits cannot occur

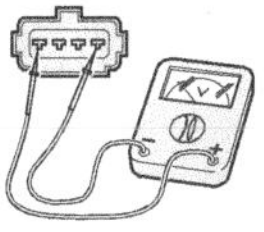

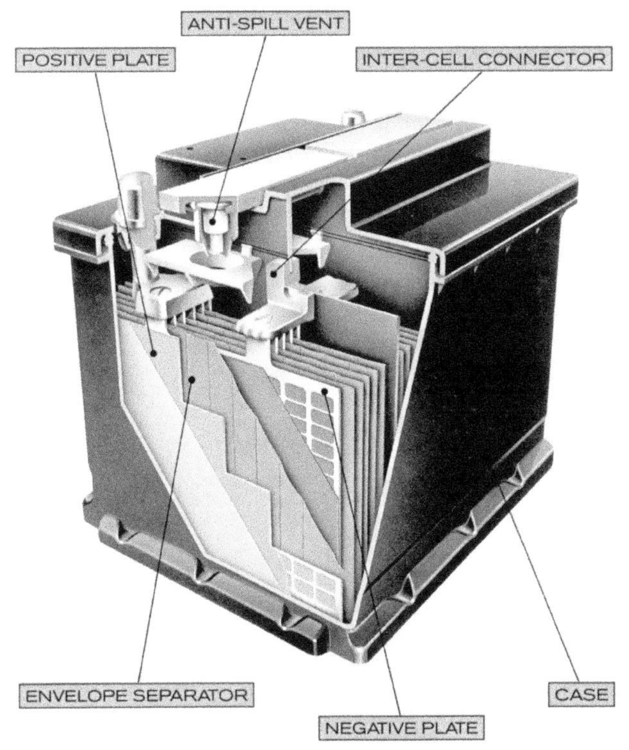


***Fig. 5.26 Construction of Fulmen Durastart maintenance-free battery***

between plates. A further improvement in construction has been the use of 'multigrids' in which thin, machine-filled grids are closely packed in a cell, giving a larger effective exposed paste area. Fulmen claim a superiority of 30% more starting power than that of a conventional battery.

**4** The Chloride-Exide Torque Starter battery is a maintenance-free battery with certain distinctive features. Using the term 'Recombination Electrolyte' the designers have achieved reduced production of hydrogen under charging conditions. Plates are separately wrapped in a glass micro-fibre separator which absorbs all the liquid electrolyte, resulting in no free battery acid being above or to the sides of the elements. Oxygen is generated from the positive plate at a point in the charging process near full charge at which stage a conventional battery would generate hydrogen.

The oxygen passes through the separator to the negative plate where lead sulphate is initially formed, changing to lead and electrolyte as charging continues. The potential of the negative plate does not achieve a value sufficient for the release of hydrogen and as a result no water is lost. The battery is fully sealed, though fitted with a pressure valve to release gas generated under abuse conditions, when the gas generated is greater than the recombination process can cope with.

**5** Another example of maintenance-free technology is the AC Delco Freedom battery in which antimony has been

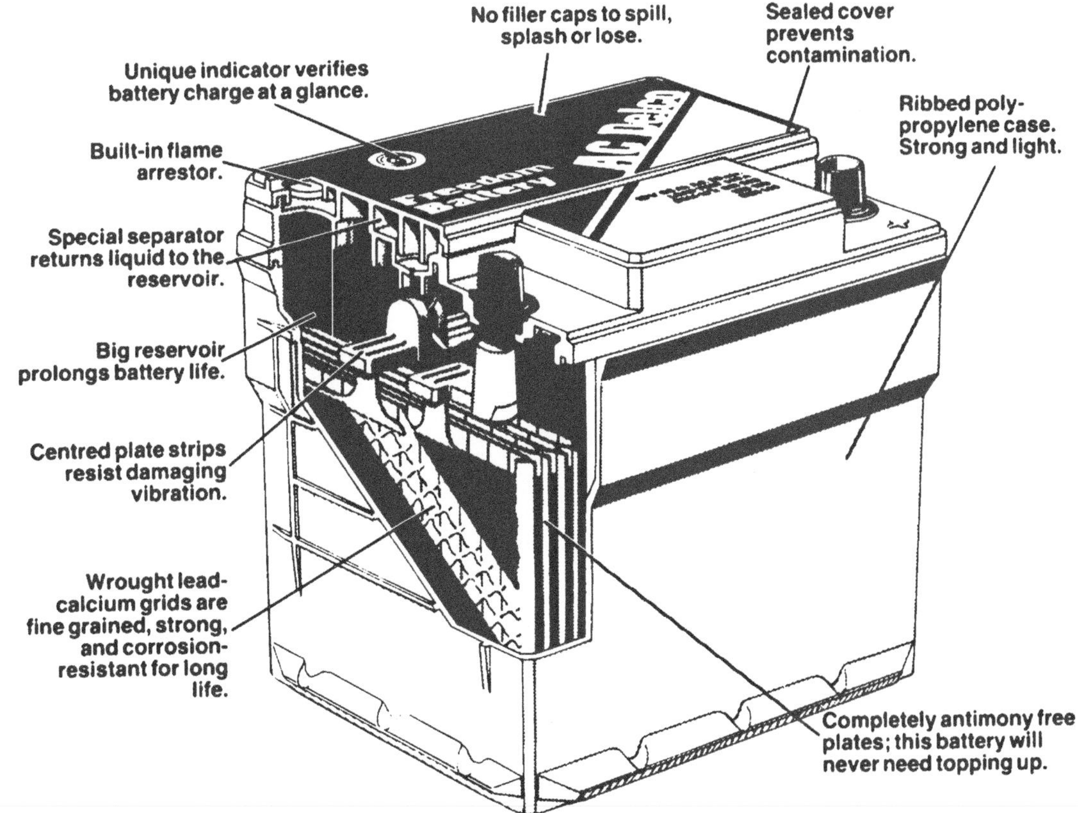


***Fig. 5.27 AC Delco 'Freedom' maintenance-free battery***

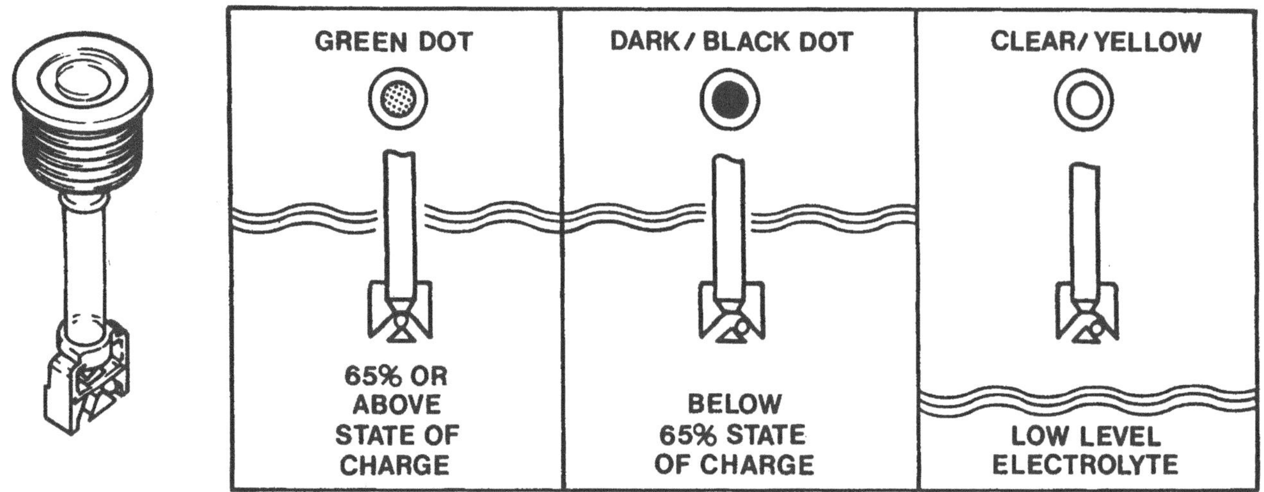


***Fig. 5.28 AC Delco 'Freedom' battery hydrometer***

replaced by calcium completely. The use of calcium in alloy with lead is difficult because calcium has no liquid state, going from solid to vapour when heated. The alloy is wrought to give a fine structure with good anti-corrosion properties.

Gassing has been reduced to a low level so that sealing except for a side vent has been possible. What gas is given off is returned to the electrolyte after reaching the liquid-gas separator cooling volume under the cover. A built-in hydrometer consists of a green ball in a plastic tube which may be observed through the cover. When the green ball can be seen the battery is charged and of correct electrolyte level. If the ball is not floated to the observation point the observed colour is black, and indicates the need for recharging. If the aperture shows clear or yellow, the electrolyte is too low and the battery must be replaced (Fig. 5.28).

# Ignition and combustion

# 6



## 1 Spark requirement for combustion

**1** Petrol engines require an electric spark at the spark plug electrodes in order to ignite the compressed air-petrol vapour. This spark must occur at a precise point in the cycle of engine operation so that maximum downward pressure on the piston occurs shortly after top dead centre. The plug voltage requirements may be anywhere within the range 5000 to 30 000 volts and depends upon several factors, including the mixture strength, the shape of the combustion chamber, the compression rate, the temperature, and the condition of the plug and its gap dimension.

**2** Once the petrol vapour breaks down under the electric stress of the plug voltage, a high intensity spark travels from the negative centre electrode to the positive earth electrode(s). The spark temperature of several thousand °C is

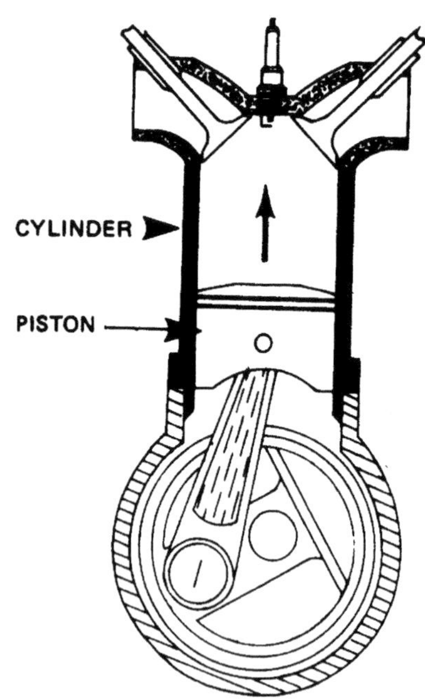


*Fig. 6.1 Compression of petrol vapour*

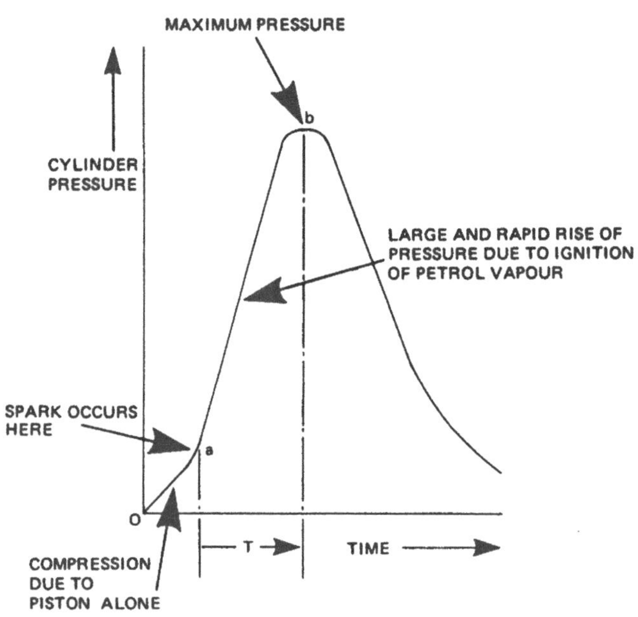


*Fig. 6.2 Pressure rise and fall in the cylinder*

sufficient to ignite the petrol vapour in the vicinity which then continues to burn by itself by the process of a travelling flame wave.

**3** In normal conditions, the spark will occur before the piston has reached TDC. Emanating from the spark region a flame front will travel across the vapour-filled space and, although combustion is completed in a fraction of a second, the gas pressure increases steadily, rises to a maximum and then falls away (Figs. 6.1 & 6.2). The time from the point of ignition to the completion of combustion is about 2 milliseconds, so the spark will be timed to occur to allow for the delay in pressure build-up. At cruising speeds a typical angle of advance (ie before TDC) is 30 to 40 degrees, but it will be seen that a particular angle of advance suits one speed only and it is essential to incorporate a form of control to vary the ignition advance angle with speed.

**4** Manufacturers' tests will determine the optimum ignition advance angle for all speeds and loads. The factors which have to be considered are:

*(a) Pollution levels of exhaust*
*(b) Absence of engine knock or detonation*
*(c) Good fuel economy*
*(d) Maximum engine power output*

**5** The energy contained in the spark discharge must be sufficient to ignite the air-fuel mixture and for an air/fuel ratio of 14.7:1 the minimum energy requirement is 0.2 millijoule (for a definition of the joule see Chapter 1). This figure rises to 3 mJ or more if the mixture is weaker or richer and, allowing for adverse conditions, a practical energy level of each spark must be about 30 mJ for reliable operation. If an ignition system cannot supply this level of energy to the spark plugs whether by design shortcomings or by electrical losses, then misfiring will occur.

## 2 Combustion factors

**1** The air/fuel ratio ($\lambda$) required in theory for complete combustion is 14.7:1. At this ratio, $\lambda = 1.0$. In practice an air deficiency of about 10% ($\lambda = 0.9$) gives maximum engine power and corresponds to fastest flame travel across the cylinder head space, but unfortunately unacceptable pollution by hydrocarbons and carbon monoxide is the result. Where excess air is supplied, that is, a weaker mixture, power falls off due to a slower flame speed. The optimum ratio for producing the cleanest exhaust is when $\lambda = 1.1$ approximately. Pollution is a subject of major interest due to regulations by governments world-wide and will be discussed at various points within this book.

**2** Power and economy are linked to the speed of the flame in the cylinder after ignition. The flame speed in turn depends upon many factors including:

**Cylinder Design.** If the compression ratio is high then, because of the greater density of the inhaled fuel charge, the flame speed is high. The location of the spark plug and the length of the spark gap come under the cylinder design. In general, the better the exposure of the cloud of fuel vapour to the igniting spark, the better the combustion performance.

**Ignition Timing.** Spark timing is crucial and must be such that gas pressure reaches a maximum to give downward piston thrust at about 12° ATDC (after top dead centre). If the spark is made to occur too early (over advanced) flame speed is so high that the charge is virtually exploded, an effect known as detonation (see later). This will damage the engine and must be avoided. Conversely, if the spark occurs too late (retarded), burning is slow and the gas pressure

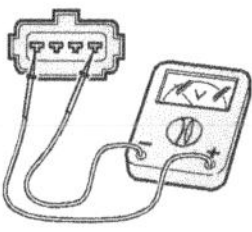

maximises too late. Low power and poor fuel consumption are the results (Fig. 6.3).

**Fuel Charge Turbulence.** In practice, the vapour cloud is not stationary when the spark occurs but is a swirling mass. Flame propagation is helped by such turbulence and cylinder heads are designed to give good fuel charge turbulence.

**Exhaust Gas Presence.** Any exhaust gas that remains in the cylinder and mixes with the incoming fresh charge will lower the flame speed and result in reducing the maximum temperature reached. From the pollution standpoint this is advantageous since the generation of undesirable oxides of nitrogen rises very rapidly with an increase in maximum combustion temperature. In fact, in some engines it is practice to pass back to the cylinder a proportion of the exhaust gases, a process that is known as Exhaust Gas Recirculation (EGR). There are limits to the amount which may be fed back, however, beyond which fuel consumption rises rapidly.

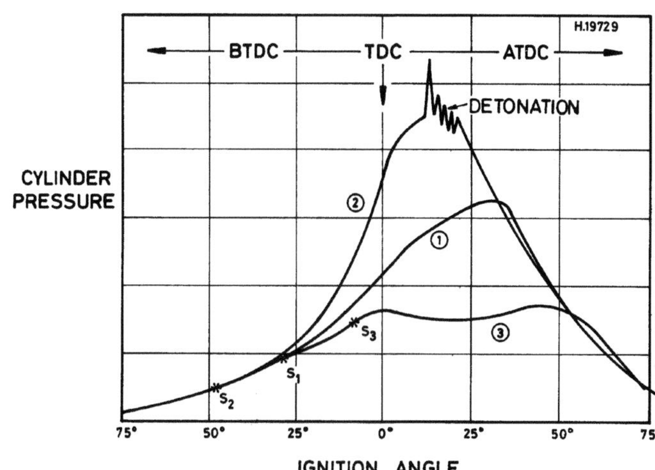


***Fig. 6.3 Effects of ignition angle***

## Detonation

**3** From the previous paragraphs it would appear that the highest possible flame front speed should be obtained in order to achieve best engine power. There is a limit, however; reached when the flame speed becomes supersonic. Under these conditions the flame does not travel across the cylinder head space steadily but the fuel charge explodes.

This is known as **detonation** and can cause serious engine damage. Detonation occurs at a particular pressure level, this being determined by petrol grade, design of cylinder head and other factors.

## Knock

**4** Before the onset of detonation another form of fuel ignition malfunction may occur. Remote from the point where the flame starts, namely at the spark plug electrodes, a volume of gas (the end gas) will be heating due to the approaching flame front. The combination of compression due to the upward piston motion and flame front heating can cause spontaneous ignition and a rapid increase in pressure. This is called **knock** and is often regarded as a combined effect with detonation but in fact the two effects are different although similar in results.

## Effects of Knock and Detonation

**5** At the onset of these phenomena, a light rattling noise known as pinking occurs and is often first noticed when the engine is heavily loaded. Because energy is expended in unwanted noise and heat, reduced power to the road wheels will occur. In serious cases and where the effect has been present for some time, the piston crown may actually melt when the power will be markedly reduced and blue exhaust smoke is given off.

Factors which may contribute to knock and detonation include:

(a) ***Poor cylinder head design.*** *Modern designs allow for efficient cooling of the cylinder head, particularly the region remote from the plug where the 'end gas' is located. Attention is given to the desirable turbulence of the induced petrol vapour charge*

(b) ***Air/fuel ratio****. A weak mixture is more likely to detonate*

(c) ***Petrol grade****. Compression ratio and grade of fuel are related – a low compression ratio engine can use a fuel with a lower octane number*

(d) ***Ignition timing****. Over-advanced timing may result in detonation*

## Knock Sensing

**6** For best efficiency an engine should be timed to run up to the limit where knock occurs. This may be achieved with the aid of electronic controls found in an increasing number of modern vehicle designs. At the onset of knock, high frequency vibrations are set up in the end-gas region. It is possible to pick up these structure-borne vibrations by a sensor which gives an electrical signal voltage proportional to the knock level. Many other vibrations are also present in a running engine but these can be filtered out, leaving the sensor knock voltage alone to be sent on to an on-board electronic control unit (ECU). When knock signals occur, the ECU retards the ignition to reduce the knock level. Such arrangements are often part of a more comprehensive system of engine management. For further details read the chapter on *Engine Management*.

## Pre-ignition

**7** A local hot point within the cylinder head volume may give rise to spontaneous fuel combustion, producing a pinking sound and a substantial loss of power. This is known as pre-ignition. The cause is frequently a deposit of carbon which heats to the incandescent point and causes the fuel to ignite before the spark occurs at the plug. Older engines needed frequent decarbonising to remove such unwanted carbon residues but modern engines and fuels have reduced the need considerably. A linked effect is that of 'running on' in which the engine continues to run after the ignition has been switched off. This is due to the hot carbon spot firing the incoming fuel charge spontaneously. Modern anti-pollution requirements have resulted in 'lean burn' engine design in which the air:fuel ratio is high (ie the mixture is weak). Weak mixture gives hotter combustion chamber temperatures than in earlier designs so measures are taken to shut off fuel supply when the ignition is switched off. This is achieved either by switching the incoming air into the manifold (and not going through the carburettor) or to block off the slow running jet in the carburettor.

## Combustion and Pollutants

**8** When air and petrol are mixed into a vapour and ignited inside the engine cylinder, combustion drives the engine and produces power at the drive wheels. There are, in addition, products of combustion which are passed out via the exhaust system. If the proportions of air and petrol are correct at about 14.7:1 by mass (the Stoichiometric ratio) then the exhaust produces carbon dioxide, water and nitrogen, all being harmless. In practice, because perfect mixing cannot be achieved there will also be carbon monoxide (CO) and oxygen present. Perfect combustion is never achieved and some of the products from incomplete burning are harmful and pollute the atmosphere. About 1% of the exhaust gas is harmful, this proportion being made up of carbon monoxide (CO), oxides of nitrogen (NOx) and hydrocarbons (HC). All three are dependent upon the air-to-fuel ratio; the problem being that if the proportion of CO and HC increases that of NOx decreases and vice versa.

**Oxides of nitrogen (NOx)** have no smell and are tasteless but as they emerge and mix with atmospheric oxygen they produce red-brown nitrogen dioxide ($NO_2$) which, if breathed in, causes irritation of the lungs. Oxides of nitrogen combine with water to produce nitric acid which precipitates as acid rain. The gas components of nitrogen oxide NO and nitrogen dioxide $NO_2$ are classified together as NOx.

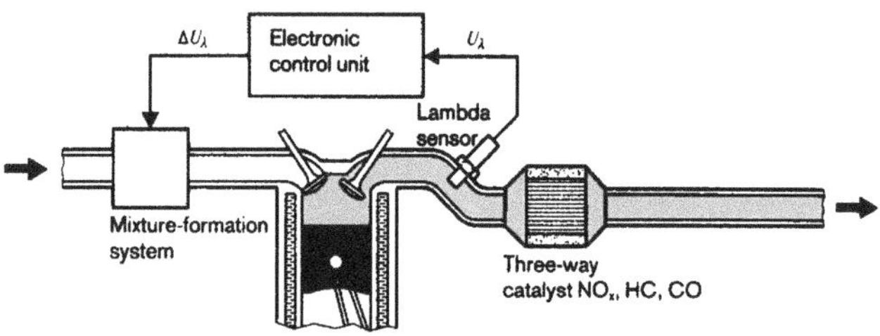


*Fig. 6.4 Single-bed three-way catalyst*

**Hydrocarbons (HC).** Exhaust gas hydrocarbons are present in various forms and all are dangerous. They emerge from parts of the cylinder volume where full combustion has not taken place and also from blow-by past the piston and into the crankcase, where they are ventilated back to the inlet manifold for recombustion. It has also been found that hydrocarbon emissions take place by evaporation from the fuel tank and the carburettor.

**Carbon Monoxide (CO)** prevents the body from absorbing oxygen into the blood stream and is highly dangerous, especially as it has no smell. It is known that as little as 0.3% of carbon monoxide in the air can cause death within 30 minutes.

**Lead**. Lead compounds deposited by vehicles as a result of combustion act as cellular poisons in blood, bone marrow and the nervous system. Lead is not a naturally occurring component of the fuel but an additive to prevent engine knock. About 75% of added lead is blown out of the exhaust and the remainder is absorbed in the engine oil.

## The Catalytic Converter

**9** The toxic components of exhaust gas can be reduced substantially by the use of a catalytic converter built into the exhaust system. Several designs have been evolved, but the type which is now mostly used is the three-way catalytic converter since it will degrade CO, HC and NOx simultaneously.

The two characteristics of the converter are:

(a) *The after burning of CO and HC is promoted reducing them to carbon dioxide ($CO_2$) and water ($H_2O$) both of which are harmless*

(b) *The converter converts the nitrogen oxides (NOx) into neutral nitrogen (N) which is a harmless constituent of air.*

The catalytic converter will reduce more than 90% of the exhaust gas toxic substances to harmless alternative substances but in order to achieve this, two conditions apply:

(a) *Lead-free petrol must be used exclusively because lead would destroy the catalytic properties of the noble metals used in the converter*

(b) *The air:fuel ratio must be held at the Stoichiometric Ratio 14.7:1 precisely (Lambda = 1.0) and this implies the use of a lambda closed-loop control system (Fig. 6.4)*

Note that on Fig. 6.4 the term single-bed here means only one box in the exhaust system. Early versions used more than one. The use of converters as after sales fittings without a Lambda closed loop control system is possible, but the best result in elimination of toxic products will not normally exceed 50%. The converter has to be located at a point in the exhaust system so that the temperature range will be within 400°C to 800°C (Fig. 6.5). Useful conversion takes place only above 250°C. Above 800°C thermal ageing of the substrate and the sintering of the noble metals used to coat the substrate will occur. Improvements in the usable temperature range are likely so that the converter positioning will not be so critical. A typical converter is

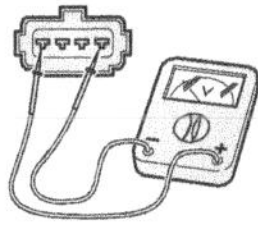

shown in Fig. 6.6. It consists of one or more ceramic blocks made of magnesium-aluminium silicate perforated by several thousand small through-holes which carry the exhaust gases.

The ceramic is, in manufacture, first washed with a coating of aluminium oxide, effectively increasing the surface area of the catalyst by several thousand times. This coating then has a surface layer deposit of the precious (noble) metals rhodium and platinum. Platinum causes oxidisation of the hydrocarbons (HC) and carbon monoxide (CO) and rhodium the reduction of oxides of nitrogen (NOx). The total weight of precious metals used in a converter is of the order of 3 grammes. Results achievable by a 3-way converter are shown graphically in Fig. 6.7 where the need for keeping the air:fuel ratio at λ = 1.0 is seen to be vital. A small rise in λ towards a weaker mixture will produce a substantial rise in the oxides of nitrogen (NOx).

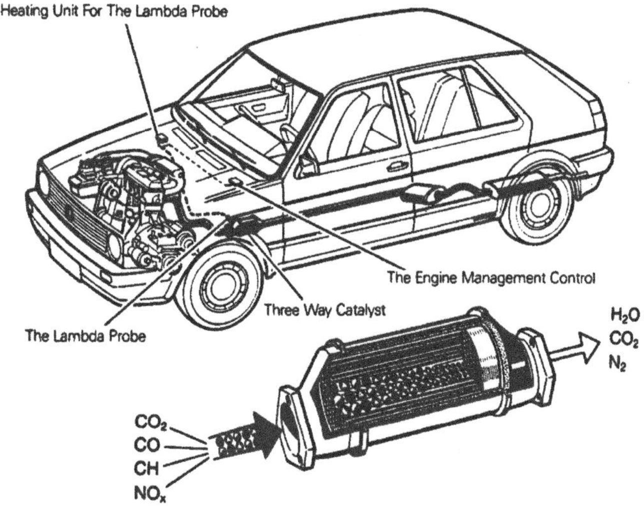


*Fig. 6.5 The location of the catalyst box is important*

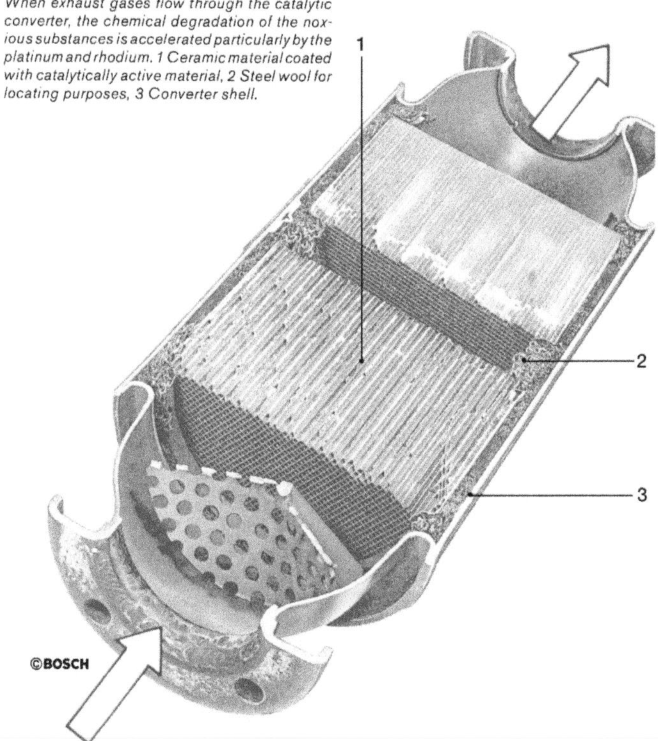


*Fig. 6.6 A catalytic converter*

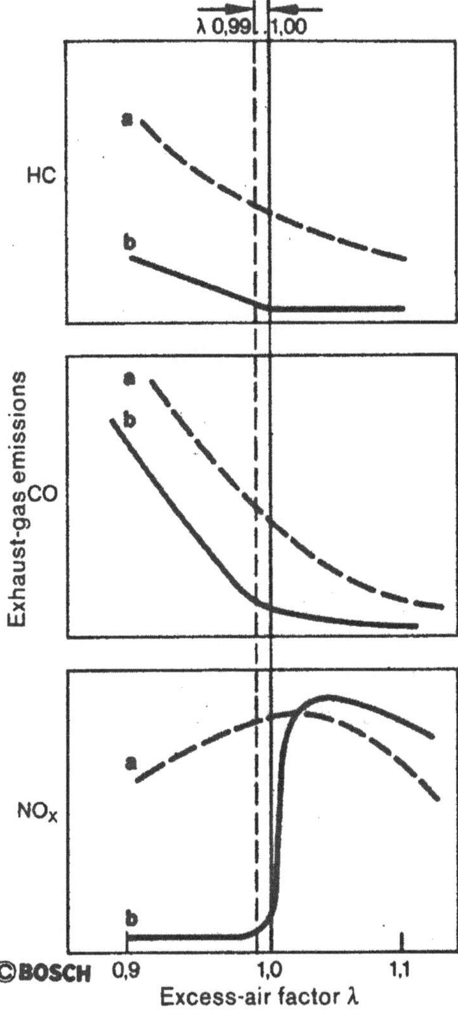


*CH hydrocarbons, CO carbon monoxide, $NO_X$ oxides of nitrogen.*
*a: without aftertreatment*
*b: with aftertreatment*
***The exhaust-gas emissions are influenced by the air-fuel mixture and by the aftertreatment. The absolute necessity for a high degree of control accuracy is shown by the pronounced increase of the noxious carbon monoxide (CO) just below the λ = 1.00 point, as well as by the sudden jump in the noxious oxides of nitrogen ($NO_X$) just above the λ = 1.00 point.***

***Fig. 6.7 Results achievable by a three-way converter***

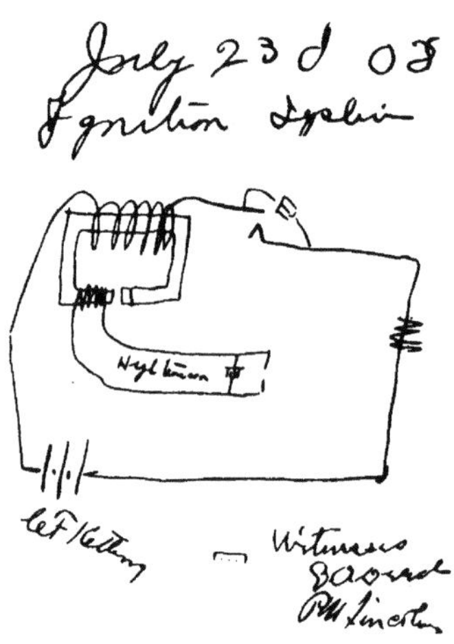

Fig. 6.8 Battery ignition system – patent sketch 1908

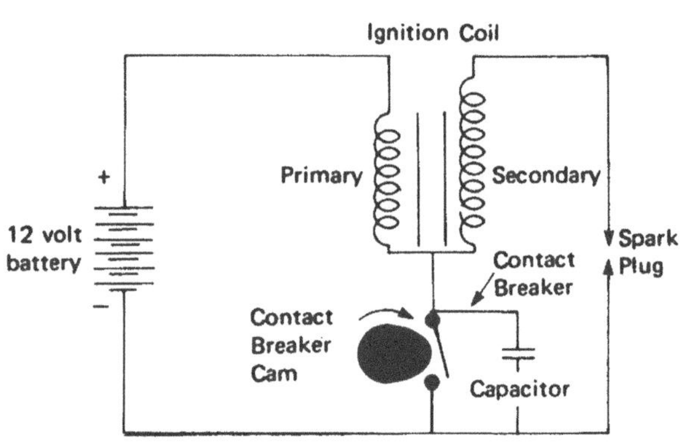


*Fig. 6.9 Present day form of coil and battery circuit*

## 3 Ignition systems

**1** For the first 20 years of the twentieth century petrol driven motor vehicles usually employed the magneto for spark production. This is a high voltage generator driven by the engine and required no battery, but as the advent of vehicle electric lighting involved the use of a storage battery, the alternative system of coil-ignition took over. This had been patented as early as 1908 by C. F. Kettering of the Dayton Engineering Laboratories Company (DELCO) and his drawing (Fig. 6.8) shows that the method has changed little in many years (Fig. 6.9).

**2** The development in electronics has brought about the end of the Kettering coil and battery ignition monopoly and in the last two decades more changes have been introduced in the design of ignition systems than in the previous 80 years. The coil and battery system is still to be found in motor vehicles and a knowledge of its operation is essential, but it now forms part of a group of other systems shown diagrammatically in Fig 6.10. The reasons for, and technology of, all these systems will be treated in this chapter but one common factor remains. For all the advances in design, the ignition coil remains. It is how it is supplied with ignition energy that has changed.

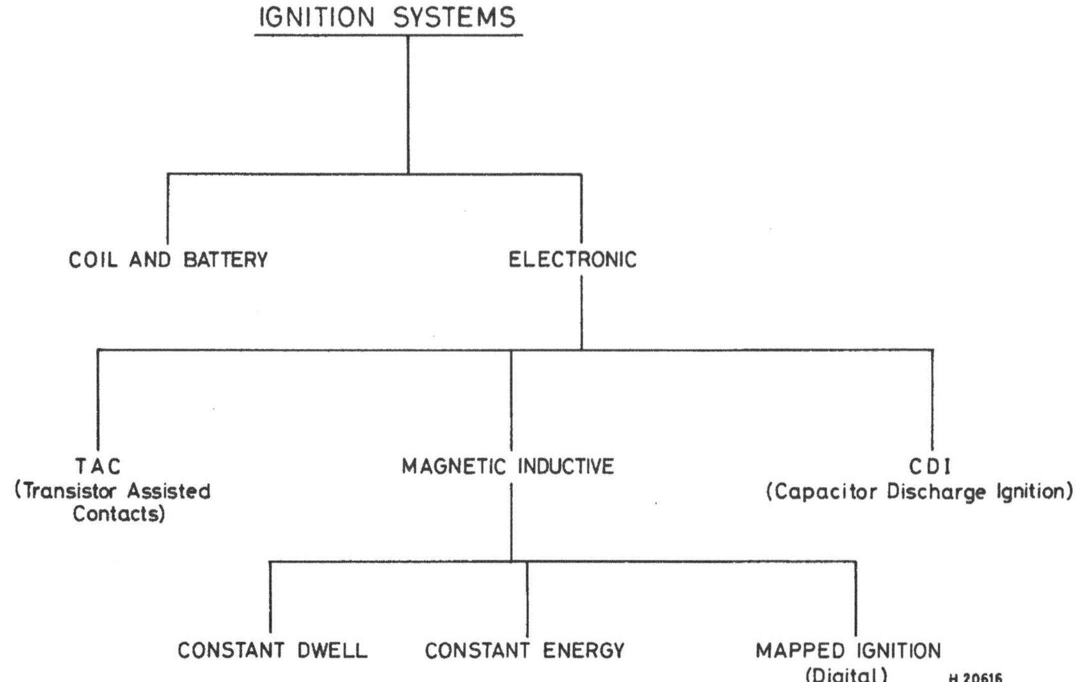


*Fig. 6.10 Classification of automobile ignition systems*

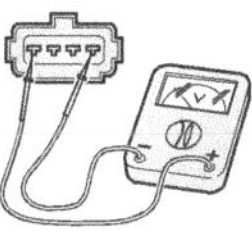

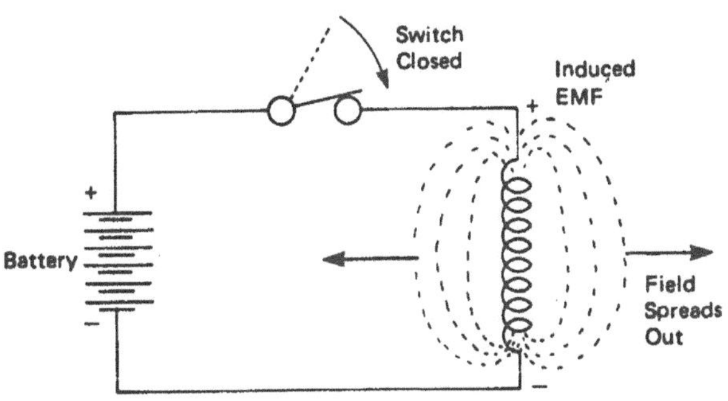


Fig. 6.11 Field build-up

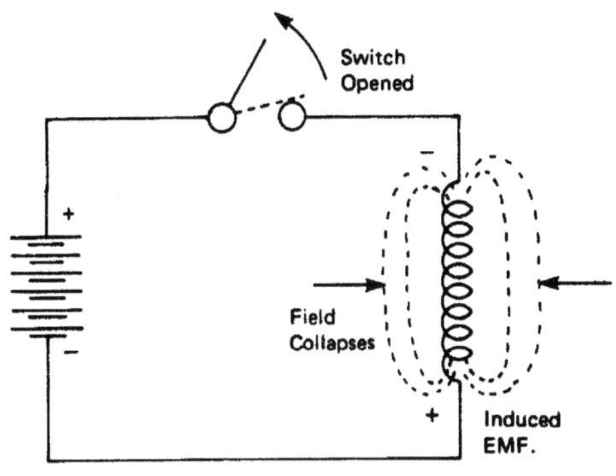


Fig. 6.12 Field collapse

## 4 Coil and battery ignition

**1** Michael Faraday discovered the laws of electromagnetic induction in 1831 – the ignition coil is a direct application. When a wire and a magnetic field move relative to each other it is found that a voltage (or electromotive force) is generated in the wire. This principle will be mentioned several times in this book, such is its importance in relation to car electrical equipment.

**2** As stated in Chapter 1 the voltage induced in the wire depends upon:

*(a) the length of the wire in the magnetic field*
*(b) the relative rate at which wire and field move*
*(c) the strength of the magnetic field*

The magnetic field could be produced by, say, a permanent bar magnet, but in the case of the ignition coil it is convenient to pass current from the battery through a primary coil, the result being a magnetic field which is similar in shape to that of a bar magnet field (Fig. 6.11).

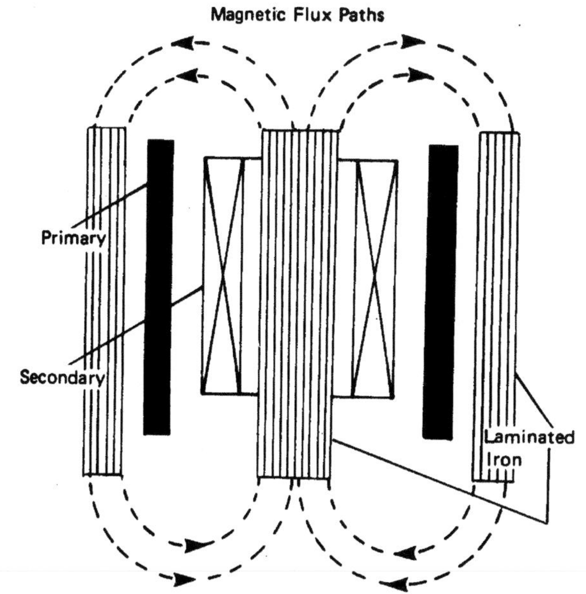


Fig. 6.13 Ignition coil windings and magnetic paths

**3** Switching on the current results in the magnetic field spreading outwards, which in effect cuts the coils, generating an electromotive force in the opposite direction to that of the battery. Now if the current is switched off, the magnetic field collapses towards the centre of the coil – that is to say we have, in both cases, relative movement between the magnetic field and the wire, hence an induced voltage (Fig. 6.12). During the very short period of time over which the magnetic field reduces to zero the induced voltage which may be measured across the coil reaches up to 300 volts.

**4** Note that this induced emf is not directly related to the 12 volt supply; the battery has simply been a means of creating the magnetic field. The switch is the means of rapidly altering the magnetic field so the coils are cut by magnetic force lines as the field either builds up or collapses.

**5** Interesting though this result is, a much bigger voltage is required at the sparking plug. The solution is to wind another coil over the first, but insulated from it, the two coils being called primary and secondary windings. The secondary winding has thousands of turns and, because it is subjected to the same magnetic field changes, will have the same induced emf per turn as the primary. The result is a voltage sufficient to produce a spark at the plugs.

**6** The practical arrangement of the ignition coil is shown in Figs. 6.13 and 6.14. The secondary coil of about 20 000 turns of thin enamelled wire is wound round a central, laminated, iron core. Over this coil is wound the primary winding of about 300 turns of enamel insulated wire of 0.5 mm diameter, sufficient to carry a primary current of

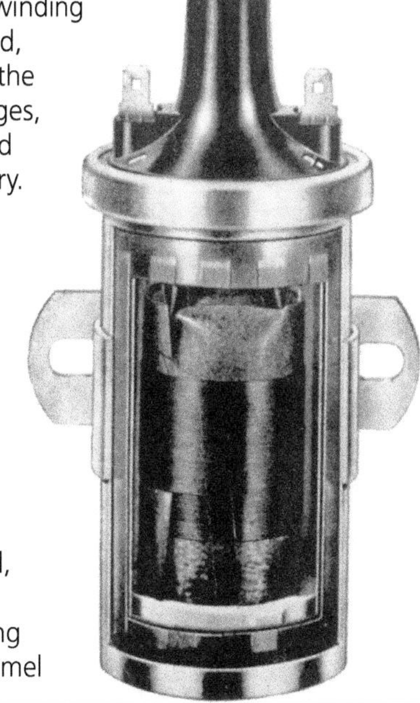

Fig. 6.14 Construction of the ignition coil

about 3 amperes from a 12 volt battery supply. The two windings are insulated from each other by layers of paper or tape and together constitute a step-up transformer of secondary to primary ratio of 66 : 1 approx. To carry the magnetic field an outer slotted iron sheath is fitted.

**7** One end of both primary and secondary windings are joined and brought out to an external terminal connector marked – or CB. The other end of the primary winding goes to an external terminal marked + or SW. Finally the other end of the secondary winding is taken to the coil tower, being the highly insulated high voltage output point of the ignition coil. The complete coil is enclosed by a seamless aluminium case or may be encapsulated in a resin jacket.

## 5 The capacitor (condenser)

**1** The capacitor connected across the contact breaker points prevents sparking at the instant when the contacts open. The effects of such sparking are:

*(a) the induced voltage in the ignition coil is reduced markedly*

*(b) metal transference from one contact to the other would cause serious erosion*

How the capacitor combats these effects is explained below.

**2** When the contact breaker (or switch) is opened, the primary current falls rapidly, so does the magnetic flux, and both primary and secondary windings will have an emf induced in them:

*(a) only as long as the current is changing*

*(b) of a magnitude which depends on how fast the flux (and therefore the current) falls*

**3** At the moment of opening, the induced primary voltage will appear across the contact breaker points and current will jump the gap. This is seen as sparking at the points. It follows that the current does not drop to zero instantly, but remains, for a few millionths of a second, in the form of a spark. Looking again at (b) above, this will reduce the emf in the secondary – just where it is needed.

**4** A capacitor connected across the contact breaker points provides an effective solution. This device is widely used in electrical equipment and is capable of storing electricity (more correctly one should say electric charge). Just as a bucket will hold a quantity of water, capable of being drained out again, so the capacitor holds electric charge. The amount of charge held depends (like the bucket) on certain dimensions, but also upon the applied voltage.

**5** An interesting feature of the capacitor is that, as it fills up with electric charge, it develops a voltage across its terminals in opposition to the original voltage which drove the charge in. If the supply is disconnected the capacitor will retain the charge and the terminal voltage for a considerable period. (Fig. 6.15).

**6** One point to note is that when charge (measured in coulombs) starts to flow down a wire the rate at which it moves is the current. Thus if 1 coulomb per second flows down a wire the current is said to be 1 ampere. Lastly, the measure of the charge handling ability of a capacitor is measured in **farads**. In practice the farad is an enormous quantity and the microfarad (μF) is used. A capacitor used in an ignition circuit (Fig. 6.16) has a capacitance of about 0.2 μF. (The microfarad is one millionth of a farad.)

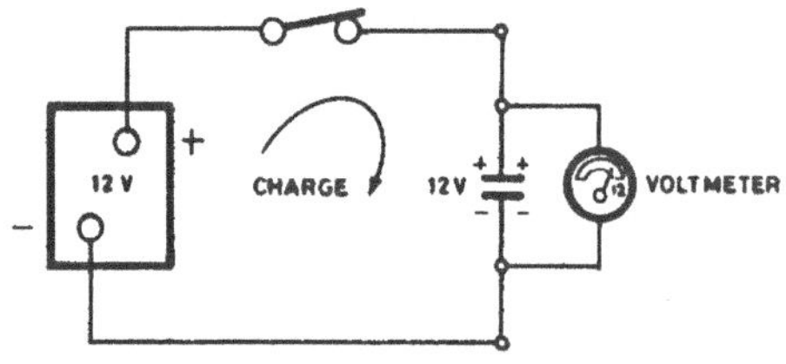


WITH SWITCH CLOSED, BATTERY CHARGES CAPACITOR LIKE A PUMP. CAPACITOR VOLTAGE BUILDS UP UNTIL, WHEN EQUAL TO BATTERY VOLTAGE, NO FURTHER CHARGE WILL FLOW.

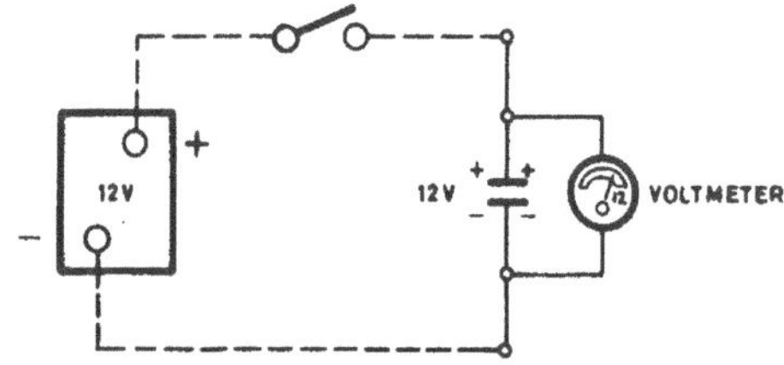


WHEN BATTERY IS DISCONNECTED BY OPENING SWITCH CHARGE AND VOLTAGE ARE RETAINED.

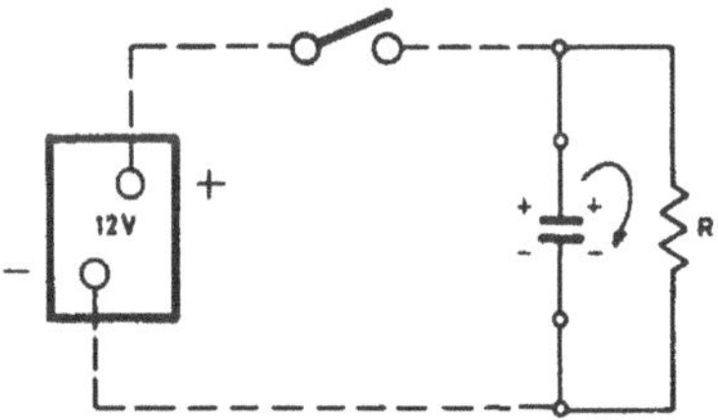


IF A RESISTOR IS CONNECTED ACROSS CAPACITOR, THE CHARGE DRAINS AWAY AND VOLTAGE FALLS. IF RESISTANCE IS HIGH, VOLTAGE FALLS SLOWLY AND VICE VERSA.

*Fig. 6.15 Charge and voltage retention of a capacitor*

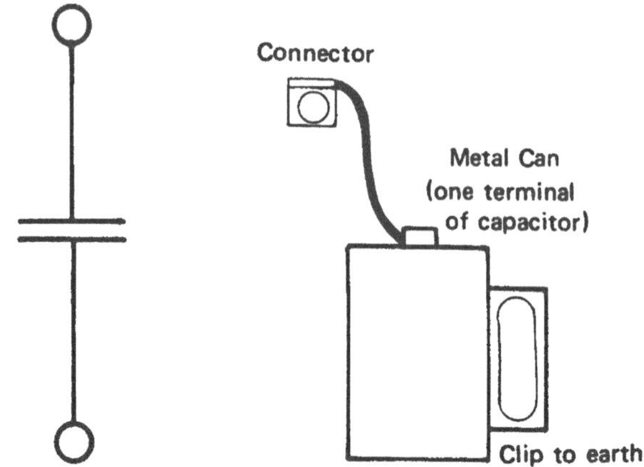


*Fig. 6.16 The ignition capacitor – symbol and actual unit*

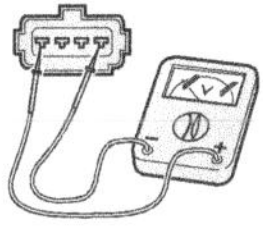

**7** When the contacts are just opening, instead of a spark jumping the gap the charge will now flow into the capacitor which quickly develops a terminal voltage, so as to oppose any further charge flow. Thus the primary current drops to zero much more quickly than without the capacitor and from this there are two consequences:

*(a) The ignition coil secondary voltage will be higher*

*(b) Because sparking does not occur at the contact breaker points, no metal erosion will take place*

In practice, (b) is never completely fulfilled.

## 6 Ballasted ignition coil

**1** When starting, the battery terminal voltage falls significantly, since cranking current for the starter motor can easily reach 300 amperes or more. This can have a serious effect on the ignition coil in very cold conditions when the engine is stiff to turn over.

**2** Some systems use a special ignition coil designed to run in series with a ballast resistor (Fig. 6.17) in the primary circuit. When the ignition key is turned on to the start position, a contact in the solenoid plunger shorts out the resistor so the battery voltage is fully applied to the coil primary. As soon as the engine fires and the driver releases the ignition switch the resistor is again in series with the coil and the system works normally. This arrangement thus gives a boost to the ignition coil primary only when the starter motor is turning over (Fig. 6.18).

**3** The ballast resistor has a resistance about equal to that of the coil primary, so when running normally, half the supply voltage appears across the coil and half across the resistor. It follows that the coil must be designed to work at a lower voltage than the system voltage. In some vehicles a resistive wire going to the primary of the coil is used instead of a special ballast resistor.

*Fig. 6.17 A typical ballast resistor*

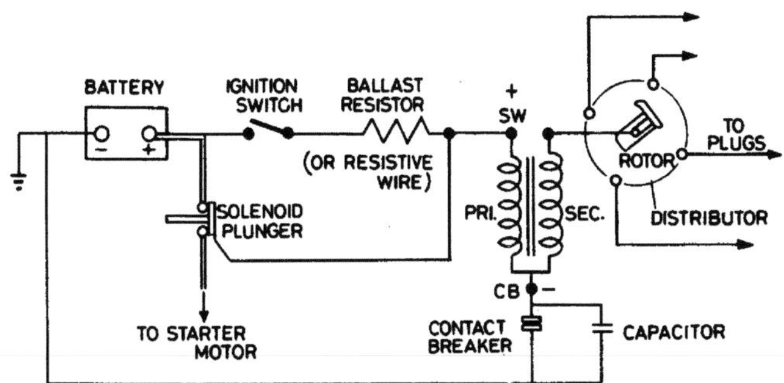


*Fig. 6.18 A ballasted ignition circuit*

**4** There are several advantages of a ballasted system:

*(a) The cold starting performance is improved*

*(b) The primary winding of the coil has a lower inductance value (see next Section) giving a more rapid rise of current when the contacts close. It follows that the ballasted coil can be used at higher engine speeds*

*(c) Because half of the circuit resistance is outside the coil, the latter runs at a lower temperature giving an improved performance*

**5** Note that on certain French vehicles, a temperature-dependent ballast resistor is used. This is made of semiconductor material that will have a low resistance when cold at switch-on, but increases in resistance when warmed by the ignition coil primary current. Thus at switch-on the whole of the supply voltage goes to the coil, but divides between the coil and the ballast resistor as the resistance of the latter rises.

## 7 Contact breaker assembly

**1** The contact breaker points are opened by a cam mounted on the shaft of the distributor (see later). The cam runs at half engine speed for all four-stroke engines. The contact breaker assembly makes provision for positioning the capacitor and also for adjustment of the contact breaker gap – a factor vital to proper ignition system performance (Fig. 6.19).

**2** The important feature of correct gap setting is to allow time for the primary coil current to build up again after the contacts close. All coils possess a feature called 'inductance' and the ignition coil is no exception. The effect of inductance is to slow down the build-up of current in the coil in much the same way as the inertia of a flywheel retards the build-up of rotational speed from standstill.

**3** It is important, therefore, that the points do not stay open too long or there will be insufficient close-time. A measure

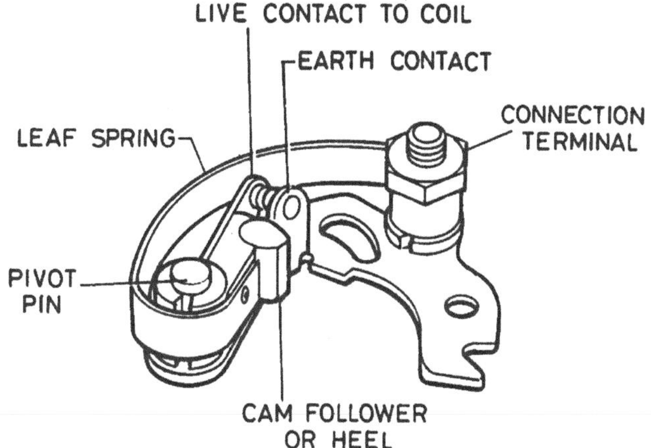


*Fig. 6.19 One-piece contact breaker set*

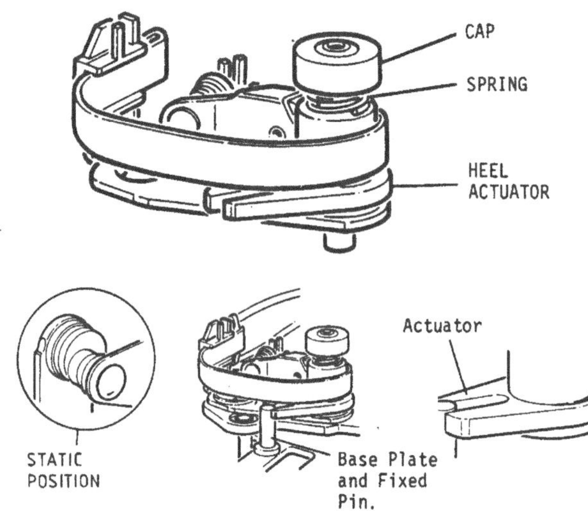


*Fig. 6.20 Sliding contact set*

of this close-time is the dwell angle and is partly determined by the cam profile and adjustable by alteration of the maximum points gap. Setting the gap by feeler gauge is, in effect, to set the dwell but is a rudimentary method because of the possibility of 'piling' of one contact, and also because the static gap setting and the gap when the engine is running may be different due to distributor wear.

**4** Some Austin Rover and Ford vehicles have been fitted with a Lucas distributor which uses a sliding contact set (Fig. 6.20). The contact breaker heel has two small ribs in its base each side of the pivot post. Each rib rests on a ramp which is cut into a forked heel actuator which also is located on the contact breaker pivot.

**5** When the vacuum unit rotates the bearing plate the heel ribs ride up the ramps, forcing the heel and the moving contact upward. The moving contact runs across the face of the larger fixed contact; this wiping action has a self-cleaning effect which reduces pitting and piling. The working life of the contact breaker is claimed to be 25 000 miles.

## 8 Dwell angle

**1** Dwell angle is defined as the number of degrees of distributor cam rotation for which the contact breaker points remain closed during one ignition cycle. The setting of this angle is most important; moving the gap wider will reduce the dwell angle. Conversely, making the gap smaller will increase the dwell angle, the reason being that the contact breaker cam follower picks up on the cam earlier or later as the case may be (see Fig. 6.21).

DWELL ANGLE

CONTACTS CLOSE

CONTACTS OPEN

ADJUSTMENT OF CONTACT GAP ALTERS DWELL

A wide gap results when the fixed point is adjusted too near cam centre (inwards). Later closing and earlier opening reduces dwell angle and advances ignition timing.

A narrow gap results when the fixed point is adjusted too far from cam centre (outwards). Earlier closing and later opening increases dwell angle and retards ignition timing.

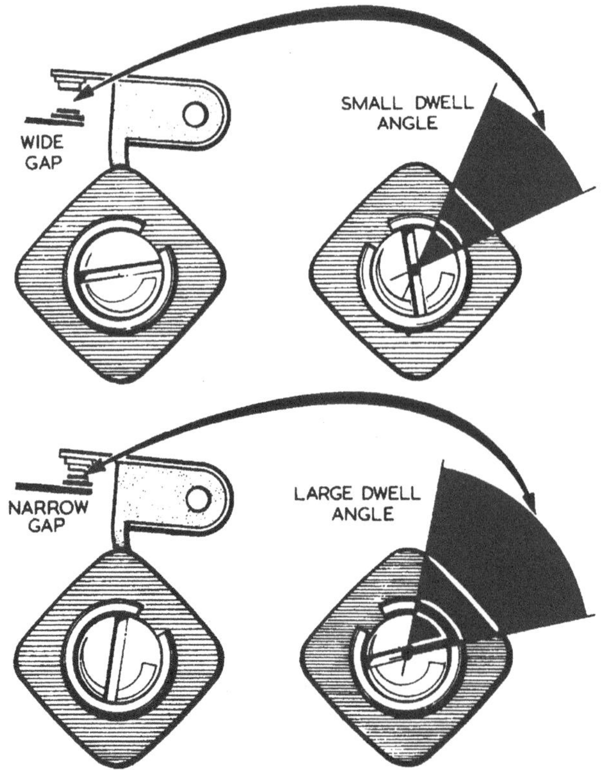


*Fig. 6.21 Illustrating dwell angle*

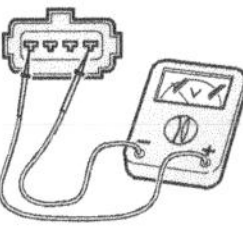

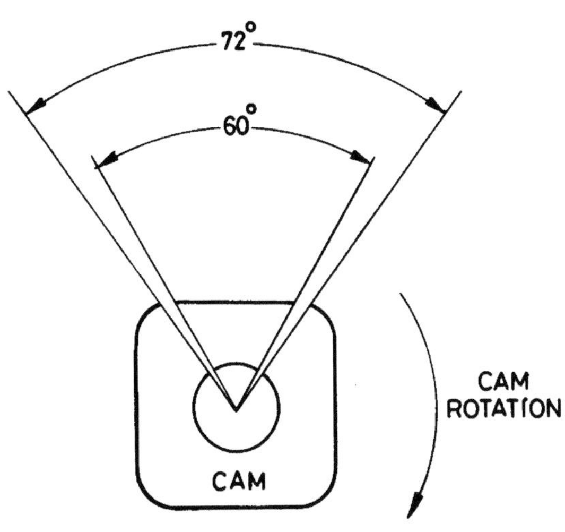


*Fig. 6.22 Dwell angle change – ignition timing change*

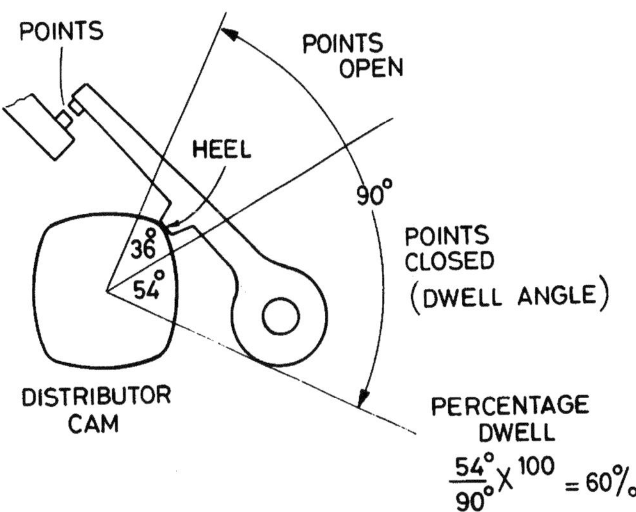


*Fig. 6.23 The relationship between dwell angle and percentage dwell*

**2** Incorrect setting can have serious consequences, for if the dwell angle is too small the coil current cannot build up enough at high speeds and the ignition may cease to work. If the dwell angle is too large then contact burning may occur.

**3** Both dwell angle and points gap should be within the maker's tolerances, and if both cannot be satisfied the distributor is faulty.

**4** A total change in degrees of dwell angle is also equal to the ignition timing change which will result. Reference to Fig. 6.22 illustrates this. Assuming a change of 12° in the dwell angle, then the instant of points opening is changed by 6°, but 6° on the distributor cam is equal to 12° on the crankshaft.

**5** Dwell can be expressed as an angle (in degrees) or as a percentage; it is useful to be able to convert from one to the other.

**Example:**

A four-lobe cam has four periods of 90° rotation and the points will open and close for a part of each period. In the case shown in Fig. 6.23 the points are closed for 54° (the dwell angle) and open for 36°. The percentage dwell is:

$$\frac{54°}{90°} \times 100 = 60\%$$

Converting back is straightforward. The dwell angle is:

$$\frac{60}{100} \times 90° = 54°$$

In fact, 54° is a typical dwell angle for a 4-cylinder engine. It is easier to use % dwell rather than dwell angle because it will not then depend upon the number of cylinders.

**6** A dwell meter can be used to accurately measure dwell angle, but with some types of meter care must be taken with interpretation of the scale reading, as one scale may be used for engines with differing numbers of cylinders. As an example, given a dwell percentage of 60% for single-cylinder, four-cylinder and six-cylinder engines, the following would apply:

Single-cylinder engine/one lobe cam – period 360°
Four-cylinder engine/four lobe cam – period 90°
Six-cylinder engine/six lobe cam – period 60°

The dwell angle readings would be:

Single-cylinder: $\frac{60}{100} \times 360° = 216°$

Four-cylinder: $\frac{60}{100} \times 90° = 54°$

Six-cylinder: $\frac{60}{100} \times 60° = 36°$

## 9 The distributor

**1** As suggested by the name, the distributor passes the spark current to each plug in turn, but it is convenient to incorporate other functions as well. Four main actions are carried out by the distributor:

*(a) To pass the spark to each plug in the correct sequence*
*(b) To make and break the ignition coil primary current*
*(c) To arrange for the timing of the spark to be varied according to engine speed*
*(d) To vary spark timing according to the engine load*

**2** The distributor shaft runs at half the engine speed for a

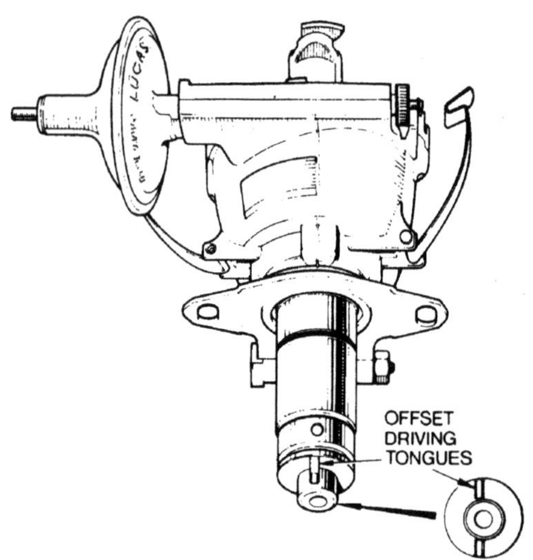


*Fig. 6.24 A distributor driven by a drive dog*

four-stroke engine and locates on the driving shaft by either an offset drive dog (Fig. 6.24) or by a gear (Fig. 6.25).

**3** The contact points are mounted on a baseplate which is able to rotate round the cam over a limited range, this rotation being controlled by a vacuum unit (Fig. 6.26) which measures the degree of vacuum in the engine inlet manifold. See Section 11 also.

**4** The heel of the moving contact is in contact with the cam which has the same number of rising lobes as the engine has cylinders. As the cam rotates the contacts are opened and closed alternately. The amount of opening of the contacts is determined partly by the rise of the cam lobe and also by the position of the fixed contact, which is adjustable and connected to earth.

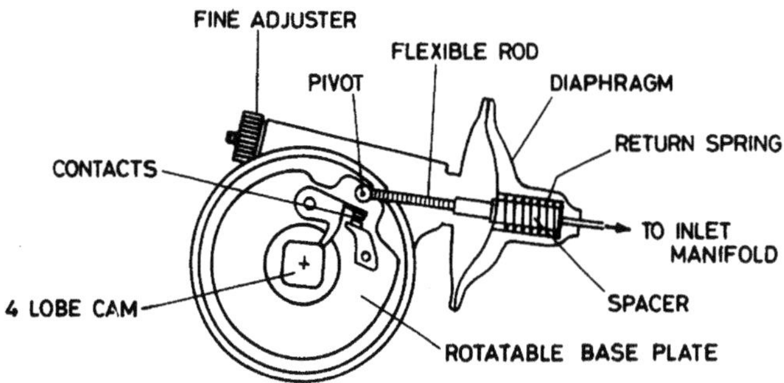


*Fig. 6.26 Vacuum advance mechanism*

*Fig. 6.27 The distributor cover – interior view*

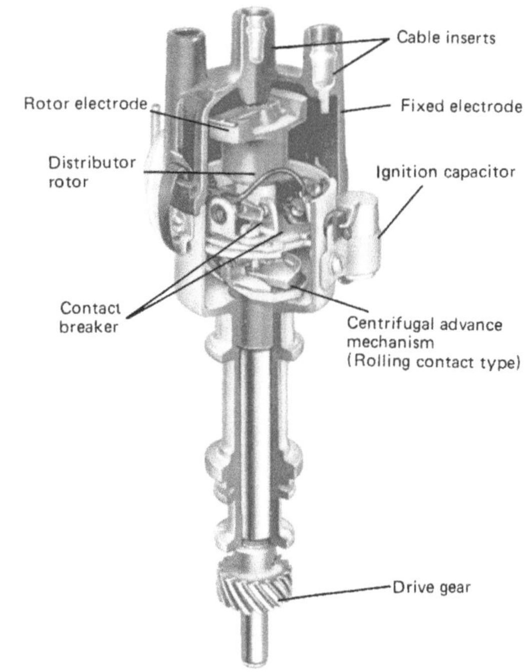


*Fig. 6.25 A distributor driven by drive gear*

**5** The cover (Fig. 6.27) is moulded from high quality bakelite, and is intended to protect the distributor interior from dust and moisture, and also to provide pick-up electrodes which take the spark current from the rotor arm (Fig. 6.28 and 6.29), located

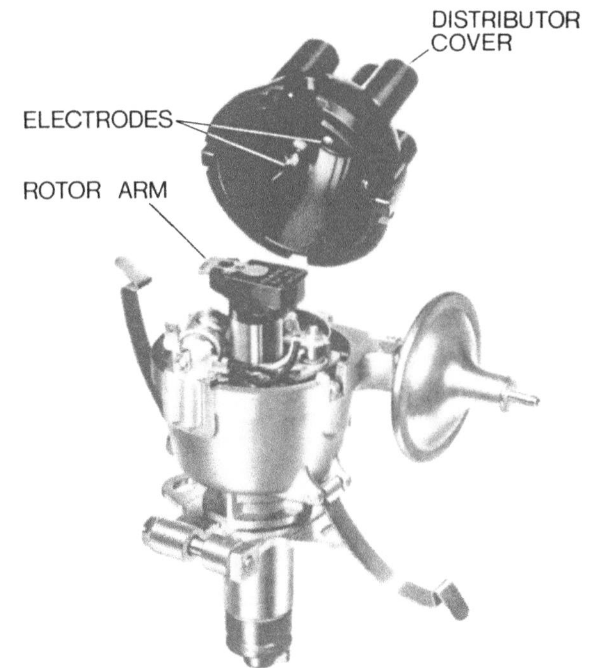


*Fig. 6.28 The distributor rotor arm and cover*

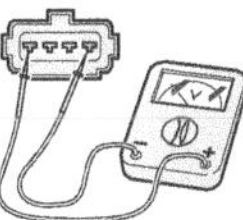

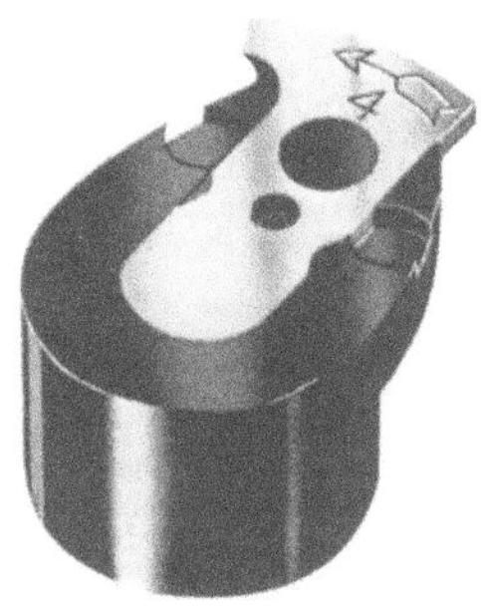

*Fig. 6.29 A typical rotor arm*

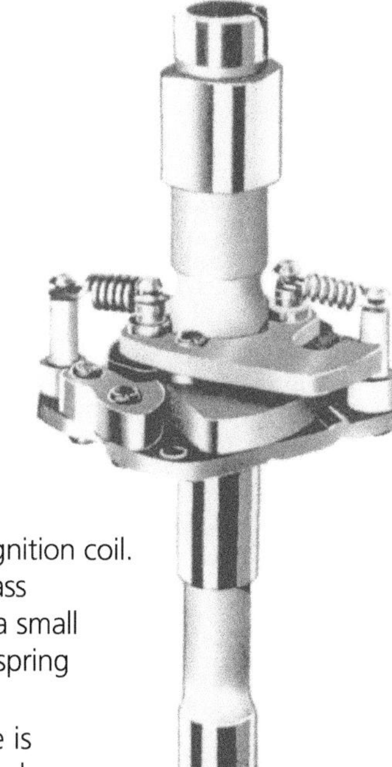

*Fig. 6.30 The auto advance mechanism*

at the top of the distributor shaft. From the cover, high tension (HT) leads go one to each plug, the centre lead being the HT input from the ignition coil. Connection is made to the brass electrode of the rotor arm by a small carbon brush or sometimes a spring loaded metal electrode.

**6** Automatic ignition advance is achieved by employing two bob weights on springs (Fig. 6.30) which fly outwards under centrifugal force and twist the camshaft relative to the driveshaft of the distributor, according to engine speed, thus making the spark occur earlier with increasing speed.

## 10 Ignition advance requirement

**1** The amount of ignition advance required for a particular engine at any speed is found experimentally by the makers, the procedure being to set the engine speed then adjust the advance until maximum power is achieved. For a typical four-stroke engine the advance curve will look something like Fig. 6.31. Ideally the distributor should give a similar response, but in practice the shape of the actual advance curve is a compromise.

**2** The springs which hold back the advance mechanism bob weights have a linear characteristic, that is to say the extension is proportional to the force stretching them. Accordingly, a distributor using two springs of identical strength will give an advance characteristic which is straight – see Fig. 6.32 (the two lines showing the acceptable limits). Note that advance ceases at about 2000 rev/min for the distributor shown (engine speed 4000 rev/min) due to the stop built into the cam which comes up against one of the fixed posts of the moving plate.

**3** A more complex curve is arranged by using two springs of different strengths, one of them also being initially loose by using an elongated loop at one end, so that it does not come into play until the bob weights are partly out in orbit. Fig. 6.33 shows the curve obtained from a distributor with a differential spring assembly.

IGNITION ADVANCE

ENGINE SPEED REV/MIN

*Fig. 6.31 A typical ignition advance curve*

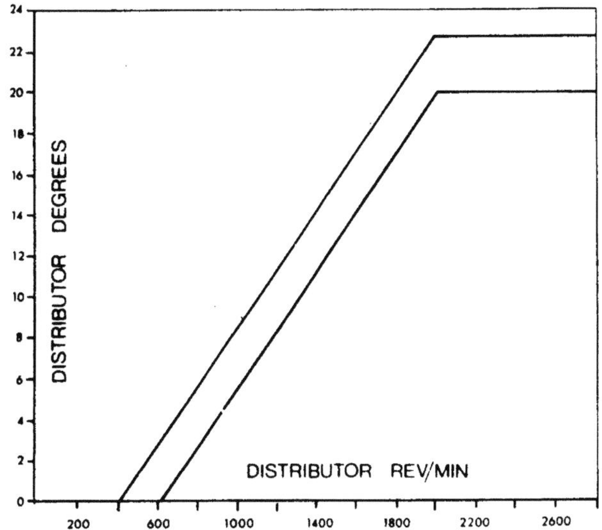


*Fig. 6.32 Typical advance curve for an equal spring assembly*

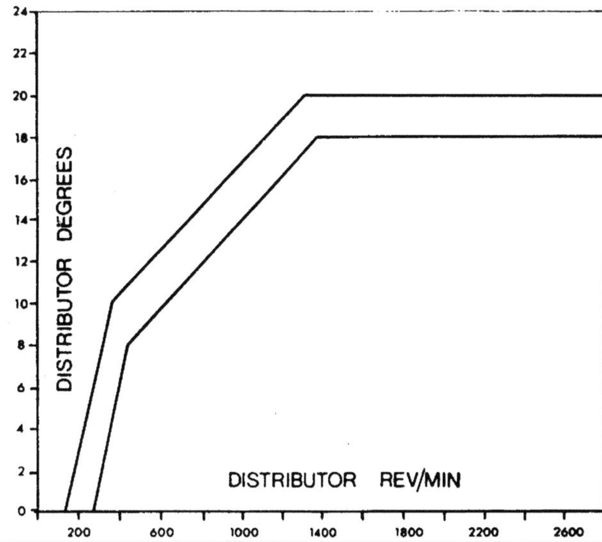


*Fig. 6.33 Typical advance curve for a differential spring assembly*

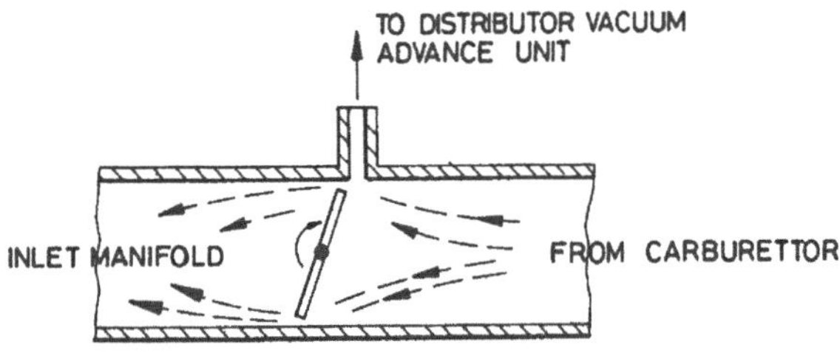


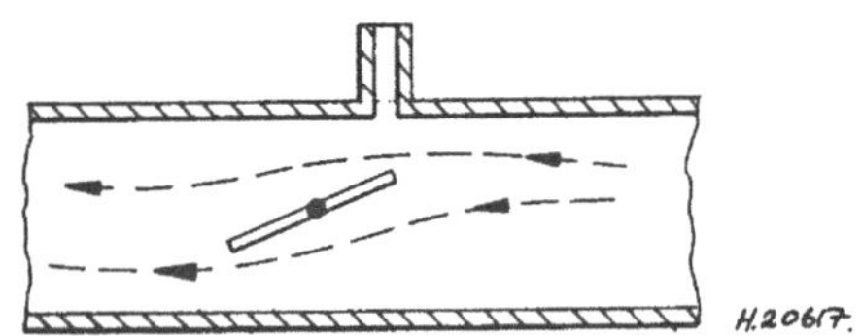


*Fig. 6.34 Vacuum in the inlet manifold*

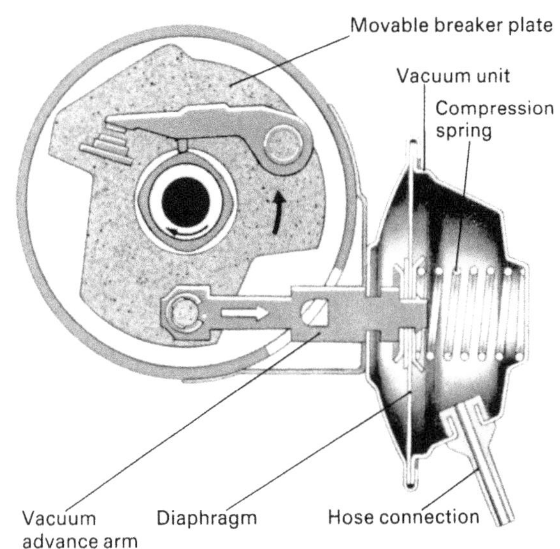


*Fig. 6.35 A vacuum advance unit*

**4** As the speed of the distributor increases there is a rapid advance of about 9° at 400 rev/min since only one spring is operating. The advance then increases more slowly until the maximum of 18° to 20° at 1350 rev/min is reached. This characteristic is typical, but variations will occur for each engine design.

**5** The delay in operation of the second spring is obtained by, as stated, having an elongated loop at one end. The loop must not be altered or a different characteristic will result and the engine performance will be sluggish.

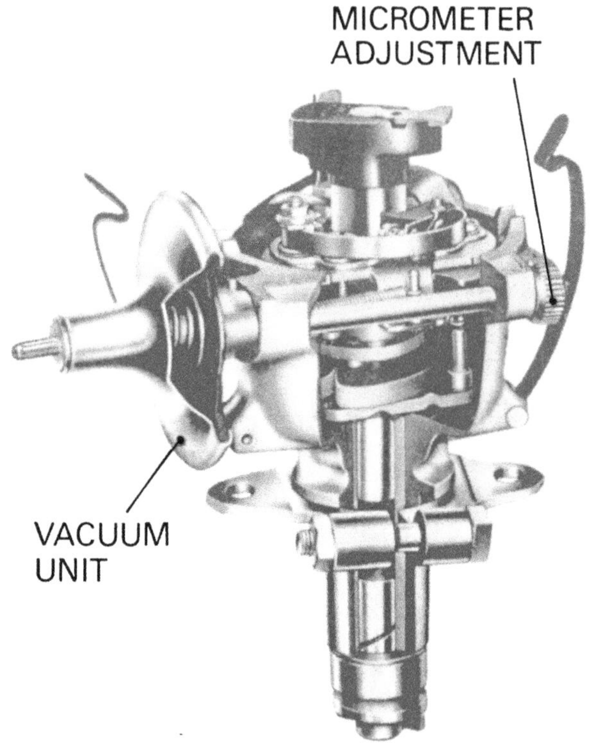


*Fig. 6.36 Micrometer control assembly and vacuum unit*

## 11 Vacuum ignition advance

**1** Centrifugal advance adjusts spark timing for an increase in speed to allow time for air/fuel mixture to burn efficiently. However, when the vehicle is cruising under light load conditions, ie not hill-climbing, the fuel intake is reduced and the fuel charge will be at lower pressure at the spark point. These conditions result in a slower burning time and further ignition advance is required.

**2** To achieve this, use is made of the fact that there will be a relatively high vacuum in the inlet manifold under light load and less vacuum under heavy load when the throttle is opened wider (Fig. 6.34).

**3** A hole in the inlet manifold near the throttle is connected by fine tubing to a vacuum advance unit which connects to a vacuum chamber and spring-loaded diaphragm. The diaphragm controls a linkage to the distributor baseplate on which the contact breaker set is mounted: when vacuum occurs the diaphragm pulls the baseplate and contacts in the opposite direction to the cam rotation, thus giving an earlier spark (Fig. 6.35). The vacuum advance will be determined by the strength of the spring (known as spring-rate) and the limit fixed by a spacer or slot in the diaphragm link. Initial setting-up of the distributor is by adjustment of the clamp unit at the base of the body; on some types a fine (micrometer) control is provided (Fig. 6.36).

**4** Conditions under which the vacuum system comes into operation are worthy of note:

*(a) At tickover speed, the degree of vacuum in the inlet manifold is large, since the throttle butterfly is nearly*

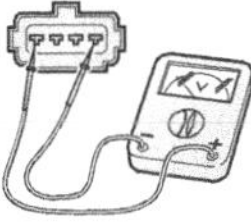

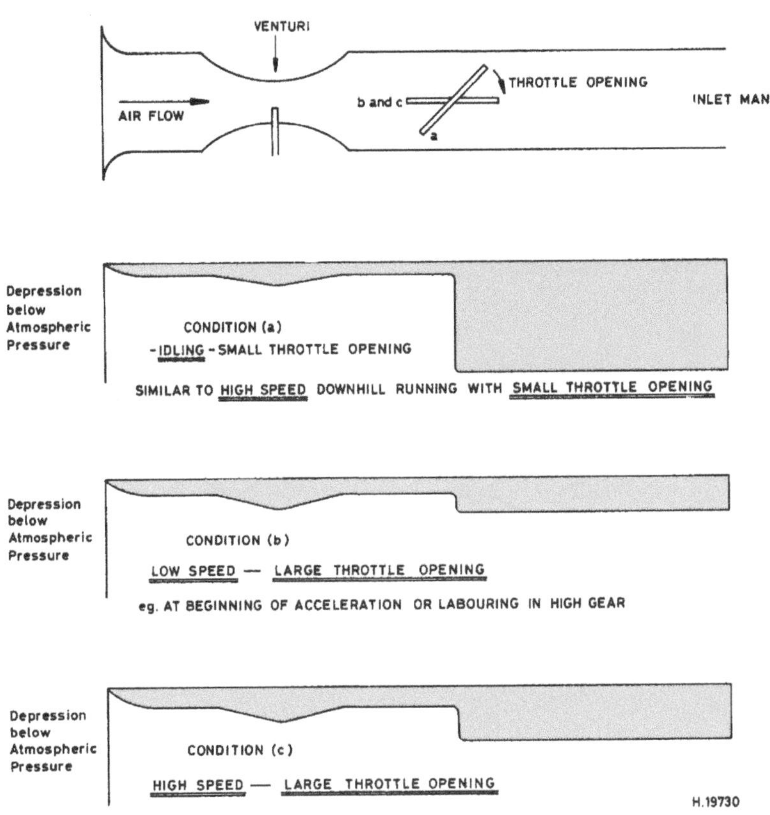


***Fig. 6.37 Induction pressures***

***Fig. 6.38 Vacuum ignition advance by moving post position***

*closed. Vacuum advance does not occur, however, because the butterfly has not exposed the vacuum tapping hole*

*(b) When cruising on the flat, the engine is on light load and the throttle only partly open. The vacuum is still large and is transmitted to the diaphragm of the advance unit. Ignition advance occurs*

*(c) When the engine comes under heavy load the driver presses the accelerator pedal and opens the throttle. The vacuum is reduced considerably, allowing the vacuum unit spring to return the contact breaker baseplate to the original position. The degree of advance is then fixed only by the centrifugal advance mechanism.*

See also Fig. 6.37 showing induction manifold pressures.

**5** An interesting method of vacuum-controlled ignition advance is used by Ducellier. As vacuum is applied, an eccentric moves the mobile contact pivot-point, thus having the effect of altering the opening and closing positions of the contacts (Fig. 6.38). Note that the contact points gap at the zero vacuum position and maximum vacuum position will differ according to the position of the cam when the initial adjustment was made.

## 12 Emission control twin diaphragm vacuum unit

**1** This type of ignition advance controller has two diaphragms operated by separate vacuum chambers. One chamber is connected by a pipe to the inlet manifold close to the throttle as in the single diaphragm unit described earlier. This is the advance or early unit. The second chamber, which is annular in form, is connected to a further point in the inlet manifold but downstream from the throttle. This is the retard or late unit. The diaphragms pull in opposite directions when subject to vacuum.

**2** It is found that lower emission pollution levels occur in the exhaust on tickover or when running downhill with the throttle closed if the engine is given ignition retardation. The high inlet manifold vacuum at tickover or overrun is shown in Fig. 6.37 and the retard unit pulls the vacuum advance arm to the left until it comes against the stop (Fig. 6.39). At part throttle, there is a degree of vacuum on both sides of the throttle and the design allows correct advance to be given over the range of throttle opening. At full throttle, both chambers are exposed to little vacuum and so the position of the vacuum advance arm is fixed by the strengths of the two springs. The secondary spring is stronger and the arm is moved to the right against the limit stop A. Thus maximum advance occurs in this situation. Under this condition the engine speed is sufficient to ensure that the centrifugal advance provides the advance control alone. Note that the overall ignition advance at any engine condition is that due to both the centrifugal and vacuum units added together.

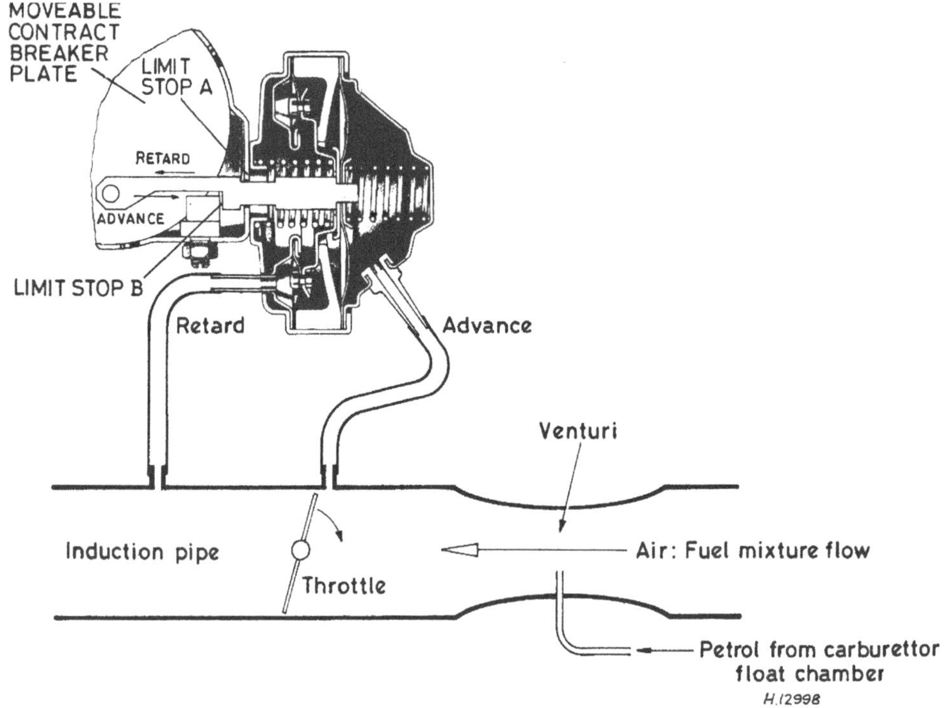


*Fig. 6.39 Emission control advance/control unit*

## 13 Spark polarity

**1** Ignition systems are designed to have negative polarity at the plug insulated electrode, and the earthed electrode positive. Electrons which in part make up the spark, leave a metallic surface of negative polarity and jump to the +ve electrode. Electrons leave some metals more easily than others, and additionally will leave a surface more readily if it is at high temperature.

**2** For these reasons the spark jumps from the centre electrode to earth, but there is also additional benefit from their arrangement. Over a long period the surface from which the sparks are emitted wears away because each spark actually conveys minute particles of metal with it. It is preferable to have the centre electrode wear away, rather than the earth electrode, especially when it comes to gap measurement by feeler gauge (Fig. 6.40). Reversed polarity also requires up to 40% higher spark voltage, and this can lead to misfiring.

**3** An interesting case is that of the Citroën 2CV where both ends of the ignition coil secondary winding are brought out to the two sparking plugs, the engine being of the horizontally opposed twin type. From Fig. 6.41 it is seen that

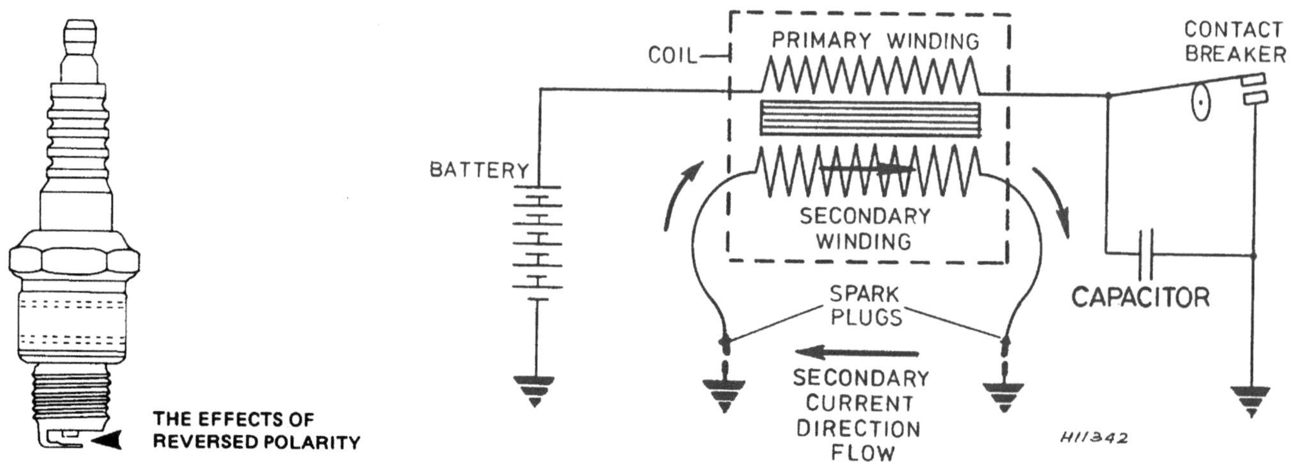


*Fig. 6.40 Electrode erosion due to reversed polarity*

*Fig. 6.41 Dual spark ignition as used in Citroën 2CV*

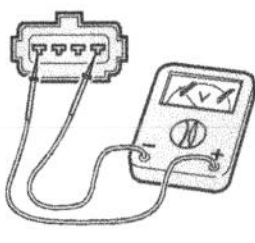

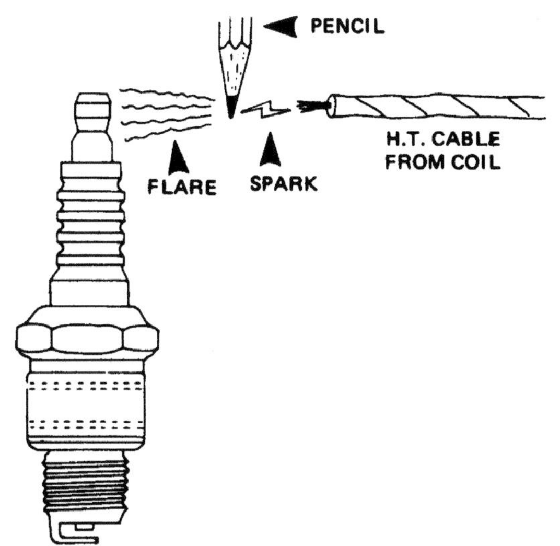


*Fig. 6.42 Polarity test for coil connections*

the secondary current (ie spark current) will flow through the two plugs, so there will be a wasted spark since only one cylinder will be ready to fire.

**4** Only one of the plugs will be working with the preferred polarity and care must be taken to ensure that they are in good condition so as to avoid misfiring on the plug with reversed polarity. This arrangement is used as an economy measure, avoiding the use of either two ignition coils or a distributor, and has reappeared in the most recent advanced distributorless ignition systems as a means of getting rid of the distributor.

## 14 Polarity test

**1** A simple test for polarity uses a lead pencil interposed between the HT wire and the plug, as shown in Fig. 6.42.

**2** The flare occurs between the pencil tip and the plug if polarity is correct, and between the HT lead and pencil tip if reversed.

## 15 Coil polarity

**1** Modern vehicles usually use negative earth, but it is always worth checking the earth polarity of any vehicle under attention. Whichever terminal of the battery is connected to earth it is essential to arrange the spark to have the correct polarity at the plug.

**2** Older Lucas coils have the low tension coils marked SW (to ignition switch) and CB (to contact breaker). Different versions of these coils were produced according to the earthing system. However, all that is necessary to change the spark polarity is to reverse the leads to the SW and CB terminals.

**3** Modern ignition coils have the LT terminals marked + and –. The same coil can then be used for both positive and negative earth systems. The + coil terminal is connected to the contact breaker lead for a positive earth system and the – coil terminal to the contact breaker lead for a negative earth system.

## 16 Servicing notes

**1** The coil ignition system is remarkably robust, requiring little maintenance except for some lubrication, adjustment for wear of the distributor's moving parts and regular cleaning.

**2** Ignition coils are mounted on or near the engine and become soiled with use. It is important to keep them clean, particularly the insulation neck that holds the secondary cable outlet to the distributor. Dirt will encourage the surface passage of spark current to earth (tracking), as will wet conditions. On a damp morning it may pay to wipe down the ignition coil neck and the HT plug leads if starting difficulties are encountered; another effect of dirt or damp tracking on the coil neck is misfiring under acceleration load.

**3** Coil connections can occasionally give trouble due to corrosion and possible looseness of the Lucar-type connectors.

**4** Resetting the contact breaker is much the same operation for any make of distributor. The engine should be turned over, either by 'blipping' the starter switch, or manually with a spanner on the crankshaft pulley nut, until the cam follower heel is in the middle of one of the lobes and the points are open.

**5** Examine the contacts for possible 'pitting and pilling', the term used to describe the metal transfer which occurs due to sparking and arcing at the break point (Fig. 6.43). The pile should be removed with fine emery cloth, or dressed with a carborundum stick, but no attempt should be made to eliminate the pit, or crater, on the moving contact. Simple cleaning up of the remaining surface is all that is required – methylated spirit will do well. However, it is now rare to clean up points in service work – a replacement set is more satisfactory and probably cost effective.

*Fig. 6.43 Pitting and piling of contacts*

**6** In general, the appearance of the contact surfaces gives an indication of the system condition, examples being:

| | | |
|---|---|---|
| *(a) Pitting and piling on clean contacts* | – | *Normal condition; Contacts may be renewed* |
| *(b) Uniform grey coating over the whole contact face* | – | *Oxidisation due to low contact pressure (weak spring) or too small a gap* |
| *(c) Severe burning or blued contacts* | – | *Defective capacitor or ignition coil* |
| *(d) Black burnt residue on and around contacts* | – | *Oil, grease or dirt has become lodged between contacts* |

**7** When the contacts are in order the gap may be measured with a feeler gauge according to the manufacturer's instructions. For most cars the gap will be between 0.35 and 0.50 mm – but check with the handbook. The stationary (fixed) contact is usually mounted on a plate which is locked in position by one or two screws. These are slackened until the movement of the fixed contact gives the correct gap and adjustment. The gap is correct when there is only a slight drag on the feeler gauge. Take care to retighten the locking screw(s), but undue force should be avoided.

**8** A similar method of gap adjustment applies to Ford (Motorcraft), Bosch and Lucas contact breaker units. Hitachi distributors use an eccentric adjusting screw to achieve the same result, while Ducellier have the facility of an adjuster nut outside the distributor body. SEV Marchal are quite different, in that the points on some distributors come in a cassette which fits over the distributor shaft and cam, the adjustment being carried out with a 3 mm Allen key through a hole in the distributor body.

**9** As referred to earlier, it is preferable to set the points to give a particular dwell angle, and today the feeler gauge method is less favoured. Several inexpensive meters are now available for this purpose.

**10** The cam face of the distributor should be given a smear (no more) of grease to reduce the cam follower wear. Remove the rotor and apply two or three drops of clean engine oil to the top of the spindle (possibly a pad will be visible).

The centrifugal advance mechanism should be lubricated with a few drops of engine oil through the gap round the spindle at the contact breaker plate. Finally the pivot post of the contact breaker should be given a light smear of grease or clean engine oil. Over-generous application of oil and grease in the distributor can cause trouble due to the contacts becoming contaminated with flying lubrication.

**11** HT leads are mostly of the push-in type, and proper seating into the distributor cap should be checked. Clean down the outer surface of the HT leads if they are soiled, if necessary with methylated spirit to remove stubborn grease.

**12** Setting the ignition timing consists of adjusting the distributor so that the ignition spark occurs at the correct point in the cycle. There are two ways, static and dynamic (stroboscopic), the latter being preferable since the centrifugal advance mechanism can be checked.

**13** Engines have timing marks (Fig. 6.44) on either the crankshaft pulley or the flywheel, and these marks must be made to align with a fixed mark on the crankcase or the flywheel housing respectively. Most engines show at least two marks, one being the top-dead-centre position and the other the correct timing mark which may be several degrees before top-dead-centre. The difference between these two marks is usually the static ignition advance expressed in degrees.

**14** Engines are mostly timed on No 1 cylinder, but to be sure consult the handbook. No 1 cylinder is normally nearest the fan, but again some manufacturers call No 1 that cylinder nearest the flywheel. In the case of V8 engines the convention used for cylinder numbers must be checked in the handbook.

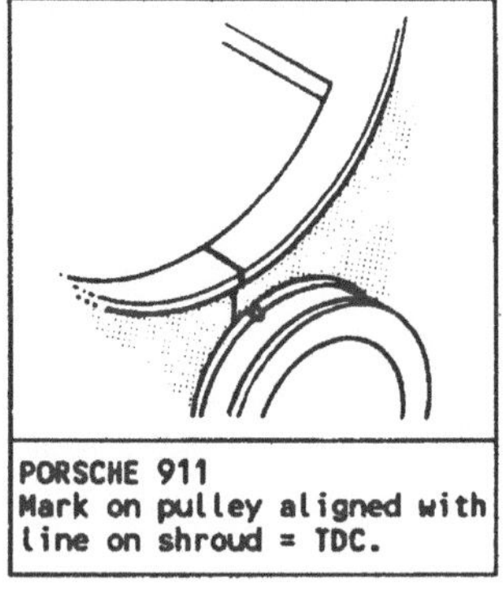

PORSCHE 911
Mark on pulley aligned with line on shroud = TDC.

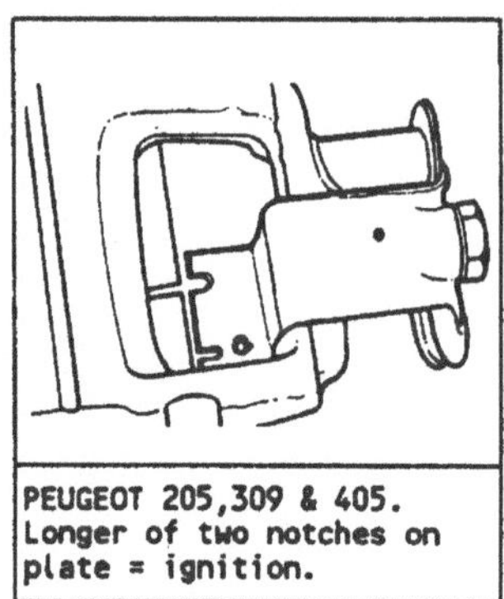

PEUGEOT 205,309 & 405.
Longer of two notches on plate = ignition.

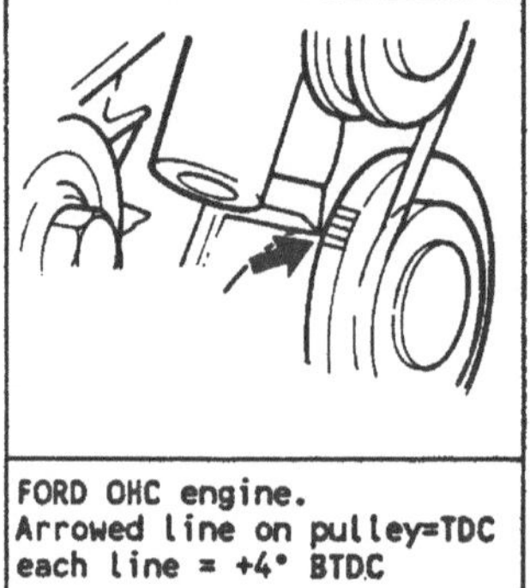

FORD OHC engine.
Arrowed line on pulley=TDC each line = +4° BTDC

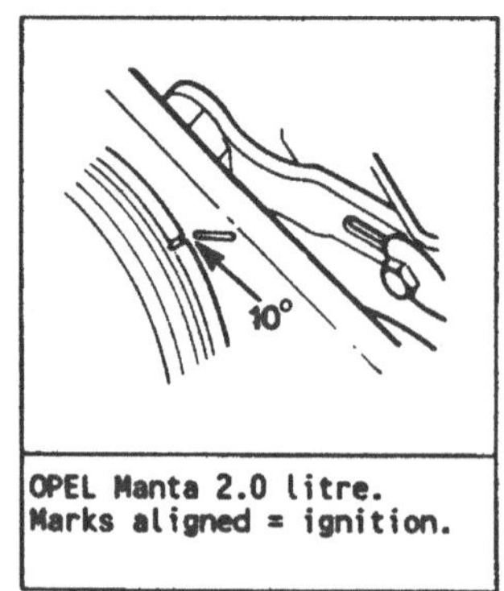


OPEL Manta 2.0 litre.
Marks aligned = ignition.

NISSAN Sunny,Micra,Prairie & Laurel.
Scale on timing cover.

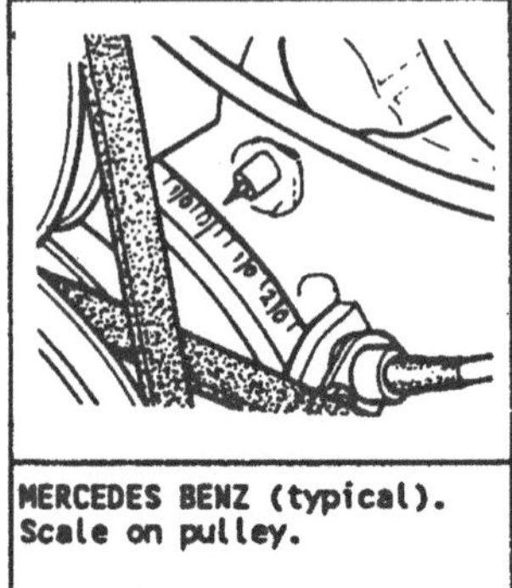

MERCEDES BENZ (typical).
Scale on pulley.

*Fig. 6.44 Typical engine timing marks*

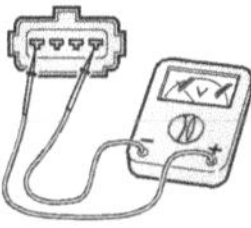

**15** Static timing is carried out as follows:

Check that the cylinder to be timed is approaching top-dead-centre on the compression stroke. Turn the crankshaft by a spanner on the pulley nut until compression can be felt by a thumb over the spark plug hole. Note that the distributor rotor is just passing the distributor cap electrode of No 1 cylinder. Line up the timing marks according to the handbook instructions. Switch on the ignition, having removed the distributor cap, and connect a 12 volt test lamp between the contact breaker terminal and earth. Slacken off the distributor clamp bolt so that the body can be swivelled, and turn it very slowly to the point where the test lamp is just lighting up, thus indicating that the contact breaker is just opening. Gently tighten up the clamp bolt and recheck. Rotate the engine crankshaft through two revolutions and check that the light-up point is still correct.

**16** Dynamic timing is carried out with the engine running and uses a stroboscope lamp. This is actuated by No 1 spark plug, the lamp being connected onto the HT wiring to No 1 and giving a short duration flash of a few microseconds, but with high intensity.

**17** Shining the flashing light onto the timing marks on the front pulley or flywheel, according to manufacture, will give an impression of the rotating mark being stationary. The marks should line up; if they do not, then the distributor body is moved round until they do. This operation is usually carried out at tickover of about 700 rev/min, the vacuum advance being disconnected and the manifold pipe blocked, but the vehicle handbook should be consulted. Revving the engine should show the timing mark moving backwards against the direction of rotation, indicating that ignition advance occurs with increasing speed. The vacuum advance is reconnected once adjustments are completed.

**Warning:** *Avoid dangling leads, neckties or loose clothing near the fan or drivebelt.*

## 17 Testing

**Test 1: Cable security**

Check conditions for tightness and cleanliness. Push home HT leads in coil neck, onto plugs and into the distributor cap.

**Test 2: Checking coil operation**

HT sparking from the coil is checked by pulling out the centre HT lead to the distributor cap. Hold it with insulated pliers close to earth (6 mm or 1/4"), crank the engine and look for regular, healthy sparks. If this is satisfactory, any fault present is likely to lie in the distributor, plugs, fuel supply or ignition timing. **Note:** *This does NOT apply to electronic ignition testing. Damage to the system may occur by breaking the HT circuit except as specified in the vehicle service instructions.*

**Test 3: Contact breaker**

If no sparking at Test 2, look at contact breaker condition and gap. Check for bad surfaces and reset gap, if necessary.

**Test 4: Coil voltage to earth**

Assuming the contacts are working satisfactorily, measure the voltage to earth at the LT feed terminal of the coil with the contacts closed. For ballasted coils the voltage should be approx 6 volts, but should be equal to the battery voltage for non-ballasted coils.

**Test 5: Ballasted coil check**

For ballasted coils only, put a temporary earth (a lead with two clips) on to the negative terminal (ie that going to the contact breaker). Measure the voltage at the + coil terminal and then crank the engine. The voltage should rise due to the action of the solenoid in shorting out the ballast resistor. If there is no increase, check the lead going from the coil to the solenoid ignition terminal.

**Test 6: Check for faulty distributor or coil**

Check the voltage at the coil -ve terminal with the contact breaker points open. The reading should be battery voltage. If, however, the voltage is zero, disconnect the LT lead to the distributor. Voltage should now rise to battery voltage, this indicating trouble in the distributor LT parts. If the voltage does not rise, the indication is a faulty coil and this should be replaced.

**Test 7: Distributor**

Assuming Test 6 showed a probable distributor LT fault, check the coil to distributor lead, then look for reasons for a short circuit to earth of the insulated contact. This can often be due to incorrect assembly of the contact breaker set after service, particularly with older vehicles where fabric insulation or plastic washers were used.

**Test 8: Check for faulty capacitor**

With the coil HT lead held close to earth, flick the contacts open and note if sparking is present and healthy. If not, next check the capacitor.

**Test 9: Checking capacitor operation**

Checking the capacitor is best done by substituting a test capacitor. It is good practice to have a spare available with clips already affixed to give rapid connections. If there is then no spark, or it is weak, replace the coil.

**Test 10: High tension system**

Assuming a good spark, if the engine still fails to start, further checks on the HT side are necessary. First check the rotor arm by holding the coil HT lead about 3 mm away from the brass insert on the top of the rotor arm. Flick the contacts open a few times. If a spark jumps more than once then the rotor arm insulation has broken down.

**Test 11: Distributor cap**

The distributor cap can sometimes break down, usually due to surface tracking or a crack in the body, the fault can be invisible and substitution is needed for a definite identification of the trouble.

**Test 12: HT leads**

Unlikely, but still worth checking, is the possibility of one or more of the HT cables being open circuit. Check with an ohmmeter or by substitution, remembering that the internal connection may be highly resistive (up to 20 000 ohms) for radio interference suppression purposes.

## 18 Deficiencies of coil and battery ignition systems

**1** Although the contact breaker plus coil and battery system has been in use for half a century at least, the shortcomings in performance and maintenance costs have long been appreciated. Mechanically, it is difficult to manufacture a cam, heel follower and spring mechanism which provide and maintain the required accuracies. Every few thousand miles it is necessary to reset the contacts to allow for heel wear; in addition the breaking of the coil primary current produces the effect of 'pitting and piling' because of metal transference with the spark.

**2** It should be noted that to obtain enough energy for spark production (about 30 millijoules are required) the coil designer will allow as large a primary current as possible, consistent with reasonable life of the contact breaker points – but for long contact life the current should be small. The graph of Fig. 6.45 shows the general effect of break current on the life of points and that the designer does not have much latitude.

**3** At high speeds, the centrifugal force acting on the moving parts of the contact breaker assembly may be sufficient to cause the gap to increase beyond the design gap, due to flinging out when the heel loses contact with the cam.

**4** The troubles mentioned above have always been present but in recent years further problems have arisen due to developments in engine design. Compression ratios have been increased, requiring a high voltage spark and higher maximum engine speeds are more common, needing a higher rate of sparking.

Limitations might now be summarized as follows:

*(a) Plug fouling: for high compression ratios, petrol additives (lead salts) are used to prevent detonation. Unfortunately these additives appear to contribute to fouling of plugs.*

*(b) Mechanical limitations of contact breakers are now severe.*

*(c) The time taken for 30 millijoules of electrical energy to build up between sparks, limits the rate to about 400 sparks per second, or time per spark 0.0025 second. This may be too low a spark rate for high-speed multi-cylinder engines.*

*(d) To overcome plug fouling, and to produce reliable sparks in cylinders of higher compression ratios, a higher spark voltage of 15 to 30 kilovolts (kV) is required. Another reason for higher ignition system voltage is to do with both economy and the achievement of low pollution emission; weaker mixtures are now used and in turn are more difficult to ignite by sparks.*

*(e) Contact breaker points pitting and burning due to the high coil primary currents used.*

*(f) Inaccuracy occurring at high speeds due to backlash and whip in the contact breaker drive mechanism.*

*(g) The fall-off of tuning with points wear is no longer acceptable since the new statutory requirements in many countries state that the emission limits must be maintained for 50 000 miles.*

It is not surprising that ignition system designers have looked for alternative methods, and the arrival of the transistor and allied semiconductor devices has provided several solutions to the problem.

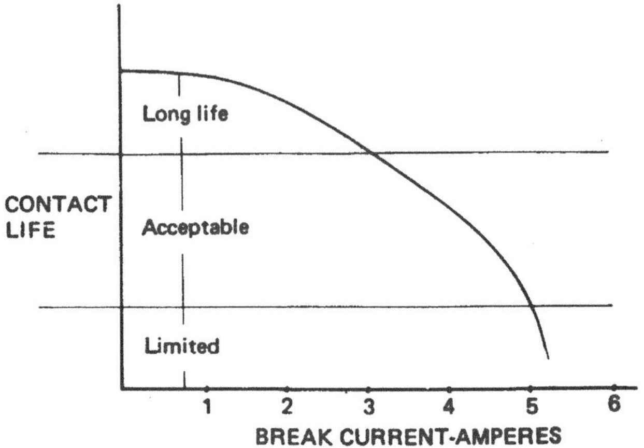


***Fig. 6.45 Contact life versus break current***

## 19 Solid-state systems

**1** 'Solid-state' is a term meaning that all amplifying and switching components in a given circuit employ semiconductor devices, eg transistors, diodes, thyristors (SCR) etc, and not the obsolete vacuum valves (called tubes in the US) which were anything but solid!

**2** It was the very fragility and bulk of electronic equipment before the advent of semiconductor devices that held back developments in automotive engineering, but gradually, from the mid-1960s, the position has changed. Now semiconductors are reliable, rugged and able to survive the harsh conditions in vehicle applications.

## 20 Types of electronic ignition circuits

**1** In a rapidly changing field of activity, three types of circuits are in use (see Fig. 6.10):

*(a) Transistor-Assisted Coil Ignition (TAC)*

*(b) Capacitor Discharge Ignition (CDI)*

*(c) Magnetic Inductive Ignition*

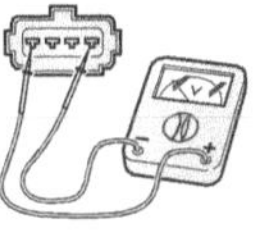

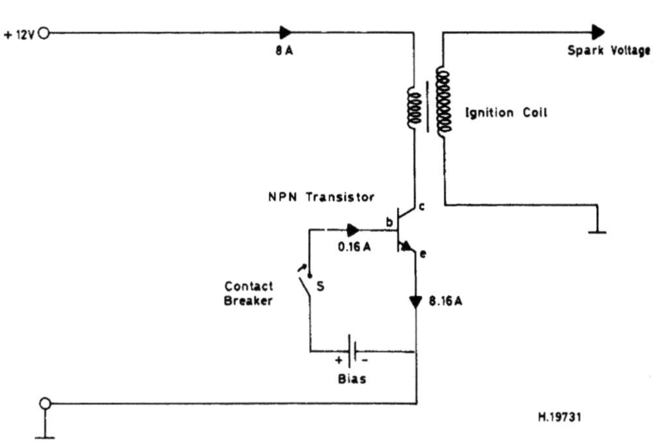


*Fig. 6.46 Base current controls main current flow*

## 21 Transistor-Assisted Contacts coil ignition (TAC)

**1** This was the first attempt to improve the shortcomings of the (then) conventional coil and battery system. Use of a transistor as a switch to break and make the ignition coil primary current was a first step; it is still necessary to turn the transistor on and off and to do this, the contact breaker is retained (S). The simple model (Fig. 6.46) shows an npn transistor connected into the ignition coil primary circuit. The load current flows from collector c to emitter e only so long as the emitter is negative relative to the base b. If the switch S is opened (this corresponds to the contact breaker) then the emitter-base current is cut off; this switches off the collector current. With the figures shown as an illustration only, it will be seen that the controlling base current of 0.16 A is only 2% of the controlled collector current of 8 A. So, the transistor can switch on or off a large current in the collector circuit by switching a much lower current in the base circuit. The circuit arrangement is not really practical because of the additional battery to bias the emitter to be – with respect to the base.

**2** Because the contacts now handle a low current, 0.16 A in this case, the life is greatly extended and, moreover, no capacitor is required since the contacts are partly isolated from the ignition coil primary. It is claimed that a set of TAC points may have a life of 100 000 miles.

**3** A factor to be considered when designing an ignition coil suitable for TAC is that of the primary coil inductance L, measured in henrys (see Chapter 1). Inductance depends, among other factors, upon the number of turns of a coil, and the energy stored in the magnetic field around the coil is:

$W = 1/2\ LI^2$

where: W = energy stored (joules)

I = coil current (amperes)

L = coil inductance (henrys)

**4** Now it is important to have the ignition coil primary current rise as quickly as possible when the contacts are closed, in order to build up energy ready for the next contact-break. Inductance in an electrical circuit is analogous to the inertia of a flywheel. As a heavy flywheel takes time to accelerate so current rise takes time in an inductive circuit (Fig. 6.47).

The primary current rise time is significantly reduced allowing a higher maximum rate of sparking (see Fig. 6.47). Designers have, therefore, taken the opportunity to set the value of the ignition coil current higher than that in conventional coils – about 8 amperes instead of 3 amperes in one particular design. This allows the inductance (and therefore number of primary turns) to be reduced and results in secondary-to-primary turns ratio about 250 : 1 or even 400 : 1 compared

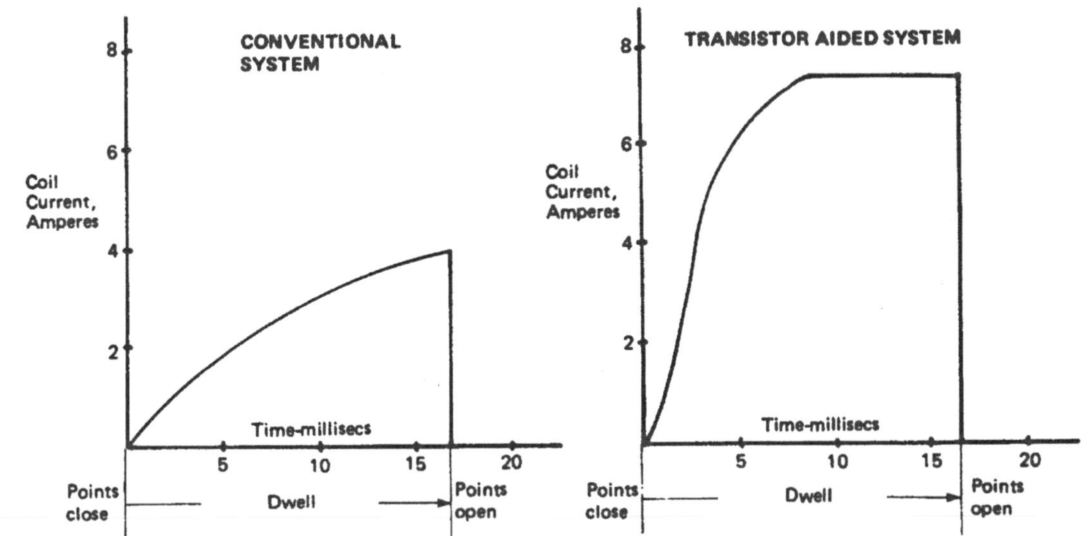


*Fig. 6.47 Rise times of coil current – comparison*

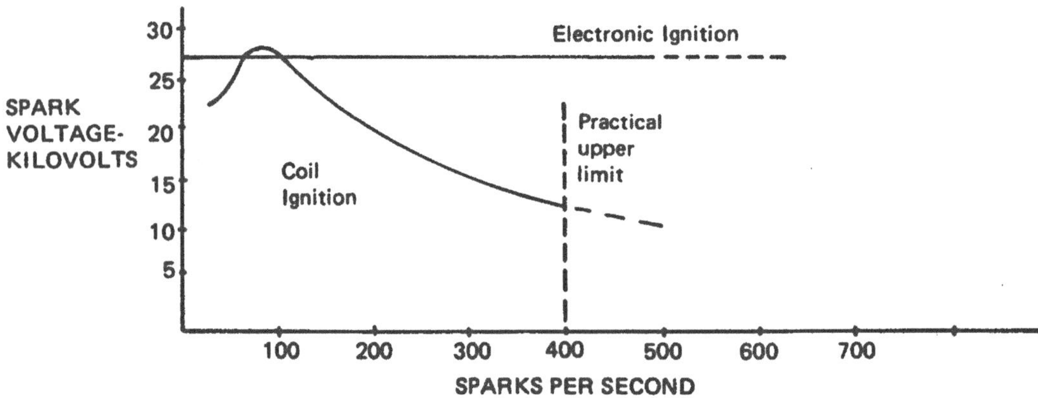


*Fig. 6.48 Performance comparison between conventional and electronic systems*

with about 66 : 1 in a conventional coil. The low primary resistance will also reduce the resistive power loss in the coil.

**5** It might reasonably be asked what other advantage this gives. The answer is that if current is changed rapidly in an inductive circuit, transient voltages are generated across the inductive coil and these could be hazardous to electronic components elsewhere in the electrical system. It is therefore of advantage to keep the primary coil inductance low.

**6** This rise-time of coil current after the contacts have closed has been a limiting factor to the maximum possible spark rate, since at high engine speeds the next spark was due before the current could rise to its maximum value. The reduced primary inductance of ignition coils driven by transistors has meant much improved performance, as shown by the typical graphs of Figs. 6.47 and 6.48. The retention of good sparking voltage at high engine speeds is required for efficiency and economy.

**7** Several advantages stem, therefore, from the use of transistor-assisted contact breaking, which include a higher maximum sparking rate, and less plug fouling and contact wear leading to longer intervals between service. The disadvantage of retaining mechanical contacts remains, however, and no vehicles are now fitted with TAC as original equipment. After sales conversion kits are still popular with the DIY market.

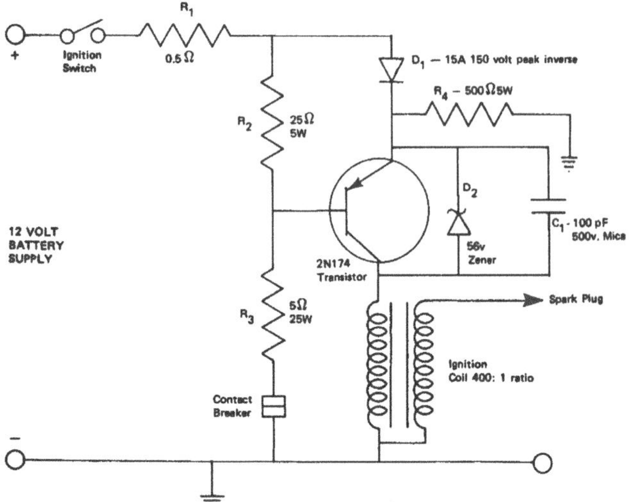


*Fig. 6.49 Single transistor TAC ignition circuit*

## 22 Basic TAC ignition circuit

**1** A drawback of the circuit of Fig. 6.46 is the need for a separate battery in the base control path. In practice the supply of current for both the base and collector branches is drawn from the same battery; all that is needed is a pair of resistors across the main battery supply, their resistance being calculated to make the centre tap correspond to the voltage required at the base. An illustration of this idea is given in the following working circuit, being a simple example of transistorised ignition (Fig. 6.49).

**2** The first approach to transistor ignition was to relieve the contact breaker of interrupting current in an inductive circuit. Fig. 6.49 shows a practical circuit using an ignition coil of 400 : 1 ratio. The transistor is protected from inductive transient voltages by the Zener diode connected across it; when the Zener conduction point is reached (56 volts) the transistor is effectively bridged by a low resistance path until the offending voltage disappears.

**3** When the points are closed, $R_1$ and $R_3$ act as a voltage divider and thus bias the transistor so that it is switched on. Current flows round the main path of $R_1$ through diode $D_1$, the transistor (emitter to collector) and through the ignition coil primary back to the battery.

**4** At break point, the chain $R_2$ and $R_3$ is broken and bias is removed from the transistor, causing it to switch off; a small current continues to flow through diode $D_1$, and $R_4$, the result being that the emitter is about 0.7 volt *negative* with respect to the base. This ensures abrupt cut-off of coil current the effect of which is to generate a spark voltage in the secondary winding. The unit must be constructed on a heat sink (an aluminium plate to disperse the heat) and can then be encapsulated in epoxy resin to give protection from damp.

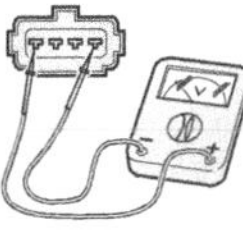

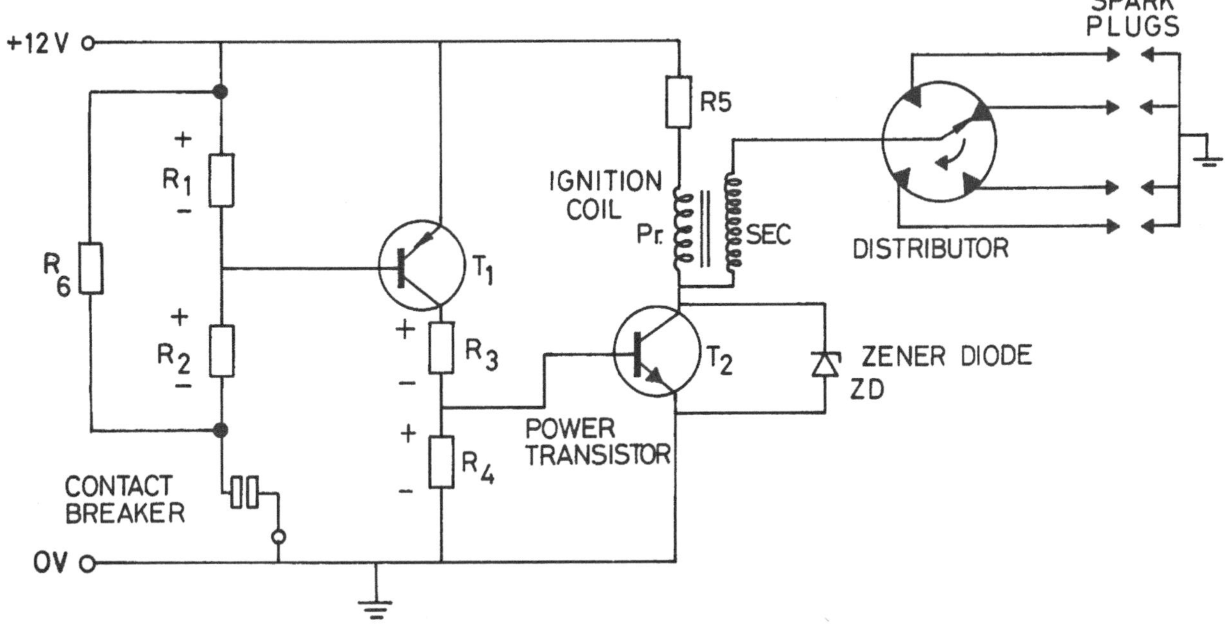


*Fig. 6.50 TAC circuit using complementary transistors*

## 23 TAC ignition – dual transistor circuits

**1** Using only one transistor of the power type is feasible but a better solution is to use a second transistor to receive the open-close signal from the contact breaker and then to drive the power transistor which controls the on-off current to the ignition coil. The main advantage of a two-transistor switch is its comparatively high switching speed, but further, it operates at a lower temperature than if a single power switching transistor is used.

**2** Two transistors $T_1$ and $T_2$ are shown in Fig. 6.50 and the direction of the arrows on their emitters show that $T_1$ is of the pnp type and $T_2$ is npn. (It should be recalled that a pnp transistor is ON when the emitter voltage is + relative to its base, and the npn transistor is ON when the emitter voltage is – relative to its base.)

**3** With the contact breaker closed, the current flow through $R_1$ and $R_2$ will produce volt-drops as shown in Fig. 6.50. The volt-drop across $R_2$ is sufficient to switch $T_1$ to ON. $T_1$ collector current will give volt-drops on $R_3$ and $R_4$. That across $R_4$ will switch $T_2$ to ON.

**4** When the contact breaker opens there is no forward bias to $T_1$ which shuts OFF. This removes the forward bias from $T_2$ which also switches OFF, so no collector current flows through the ignition coil primary. The induced voltage in the secondary winding of the ignition coil provides the spark at the plugs via the distributor.

**5** At the point when ignition occurs, there will be a high emf generated in the ignition coil primary of the order of a few hundred volts, enough to destroy transistor $T_2$. The Zener diode ZD is chosen to conduct at about 100 volts and so protects $T_2$ from large voltage spikes. The bias chain $R_1R_2$ is made up of resistor values to give correct bias to $T_1$. $R_6$ sets the contact breaker current to about 250 mA, sufficient to burn off dirt and corrosion. $R_5$ is a ballast resistor to limit primary coil current.

**6** Many variations of this circuit have been used, but although good results may be obtained with TAC, the drawback of mechanical contacts to generate the ignition signal remain. The drawbacks are:

(a) *Need for regular servicing due to cam-follower heel wear*
(b) *Contact bounce at high speeds*
(c) *Relatively high manufacturing cost*

The next stage in solid state transistor ignition involved getting rid of mechanical contacts.

**7** The Sparkrite 2000 is an example of an electronic conversion kit which uses mechanical contacts and retains the original ignition coil (Fig. 6.51). In this set, both

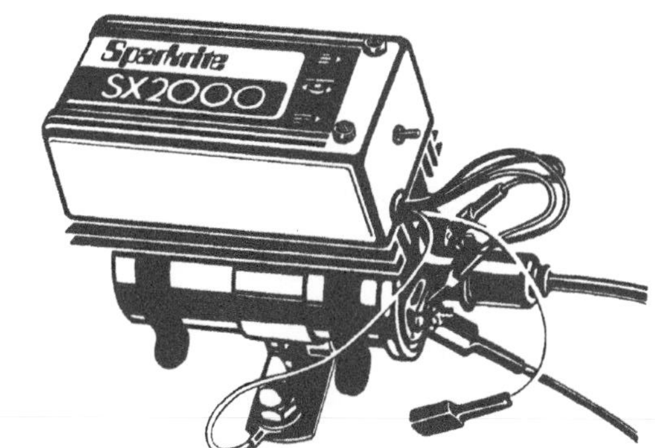


*Fig. 6.51 Sparkrite SX2000 ignition set*

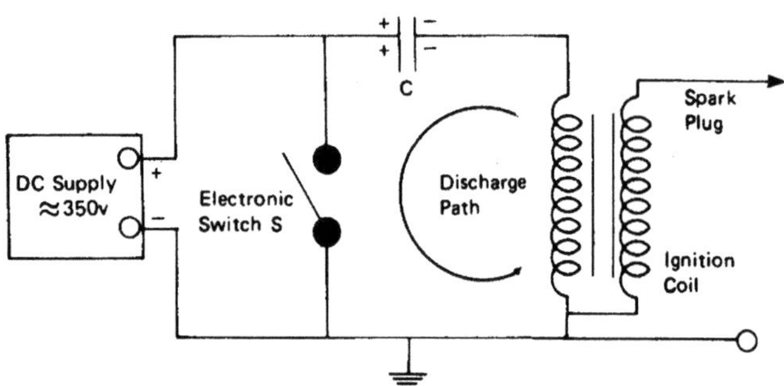


*Fig. 6.52 Principle of capacitor discharge*

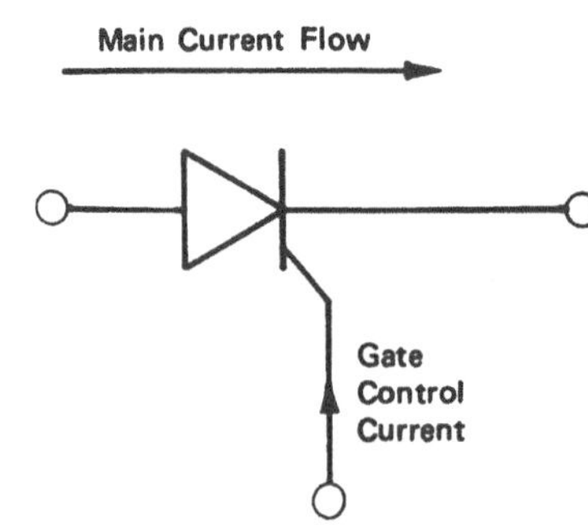


*Fig. 6.53 Thyristor symbol – silicon-controlled rectifier (SCR)*

capacitive and inductive energy is used for sparking, giving the characteristic long burn time of the inductive (ie standard ignition coil) system and the fast rise time of the capacitor discharge. An explanation of capacitor discharge appears later in this chapter.

**8** The overall result is claimed to be successful ignition of weak mixtures under all load and speed conditions, but another advantage to drivers is that a switch to go back to conventional ignition is provided, most useful in the unlikely event of a failure in the electronics box.

**9** Where diagnostic equipment is used it is best with the Sparkrite set to carry out all tests and adjustments with the switch set to 'conventional' ignition. Once timing has been set correctly, switching over to the electronic section will give the same timing accuracy. Initial ionisation voltage at the plug tip is positive, and so readings of the spark voltage with the oscilloscope parade display will not be possible with the switch in the 'electronic' position.

## 24 Capacitor Discharge Ignition (CDI)

**1** This type of system stores electrical energy in a capacitor which is then discharged through the primary winding of the ignition coil when the spark is required. In other systems described in this book, the spark energy is derived from the magnetic field of the ignition coil but with CDI the energy stored in the discharge capacitor is predominant and is given by:

Energy = $1/2\ CV^2$ joules

where C = capacitance in farads

V = charge voltage of capacitor

It will be seen that a high voltage is desirable for charging the capacitor in order to achieve adequate stored energy. The ignition coil is of different design from that used in other systems and is a pulse transformer, although it has still primary and secondary windings.

**2** The principle of CDI is illustrated in Fig. 6.52. If it is assumed that a dc supply is available to charge capacitor C to about 350 volts, then at the instant when a spark is required, the electronic switch closes and capacitor C is discharged rapidly through the ignition coil primary winding. This pulse of current results in a high voltage to the secondary winding in excess of 40 kV to give a high intensity spark of short duration.

**3** The electronic switching is invariably carried out by a power thyristor (sometimes called a silicon controlled rectifier SCR) and this device is described in Chapter 1. It is essentially a 4-layer semiconductor which blocks current flow until a control signal current is applied to the gate terminal (Fig. 6.53). When the control signal is applied, the thyristor abruptly goes from the non-conducting to the conducting state, much like an electrical switch. When the voltage across its main terminals falls to a low level, the thyristor resumes the non-conducting condition. The gate current required to switch the thyristor is very small and need be of short duration only. Thus the thyristor is a highly efficient electronic power-switching device.

**4** Referring again to Fig. 6.52, it might be asked why the thyristor does not short-circuit the power supply. It does, in fact, but the internal resistance of the power supply limits the current from it to negligible proportions compared with the capacitor discharge current through the ignition coil primary.

**5** Triggering of the spark can be obtained by a mechanical contact breaker but preferably by a pulse generator of the magnetic, Hall Effect or optical types (see later). If mechanical contacts are used, some provision must be made to eliminate spurious signals due to contact bounce which may occur at higher speeds. All triggering systems need to have signal processing so that the signal arriving at the thyristor gate terminal is a clean step-wave.

**6** The short charging time of the capacitor (of the order of 250 microseconds) means that dwell angle control is not required since there is no dependence on engine speed. Conventional and CDI ignition coils are not interchangeable since CDI units have low primary inductance to allow rapid capacitor discharge.

**7** The CDI system has the advantage of rapid rise time for the spark voltage and is some 10 times faster than Kettering coil and battery ignition.

The advantages of fast rise time are:

*(a) Leakage of spark charge on the HT side becomes unimportant because there is insufficient time for*

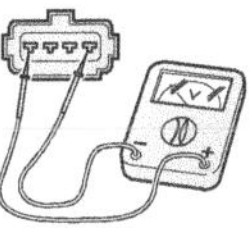

*current to drain away before the spark pulse is completed, ie the shunt (parallel) resistive paths due to carbon, damp etc are of negligible effect*

*(b) The rapidity of capacitor discharge 'punches' through accumulations on dirty spark plugs and as a result service periods for plugs can be much longer, and the ultimate plug life is significantly greater. A 50 000 mile plug service interval should be easily attainable*

**8** While the pulse rise time is commendably fast, the spark duration is short, being 100 to 300 microseconds. This is too short to ignite the air-fuel mixture reliably, but in partial compensation, larger plug gaps may be used to give greater spark exposure. Nevertheless, the CDI system has not competed well against inductive-discharge electronic systems and is not generally in use, but found in certain high performance engines, eg Porsche, and for special designs.

## 25 Battery CDI system

**1** Referring back to Fig. 6.52 it will be seen that a dc supply of about 350 volts is required to charge the capacitor. To achieve this a transistor oscillator is used. This works off the 12 volt vehicle supply and produces an alternating voltage which may be stepped up to the final voltage required by means of a transformer (often part of the oscillator circuit). The alternating output is then rectified to give a direct voltage for supplying the discharge. The schematic arrangement is shown in Fig. 6.54.

***Fig. 6.54 DC inverter CDI system***

**2** Such an oscillator is made up of one or more transistors connected to a small transformer which feeds back energy from the transistor amplifier output to the input, so that, being self-feeding, oscillations of a sine wave form will be generated. The transformer which is used for passing back this energy also has a third winding which steps up the alternating voltage to be suitable for feeding the capacitor C after rectification (Fig. 6.55).

**3** The frequency of the oscillations is determined mainly by inductance and capacitance values used in the oscillatory circuit. To use low frequencies would require large sizes of oscillator coil and capacitors, and high frequencies might give rise to radiation and conduction interference with radio and other equipment. In practice, the operational frequency may be at the top end of the audio range and sometimes the oscillator can be heard, corresponding to a frequency of about 500 Hz.

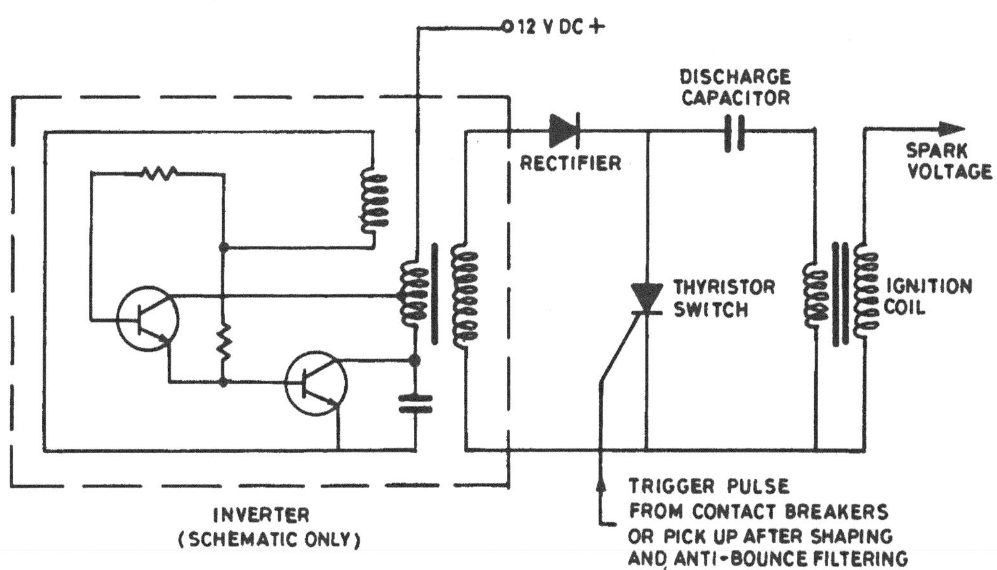


***Fig. 6.55 Schematic diagram of a CDI inverter***

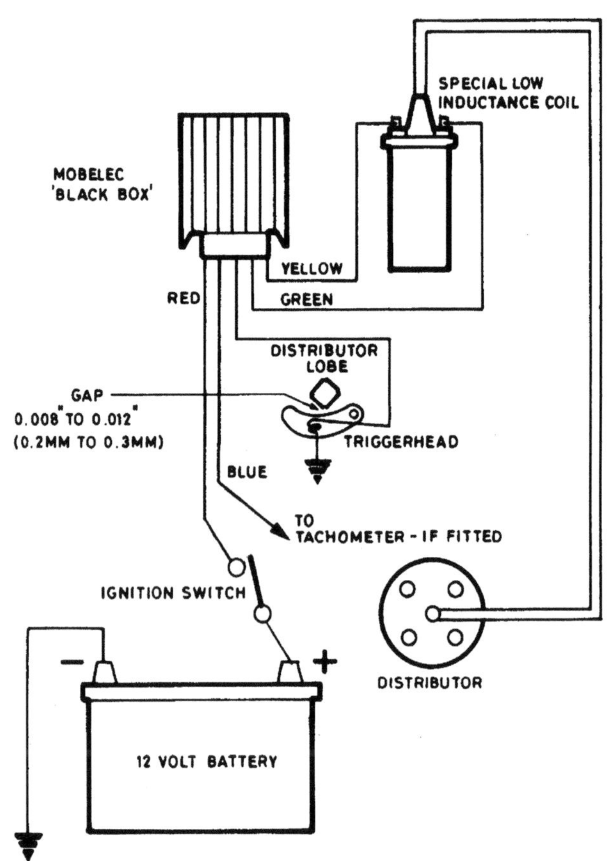


*Fig. 6.56 Mobelec CDI system*

**4** As a general rule, radio interference suppression is built into CDI units, and the use of additional capacitors in the ignition coil will result in damage to the CDI. **No radio interference capacitors should, therefore, be used with CDI.**

## 26 Mobelec CDI system

**1** This is a kit using the existing distributor cam on which an adaptor is fitted as part of the triggering system. The triggerhead fits in Lucas four- and six-cylinder distributors and can be made to fit others; the fitting is to the distributor baseplate after contact points and capacitor have been removed.

**2** Fig. 6.56 shows the layout of the Mobelec CDI system, and from it the gap between the triggerhead sensor and cam lobe peak is seen. It is important that contact does not occur between the sensor tip and the lobe, due to the sensitivity of the sensor tip.

**3** In order to achieve rapid discharge through the ignition coil primary, a specially designed ignition coil is supplied. This will have low primary inductance, but with a higher turns ratio than a conventional coil. Such coils are not interchangeable.

## 27 Magneto-generator CDI

**1** CDI is a convenient form of ignition for motorcycles, lawnmowers, chain saws and other small utility engines. In these cases, no battery is involved and to energise the discharge capacitor, a flywheel magneto generator is used (Fig. 6.57). The pulse coil is sometimes adjustable to vary the ignition timing.

**2** Hitachi, Femsa and Motoplat have marketed a range of flywheel electronic ignition systems which have certain common features; sparking will begin at speeds from 200 rpm to 500 rpm, depending on the make, and all depend on good electrical connections between the engine, the electronics boxes (usually housing the ignition coil and CDI components) and the generator.

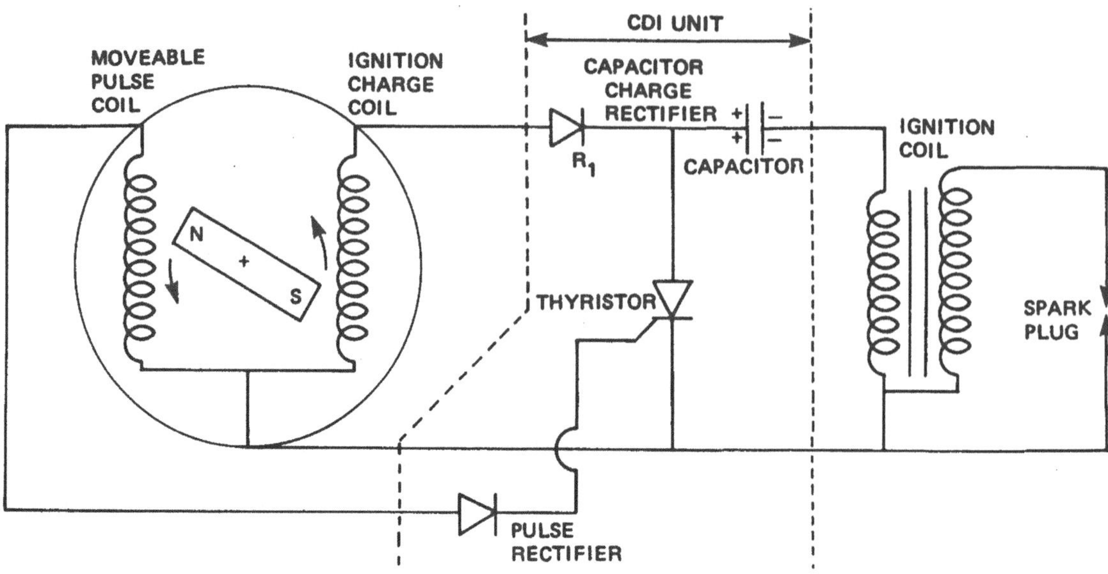


*Fig. 6.57 Simplified CDI circuit using a flywheel generator*

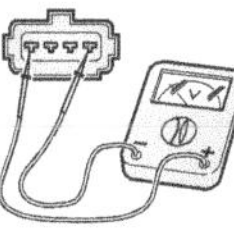

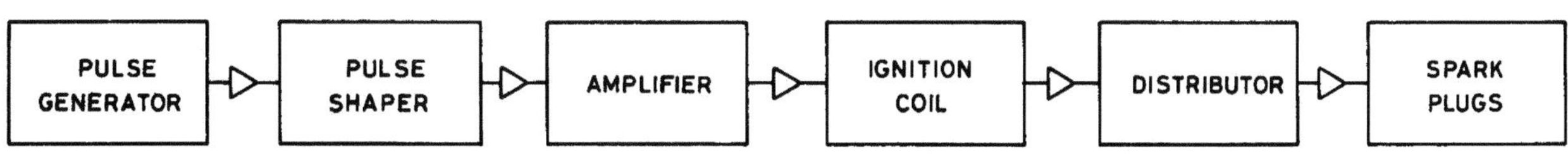


*Fig. 6.58 Pulse-triggered electronic ignition*

## 28 Breakerless triggering

**1** To trigger the spark some form of sensor is required to produce a signal at the instant when the spark is required. The contact breaker is a crude sensor which carries out this function, but a non-contact triggering device has the advantages:

(a) *Elimination of contact wear, bounce or mechanical free play*

(b) *As a result of (a) the timing will remain accurate*

(c) *Spark timing can be made accurate over all speed and load conditions by electronic control*

(d) *The fall-off of spark energy with speed can be eliminated by electronic control of the dwell period*

The sensing device is sometimes called a **pulse generator** or a **signal generator**.

**2** Pulse generators fall usually into 3 types:

(a) *Optical*

(b) *Hall effect*

(c) *Variable reluctance*

A block diagram (Fig. 6.58) shows how the pulse signal goes through a conditioning process before triggering the power transistor which drives the ignition coil (or coils in some arrangements).

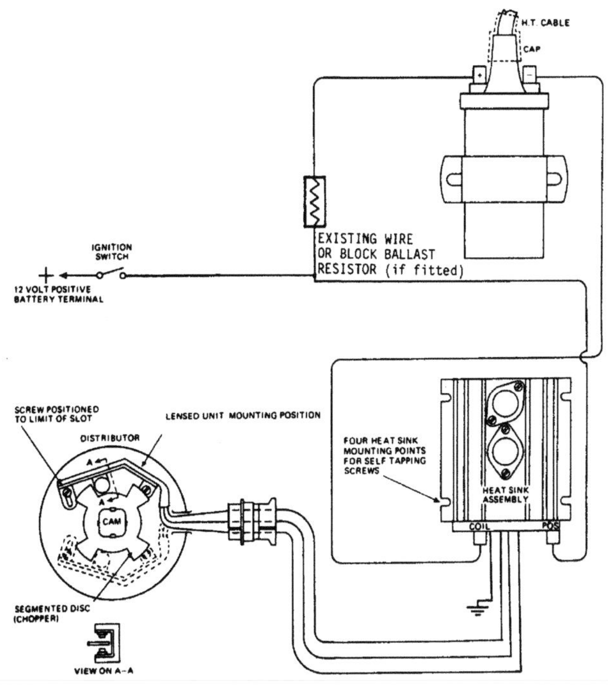


*Fig. 6.60 Lumenition ignition system*

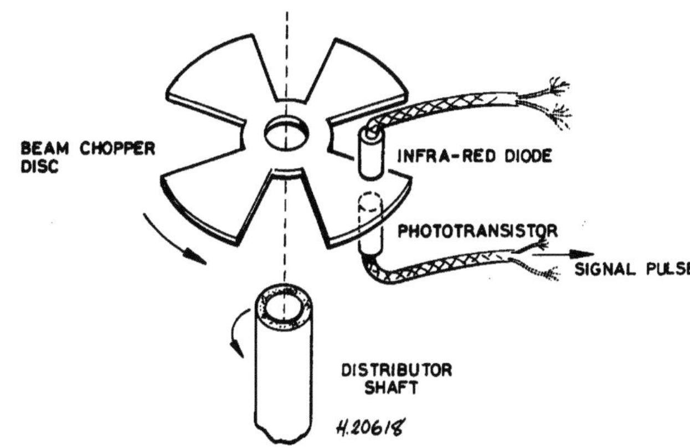


*Fig. 6.59 Optical pulse generator*

### Optical pulse generator

A segmented disc fitted to the distributor shaft breaks an infra-red beam normally focused onto a phototransistor (Fig. 6.59). During the period when the beam is on the phototransistor the coil is on; as a vane cuts the beam, the phototransistor sends a pulse which shuts off the coil primary current and the spark is generated at the plug. The infra-red is produced by a gallium-arsenide semiconductor diode. Several variations of this arrangement exist; the pulse may be generated when the vane allows the beam to pass or again in place of an infra-red diode, a light-emitting diode (LED) source may be used. Lumenition have developed this system; the layout shown in Fig. 6.60 uses a standard ignition coil.

Fig. 6.61 shows an optical pulse generator for an 8-cylinder engine and the segmented disc mounted on the

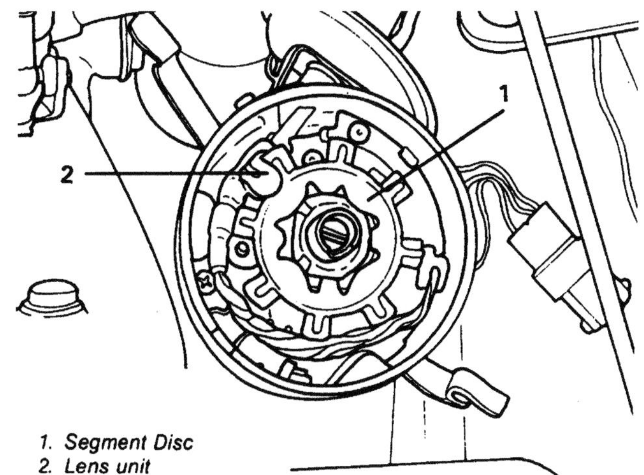


*Fig. 6.61 Distributor fitted with optical pulse generator*
*Courtesy FKI Crypton Ltd*

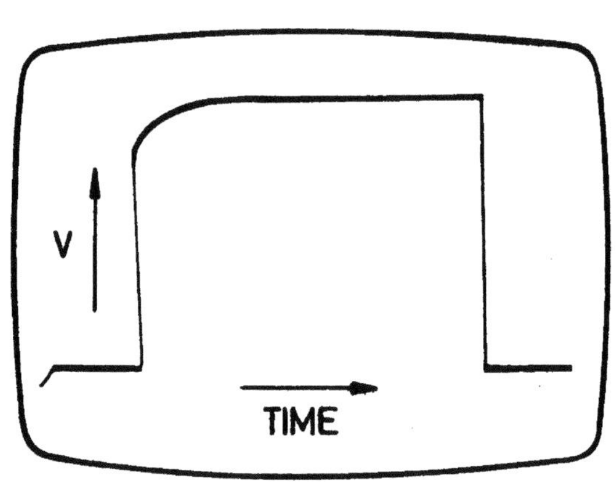


*Fig. 6.62 Trace produced by optical generator*
*Courtesy FKI Crypton Ltd*

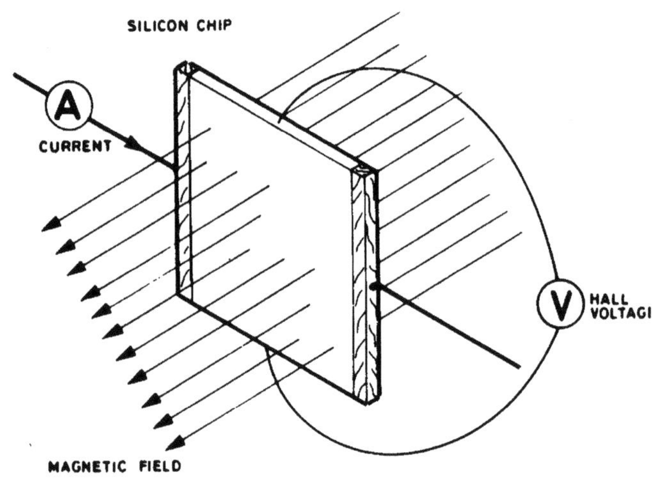


*Fig. 6.63 Illustrating Hall effect voltage*

distributor shaft, while Fig. 6.62 gives the shape of the pulse generator wave form. Generally, these systems produce a fixed dwell angle but do not suffer from the high speed limitations associated with contact breaker systems owing to the large dwell angle achieved with the segmented disc.

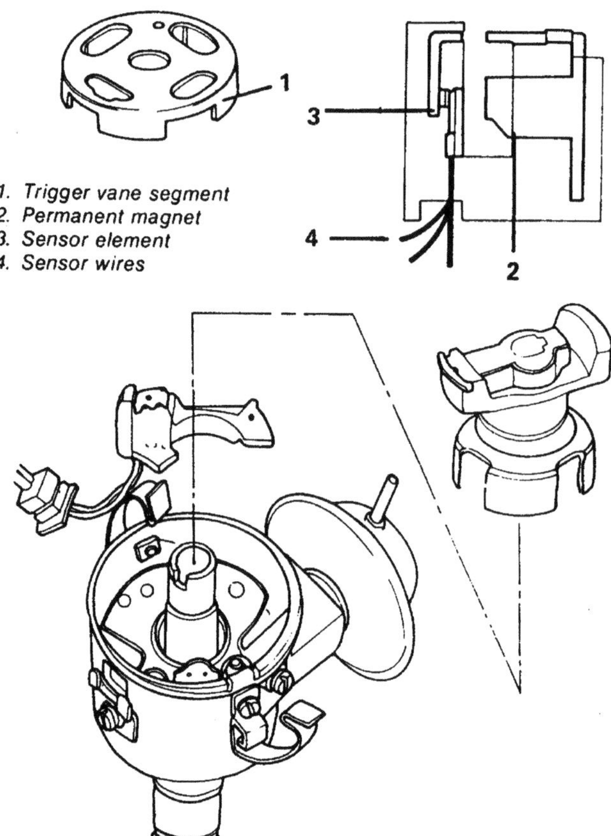


*Fig. 6.64 Practical Hall generator arrangement*
*Courtesy FKI Crypton Ltd*

## Hall effect pulse generator

This device consists of a silicon chip through which a small current is passed between opposite edges. When a magnetic field passes through the major surface of the chip, a voltage appears between the other two edges (Fig. 6.63).

This is the Hall voltage and is used to trigger the ignition spark when the magnetic field is changed, this being achieved by a metallic chopper disc driven by the cam shaft of a distributor (Fig. 6.64). The magnetic field is usually provided by a small permanent magnet on the opposite side of the gap from the Hall chip. Typically the chip will take a current of about 30 mA, delivering a 2 mV Hall voltage signal with a positive temperature coefficient, ie the Hall voltage increases with an increase of temperature. The chip is usually built into an integrated circuit, providing signal shaping and amplification. Fig. 6.65 shows that at A the magnetic field crosses the air gap when the vane is not in between the gap faces and the Hall chip gives an output voltage; at B the vane is between the air gap faces and provides a path for the magnetic flux, shielding the Hall chip so the output voltage falls to a low level (Fig. 6.66). The voltage waveform is roughly rectangular and is processed by the integrated circuit to give a sharp ON-OFF output. The

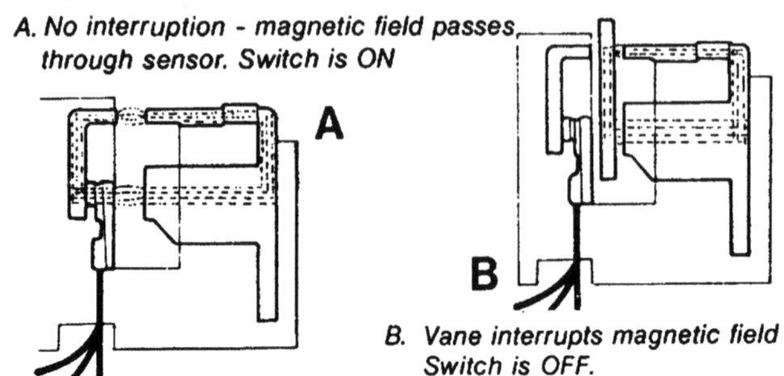


*Fig. 6.65 Effect of trigger vane on magnetic field*
*Courtesy FKI Crypton Ltd*

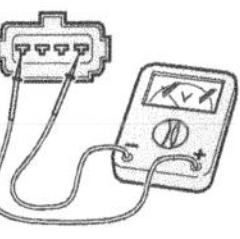

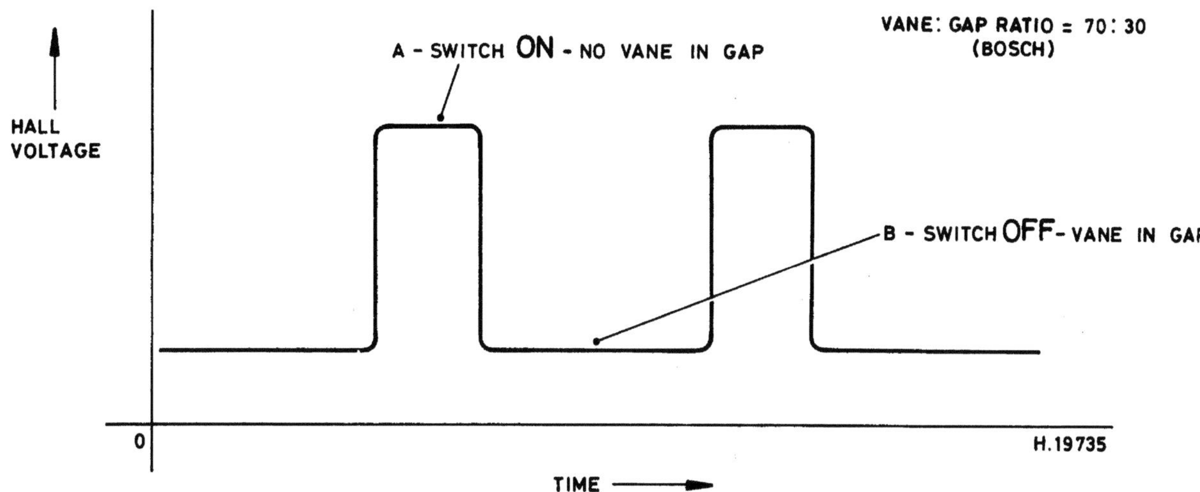


*Fig. 6.66 Output waveform of Hall pulse generator*

Bosch rotor vane has a ratio of 70:30 vane to air gap length and this gives a preset dwell angle which may be varied by the electronic circuitry into which the signal is fed. Finally when the Hall voltage is ON (= high) the ignition coil current is switched OFF generating a spark at the plug so: *The spark occurs as the vane passes out of the air gap.*

Hall pulse generators have a high reliability and have the advantage over the optical type where dirt may affect the LED light or infra-red path.

IT SHOULD BE NOTED THAT IT IS POSSIBLE TO PRODUCE SPARK VOLTAGE WHEN WORKING ON A HALL SYSTEM EVEN THOUGH THE ENGINE IS STATIONARY, AND THE ENERGY DELIVERED IS DANGEROUS!

## Variable reluctance pulse generator

Going back to fundamentals of electromagnetism, it will be remembered that, if a coil is subjected to a change of magnetic field, voltage will be induced. The voltage generated will depend upon:

- *(a) The rate at which the magnetic field changes*
- *(b) The number of turns of wire in the coil*
- *(c) The direction of flux change, ie increase or decrease*

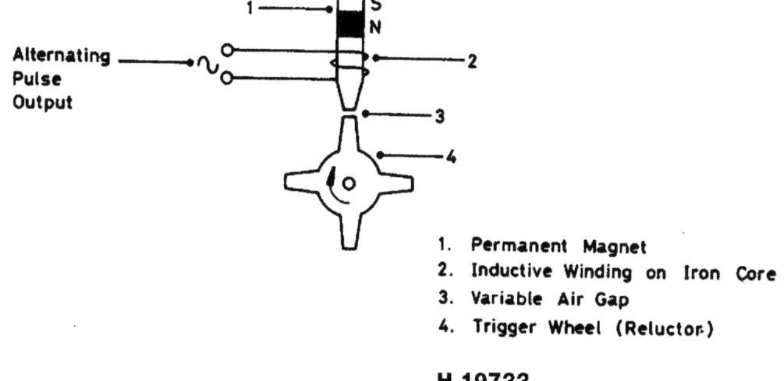


*Fig. 6.67 Schematic permanent magnet pulse generator*

This principle is used in a device to trigger an ignition spark. The magnetic field is varied by altering the reluctance of the magnetic circuit, and Fig. 6.67 shows the schematic arrangement. As a trigger wheel tooth approaches the iron core of the pick-up winding, the flux rises rapidly only to fall as rapidly as the tooth moves away. The maximum voltage is generated just before and just after the teeth are opposite each other. The output is a form of alternating voltage (Fig. 6.68) which is passed through a pulse shaping circuit

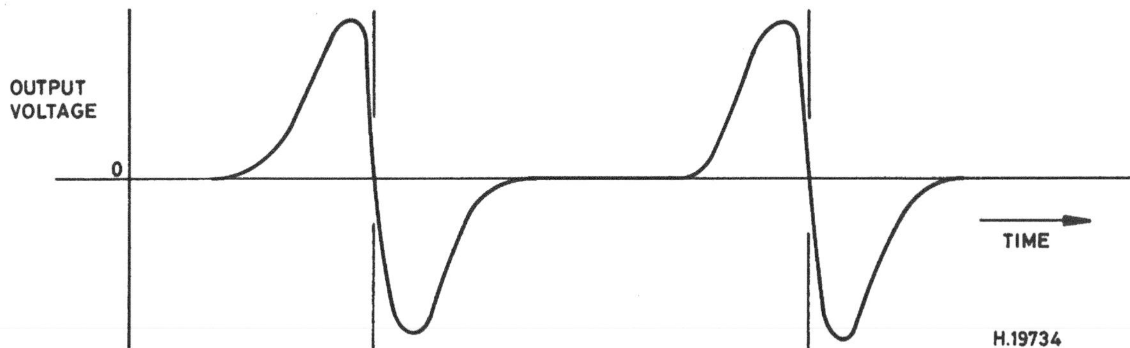


*Fig. 6.68 Variable-reluctance pulse generator output*

and on to the power transistor switch controlling the ignition coil current. A practical arrangement is shown in Fig. 6.69. The output voltage will vary in two ways with a speed increase:

(a) *The frequency will increase*

(b) *The magnitude will increase from a fraction of a volt up to 100V*

Both these changes can be sensed and used by the electronic module into which the pulse generator output is fed.

Bosch use a different arrangement utilising the same principle. A flat circular stationary plate has 4 soft iron pole pieces (for a 4-cylinder engine) magnetically energised by built-in high efficiency permanent magnets. Attached to the distributor shaft is a trigger wheel with 4 projections which pass close (0.5 mm) to the stationary pole pieces generating pulses in a single coil wound round the distributor shaft (Fig. 6.70). The advantages are the use of a single concentric coil and the symmetry of the magnetic pole piece arrangement. Other arrangements do not always use a distributor but the flywheel to which a target slug is bolted. A sensor containing a permanent magnet and a pick-up coil is located so that the slug passes by at the point of ignition. The idea of using the flywheel teeth is also used, in which a sensor counts the teeth as a series of impulses and can then pass this information to the computer module to read speed and estimate advance required.

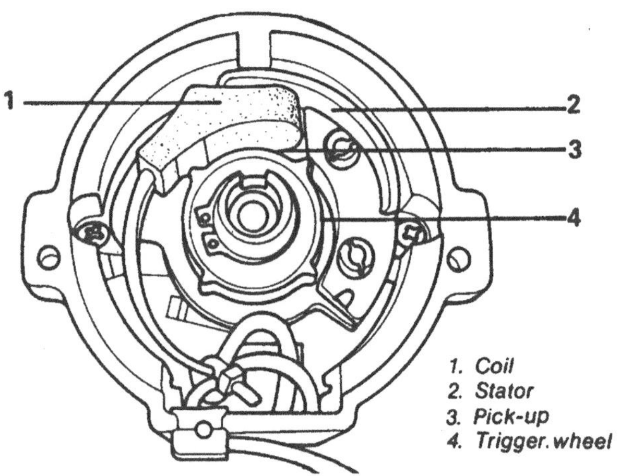


***Fig. 6.69 Typical Lucas permanent magnet pulse generator distributor***
*Courtesy FKI Crypton Ltd*

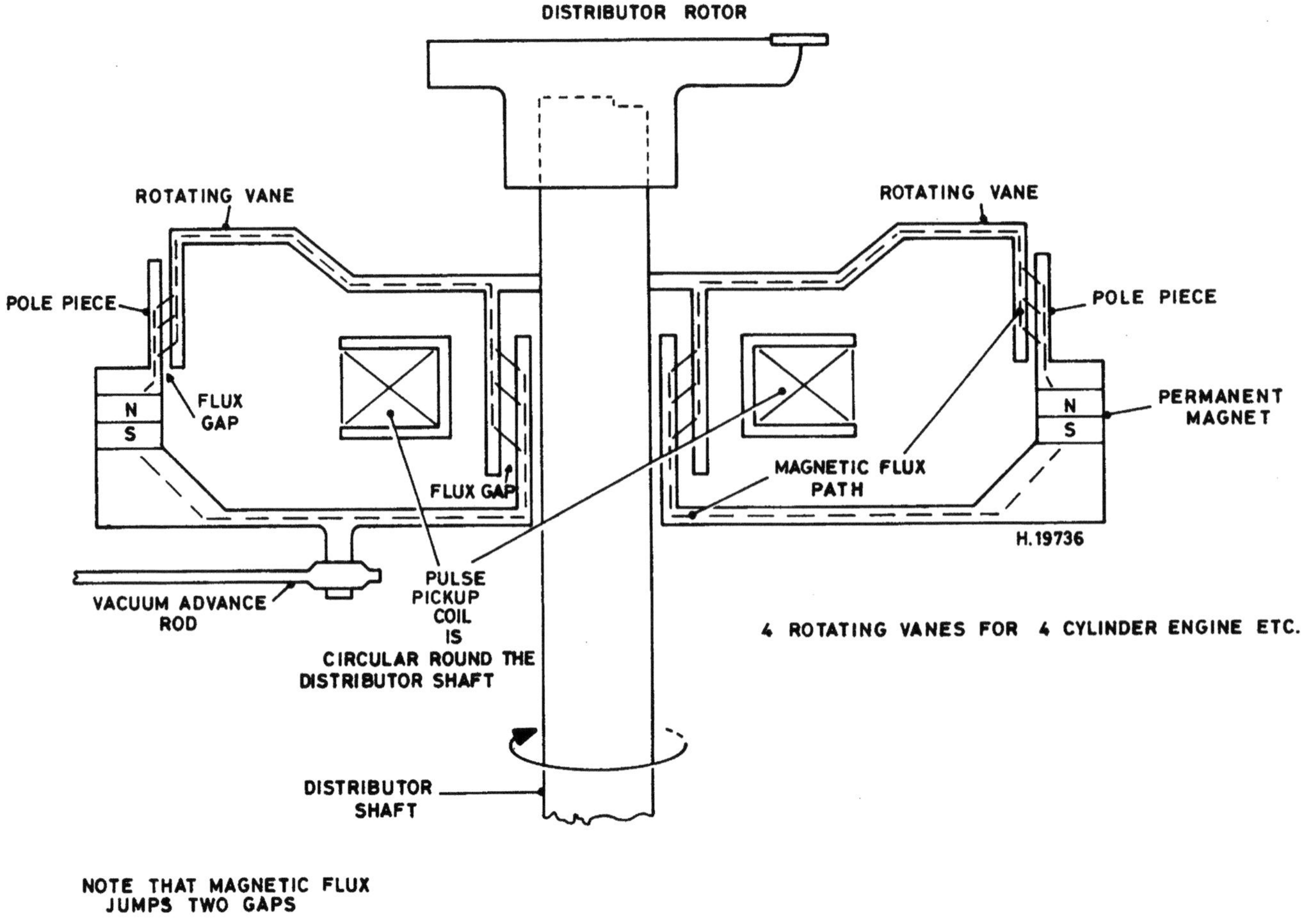

DISTRIBUTOR ROTOR
ROTATING VANE
ROTATING VANE
POLE PIECE
POLE PIECE
N
S
FLUX GAP
N
S
PERMANENT MAGNET
FLUX GAP
MAGNETIC FLUX PATH
H.19736
PULSE PICKUP COIL IS CIRCULAR ROUND THE DISTRIBUTOR SHAFT
VACUUM ADVANCE ROD
4 ROTATING VANES FOR 4 CYLINDER ENGINE ETC.
DISTRIBUTOR SHAFT
NOTE THAT MAGNETIC FLUX JUMPS TWO GAPS

***Fig. 6.70 Bosch-type variable reluctance ignition pulse generator***

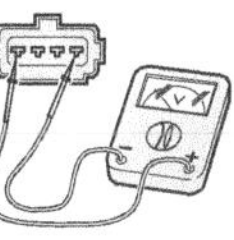

## 29 Electronic ignition with variable reluctance pulse generator

**1** Typical systems comprise:

(a) *An ignition coil of low primary inductance and resistance of less than 1 ohm.*

(b) *A ballast resistor in series with the battery supply to the primary. This is temperature dependent and limits the primary current. When cold, the resistance is low, giving a high primary current and a high energy spark. When the engine runs fast the primary is switched on for a shorter period so the resistor value remains low and high spark voltage is retained.*
*At cranking the resistor is shorted out to give good starting with low battery voltage.*

(c) *A distributor which will contain all or part of the pulse generator together with a conventional cap, distributor rotor and centrifugal/vacuum advance mechanisms.*

(d) *An electronic control unit (ECU) – this consists of a circuit to shape the pulse coming in from the pulse generator, another circuit which controls the dwell period and finally the electronic switch to turn the ignition primary current off and on.*

Modern practice now employs closed-loop controls for dwell and primary current limiting, to be described later in this chapter.

### Pulse shaping

**2** The object is to convert the input signals from the pulse generator into a train of square wave pulses all of the same height. To do this a standard 'building-block' from electronic logic circuitry is used, known as the Schmitt Trigger. The Schmitt Trigger employs two transistors in which voltage

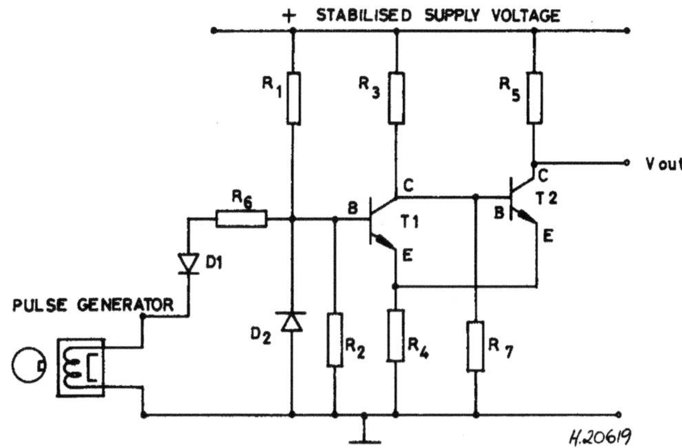


*Fig. 6.71 Schmitt Trigger*

signals from the second are sent back to the first. This is known as feedback and in this case results in an extremely rapid switching action from OFF to ON and *vice versa.*

A schematic circuit is shown in Fig. 6.71. Circuit operation:

(a) *With no pulse signal, transistor $T_1$ is ON; base current will flow through $R_1$ to give this condition.*
*With $T_1$ ON the voltage at its collector c will hold transistor $T_2$ OFF.*
*Because no collector current drop occurs across $R_5$ the output of $T_2$ is high at approximately the level of the stabilized supply voltage.*

(b) *Whenever the base voltage of $T_1$ is more negative than –0.7V (eg –0.8 V) the collector current will cut off. This happens when the pulse voltage reaches point A in Fig. 6.72; $T_1$ is cut OFF and this causes $T_2$ to switch ON. The voltage drop across $R_5$ causes a drop in output voltage $V_{OUT}$. The rise in current through $T_2$ gives a volt-drop*

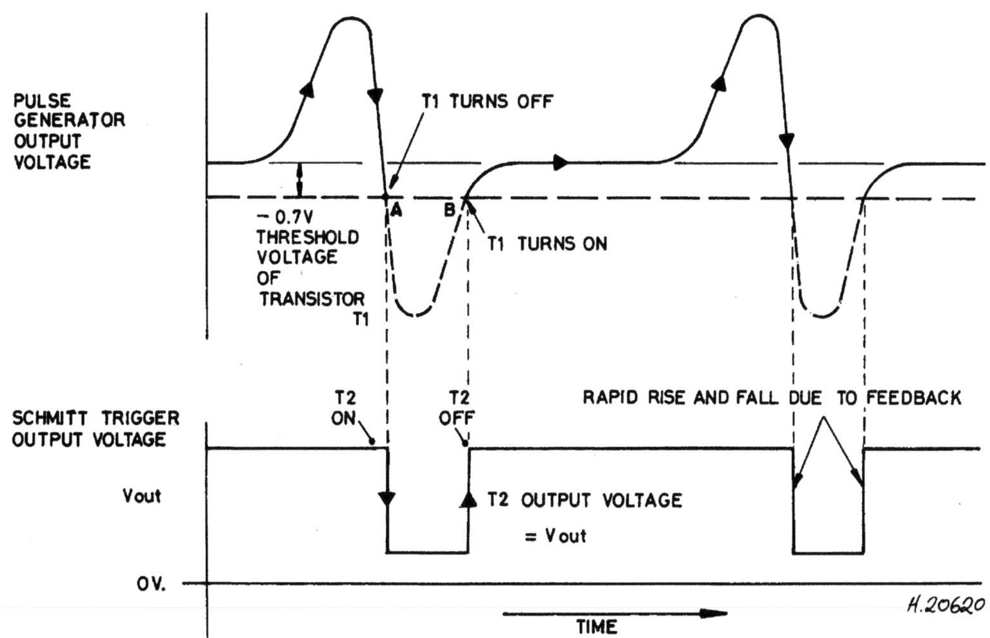


*Fig. 6.72 Input/output of Schmitt Trigger*

*across $R_4$ which is sensed by $T_1$ causing it to switch off very rapidly – an example of feedback.*

(c) *As the signal pulse returns to the $T_1$ threshold voltage of –0.7 volt, current will begin to flow through $T_1$. The volt-drop across $R_3$ will reduce current flow in $T_2$ – a smaller volt-drop will occur in $R_4$ causing $T_1$ to switch ON harder and so the circuit will snap the output voltage $V_{OUT}$ again up to the supply voltage level as $T_2$ shuts OFF.*

The Schmitt Trigger has shaped the pulse signal to a square topped wave which will occur at the same rate as the incoming pulses. Note that diode $D_1$ prevents positive-going pulses from reaching the base of $T_1$ and diode D2 will effectively short out high negative pulses which will occur as the engine speed rises. Some variable reluctance pulses generators can deliver peak voltage of the order of 100 V at high engine revolutions because the induced emf in the pick-up is proportional to the RATE of change of magnetic flux. A fully detailed practical circuit would include temperature control diodes in series with $R_1$, but are omitted here for clarity.

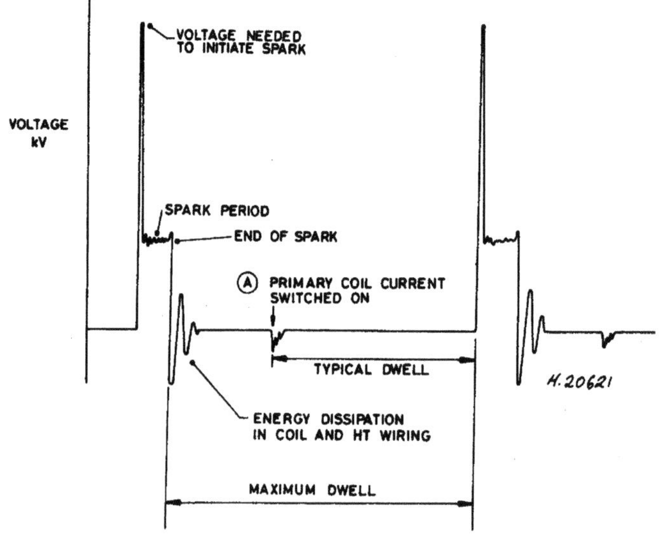


***Fig. 6.73 Coil secondary voltage***

## Dwell period control

**3** In contact-breaker ignition, the DWELL ANGLE (the angle over which the contacts are closed and coil current is building up) is fixed by the shape of the distributor shaft lobes and the gap setting of the contact breaker points. However, the DWELL PERIOD is not fixed and decreases as the engine speed rises, and it is the dwell period in time that determines how far the coil current builds up before the next spark; at high speeds in multi-cylinder engines there will be insufficient time for coil current build-up. Referring to Fig. 6.73, a simplified form of the coil secondary voltage is shown. The high peak is the voltage provided by the ignition coil secondary; once the spark has begun, a lower, flat, voltage plateau shows the voltage required to maintain the spark. At the end of the spark a decaying oscillatory voltage represents the remaining energy dissipation as it passes through the coil inductance and the capacitance of the coil and HT wiring. At point A, the coil primary is switched on and the normal dwell period begins. Extension of the dwell period is achieved by moving point A to the left, the limit being at the point of time when the spark ends. Electronic control of the dwell period is possible with simple circuitry, one example being shown in Fig. 6.74. This shows the second transistor $T_2$ of the Schmitt Trigger coupled to a further transistor $T_3$ by capacitor C. For ease of explanation $T_2$ base may be considered as at earth potential. The purpose is to make $T_3$ conduct ( = ON) longer at high engine speed in order to give the ignition coil (not shown) time to build up primary current and hence magnetic stored energy for spark production.

Operation:

**Note:** When $T_3$ switches OFF, ignition occurs.

(a) *Let T2 be just switching OFF*

*At low speed capacitor C charges up through $R_5$ and $T_3$ base/emitter to nearly the full supply voltage; note polarity (Fig. 6.75). Because base-emitter current flows,*

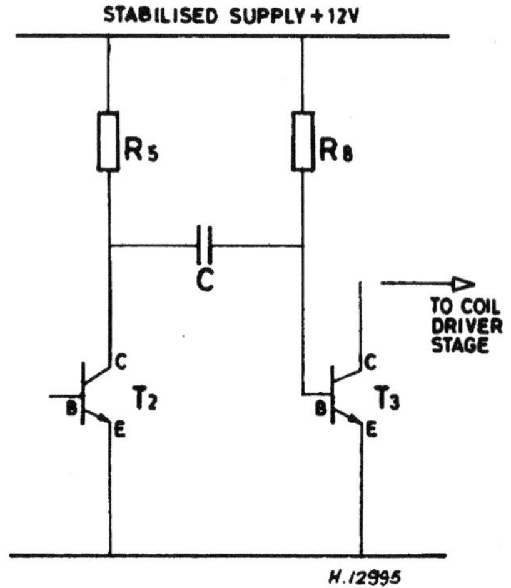


***Fig. 6.74 Dwell control***

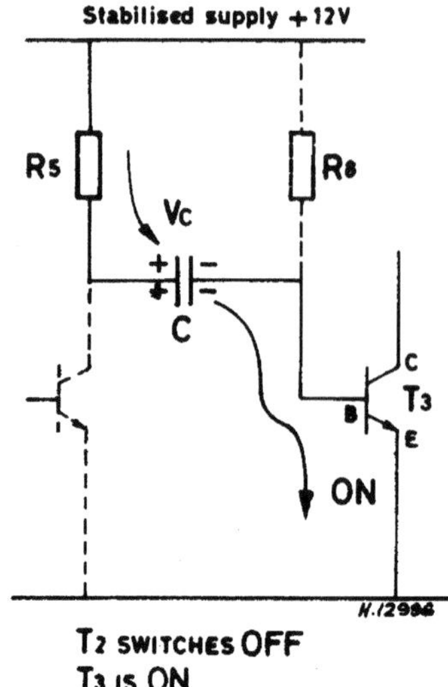


***Fig. 6.75 Dwell control operation – $T_2$ just switching off***

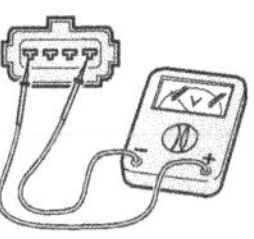

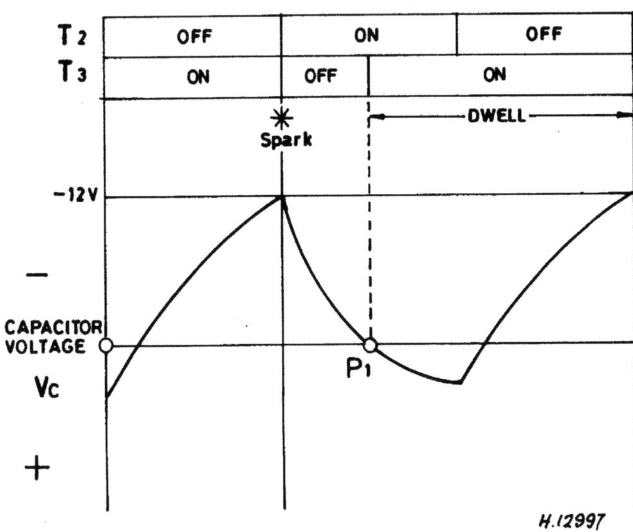


*Fig. 6.76 Dwell at low speed*

$T_3$ is ON and therefore also is the coil primary current; see Fig.6.76.

(b) $T_2$ switches ON – ignition spark point
When $T_2$ is switched ON it provides a path to earth for the capacitor which starts to discharge (Fig. 6.77). Note that if the collector-emitter small volt-drop of $T_2$ is ignored, the capacitor voltage is applied to the base-emitter of $T_3$ and is of polarity to switch $T_3$ OFF, giving ignition.

(c) $T_3$ turns ON at point $P_1$ (Fig. 6.76)
As C discharges through $R_8$ and $T_2$ it reaches zero voltage and will begin to charge in the opposite direction. Shortly after the zero point, $T_3$ will be switched ON and current again flows in the ignition coil primary winding (Fig. 6.78). This state continues up to the point where $T_2$ is switched OFF.

(d) $T_2$ switches OFF
The cycle is now completed; C now charges towards the 12V point, leaving $T_3$ conducting until $T_2$ switches ON again.

(e) At high speed.
Now C does not have time to charge as fully as at low speed (Fig. 6.79). However, it also discharges to zero in a shorter time to cause $T_3$ to switch ON earlier.

(f) Spark duration limiter
With a multi-cylinder engine running at high speed there is the likelihood that this circuit would push the coil current switch-on point so early that it would interfere with the length of spark which should never be allowed shorter than 500 microsecond. The simple circuit shown will have a limiter which ensures that the dwell period remains fixed above a certain sparking rate.

## Ignition coil power switch

**4** A common arrangement where high input resistance and high current gain are required is known as the Darlington pair (or super alpha pair).

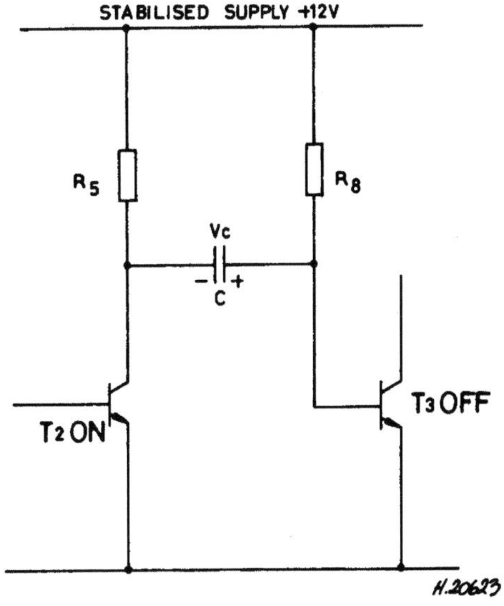


***Fig. 6.77 Dwell control operation – $T_2$ switches ON***
*At the instant when $T_2$ switches ON, the full voltage of C appears across base and emitter of $T_3$, switching $T_3$ OFF and creating an ignition spark Ignore the volt drop across collector-emitter of $T_2$*

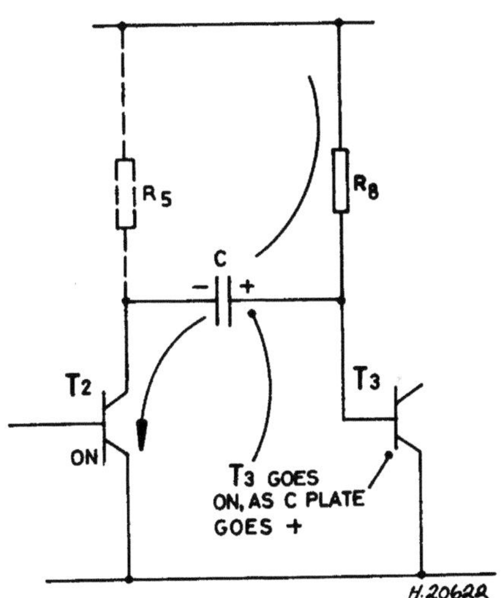


***Fig. 6.78 Dwell starts as C reverses polarity***

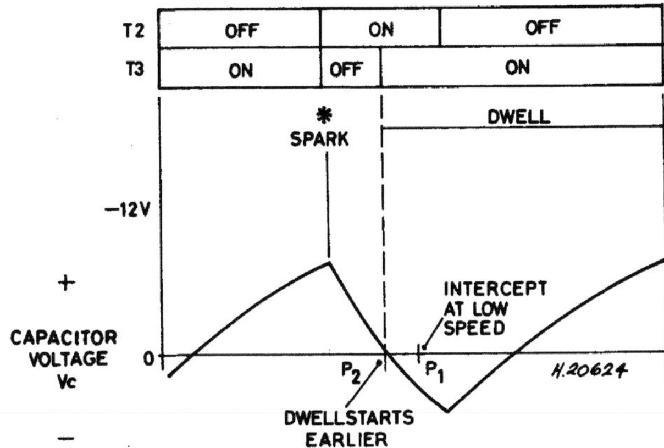


***Fig. 6.79 Dwell at high speed***

This consists of two transistors directly coupled; the second transistor can be a power type and the two are available in one package (Fig. 6.80). The action of the transistor $T_3$ from the previous dwell control stage switches a driver transistor $T_4$ on and off (Fig. 6.81). The emitter resistor chain provides current drive for the first of the Darlington pair transistors, resulting in rapid power switching as $T_3$ goes OFF. The simplified circuit will have additional components such as a diode connected from the ignition coil primary to earth in order to absorb rapidly-changing voltage spikes which occur when the coil current is broken abruptly. A radio interference capacitor will be similarly connected, and this parallels closely the points capacitor in a Kettering system. In some arrangements, feedback resistors are connected from the Darlington collector output terminal back to the base input, thus speeding up the switching process.

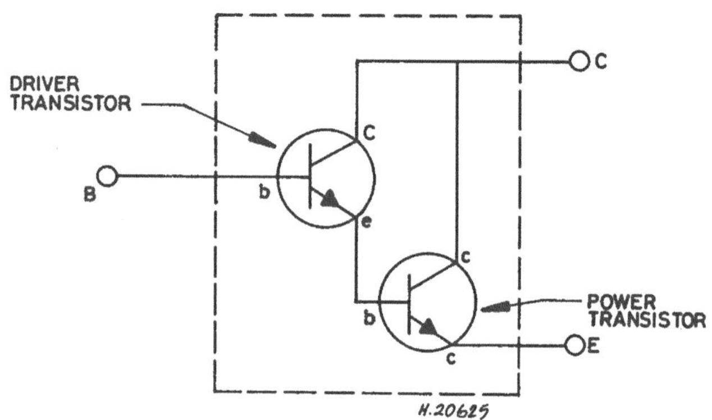


*Fig. 6.80 Darlington pair package*

## 30 Constant energy system with magnetic pulse generator

**1** Constant Energy is a term in use to describe a further development in which more sophisticated control of the primary coil current is employed. Voltage feedback in a closed-loop circuit is used to control the Darlington power switch so that the correct value of coil primary current flows under all engine conditions and supply voltage variations. A further feature usually included is a switching device which will cut off the coil primary current when the engine stops but with the ignition still on.

### Current regulation

**2** The means of sensing the coil primary current is to include a low value resistor R between the coil primary and earth. A voltage drop will occur proportional to current flow (remember Ohm's Law) and this is sent back to be compared with a standard reference volt-drop that would correspond to correct current in the primary winding (Fig. 6.82). If the actual voltage drop across the resistor is less than the standard reference voltage then the difference is measured as a + voltage which is then passed to the Darlington driver requiring this stage to pass more current via the power stage to the coil primary and *vice versa* if the measured voltage is too high.

### Closed loop dwell control

**3** Here a dwell period control circuit senses:

(a) *Whether the comparator checking the coil current is limiting or not, ie whether the coil current is reaching its correct value or not*

(b) *The frequency of the pulses from the magnetic variable reluctance pulse generator indicating engine speed*

It combines the two to a direct voltage bias to the pulse shaper circuit which causes it to switch on earlier or later according to the dc bias (Fig. 6.83). The two points

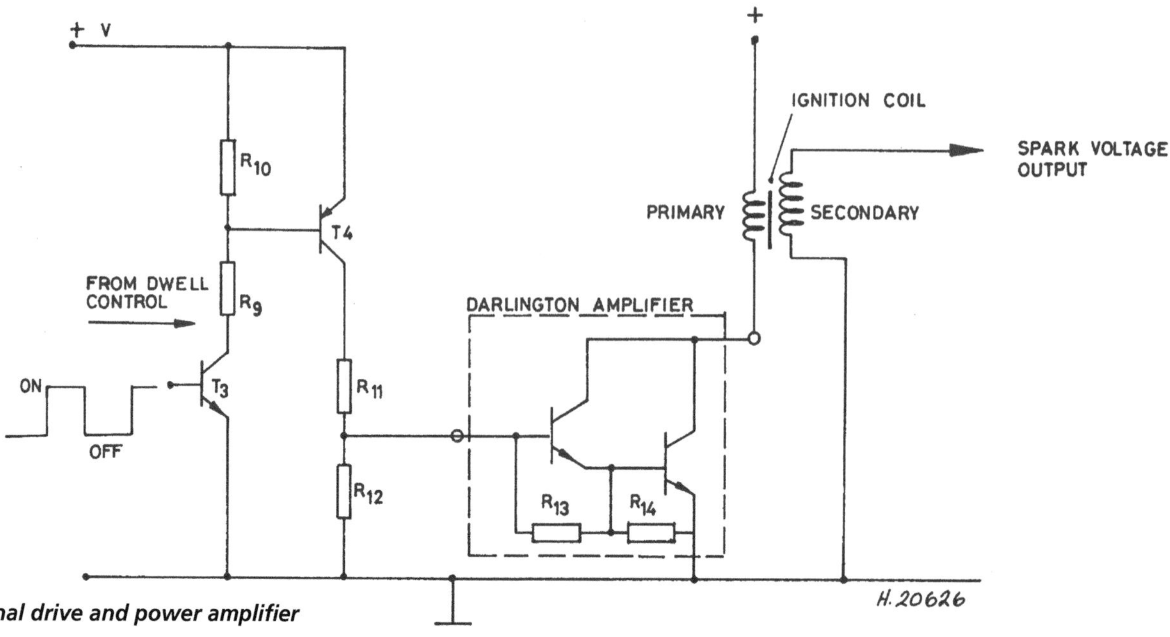


*Fig. 6.81 Final drive and power amplifier*

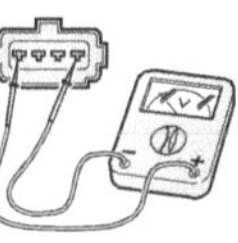

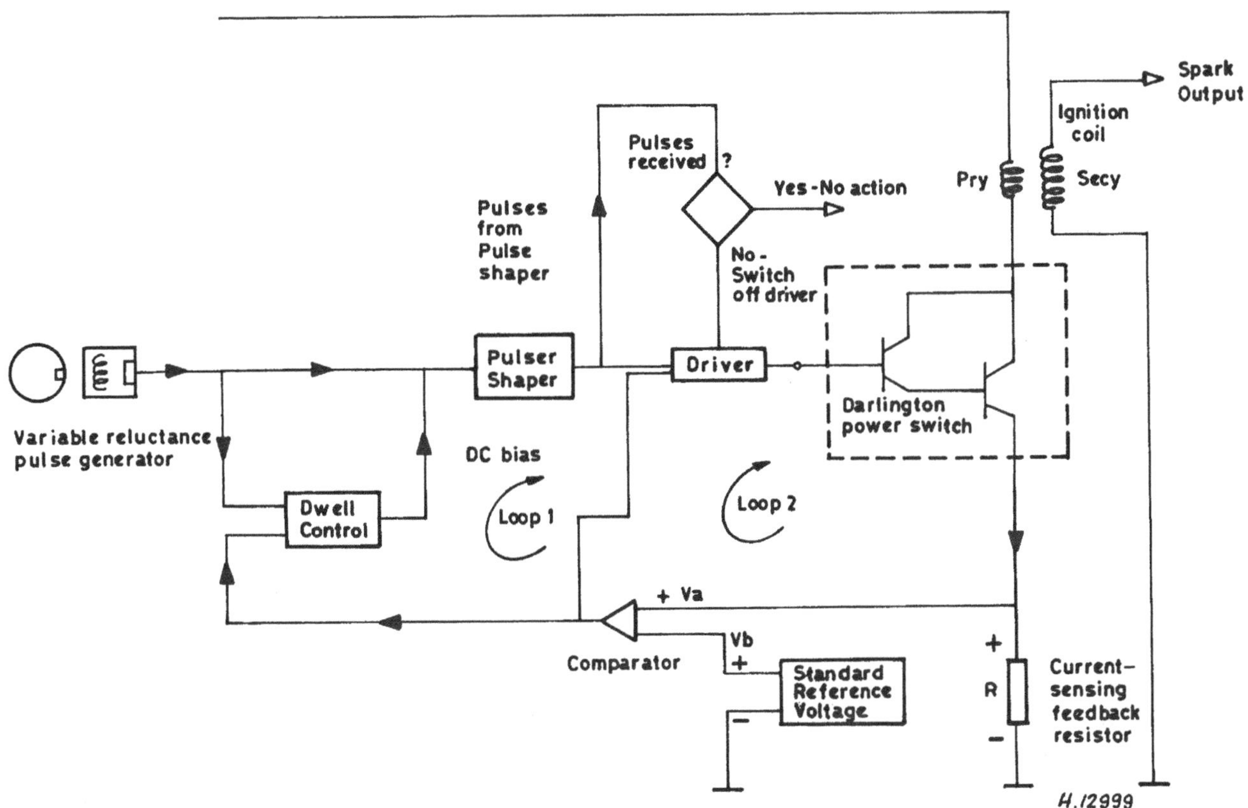


*Fig. 6.82 Constant energy system with magnetic pulse generator*

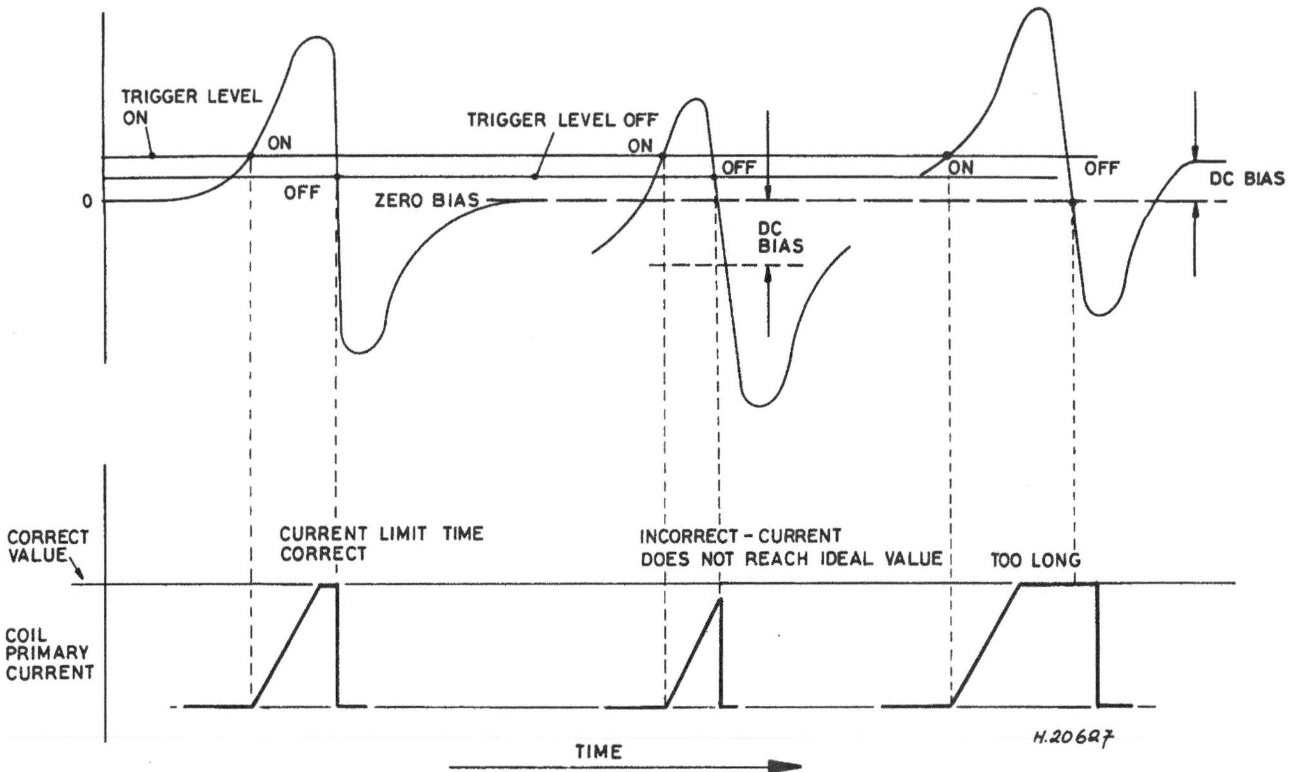


*Fig. 6.83 Closed loop dc bias dwell control*

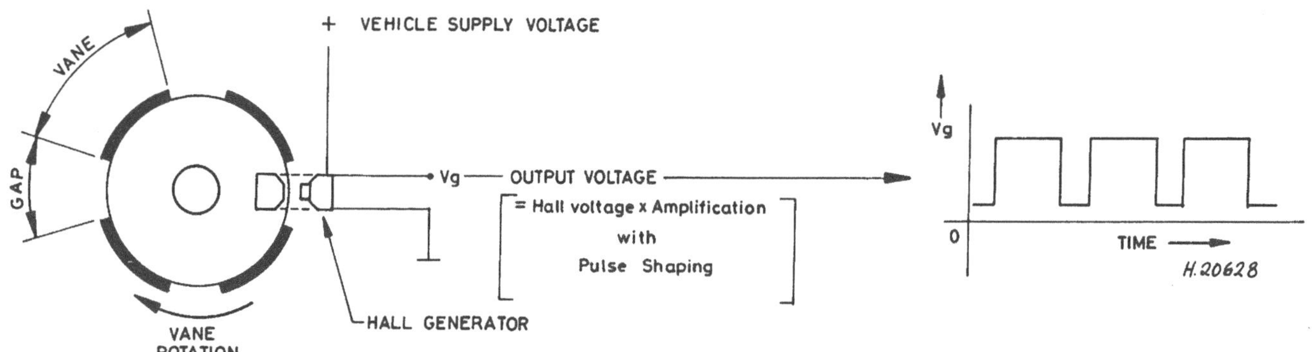


*Fig. 6.84 Hall generator and output voltage waveform*

corresponding to ON and OFF on the pulse generator signal voltages are not quite at the same level, an effect known as hysteresis – unimportant in this discussion.

**4** The superior results obtained by closed loop systems have meant their widespread adoption in current vehicle models. Summarising, those results are:

(a) *A constant quantity of electrical energy is available at the coil for spark production at all vehicle speeds and over a wide range of supply voltage*

(b) *The additional feature of stationary-engine current cut-off control means a low drain on the battery with ignition switched on*

If desired, radio or other accessories can now be ignition switch controlled without, as formerly, heavy ignition coil current drain.

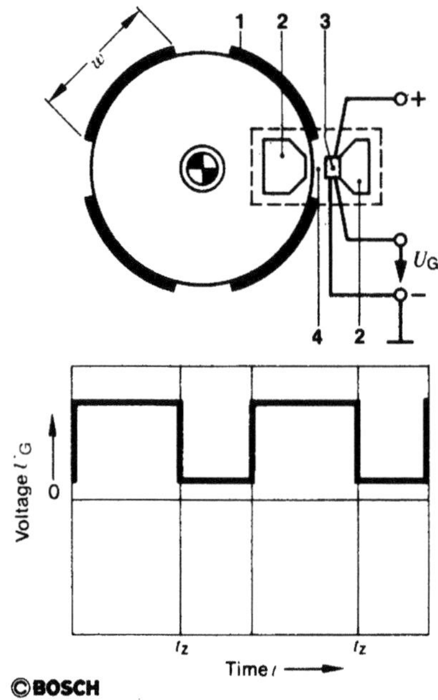


*Fig. 6.85 Hall generator in the distributor*

*1 Vane with width W*
*2 Soft magnetic conductive elements*
*3 Hall IC*
*4 Air gap*
*Ug Generator voltage*

## 31 Electronic ignition with Hall generator

**1** In principle, the output of the Hall generator could be used in much the same way as the variable reluctance generator, namely to produce, after Schmitt trigger processing, a rectangular wave to switch the ignition coil power stage on and off for spark production.

**2** The output of the Hall generator is lower than that of variable-reluctance types and it is practice to amplify and shape the Hall voltage in an integrated circuit (IC), this usually being located in the distributor (Fig. 6.84). The IC will also stabilise the supply voltage and provide compensation against temperature variation. Note that the distributor rotor and vane are one component in the diagram which shows a conversion set (Fig. 6.85).

**3** Dwell is fixed by the rotating vane and could be used through the electronic system, but fixed dwell is a disadvantage in a high performance engine where rapid ignition coil primary current rise is required. However, the Hall vane does give precise dwell and requires no setting (or re-setting with service life) as would be the case with the contact breaker system.

## 32 Constant energy system with Hall generator

**1** Again the development of this constant energy system is to ensure that the correct level of current is flowing through the ignition coil primary under all engine conditions and with all variations of battery voltage. As with the vari-reluctance system this implies:

(a) *Primary current reaches a safe maximum value for a defined period and is limited to this value*

(b) *Spark voltage is almost constant throughout the engine performance range*

(c) *No ballast resistors are used*

Often accompanying these is the provision for primary current cut-off when the engine is stationary but with the

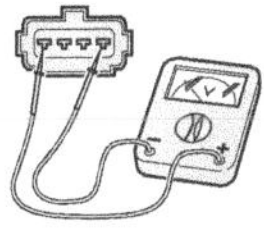

ignition switched on. Achievement of (a), (b) and (c) is obtained by closed-loop control of dwell period and coil current regulation.

## Dwell period closed-loop control

**2** In the case of the variable-reluctance generator the shape of the waveform lends itself to variations by means of a dc bias (Fig. 6.83) but the square waveform of the Hall generator does not. In analogue control systems (as distinct from digital ON-OFF conditions) switching is carried out at different threshold levels. To identify different levels the rectangular waveform output of the Hall amplifier (which will be larger than that of the Hall generator and probably inverted) is fed into a resistor-capacitor pulse shaper to give a triangular voltage (Fig. 6.86). A direct-voltage bias derived from a comparator sets the trigger level at which the ramp voltage will switch on the Darlington power stage controlling the primary current. This trigger level is such that the primary current reaches the correct design value and levels off for a period t. This short period over which the current flattens out to a maximum value is the lead-time t and is required to cope with the dynamic conditions when the engine accelerates. The ON point is the start of the dwell period; OFF corresponds to the ignition spark point.

Variations in output from the comparator result in either:

*(a) Too short a period for the primary current to reach the correct level, or*

*(b) Too long a period*

In the case (a) the voltage across the current-sensing feedback resistor will cause the comparator to adjust the trigger level to give an earlier switch on and *vice versa* in the case of (b).

## Peak current closed-loop control

The signal from the current sensing feedback resistor will contain information on the peak current flowing in the coil primary. The comparator will measure this peak value with a standard derived voltage and produce an output which will control the driver stage. If the maximum current has been reached the comparator reduces the output of the driver, forcing the Darlington stage off. Thus the feedback loop ensures that the maximum value of primary current is not exceeded and acts as a cut-off regulator.

# 33 Digital ignition

**1** The change to digital electronics for ignition was a major step forward, since it dispensed with centrifugal and vacuum advance devices. Still retaining the ignition coil, the system

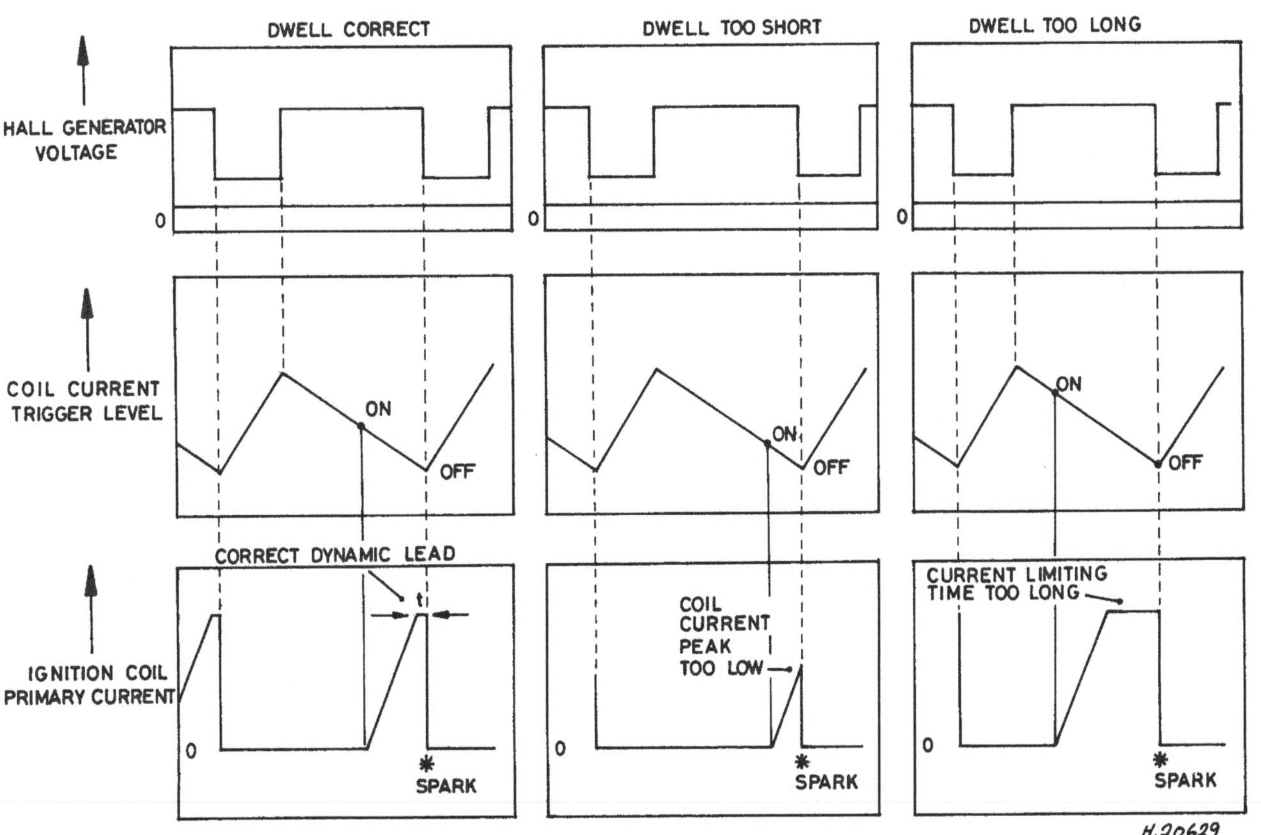


*Fig. 6.86 Trigger level control of dwell in constant energy Hall generator ignition*

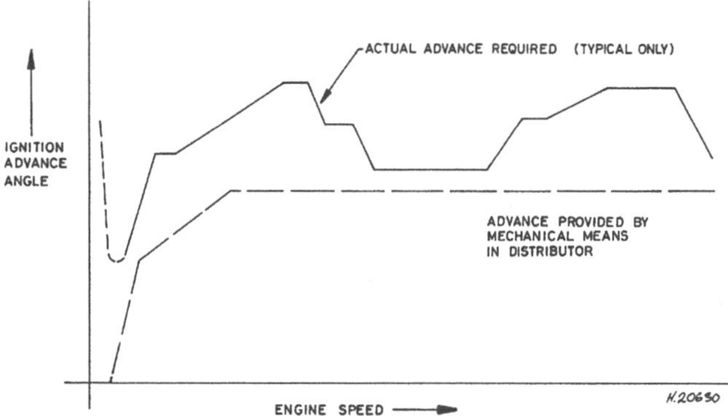


*Fig. 6.87 A shortcoming of distributor advance mechanisms*

provides for constant energy and coil current-limiting. A micro-computer is used to select the correct ignition point and takes into account the principal features, engine speed and load.

**2** With the adaptability of the micro-computer it is now possible to measure and evaluate a range of variables which give information on the engine and vehicle but importantly the end results are:

(a) *Constant spark energy is available to the modern lean-burn engine over the complete speed range*

(b) *Ignition advance can be taken to the point where knock is about to start – since the greatest advance short of knocking gives best power output*

**3** The advantage of accuracy in ignition advance setting with allowance for speed, engine temperature and load ensures good fuel economy and low exhaust pollution. There is no mechanical wear to require frequent service; factors such as idle-speed stabilization and good starting under adverse conditions more than compensate for additional complexity. Cost of micro electronic equipment continues to fall and it is now established that digital ignition is the norm for future designs.

**4** At this point it is worth noting that digital ignition can be employed independently of the fuel system but current designs treat both ignition and fuelling together as a total engine management system. More will be said of this later.

## 34 Ignition advance v engine parameters

**1** When an engine is designed, the manufacturer will run it in the test house over the whole load and speed range. At every spot value of load and speed the ignition advance required is noted and graphs plotted. The ignition advance selected is a compromise and at a specific point takes into account fuel consumption, safety margin from the knock level, exhaust gas content, torque and engine temperature, and it is not surprising that the graph is of jagged shape. It bears only a general resemblance to the graph of advance angle provided by distributor centrifugal weights and the vacuum unit as shown in the two-dimensional graph (Fig. 6.87).

**2** In order to display the required advance against engine speed and load, a three-axis graph is required (Fig. 6.88) and if all the points are imagined to be joined together a surface is made. Erecting a vertical at any combination of load and engine speed will give the required ignition advance. The surface is like a 3-dimensional contour map and for this reason is sometimes known as **mapped ignition**. If the base or floor of the ignition map can be imagined as being divided along the speed and load axes, then they provide intersection points at which values of ignition advance are stored (Fig. 6.89). The figure shows a simple matrix giving intersection points at which the angle of advance is stored in the computer memory. In practice the entire ignition advance map might contain between 1000 and 4000 individual recallable ignition advance angle points.

**3** The opportunity will be taken by the manufacturer to build in extra advance for engine speeds below the nominal engine

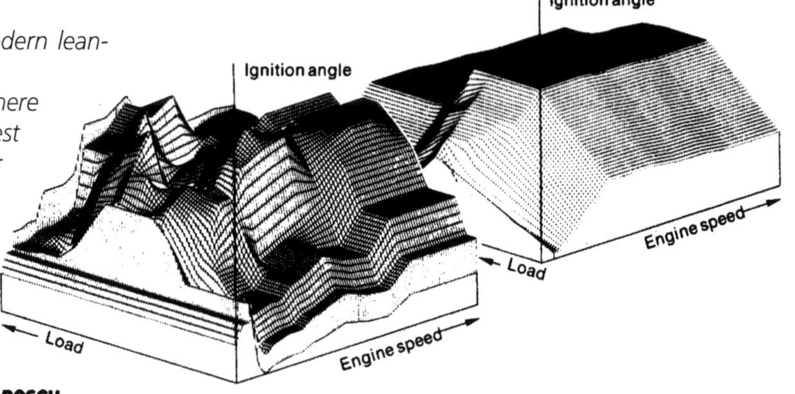


***Fig. 6.88 Optimized electronic ignition advance map (left) compared with the ignition advance map of a mechanical spark advance system (right)***

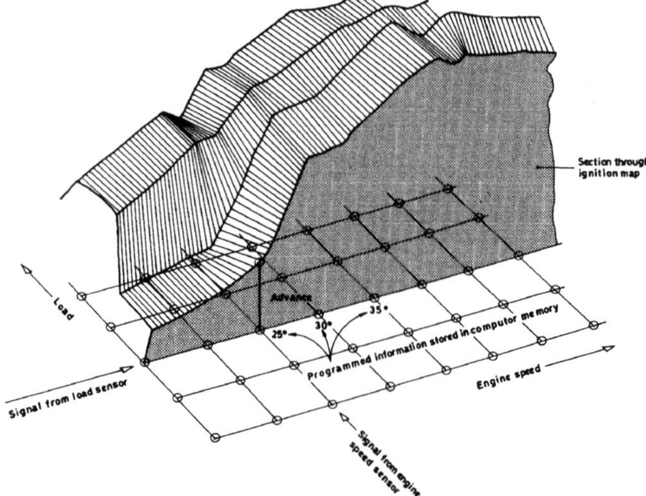


***Fig. 6.89 Ignition map and stored information concept***

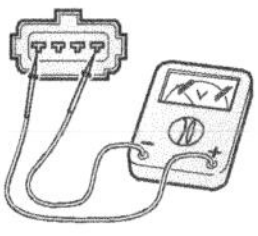

idle speed to give stabilisation by increasing the torque. The condition of overrun is also programmed specially, in respect of information received on exhaust content and driveability, and a switch to signal these conditions is linked to the accelerator pedal. Finally the full-load curve is programmed to follow closely, but not exceed, the knock limit.

## 35 Computerised ignition processing

**1** The micro-computer has been adapted for vehicle service and is programmed with the above data (Section 34). Information is fed into the computer in the form of electrical signals representing, in a typical system:

1 Engine speed
2 Engine load
3 Coolant temperature
4 Knock condition
5 Crankshaft position
6 Battery voltage

**2** Information is provided for the computer from a variety of transducers which measure a quantity such as temperature, pressure, speed etc and give out an electrical signal proportional to the magnitude of the measured quantity. These devices have taken the name of **sensors**.

**3** The sensors deliver signals to the computer (sometimes called the Electronic Control unit, ECU), at the heart of which is a micro-processor. The computer will firstly convert all the incoming analogue signals to digital forms (ie a series of on/off pulses) since computers can handle only digital quantities. Certain measured quantities such as the crankshaft-derived pulses giving engine speed and crankshaft position will already be in digital form, but signals from the manifold pressure, engine water temperature and battery voltage sensors will be in a continuously present, but changing, form. These are analogue signals and are changed in the computer into digital signals by an analogue-to-digital (A–D) converter, described later.

**4** Referring to the ringed numbers in Fig. 6.90:

**1. Load.** Intake manifold pressure gives a measure of engine load and a pressure sensor of the aneroid capsule or semiconductor piezo strain gauge types might be used. The signal is an indirect method of measuring air flow and so is linked to the load conditions of the engine. An air temperature sensor may be used as a further provider of information to the computer (ECU) to allow for air density variation with temperatures, and is used particularly with fuel injection engines. Alternatively, air mass flow may be measured directly by a hot-wire or hot surface airflow sensor, these devices being designed to take into account air temperature and density. The signal produced will be in analogue form and will be changed to a series of digital pulses in the AD converter.

**2. Knock** is sensed by a piezo accelerometer which means it is a slice of piezo quartz held down to a suitable engine point between cylinders and in contact with a heavy disc (a seismic disc, ie having some significant **mass**) (Fig. 6.91). The piezo crystal gives a voltage at opposite edges proportional to change of stress on the face of the crystal. When the onset of knock is reached, the structural vibration of the engine block causes the mass to stress the piezo crystal. The electrical signal so generated passes to a circuit for evaluation. A set level is formed for each cylinder, based on the average of previous combustion cycles; this level is

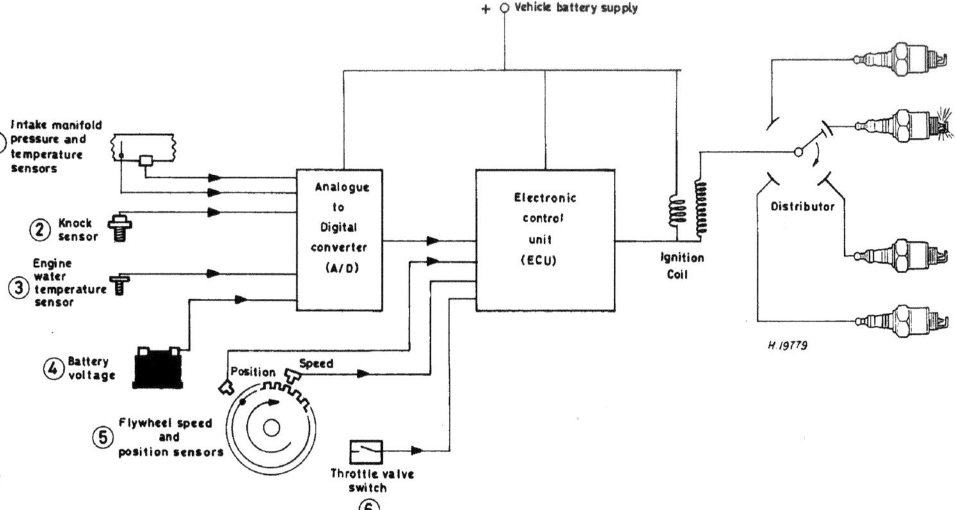


*Fig. 6.90 Schematic layout of digital electronic ignition system*

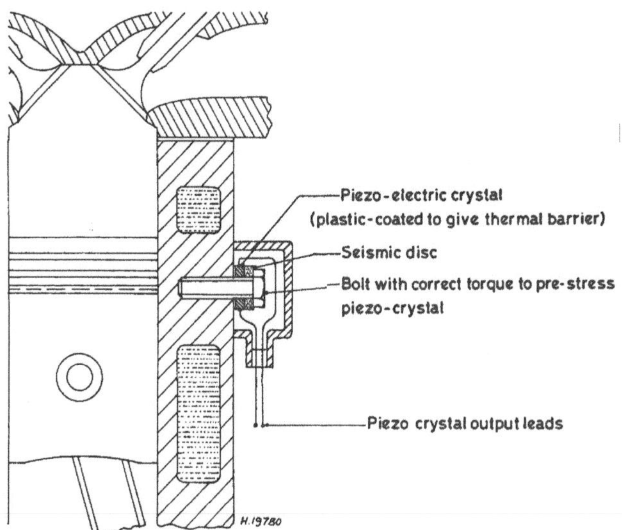


*Fig. 6.91 Knock sensor using piezo crystal*

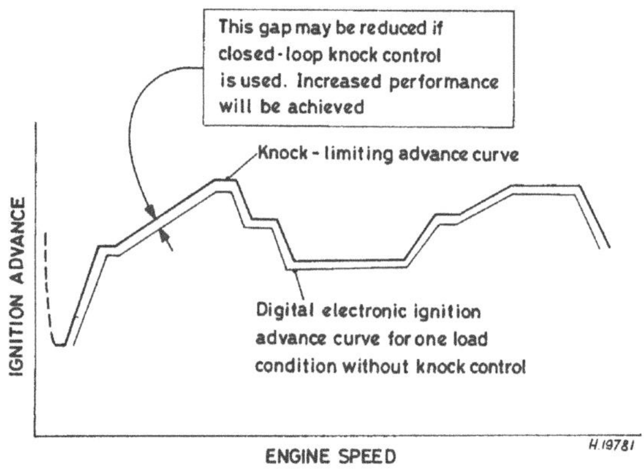


*Fig. 6.92 Increased performance with knock control*

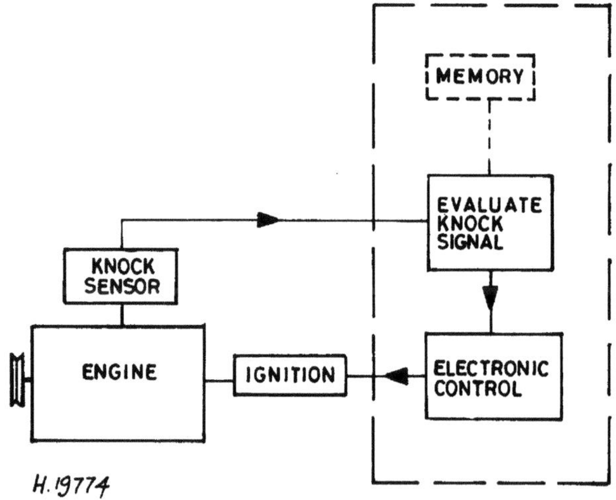


*Fig. 6.93 Knock control closed loop system*

continuously adapted for operating conditions. This is then compared with the knock sensor signal for every spark and, if the comparator shows the knock level to be exceeded, it will then retard the ignition point by a fixed angle, say 1.5 degrees, for THAT PARTICULAR CYLINDER.

The process is repeated for every cylinder and if no further knocking is detected, the micro-processor advances the ignition in small discrete steps until the advance angle is as it should be according to the ignition map stored in memory.

The result is that each cylinder is monitored continuously and the ignition angle separately adjusted giving the optimum for both engine efficiency and consumption, since it is known that these conditions are achieved with the largest advance possible short of the knock condition (Fig. 6.92). Since each cylinder has its own characteristic noise, one sensor will suffice to deal with four cylinders. A six-cylinder engine will have two sensors which are switched according to firing sequence. This process is an example of closed loop control shown schematically in Fig. 6.93. Should a circuit failure occur, such as in the sensor or a wiring break, the ignition is retarded to a safe value and a warning light is switched on.

**3. Engine temperature.** Temperature sensors are usually of the semiconductor type, known as thermistors, which have displaced earlier thermocouple units for situations below 200°C. The bead of semiconductor material has a marked negative temperature coefficient of resistance (Fig. 6.94), and a working range of at least –20°C to + 130°C. It is suitable for measuring coolant temperature and is mounted in a screw-in capsule (Fig. 6.95) in a water channel in the engine block. The sensitivity is good for accurate temperature measurements to within 0.05°C. Information on

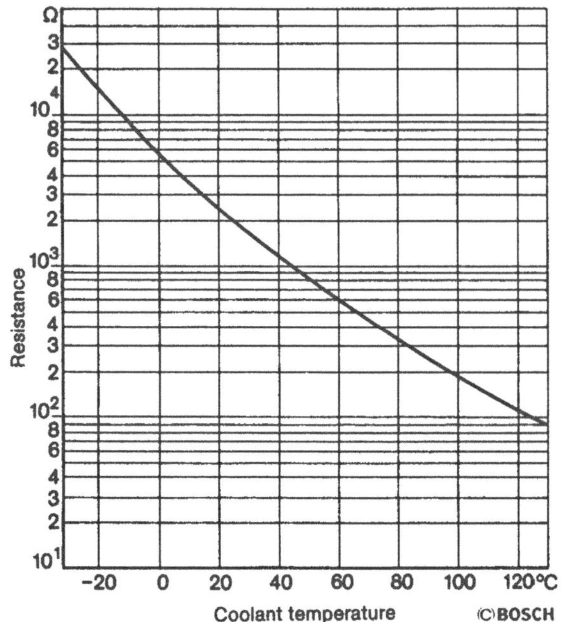


*Fig. 6.94 Resistance change with temperature of NTC bead (negative temperature coefficient)*

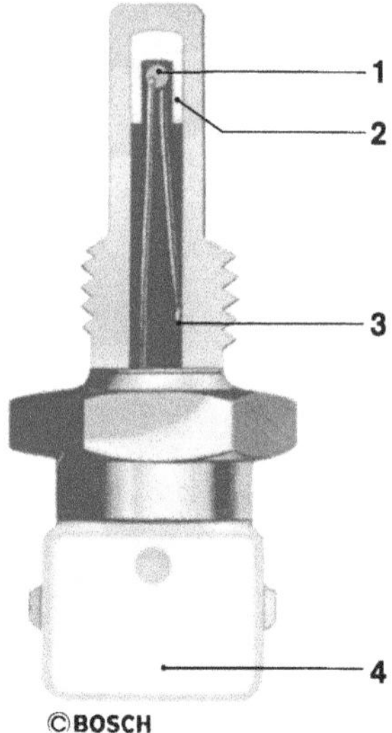


*Fig. 6.95 Engine temperature sensor*

*1 Negative temperature coefficient semiconductor resistor (NTC bead)*
*2 Insulation*
*3 Sealing compound*
*4 Electrical connection*

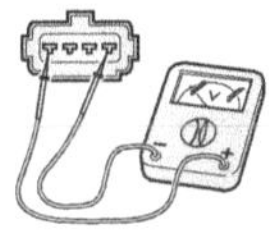

coolant temperature is processed in the ECU as an additional variable in finding the correct operating point on the engine load/engine temperature ignition advance map (Fig. 6.96). When the engine is cold, starting and driveability are more important than economy or efficiency.

**4. Battery voltage.** This is a correcting quantity; if the battery voltage deviates from a set standard, the time allowed for energising the coil (dwell period) is lengthened or shortened so that constant energy conditions obtain.

**5. Engine speed and crankshaft position.** The engine speed may be read by counting the number of teeth on a toothed ring gear mounted on the crankshaft. An induction type sensor is often used for this purpose on the same principle as in Fig. 6.67, here shown in production form in Fig. 6.97. It is necessary to give a datum point usually to show the position of the piston – often 90° BTDC. This may be picked up by another sensor from a projection on the ring gear; sometimes the flywheel teeth are used instead of a purpose built tooth-wheel. Speed and crankshaft position could, alternatively, be measured at the distributor by a Hall generator but this is not so accurate as using direct crankshaft measurements. Instead of using two separate sensors, one sensor can be used for speed and crankshaft position if a special marker is used, eg one tooth missing. Finally, although the inductive sensor is in common use, it does have the disadvantage that its output depends on speed, so slow rotation is not measurable.

**6. Throttle valve switch.** This is used to send a signal to the ECU at idle and full load positions, and so switch on to special characteristic advance curves on the ignition map. As will be seen later, some designs shut off fuel on overrun and this switch gives the required control signal (Fig. 6.98).

## The Electronic Control Unit (ECU)

**5** Fig. 6.90 shows the sensors feeding information to the ECU with the end result of producing an ignition of correct timing and energy. The structure of the ECU is shown in Fig. 6.99 and the function of the separate parts is:

**Interface unit.** Incoming signals from the sensors are processed into a form which can be handled by the computer, ie as a series of on-off pulses to which the symbols:

ON = 1 and OFF = 0

are allocated.

This method of displaying quantities is the binary notation. Where a signal is in analogue form, eg battery voltage, this is made into binary equivalent by an analogue-to-digital converter. The interface unit will also contain circuitry to handle the knock sensor input in which it is compared with the average level of previous combustion cycles.

**Input/output unit (I/O).** This handles incoming signals at whatever rate they are fed in and outputs them at the required processing speed and in the correct sequence, or alternatively will send them for storage in RAM (random access memory) until required.

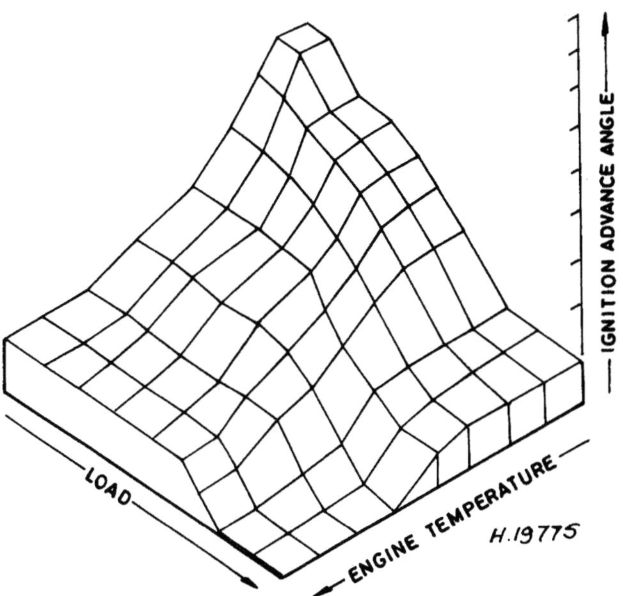


*Fig. 6.96 Simple matrix map. Ignition advance map for load and temperature variables*

©BOSCH

*Fig. 6.97 Induction pulse sensor on crankshaft toothed wheel*

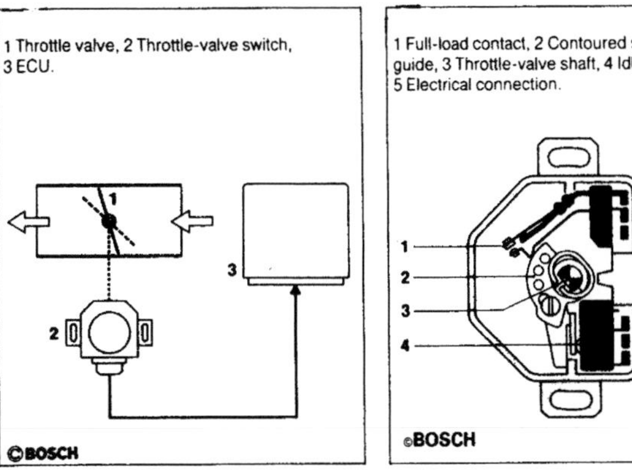


*Fig. 6.98 Throttle valve switch*

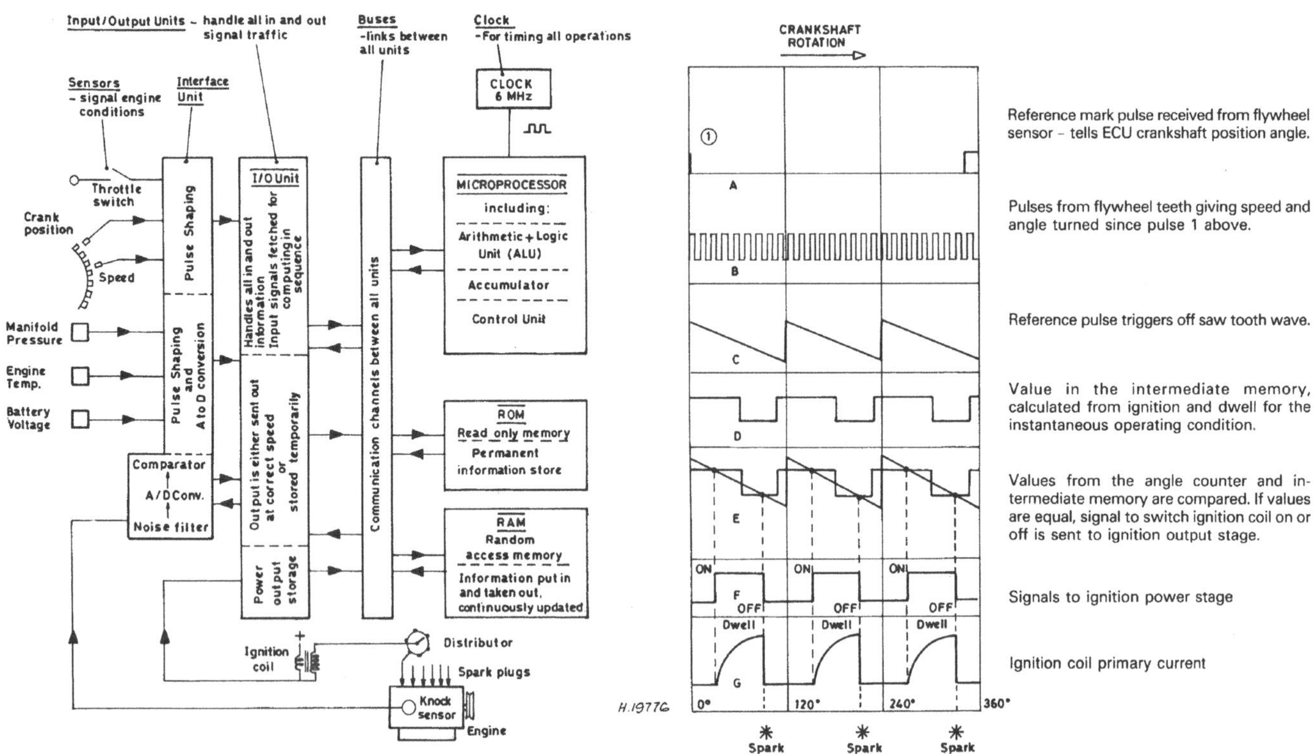


***Fig. 6.99 Digital electronic system***

**Clock.** The computer handles information in sequence as a function of time. It is a crystal-controlled pulse generator of high stability.

**Bus.** All sections of the computer are linked by connecting links shown as buses. The buses provide all units with data (databus), memory addresses (address bus) and control signals (control bus).

**Micro-processor or central processing unit**. The micro-processor (ALU) is that part of the computer which carries out calculations. Arithmetic functions of add, subtract, multiply and divide are all it can do and problems must be presented to it in these forms; it can also perform logic operations (see Chapter 1). An accumulator is a small temporary store for the ALU whilst calculating. The Control Unit directs the computing by ordering the movement of data between units of the computer and orders the timing and sequence of the Arithmetic and Logic (ALU) operation.

**Read Only Memory (ROM).** This is a memory which can only give out stored information and this stored information is permanent or non-volatile. That is to say the content remains even if there is a power failure. It is not possible to feed in new information for storage in this type of memory. The memory may contain data such as engine map values in tabular form, coding instruction, control programme etc. and this is programmed in advance by the manufacturer. A subgroup of the ROM family includes REPROM (reprogrammable ROM) and the EPROM (erasable ROM). These find application in automotive electronics for manufacturers can update or change the information stored.

**Random Access Memory (RAM).** Data supplied by the sensors are stored in RAM until fetched to the CPU or overwritten by updated signals from the sensors. RAM loses its information when the system is switched off.

## Micro-computer operation

**6** Information about the engine characteristics is stored in the computer memory in the form of tables of values, called look-up tables (or maps), and are derived from the three-axis ignition advance map and also that for dwell. Look-up tables will be memorized in the computer for several variables but essentially for engine speed, manifold air pressure, engine temperature and probably battery voltage. Each look-up table will give an output calling for an ignition angle and the several results are added together to give an overall ignition angle to meet the given input information. A similar arrangement will be embodied for dwell. When the system is switched on, the micro-processor sends a digital address code which fixes which memory location is to be worked. Next comes a control signal which instructs how data is to move, whether in or out of the micro-processor, and when. Lastly, data in binary digital form is sent to and from the micro-processor. All these actions stem from memory which guides the micro-processor. The action within the micro-processor is a series in which data is fetched, then decoded and executed. The 'execute' operation is by memory instruction in which digital information may be used in arithmetic, logic or storage actions. Finally, the control unit will send out instruction signals to the ignition power stage

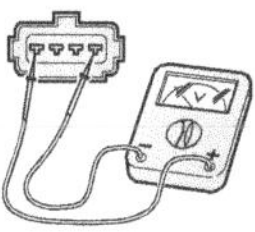

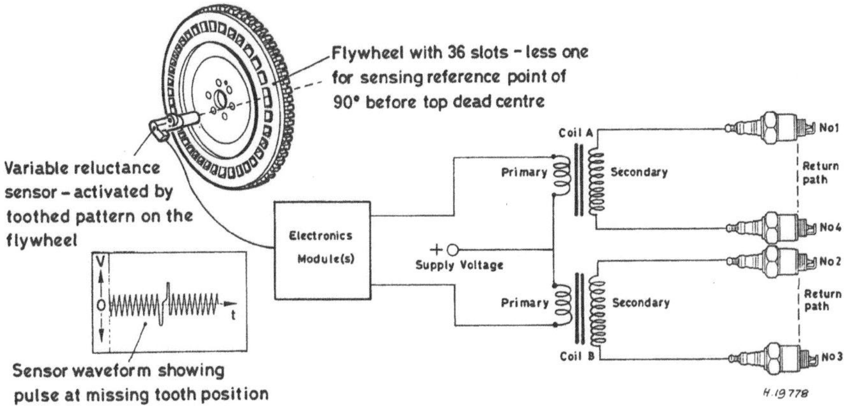


*Fig. 6.100 Distributorless ignition system (Ford)*

to switch ON and OFF the coil primary current so that dwell and spark timing meet the engine conditions. In a system which does not have knock sensing, the ECU will give an advance value which follows closely the contour of the ignition maps but with a margin (Fig. 6.92). This is good for an engine in perfect condition but cannot take into effect changes in performance with wear, fuel quality, etc – in other words, there is no feedback on the result of applying a given value of advance and dwell. With knock sensing, there is feedback which tells the ECU when the knock limit is reached and this then gives a closed-loop system. Later, the technology of exhaust control will be described and will give another quantity to the ECU – the pollution level. This forms another closed-loop control element.

## Distributorless ignition

**7** With the development of electronic ignition the first undesirable item to be replaced was the contact breaker followed by the elimination of the centrifugal advance mechanism. The distributor was left with the sole function of passing the spark in correct sequence to the plugs, but now this mechanical device can be replaced by an ignition coil with 4 HT outlets for a 4-cylinder engine. Ford use such a system on their HCS Valencia engines for the 1989 Escort/Orion range in which the distribution of HT is achieved by two dual-ended coils. This concept is not new since it has been used on Citroën 2CV and Visa engines but with the help of electronic ignition circuitry it has been applied here to four-cylinder engines. Each time a coil receives an ignition signal, two sparks are produced, one at either end of a secondary winding (Fig. 6.100). One spark goes to a cylinder on the compression stroke and the other to the corresponding cylinder on the exhaust stroke. The first will give the correct power stroke but the second spark produces no effect since it occurs during exhaust conditions. The Ford ignition gives a minimum 37.0 kilovolt output and this is more than adequate to fire two plugs in series. Note that the current will flow the correct way through one plug but the 'wrong' way through the other (Fig. 6.101), remembering that ideally the plug centre electrode should be negative so that erosion will take place from it and not the earthed electrode (see Section 13 of this Chapter). The firing order is 1-2-4-3 and standard spark plugs are used, but should be discarded at normal service intervals of 12 000 miles (20 000 km). The primary windings have a resistance of 0.5 ± 0.05 ohm and the secondary windings 11 to 16 kilohms. Micro-processor control calculates the required spark advance from all module inputs which include inlet manifold pressure, engine speed, crank position and coolant temperature. It then signals the coil drive circuit to turn off the coil current to generate the spark at the correct time for one pair of cylinders simultaneously. Should the micro-processor fail, the system switches automatically to a fixed 10° BTDC which enables the vehicle to continue working

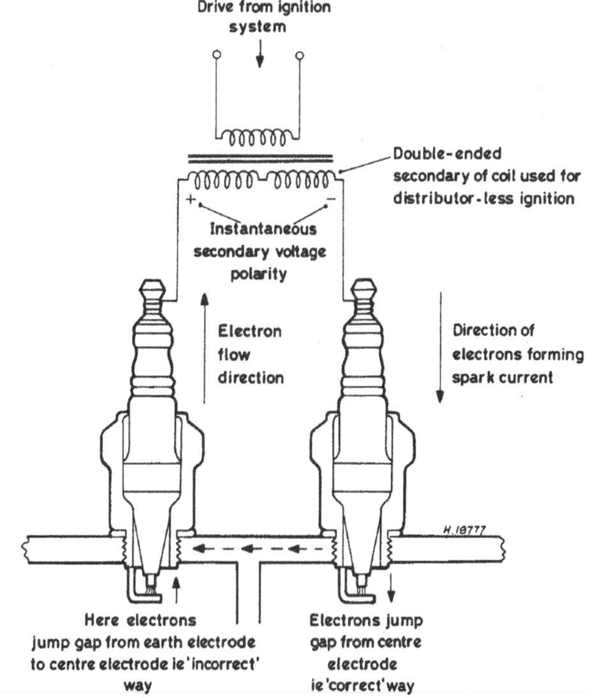


*Fig. 6.101 Plug current flow in distributorless ignition system*

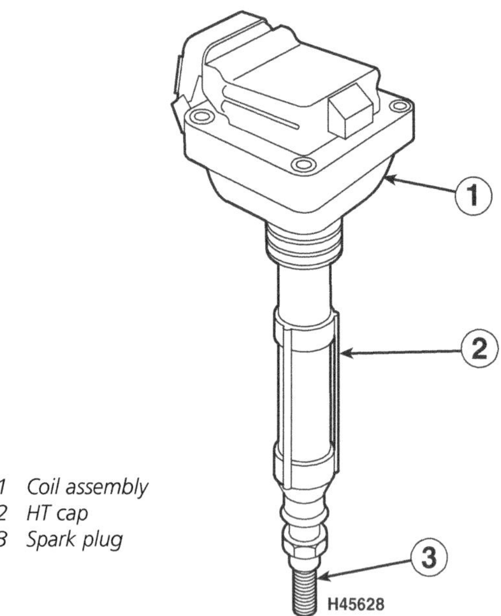


1 Coil assembly
2 HT cap
3 Spark plug

***Fig. 6.102a Single spark coil-per-plug***

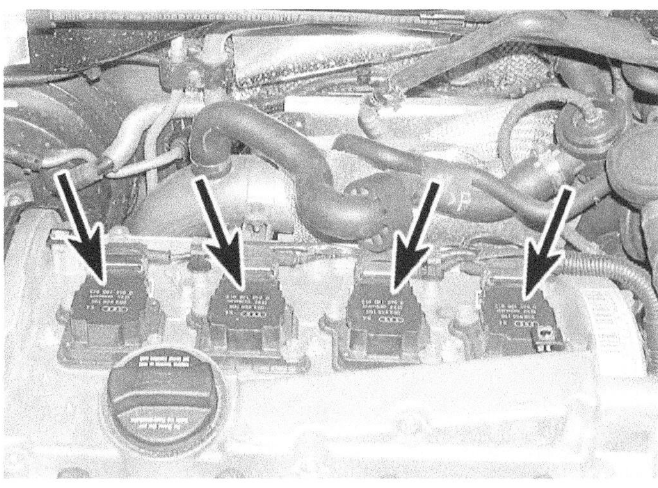

***Fig. 6.102b Ignition coils (arrowed) mounted directly over the spark plugs***

until it can be serviced. To meet new EC emission levels the 1.3 HC 2V Valencia engine also has a thermistor sensor mounted in the air cleaner (clean air side) to register air charge temperature. At high load with either high air charge temperature or high coolant temperature the electronics module retards spark timing to avoid knock. The amount of retard is calculated from the stored map of engine speed, load and the actual temperature as measured by the appropriate sensor.

## Coil per plug ignition

**8** In order to increase control over the combustion ignition function, reduce exhaust emissions, decrease fuel consumption and increase performance, recent vehicles have been fitted with a system where a single spark coil is used for each spark plug (Fig. 6.102a and 6.102b).

This system allows the engine management ECU to control the timing and duration of the ignition spark for each cylinder on each power stroke, based on information from the knock sensor, crankshaft position sensor, air mass flow sensor, throttle position sensor and the coolant temperature sensor. The output stage and ignition coil are combined in one unit normally fitted directly above the relevant spark plug at the top of the camshaft cover. This arrangement eliminates the use of secondary HT leads as the HT cap extends from the base of the coil assembly and fits directly onto the spark plug.

On some systems, the coils are manufactured as an assembly and mounted away from the spark plugs, utilising traditional HT leads (Fig. 6.103), or as assembly mounted above the spark plugs (Fig. 6.104).

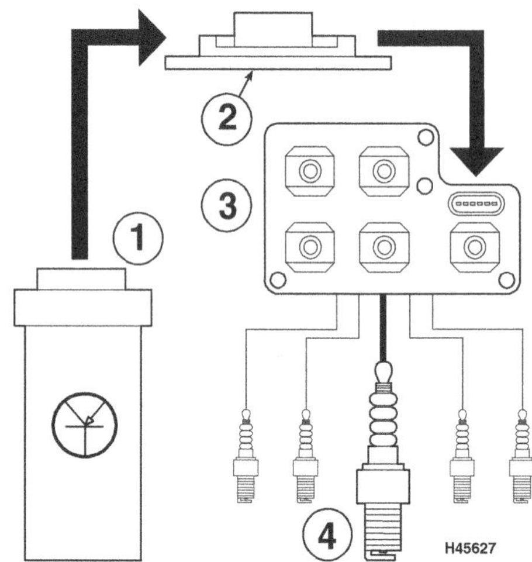


***Fig. 6.103 Coil-per-plug system layout – VW VR5 engine***

1 Engine management ECU
2 Output stage amplifier
3 Ignition coil assembly
4 Spark plugs

***Fig. 6.104 The ignition module assembly fitted to a Vauxhall Z22SE engine***

# Fuelling

# 7



## 1 Fuel metering

**1** The petrol engine normally requires a supply of fuel in the form of a vapour of air and petrol in a ratio within the range 12:1 to 17:1, the first being a rich mixture and the second a weak or lean mixture. From the beginning of automobile technology this has been achieved, not always with precision, by the carburettor. Now anti-pollution regulations require exact metering of fuel, particularly where catalytic converters are used.

**2** Although the carburettor has been available with electronic controls to improve precision of fuel metering, the alternative of fuel injection is now almost universally employed.

Principal advantages of fuel injection are:

*(a) Increased power output per unit of displacement*
*(b) Higher torque at low engine speeds*
*(c) Improved cold start, warm-up and acceleration*
*(d) Lower pollution levels from the exhaust*
*(e) Lower fuel consumption*

The disadvantages of carburettors are:

*(a) Volumetric efficiency is limited by the venturi constriction and fuel mixture pre-heating requirement. NB volumetric efficiency is the ratio:*
*Volume of mixture actually taken in:Swept volume*
*and is about 70% using conventional carburation.*

*(b) It is virtually impossible to distribute the mixture evenly between cylinders. One result is the use of a richer mixture than might otherwise be required so that the cylinder(s) receiving the weakest mixture do not suffer from detonation.*

*(c) In cold conditions, fuel wets the walls of the induction manifold causing running difficulties.*

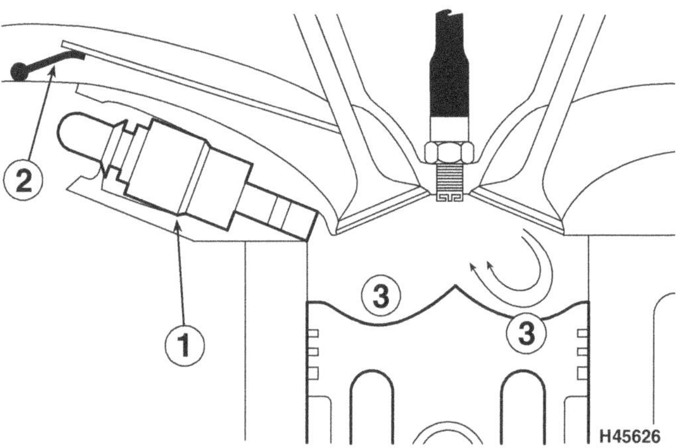


*Fig. 7.1a* ***Direct petrol injection***
*1 High-pressure injector*
*2 Intake manifold flap change-over mechanism*
*3 Piston crown recesses*

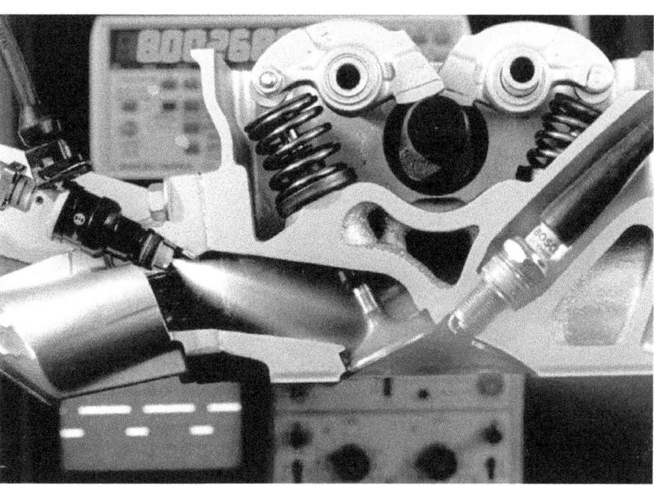

*Fig. 7.1b* ***Indirect petrol injection***
*Bosch press photo*

## 2 Petrol fuel injection

**1** There are several ways in which fuel may be injected; the first consideration is whether injection should be directly into each cylinder (direct injection) (Fig. 7.1a) or into the airstream before entering the cylinder via the inlet valve(s) (indirect injection) (Fig. 7.1b).

**Direct injection** has been recently introduced to by car manufactures. Fuel is injected directly into the combustion chamber at high pressure by an engine driven pump, and the sequential injection pulses are synchronised with the engine cycle. The result is much lower exhaust emissions, lower fuel consumption and improved performance - see Section 14.

**Indirect injection** in which the fuel is sprayed at one or more points in the air intake system operates at lower pressures, and the injectors can be triggered either simultaneously, or sequentially with engine-cycle synchronisation.

**2** There are two types of indirect injection:

**Continuous Injection.** Fuel is sprayed continuously while the engine is running, the quantity of fuel being governed by changes in the fuel pressure. However, the ratio of idle to full load fuel consumption can be 1:60 with high accuracy at the low end being required. Exhaust emissions and economy are only marginally better than using carburettors.

**Intermittent injection.** Fuel is sprayed at regular intervals at constant pressure (see later). The quantity of fuel is determined by the length of spraying time. These spraying pulses may take place EITHER without regard to the opening of the inlet valves (simultaneous) OR being correctly phased in relation to the opening of the inlet valve (sequential).

**3** Finally, designers had the choice to make between the use of only one injector per engine (single point injection) or one injector for each cylinder (multiple point injection) (Fig. 7.2).

**4** The single point injector valve is located above the throttle

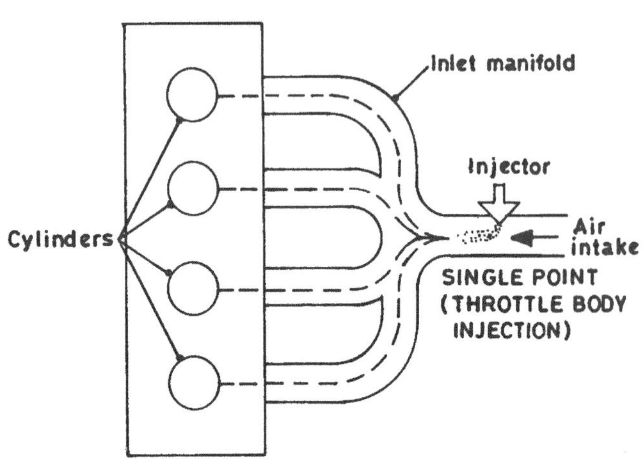


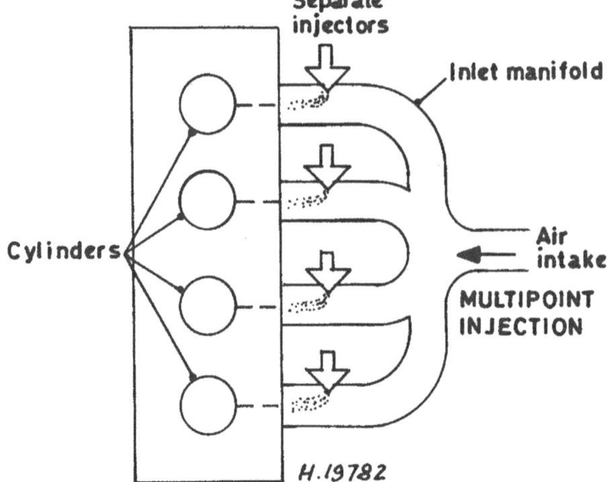


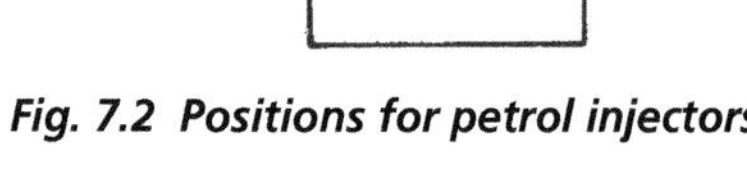

*Fig. 7.2* ***Positions for petrol injectors***

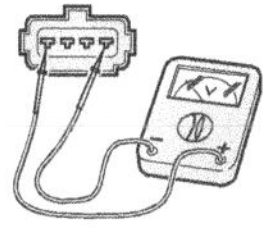



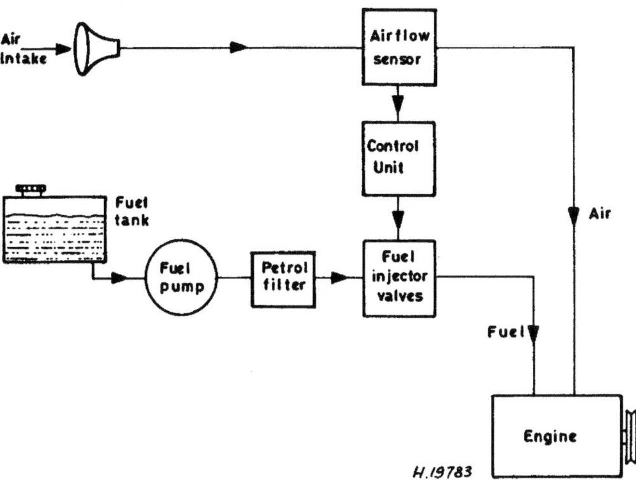


*Fig. 7.3 Principle of fuel injection*

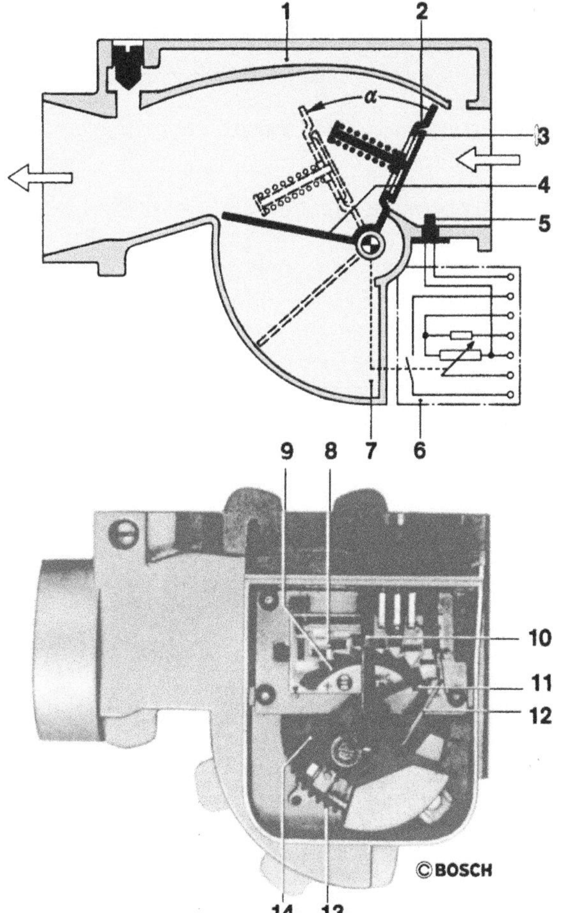


***Fig. 7.4 Air flow sensor (air flap type)***

*1 Bypass*
*2 Airflow sensor flap*
*3 Non-return valve*
*4 Compensation flap*
*5 Temperature sensor*
*6 Potentiometer circuit*
*7 Damping chamber*
*8 Ceramic substrate with resistors R0 . . . R10 and conductor straps*
*9 Wiper track*
*10 Wiper tap*
*11 Wiper*
*12 Safety switch for the fuel pump. Off position at a = 0°*
*13 Ring gear for spring preloading*
*14 Return spring*

valve and is a relatively low-cost system. Because the injector is so located it is sometimes known as throttle-body injection (TBI). Multiple point injection is in use in the majority of systems, particularly where the extra cost is not an overriding consideration. Whichever method is used, the basic principle is illustrated in Fig. 7.3.

## 3 Flap sensor air metering

**1** In order that the electronic control system can provide the correct amount of fuel it is necessary to measure the amount of air taken by the engine. The airflow (flap) sensor in use for some years is shown in Fig. 7.4. It is located in the air intake and the flap (2) will rotate due to airflow against a spring return. It is balanced by a similar flap in a damping chamber which not only balances the main flap but damps out any tendency to oscillate. On the flap spindle outside the airflow chamber is an arm with a wiping contact on a resistor potentiometer (Fig. 7.5). The voltage picked up by this wiping contact corresponds to the angle of the flap and this in turn measures the airflow. The signal voltage is fed into the electronic control unit along with signals from other sensors to determine the fuel injection. The potentiometer is made up of a series of resistors R0 to R10 and are ceramic-metal (cermet) connected by narrow conductors to the wiper track which is of high impedance and hard wearing. Signal voltage is high as the air quantity Q goes down resulting in the graph shown in Fig. 7.5.

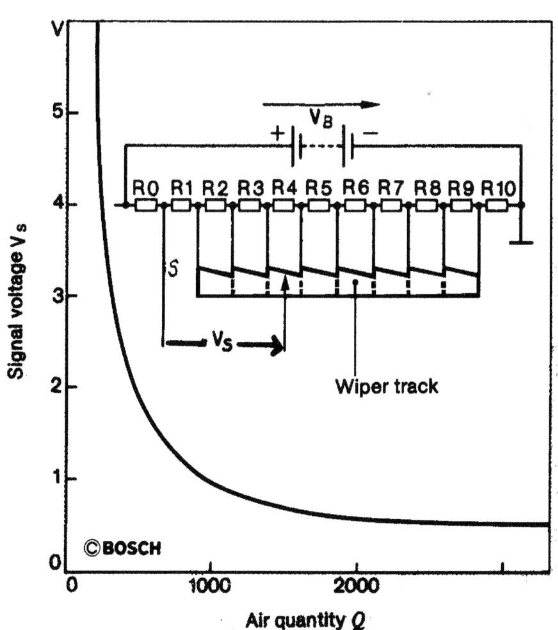


***Fig. 7.5 Air flow meter output characteristic***

*Potentiometer circuit and voltage characteristic of the airflow sensor*
*The characteristic is a hyperbola since Vs ª 1/Q*
*S Conductor straps*
*$V_B$ Supply voltage*
*Vs Tapping point voltage*

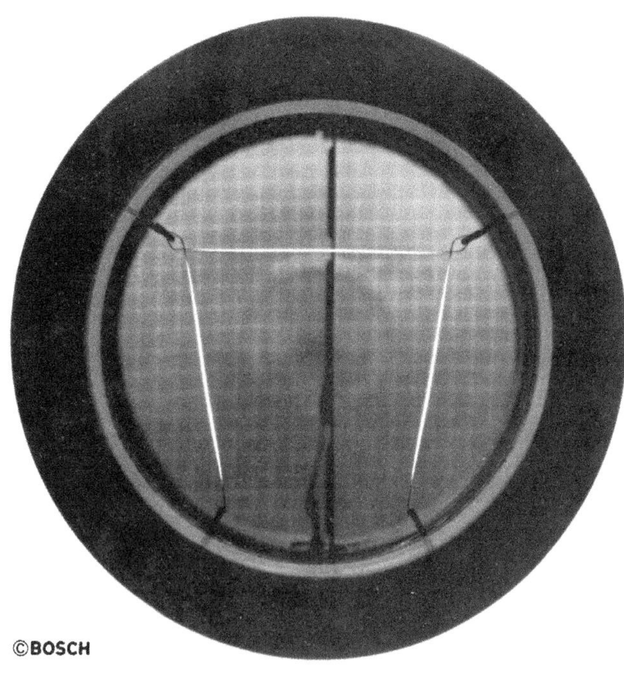


*Fig. 7.6 Hot wire air mass flow meter*

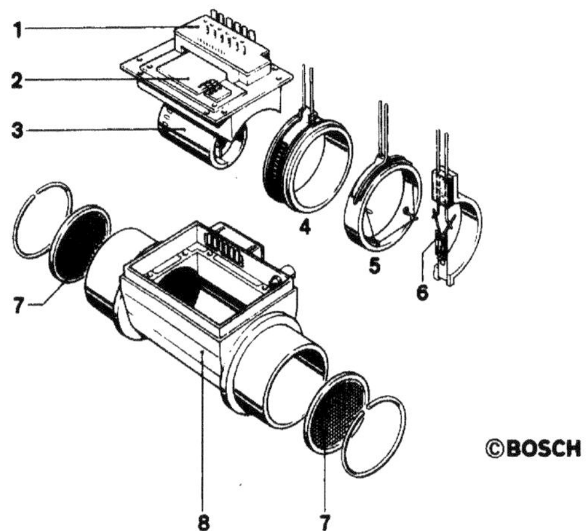


*Fig. 7.7 Hot wire air mass flow meter assembly*

1 *Printed board*
2 *Hybrid circuit. In addition to the resistors of the bridge circuit, it also contains the control circuit for maintaining a constant temperature and the self-cleaning circuit*
3 *Inner tube*
4 *Precision resistor*
5 *Hot wire element*
6 *Temperature compensation resistor*
7 *Guard*
8 *Housing*

**2** The airflap sensor is simple and reliable but suffers from the disadvantage that it measures the volume of intake air. Air to fuel ratios are in terms of mass (weight) and the flap meter readings will require correction for air density. An air temperature sensor is mounted at the air intake to the flap sensor, the signal being processed by the electronic control unit (ECU).

**3** The flap is bypassed by a channel for idle air and an adjusting screw partially closes an orifice to regulate the idle mixture (Fig. 7.4).

## 4 Hot wire air mass sensor

**1** The disadvantages of the airflap sensor lie in the fact that it measures volume of air intake, and what is really needed is the mass. Errors are introduced according to altitude (since the density of air will change) and, in addition, the airflap sensor is subject to slight pulsation errors arising from the sudden opening and closing of inlet valves. (Remembering: Mass = Volume x Density.)

**2** A solution lies in the hot wire air mass meter which will measure the air mass directly, independent of air density changes. In addition, there is no pulsation error (Figs. 7.6 and 7.7). In this type of sensor, a heated wire of 70µm diameter is mounted in a measuring tube placed in the incoming airstream before the throttle valve.

**3** The hot wire air mass meter works on the constant temperature principle. The hot platinum wire, located in the incoming airstream, is one arm of a Wheatstone Bridge and the bridge is kept in balance by changing the heating current so that the temperature (around 100°C) of the hot wire is a constant amount above that of the incoming air (Fig. 7.8a). As airflow increases, the wire cools and the resistance falls. This unbalances the bridge, the difference voltage at A and B being fed into an amplifier, the output of which supplies the bridge, so heating up the wire and increasing its resistance again until balance is restored. The range of heating current is from 500 mA to 1200 mA. The increase of current will also flow through the precision resistor $R_3$ and the voltage so developed acts as a signal to the ECU in calculation of the fuel to be injected.

**4** Air temperature changes are compensated by $R_c$ which is a platinum film resistor located in the airstream but with a high resistance of about 500 ohms. Variations in air

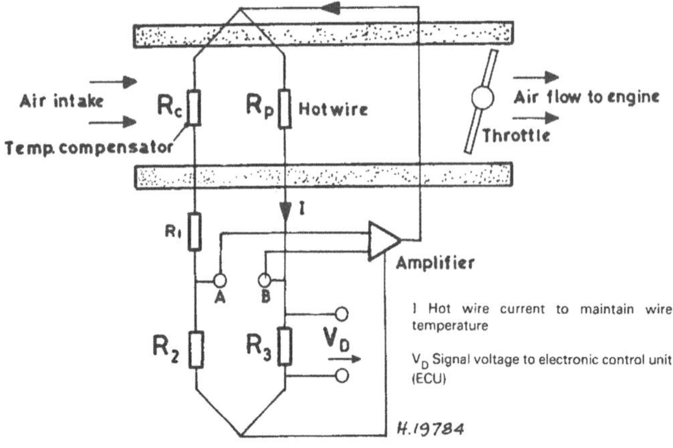


*Fig. 7.8a Hot wire air mass meter electrical circuit*

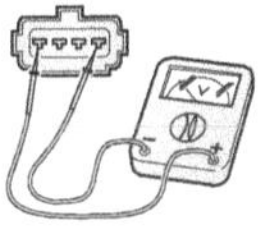



temperature will affect $R_c$ and the hot wire simultaneously, so compensating for air temperature changes.

**5** As the meter is used, the hot wire will become dirty and to avoid this the wire is heated to incandescence (about 1000°C) for one second when the engine is switched off. This burns off any dirt on the hot wire, the burn-off current being controlled by the electronic control unit.

**6** Lucas EFI and Bosch LH Jetronic systems use the hot wire air mass sensor.

## 5 Hot film air mass sensor

**1** In common use is the Bosch developed hot film air mass flow sensor in which a heated film, together with temperature compensator and precision measurement resistors are located on a ceramic substance as thick-film components (Fig. 7.8b). The unit is more robust and accurate than the hot wire sensor and of lower manufacturing cost.

The principle of operation is very similar to the hot wire sensor, but instead of a wire element being placed in the airflow, a 'thin film' element is used. The film is heated to a constant temperature by the sensor control electronics, and the current needed to maintain this temperature is proportional to the mass of air flowing over it. By measuring this current the sensor can produce a signal for the ECM proportional to the air mass.

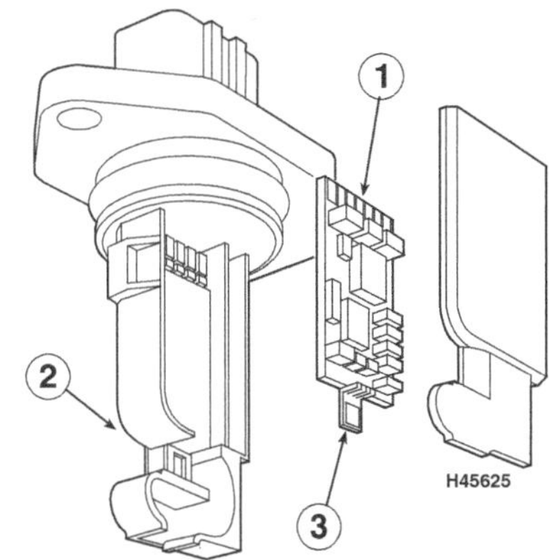


***Fig. 7.8b Hot film air mass sensor***
*1 Evaluation electronics 2 Measuring channel 3 Sensor element*

***Fig. 7.8c Pressure sensor for air mass flow measurement (thick-film air pressure sensor)***
*Bosch press photo*

## 6 Thick-film pressure sensor

**1** This airflow sensor is a pressure device which uses a bubble encased by thick-film diaphragm and mounted on a ceramic substrate. The strain measuring elements are bonded into the thick-film and expansion of the bubble will be a measure of the vacuum in the inlet manifold. The active electronic components are bonded in as shown in Figs. 7.8c and d. The bubble is fitted in the intake where it will be a pressure/vacuum sensor with rapid response.

**2** Other types of sensor have been used to measure air mass flow but have largely given way to either airflap or hot wire/film units. Alternatives include the pressure sensor, usually an aneroid capsule to measure manifold depression; another being the vortex airflow sensor in which air passing through a channel passes over a triangular strut and generates vortices behind the strut. The frequency of these vortices is nearly proportional to the air velocity and so air mass flow may be indirectly measured. The vortex frequency is measured by the use of an ultrasonic generator, the signals of which are changed or modulated by the vortices. A receiver picks up the generated wave passing through the channel and after processing this gives the vortex frequency.

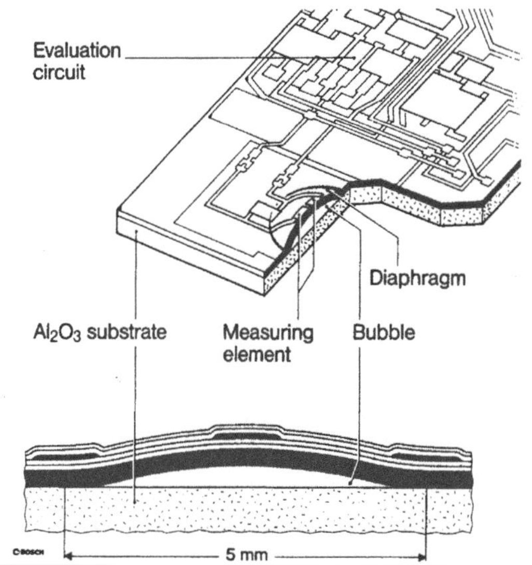


***Fig. 7.8d Pressure sensor for air mass flow measurement***
*Bosch press photo*

# Chapter 7

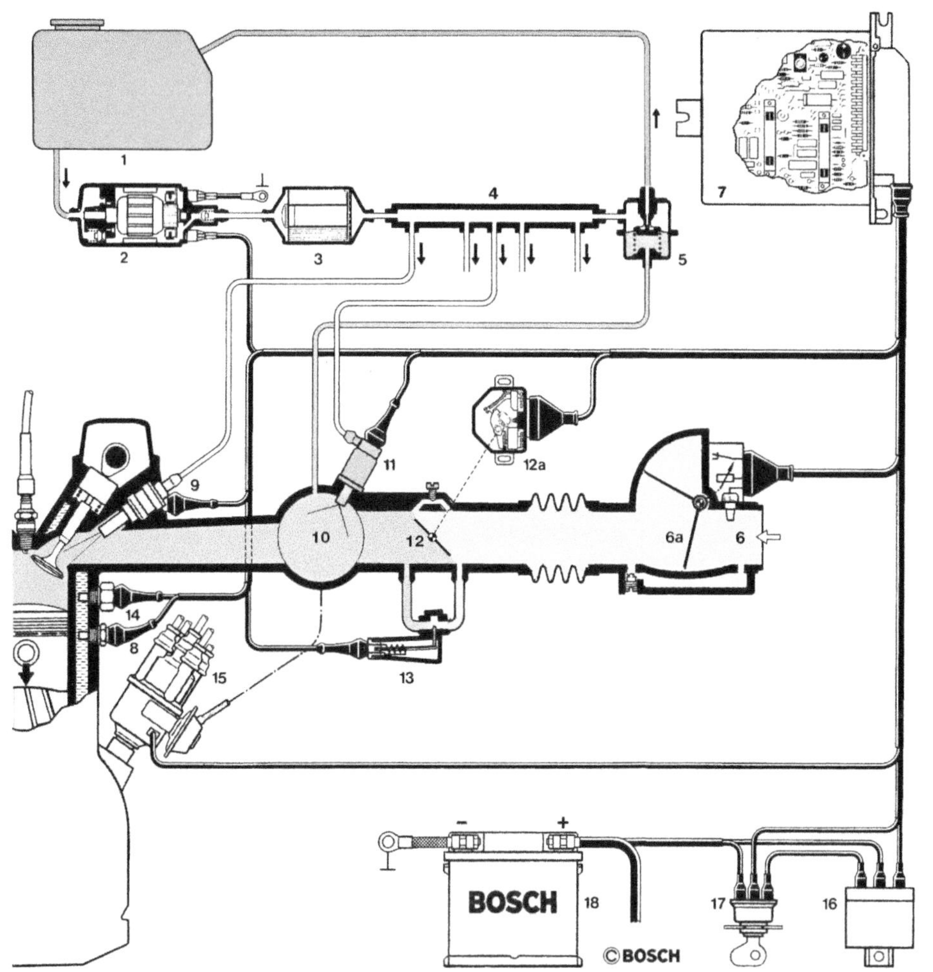


*Pressures and components of the L-Jetronic*

- *System pressure*
- *Suction line or return line*
- *Atmospheric pressure*
- *Intake manifold pressure*

*1 Fuel tank*
*2 Electric fuel pump*
*3 Fine-mesh filter*
*4 Distribution pipe*
*5 Pressure regulator*
*6 Air-flow sensor with flap (6a)*
*7 Control unit*
*8 Temperature sensor*
*9 Injection valve*
*10 Intake manifold*
*11 Cold-start valve*
*12 Throttle valve with switch (12a)*
*13 Auxiliary air valve*
*14 Thermo time switch*
*15 Ignition distributor*
*16 Relay set*
*17 Ignition starting switch*
*18 Battery*

***Fig. 7.9 Bosch L Jetronic system***

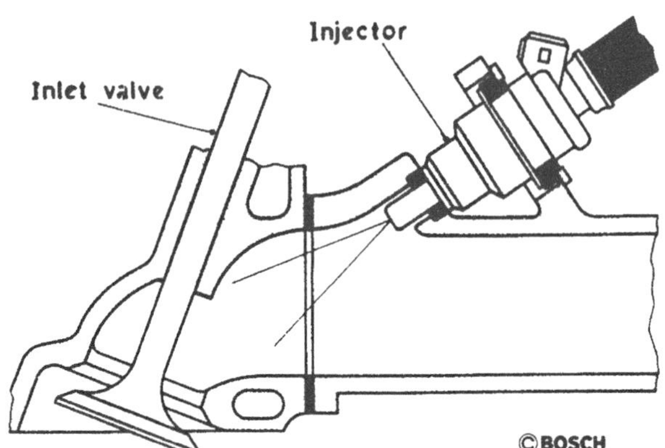


***Fig. 7.10 Multipoint indirect petrol injection***

## 7 Multipoint electronic fuel injection system

**1** The Bosch L Jetronic is taken as a model here to explain the principles of intermittent, multipoint fuel injection. Fig. 7.9 shows a layout which includes airflap metering and ignition pulses, received from a distributor, as a timing signal.

**2** Closely related to L Jetronic is the LH Jetronic system in which air metering is by hot wire sensor.

**3** Looking again at the principle of L Jetronic with the aid of a block diagram (Fig. 7.3) two inputs, fuel and air, arrive at the engine so combined to give the required air:fuel ratio for all conditions and that the timing and length of fuel pulses are correct. Multipoint injection requires an injector valve for each cylinder, being located behind the inlet valve. When the valve opens the cloud of fuel is drawn along with the incoming air and an ignitable mixture formed by swirling action (Fig. 7.10).

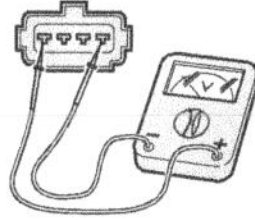

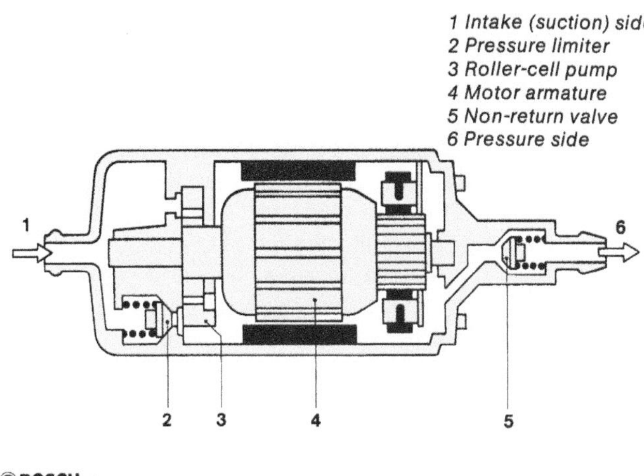


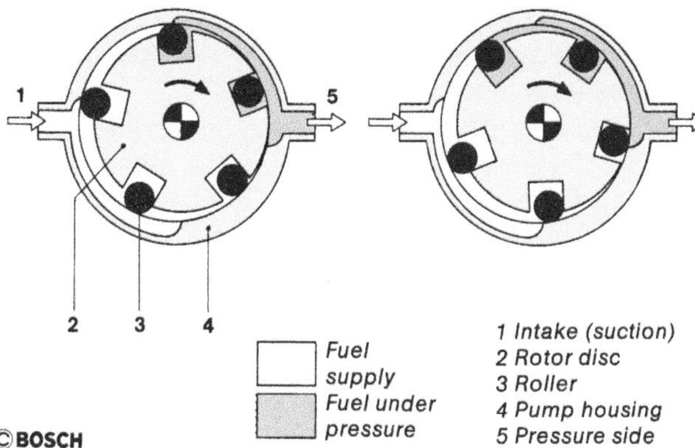


***Fig. 7.11 Roller cell fuel pump***

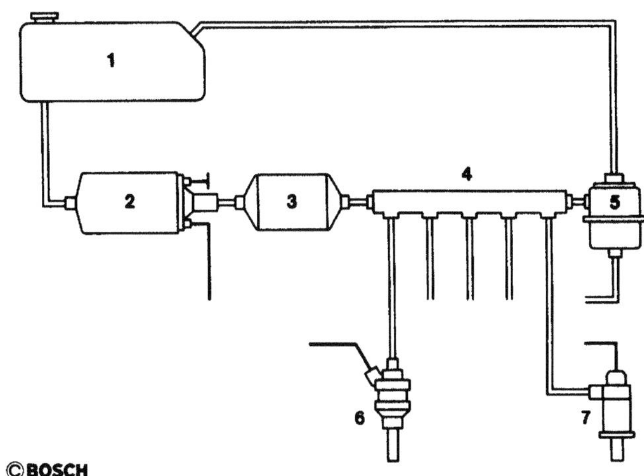


***Fig. 7.12 Diagrammatic layout of fuel injection system (Bosch L Jetronic)***

*1 Fuel tank*
*2 Fuel pump*
*3 Fuel filter*
*4 Distributor pipe*
*5 Pressure regulator*
*6 Fuel injection valve*
*7 Start valve*

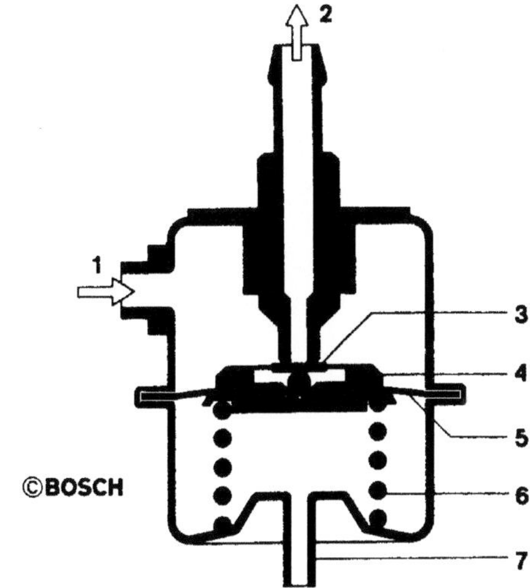


***Fig. 7.13 Pressure regulator***

*1 Fuel connection*
*2 Fuel return connection*
*3 Valve plate*
*4 Valve holder*
*5 Diaphragm*
*6 Compression spring*
*7 Vacuum connection*

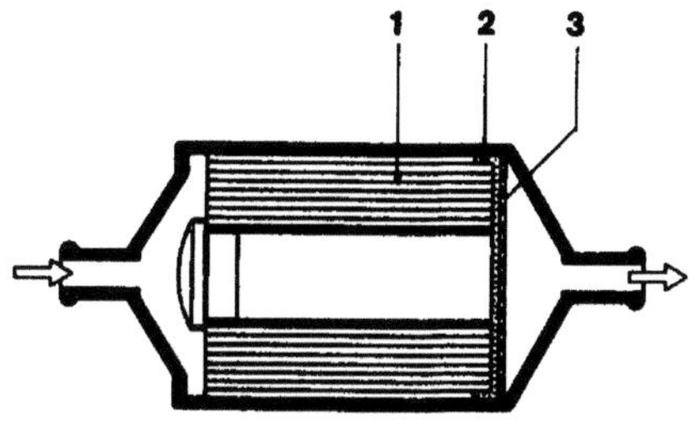


***Fig. 7.14 Fuel filter***

*1 Paper filter*
*2 Strainer*
*3 Support plate*

## Operation

**4 The fuel** is pumped by a roller-cell pump (Figs. 7.11 and 7.12) at a pressure of 2.5 bar (36 lbf/in$^2$) through a filter into a distribution pipe at the end of which is a pressure regulator which keeps the injector pressure at a constant differential level. The spring chamber of the pressure regulator (Fig. 7.13) is connected by a fuel line to the intake manifold past the throttle valve. It picks up the manifold depression and results in the pressure to the injectors (Fig. 7.14) being at a constant value ABOVE that of the inlet manifold, normally 0.5 bar. More fuel is pumped than is needed and when the pressure reaches the set level the pressure regulator sends excess fuel back to the petrol tank. This flushing through continuously keeps the fuel cool and avoids the formation of pockets of fuel vapour. Filtering of the fuel is important in case dirty petrol gets into the tank. The filter has a 10 μm pore size paper cartridge, the whole filter requiring replacement at 25 000 to 60 000 miles depending on filter size (Fig. 7.14). The distribution pipe is otherwise

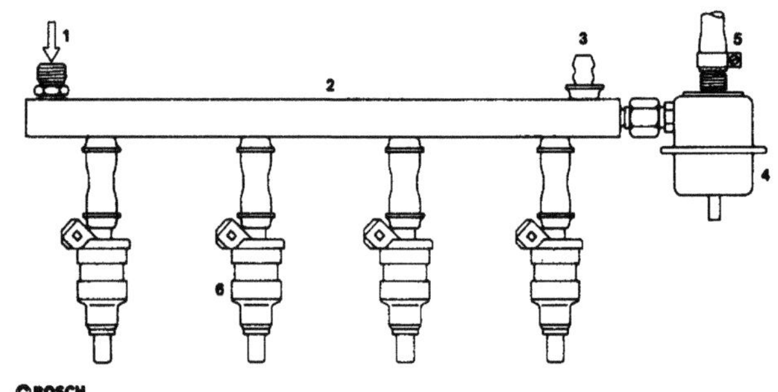


*Fig. 7.15 Fuel rail*

*1 Fuel inlet*
*2 Fuel rail*
*3 Connection for start valve*
*4 Pressure regulator*
*5 Return line*
*6 Injection valves*

known as a fuel rail from which fuel to the injectors is tapped (Fig. 7.15).

**5 Fuel injection valves** (Fig. 7.16) are solenoid operated, one for each cylinder, and are opened and closed by power pulses from the control unit. With no current in the winding, the needle valve is held against its seat by a spring. When the solenoid is energised the needle valve is lifted by 0.1 mm and fuel sprays out through an orifice. A ground pintle at the front end of the needle valve serves to atomize the fuel into a fine spray. The pull-on and release times of the valve are between 1.0 and 1.5 millisecond, and will stay open, according to signals from the ECU, for 1.5 to 10 milliseconds approx. The valves are held in rubber mountings as heat insulators to avoid fuel vapour bubbles and to assist in good hot-starting.

**6 Cold starting**. Corresponding to the use of a choke in a carburettor system, fuel injection provides for extra fuel at cold starting. Cold start enrichment is timed by the thermotime switch (Figs. 7.9 and 7.17) sensing the coolant temperature, and consists of a bimetal switch which opens or closes a contact according to temperature. The switch has a built-in heater so that the switch will operate eventually (8 seconds at –20°C) to limit the time of enrichment and prevent flooding. While the time-switch is on, a start valve (II) located in the inlet manifold sprays extra fuel to provide enrichment (Figs. 7.9 and 7.18). Later versions do not use a separate start valve but instead lengthen the period of main injector operation.

**7 Warm-up.** After starting, fuel enrichment is still necessary to overcome fuel condensing on the cold cylinder walls. After-start enrichment varies with time but in the first 30 seconds between 30% and 60% more fuel is needed (Fig. 7.19). The control procedure is determined by the engine temperature and this is measured by a temperature sensor which is screwed into the block and exposed to coolant. This sensor is a resistor with a negative temperature coefficient of resistance.

**8 Idle speed control**. To overcome cold friction effects an auxiliary air device admits more air into the engine to go with the extra fuel of cold enrichment. This device is a bimetal strip which will bend so as to gradually open or close an air bypass round the throttle valve (Fig. 7.20). While it is located so as to sense temperature, it also has its own heater to limit the time of operation.

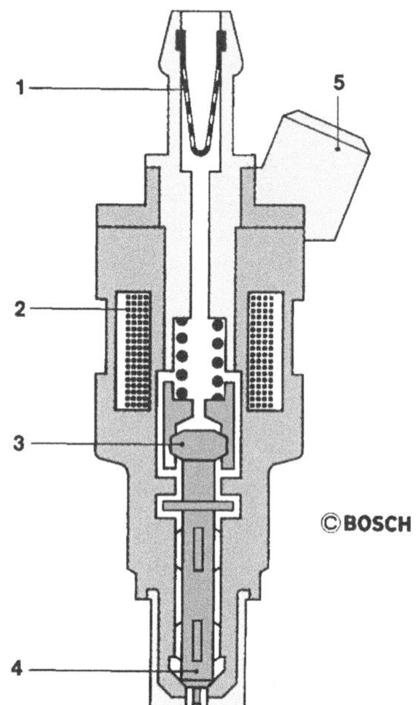


***Fig. 7.16 Injection valve***

*1 Filter*
*2 Solenoid winding*
*3 Solenoid armature*
*4 Needle valve*
*5 Electrical connection*

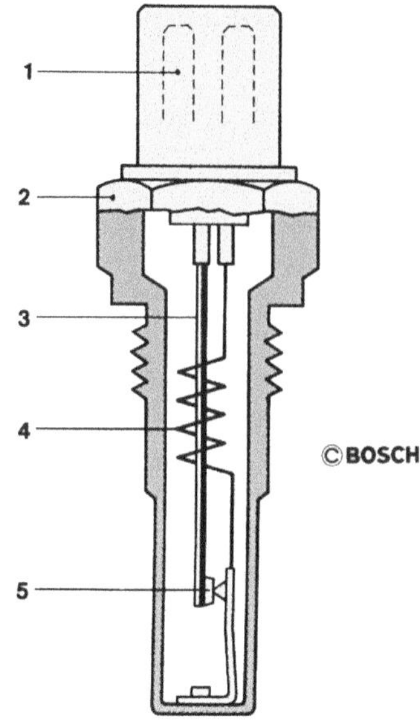


***Fig. 7.17 Thermotime switch***

*1 Electrical connection*
*2 Housing*
*3 Bimetal strip*
*4 Heating winding*
*5 Switch contact*

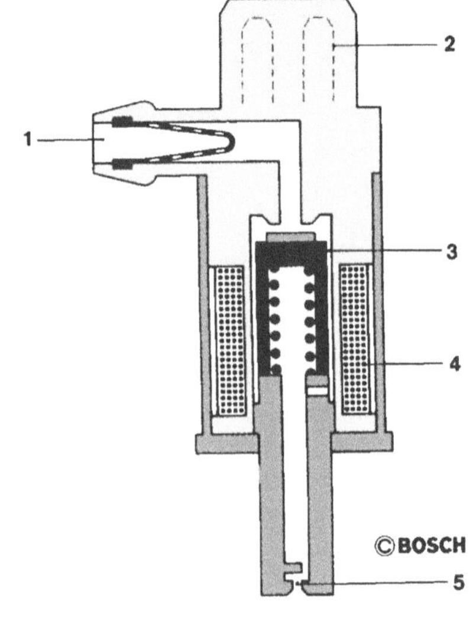


***Fig. 7.18 Start valve***

*1 Fuel inlet*
*2 Electrical connection*
*3 Solenoid armature*
*4 Solenoid winding*
*5 Swirl nozzle*

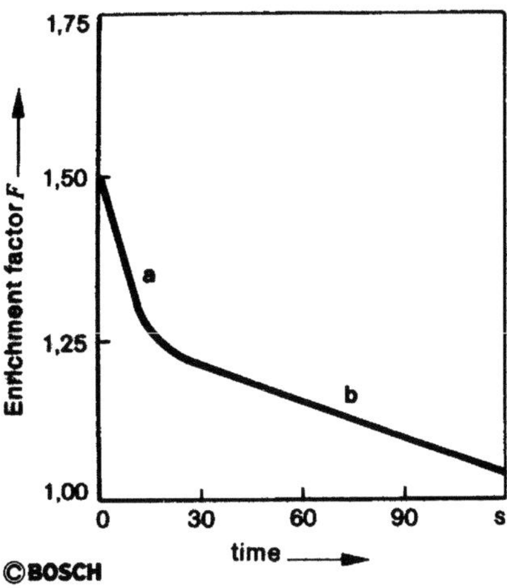


*Fig. 7.19* ***Warm-up enrichment curve***
*Enrichment factor as a function of time, 'a' proportion mainly dependent on time, 'b' proportion mainly dependent on engine temperature*

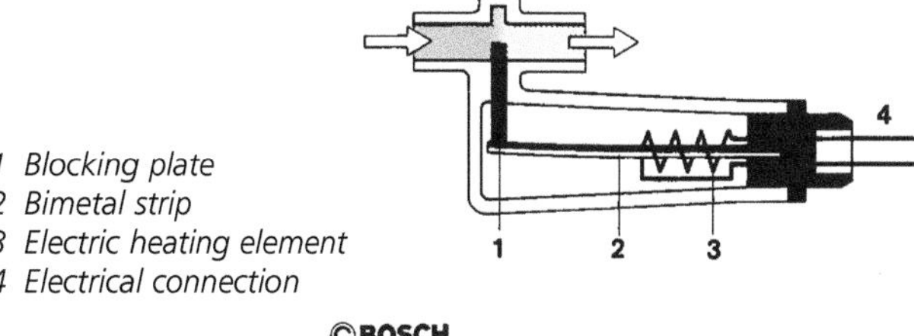


1 *Blocking plate*
2 *Bimetal strip*
3 *Electric heating element*
4 *Electrical connection*

*Fig. 7.20* ***Auxiliary air device***

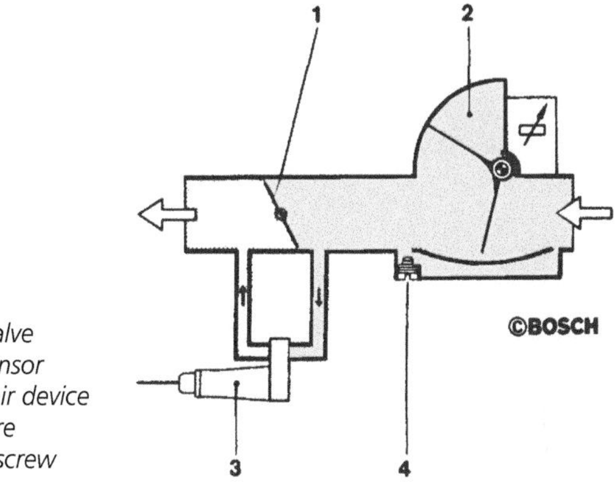


1 *Throttle valve*
2 *Airflow sensor*
3 *Auxiliary air device*
4 *Idle mixture adjusting screw*

*Fig. 7.21* ***Idle speed control***

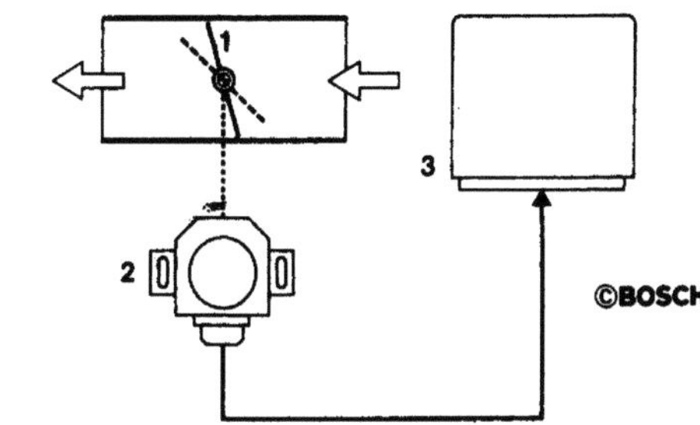


1 *Throttle valve*
2 *Throttle valve switch*
3 *Control unit*

*Fig. 7.22* ***Idle/full load correction***

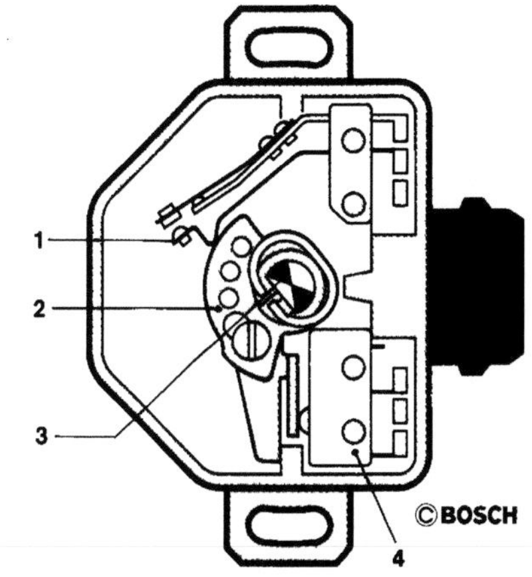


1 *Full load contact*
2 *Contact path*
3 *Throttle valve shaft*
4 *Idle contact*

*Fig. 7.23* ***Throttle valve switch***

## Load adaptations

**9** If the air:fuel mixture is too weak when idling this can result in misfiring. If necessary, therefore, the mixture should be enriched for this operating condition. An adjustable bypass is provided in the airflow sensor for adjusting the mixture (Fig. 7.21). In the case of a control system using the hot wire sensor, the ECU will set the air:fuel ratio to give efficient idle tickover.

**Part load.** For most of the running time the engine will be on part load. The fuel requirement is programmed in the ECU and is designed to give a low fuel consumption on part load.

**Full load.** To achieve maximum output the engine must have a richer mixture than that of part load. To signal to the ECU that full load enrichment is required, a contact is closed in the throttle valve switch unit (Figs. 7.22 and 7.23).

**Acceleration.** Extra fuel must be injected during acceleration. When the accelerator pedal is pressed down, the throttle opens and the flap on the air sensor swings open. It will overshoot briefly and this action will increase the metered fuel giving a good transitional response in going from one roadspeed to a higher. When the engine is still warming up, this enrichment may be insufficient. The ECU will detect the RATE at which the throttle potentiometer deflects and make the necessary provision for extra fuel. Under deceleration the reverse process occurs, leading to a fuel weakening or over-run cut-off.

## Air temperature correction

**10** As explained in Section 3, paragraph 2 of this Chapter, the air flap airflow meter readings are subject to correction for temperature, but the hot wire/film air mass meter is not: airflap meters have an air temperature sensor mounted at the air inlet, the signal from which is taken to the ECU where a correction is calculated according to air temperature.

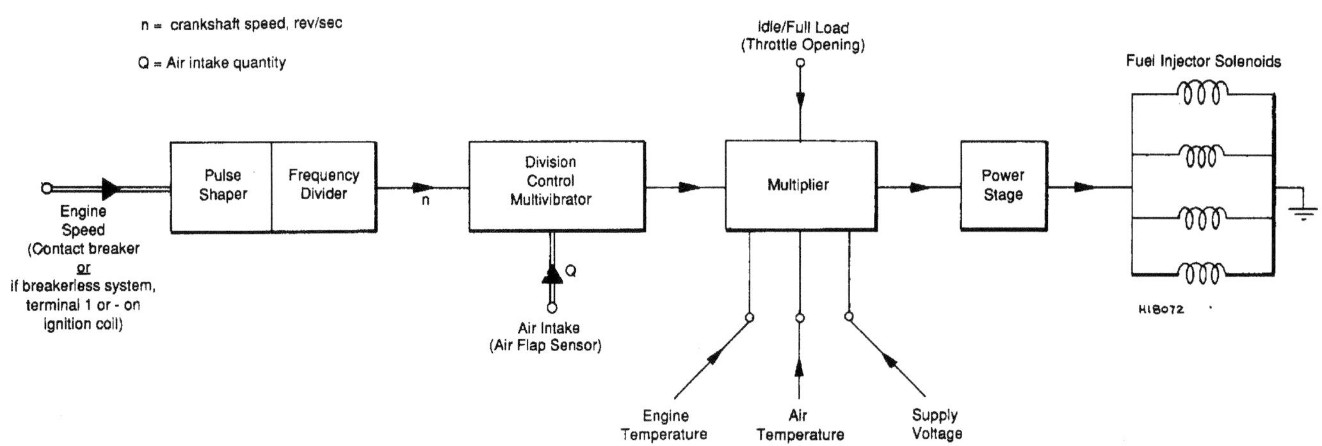


*Fig. 7.24 Operation of Electronic Control Unit (L Jetronic)*

## Other adaptations

**Overspeeding** of an engine is limited by the ECU. However, cutting ignition alone would pass unburned fuel into the exhaust. If a catalytic convertor were fitted in the exhaust system, this would lead to an expensive failure. Accordingly, the ECU cuts off fuel to the injector.

**Overrun** condition exists when the driver shuts off the accelerator pedal downhill and has the penalties of waste of fuel and bad exhaust emissions.

The ECU will shut off fuel given the following conditions (which are approximate and temperature dependent):

(a) *The throttle is shut off*
(b) *Engine speed is above 1200 rev/min*
(c) *Coolant temperature is above (about) 25°C. (This is adaptive however – a cold engine would have cut-off only at a higher engine speed.)*

When the engine overruns, the throttle valve is closed and a high vacuum is produced in the inlet manifold and thereby in the combustion chamber. The mixture is difficult to ignite. Combustion is incomplete and leads to emissions of unburned hydrocarbons and carbon monoxide. Cutting off the fuel will prevent this; if the engine speed falls below a set level or the idle contact in the throttle valve switch opens, fuel supply is resumed.

## 8 The Electronic Control Unit ECU

**1** The ECU is the central unit of the system and its purpose is to evaluate the sensor signals, and from them to make up control pulses for the fuel injector valves. The quantity of fuel delivered to the engine is determined by the length of time that the injectors are opened.

**2** In all, five sections make up the ECU using printed circuit boards and integrated circuits, while the output power stage components are mounted on the metal frame of the ECU to ensure good heat dissipation. Fig. 7.24 shows the block diagram layout.

**3** The circuit to be described arranges:

(a) *For each turn of the crankshaft each injector valve injects fuel once, irrespective of the position of the intake valves. If an intake valve is closed when the injector operates, the fuel is let in with air the next time the intake valve opens*
(b) *All injector valves to open and close simultaneously, semi-sequentially or sequentially depending on the system.*
(c) *That the duration of injection depends upon the quantity of air measured by the air sensor and the engine speed. This duration is subject to corrections for various engine and ambient conditions*

## Operation

*See Fig. 7.25 for time sequences*

**Line 2 – Ignition pulses**

The rotational speed of the engine is picked up from the contact breaker terminal of the distributor. the No 1 or minus terminal of the ignition coil if a breakerless system is in use or the crankshaft position (TDC) sensor. These ignition pulses show a sharp rising voltage spike which dies away in a damped oscillation. The number of pulses per second will be TWICE the number of crankshaft revolutions per second, remembering that the distributor runs at 1/2 x engine speed but has four breaker lobes (for a four-cylinder engine).

**Line 3 – Pulse shaping**

The low tension ignition spiky wave form is fed into a pulse shaping circuit to produce a flat-topped pulse of the same repetition frequency. This is a similar process used in electronic ignition systems. These pulses determine the timing of the fuel injection process.

**Line 4 – Frequency divider**

It is necessary to halve the repetition frequency of the pulses to produce one operation of the injectors for each turn of the crankshaft. This is achieved by the use of a bistable multivibrator which serves as a frequency divider so that one pulse appears at the output for every two at the input.

### Line 5 – Division control multivibrator

This part of the circuit takes in the speed data, namely the pulses from the frequency divider, together with data from the airflow sensor. The airflow sensor voltage is converted into a rectangular pulse wave, the time duration of which is proportional to the air intake volume Q divided by the crankshaft speed n. This gives a measure of the cylinder air intake per induction stroke. The quantity Q/n is calculated electrically by alternately charging and discharging a capacitor. Charging is carried out at a constant current for a time which is dependent (inversely) upon engine speed and discharged with a current which is dependent (again inversely) upon air quantity. The result of these calculations is a generated pulse which defines, from the start of the discharge, the duration of the injection period without any correction factor. This period $t_p$ is the basic duration of injection. The definition of the basic duration as calculated will ensure correct air:fuel ratio for all engine speeds and loads.

### Line 6 – Multiplier

The basic injection duration needs to be modified to meet special circumstances such as cold starting, warm-up, acceleration, etc. This modification is carried out in the multiplier stage which takes in information from temperature sensors, the throttle position and the start switch, and adjusts the injection duration pulse to suit. The same principle of charge and discharge of a capacitor is used in the multiplier, for the capacitor charge and discharge currents depend upon signals from the sensors supplying the multiplier with data. As an example, a low coolant temperature has a considerable influence on the discharge time and therefore upon the injection duration. The additional injection time to allow for these extra factors is added to the basic duration of injection, but one further effect must be taken into account before the precise result is obtained – this is the effect of variations in supply voltage which are also handled by the multiplier unit. Injector solenoids are inductive and will give rise to a delay in operating and releasing. These times are voltage dependent, particularly the operating time delay, and so the lower the battery voltage the shorter will be the time of injection. Battery voltage is fed in to the multiplier as a control parameter and variations about a standard will result in an extension of operating pulse time equal to the delay of the injector. Note that although the injectors will pull in later than the start of the driving current pulse, the time of operation is correct (Fig. 7.25) because of extra time Tu given to the injection period according to battery voltage. The detail of this compensation is shown in Fig. 7.26.

## Final stage (ballast resistor type)

The injector valves require considerably more power to operate than could be delivered by the multiplier stage.

A power amplifier stage takes in the multiplier signals and drives the injector valves all simultaneously, requiring the injectors to be connected in parallel. A current of the order of 6 A is

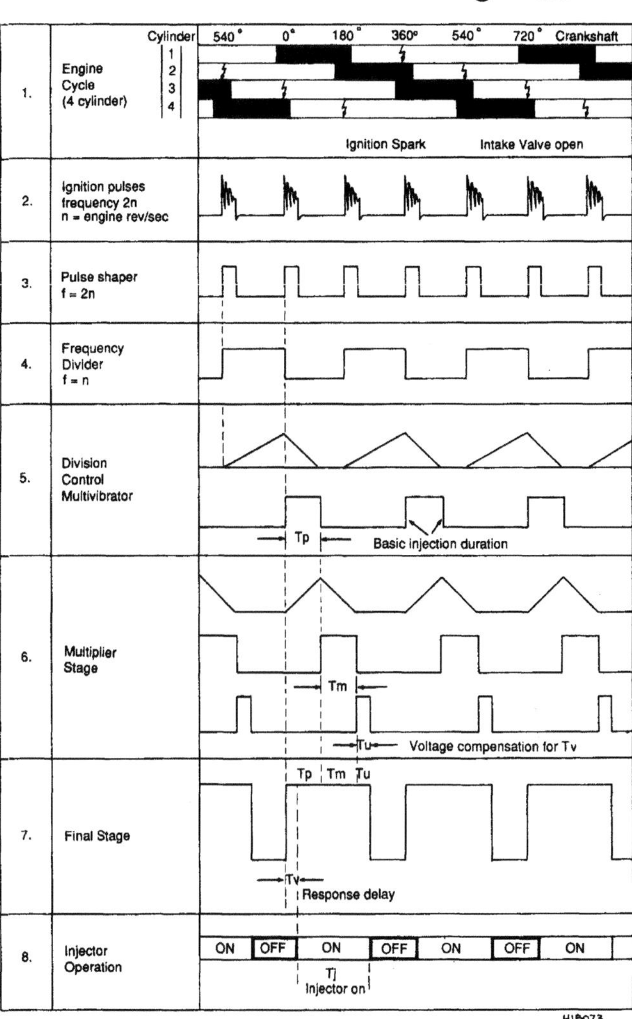


*Fig. 7.25 Time sequence for four-cylinder injection*

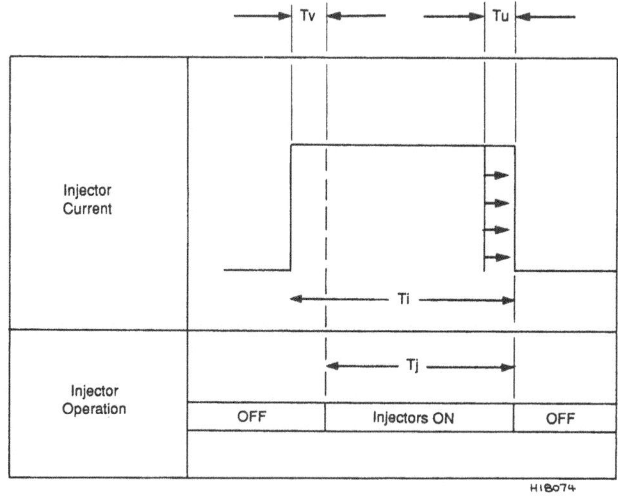


***Fig. 7.26 Voltage compensation for injectors***

*Tv Response delay in injector operation*
*Tu Compensation time (Tu = Tv)*
*Ti Pulse duration of injector current*
*Tj Duration of injection*

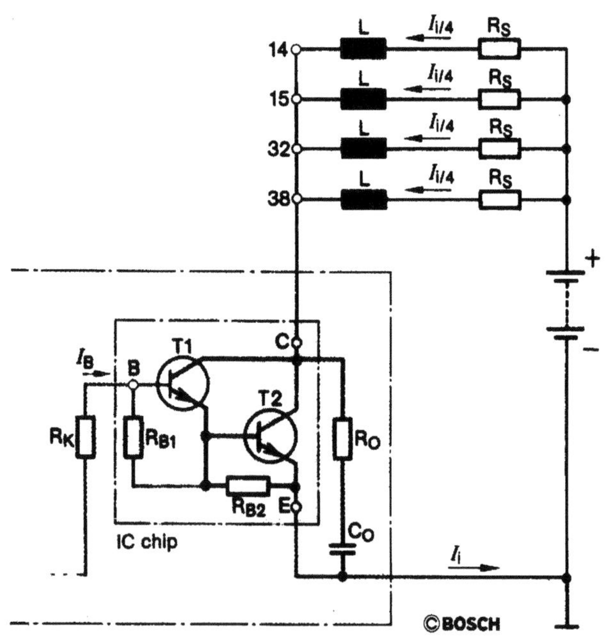


***Fig. 7.27 Final stage driving four injectors – ballast resistor current limiting***

*L Injector winding*
*I Current for four injectors (variable with time)*
*Rs Ballast resistor*
*T1, T2 Darlington pair power amplifier*

necessary to open four parallel valves rapidly. To do this a Darlington pair is located on one silicon chip, the pulses being applied to the input through a coupling resistor $R_K$ (Fig. 7.27).

*Base current* $I_B$ switches on transistors T1 and T2 simultaneously; T2 being the power transistor. Each injector winding has a series ballast resistor $R_s$ to limit the current to about 1.7 A from a 14 volt supply, which current can be estimated, neglecting the volt-drop across T2, from the resistance of each coil 2.4 ohms and the ballast resistors of 6 ohms each:

$$I\ max = \frac{14}{2.4+6} = 1.7\text{A per injector}$$

The components $R_o$ and $C_o$ give protection for the Darlington transistors against rapid-switching transient voltages. Control units for six-cylinder engines would use two final stages driving three injectors each and an eight-cylinder engine two final stages of four injectors each. The whole design provides one injection to each inlet valve for every crankshaft revolution, giving one half of the required petrol per complete cycle.

## Final stage (current regulated type)

Power is lost in each ballast resistor in the circuit of Fig. 7.27. In order to avoid this loss and to run the injector on a low hold-in current once they have operated, a current regulator circuit is usually employed (Fig. 7.28). The current regulator eliminates the need for ballast resistors and provides an initial current which rises more quickly than the current rise

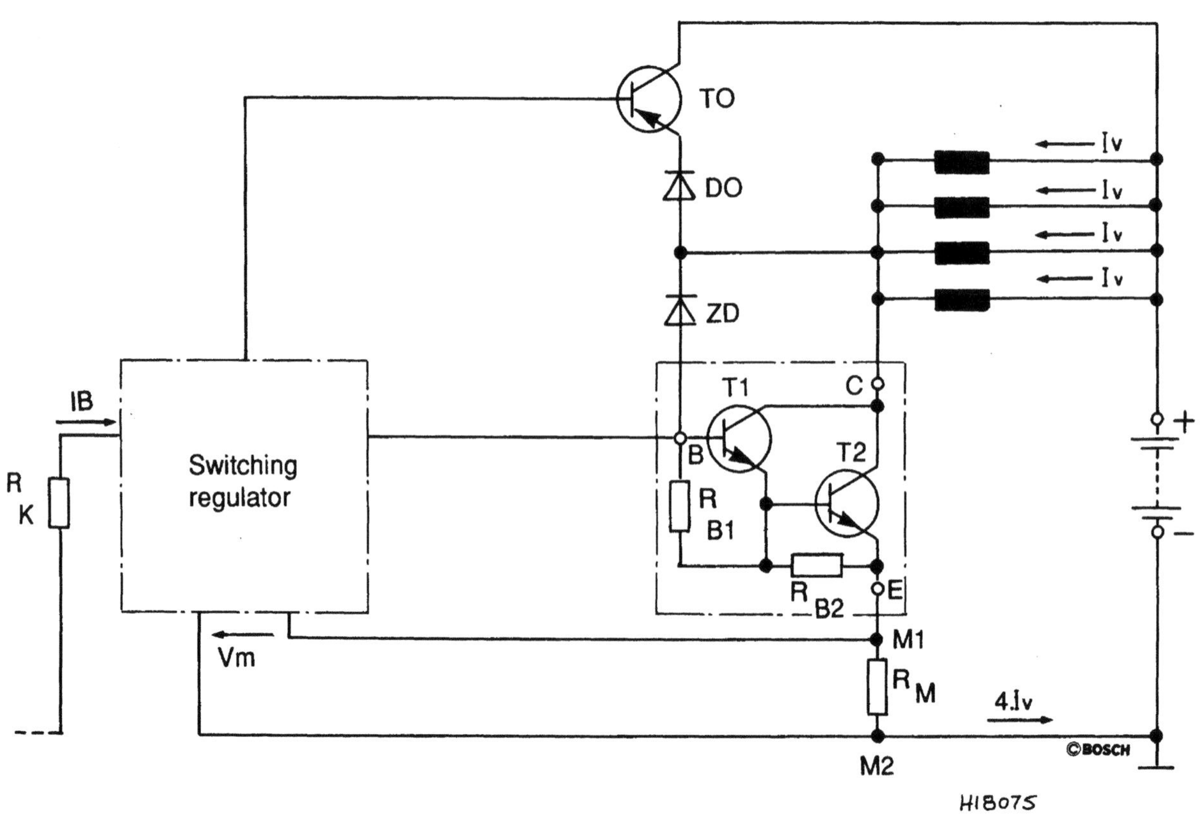


***Fig. 7.28 Final stage driving four injectors – electronic current limiting***

*D0 Free-wheeling diode* *Iv Control current* *R Resistances* *Vm Time dependent voltage signal* *ZD Zener diode*

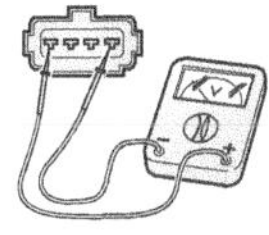

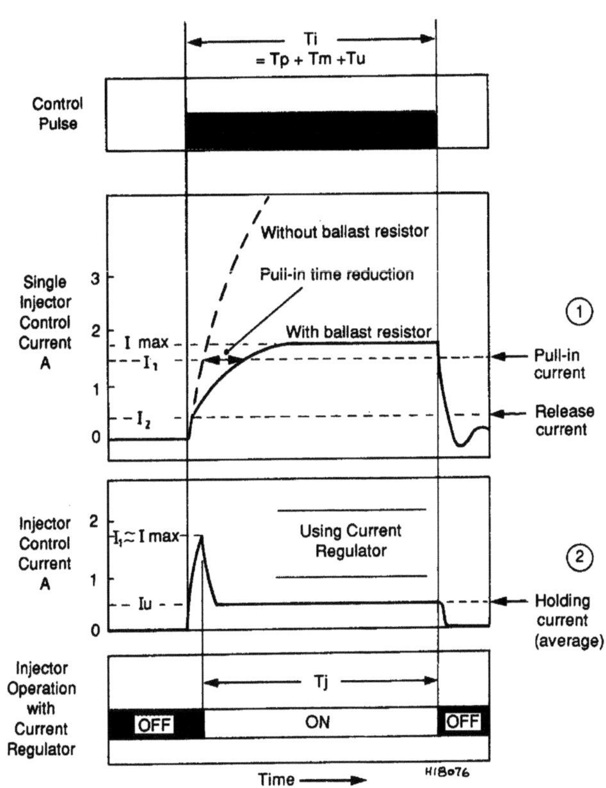


*Fig. 7.29* ***Injector operation***
*1 With ballast resistor 2 With current regulator*

with ballast resistors (Fig. 7.29). Once the injector has operated, the current is reduced to enough current to hold the injector valve on (holding current). The circuit switches the final stage on and off rapidly to give an average current equalling the holding current, about 0.5 ampere per injector. The action of the switching regulator is similar in principle to an alternator regulator. Diode D0 and transistor T0 allow a path for the decay current when the power diode T2 switches off. At the end of the injection period the current falls and when it goes below the release level (about 0.25 A per injector) the armature of each injector valve releases.

The advantages of using a current regulator are:

*(a) Reduced power consumption*
*(b) Reduced response delay in injector opening and closing*
*(c) The final stage can switch up to 12 injectors simultaneously*
*(d) The final stage can work over a wide range of supply voltage from 6 V to 16 V*
*(e) Fewer components, wiring and terminals*

## 9 Single point (throttle body) injection

**1** In response to car manufacturers' requests for a cheaper injection system, Bosch produced a single point injection arrangement which was first used in certain markets in the VW Polo in 1985 and 1987 in the Fiat FIRE (Fully Integrated Robotised Engine) 1000 cc engine for Panda and Uno models.

**2** Research showed that the best place to locate the injector was above and close to the throttle valve where the high air intake speed gave best possible atomization of the sprayed fuel. (Fig. 7.30).

**3** The throttle body houses a fuel pressure regulator

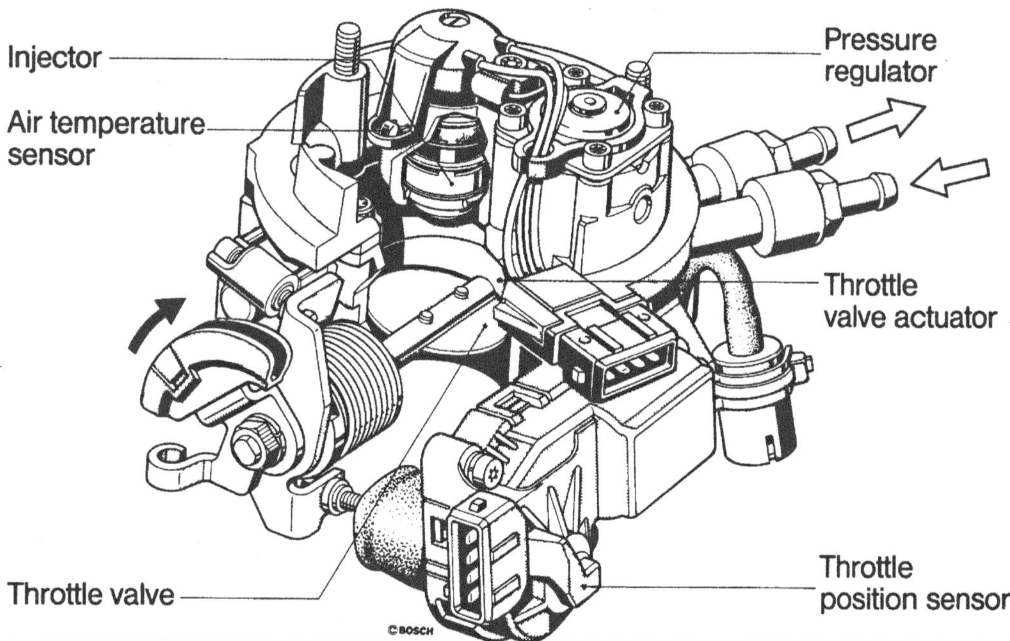


***Fig. 7.30 Central injection unit of the Mono Jetronic***
*Bosch press photo*

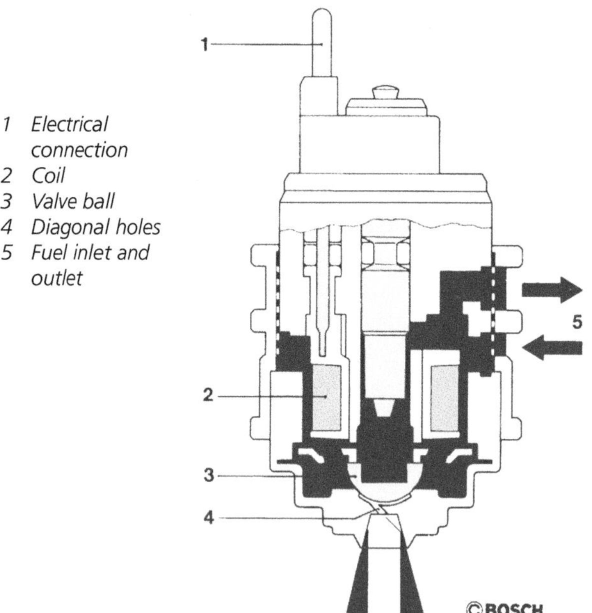


*Fig. 7.31 Low pressure fuel injection valve for single point fuel injection system*

delivering at a constant pressure of about 1 bar (14.7 lbf/in$^2$) and a special fast-operating fuel injection valve located centrally in the airstream (Fig. 7.31). Also in the throttle body is the idle speed regulator, throttle valve switch and an air temperature sensor which is located in the intake passage.

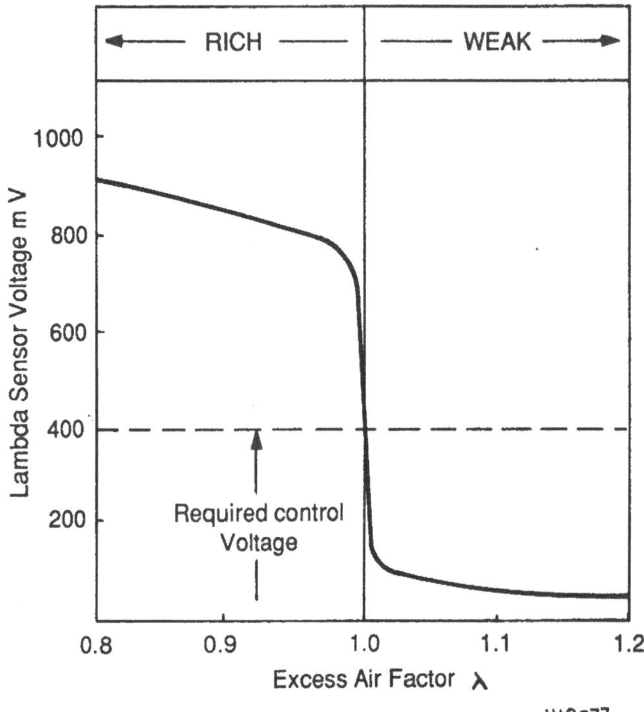


*Fig. 7.32 Lambda sensor voltage characteristic at 600°C*

**4** Air quantity Q is measured by the throttle valve angle, the position of which is signalled by a potentiometer attached to the throttle shaft. Engine speed n is measured by ignition pulses or the crankshaft position (TDC) sensor. The figure of Q/n determines the duration of injection and this is calculated by the ECU.

**5** Electronic control is by an ECU which contains a microcomputer, a programme memory, a data memory and an analogue-to-digital converter. The control unit generates basic injection durations using as a base engine speed and throttle angle information, and for this purpose a characteristic map is stored with 15 throttle angle and 15 engine speed data points. Superimposed on this 15 x 15 map is a further adaptive map and correction values to injection duration are generated if results from the two maps differ by more than a set amount.

**6** The control system can be programmed to include enrichment for cold start, warm-up mixture correction, acceleration and full load enrichment and deceleration fuel cut-off. It also may make provision for closed loop lambda control of air:fuel ratio (described in the next Section). A further provision is that of a closed loop control of an idle speed system, using a servo motor which supplies the engine with more or less air by control of the throttle valve opening.

## 10 Lambda closed-loop control

**1** In Chapter 6, the pollutant products of combustion were discussed and the catalytic converter was shown to be a highly successful solution in reducing toxic outputs to within the limits specified by most countries. It is an overriding proviso that an engine fitted with a three-way catalytic converter must be run with an air/fuel ratio at which combustion will be theoretically complete. This Stoichiometric ratio is 14.7:1 by mass, meaning 14.7 kg of air to 1 kg of fuel. It is perhaps more convenient to give this ratio the figure of 1.0 and the symbol (lambda) λ. A comparison between actual numerical ratios and the corresponding lambda figure is shown below. The term Excess Air Factor is used for the lambda figure (see table).

**2** So far, the injection systems described have no check on the results of injector control as far as exhaust emissions are concerned. Working figures for injection are based on an engine in good condition only, and cannot take into account wear in valves and cylinders. Such an arrangement is called open-loop control.

**3** To give information on the state of exhaust gases, a lambda sensor is fitted in the exhaust pipe. This sensor measures the oxygen left unburned in the exhaust gases (a measure of excess air factor λ) and generates a signal voltage (Fig. 7.32) which is fed back to the electronic control unit as an additional unit of information. In turn the ECU will correct the fuel injection to ensure that the excess air factor λ is within a narrow range of around unity; this range being

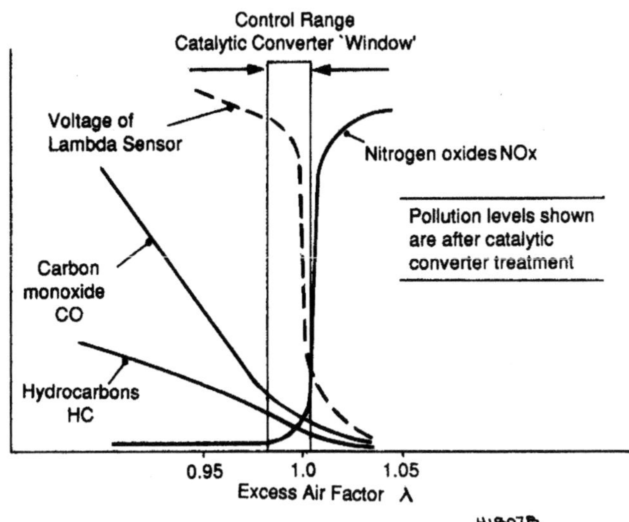


*Fig. 7.33 Lambda sensor voltage curve and pollutants in exhaust*

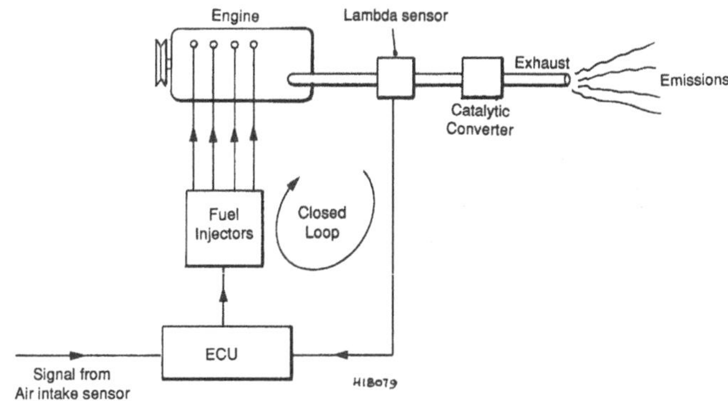


*Fig. 7.34 Lambda closed-loop excess air factor control*

called the catalytic converter window (Fig. 7.33). Because the output information (ie state of exhaust gas) is fed back to the ECU which in turn controls the output, this arrangement is **closed-loop control** and is common in many branches of engineering (Fig. 7.34).

**4** Graphs in Fig. 7.33 show that carbon monoxide quantities rise sharply just below $\lambda = 1.0$ and nitrogen oxides rise rapidly just above $\lambda = 1.0$. From this it will be seen that maintaining the Stoichiometric ratio at $\lambda = 1.0$ is vital to the success of the catalytic converter.

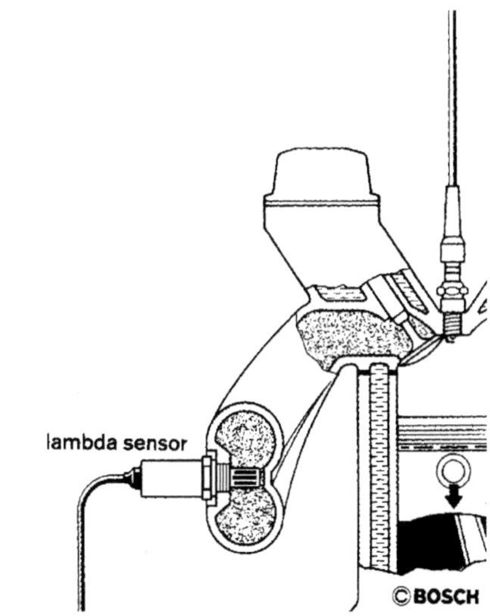


*Fig. 7.35 Lambda sensor in dual exhaust system*

## 11 Operation of the Lambda sensor

**1** The sensor is an exhaust gas oxygen measuring device which works like a small battery. It is about the size of a spark plug, screws into the exhaust pipe and is exposed to the full flow of exhaust gases (Fig. 7.35). The presence of oxygen in the exhaust gases means that the mixture is weak ($\lambda$ greater than 1.0) but no oxygen indicates a rich mixture ($\lambda$ less than 1.0).

**2** The lambda sensor (or exhaust gas oxygen sensor EGO) uses a ceramic body made of zirconium dioxide ($ZrO_2$) in the shape of a long thimble; the outer surface is exposed to the exhaust gases and the inner surface is in contact with the outside air (Fig. 7.36). The zirconium dioxide is covered inside and out with two thin layers of porous platinum as electrodes from which the output signal voltage is taken. Extra protection is given by coating the surface exposed to the exhaust with a layer of porous alumina through which the exhaust gas can penetrate. The zirconium dioxide acts as the (solid) electrolyte; the inside surface is exposed to air which has 21% oxygen content and the outer surface is exposed to the exhaust gas. The sensor develops a voltage between the inner and outer surfaces according to the

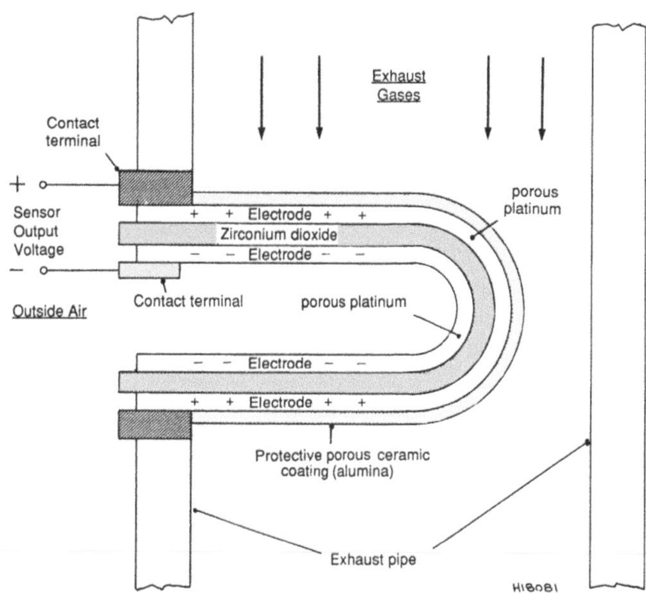


*Fig. 7.36 Schematic of Lambda sensor*

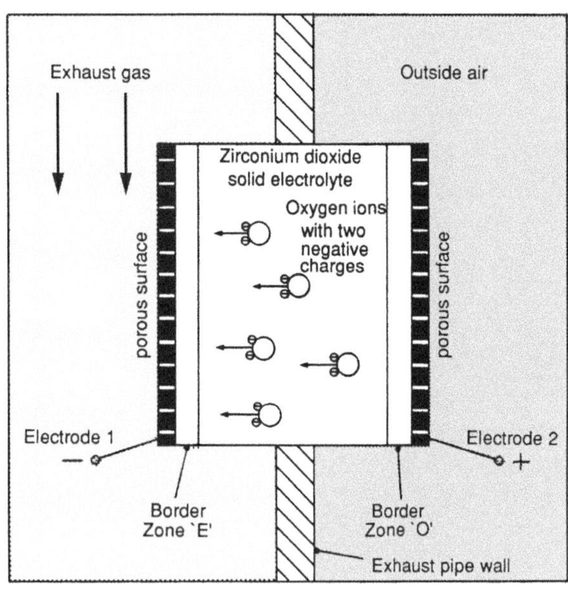


*Fig. 7.37* **Lambda sensor operation**

*When in the vicinity of the electrode surface, residual oxygen is bound to hydrogen, carbon monoxide and hydrocarbons. If the mixture goes from weak to rich, border zone E becomes depleted of oxygen. Large numbers of oxygen ions migrate to electrode 1, causing this to go negative relative to electrode 2. This gives the sensor voltage used in the Lambda closed-loop control system*

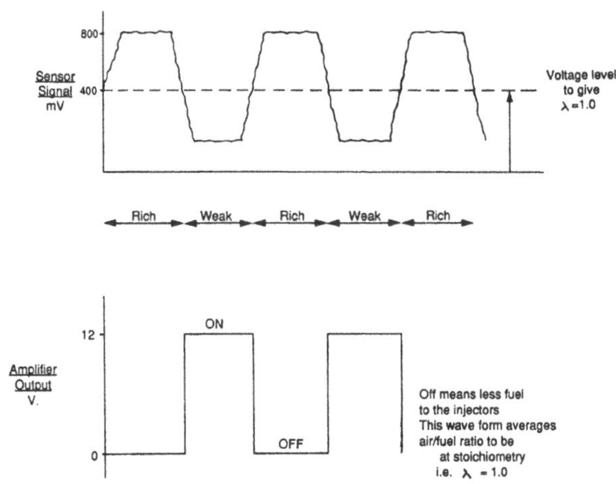


***Fig. 7.38* Control waveforms in Lambda control system**

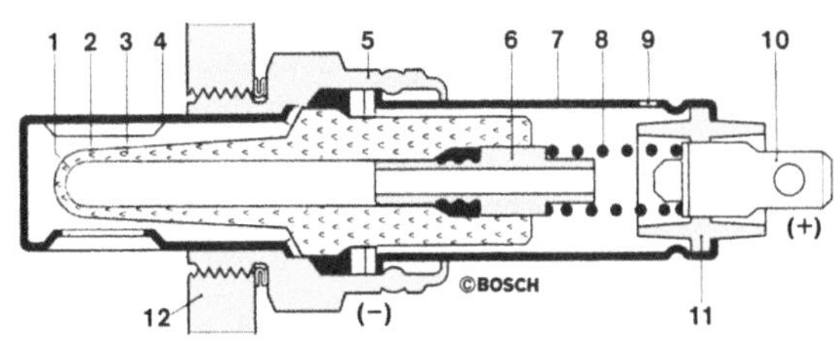

***Fig. 7.39* Bosch Lambda sensor**

*1 Electrode (+)*
*2 Electrode (–)*
*3 Ceramic body*
*4 Protective tube (exhaust -gas side)*
*5 Housing (–)*
*6 Contact bushing*
*7 Protective sleeve (air side)*
*8 Contact spring*
*9 Ventilation opening*
*10 Electrical connection*
*11 Insulating part*
*12 Exhaust pipe wall*
*Left: exhaust gas side*

difference of oxygen concentration and the voltage is collected at the two platinum electrodes (Fig. 7.37).

**3** When the engine is working with a rich mixture the voltage generated will be about 900 millivolts (mV). This drops abruptly at the Stoichiometric point and levels off to about 50 mV in the weak region. The change is abrupt so that the sensor acts almost like an on-off switch and the signals it sends to the ECU, together with wave re-shaping and the rapid correction produced by the ECU, mean that the signal is like an on-off square wave maintaining the excess air factor at very close to $\lambda = 1.0$ (Fig. 7.38).

**4** The output voltage is strongly influenced by temperature since the electrolyte $ZrO_2$ does not become conductive below 300°C; ideally the sensor should work at about 600°C. In addition the response time at 300°C is several seconds but at 600°C the sensor reacts in less than 50 ms. For these reasons the location of the sensor was critical in early models – too far away from the engine and the sensor would not work, too near and on long hot runs the sensor would be destroyed. (Note – maximum temperature should not exceed 850°C). A Lambda sensor is shown in Fig. 7.39. Later units have a built in heater (Fig. 7.40) for use under low engine load conditions; the heater is switched off on high loading. The location is still important but the lambda control is up to temperature and working after 25 seconds. Properly installed the heated lambda sensor has an expected life of 100 000 km. Lead-free fuel must be used to avoid damage to the active outer platinum electrode.

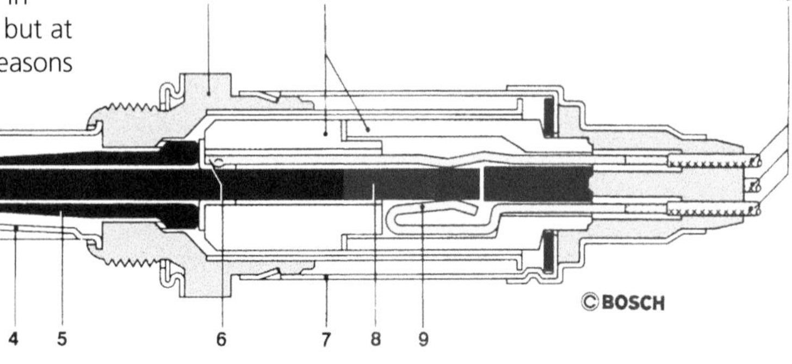


***Fig. 7.40* Lambda sensor with heater**

*1 Sensor housing*
*2 Protective ceramic tube*
*3 Connection cable*
*4 Protective tube with slots*
*5 Active sensor ceramic*
*6 Contact section*
*7 Protective sleeve*
*8 Heating element*
*9 Clamp terminals for heating element*

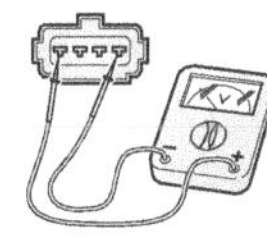

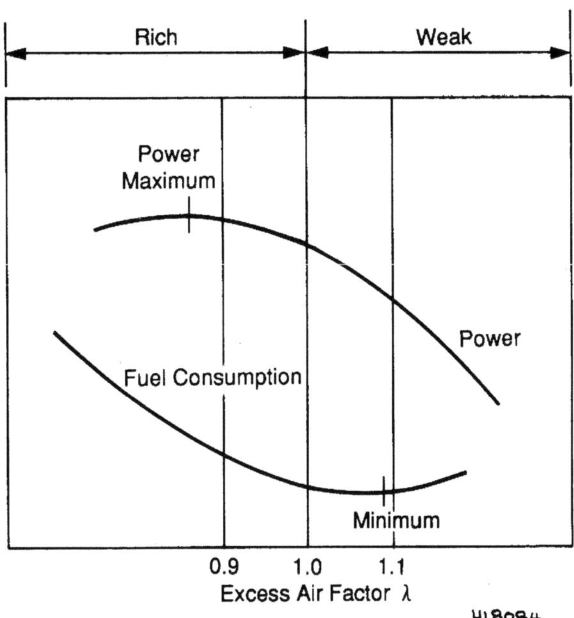


***Fig. 7.41 Fuel consumption and power output in relation to excess air factor***

## 12 Electronically controlled carburettors

**1** The carburettor had been developed continuously since the early days of the automobile. However due to ever increasingly stringent exhaust emission legislation, the carburettor is no longer in common use. Although for a while manufacturers produced carburettors with electronic control systems designed to allow then to work with closed loop fuel systems, the increasing complexity and cost meant it could not compete with fuel injection.

**2** Both carburettor and fuel injection are designed to meet emission requirements and to provide optimum power output with fuel economy. The last two factors are not compatible as shown in Fig. 7.41. Lower pollution levels are given with a weak (or lean) mixture as was seen in Fig. 7.33 and some manufacturers supply a lean-burn engine since the paramount factor is lower pollution.

**3** Lean-burn engines bring inherent difficulties including:

*(a) Tendency to detonation*
*(b) Overheating due to slower burning of fuel*

Additionally regulations require that an engine stays in tune for a lengthy period. Electronic control had proved to be effective in maintaining the correct air:fuel ratio over all conditions with modern carburettor designs for a while, but the complexity and cost issued could not be overcome.

**4** Electronically controlled carburettors attempted performed the following functions:

*(a) Air:fuel ratio maintained at correct value for all engine conditions*
*(b) Cold-start choke is automatic and can result in an improvement of up to 5% over a manual choke*
*(c) Idle speed regulated for all temperatures and can be kept to 100 rev/min below normal rate without cutting out the engine, giving worthwhile petrol saving*
*(d) Deceleration fuel cut-off saves fuel on override. Fuel is switched on and off rapidly to keep the engine running.*

These functions were carried out by an electronic control unit which sent signals to actuators attached to the carburettor. Several manufacturers, including Weber, Austin Rover (SU) and Bosch-Pierburg made electronic carburettors which all performed the same range of functions using some different methods.

## 13 Bosch-Pierburg electronic carburettor (Ecotronic)

**1** As an example of electronic controls applied to carburettors, the Bosch-Pierburg Ecotronic will be described.

**2** Reference to Fig. 7.42 shows the principal components which are:

*(a) A throttle butterfly potentiometer*
*(b) A throttle valve actuator with idle switch*
*(c) A choke actuator*
*(d) An engine speed sensor*
*(e) A coolant temperature sensor*
*(f) A digital electronic control unit (ECU)*

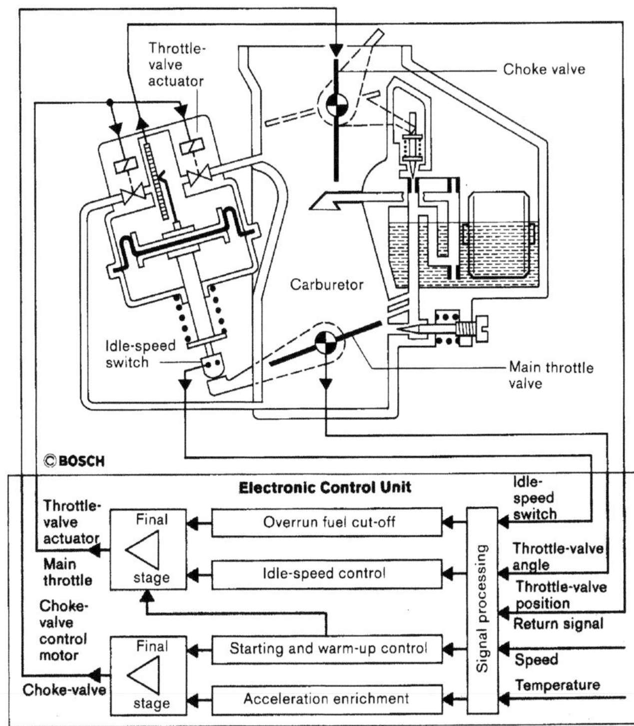


***Fig. 7.42 Electronically controlled carburettor (Ecotronic)***

**3** The **throttle butterfly valve potentiometer** picks up the position and any movement which is passed to the ECU.

**4** The **throttle butterfly valve actuator** is of the electropneumatic type and acts on the butterfly valve by means of a plunger to maintain correct idling under all conditions. The plunger pressure is controlled by two solenoid-operated valves, one of which is open to atmospheric pressure and the other to the manifold vacuum. Both solenoids are operated by the ECU to control the actuator movement and hence the position of the butterfly. When the throttle is in the idle position a switch on the actuator plunger closes, this closure being fed as information to the ECU.

**5** **Choke actuation** is by a torque motor acting against a return spring. The purposes are to give enrichment during cold start and warm-up periods. Because the torque motor is quick acting the enrichment needed for acceleration is obtained by partial choke closure. Equally the choke position is used for adjustment of the air:fuel ratio in the part load range.

**6** **Engine speed sensing** is obtained from the ignition system pulses.

**7** **Temperature sensing** of the coolant and of the inlet manifold temperatures is by semiconductor thermistor and thermocouple respectively.

**8** The **electronic control unit ECU** consists of an 8-bit microprocessor, an analogue to digital (A–D) converter to change the incoming sensor analogue signals to digital form, and power output stages to operate the actuators. The digitized signals are supplied to the micro-processor which calculates output values from the input signals and the pre-programmed information stored in the ROM memory. A correct sequence of instructions programmed into the micro-processor obtains the necessary output values which are then converted into power to control the actuators. A fail-safe provision is made in that should the ECU fail the carburettor settings without control will permit the 'limp home' condition.

### Operational notes

**9** With acceleration kickdown the throttle potentiometer ECU input partially closes the choke at a rate depending on other factors of engine speed, the existing position of the throttle valve and the engine temperature. Idle speed is maintained constant to within 10 rev/min irrespective of ambient temperature, pressure or carburettor wear. The actual idle speed is compared with the value in the computer memory and a correction is made to the valve opening by the throttle valve actuator. Over-run is sensed when the throttle is closed (automatic idle switch) and the engine speed is above 1400 rev/min; given both conditions, fuel is cut off. When the engine is switched off the throttle moves so as to cut off fuel but when the engine comes to rest the throttle is re-opened to the usual starting position. This avoids run-on which can occur, especially with lean-burn engines due to hot cylinder head internal surfaces.

## 14 Direct petrol injection

**1** Ever increasingly stringent exhaust emission legislation and spiralling fuel cost have forced manufacturers to develop direct petrol injection technology. With this system, fuel is injected directly into the combustion chamber - to be precise, it's injected directly into the piston crown. This allows incredibility fine control over the combustion process, since the fuel can be concentrated in area immediately surrounding the spark plug electrodes. With this level of control, the engine is able to run extremely lean air:fuel mixtures under low engine load/speed conditions (Stratified Charge), and normal mixtures under higher load/speed conditions (Homogenous Charge). Once thought to be practically impossible, direct petrol injection is now common place and offers the following advantages:

1. *Up to 15% reduction in fuel consumption compared with late sequential indirect systems.*
2. *Higher thermal efficiency (quicker engine/catalyst warm-up) due to less heat loss through the cylinder walls.*
3. *Higher gas recirculation rate, resulting in lower emissions.*
4. *Faster throttle response.*

**2** In order to achieve the level of control for this technology to be practical, many sensors, control units, and actuators are necessary (see Fig. 8.5b in the next Chapter).

# Engine management and emission control

## 1 Combined control of ignition and fuelling

**1** The motor vehicle spark ignition engine has two supplying units for the production of power, one being the supply of atomised fuel in correct quantity and air:fuel ratio, the other being the supply of an igniting spark at the correct timing. For most of last century, covering the span of motor vehicle design, these two provisions of fuelling and sparks have been dealt with separately. Chapters 6 and 7 of this book have described ignition and fuelling. It will be noted that performance requirements, in line with emission regulations show that these are not separate subjects but are inter-dependent; the fact that a change in air:fuel ratio should have a corresponding change in ignition timing is an example.

**2** Digital electronic ignition circuits use a micro-processor (computer) for control of ignition sparks, and fuel injection also uses a micro-processor. There is spare capacity on one micro-processor, however, to analyse Inputs and control outputs for both ignition and fuelling, this being the basis for an engine management system.

**3** Using one central micro-processor for the control of other operations in addition to ignition and fuelling leads to the concept of a total electronic management system in which, for example, the computing facility is applied to steering and suspension, gear change in automatic boxes, automatic fault diagnosis and control of clutch lock-up operation.

**4** The single computer control of ignition and fuelling is the main purpose of this Chapter, however, for such a system is now in wide use.

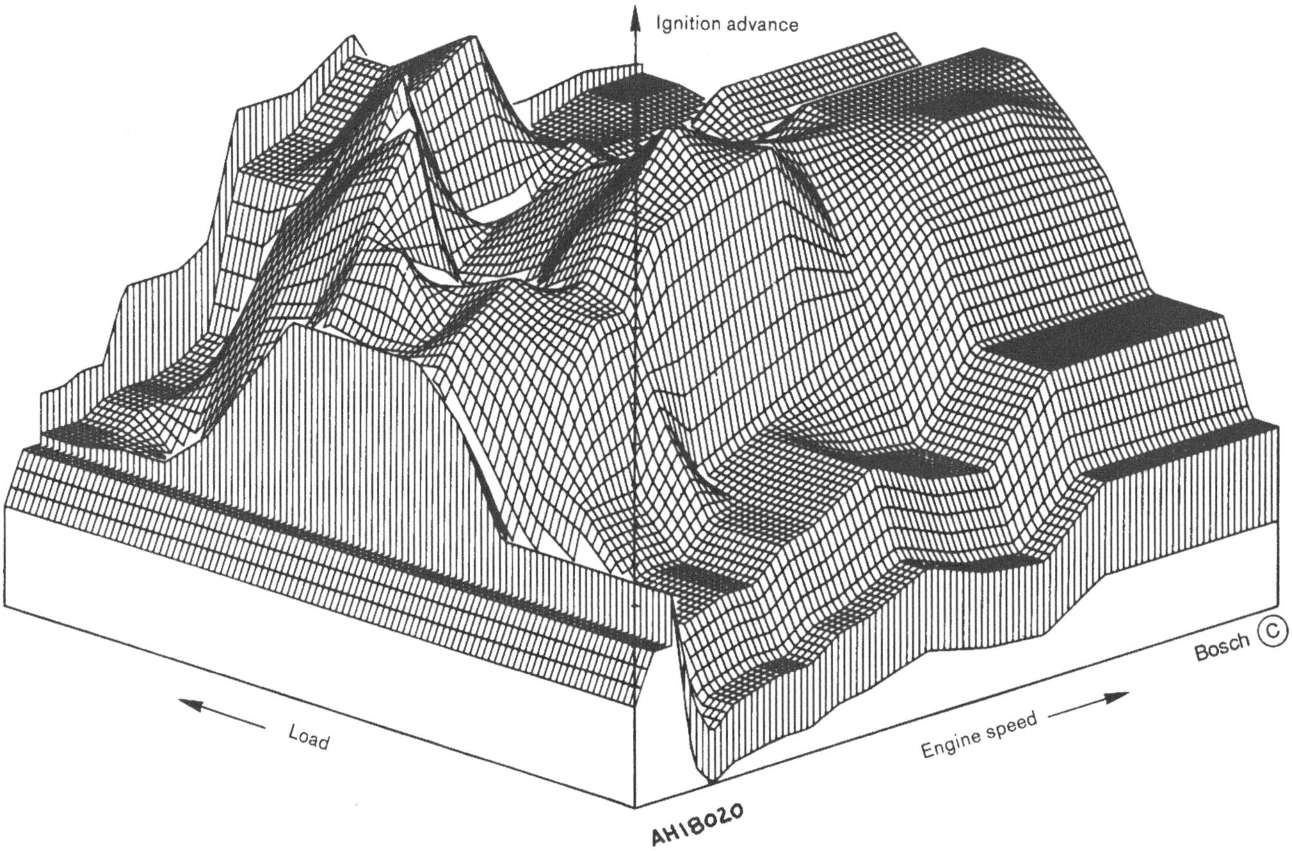

*8.1 Map linking load, speed and ignition advance*

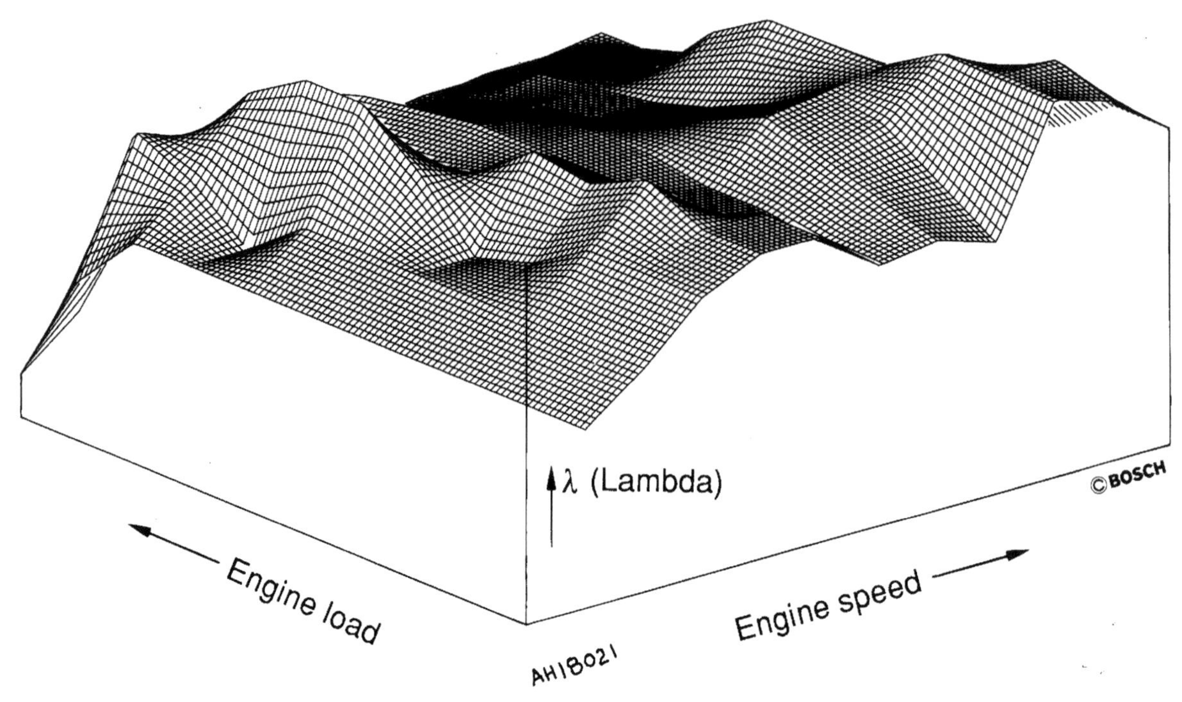


*8.2 Lambda map*

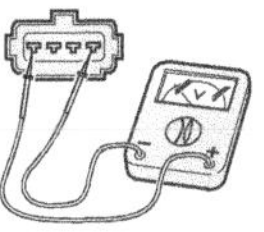

## 2 Performance mapping

**1** This topic has been mentioned earlier in relation to knock sensing and lambda control of exhaust emissions.

**2** When an engine is under development, comprehensive tests will take place relating the variables that bear on the output of an engine and the by-products in the exhaust. The engine is mounted on a dynamometer, a test bed device that can place the complete range of loads upon the engine and then measure all the relevant quantities including power output, torque, best idle speeds and exhaust emissions. Performance graphs are then plotted when the engine is subjected to variations in speed, throttle opening (load), ignition timing, air:fuel ratio and a range of coolant and air temperatures. Drawing these graphs in two dimensions involves a vast number of graphs and so, by plotting in three dimensions much more information can be portrayed, and are referred to as engine performance maps.

**3** Two such maps are shown in Figs. 8.1 and 8.2 each showing a family of curves which result in an irregular surface.

One shows the relationship between engine load ignition advance and engine speed while the other shows the lambda map relating engine load, engine speed and the excess air factor $\lambda$ (air:fuel ratio).

**4** These maps provide fundamental information on engine performance but several others will be used in a comprehensive control system. Examples are Fig. 8.3 which shows how dwell angle is related to engine speed and battery voltage; Fig. 8.4 plots the relationship of warm-up time against load and speed.

**5** The sensors which measure all these variables are often the same type used in ignition and fuel-injection equipment. It is a matter of natural development that one set of sensors and one micro-processor should suffice to control both ignition and fuelling. Before looking at such a system, the matter of open and closed-loop control should be considered again.

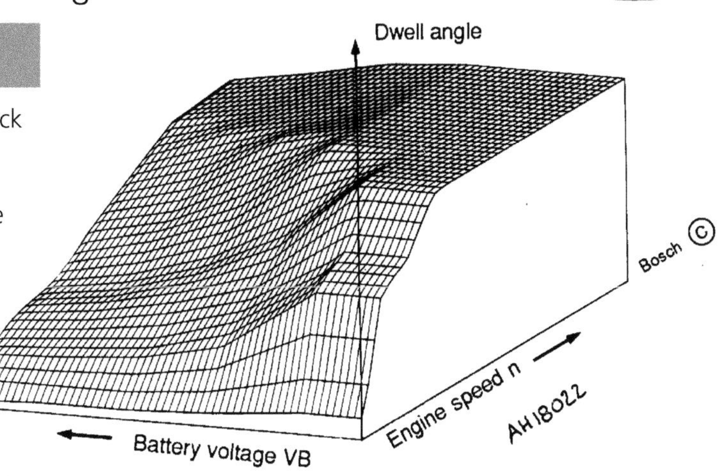


***8.3 Dwell map***

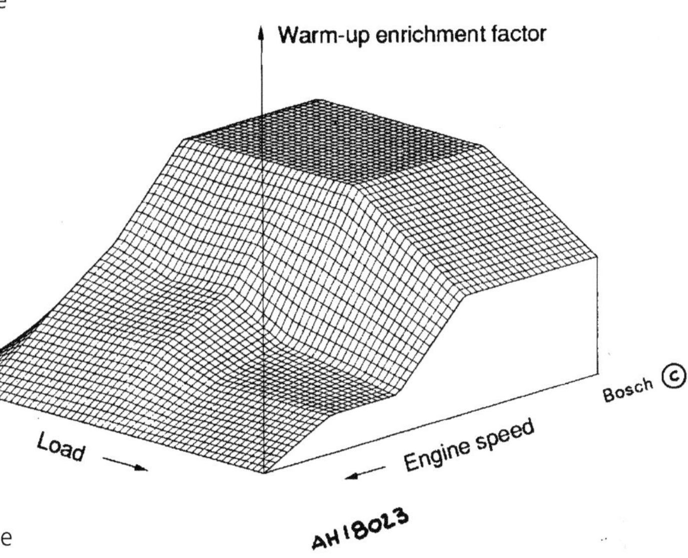


***8.4 Warm-up time map***

## 3 Definition of the engine management system

### Petrol engines

An engine management system (EMS) is essentially an electronic control system whereby the engine ignition, fuelling and idle speed functions are controlled by an electronic control module (ECU). The distributor, when used, is provided purely to distribute the HT spark to the correct cylinder in firing order. It is important to understand that the EMS does not control these functions separately. During the different engine control operations, the ECU synchronises timing and injection so that the various inputs and outputs work hand in hand, and not as separate entities (Fig. 8.5a and 8.5b overleaf).

The modern EMS employs digital technology and has a high degree of self-diagnostic capability. In addition, an EMS may also control other vehicle functions such as the air conditioning and communicate with other vehicle ECUs such as those controlling the ABS, automatic transmission or traction control when fitted.

However, in early systems the ECU did not always control the idle speed and the self-diagnostic function was often of limited performance.

### Diesel engines

For many years diesel engines were loved and loathed for being essentially crude mechanical devices, relying on solid engineering to function in a workman like manner, with the minimal of electronic/electric components. However,

# Chapter 8

1 Fuel tank
2 Electric fuel pump
3 Fuel filter
4 Pressure regulator
5 Control unit
6 Ignition coil
7 High tension distributor
8 Spark plug
9 Fuel injection valves
10 Throttle valve
11 Throttle valve switch
12 Airflow sensor
13 Potentiometer and air temperature sensor
14 Lambda sensor
15 Engine temperature sensor
16 Rotary idle actuator
17 Engine speed and reference mark sensor
18 Battery
19 Ignition and starting switch
20 Air conditioning switch

©BOSCH

**8.5a Typical petrol engine block diagram**

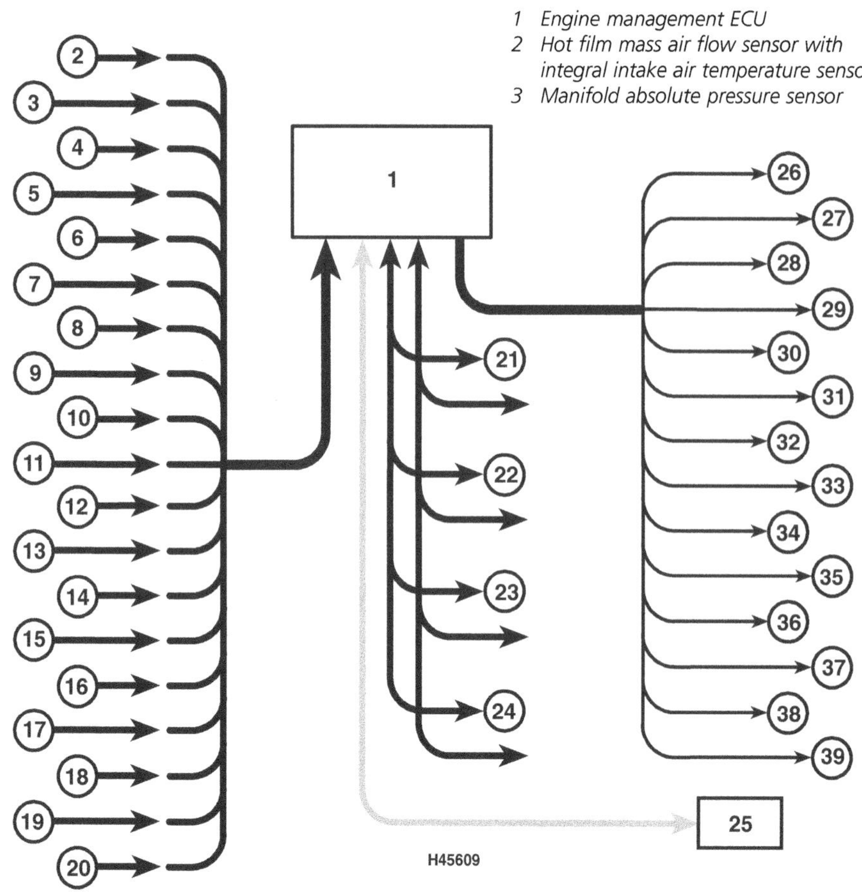


1 Engine management ECU
2 Hot film mass air flow sensor with integral intake air temperature sensor
3 Manifold absolute pressure sensor
4 Engine speed sensor (crankshaft position)
5 Camshaft position sensor
6 Throttle valve positioner
7 Accelerator pedal position sensor
8 Brake light switch
9 Clutch pedal switch
10 Fuel pressure sensor
11 Intake manifold flap potentiometer
12 Knock sensor
13 Coolant temperature sensor
14 Coolant temperature sensor – radiator outlet
15 Cabin temperature selector potentiometer
16 EGR potentiometer
17 Lambda (oxygen sensor)
18 Exhaust gas temperature sensor
19 NOx sensor and control unit
20 Brake servo pressure sensor
21 Gearbox ECU
22 Airbag ECU
23 Instrument cluster
24 ABS ECU
25 Diagnostic connector
26 Fuel pump and relay
27 Fuel injectors
28 Ignition coils
29 Throttle valve positioner
30 Engine management ECU supply relay
31 Fuel pressure regulating valve
32 Fuel metering valve
33 EVAP system solenoid valve
34 Intake manifold flap air flow control valve
35 Inlet camshaft timing adjustment valve
36 Mapped engine cooling thermostat
37 EGR valve
38 Lambda (oxygen) sensor heater
39 NOx sensor heater

**Fig. 8.5b VW's FSI direct petrol injection system**

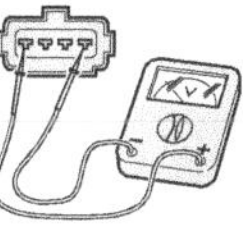

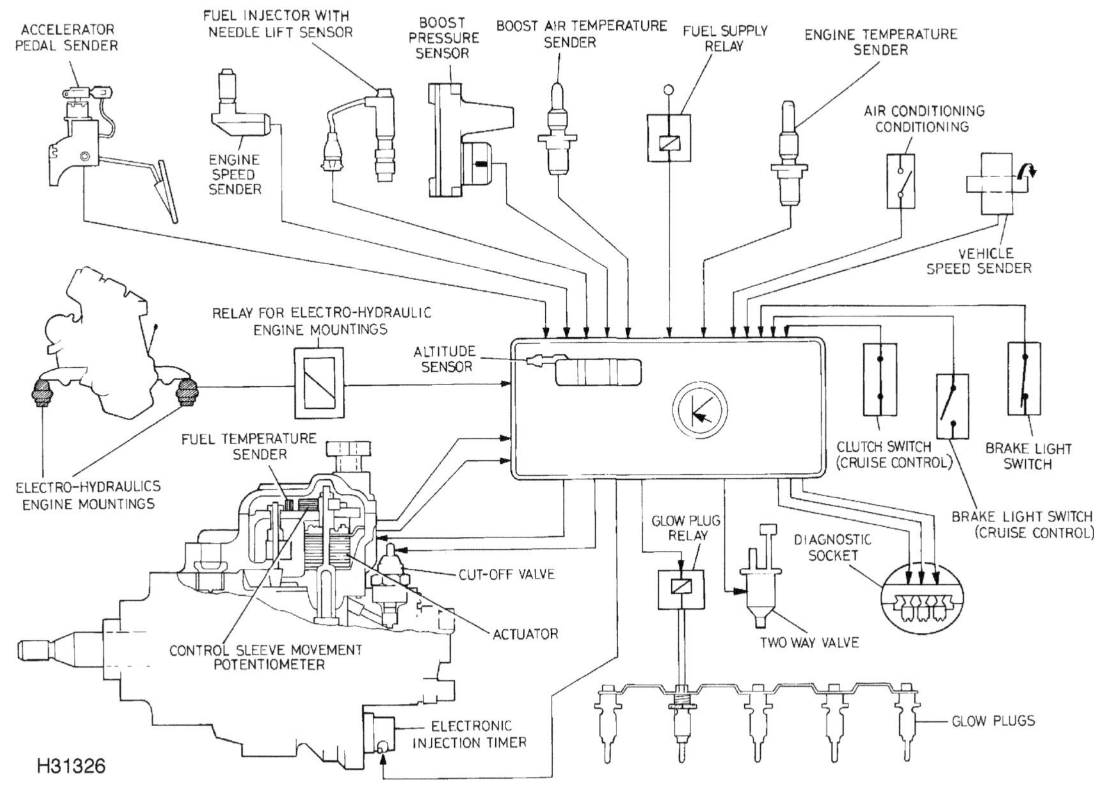


***8.6 Electronic diesel control system components fitted to an Audi 2.5 litre engine***

environmental pressures and spiralling fuel costs have forced the development of the diesel engine to the point where now, it can be argued that now they are more complex than their petrol equivalents.

### Electronic control using a conventional diesel injection pump

The function of the fuel injection pump is to supply fuel to the injectors at the correct pressure, at the correct moment in the combustion cycle, and for the length of time necessary to ensure efficient combustion. A conventional (mechanically-controlled) fuel injection pump uses an accelerator cable (connected to the driver's accelerator pedal), and various mechanical add-on devices (such as cold start injection advance, fast idle units, turbo boost pressure sensors, etc) to provide control of the fuel injection timing and the quantity of fuel injected. Even with these add-on devices, it has become increasingly difficult for a mechanical diesel control system to keep pace with modern demands on engine refinement and exhaust emission control.

Many electronic diesel engine control systems use a conventional in-line or distributor fuel injection pump, but the injection pump timing and the quantity of fuel injected are controlled electronically instead of mechanically. Various electronic sensors are used to measure variables such as accelerator pedal position, engine crankshaft speed, engine camshaft position, the mass of air passing into the engine, turbocharger boost pressure, engine coolant temperature, ambient air temperature, etc (Fig. 8.6 and 8.7).

The information from the various sensors is passed to an electronic control unit (ECU), which evaluates the signals. The ECU memory contains a series of mapped values for injected fuel quantity, and start-of-injection point. The ECU

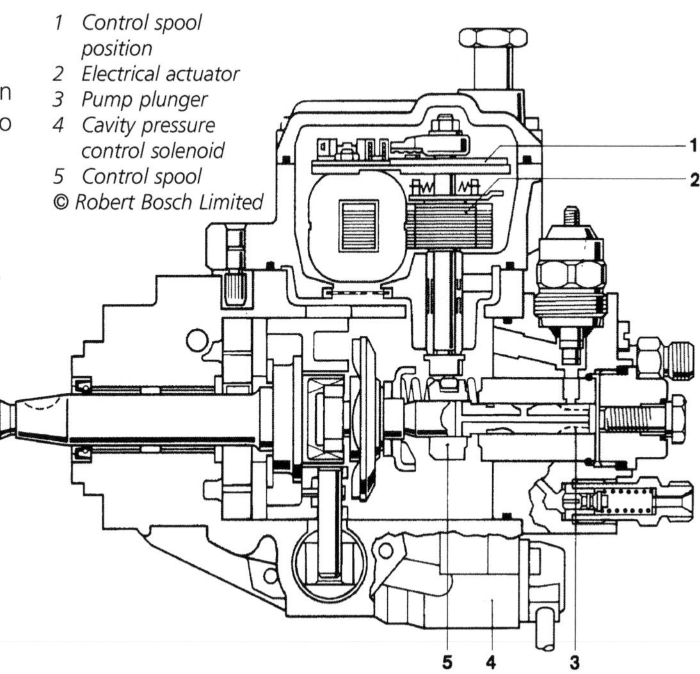


*1 Control spool position*
*2 Electrical actuator*
*3 Pump plunger*
*4 Cavity pressure control solenoid*
*5 Control spool*
*© Robert Bosch Limited*

***8.7 Bosch VE injection pump with electronic diesel control***

performs a number of calculations based on the information provided by the sensors, and selects the most appropriate values for the fuel quantity and start-of-injection point from its stored values. The ECU is capable of analysing the data and performing calculations many times per second, which allows very accurate control over the operation of the engine.

### Common rail diesel injection systems

The most widespread common rail system in current use is the Bosch system. Although there are other types of common rail system (eg, Caterpillar system), we will use the Bosch type as a typical example to explain the principles involved.

The common rail system derives its name from the fact that a common rail, or fuel reservoir, is used to supply fuel to all the fuel injectors. Instead of an in-line or distributor fuel pump, which distributes the fuel directly to each injector, a high-pressure pump is used, which generates a very high fuel pressure (up to 1350 bar on some systems) in the accumulator rail. The accumulator rail stores fuel, and maintains a constant fuel pressure, with the aid of a pressure control valve. Each injector is supplied with high-pressure fuel from the accumulator rail, and the injectors are individually controlled via signals from the system electronic control unit. The injectors are electromagnetically-operated.

In addition to the various sensors used on models with a conventional fuel injection pump, common rail systems also have a fuel pressure sensor. The fuel pressure sensor allows the electronic control unit to maintain the required fuel pressure, via the pressure control valve.

For the purposes of describing the operation of a common rail injection system, the components can be divided into three sub-systems; the low-pressure fuel system, the high-pressure fuel system and the electronic control system.

### Low-pressure fuel system

The low-pressure fuel system may consist of the following components:

*Fuel tank.*
*Fuel lift pump.*
*Fuel filter/water trap.*
*Low-pressure fuel lines.*
*Fuel cooler*

*The low-pressure system (fuel supply system) is responsible for supplying clean fuel to the high-pressure fuel circuit.*

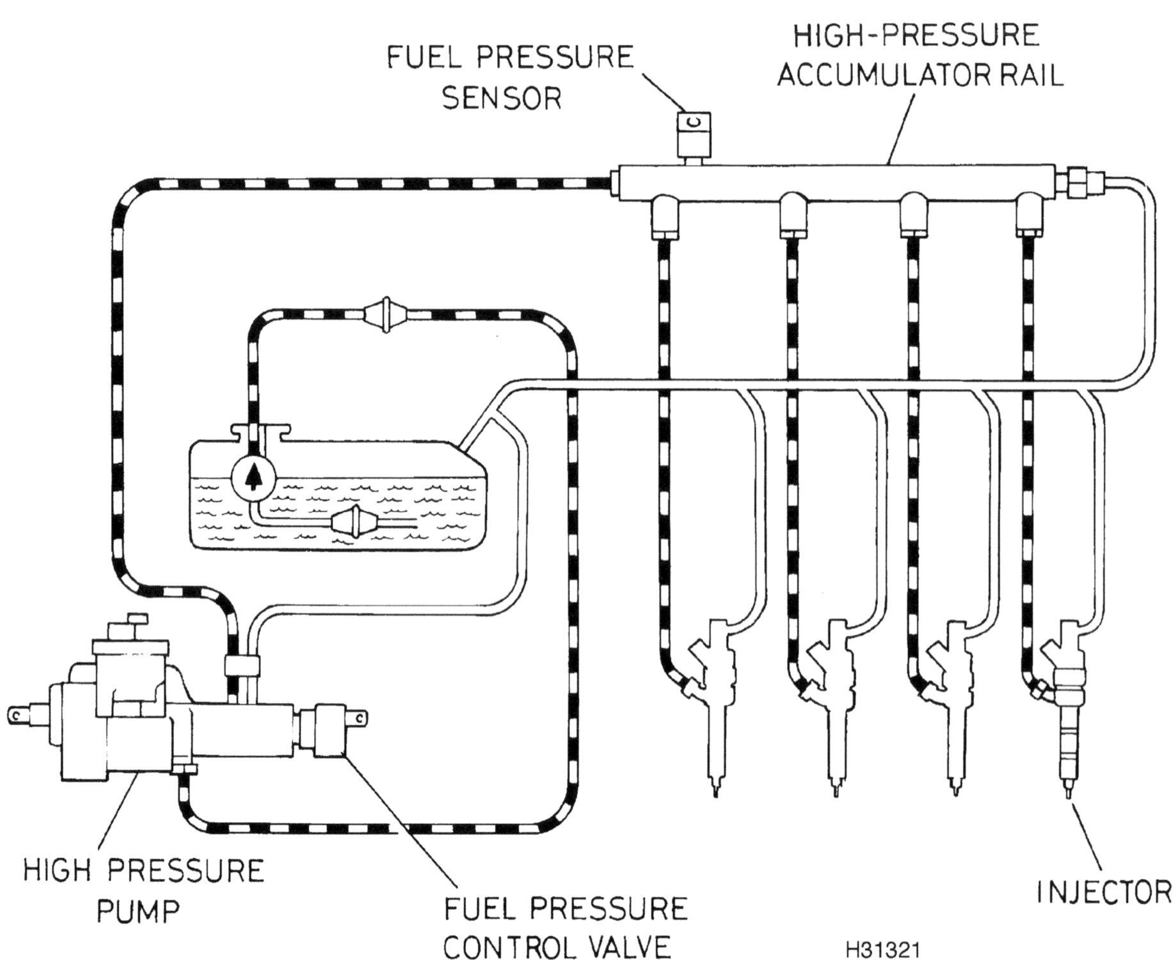


***8.8 Schematic view of a high-pressure fuel system – Bosch common rail***

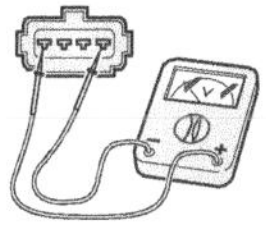

**High-pressure fuel system**

The high-pressure fuel system consists of the following components (Fig. 8.8):

*High-pressure fuel pump with pressure control valve.*
*High-pressure accumulator rail with fuel pressure regulator.*
*Fuel injectors.*
*High-pressure fuel lines.*

After passing through the fuel filter, the fuel reaches the high-pressure pump, which forces it into the accumulator rail, generating pressures of up to 1350 bar. As diesel fuel has a certain elasticity, the pressure in the accumulator rail remains constant, even though fuel leaves the rail each time one of the injectors operates: additionally, a pressure control valve mounted on the high-pressure pump ensures that the fuel pressure is maintained within pre-set limits.

The *pressure control valve* is operated by the ECU. When the valve is opened, fuel is returned from the high-pressure pump to the tank, via the fuel return lines, and the pressure in the accumulator rail falls. To enable the ECU to trigger the pressure control valve correctly, the pressure in the accumulator rail is measured by a *fuel pressure sensor*.

The electromagnetically-controlled fuel injectors are operated individually, via signals from the ECU, and each injector injects fuel directly into the relevant combustion chamber. The fact that high fuel pressure is always available allows very precise and highly flexible injection in comparison to a conventional injection pump: for example combustion during the main injection process can be improved considerably by the pre-injection of a very small quantity of fuel.

**Electronic control system**

The electronic control system consists typically of the following components:

*Electronic control unit (ECU).*
*Fuel lift pump.*
*Crankshaft speed/position sensor.*
*Camshaft position sensor.*
*Accelerator pedal position sensor.*
*Turbocharger boost pressure sensor.*
*Air temperature sensor.*
*Coolant temperature sensor.*
*Air mass meter.*
*Fuel pressure sensor.*
*Fuel injectors.*
*Fuel pressure control valve.*
*Preheating control circuit.*
*EGR valve actuator.*

The information from the various sensors is passed to the ECU, which evaluates the signals. The ECU contains electronic 'maps' which enable it to calculate the optimum quantity of fuel to inject, the appropriate start of injection, and even pre- and post injection fuel quantities, for each individual engine cylinder under any given condition of engine operation.

Additionally, the ECU carries out monitoring and self-diagnostic functions. Any faults in the system are stored in the ECU memory, which enables quick and accurate fault diagnosis using appropriate diagnostic equipment (such as a suitable fault code reader).

## 4 Engine Management Sytems (EMS) – typical operation

### Basic electronic control module (ECU) operation

This section describes the operation of a typical EMS. Although the components of each specific system may vary, the principles involved are fairly constant and this description is relevant to many of the modern systems.

### Sensors and actuators

A sensor is an input device that provides variable information on an engine function. Examples include the airflow sensor (AFS), crank angle sensor (CAS), coolant temperature sensor (CTS), throttle potentiometer sensor (TPS) etc, and these provide data on load, rpm, temperature, throttle opening etc. This data is signalled to the ECU, which then analyses the results and computes an output signal. The output signal is used to actuate an output device. An actuator is a device that is switched or actuated by the ECU for a period of time depending on the input signal. Examples include the fuel injector, idle speed control valve (ISCV), EGR valve, fuel pressure regulating valve, carbon filter solenoid valve (CFSV), relay driver etc.

Put in simple computer terms, the process is summed up as input, compute, and output. Input is determined by the signals from the engine sensors, the ECU computes the actuator values required, and an appropriate signal is output to switch actuator components such as the injector, coil negative terminal, idle system, emission system, air conditioning etc. This process is repeated many times per second.

### ECU power supplies and earths

A permanent voltage supply is usually applied from the vehicle battery to one of the ECU pins. This allows the self-diagnostic function to retain data of an intermittent nature. Once the ignition is switched on, a voltage supply is made to the ECU, ignition coil(s), injectors, ISCV and other devices. The voltage supplies may be made direct from the ignition switch or come from the system relay/fusebox. The ignition 'on' supply to the ECU effectively powers up the ECU so that it is ready to go about its business.

When a petrol engine is cranked or run, a signal from the ignition causes the ECU to earth the fuel pump relay so that the fuel pump will run. Ignition and injection functions are also activated. Actuators such as the injectors and ISCV are supplied with nbv from the main relay or ignition switch and the ECU completes the circuit by pulsing the relevant actuator wire to earth (Fig. 8.9). The same process occurs with a modern diesel engine, except that EGR is activated (temperature dependant), and most common-rail systems do not have a lift pump between the fuel tank and high-pressure pump.

There are normally several earth connections to the ECU. However, only one or two will normally be used as the actual ECU system earth. The other earth connections are provided to allow the ECU to complete various sensor and actuator circuits. In effect, these earth paths are secondary paths and only used when the ECU switches an actuator.

For example, to create an injection pulse, the ECU will use an earth to complete the circuit for the instant required to give correct pulse duration. The circuit to earth will then be broken until the next pulse is required. This practice occurs many times a second.

In some systems, an inertia switch is used as a safety device to break the power supply to the relay or to the fuel pump.

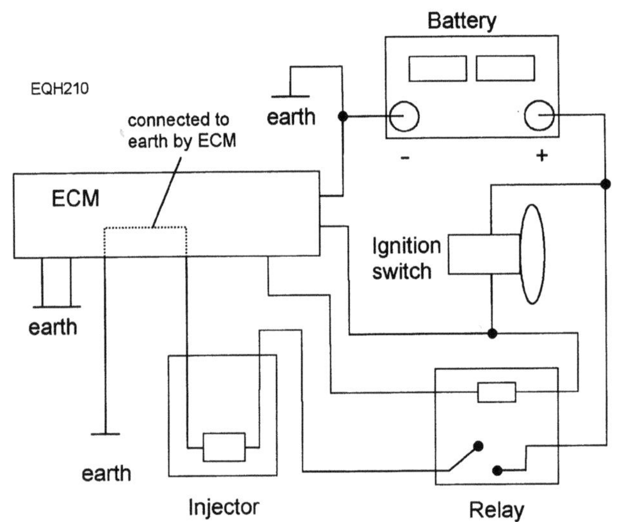


*8.9 Typical ECM earth and voltage supplies*

## Reference voltage

During normal engine operation, battery voltage could vary between 9.5 (cranking) and 14.5 (running). To minimise the effect on engine sensors (for which the ECU would need to compensate), the voltage supplies from the ECU to the engine sensors are made at a constant voltage (known as a reference voltage) of 5.0 volts (Fig. 8.10).

Once the ECU has powered up then, the majority of sensors (other than those that generate a voltage such the CAS and OS), are supplied with the 5.0 volt reference.

In most instances the engine sensors are not directly connected to earth. Rather, the sensor earth path is connected to one or two common earth return connections that connect directly to the ECU. This ECU pin is not usually connected directly to earth. The ECU internally connects that pin to earth via one of the ECU pins that are directly connected to earth.

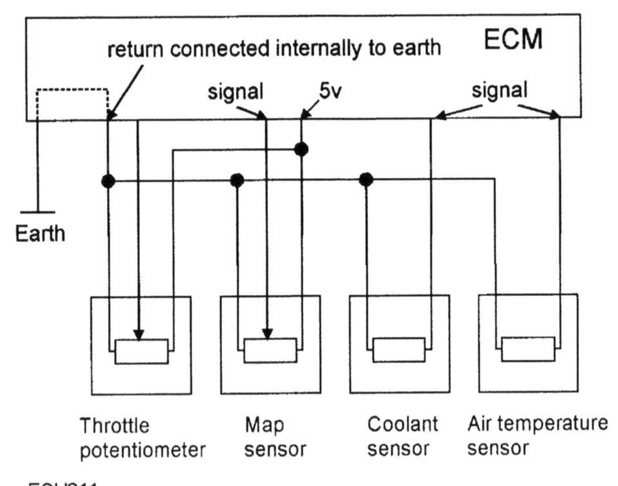


*8.10 Typical sensor wiring*

## Signal shielding

To reduce radio frequency interference or RFI, some signals are protected with a shielded cable. The shielded cable is often connected to the main ECU earth pin, so that interference is reduced to a minimum (Fig. 8.11).

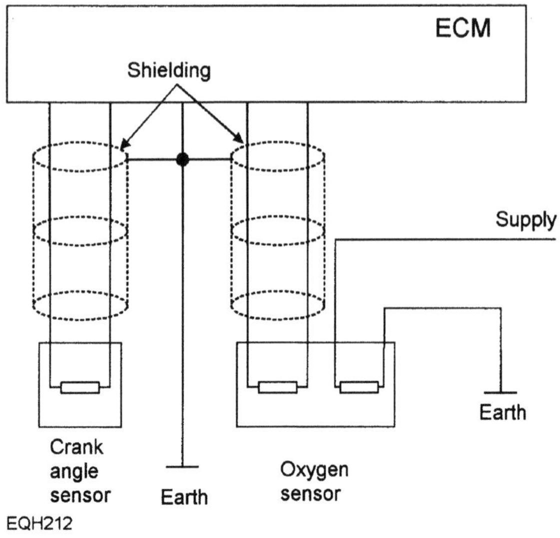


*8.11 Sensor shielding to reduce RFI*

## Signal processing

Basic data on dwell angle, ignition timing, fuel pressure, and injection duration/timing are stored internally in the ECU in a number of two- or three-dimensional maps. These maps or look-up tables allow the ECU to look-up the correct ignition timing and injection duration/timing according to speed, temperature and load.

Accessing data from a table is a far quicker method of selecting data than by computing it. If the system is well designed, the map will contain settings for almost every possible engine load and speed. Even so, the map would be enormous if every single rpm or load setting was listed, and

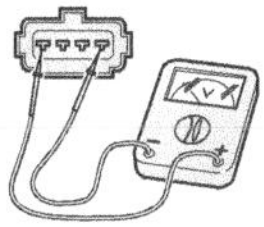

rpm may be mapped every 5 rpm and the load logged in a similar fashion. The ECU will interpolate in-between values so that most operating conditions are extensively covered. Some early systems were not always well mapped, and this created a 'black hole' for some operating conditions with consequent deterioration of performance.

In addition, on petrol engines, the ignition point and injection duration are jointly processed by the ECU so that the best moment for ignition and fuelling are determined for every operating condition.

The main engine load sensor is either the AFS or MAP sensor and engine speed is determined from the Crankshaft Position Sensor or CAS. Correction factors are then applied for starting, idle, deceleration and part and full-load operation. The main correction factor is engine temperature from the CTS. On petrol engines, minor corrections to timing and air-fuel ratio (AFR) are made with reference to the battery voltage, ATS and TPS signals. On diesel engines, alterations to injection timing and duration are made with reference to the coolant temperature, intake air temperature, fuel temperature, and accelerator pedal position sensor.

In petrol models with an ISCV or a stepper motor, the ECU accesses a different map for idle running conditions, and this map is implemented whenever the engine speed is at idle. Idle speed during warm-up and normal hot running conditions are maintained automatically by the idle control function. However, in most systems the ECU makes small adjustments to the idle speed by advancing or retarding the timing, and this results in an ignition timing that is forever changing during engine idle.

In petrol models with an catalytic converter and OS, the ECU monitors the OS signal and controls the injection pulse so that the AFR is always around Lambda = 1.0 (0.97 to 1.03 is a typical range for Lambda control). Lambda is represented by the Greek symbol '$\lambda$'. This mode of operation is known as 'closed-loop'. If the AFR was placed into closed-loop under all operating conditions, the vehicle would be pretty much undriveable during certain driving situations. For this reason, during cold start and warm-up, sharp acceleration and wide-open throttle conditions, the ECU slips into open-loop operation when the AFR is allowed to move outside of the Lambda operating range.

If the engine speed exceeds a pre-designated engine rpm, the ECU cuts off injector operation as a safety precaution. Fuel is also cut during deceleration to maintain smooth running and as an economy measure. Fuel is re-introduced when the deceleration speed falls below a certain rpm. After a period of closed throttle running; when the throttle is opened again, the ECU re-introduces fuel injection in a controlled manner to prevent a loss of smoothness.

## Self-diagnostic function

The modern engine management system has a self-test capability that regularly examines the signals from the engine sensors and in some instances the actuators. In the event of a fault being present the ECU internally logs a code. This code can be extracted from an output terminal, known as a diagnostic plug/socket or serial port, by a suitable fault code reader (Fig. 8.12).

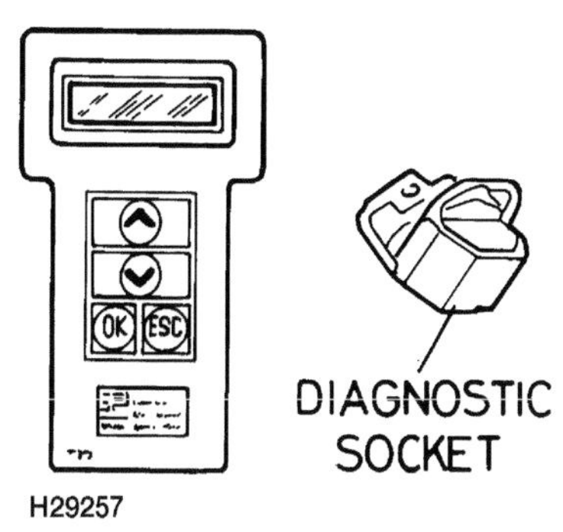


***8.12 FCR and typical serial port/diagnostic socket***

To a large degree, the format and type of data to be output used to be determined by the vehicle manufacturer (VM). The function of the fault code reader (FCR) is to initiate the VM's program and to make the best of what is actually available. In other words, if the VM does not make certain information available, then it is not possible to access such information through the serial port. For example, apart from reading fault codes and clearing fault codes, it may be possible to obtain datastream information on the signal output from the sensors, or make adjustments to CO or timing, or fire the injector, ISCV, relays and other actuators or log sensor data during a road test. But these functions will only be available if the VM has made them available.

Some vehicles are provided with a dash-mounted warning lamp. When the ECU detects that a major fault is present, it earths a dedicated ECU pin and the warning lamp on the dash will light whilst the engine is running. The lamp remain lit until the fault is no longer present. If the fault clears, the code will remain logged until wiped clean with a suitable FCR, or when the battery is disconnected. However, not all vehicles utilise a warning lamp; those without one will require interrogation by a FCR to determine whether a fault is logged or not. Some ECUs retain codes for faults of an intermittent nature, and this is a valuable aid to fault diagnosis.

Codes emitted by an ECU may be designated as 'slow codes' or 'fast codes'. Slow codes (sometimes termed flash codes) are fault codes emitted by an EMS that are slow enough to be displayed on an LED lamp or on a dash-mounted warning lamp. Fast codes are digital fault codes emitted by an EMS that are too fast to be displayed on an LED lamp or on a dash-mounted warning lamp. A digital FCR instrument is required for capturing fast codes.

## European On-Board Diagnosis (EOBD)

All new petrol engined models sold after 01/01/2000, all existing models with petrol engines from 01/01/2001, and all diesel engined models sold after 2005 in Europe, must be equipped with EOBD. This is a higher standard of system monitoring, where any emission related faults must be notified to the driver by illuminating the MIL (Malfunction Indicator Light) in the instrument cluster, the fault (and the distance travelled since the fault occurred) must be recorded for later retrieval.

EOBD also attempts to standardise the type of diagnostic

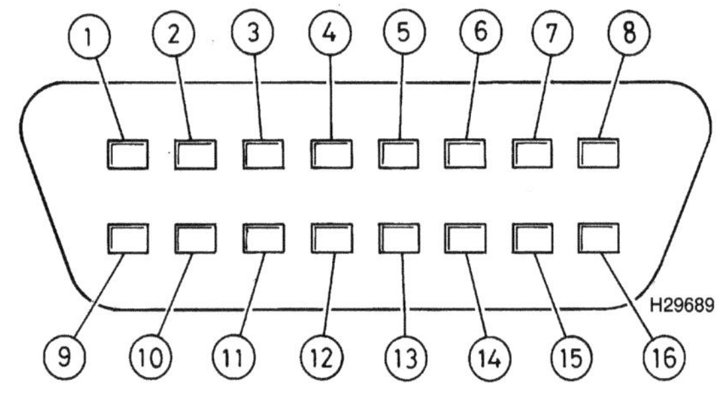


*8.13 EOBD 16-pin diagnostic connector details*

plug (16-pin J1962), the plug position, and the configuration of the plug terminals. The diagnostic plug must be within reach of the drivers seat, tools must not be required to reveal the plug, although it may have a removable cover.

The different pins of the plug (Fig. 8.13) are used by different manufacturers in different ways, depending on which communication protocol is used. There are four protocols available:

| **Protocol** | **Connector pins used** |
|---|---|
| J1850 VPW | 2, 4, 5 and 16 |
| ISO 9141 – 2 | 4, 5, 7, 15 and 16 |
| J1850 PWM | 2, 4, 5, 10 and 16 |
| KWP2000 (ISO14230) | 4, 5, 7, 15 and 16 |

Generally speaking, European and Asian manufacturers use ISO / KWP protocols, whilst General Motors (Vauxhall/Opel) use J1850 VPW, and Ford use J1850 PWM.

The plugs pins are configured as follows:

| **Pin** | |
|---|---|
| 2 | J1850 BUS+ |
| 4 | Chassis ground |
| 5 | Signal ground |
| 6 | CAN High (J-2284) |
| 7 | K-line |
| 10 | J1850 BUS |
| 14 | CAN Low (J-2284) |
| 15 | L-line |
| 16 | Battery power |

Manufacturers may use additional pins for other purposes.

To a certain extent, EOBD standardises the fault codes generated by the self-diagnosis system. These five digit alphanumeric codes are made up as follows:

| **Letter** | **System** |
|---|---|
| B | Body |
| C | Chassis |
| P | Powertrain |
| U | Network |

The second digit determines whether the code is a generic EOBD code (where the definition of the code is stated in the EOBD regulations, and will be the same for all manufacturers), or a Manufacturer specific code (where definition of the code is determined by the vehicle manufacturer).

**Powertrain codes**

P0xxx – Generic
P1xxx – Manufacturer specific
P2xxx – Generic
P30xx – Manufacturer specific
P34xx – Generic

**Chassis codes**

C0xxx – Generic
C1xxx – Manufacturer specific
C2xxx – Manufacturer specific
C3xxx – Generic

**Body codes**

B0xxx – Generic
B1xxx – Manufacturer specific
B2xxx – Manufacturer specific
B3xxx – Generic

**Network communication codes**

U0xxx – Generic
U1xxx – Manufacturer specific
U2xxx – Manufacturer specific
U3xxx – Generic

The third digit determines the specific system/sub-system within the vehicle that is associated with the recorded fault code:

| **Digit** | **System/sub-system** |
|---|---|
| 1 | Fuel and Air metering |
| 2 | Fuel and Air metering (injector circuit only) |
| 3 | Ignition system or misfire |
| 4 | Auxiliary emission control system |
| 5 | Vehicle speed control and idle control system |
| 6 | Computer output circuits |
| 7 | Transmission |
| 8 | Transmission |

**Note:** *Manufacturers are not obliged to adhere to the above table for their manufacturer specific codes.*

The forth and fifth digits of the code identify the section related to the code generation.

## Limited operating strategy (LOS)

In addition to the self-test capability, the modern EMS normally contains a 'limp-home' facility that is usually termed LOS or Limited Operating Strategy. This means that in the event of a serious fault in one or more of the sensor circuits, and the system perceives that a sensor is operating outside of its design parameters, the EMS will substitute a fixed default value in place of the defective sensor. A fault that puts the circuit outside of its design parameters would normally be a short circuit or when the circuit is virtually open. Other sensor faults may not necessarily cause a code to be logged.

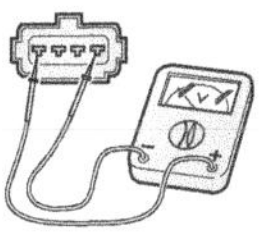

The LOS is a safety system which allows the engine to operate at a reduced efficiency level. and allows the vehicle to be driven to a service area. Some LOS systems are so smart that the driver may be unaware that a fault has occurred during most of the vehicle's operating conditions.

However, since the substituted values are usually those of a hot (sometimes warm) engine, cold starting and running during the warm-up period may be less than satisfactory. Also, failure of a major sensor, ie the AFS or the MAP sensor, will tend to make driving conditions less easy.

The instrument panel warning light (where fitted) is switched on to indicate that a fault has occurred. Some systems (for example Ford) may also lock the timing to a set figure (with no timing advance) and allow the fuel pump to run continuously.

## Adaptive systems

The ECU is adaptive to changing engine operating characteristics, and constantly monitors the data from the various sensors (ie AFS or MAP, ATS, CTS. TPS etc). As the engine or its components wear, the ECU reacts to new circumstances by adopting the changed values as a correction to the basic map.

When the adaptive map is used in conjunction with the oxygen sensor (OS) on petrol engines, the ECU is able to respond much more quickly and retain tighter control over the changing gases in the exhaust system. During closed-loop operation, the basic injection value is determined by the values stored in the map for a specific rpm and load. If the basic injection value causes exhaust emissions outside of the Lambda value (ie 0.97 to 1.03 AFR) the mixture would be too rich or too lean and the OS would signal the ECU, which in turn will correct the mixture. However, this response takes a little time and so the ECU learns a correction value and adds this 'adaptive' values to the basic map. From now on, under most operating conditions, the emissions will be very close to Lambda and so, after reference to the OS signal, the ECU will only need to make small corrections to keep it that way.

Adaptation and correction of the map occurs during the following engine operations.

*a) CFSV operation*
*b) ISCV operation*
*c) Idle speed and mixture adjustment*
*d) Part-load mixture adjustment*

Operation of the CFSV introduces a combustible mixture to the engine that is compensated for by the fuel evaporation adaptive correction values after detection by the OS.

At idle speed the system will settle down to idle at the best speed for each individual application. Most adaptive systems will lose their settings if the battery is disconnected. Once the battery is reconnected and the engine is restarted, the system will need to go through a relearning curve. This usually occurs fairly quickly, although idle quality may be poor until the adaptive process is completed.

Not all systems are affected by battery disconnection, and the Rover MEMS is an example of a system that uses non-volatile memory to retain adaptive settings when the battery is disconnected.

When one or more system components have been renewed, the ECU will need to relearn the new values, and this can sometimes create operating problems until the ECU has completed the process.

### Rogue adaptive function

The danger with an adaptive function is that sometimes an erroneous signal may be adopted as a valid measurement, and this may create an operating problem. If the erroneous signal is not serious enough to generate a fault code, the fault may remain undetected.

In some instances the ECU can become confused, and the adaptive values could become corrupted. This may cause operational problems and a system check will reveal 'no fault found'. Disconnecting the vehicle battery may effect a cure, since the re-calibration will reset the ECU default base values.

# 5 Catalytic converter and emission control systems

## General

All new petrol vehicles sold in the UK from January 1st 1993 onwards are equipped with a catalytic converter, and implement a closed-loop control system so that exhaust emissions may be reduced. Many diesel vehicles are fitted with a catalytic converter, but a closed loop system similar to that fitted to petrol engines, cannot be used because a diesel engine always operates with excess air, and hence oxygen, in the exhaust gas.

## Catalytic converter

A catalyst is something which promotes a chemical reaction, but itself remains unaffected by the reaction. The catalytic converter consists of a stainless steel housing containing a ceramic monolith element with a honeycomb of passages called cells. There are 400 cells per square inch, giving an internal surface area of 3.55 metres. The element is coated with a rough-surfaced aluminium oxide washcoat and fired in a kiln to give a surface area of 1-2 football pitches (depending on catalyst size). The washcoat is coated with a microscopically-thin layer containing 2-3 grams of the precious metals platinum and rhodium (Fig. 8.14).

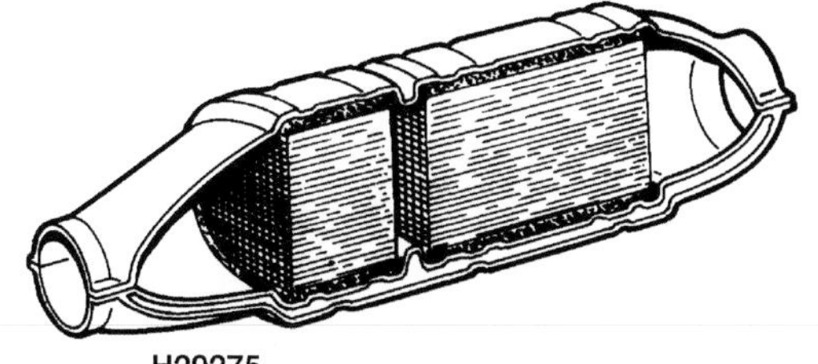


***8.14 Catalytic converter***

A steel mesh blanket is used to protect the monolith from heat and road vibrations. Some form of heat shielding is placed between the vehicle underbody and exhaust, and thus the passenger compartment is heat-insulated from the high operating temperature of the converter.

The catalyst is like a secondary combustion chamber, and CO and HC are oxidised into $H_2O$ and $CO_2$. NOx is oxidised by a process known as reduction, where oxygen and nitrogen are forced apart. The oxygen combines with CO to produce $CO_2$ and $N_2$.

A weak mixture with a high level of $O_2$ is good for the efficient oxidation of CO and HC. On the other hand, a relatively rich mixture with some CO aids the reduction of NOx. A compromise is reached by adjusting the air-fuel ratio of the catalyst-equipped engine to the stoichiometric ratio of 14:1. This means that the engine is perhaps adjusted slightly richer than desirable, and will therefore use more fuel (Fig. 8.15).

A catalyst needs to reach a minimum temperature of 300°C before it begins to work efficiently, and a working temperature of 400-800°C is more desirable. As the temperature rises over 800-1000°C, the precious metals will begin to break down. Above 1000°C, the catalyst will melt. Excess fuel or misfires causes overheating. Leaded petrol and excessive oil residue also destroys the catalyst. Here the lead compounds clog the pores of the washcoat, and coat the

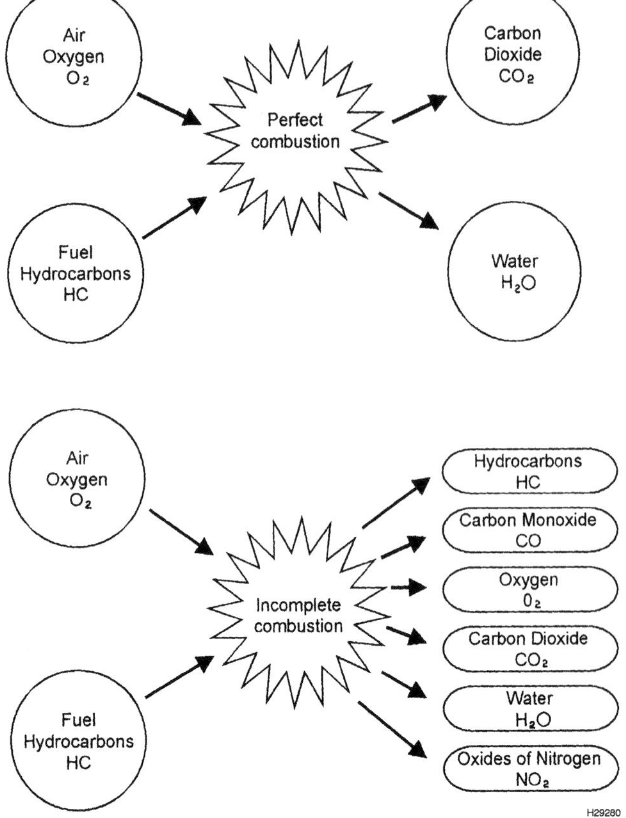


***8.15 Combustion chart***

precious metals, thus reducing the conversion rate and eventually rendering it useless. The fuel filler pipe in a catalyst-equipped vehicle is restricted to prevent the use of anything other than unleaded petrol.

When new, the catalyst may emit $H_2S$ (hydrogen sulphide) gas. This smells like rotten eggs, and is caused by the sulphur contained in petrol. Under deceleration when the AFR is lean, sulphur trioxide is stored in the catalyst. After deceleration, when the AFR enriches, this sulphur trioxide reacts with hydrogen in the exhaust to be emitted as $H_2S$. Although $H_2S$ is toxic, the emission is considered to be quite safe. Generally, the smell becomes less pronounced after a few thousand miles.

An engine with a catalytic converter, but without an ECU and an oxygen/Lambda sensor and therefore operating in 'open-loop' control, will convert approximately 50% of emissions. However, in an engine with a catalytic converter, and with an ECU and oxygen/Lambda sensor ('closed-loop' control), the emission conversion rate is likely to be more than 90%.

**Precautions**

**DO NOT**

*a) Turn the engine off at engine speeds above idle rpm.*
*b) Start the vehicle by towing.*
*c) Use fuel or oil additives.*
*d) Drive when the engine burns oil.*
*e) Park over dry leaves or long grass.*

It is essential that an engine with a catalyst is operating correctly at all times. Any engine problem or misfire that results in unburnt fuel passing into the catalyst will destroy it in very quick order. The unburnt fuel causes the catalyst to overheat. Once temperatures over 900°C are attained, the catalyst substrate will melt. This will destroy the catalyst, and a blocked exhaust is also highly likely. The blocked exhaust will cause lack of power and starting problems, and this will almost certainly become a common occurrence.

## 'Closed-loop' control

'Closed-loop' systems are equipped with an oxygen sensor which monitors the exhaust gas for oxygen content. A low oxygen level in the exhaust signifies a rich mixture. A high oxygen level in the exhaust signifies a weak mixture.

When the engine is operating in closed-loop control, the OS signal causes the ECU to modify the injector pulse so that the AFR is maintained close to the stoichiometric ratio. By controlling the injection pulse, during most operating conditions, so that the air/ fuel ratio is always in a small 'window' around the Lambda point (ie Lambda = 0.97 to 1.03), almost perfect combustion could be achieved. Thus the catalyst has less work to do, and it will last longer with fewer emissions at the tail pipe (Fig. 8.16).

The closed-loop control is implemented during engine operation at coolant temperatures near normal operating temperature. When the coolant temperature is low, or the engine is at full-load or on the overrun, the ECU will operate

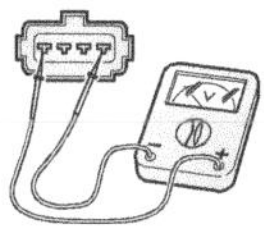

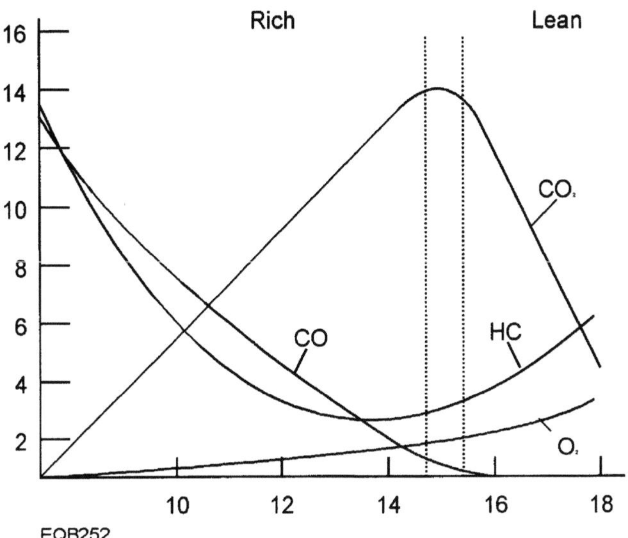


*8.16 AFR chart*

in 'open-loop'. When operating in open-loop, the ECU allows a richer or leaner AFR than the stoichiometric ratio. This prevents engine hesitation, for example, during acceleration with a wide-open throttle.

## Oxygen sensor (OS)

An oxygen sensor is a ceramic device placed in the exhaust manifold on the engine side of the catalytic converter on petrol vehicles. Various names have been given to this sensor, and it could equally be called a Lambda sensor, oxygen sensor or even an exhaust gas oxygen sensor (EGOS) (Fig. 8.17).

The quantity of oxygen remaining after combustion is an excellent indicator of a deficit or surplus of air (rich or weak mixture). The oxygen sensor returns a signal to the ECU, which can almost instantaneously (within 50 ms) adjust the injection duration. By controlling the engine electronically so that the AFR is always at the Lambda point, no matter the load or speed, almost perfect combustion could be achieved.

Essentially, the OS contains two porous platinum electrodes. The outer surface electrode is exposed to exhaust air and coated in porous ceramic. The inner surface electrode is exposed to ambient atmospheric air.

There are now two different types of OS in use. The first

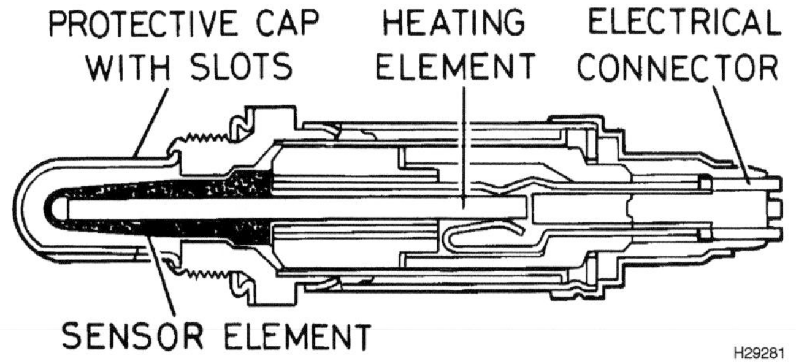


*8.17 Oxygen sensor (OS)*

and most commonly used OS utilises a zirconia element. A voltage signal is generated by the difference in oxygen levels at the two electrodes, and this is transmitted to the ECU. This voltage is inversely proportional to the level of oxygen in the exhaust manifold. The ECU uses this signal to adjust the injector opening time to maintain Lambda = 1.0 ± 0.02.

The OS closed-loop voltage is quite low, and switches between 100 millivolts (weak) to 1.0 volt (rich). The signal actually takes the form of a switch, and switches very quickly from weak to rich.

The second type of OS is made from titania, and functions by a change in resistance which alters a digital signal that originates from the ECU. Response of the titania OS is much faster than those made from zirconia, and the signal is much more stable over a range of exhaust temperatures.

Unfortunately, driveability would be impaired if the engine was set at Lambda for its entire driving cycle. Controlling the engine to the Lambda ideal would cause hesitation, flat spots and a lack of smoothness that would make a car pretty near undriveable. Therefore, when the engine is under Lambda control (ie cruising) it is in 'closed-loop' operation. Under acceleration or during the warm-up period, the system goes into 'open-loop' operation, and a richer mixture is allowed to prevent hesitation.

### Heated OS

The OS only produces a signal when the exhaust gas, has reached a minimum temperature of approximately 300°C. In order that the OS will reach optimum operating temperature as quickly as possible after the engine has started, the OS contains a heating element. The OS heater supply is usually applied from the fuel pump relay output terminal. This ensures that the heater will only operate whilst the engine is running.

## Engine faults

Although the oxygen sensor method of regulating the AFR works perfectly well with a properly operating engine, things go awry once faults develop. Almost any problem that affects combustion will see an increase of $O_2$ in the exhaust. For example, a misfire due to an ignition or mechanical problem means that combustion is incomplete, and the level of $O_2$ in the exhaust will rise.

The ECU will interpret this as a lean mixture and increase the fuel injection duration. When the fuel injection method is Multi-point simultaneous injection or single point injection, all cylinders will be enriched. This is the main reason why use of the sequential injection method will almost certainly increase. With sequential injection, only the afflicted cylinder will receive more fuel.

## Evaporation control (activated carbon filter and control valve)

An activated carbon canister is employed in catalyst equipped vehicles to aid evaporative emission control on petrol vehicles. The carbon canister stores fuel vapours and a control valve (CFSV) or (CFCV) is used to control the vapours stored in the canister. Depending upon the system, the control valve may be actuated by the ECU, or mechanically actuated according to temperature. Once the control valve is actuated, fuel vapours are drawn into the inlet manifold to be burnt by the engine during normal combustion. Alternatively, a very simple evaporative purge system may simply be operated by the position of the throttle (Fig. 8.18).

#### ECU-actuated

When the engine is stopped, the carbon filter solenoid valve (CFSV) is open. As soon as the ignition is switched 'on' the CFSV closes. So that engine performance will not be affected, the CFSV remains closed during cold engine operation and also during engine idle. Once the engine coolant temperature reaches normal operating temperature and the throttle is partially open (normal cruise conditions with a hot engine) the CFSV will be modulated (pulsed) on and off by the ECU. Once the CFSV is actuated by the ECU, fuel vapours are drawn into the inlet manifold to be burnt by the engine during normal combustion.

#### Mechanically-actuated

Vacuum is usually applied to the carbon filter control valve (CFCV) through a thermistor. The CFCV remains closed during cold engine operation, so that engine performance will not be affected, and the vacuum supply is arranged so that vacuum to the CFCV is not available during engine idle. Once the engine coolant temperature reaches normal operating temperature and the throttle is partially open (normal cruise conditions with a hot engine) vacuum is applied to the CFCV so that fuel vapours are drawn into the inlet manifold to be burnt by the engine during normal combustion.

#### Throttle-actuated

When the throttle is closed, the purge line to the canister is closed. After the engine is started and the throttle is opened, vacuum acts upon the canister to draw the vapours into the inlet manifold, to be burnt by the engine during normal combustion.

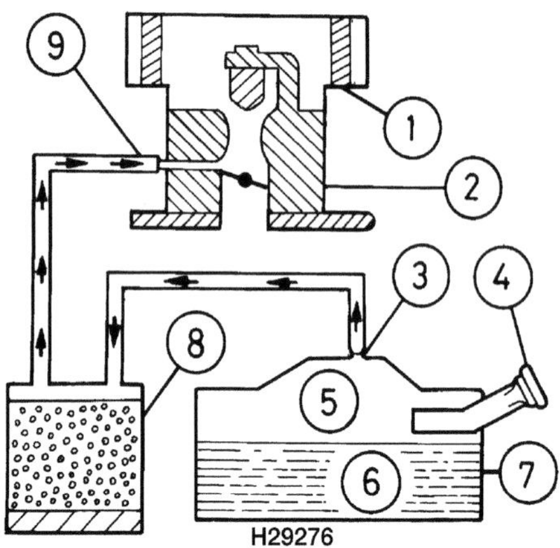


***8.18 Mechanically-controlled evaporation circuit***

*1 Air filter*
*2 Throttle body*
*3 Restrictor*
*4 Sealed fuel cap*
*5 Fuel vapour*
*6 Fuel*
*7 Fuel tank*
*8 Charcoal canister*
*9 Purge hose*

## Analysis of exhaust gases

#### Oxygen ($O_2$)

Oxygen is a harmless gas that is present in about 21% of air, and is necessary for proper combustion. O2 consists of two oxygen atoms and is measured in % volume. A small proportion of oxygen (1 – 2%) will be left after proper combustion. Too much or too little would indicate an incorrect air/fuel ratio, ignition or mechanical problems, or an exhaust leak. The amount of O2 that is expelled into the exhaust is that which is left over after combustion, and is a good indicator of the AFR – so long as the engine is operating correctly.

#### Carbon monoxide (CO)

Carbon monoxide is formed by the partial burning of the fuel due to a lack of oxygen. A low proportion of CO in the exhaust indicates how well the air/fuel ratio is maintained. A high proportion of CO in the exhaust indicates a rich fuel mixture, choked air filter, choked PCV valve or low idle speed. Low CO would indicate a lean fuel mixture or a vacuum leak, or even an exhaust leak. CO (and HC) emissions decrease as load (heat and temperature) rises to give a more efficient engine.

The CO content in the exhaust is an indicator of the AFR, but only when the engine is functioning normally. Any engine condition that causes a misfire will reduce the amount of CO that is burnt. CO is produced from the partial burning of fuel, and if you don't burn the fuel you won't produce the CO.

It is therefore obvious that an engine with a burnt valve or a dead spark plug would produce less CO. In this instance, any attempt to adjust the fuel mixture would result in an over-rich mixture, even though the gas analyser indicated a lean mixture. Only a gas analyser that could calculate a 'corrected' CO reading would provide the complete picture. It is essential therefore that all mechanical and ignition faults are corrected before making fuel adjustments.

CO is a poisonous, tasteless, colourless and odourless gas. It is a serious health hazard in dense city traffic or in semi-enclosed areas. A concentration of 0.3% can be fatal if breathed in continually for 30 minutes. CO combines with red blood cells at the expense of oxygen, and causes suffocation. By weight, CO accounts for about 47% of air pollution, but is thought to have little effect on the environment. One molecule of CO contains one atom of carbon and one of oxygen, and it is measured in % volume. CO is inversely proportional to the AFR – the less fuel, the lower the CO.

#### Carbon dioxide ($CO_2$)

$CO_2$ is the product of an efficient engine. With low CO and HC levels, the percentage of $CO_2$ in the exhaust is likely to be 13 to 15%. Less than 8% $CO_2$ indicates an incorrect AFR, or a

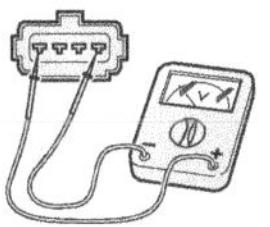

misfire or leaky exhaust. $CO_2$ is directly proportional to the AFR, but inversely proportional to CO. The less fuel, the higher the $CO_2$. At speeds over 2000 rpm, the level will be 1-2% higher than at idle, due to an increase in engine efficiency.

One molecule of $CO_2$ contains one atom of carbon and two of oxygen. $CO_2$ is chemically stable, and does not easily react with other substances. Not poisonous, it is produced by all breathing animals, including fish. Oxygen is inhaled and $CO_2$ exhaled at a concentration of about 5%. $CO_2$ is absorbed by all green plants by a process called 'photo-synthesis', which only happens in daylight, and which also releases $O_2$ into the atmosphere.

Any burning process produces $CO_2$, and the contribution from automotive sources is said to be less than half that of industrial and domestic sources. The contribution from people and animals is insignificant. A heavy concentration of $CO_2$ is like placing a blanket over the atmosphere, and this prevents heat loss by radiation. At present, more $CO_2$ is being produced than is being consumed, and the disappearance of the rain forests is another significant factor. As the forests fade away, less $CO_2$ is absorbed; the increase in atmospheric concentration is said to contribute towards 'global warming' and the so-called 'greenhouse effect'.

In the automobile, the only way to produce less $CO_2$ is to burn less petrol, or even none at all. This means an efficient engine with good economy (a lean-burn engine), or a diesel engine with high economy, or even a car with no engine – ie an electric motor. But electric cars need electricity, and electricity is produced by power stations, and most power stations also produce $CO_2$.

### Hydrocarbons (HC)

Composed of 15% hydrogen and 85% carbon, petrol is almost pure hydrocarbons. HC is a generic term, and refers to unburnt and partially-burnt hydrocarbon fuel. It is measured in PPM – parts per million. There are many different kinds of HC in the exhaust and HC is generally capable of serious damage to eyes, nose and lungs. When mixed with NOx and in the presence of bright sunshine, photochemical smog is formed. HC is also said to be a reason for the death of the forests.

During combustion, the hydrogen atoms combine with the $O_2$ atoms to produce $H_2O$. The carbon atoms combine with $O_2$ atoms to produce $CO_2$. High levels of HC in the exhaust signifies ignition problems such as defective plugs or HT leads, incorrect timing, vacuum leaks, incorrect air/fuel ratio or engine mechanical faults. In fact, anything that causes inefficient engine operation will increase the level of unburnt HC in the exhaust.

**As the AFR weakens, the HC emissions increase due to a lean misfire. This is why a black exhaust is often the result of a too-lean idle mixture. Careful design of the combustion chamber can overcome this problem.**

### Oxides of nitrogen (NOx)

NOx is a term for a group of poisonous gases formed due to high temperatures (exceeding 1300°C). and high compression. There are many different kinds of NOx (ie NO, $NO_2$, $NO_3$ etc) and they are all lumped together under the term NOx, the N representing one nitrogen atom and Ox representing any number of oxygen atoms.

The nitrogen content of air passes through the combustion process unchanged until high temperature (more than 1370°C) and high pressures are reached. Under these conditions, nitrogen and oxygen react to form nitrogen monoxide – sometimes called Nitric oxide – (NO). The breeding conditions for NOx are wide-open throttle, acceleration and high-speed cruising. When NO is produced in the presence of strong sunshine, $NO_2$ (nitrogen dioxide), ozone ($O_3$) and $NO_3$ (nitrogen nitrate) are the result. $NO_2$ is a light brown gas commonly called 'smog'. Unfortunately, NOx emissions reach their peak at Lambda = 1, the so-called perfect combustion point.

## Exhaust gas re-circulation (EGR)

Modern engines that run at a high temperature with high compression tend to produce an excessive level of NOx. NOx production can be reduced by recycling a small amount of exhaust gas into the combustion chamber. This procedure effectively lowers the combustion temperature, and reduces the incidence of NOx. So long as the recycling of the exhaust gas is properly controlled, engine operation will be little affected.

EGR operation in modern engines is controlled by the ECU, as distinct from earlier vehicles which used mechanical means. EGR control only occurs after the engine has attained normal operating temperature and the engine is operating under part-load conditions. The ECU monitors the voltage returned from the EGR sensor, and adjusts the signal to actuate the EGR vacuum control. The vacuum control device opens the EGR valve, which allows a finely-metered supply of exhaust gas to be introduced into the inlet manifold (Figs. 8.19 and 8.20).

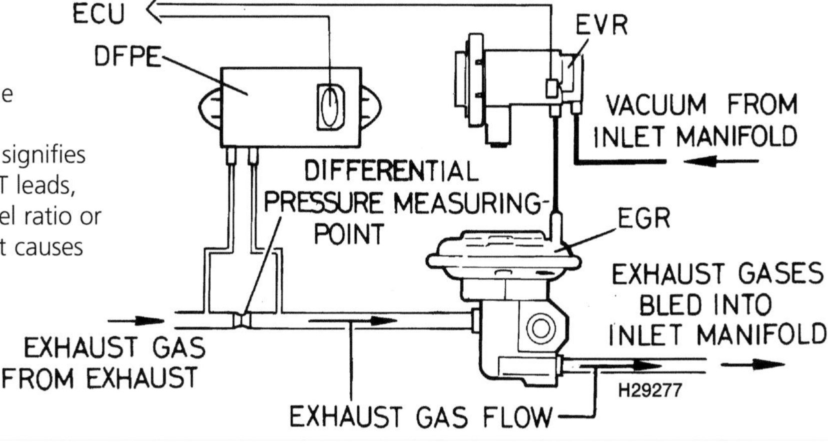


*8.19 Typical ECU-actuated exhaust gas re-circulation (EGR) system*

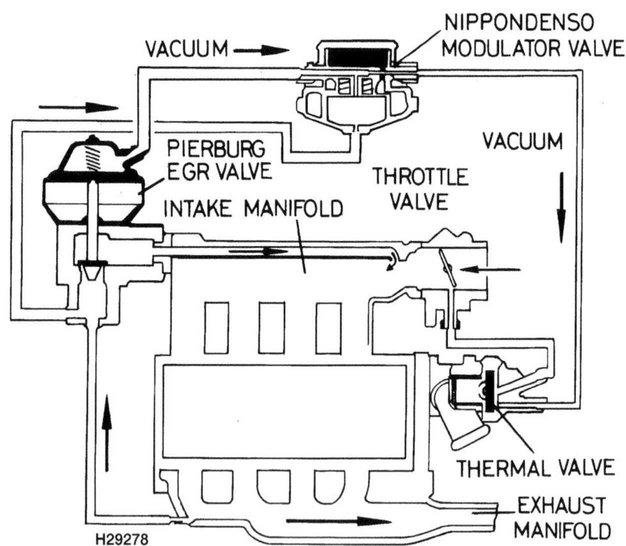


***8.20 Typical mechanically-actuated exhaust gas re-circulation (EGR) system***

## Particle filter systems – diesel vehicles

Particle filters and traps reduce the level of smoke particles released into the air by the diesel engine exhaust. this is an evolving technology; not all vehicle manufacturers use particle filters, but they still manage to satisfy the 'Euro 4' emission standards (mandatory in 2005).

The particle filter used by Peugeot and Citroën (PSA) is of the soot burn-off type. It works as follows (Fig. 8.21).

The soot particles are trapped in a block of filter material. The filter is carefully designed to allow the exhaust gases to flow through it, whilst trapping the soot particles; however there obviously comes a point when the filter will become blocked due to the large number of particles trapped. As the trapped particles in the filter build up, there will be a resistance to the exhaust gas flow. Pressure sensors on either side of the filter detect this resistance; when it exceeds a certain level the ECU triggers a cleaning cycle.

Because the diesel engine always operates with excess air, the exhaust gas contains enough oxygen that at temperatures above 550°C, soot will burn off of its own accord. The exhaust gas temperature in a diesel engine is normally between 150°C and 200°C, which is not high enough to burn off the soot. When the cleaning cycle is triggered, an additive is injected into the fuel which increases the exhaust gas temperature and burns off the soot. The additive is stored in a container next to the fuel tank.

If the filter is still clogged following a cleaning cycle, the ECU will go into 'limp home' mode and engine performance will be severely impaired. The filter must then be cleaned by a dealer workshop or diesel specialist using a special diagnostic tool in conjunction with the system's ECU (this cleaning may also be specified as a routine maintenance operation, typically every 48 000 miles). The engine's high pressure injection system is utilized to inject fuel into the exhaust gases during the post injection period; this causes the filter temperature to increase sufficiently to oxidize the particulates, leaving an ash residue. The filter is then removed from the exhaust system, and the ash residue flushed away with water.

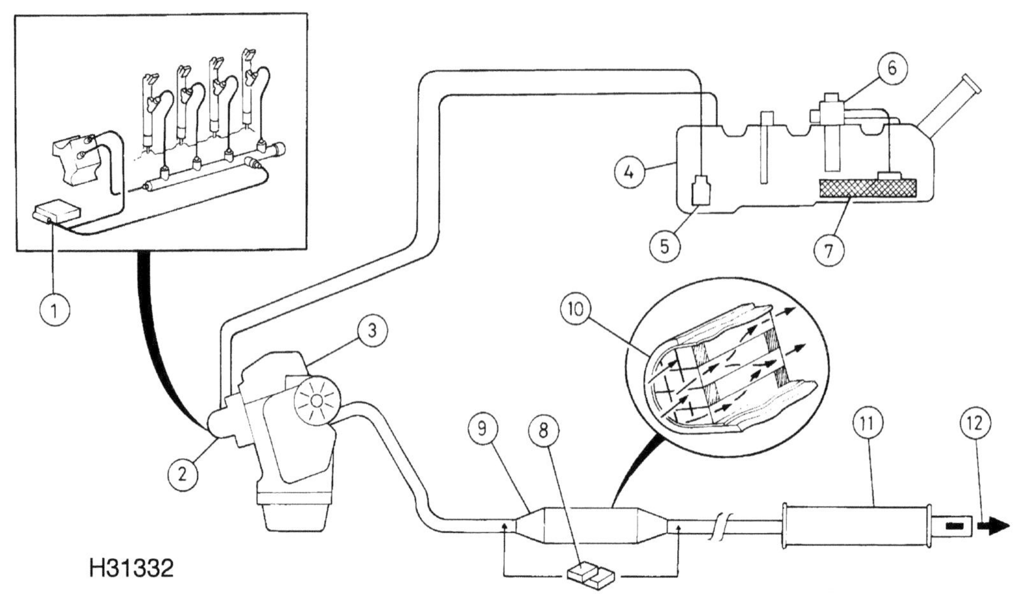


***8.21 Schematic view of emission control system using soot burn-off filter***

*1 Common rail injection system*
*2 High pressure fuel pump*
*3 Engine*
*4 Fuel tank*
*5 Fuel lift pump*
*6 Additive injector and regulator*
*7 Additive tank*
*8 Exhaust gas pressure sensors*
*9 Catalytic converter*
*10 Burn-off filter*
*11 Silencer*
*12 Exhaust gases*

# Spark plugs

## 1 The spark plug

**1** In principle, the spark plug is a simple device for providing electrodes within the cylinder space. A high voltage provided by the ignition system is applied to the electrodes causing a spark at the correct time and in the correct position to ignite the petrol-air vapour. It was invented by Jean Lenoir in 1860 and remains the same in principle, but in practice is the result of much research and technological innovation.

**2** A spark plug operates in the combustion chamber of the engine under severe conditions. For example, the combustion chamber temperature can reach 2500°C and pressures of 700 lbf/in$^2$ (50 kg/cm$^2$). The plug is exposed to sudden changes in temperature and pressure; going abruptly from the temperature of burning fuel to the relatively low temperature of the incoming petrol mixture. It must endure high voltage, mechanical vibration and corrosion attack from the combustion gases.

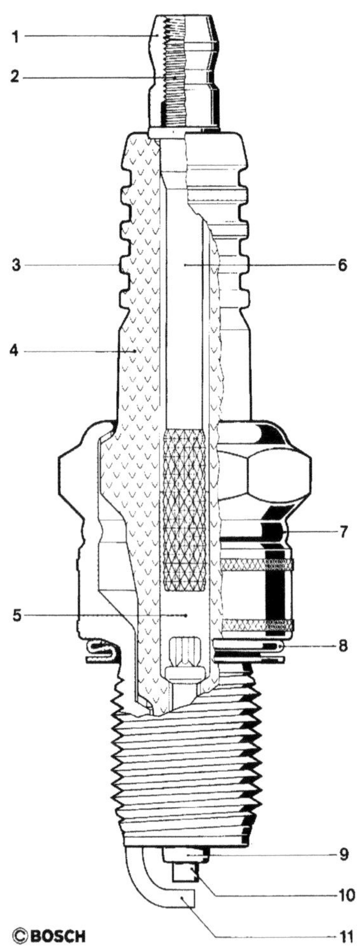


*Fig. 9.1 Spark plug construction*

1 *Terminal nut*
2 *Connection thread*
3 *Leakage-current barrier*
4 *Insulator ($Al_2O_3$)*
5 *Special conductive glass seal*
6 *Terminal stud*
7 *Swaged and heat-shrunk fitting*
8 *Captive outer gasket (in the case of flat seal)*
9 *Insulator tip*
10 *Centre electrode*
11 *Ground electrode*

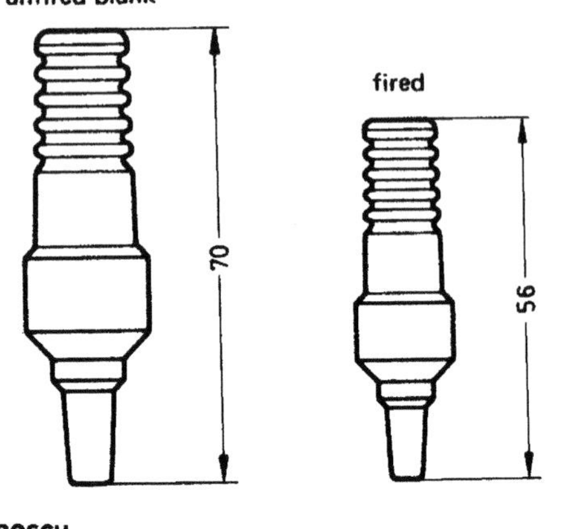


*Fig. 9.2 Spark plug insulator before and after firing*

## 2 Construction

**1** Plugs are made up of three main components – the shell, electrodes and insulator (Fig. 9.1).

### Insulator

The job of the insulator is to ensure that the high voltage pulse will not leak to earth within the plug body. It also has an effect on heat dissipation and partly determines the 'heat range' of the plug. Alumina ($Al_2 O_3$) plus a filling agent is used to form the insulator which starts as a blank which is then fired in a high temperature furnace, during which a shrinkage of 20% takes place (Fig. 9.2). The exposed surface is glazed to prevent adherence of dirt, which could provide a leakage path. The effective length is increased by providing five ribs over which leakage current would have to travel. The insulator houses the centre electrode and the terminal stud.

In summary the insulator must possess:

*(a) Mechanical strength*
*(b) High insulation resistance*
*(c) Good thermal conductivity*

### Shell

Made of steel, the shell has a thread to screw it into the cylinder head while the upper part has a hexagon. The surface is electroplated nickel to deter corrosion, keep the thread free and to prevent seizure, the last being most important with alloy cylinder heads. The insulator is inserted into the spark plug shell then swaged and heat-shrunk in position by inductive heating under high pressure.

### Electrodes

The electrode materials are vital to correct plug operation for they must be suitable for easy spark emission, and resistant to high temperature and chemical corrosion. The centre electrode is held in place in one of several ways. Bosch use a conducting glass seal, and NGK and Champion use a powdered seal which caulks the electrode/insulator and insulator/steel body gaps. Nickel alloys are suitable for electrodes but in some plugs the nickel alloy has a core of copper or platinum to assist in conducting away the heat. The earthed electrode(s) is welded to the steel body and is commonly of rectangular section. The Champion double copper plugs have a copper core for both the centre and earthed electrode, the latter having a trapezoidal cross-section to give a larger area over which the spark may jump. It is claimed that this plug runs 100°C cooler than plugs with a solid nickel-alloy earth electrode (Fig. 9.3) and because the wear rate of the copper-cored earth electrode is reduced, it is possible to use electrode gaps of up to 0.15 mm greater than with conventional solid earth electrode plugs. It is now accepted that a wider spark plug gap improves both the engine start-up characteristic and the ability to give efficient ignition to leaner fuel:air mixtures.

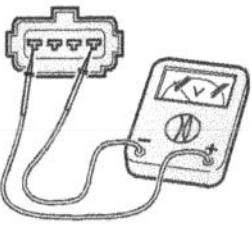

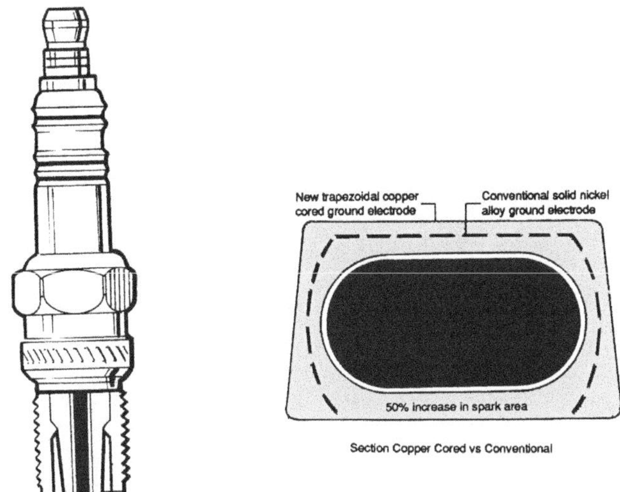


***Fig. 9.3 Champion double copper plug***

## 3 Heat range

**1** The firing end of a spark plug must operate between the temperature limits of 400°C and 800°C approximately. Below 400°C the plug cannot burn off the carbon deposits generated by combustion, and much above 800°C there is increasing oxide fouling and electrode burning. At 950°C the plug tip becomes so incandescent that premature igniting of the petrol vapour occurs – pre-ignition – resulting in damage to the piston and the plug itself (Figs. 9.4, 9.5 and 9.6).

**2** Heat flow from the plug has been measured by manufacturers with some accuracy and it is known that some 91% is transmitted via the screw thread and gasket to the engine body with the remaining 9% lost by radiation and convection from the plug shell and the exposed insulator (Fig. 9.7).

**3** The figures do not take into account the cooling effect of the fresh inflowing vapour, but do give an informative

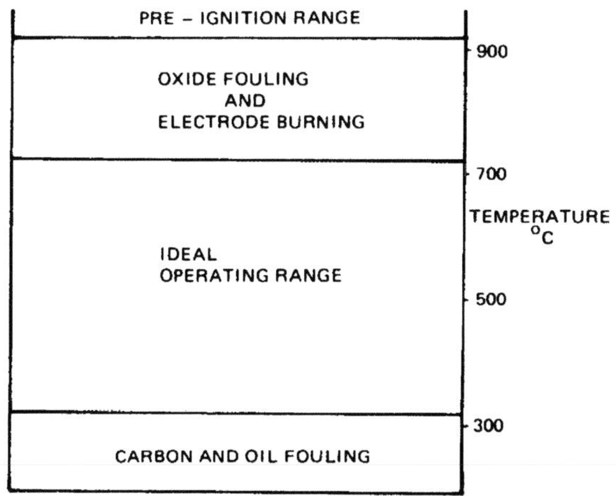


***Fig. 9.6 Plug operating temperatures***

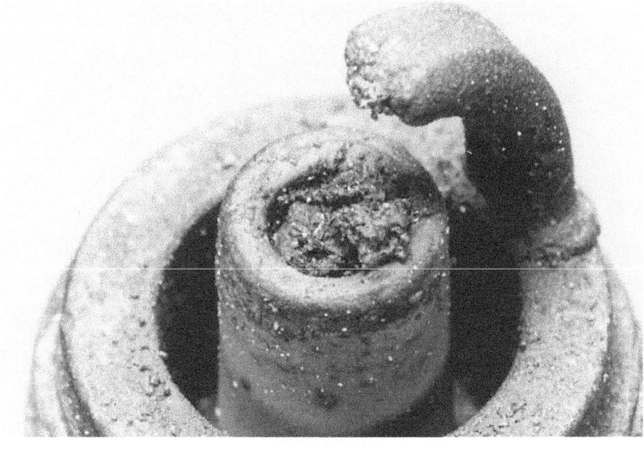

***Fig. 9.4 Pre-ignition damage to plug***

***Fig. 9.5 Piston crown holed by pre-ignition***

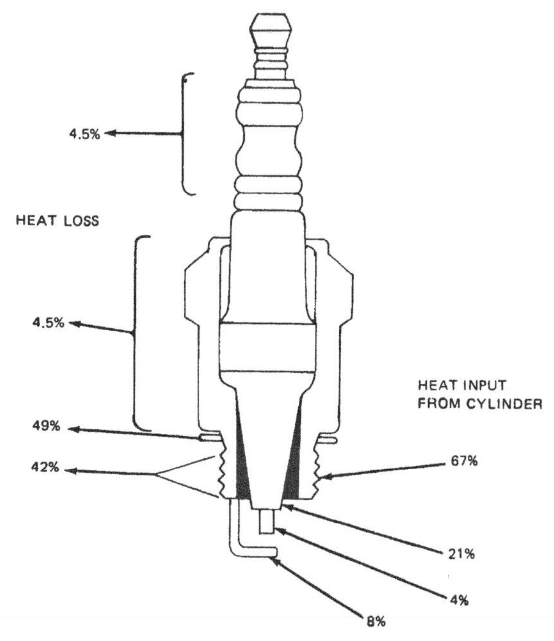


***Fig. 9.7 Heat flow in a sparking plug***

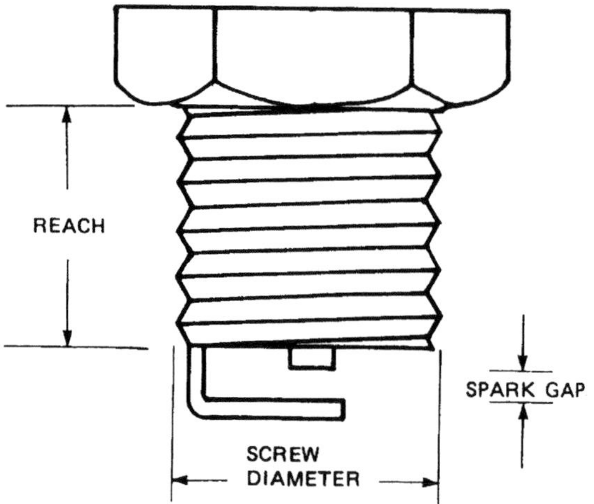


*Fig. 9.8 Vital dimensions of a sparking plug*

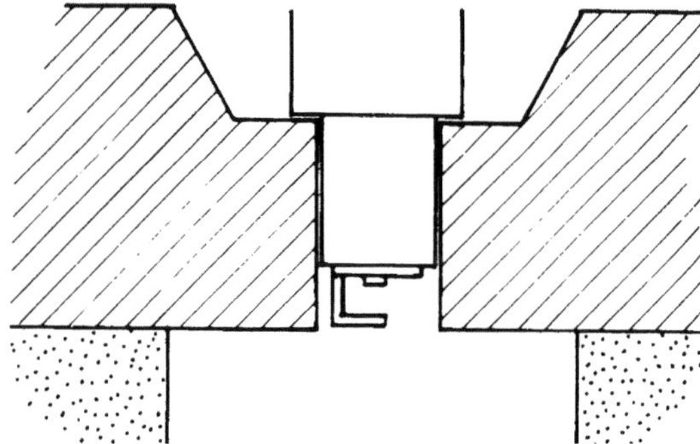

*Fig. 9.9a Reach too short*

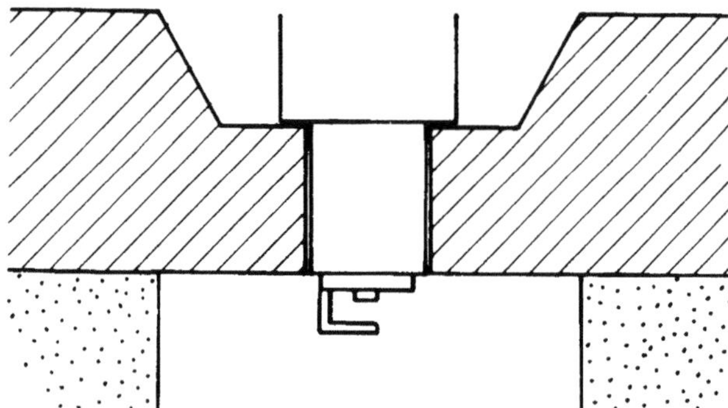

*Fig. 9.9b Reach correct*

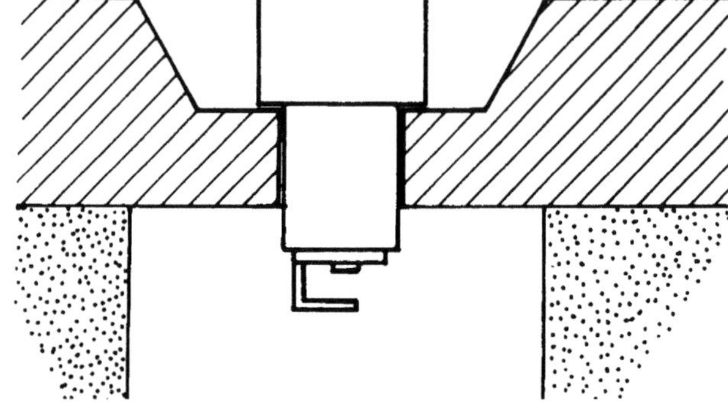

*Fig. 9.9c Reach too long*

picture. It is clear, for instance, that correct fitting and tightening down is vital, since the attached gasket is responsible for nearly half of the heat transmission – failure to maintain good seating contact could result in an overheated plug.

**4** Clearly no one plug can be correct for all operating conditions and some manufacturers distinguish between plug choice for round-town work or for sustained motorway travel. Most important dimensions of a spark plug are at the bottom end, and Fig. 9.8 shows vital statistics that MUST be correct.

**5** It is essential for correct plug tip temperatures that the electrodes should JUST project into the cylinder. If the plug reach is too short, the spark is shielded from the petrol vapour, and bad misfiring will result and be accompanied by carbon build-up: too long, and the electrodes will run hot and there is also the chance that the screw threads of cylinder and plug may be damaged by overheating (Fig. 9.9).

**6** Plugs dissipate heat from the centre electrode via the nose of the insulator surrounding it: a short insulator will pass heat to the steel shell more readily than a nose insulator which is relatively long and thin (Fig. 9.10).

**7** A high compression engine generally has hot operating conditions, and so a plug with best heat dissipation would be required. Conversely, a low compression engine has lower combustion chamber temperature and so a hotter grade of plug would be chosen so that the plug tip temperature could be maintained above the oil fouling level (Fig. 9.6). The rule is, therefore:

A hot engine uses a cold plug
A cold engine uses a hot plug

Note that sometimes hot plugs are referred to as 'soft' and cold plugs as 'hard'.

**8** The working temperature of a plug (heat range) depends upon four factors – see Fig. 9.11:

*(a) Choice of material used for the insulator and the design of electrodes. Electrodes with materials of high thermal conductivity or copper cored types will conduct heat well*

*(b) Insulator nose length will affect tip temperature. It is the*

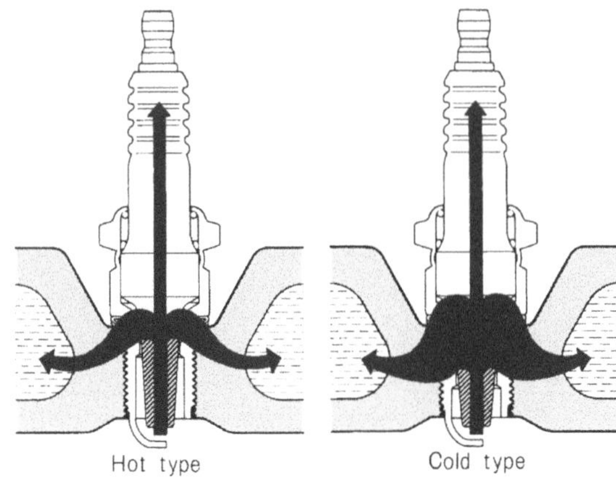


*Fig. 9.10 Heat flow in hot and cold plugs*

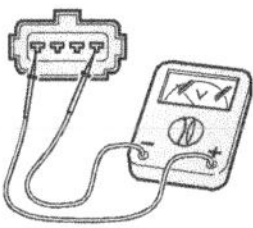

length from the tip of the insulator to the point where it can transfer conducted heat to the body

(c) *Insulator projection into the combustion chamber is linked to the cooling effect of the incoming petrol vapour. The term 'turbo action' is used to describe the effect of the incoming charge and better resistance to fouling is claimed*

(d) *Insulator/shell space is important because gas circulates in this 'gas volume'. Exchanges of heat between incoming vapour and outgoing gas will take place here.*

Enlarging this volume improves the ability of the plug to resist low temperature fouling. Due to the clearance gap there is improvement in charge cooling effect on the insulator nose and allows the use of a longer insulator nose. Enlarging the clearance also increases the amount of deposits that can be accepted before the fouled plug condition occurs.

## 4 Plug examination

**1** Examination of the spark plugs will give a good indication of the condition of the engine. If the insulator nose of the spark plug is clean and white, with no deposits, this is indicative of a weak mixture or too hot a plug (a hot plug transfers heat away from the electrode slowly, a cold plug transfers heat away quickly).

**2** If the tip and insulator nose are covered with hard black-looking deposits, then this is indicative that the mixture is too rich. Should the plug be black and oily, then it is likely that the engine is fairly worn, as well as the mixture being too rich.

**3** If the insulator nose is covered with light tan to greyish-brown deposits, then the mixture is correct and it is likely that the engine is in good condition.

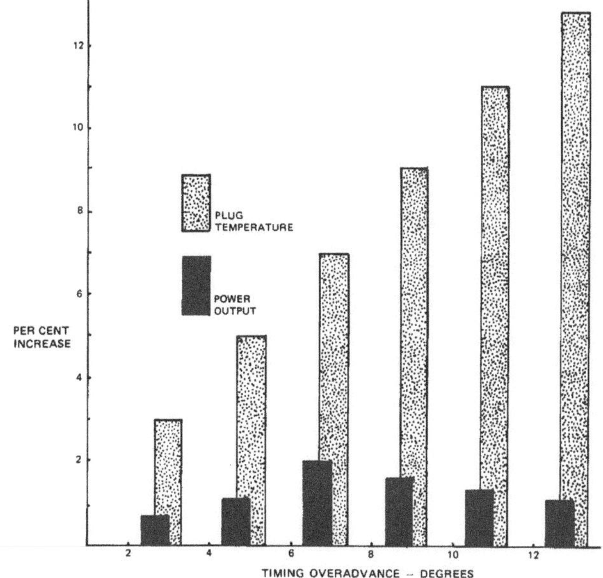


*Fig. 9.12 Effects of ignition advance*

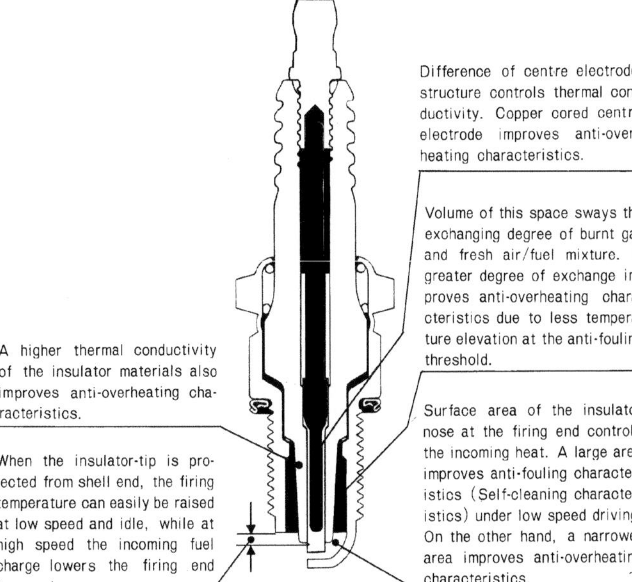


***Fig. 9.11 Influence of design on the heat range of a spark plug***

## 5 Ignition timing

**1** Incorrect ignition timing will have a marked effect on plug temperatures. While advancing ignition beyond manufacturer's figures may show a small power increase, the temperature rise will be disproportionally greater, giving rise to problems on sustained full load (Fig. 9.12).

## 6 Types of spark plug

**1** Plugs have seats which are either flat or conical (Fig. 9.13). The **flat seat** uses a gasket washer which is attached permanently to the plug body, and it is important that the

***Fig. 9.13 Spark plugs with flat (left) and conical seats***

*Fig. 9.14 Spark plug types*
*A Standard type*
*B P type (projected insulator nose)*
*C Resistor type*
*D Multiple earth electrodes*
*E Surface discharge plug*

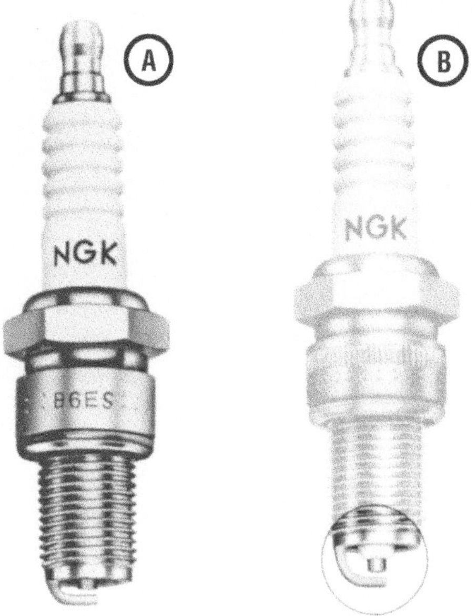


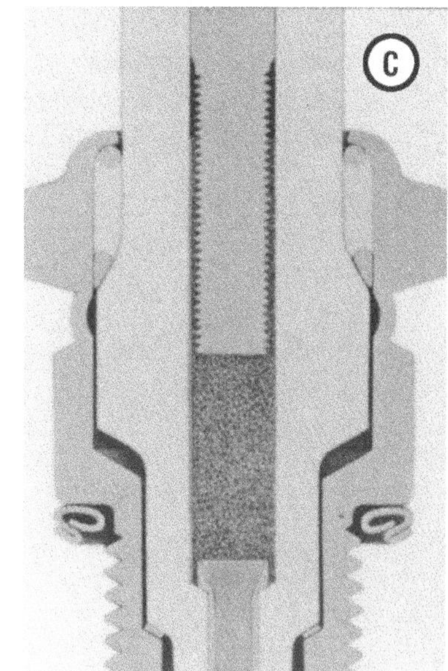


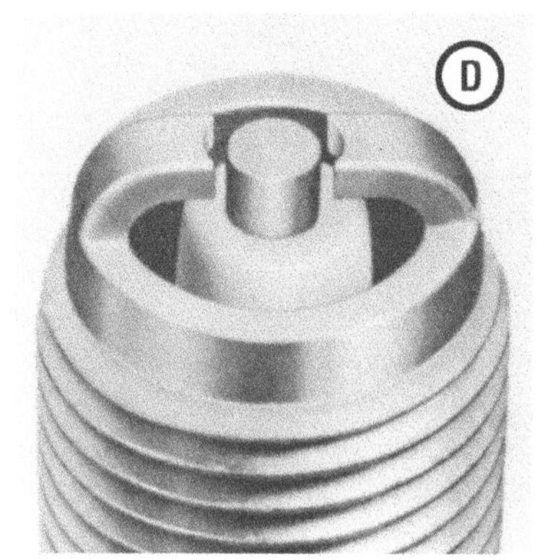


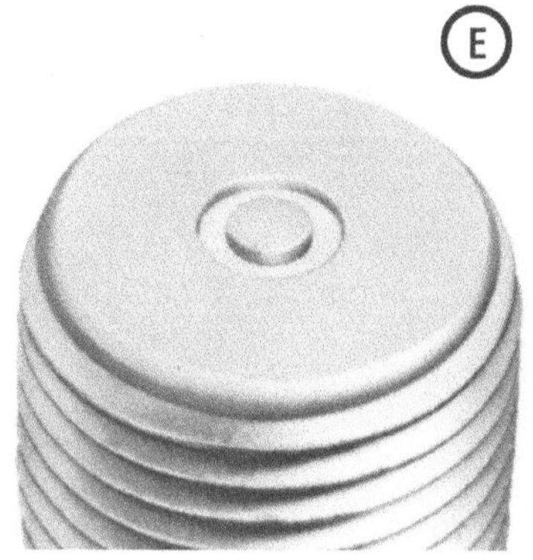


plug is screwed properly into the cylinder head. Too loose and the effect can be pre-ignition because there is no proper conductive path for heat; too tight and threads of both plug and cylinder head could be damaged. (For correct fitting notes see Section on plug servicing.)

**Conical** (or taper) seating plugs do not use gaskets and can be made with a smaller body shell; they are becoming increasingly popular. Special care must be taken when fitting (see plug servicing Section).

**2** The **standard** plug has the spark gap just protruding from the bottom of the plug thread (Fig. 9.14a).

The standard insulator nose plug is suitable for older engine design.

**3 P types** (an NGK term) refers to plugs with a projecting insulator nose (Fig. 9.14b). Better fouling protection and anti-pre-ignition characteristics are claimed for this type of plug, since the nose temperature is raised quickly at idle and low speeds to be within the self cleaning heat band. At high speeds the incoming charge has a cooling effect. This type of plug is suited to modern engine design.

**4 Resistor** types have a carbon compound resistor often of about 5 kΩ resistance in the centre core. This gives good radio interference suppression for it is more effective to have a suppression resistor close to the source of radiation – namely the spark (Fig. 9.14c). This type of spark plug has been standard original-equipment (OE) fitting in General Motors and Ford cars in the USA for several years.

**5 Multiple earth electrode plugs** are now standard fitment by many engine manufacturers (Fig. 9.14d). The Bosch Super 4 has four thin ground earth electrodes and a pointed, silver plated centre electrode. Depending on the engine loading and degree of wear of the plug, the spark 'selects' the best path to earth. the manufacturers claim the efficiency of the plug is improved by upto 60%. No gap adjustment is needed.

**6 Surface discharge plugs** are designed for CDI (capacitor discharge) ignition systems and will give good sparking even under conditions of fouling (Fig. 9.14e).

**7 Yttrium plugs** are manufactured by Bosch. This rare metal forms an adhesive oxide layer around the central electrode, and gives improved heat and wear characteristics.

## 7 Corona discharge and flashover

**1** If conditions are damp or the plug ribbed insulator is dirty, then in the dark a pale blue light may be seen around the HT cable connector and/or the plug insulator when the engine is running. This is due to ionization of the air which splits up into free electrons and positively charged ions in the area of high electric stress. It is known as Corona discharge.

**2** The effect on ignition is minimal unless the Corona reaches the terminal stud allowing flashover to the metal shell. This gives an engine misfire (Fig. 9.15).

**3** Sometimes a plug has a stain on the insulator which appears to be due to a gas leak. It is actually Corona stain

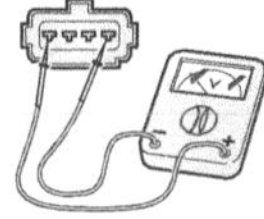

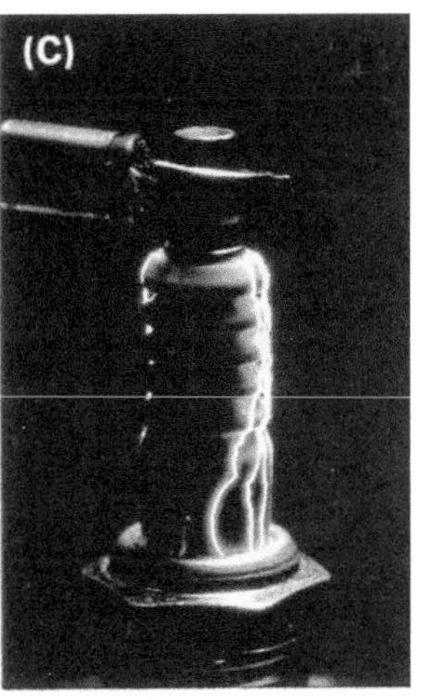


***Fig. 9.15 Corona discharge and flashover***

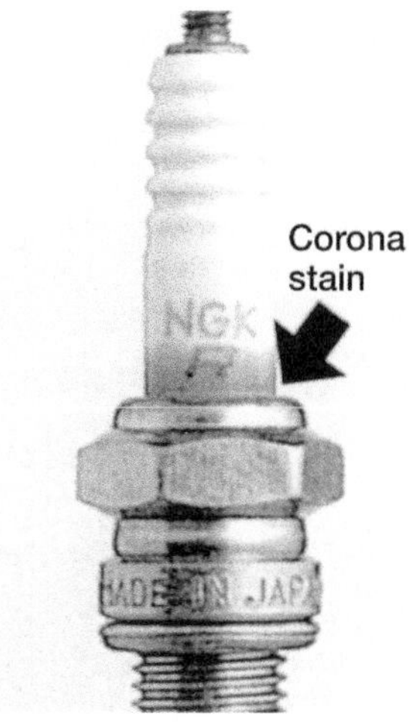


***Fig. 9.16 Corona staining of insulator***

due to the attraction of oil vapour particles around the engine, but due to the high insulation resistance of the oil, will not cause deterioration of the plug performance (Fig. 9.16).

## 8 Spark plug servicing

**1** Plugs used to have to be checked regularly at 3000 mile intervals for performance to be maintained at peak and even properly serviced plugs have a gradual deterioration and a finite life. Depending upon the way in which a car is used the economical limit of plug life is 10 000 miles. However, some of the platinum types plugs have a specified service life in excess of 50 000 miles! Check with your Service and Repair Manual.

**2** Plug cleaning used to be carried out by hand or by workshops using an abrasive grit blast machine. However, since the almost universal usage of unleaded petrol, plug cleaning has become unnecessary. If a plug looks unserviceable, replace it.

**3** However, on vintage or classic vehicles cleaning may be necessary. Cleaning manually is best carried out with a fine wire brush, going over external thread, plug tip and earth electrode CAREFULLY. A harsh abrasive brush may damage the plug and in any event check that no whiskers from the wire brush remain in the plug. Finally clean the insulator with a methylated spirits-soaked rag to prevent spark tracking paths from developing.

**4** When removing the plug, unscrew a few turns and blow or brush away any grit or rust particles lying round the plug well. Do not, under any circumstances, allow foreign matter to drop into the engine through the plug hole.

**5** Refitting needs care, especially with alloy heads. After cleaning the plug thread with a brass wire brush smear a TRACE of a suitable grease on the thread and start the plug carefully by hand. Withdraw immediately if unusual resistance is felt – this may be due to cross threading. One manufacturer (Bosch) states that their NEW plugs are already lubricated but grease should be used for all used plugs. Plugs should ideally be fitted to correct torque spanner values but in practice this is rarely done. The following rules will be satisfactory if a torque spanner is not used (Fig. 9.17):

(a) ***Flat seat plugs****. Screw the plug in by hand as far as it will go. Apply and turn the plug spanner until first resistance is felt and then for a NEW plug turn through 90°. USED plugs should be turned 30° only to tighten, since the gasket will have been compressed previously.*

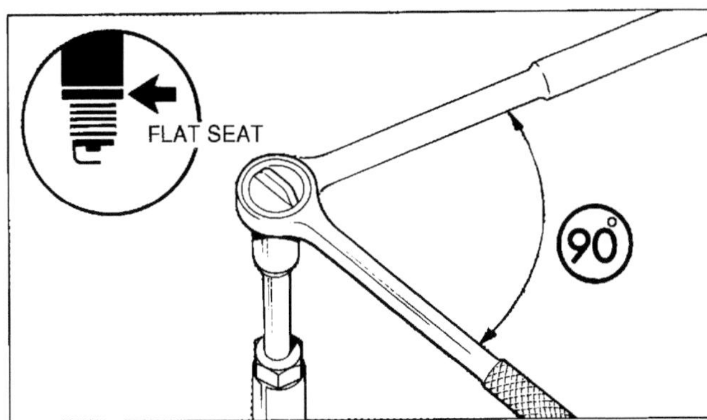


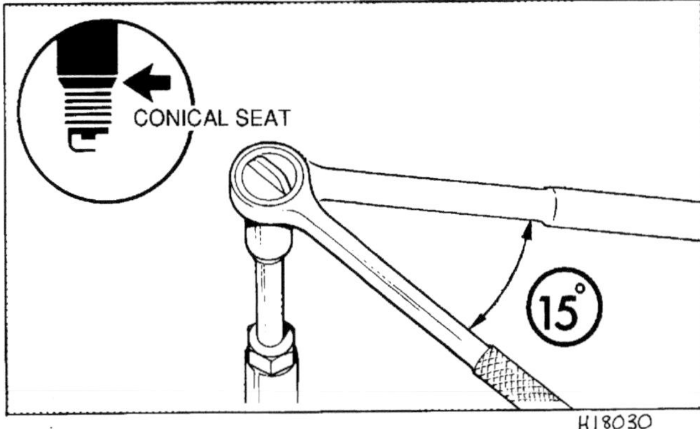


***Fig. 9.17 Spark plug tightening***

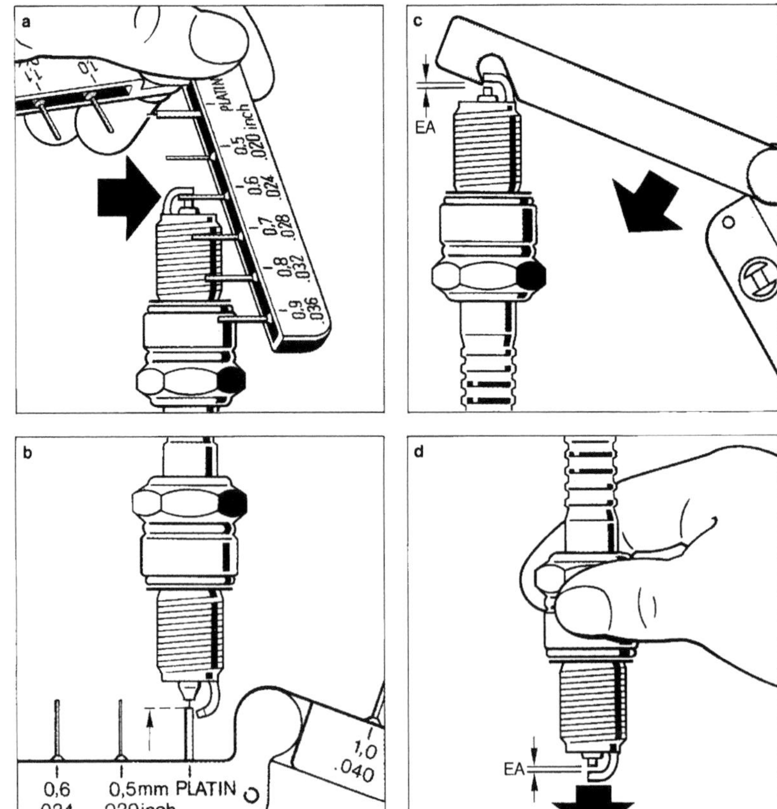


***Fig. 9.18 Using Bosch spark plug gauge***

*a) Measuring the electrode gap (EA). The appropriate measuring wire must pass between the electrodes with hardly noticeable resistance*

*b) Checking for wear. With the ground electrode bent back, the measuring wire for platinum spark plugs is introduced into the hole in the insulator nose. The wear limit has been reached when the wire goes in as far as the plastic stop (see arrow)*

*c) Widening the electrode gap: bend open with bending device*

*d) Holding the spark plug as shown, lightly and carefully tap the ground electrode vertically in the direction of the arrow on a hard, smooth surface*

*(b)**Conical seat plugs** should be turned by 15° after the first resistance is felt. This applies to new and used plugs.*

**6** Gap resetting should be carried out with a combination tool with an electrode adjuster and feeler gauge. Flat feeler gauges are not ideal for this job in case of irregular electrode wear. The Bosch set has a special thin wire which is inserted into the centre electrode of the platinum plug. When the wire goes in as far as the plastic stop the plug should be replaced. Fig. 9.18 shows the Bosch plug gauge in use.

## 9 Diesel glow plugs

**1** The diesel engine does not require a sparking plug to ignite the fuel since this is achieved by compressing air in the cylinder to give the required temperature for ignition when the fuel oil is injected by nozzle.

**2** However, it is advantageous for cold-start conditions to heat either the air in the engine intake manifold, or the fuel-air mixture in the combustion chamber.

**3** Glow plugs (Fig. 9.19) have a built-in electric resistance coil which is energised from the battery. Once the engine is running the electrical supply is automatically switched off. The AG2 and CH2 plug is a manifold heater type and is designed to heat a large volume of air as quickly as possible. AG4 and CH4 are pre-chamber glow plugs (combustion chamber plugs). The wire element is robust and of low resistance, working off only 1 or 2 volts. Consequently, such plugs are connected in series with each other and with a volt drop resistor. AG60and CH60 are sheathed, having higher resistance and may work off the vehicle supply voltage.

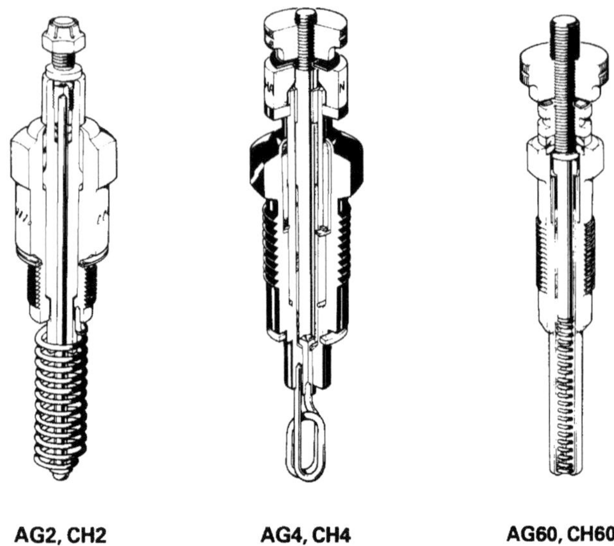


***Fig. 9.19 Typical diesel glow plugs***

# Signals and wipers

# 10



## 1 Direction indicators

**1** Flashing warning lights on front, rear and sides of a vehicle are required on all new vehicles manufactured after 1986. These lights should be amber coloured and flash on and off simultaneously at a rate of 60 to 100 operations per minute. A signal warning indicator lamp should be fitted so that it can be seen by the driver and flash at the same rate as the external turn signal lights. Bulb ratings should be within the range of 15 to 36 watts for each of the front and rear lamps, and the side-mounted repeater lamp is about 6 watts. In the event of an emergency, such as a roadside breakdown, all the lamps should be capable of working simultaneously, when they are called 'hazard warning lights'. A separate switch is used for this purpose. Provision should be made to show if lamp failure occurs, and this often takes the form of the remaining lamps working at a different rate. An outline of a directional indicator circuit is shown in Fig. 10.1 and a hazard warning circuit in Fig. 10.2.

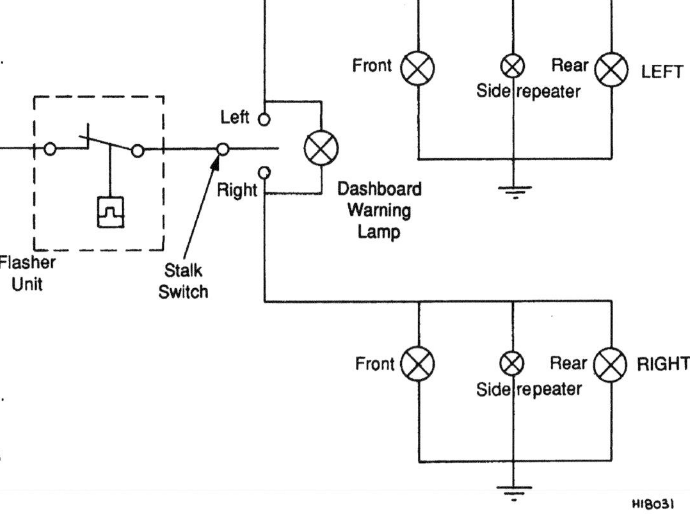


*Fig. 10.1 Direction indicator circuit*

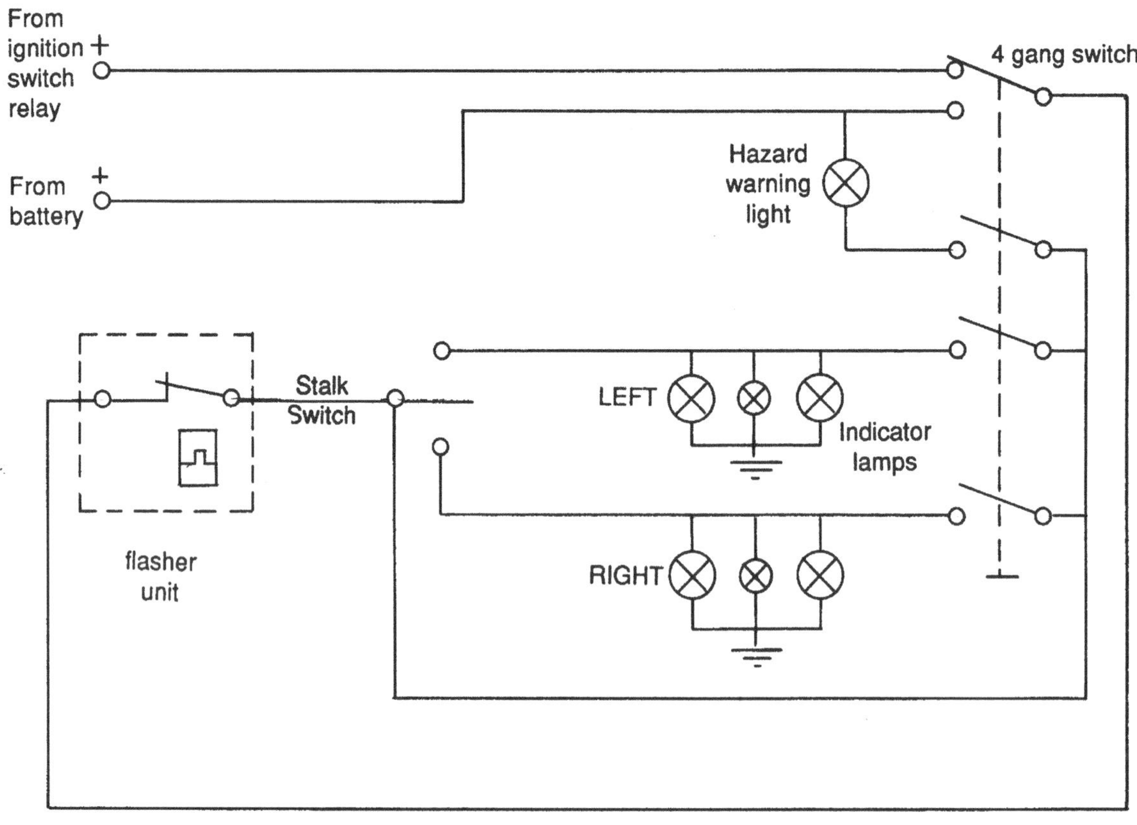


*Fig. 10.2 Hazard warning lamp circuit*

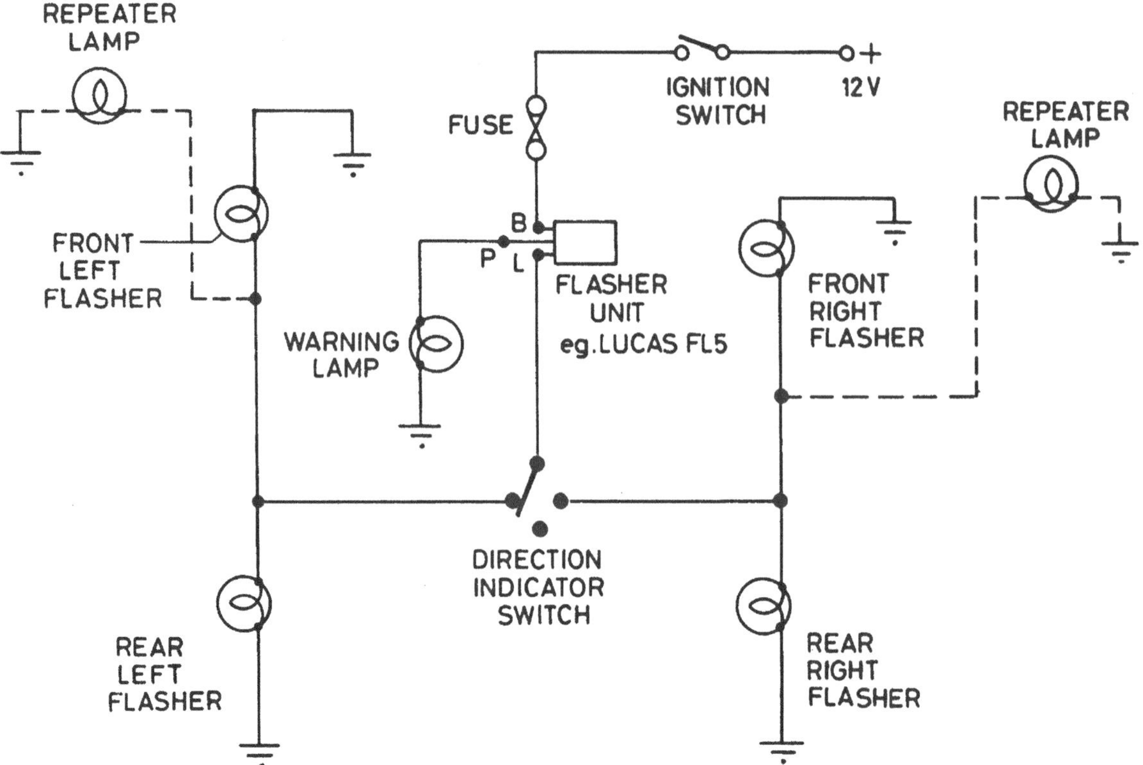


*Fig. 10.3 Three-terminal flasher unit and connections*

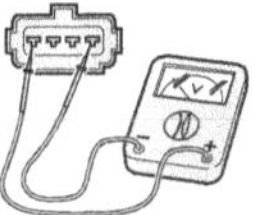

**2** Three types of flasher units may be found in vehicles:

*(a) Electronic*

*(b) Thermal*

*(c) Capacitor*

Of these, the electronic flasher is now virtually standard fitting on new and recent vehicles but many thermal flasher units are still in service; capacitor types are of various designs and now of minor importance. Fig. 10.1 shows a flasher unit with two active terminals, but in some older vehicles a three-terminal type may be met, a circuit for which is shown in Fig. 10.3. This may now be regarded as obsolete.

Many modern vehicles have indicator timing and other functions controlled by a central timer unit. This unit also controls the intermittent action of the wipers, the heater rear/front window auto cut-out, courtesy light operation and any other system requiring a timed function. For more information see Section 14.

## 2 Thermal flasher units

### Vane type

**1** Most common is the two-terminal 'clicker' type of flasher unit, having almost entirely replaced the older hot-wire three-terminal model, and itself has given way to electronic units.

**2** Fig. 10.4 show its construction. A vane or diaphragm of spring steel is normally in the 'bent' position shown and held in place by a taut metal resistive ribbon. When the flashers are switched on the resistance ribbon, which carries the lamp current, expands and allows the spring steel diaphragm to snap straight with an audible click. This also opens the main contacts, cutting off the heater current, the heater cools and at a particular point the spring steel bends suddenly back to its original shape with another click. This unit operates the flashing lights immediately the switch is closed.

**3** This flasher has only two terminals. If one bulb fails the click action usually stops, the pilot light and remaining lamp stay on but do not flash.

### Hot-wire type

**4** The hot-wire flasher is still found on some vehicles, and is illustrated in Fig. 10.5. When the direction indicator switch is on, current flows through the heater wire and the coil. As the heater wire expands, the main armature moves under spring tension to close the main contacts. During heating the limiting resistance prevents lighting of the indicator lamps, but when the contacts close this resistance is short-circuited and connects the indicator lamps straight on to the 12 volt supply via the coil.

**5** The higher current in the coil then magnetises the iron core and attracts the armature so that the contacts close firmly. This magnetism also attracts the secondary armature so as to close the pilot light contacts.

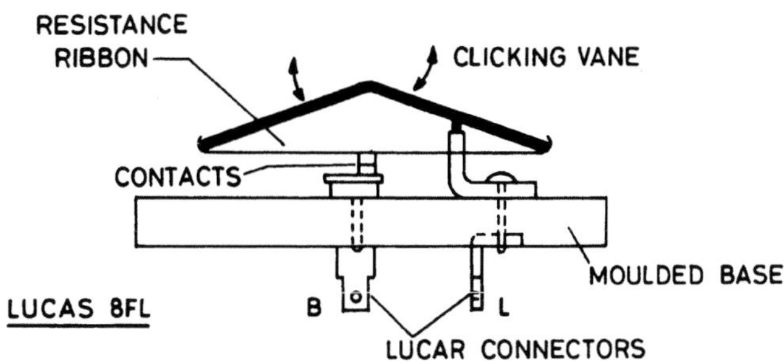


*Fig. 10.4 Vane (or diaphragm) flasher unit*

**6** As the short circuited heater wire cools, it contracts and the contacts open. The magnetism drops to a low value and the main and secondary armatures return to original positions.

**7** If an indicator lamps fails the current drawn is lower and the flashing frequency will rise. Additionally, it may be that the secondary armature will not close at all, so no dashboard warning light will come on.

## 3 Electronic flasher units

**1** Using a multivibrator oscillator to produce ON-OFF square wave pulses, this type of flasher unit has become standard for original equipment in passenger cars. There are several advantages over thermal types, including constant repetition rate of flashing irrespective of bulb loading, the provision of audible or visual warning of bulb failure (which is signalled by a doubling of flashing frequency seen on the dashboard warning lamp) and the ability to give hazard light warning over a long period.

**2** The astable multivibrator is, in principle, a square-wave

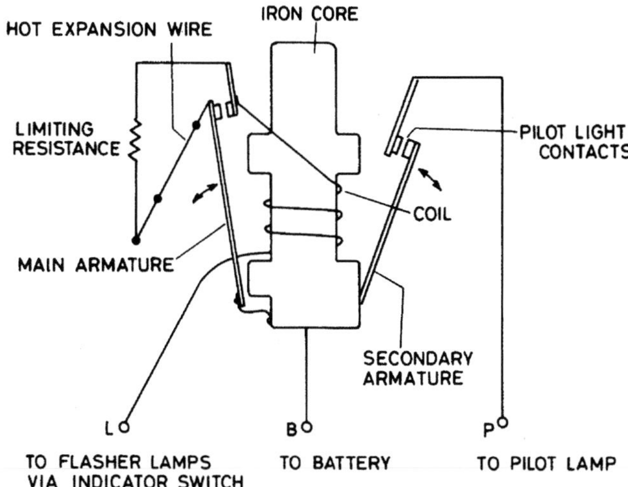


*Fig. 10.5 Hot wire flasher unit*

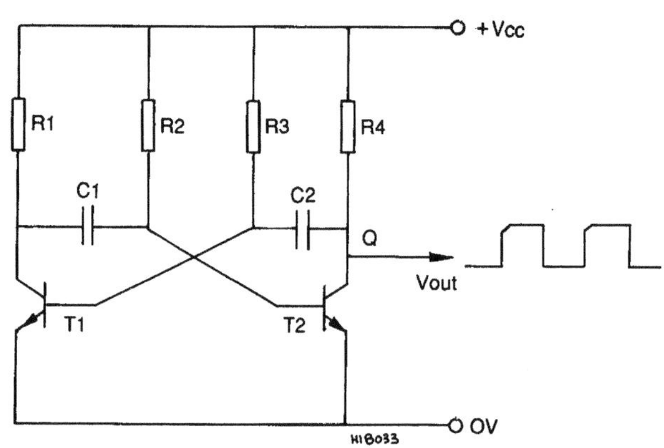


Fig. 10.6a Simple multivibrator oscillator

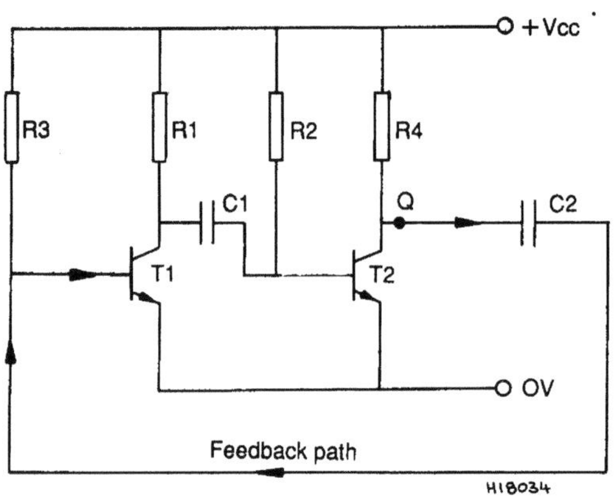


Fig. 10.6b Multivibrator as feedback amplifier

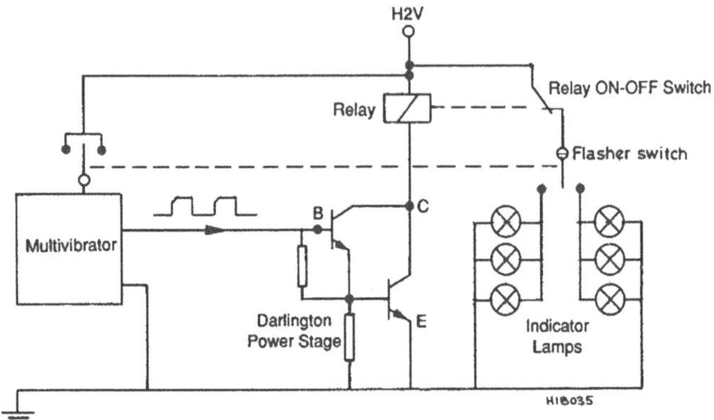


Fig. 10.7 Darlington driver stage to operate flasher switch (principle only)

oscillator using two transistors in its simplest form (Fig. 10.6a). It is really two amplifying stages in which the output of the second is fed back to the input of the first (Fig. 10.6b).

The output at point Q is (nearly) a square wave and in the flasher unit this is passed to the input of a Darlington power stage, the load of which is a relay winding which switches the turn indicator lights on and off (Fig. 10.7).

**3** In practice, the circuit is more refined than the basic multivibrator shown and comprises an integrated circuit (Fig. 10.8) with external R and C components wired to it. The relay is housed in the same unit and is used to make and break the lamp current (Fig. 10.9). It is preferable to use a relay rather than a power transistor because the bulbs take a large initial current which falls rapidly as the filaments heat up due to their increase of resistance with temperature. Such current spikes would destroy the transistor. The switch on

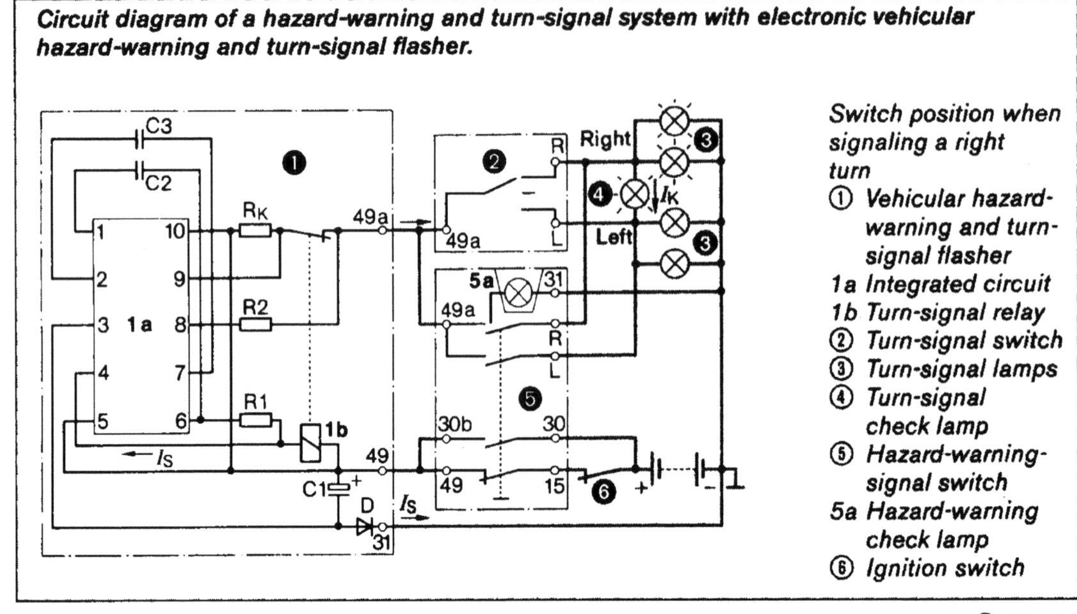


Fig. 10.8 Turn signal and hazard warning integrated circuit

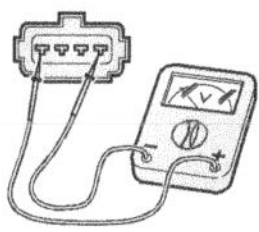

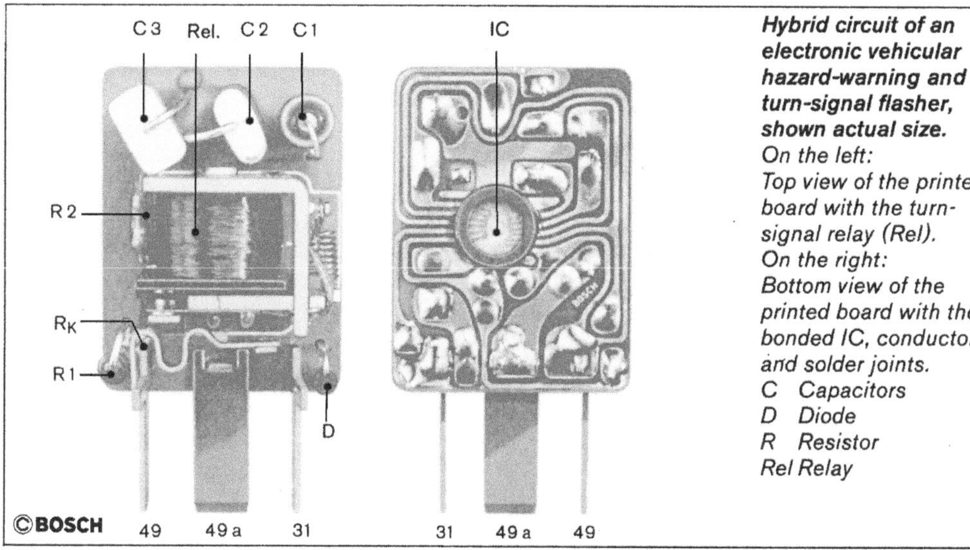


***Hybrid circuit of an electronic vehicular hazard-warning and turn-signal flasher, shown actual size.***
*On the left:*
*Top view of the printed board with the turn-signal relay (Rel).*
*On the right:*
*Bottom view of the printed board with the bonded IC, conductors and solder joints.*
*C Capacitors*
*D Diode*
*R Resistor*
*Rel Relay*

***Fig. 10.9 IC and relay of turn and hazard signal unit***

current of a 21 watt bulb is 3.63 A, falling to 1.95 A when the bulb is hot. Another reason for using a relay is the low volt-drop across the closed contacts on load – about 0.1 volt. If a power transistor were used directly to light the lamps, the volt-drop across the transistor would be of the order of 1 volt and would also result in high power loss in the transistor.

**4** The integrated circuit affords two further facilities:

(a) *It has a built-in voltage regulator which ensures a constant flashing rate over the range of 9 to 15 volt supply*

(b) *A built-in monitor to detect if a bulb fails. A low resistor Rk of 30 milliohms carries the bulb current and the volt-drop across it is connected to a comparator. If a bulb fails, the volt-drop across the resistor is halved and this causes a resistor to be connected in parallel with the resistor of the R1–C2 combination which fixes the flashing frequencies. The result is that the frequency of flashing is doubled in the event of bulb failure and this is easily noticed by the driver.*

**5** Referring again to Fig. 10.8, capacitors $C_1$ and $C_3$ absorb voltage transients from the inductive coil of the relay and act as radio interference suppressors. Diode D cuts off the unit should the supply voltage be connected the wrong way round and so protects the IC. Flashing lamp output power comes from terminal 49a and goes to (a) the turn signal switch (R) usually located on a stalk on the steering column, and (b) the hazard warning signal switch (5) which is a 4-gang type. Two terminals L and R serve to switch all the warning lights on simultaneously, including internal tell-tale lamp (5a).

Terminal 15 is a normally-closed switch which is opened on switching on the hazard lights. The switch connected from 30 to 30b, however, connects the flasher unit straight to the battery, bypassing the ignition switch.

**6** Flashing lamp failure is not rare, probably because of the continuous heating cycles, but, just as often, failure to flash is due to a poor connection to earth. Bulbs sometimes suffer corrosion due to damp or even actual ingress of water; bases can be lightly cleaned with fine emery paper and re-used. A THIN smear of grease helps to prevent further trouble.

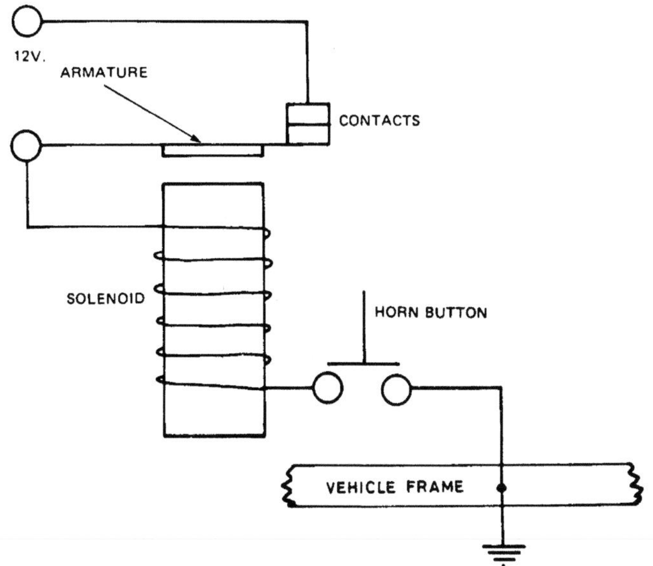


***Fig. 10.10 The electromagnetic vibrator principle***

## 4 Horns

**1** A horn is a legal requirement on motor vehicles in most countries. In general, three types of horn may be met:

(a) *High frequency horns*

(b) *Wind-tone horns*

(c) *Air horns*

**2** With the exception of the air horn, vibratory motion of a diaphragm to create sound waves is produced by a form of electric bell mechanism, in which an iron armature is attracted to the iron core of a solenoid working off the vehicle 12 volt supply. The movement of the armature breaks open the contacts so current and magnetic attraction cease; the armature returns to its original position under spring tension and the cycle repeats (Fig. 10.10). This principle of operation applies to both high frequency (HF) and wind-tone horns.

### The high frequency (HF) horn

**3** The HF horn has been in existence since the 1920s with

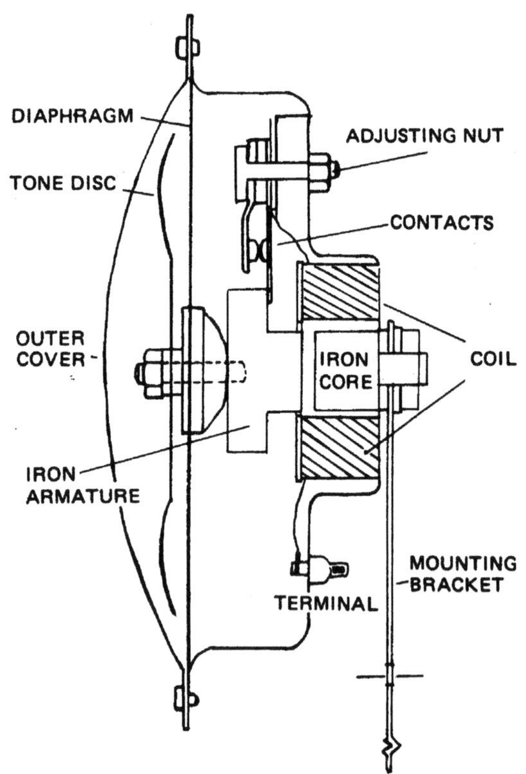


*Fig. 10.11 High frequency horn*

little change (Fig. 10.11). A vibratory circuit drives a thin diaphragm to give a low frequency note of about 300 vibrations per second (300 hertz). A second vibrator called a tone disc is also driven, but will give rise to a high frequency sound of about 2000 vibrations per second (2000 hertz). The low notes have the property of distance penetration while the high notes can be heard above traffic roar.

**4** When the horn button is pressed, the coil energises the electromagnet, the armature is attracted to it and hits it (see Fig. 10.11). The movement breaks the contacts, the armature releases and the contacts again close – a repeating process for so long as the horn button is pressed.

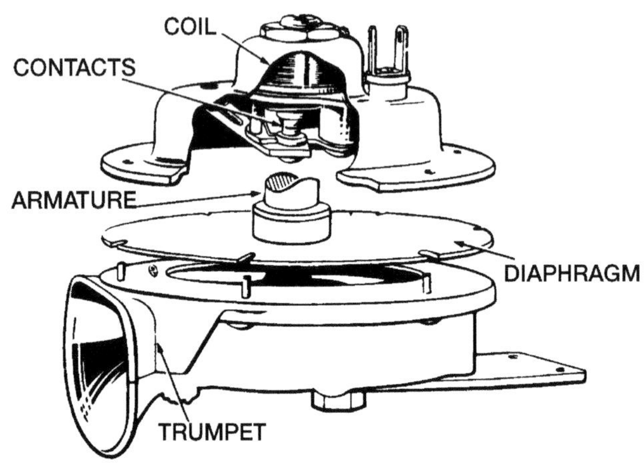


*Fig. 10.13 Wind-tone horn*

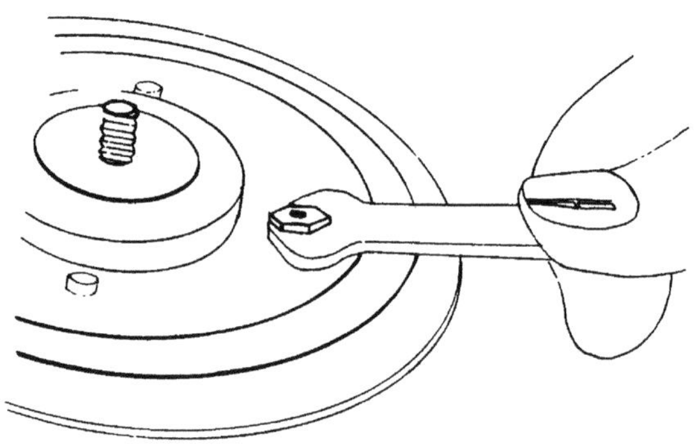

*Fig. 10.12 Horn adjustment*

**5** The mechanical shock of the armature/magnet impact makes the tone disc ring. The tone disc vibrates at an overtone frequency with the diaphragm, so that the two tones produce a resultant sound which has penetration without being too harsh.

**6** It is possible to connect two or more horns in parallel to produce a greater sound level and to mix tones for a pleasing effect.

**7** Adjustment is usually effected at the rear of the HF horn (Fig. 10.12) either until the current is as recommended or until it gives a clear note.

## Wind-tone horns

**8** The operating mechanism is basically the same as for the HF horn, but the sound is passed into a horn wound in a spiral like a snail shell (Fig. 10.13). The dimensions and the flare of the horn trumpet have been carefully calculated to give a mellow tone in the same manner as an orchestral wind instrument.

**9** To obtain a good note, wind-tone horns are often operated in pairs. The current load is high, and so a relay may be used to keep heavy cables out of the car interior and minimize voltage drop (Fig. 10.14).

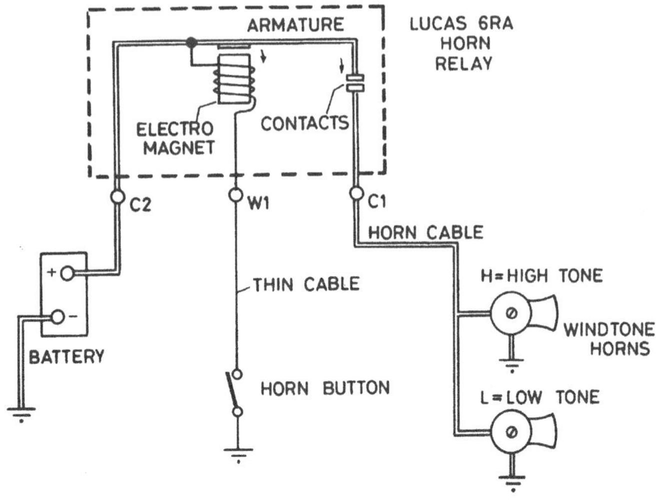


*Fig. 10.14 Relay operated wind-tone horns*

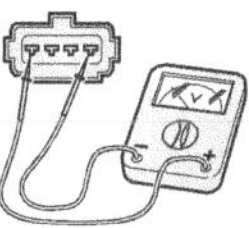

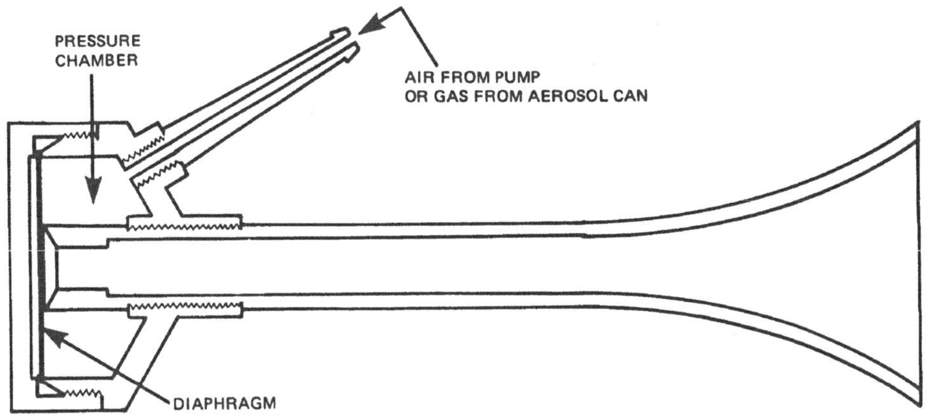


***Fig. 10.15 Simple air horn***

## Air horns

**10** Air horns are simple in principle. Air or gas is pumped under pressure to a chamber which is closed at one end by a diaphragm; the diaphragm pressure against the annular end of the horn prevents the escape of the air or gas.

**11** When the pressure is high enough the diaphragm is pushed to the left (Fig. 10.15), and air/gas is released into the horn. The pressure drops and the diaphragm closes – the cycle repeats. If the pressure is supplied by a pump then the horn button controls the pump motor either directly or by a relay.

**12** Pumps can be simple in just supplying pressure to the horn, but can also be led out to various timed horns in sequence by a rotary valve in order to play a tune. Such equipment is on sale, but it should be pointed out that the use of a horn combination producing notes separately is illegal in the UK.

# 5 Screen wipers and washers

**1** A working, efficient windscreen wiper is required by law, and the minimum fulfilling standard would be a single blade, single speed wiper together with a screen washer.

In practice, most vehicles have two blades driven by a motor which works at two or more speeds, with provision for intermittent operation. Usually, on the same stalk switch, a means of operating a windscreen washer is provided. Upon using the washer the wiper may be activated to wipe away grime and then continue after the wash jet has stopped for long enough to dry the screen.

**2** The hatchback body design often results in an airflow which deposits dirt and roadspray on the rear window. It is usual (and almost essential) to have a wiper, usually single blade, single speed, plus a washer on the rear window. Many cars also have a wash/wiper provision on the headlamps.

# 6 Wiper motors

**1** Wiper motors are mainly of the permanent magnet field type (Fig. 10.16) with earlier vehicles using a shunt wound field form (Fig. 10.17). Permanent magnets are now well developed and are of the high-energy ceramic type set in a cylindrical yoke of laminated steel. The advantages of permanent magnet motors are that the cost of a wound field is eliminated with the gain of lower input current requirement and greater reliability.

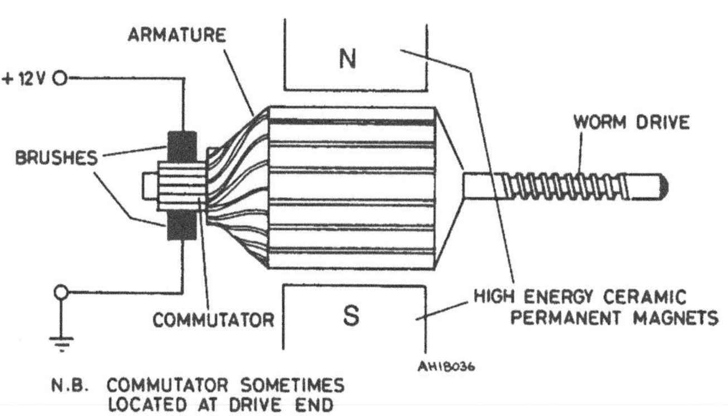


***Fig. 10.16 Permanent magnet wiper motor***

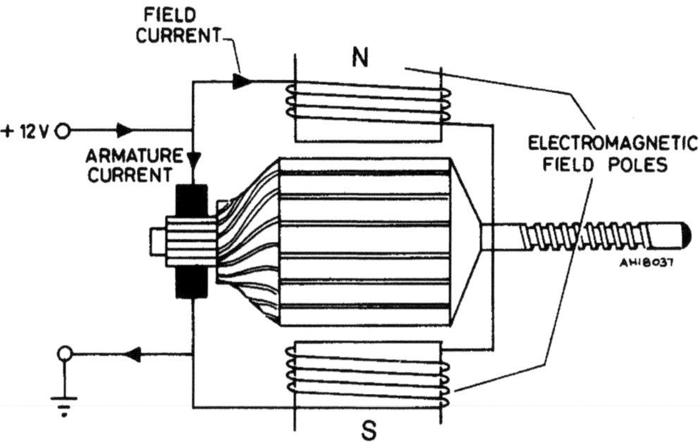


***Fig. 10.17 Shunt wound field wiper motor***

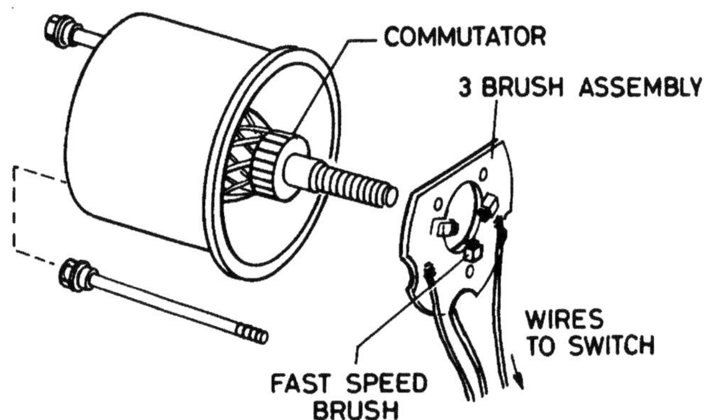


*Fig. 10.18 Two-speed permanent magnet motor*

**2** Permanent magnet motors may be single-speed or two-speed. Single-speed motors have a pair of commutator brushes 180° apart, but the two-speed motor has three brushes, the additional brush being set at a small angle from one of the others and identifiable by being narrower at the top than the other two. The supply voltage is switched to this third brush to obtain high speed wiping (Fig. 10.18).

**3** Two-speed operation of a shunt wound motor is possible by the inclusion of a switchable series resistor in the shunt, or by including a resistor in the main supply lead (Fig. 10.19).

**4** Normally the wiper motor is connected directly to an auxiliary output fuse so that it becomes live when the ignition is on. Special arrangements are made to bring the wiper blades to a park position on switching off.

**5** Protection of the wiper motor is desirable under conditions of overload which might occur, for example, if the wiper blades are frozen to the windscreen. Since the motor would be prevented from rotating there would be no back emf, and consequently a heavy current would overheat the armature. A thermal switch working on the bimetal principle is sometimes found connected in series with the supply to the wiper motor. Under sustained overload the bimetal strip heats and bends, thus opening a pair of contacts, switching off the motor. As the switch cools, the supply is reconnected; the motor is switched on and off cyclically until the fault cause is cleared.

**6** In British designs, permanent magnet motor wipers are cylindrical and wound-field types are of rectangular cross-section – an easy method of identification.

**7** Two types of drive from the motor to the wiper blades are in use:

(a) *The pushrod system (Fig. 10.20)*

(b) *The rack drive (Fig. 10.21)*

In both cases the motor drive operates through a worm gear to develop the necessary torque at a suitable speed for the windscreen, ie about 50 wipes per minute for single-speed motors and 50 and 70 wipes per minute for two-speed motors. Here a 'wipe' is defined as one go-and-return movement, or one complete cycle.

**8** The pushrod systems are more efficient than the rack drive, but suffer the disadvantage of being difficult to house under the dashboard. The less efficient rack drive is often used because of this problem. On some installations the rack is fairly flexible, but others have the rack running in a rigid tube preformed to the shape required for a particular vehicle.

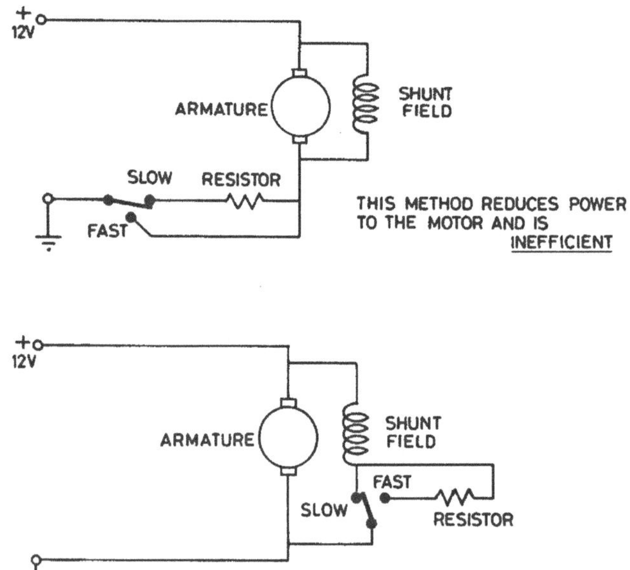


*Fig. 10.19 Speed change methods for a shunt motor*

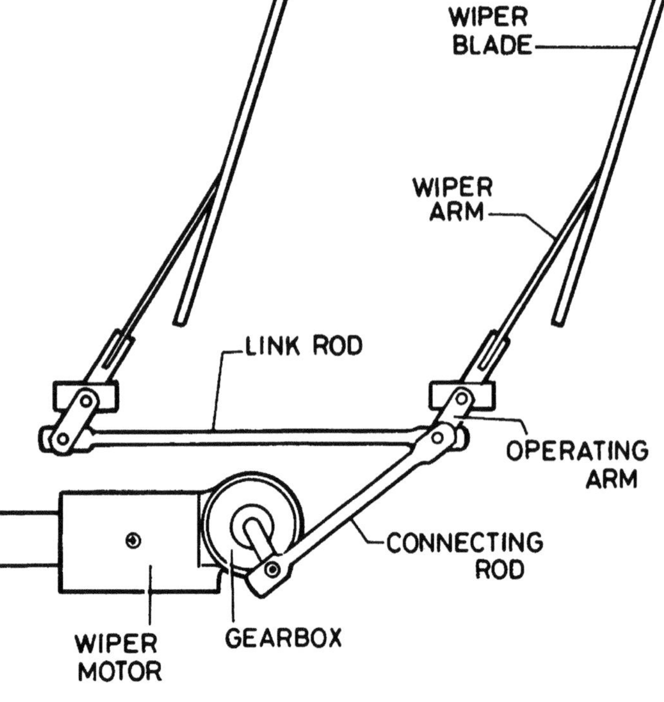


*Fig. 10.20 Pushrod system for wiper drive*

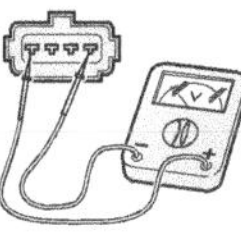

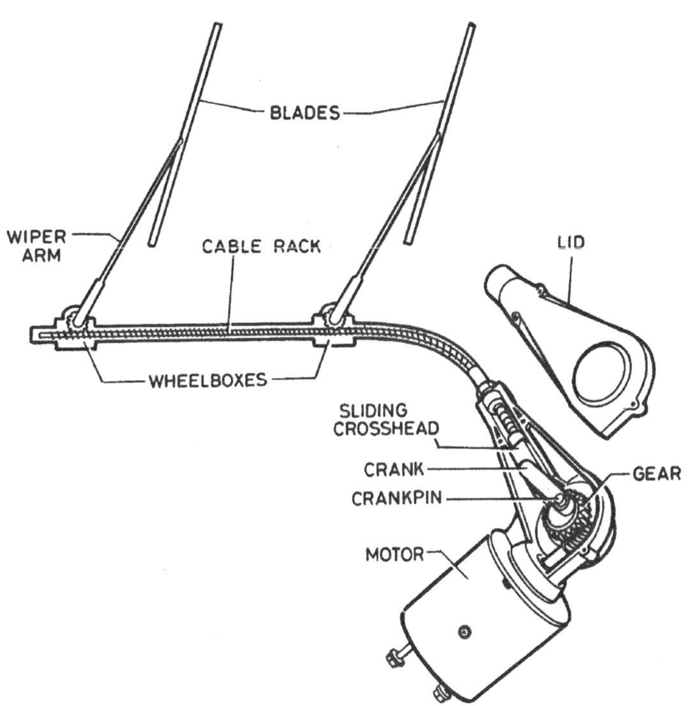


*Fig. 10.21 Rack system for wiper drive*

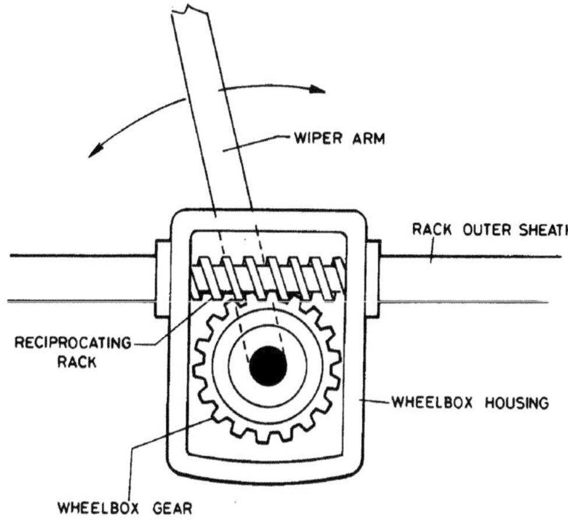


*Fig. 10.22 Wiper wheelbox*

**9** Reference to Fig. 10.21 will show the rack passing through small gearboxes (wheelboxes); these are the take-off points for the wiper arms. The rack is pushed and pulled alternately by the action of the crankpin, connecting rod and main gearwheel.

**10** Fig. 10.23 shows a variation of the pushrod design (Austin Metro) in which the motor is centrally mounted and operates a separate pushrod to each wiper.

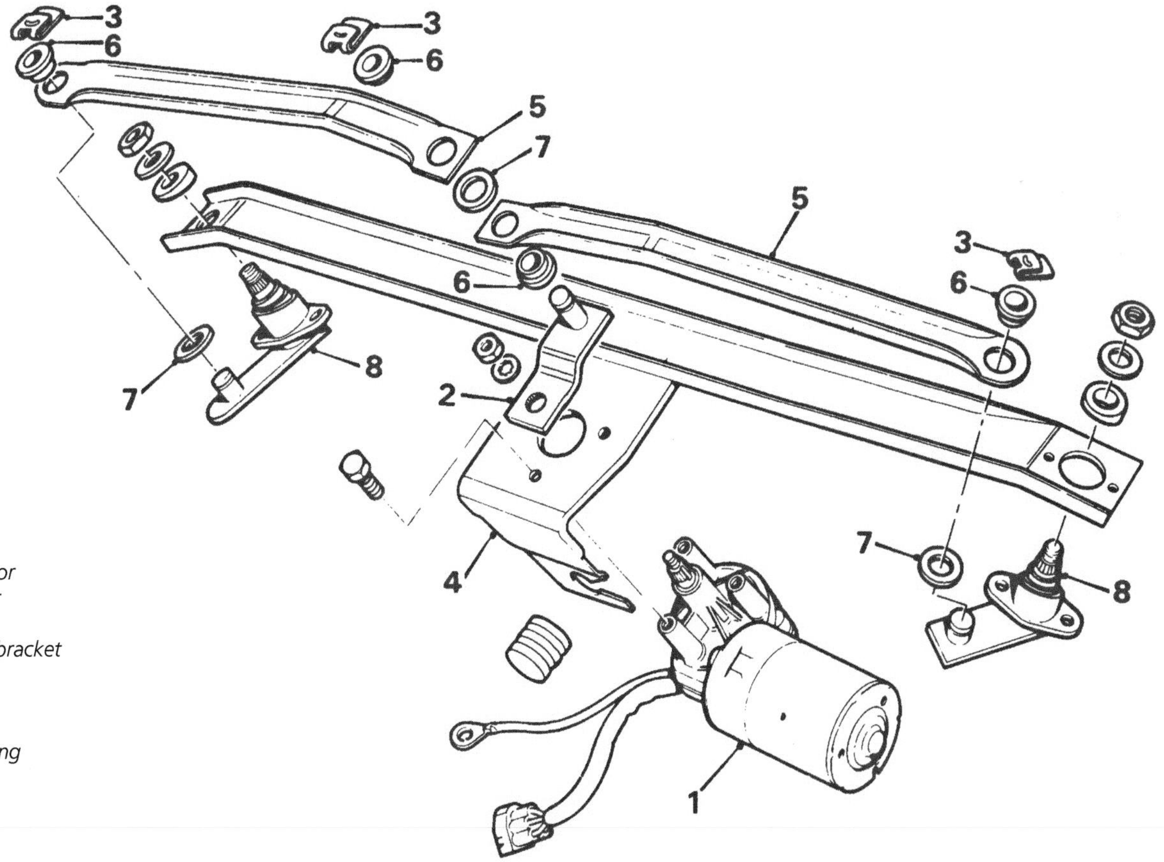

1 *Wiper motor*
2 *Crank lever*
3 *Clip*
4 *Mounting bracket*
5 *Link*
6 *Bush*
7 *Washer*
8 *Pivot housing*

*Fig. 10.23 Double pushrod system for wiper drive*

## 7 Park switching

**1** It is an undesirable task for the driver to have to switch off the wipers at the end of a stroke, and an automatic park switch is always incorporated in the motor linkage housing. Fig. 10.24 shows the principle in which the motor stays connected to the battery supply after the driver has switched off until the wiper driven cam opens the limit switch.

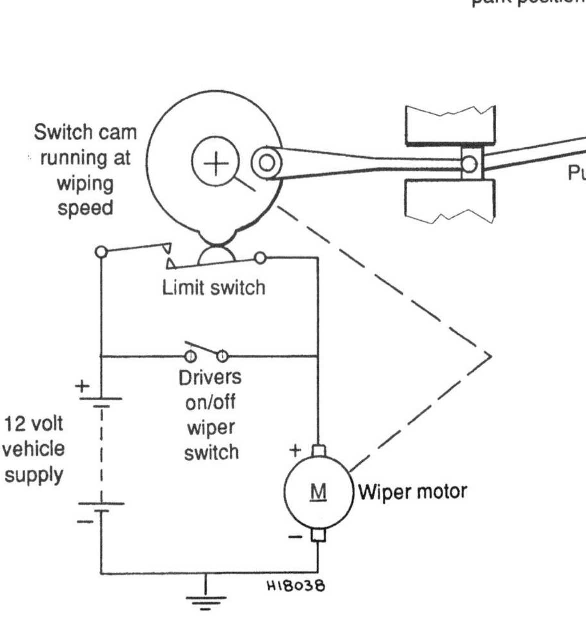


*Fig. 10.24 Limit switch in wiper motor*

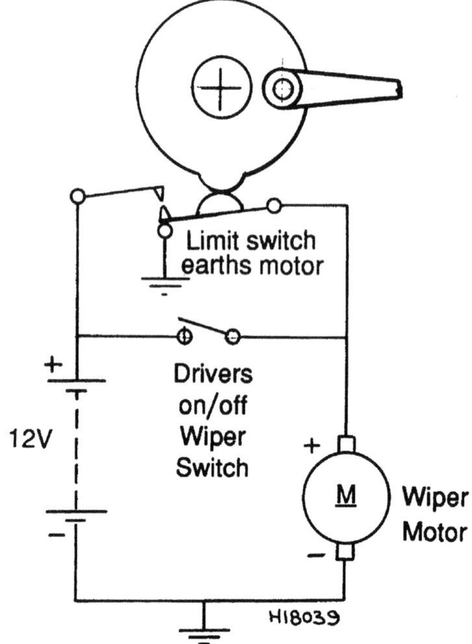


*Fig. 10.25 Motor braking by regenerative action*

**2** Even this simple arrangement can be insufficient to stop the blades at the right place on the windscreen. When the motor is hot and running freely, and the screen is wet giving low friction, the wiper speed can be sufficient to over-run the park position.

To meet this problem the limit switch earths the positive terminal of the motor. At this point the motor armature is turning through its own magnetic field and is generating an emf. Shorting this to earth causes the armature to drive power out (to earth) and because this power is derived from the energy of rotation, the armature decelerates to zero abruptly. This is the principle of regenerative braking (Fig. 10.25).

**3** Park switching with regenerative braking of a 2-speed permanent magnet motor is shown in Fig. 10.26. On the underside of the gearbox gearwheel is a two-stage limit switch with contacts A and B which are

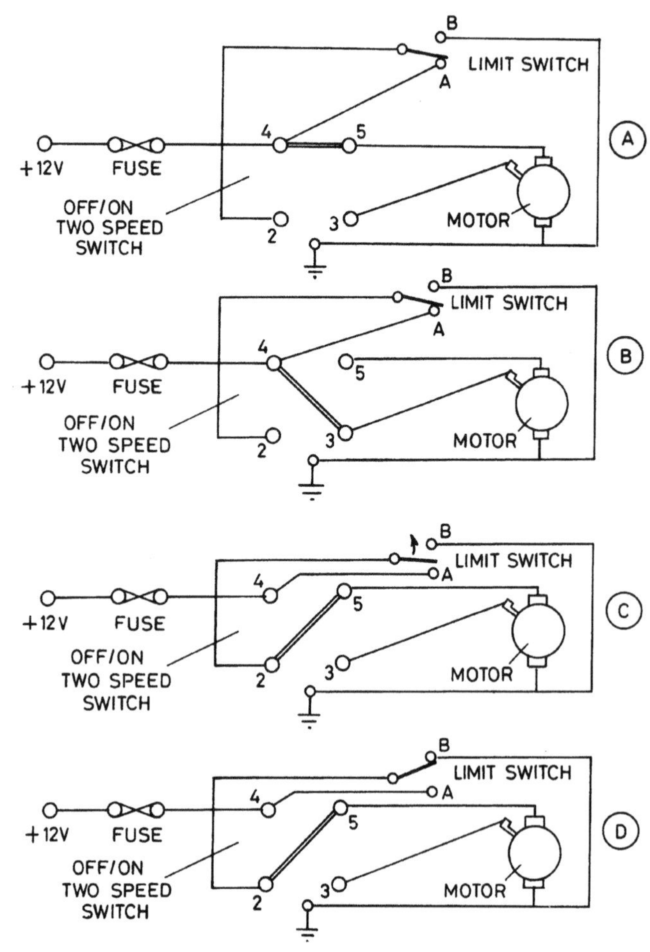


***Fig. 10.26 Park and on/off switching of a two-speed permanent magnet wiper motor***

*A Normal speed wipe*
*B High-speed wipe*
*C Off – switch blade has left terminal A, but not reached terminal B*
*D Off – switch blade contacts terminal B. The motor brakes regeneratively*

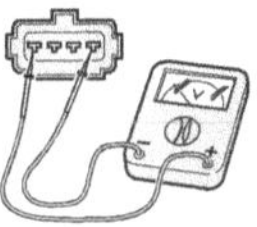

so arranged that the cam first switches the blade away from contact A followed by a small gap when the blade is not in contact with A or B, then finally makes contact with B. When the driver switches off the wiper, contacts 2 and 5 are made and current will still flow to the armature because the switch blade is still in contact with terminal A. As the gearwheel proceeds, the cam breaks the switch contact with A resulting in the motor slowing down. At this stage there is no supply to the motor. The motor will have sufficient momentum to run on until the blade touches contact B at which point the rotating armature is decelerated rapidly by the regenerative action.

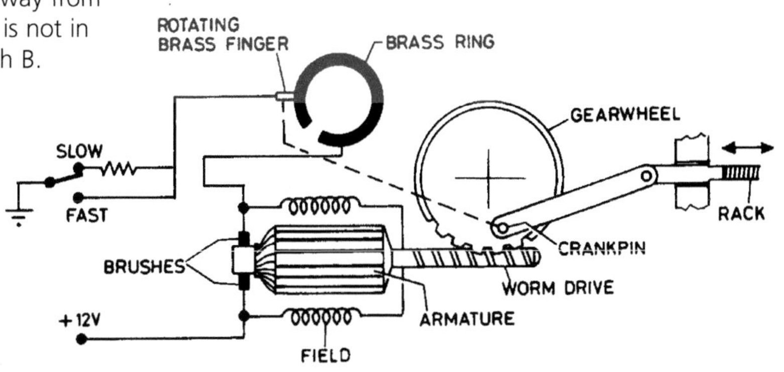


*Fig. 10.27 Wound field two-speed wiper motor*

**4 Park switching – wound field motors.** Self-parking of wiper blades is due to a park switch housed in the wiper gearbox. The cover has an insulated disc on its underside, and set in this disc is a brass circular track with a small cut-out so that it does not form a complete circle. A spring finger is attached to the rotating crankpin and the finger runs in contact with the brass track (Fig. 10.27). When the driver switches the wiper switch off the motor continues to drive until:

*(a) The rotating finger comes to the gap in the brass track and switches the motor off*

*(b) The wiper blades have reached the park position*

The insulated disc is adjustable (Fig. 10.28) to make condition (a) coincide with (b).

**5** A distinction should be drawn between the self-switching action described above in which the blades stop at the end of the normal wiping arc and the self-parking motor. The latter, when switched off, will reverse its rotation, operate an eccentric coupling and extend its length of stroke to park beyond the normal wiping arc, usually off the screen.

## 8 Intermittent wiping – principle

**1** The requirement for intermittent wipe is most felt on those days when the rain has ceased but the roads are still wet. Nearby traffic throws up dirty specks which do not call for continuous wiper action. Under these circumstances an occasional wipe of the screen is required.

**2** It is possible for the driver to switch on the wiper motor momentarily with a spring-loaded switch, but this works only with the wound-field type of motor. The permanent magnet motor will have a short circuit across the armature in the rest position (see Fig. 10.25) and will not start if pulsed by a simple switch.

**3** In any case, the continual switching on for one wipe stroke is tiresome, and in practice an electronic switch is used with a pulse output to a relay. The delay between pulses is fixed by the charge or discharge time of a resistor-capacitor RC combination and is often a fixed delay set by the manufacturer, typically 4 to 6 seconds. In some designs, delay may be varied by the driver using a dashboard-mounted variable resistor.

**4** On many modern vehicles, the intermittent action of the wipers is controlled by the central timer unit. This electronic module controls many of the vehicles electrical items that have a timed function – Wipers, Indicators, Heated rear/front windows, Central locking, etc. For more information see Section 14.

## 9 Intermittent wiping – practical arrangement

**1** One method of achieving an intermittent wipe operation with a permanent magnet motor wiper is shown in Fig. 10.29 overleaf.

### Interval timer

Pause interval between single wipes is set by the time taken for capacitor C to charge via resistor R after switching on

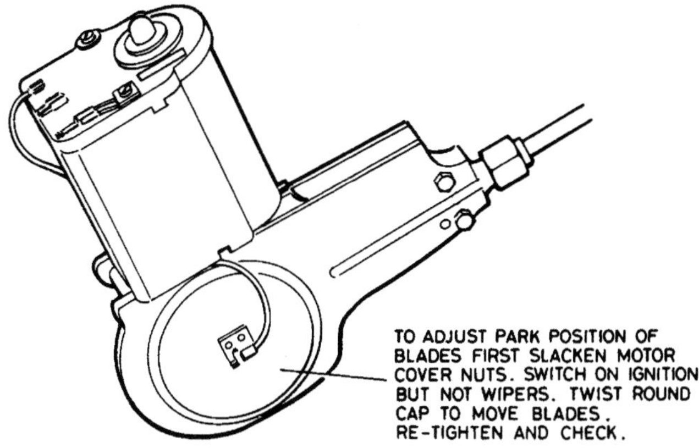


*Fig. 10.28 Adjustment of park position for the wound field motor*

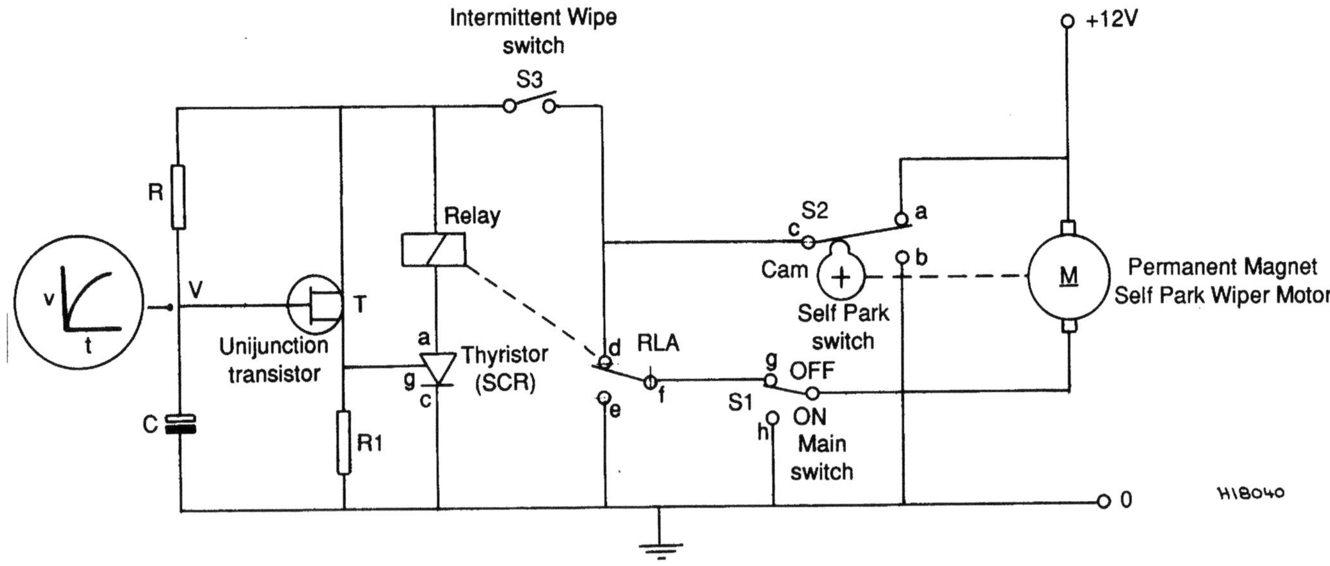


*Fig. 10.29 Intermittent wiping control*

intermittent wipe switch S3. The voltage V rises exponentially (ie in a curved fashion – see Chapter 1) and when it reaches a certain value, the unijunction transistor T starts to conduct. When this happens the volt-drop across R, serves as a gate-voltage to the thyristor which switches on, operating the relay to change over the contact f from d to e.

### Motor

In normal operation (ie with no intermittent wipe) the driver controls the main switch S1. When S1 is ON the motor is across the 12 V supply and wipes continuously. When S1 is switched OFF, switch S2 has contacts c and b joined so the motor continues to run until the self-park switch cam switches S2 over so that c and a are joined. The motor armature is shorted out and regenerative braking occurs.

### Operation

If the driver now switches on the intermittent wipe switch S3, the relay operates after the time interval. This changes over switch RLA so that f and e are joined and the wiper motor starts. As the cam rotates c and b are joined on S2 and the interval controller switches OFF. The motor continues to run because although f is now joined to d, the earth path is made from c to b in switch S2. When the cam opens S2 so that c and a are joined the motor stops and the interval timer starts to charge R and C again. The cycle repeats.

**2** Other forms of interval timer are in use including a multivibrator which gives a rectangular pulse output to a relay which then performs the same operation as the example explained above.

**3** On many modern vehicles, the intermittent action of the wipers is controlled by the central timer unit. This electronic module controls many of the vehicles electrical items that have a timed function – Wipers, Indicators, Heated rear/front windows, Central locking, etc. For more information see Section 14.

## 10 Wash/wipe equipment

**1** The ideal solution to the cleaning of windscreens is to employ a combined wash and wipe arrangement with the following provision:

*(a) Wash screen (driver operates washer switch)*
*(b) Delay before wiping begins to allow wetting of screen (about 1 to 2 seconds)*
*(c) Wipe clean*
*(d) Wash ceases (when driver releases washer switch)*
*(e) Wipe continues so as to dry the screen (5 strokes)*

In some vehicles such a system is linked with simultaneous wash and wipe of headlamps.

**2** Wash is performed by a small 12 volt permanent magnet motor driving a centrifugal water pump and may be mounted on the wash fluid container or located separately. The pump is self-priming and has an inlet tube filter. It is designed to work from –20°C to +80°C, assuming that the washing fluid is protected by an antifreeze. The performance is typically such that at a current loading of 2.8 A at 13.5 V, the pump will deliver 1.3 pints per minute at a pressure of 10 lbf/in$^2$.Little can be done to service washer motors and replacement of a faulty unit is necessary.

## 11 Wiper service

**1** A number of wiper motors are sealed and are not intended for repair in the event of trouble. It may be possible to take such motors apart, but unfortunately dealers will not stock any spares, although it may be possible to replace brushes by filing down a set intended for other equipment.

**2** A most common fault with wipers is that of worn brushes, which should typically be about 5 mm long. The high speed

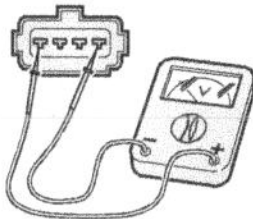

brush should not be worn so that the narrow section has disappeared (Fig. 10.30).

**3** Permanent magnet motor brush sets are available mounted on a plastic board (Fig. 10.18) and for the wound field motor brushes are set in two holders linked by a pressure spring.

**4 Armatures** are not easily repaired, and if inspection shows signs of blackening, or the commutator has worn through (it is too thin to lathe-skim) then a replacement armature will be required. Stripping down requires care and the procedure varies according to make, but in general look out for the parking switch wires which can be jammed inside the motor during disassembly. Mark the correct position of the parking switch in order that it can be reassembled correctly, and check that there is armature endfloat of about 0.25 mm (0.01 inch). Endfloat can be adjusted on some models by shim washers, or by an adjuster screw which should be locked by a nut and/or a thread-locking compound.

**5 Gearboxes** can be checked for obvious stripped gears. Check that the packing grease is actually around the gear; after a period of operating the gear cuts a hole in the grease which then surrounds but does not touch the gear.

**6** If a main gearwheel has to be renewed, ensure that the correct one is purchased, since the angle of wipe depends on the location of the crankpin hole. A number on the wheel gives the angle of wipe, eg 130°.

**7** It is important to replace the washers associated with the gearwheel exactly as they were, especially the crinkled washer underneath the gear. Ideally the special grease recommended by the manufacturers should be used.

**8** Motor fails to switch off is not an uncommon fault, and is often due to a faulty parking switch or possibly the parking switch/motor wire shorting to earth. Sometimes a motor will switch off under heavy load conditions, eg with a dry screen or low battery voltage, but refuses to switch off perhaps when running fast on a slippery screen. It is worth trying an adjustment of the parking switch before condemning it, however.

**9 Slow or no operation** of the blades can be due to a jammed rack or, in the case of a linkage mechanism, a linkage member dropping off. In the latter case a free rod flailing about has been known to go right through the bodywork.

**10** To check the rack, remove the gearbox cover and disconnect the rack from the gear-drive. Then push and pull the rack to see if the wipers move; if the rack operates the wipers, only a moderate force (about 6 lbf) should be needed. If the system is stiff the rack should be pulled out (remove the blades first) and greased with high melting point (HMP) grease. An occasional spot of glycerine (not oil) on the shaft where it emerges from the body is beneficial (Fig. 10.32).

**11 A worn rack and pinion** can result in slack movement of the wiper arms causing the blades to hit the screen trim at the bottom end of travel or even to fail to work completely, although the motor will be heard operating fast. The rack and pinion in a wiper wheelbox (ie behind the blade) operate over a fixed and limited range, and it is possible to defer the day for complete renewal by turning the pinion through a half turn and by turning over the rack. This way both will engage on unworn sections.

**12** To do this, first remove the wiper arms and blades. In the wiper gearbox remove the circlip holding the connecting rod

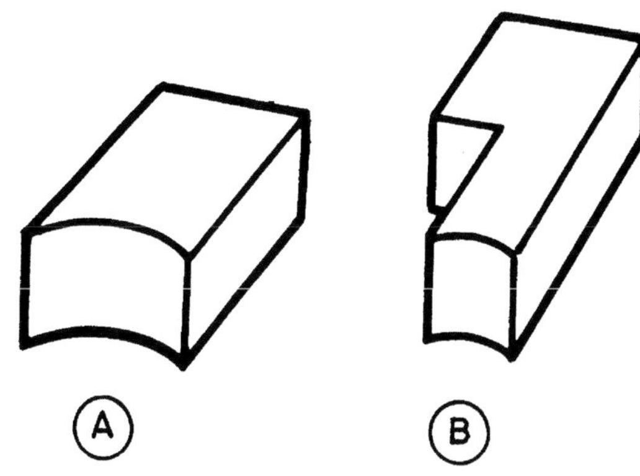


***Fig. 10.30 Wiper motor brushes***
*A Normal speed brush B High-speed brush*

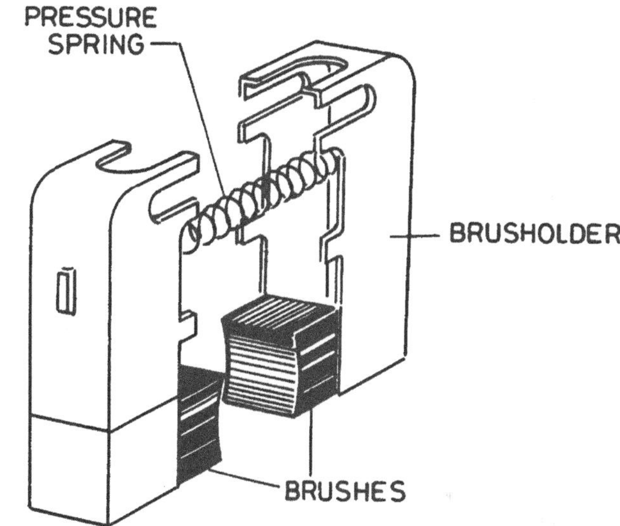


***Fig. 10.31 Wiper motor brush set***

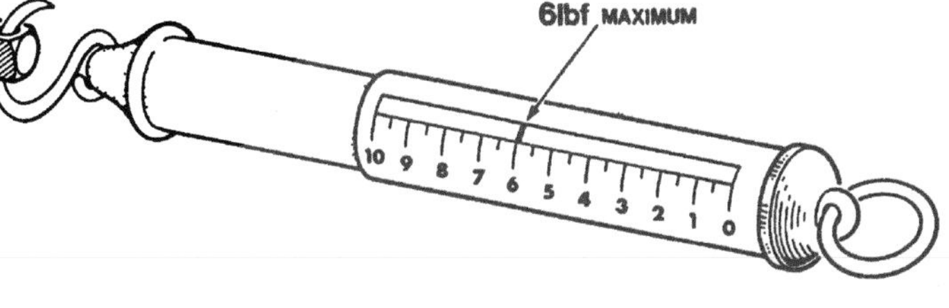


***Fig. 10.32 Checking rack for friction***

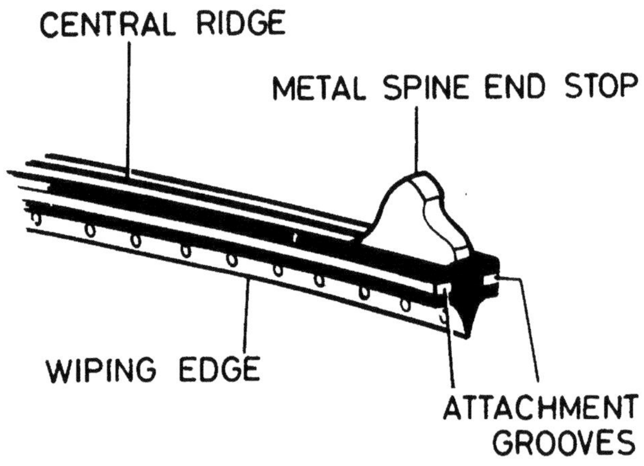


*Fig. 10.33 Shape of wiper rubber*

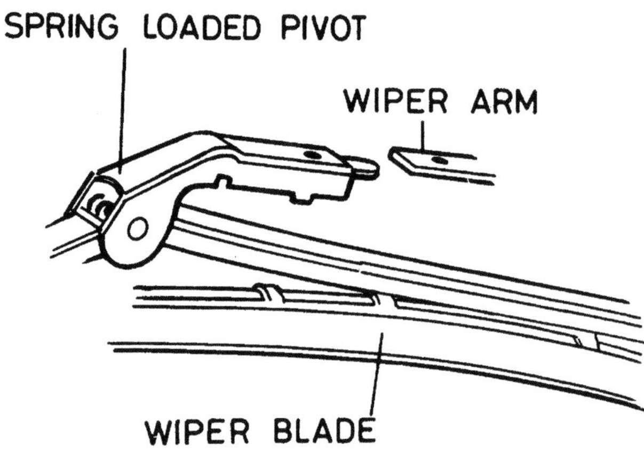


*Fig. 10.34 Bayonet-type wiper arm fixing*

to the crankpin located in the main gear. Lift off the connecting rod and, after pulling the rack back far enough to clear both wheelboxes, that is when no longer engaging the pinions, turn the rack over 180° and refit after turning the wiper spindles by 180° each also. Since pulling back the rack will rotate the wiper spindles by several turns, make alignment marks for the starting point of the gear engagement with the rack (Fig. 10.21).

**13** If the gears in the wheelboxes are too far worn, then replacements may be available, the boxes being fixed by the nut behind the wiper arm.

## 12 Wiper blades

**1** The deterioration of blades is gradual and it is only when replacements are fitted that the fall-off in performance can be appreciated. Clues to the need for replacement are streaking marks, showing that the thin wipe edge has been cut and is ragged, and also areas of the screen which are missed altogether.

**2** It is recommended that blades are changed annually, and the choice is between complete blades units or refills. Before opting for the cheaper refill it is worth checking to see if the remainder of the blade is worth using again. Pins and fixings in the blades can become badly worn, giving rise to sloppy action on the screen, which can ultimately result in the metal parts coming into contact with the glass and causing scratches. When replacement rubbers are bought, it is as well to buy them with the metal backing strips, since these have a significant effect in keeping the rubber in contact with the glass. Check that the blades are of the same type, fitting and length as those being replaced (Figs. 10.33 and 10.34).

**3** Springs built into the wiper arms will weaken in time and replacement is advisable if there is any suspicion of tension loss. The designers place regard on these often forgotten items for, if the tension is too great, the rubber drag is too much for the motor, but if too weak the blades will lift off the screen, especially in windy conditions.

**4** Wiper judder is very annoying and can be tracked down to several causes, but most probably is due to the lack of parallelism of the wiper arm with the screen, resulting in the blade being pulled one way but pushed the other way. To check, remove the blades and look at the arm end; this should be parallel with the glass surface at mid-wipe position. It is worth trying a judicial bending of the arm to achieve this condition.

## 13 Wiper motor testing

**1** Most wipers have the outcoming wires terminated in a socket; for testing it is useful to make up a corresponding plug (Fig. 10.35).

**2** To test, remove the wiper motor plug on the vehicle and connect a 12 volt fused supply via an ammeter of suitable range to the wiper motor terminals as shown in Fig. 10.36. In choosing an ammeter range note that wipers will take between 2 and 4 amperes if working correctly.

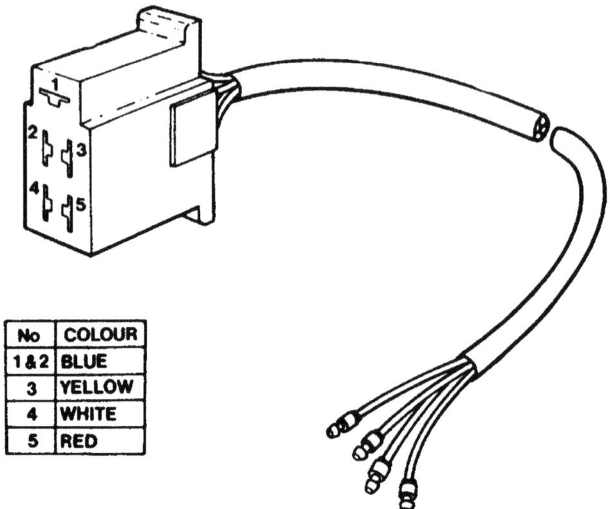


| No | COLOUR |
|---|---|
| 1&2 | BLUE |
| 3 | YELLOW |
| 4 | WHITE |
| 5 | RED |

*Fig. 10.35 Test plug for Lucas wiper motors*

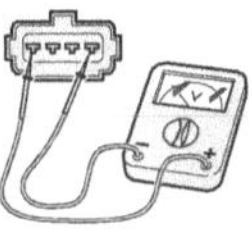

| CONNECTIONS BATT. '+' | BATT. '–' | TYPE OF MOTOR | RESULT |
|---|---|---|---|
| *TEST 1 Red/Green | Brown/Green | All types | Motor should run at normal speed |
| *TEST 2 Blue/Green | Brown/Green | 2-speed motors only | Motor should run at high speed |
| TEST 3 Red/green | Green | Self-switching types only | Motor should run to park position then stop |
| TEST 4 Green | Red/Green | Self-parking types only | Motor should run to extended park position then stop |

* Do not disconnect battery supply from plug while the wiper blades are in the parked position.

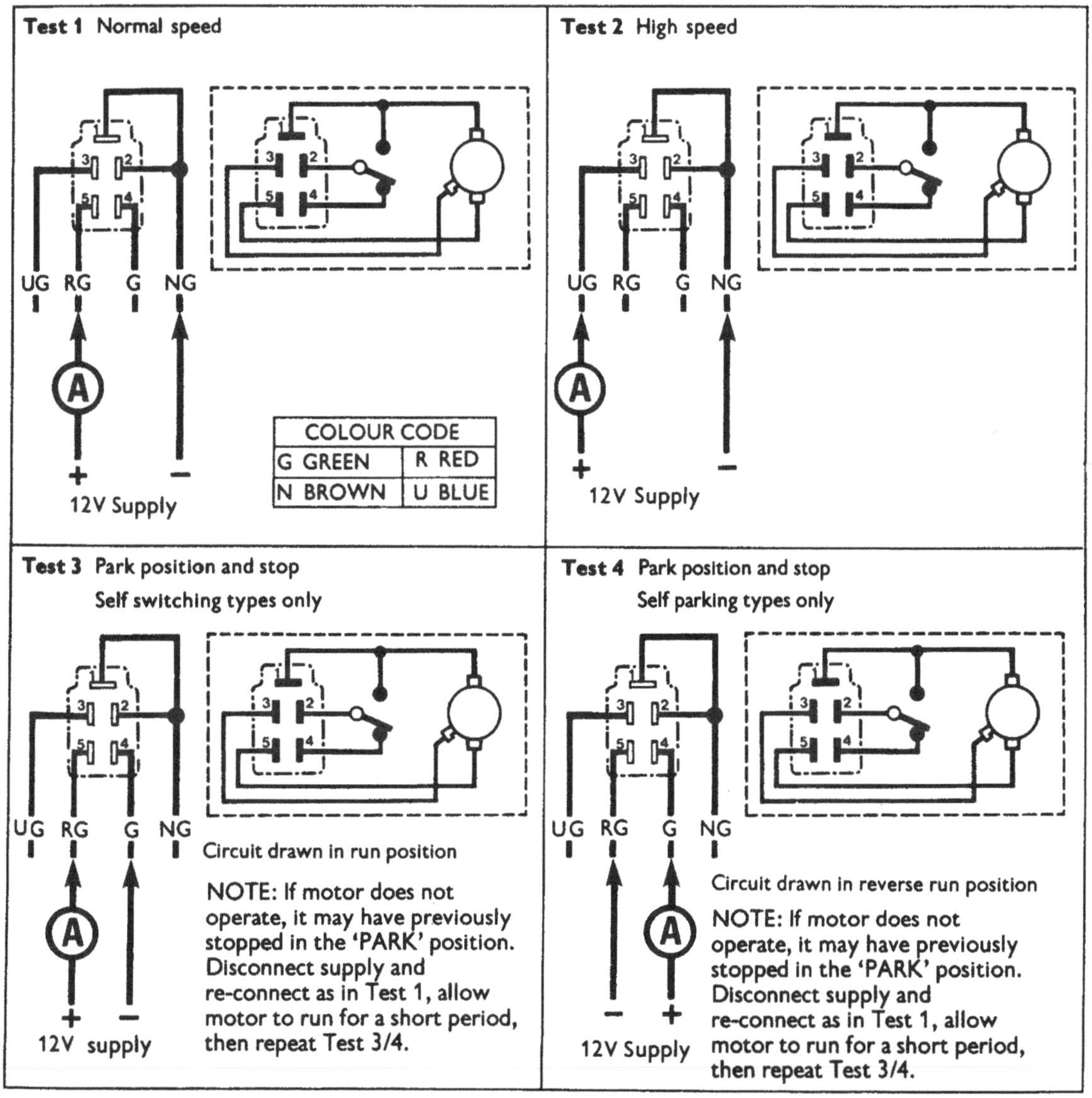

***Fig. 10.36 Wiper motor tests (colour-coding applies to Lucas motors)***
*All tests performed with screen wet*

### Additional tests

**Note:** *It is most important to observe correct polarity and connections.*

If the motor fails to function in any one or more of the previous tests, a faulty motor is indicated. If, however, the motor is satisfactory, the fault lies in the switch or wiring on the vehicle. Should the current consumption during the tests exceed 4 amperes, remove the wiper arms and blades and repeat test. If the current is still high this could indicate excessive friction in the rack or link drive mechanism. Disconnect the drive from the motor and again check current consumption. A high current reading now indicates a faulty motor. On the rack-type drive a pull of 6 lbf applied to the crosshead with a spring balance should be sufficient to move the crosshead within the outer casing. If not, the assembly must be examined for faults.

**Note:** It should be remembered that where excessive friction exists, overloading will result. Replacing the motor will *not* solve the problem.

In cases where removal of the arms and blades lowers the current consumption the fault is due to either a contaminated screen or faulty arms or blades.

## 14 Central Timer Unit/GEM

**1** This term, pioneered by Ford, refers to an electronic module which controls the timed functions of many of a modern vehicle electrical systems (Fig. 10.37). The unit is also referred to as a 'Generic electronic module' (GEM). It controls the following:

*a) Battery saver – the interior lights and chimes are automatically shut-off after a predetermined period of inactivity.*
*b) Turn signals and hazard lights*
*c) Courtesy lighting*
*d) Heated windscreen*
*e) Heated rear window*
*f) Heated mirrors*
*g) Windscreen wiping/washing*
*h) Rear wiper/washing*
*i) Seat belt warning*
*j) Lights-on warning*
*k) Door ajar warning*
*l) Chimes warnings*
*m) Central locking*
*n) Tailgate/boot lid release*
*o) Alarm systems*

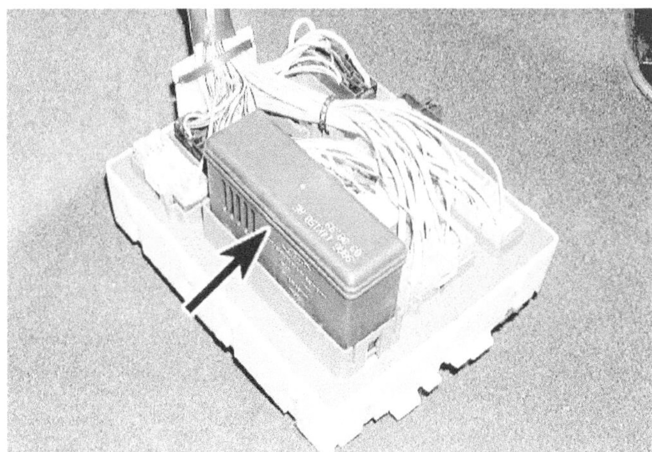

**10.37 On the Ford Focus, the Central Timer Unit (arrowed) is fitted to the rear of the fusebox**

## 15 Rain sensor

**1** On some modern vehicles, automatic wiping, is available as an option. With this system a rain sensor, mounted behind the windscreen detects rain drops on the screen and operates the wipers accordingly. The VW system works on the principle of water droplets on the screen surface will refract light directed at it, thereby reducing the amount reflected – see Fig. 10.38. The LEDs of the sensor emit a light beam, which when the windscreen is dry, are reflected by the outer surface of the windscreen. The reflected light is recorded by a photodiode. However, when drops of rain are on the windscreen surface, some of the light from the LEDs is refracted differently, so less light is reflected to the photodiode, which sends a signal to the wiper control unit, and the wipers operate.

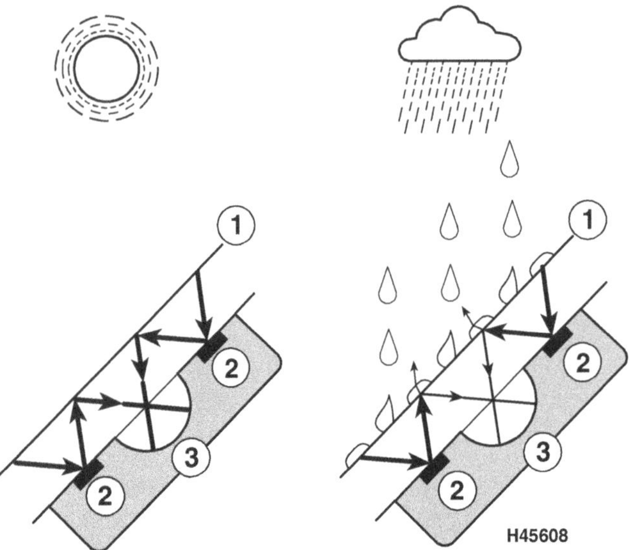


**10.38 Rain sensor in the dry (left) and in the rain (right)**
*1 Windscreen surface 2 LEDs 3 Photodiode*

# Lighting

# 11



## 1 Lighting arrangements

**1** In European countries which belong to the EC (European Community) agreement has been reached on mutual recognition of motor vehicle equipment and parts. Guideline 76/756 regulates the installation and optical signalling devices on the motor vehicle.

**2** Most countries will additionally have local regulations which will specify that a motor car must have two forward facing lights, two red lights at the rear, two red reflectors at the rear and that the number plate (US = license plate) should be illuminated. In France the forward facing lights are yellow but in most other cases they are white.

**3** In the UK, obligatory front lamps must be at the same height and, if the bulbs are over 7 watts, must be capable of being dipped to avoid dazzle to oncoming vehicle drivers. Both headlights should be of the same colour and wattage rating; additionally they will be mounted equidistant from the centre-line of the car.

**4** Rear lights will have a minimum rating of 5 watts. Usually the rear light has a reflective red lens built in to the unit to give a reflected light as a safety precaution in the event of bulb failure.

**5** Two brake lights of 21 W rating each will be mounted in the rear lamp cluster.

**6** At the front and rear, pairs of 21 W amber flashing lamps are mounted as turn signal indicators. Repeater lamps of approx 5 W rating are located on the sides of the front wings.

**7** Reversing lamps are now normal original equipment. A maximum of two reversing lamps is permitted, each usually of 21 W rating and are activated by a gearbox or selector mechanism switch which closes when reverse is selected.

**8** In order to achieve improved illumination to the rear, designers now usually mount all the rear facing lamps in a cluster, being housed in a separate large plastic box for each side. This allows the use of large internal reflectors. Lenses are designed for light scatter to give an even spread to outgoing light, the inside surface being a series of tiny wedges. The outside of the lens is shaped into a series of long horizontal wedges to break up the flow of air over the lens surface. It is claimed that this reduces the dirt deposited on the lens surface.

**9** Lamps are always connected in parallel across the battery supply so that the total current drawn is the sum of all the lamp currents when switched on.

**10** Auxiliary driving lamps (spot lamps) are long range and are connected on the high beam position of the dip switch, since they must be switched out when other vehicles are met. Relays are used to handle the considerable current loading of this type of lamp.

**11** High-intensity rear foglamps are permitted only in conditions of poor visibility and are connected only on the dip position of the headlamp switch. A warning indicator must be fitted to inform the driver that the rear foglamps are on.

## 2 Circuits and switching

**1** Lighting circuit diagrams may be drawn either:

*(a) So as to show the electrical circuit and the approximate location on the car, or*

*(b) In a convenient form to show electrical connections but not the component location*

**2** Fig. 11.1 shows a simple arrangement of lighting and the necessary switches. A number of lighting loads are switched by means of relays so that only small cross section cables need be brought to the operating switches. Often relays are

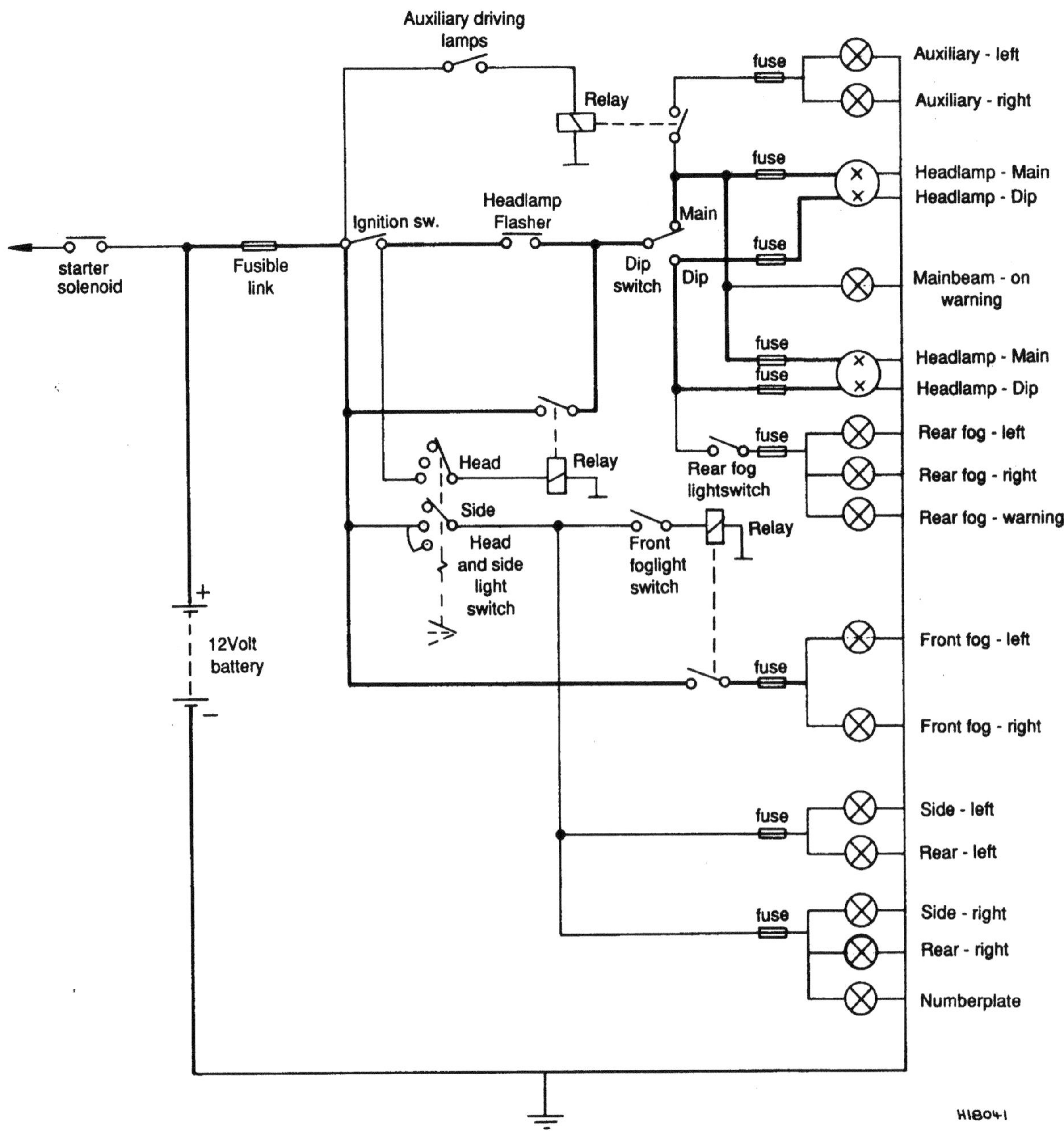


***Fig. 11.1 Simplified lighting circuit***

*NB This circuit does not show dim-dip provision, compulsory on new vehicles since April 1st 1987 – see text for details*

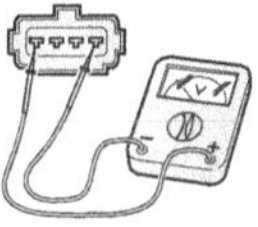

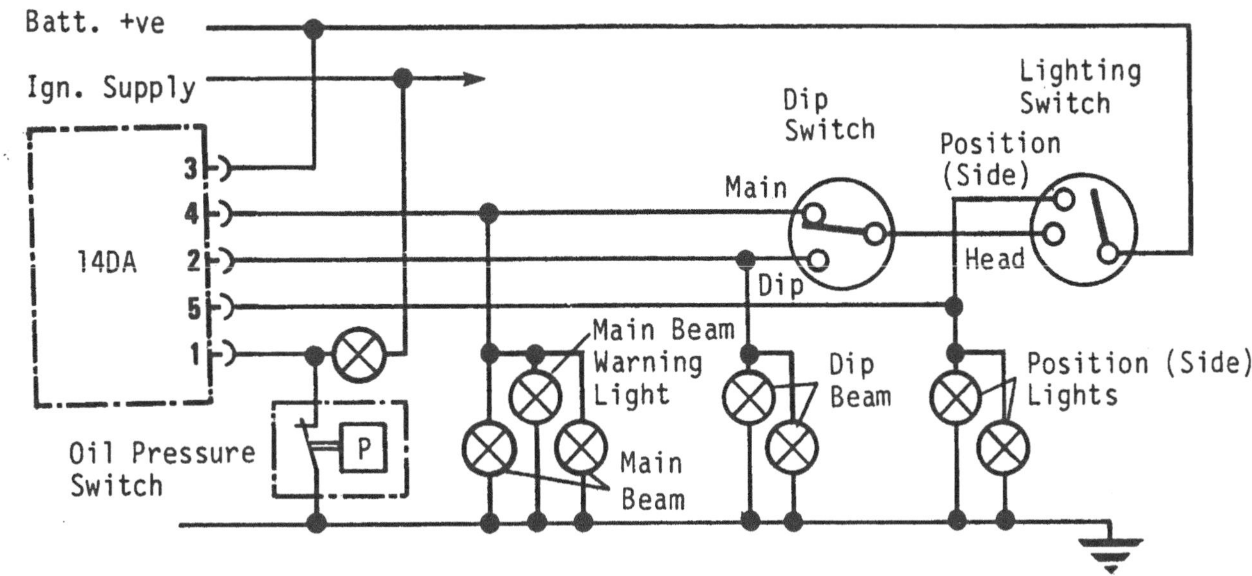


*Fig. 11.2 Dim-dip by electronic chopper (Lucas 14DA)*

housed in the fusebox and are used much more in modern cars than in earlier designs.

**3** It is debatable whether lighting circuits should be fused since a sudden blackout of lights when driving is dangerous. In the example circuit of Fig. 11.1, fuses are shown to each lighting load so that a local fault will blow its own fuse leaving the remainder working. Another solution is to use a thermostatic interruptor. It consists of a bimetal strip with a heater coil which carries the lighting load current. If a fault occurs the high current causes the bimetal strip to bend, opening a pair of contacts which cuts off the current. The strip cools, the contacts close and the lights come on again. This happens fairly rapidly allowing a low-average current to flow. The lights work dimly but give enough light to 'limp home'.

**4** Note the use of a fusible link in Fig. 11.1. This is installed on the battery live side so as to protect all the car electrical systems except the starting circuit. The fusible link consists of a plug-in section of resistance wires which heat and melt if made to carry a large fault current.

## 3 Dim-dip lighting

**1** Dim-dip lighting means the operation of dip beam filaments at a lower intensity when driving with the light switch in the side-lights position. The dim-dip light intensity should be: for halogen lights 10% of normal dipped light intensity, and 15% for normal bulbs. Since 1st April, 1987, British vehicles registered for the first time must be fitted with dim-dip lighting; this ensures that cars cannot be driven on side-lights alone. The obligatory fitment of Dim-dip lighting ceased in the mid 1990's.

When the car is parked, side-lights alone can be used provided the ignition is off or the engine is not running. This does not affect the use of normal intensity dip beam driving when the headlamps are ON and switched to the dip position. Exemptions include vehicles with a maximum speed not exceeding 25 miles/hour, military vehicles and motorcycles (solos and combinations).

**2** Two methods of achieving the dim-dip requirement are available:

### Electronic voltage chopper (Lucas 14DA)

Referring to Fig. 11.2, when the side-lights are on and the engine running both dip beam filaments will be lit at reduced intensity by connections at terminal 2. The chopper reduces the average voltage to the required level. The oil pressure switch must be open, ie engine running in order to obtain the dim-dip output from terminal 2.

### Resistor method (Lucas 13DA)

This circuit consists of a volt dropping resistor (14BR in Fig. 11.3) which is switched in series with the dip beam filaments by a relay with integral electronic circuitry, the resistor being mounted remotely. With the ignition on and the lighting switch at the side-lights position, the relay operates connecting resistor 14BR in series with the dip beam filaments. Selection of headlights at the lighting switch overrides this condition to provide full illumination of the dip or main beam as selected at the dip switch.

## 4 Bulbs

**1** The filament of an automobile bulb is generally made of tungsten, and is heated by electric current from the vehicle to a temperature of about 2300°C.

**2** Early bulbs had filaments working in a near vacuum, but many today are gas-filled. This gives greater light efficiency

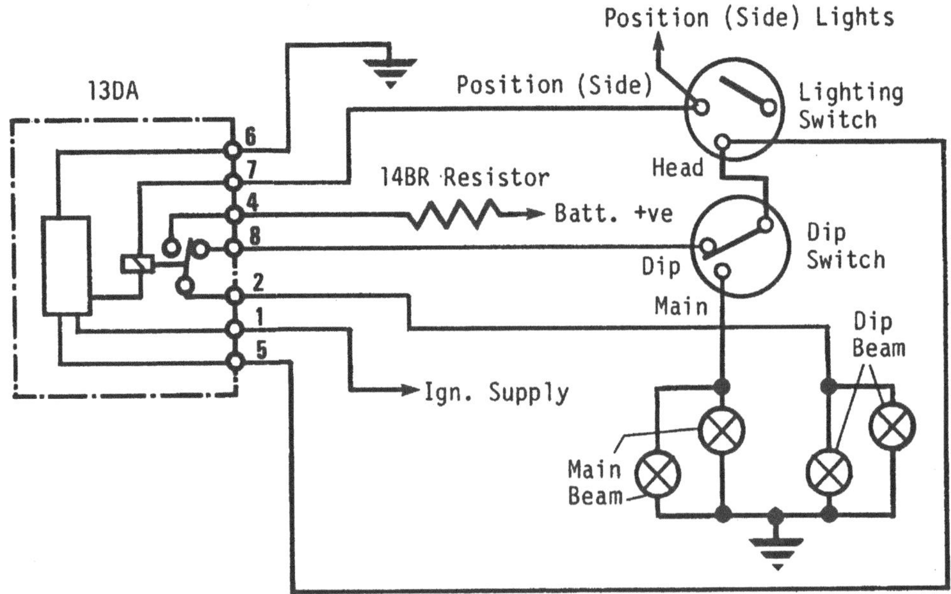


*Fig. 11.3 Dim-dip by volt-drop resistor (Lucas 13DA)*

and, since inert gases are used, eg argon, there is no reaction between the gas and the filament. Filaments are wound in the form of a tight spiral to give better efficiency, since there will be less heat loss due to convection in the gas filling.

**3** Headlamp bulbs usually house two filaments, one for main beam and one for dipped beam (see Figs. 11.4, 11.5 and 11.6). The two usual arrangements for the dipped beam filament are:

(a) *Offset filament – in which the filament is set above and to one side of the focal point of the associated reflector.*

(b) *Shielded filament – here the dip filament is covered with a small shield which deflects the light to one side of the reflector only. The shield has an effect on the main beam in that the centre of the parallel rays is missing. Also, on dip, only one half of the reflector is utilised and projects light downwards.*

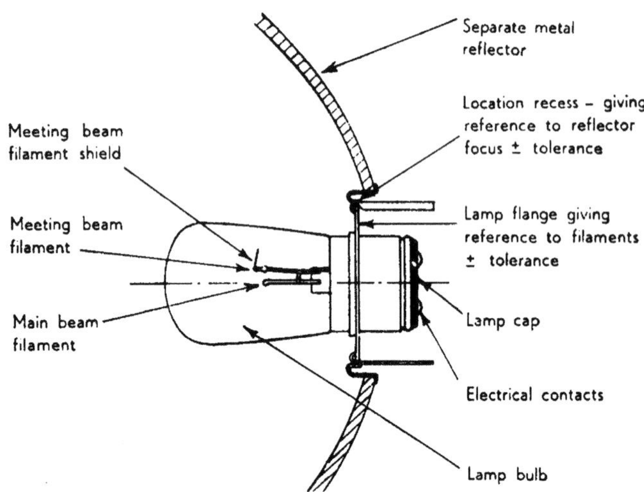


*Fig. 11.4 Prefocus bulb located in the reflector*

**4** Recent innovations in bulb design has resulted in greater light output without increased power consumption. Tungsten bulbs filled with Xenon gas project a brilliant daylight white light, although the bulb glass is blue in colour. These inexpensive replacements for standard halogen bulbs are rated at 3900K.

**5** Further developments have seen LED bulbs fitted as original equipment, and available as replacements for standard bulbs. There are several advantages to LED bulbs:

a) *50 000 hour bulb life.*
b) *Very low power consumption (1 watt typically).*
c) *Greater resistance to vibration.*
d) *Immediate on/off response.*

However, when replacing standard bulbs with LED items, because of the low power consumption, the vehicles electrical system may indicated a 'blown' bulb - either by a dashboard bulb monitoring system, or by increased indicator flash rate (or not flashing at all). To remedy this, it's necessary to place appropriate value resistors in series with the LED bulb, to mimic the electrical load of the standard bulb.

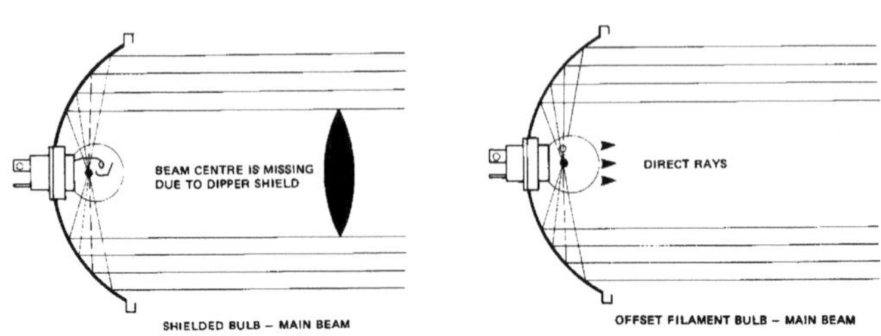


*Fig. 11.5 Main beam patterns for shielded and offset filament bulbs*

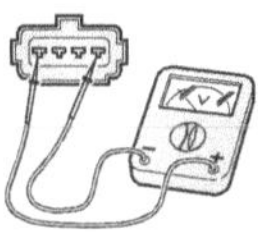

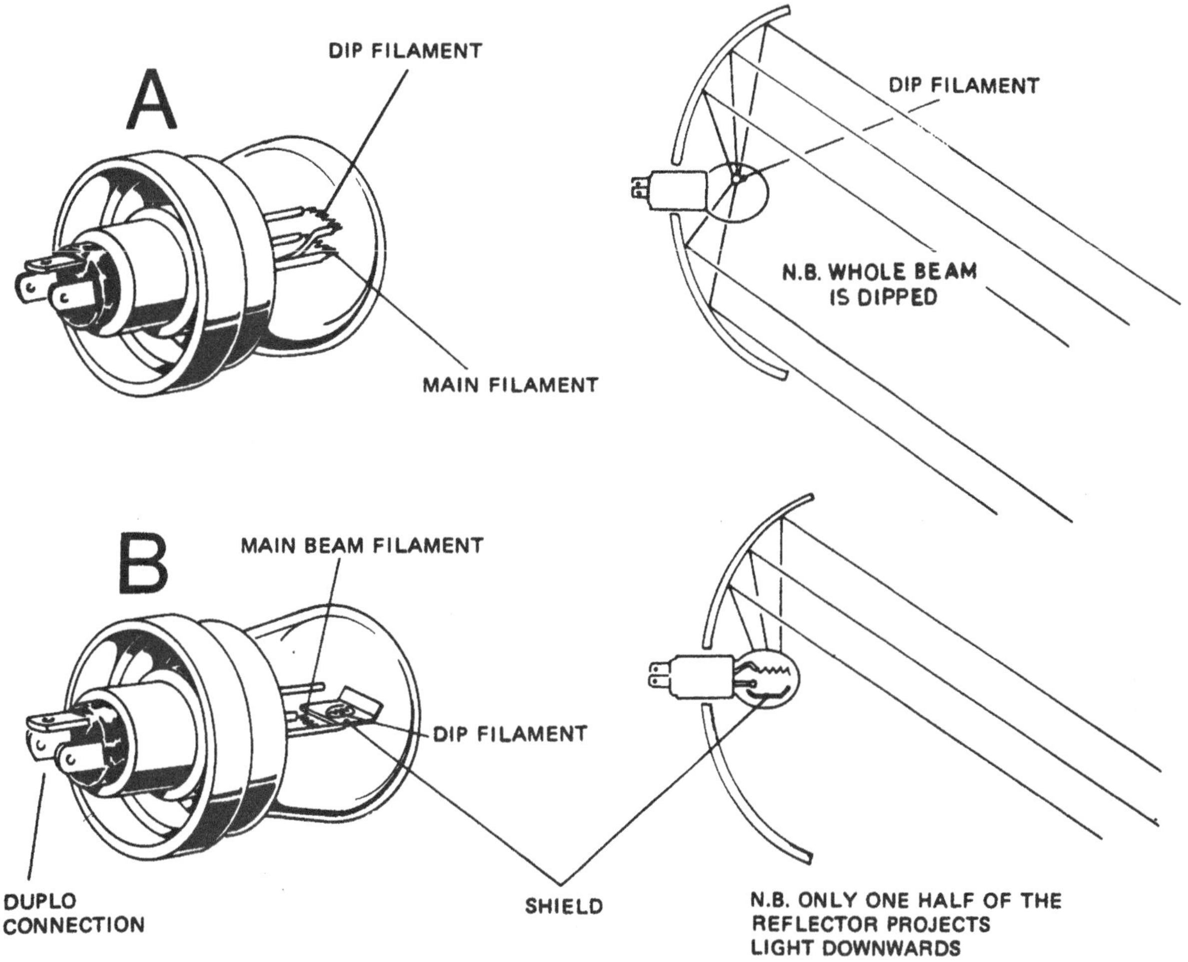

A

DIP FILAMENT

MAIN FILAMENT

DIP FILAMENT

N.B. WHOLE BEAM IS DIPPED

B

MAIN BEAM FILAMENT

DIP FILAMENT

DUPLO CONNECTION

SHIELD

N.B. ONLY ONE HALF OF THE REFLECTOR PROJECTS LIGHT DOWNWARDS

***Fig. 11.6 Headlamp bulbs***
*A Offset dip filament B Shield dip filament*

## 5 Disadvantages of a separate bulb and reflector

**1** The makeup of the main and dipped beams is primarily dependent upon the filament position relative to the focal point of the reflector, and for many years road vehicles used the prefocus bulb in which the filaments were welded in place with precision.

**2** Even the close tolerances to which this design could be made were too wide for proper beam control. To them should be added the tolerances between the lamps seating in the reflector and the focal point (Fig. 11.7). Additionally, about 20% of light from the filament is lost due to

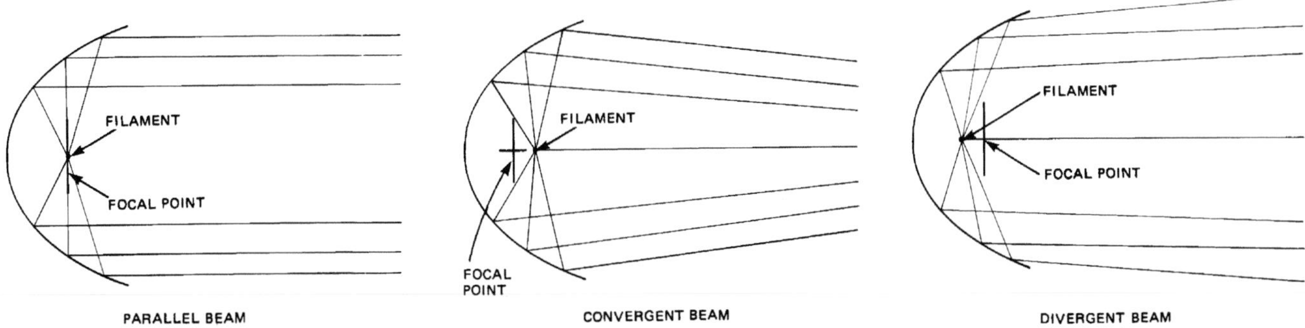


***Fig. 11.7 Filament location should be at the focal point of the reflector***

obscuration by the bulb and cap; also in service the evaporated tungsten from the filament settles on the upper surface of the bulb, and although the total light from the lamp is reduced by only 10 to 15% at half-life (about two years, say) the obscuration presented to a large section of the reflector is of serious consequence and the beam is disturbed (Fig. 11.8).

**3** Finally, due to oxidation and the effects of dust and dirt, the reflector loses efficiency so that after four years' service the beam intensity may be reduced to about 60% of the original value. Most of the troubles mentioned occur because, in the design, the reflector and bulb were considered as separate entities. When combined into a single sealed beam unit a considerable improvement is obtained.

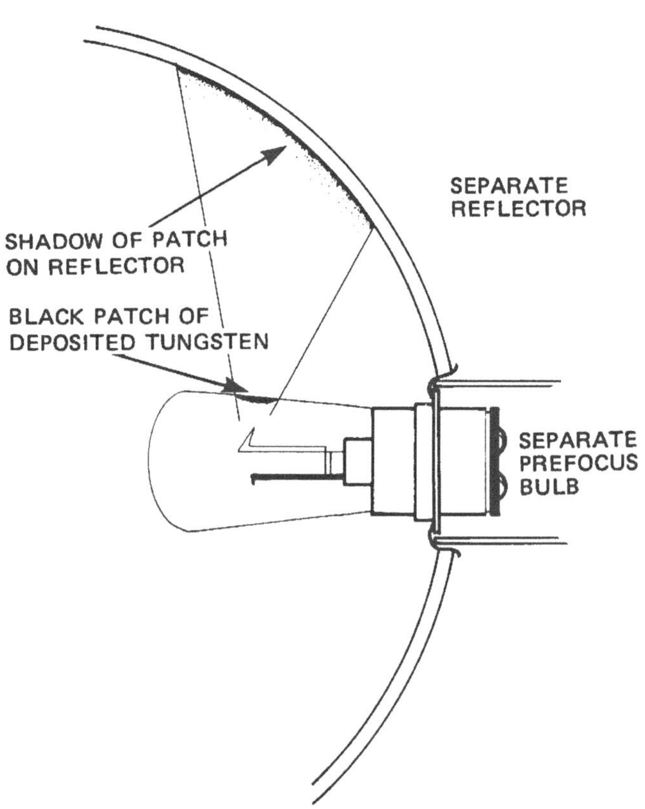


*Fig. 11.8 Obscuration due to lamp blackening*

## 6 Service life and light output of bulbs

**1** The life of a typical standard filament bulb when used in a vehicle will depend upon two main factors – (a) actual voltage applied and (b) vibration. Vibration effects will become less significant with developments in suspension design, and the greater precision of alternator voltage regulators has led to longer filament life. The effects of voltages other than standard are shown below. An over-voltage of only 5% will reduce the filament life by 50% – the significance of correct voltage regulation will readily be seen.

| **Applied voltage (V)** | 11.48 | 12.15 | 12.83 | 13.5 | 14.18 | 14.85 | 15.2 |
|---|---|---|---|---|---|---|---|
| **Applied voltage (%)** | 85 | 90 | 95 | 100 | 105 | 110 | 120 |
| **Relative light output(%)** | 53 | 67 | 83 | 100 | 120 | 145 | 200 |
| **Relative life expectancy** | 1000 | 440 | 210 | 100 | 50 | 28 | 6 |

**2** The normal wearing-out of a conventional filament bulb is due to the evaporation of tungsten from the filament surface (for a mental picture of evaporation think of steam coming from the surface of water). As the filament temperature is raised then evaporation increases rapidly and not only does the filament become thinner but the tungsten vapour also blackens the inside of the bulb and illumination decreases.

## 7 Tungsten-halogen type bulbs

**1** In the last two decades a new form of bulb has found wide use and is now fitted as standard in many vehicles. The tungsten-halogen bulb goes under various other names, ie quartz-iodine, quartz-halogen or tungsten-iodine, but all are really the same thing, namely, a bulb giving a much higher illumination and longer life than a conventional type. Several considerations determine the high efficiency, shape and life of tungsten-halogen lamps.

**3** It is found that if one of a group of chemical elements known as halogens is added in precise quantity to the normal inert gas filling of a bulb, great improvements are possible in terms of life and illumination. (Halogens are elements that compound themselves to form salts.)

**4** When tungsten vapour leaves the filament surface it works its way towards the glass envelope. Between the filament and the glass there exists a temperature gradient; when the tungsten atoms reach the zone of about 1450°C the halogen combines with tungsten to form tungsten halides (Fig. 11.9) and these diffuse back to the region of the filament without the glass-blackening effect taking place.

**5** As the filament is approached, the temperature rises again towards 2000°C (the surface temperature) and the tungsten halides break up again into tungsten and halogen at the 1450°C boundary. The halogen goes back to the gaseous area whilst the tungsten atoms return to the filament, although some surround the filament and tend to reduce evaporation. Because evaporation is thus reduced it is

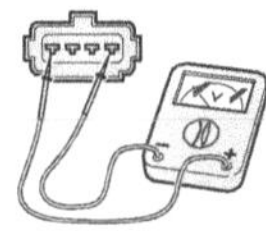

possible to have a hotter filament and so there is a corresponding increase in illumination; also because the filament is being constantly replenished with tungsten atoms it has a very long life and, as stated, because the tungsten atoms do not reach the glass there is no blackening of the inner surface.

**6** One final point – the usual halogen is presently iodine, and the tungsten-halogen formed with it is gaseous only above 250°C. For this reason the bulb must be small so as to stay hot, and so not only are the bulbs much smaller in volume but also they are made of quartz to withstand the temperature. Because quartz is stronger than normal bulb glass, designers increase the gas pressure which in turn reduces the amount of evaporation.

**7** The increase in gas pressure and the halogen cycle of returning tungsten to the filament produces a lamp of high luminous power which is almost constant throughout the life of the lamp.

**8** Two disadvantages should be noted:

*(i) The bulb should not be handled because the salt from body perspiration will stain the quartz: should the bulb be accidentally touched it may be wiped carefully, whilst cold, with methylated spirit and allowed to dry before use again*

*(ii) Life is reduced rapidly if the quartz bulb and the gas filling are not maintained at the correct working temperature. A low supply voltage results not only in a drop in luminous power but also a serious fall in service life*

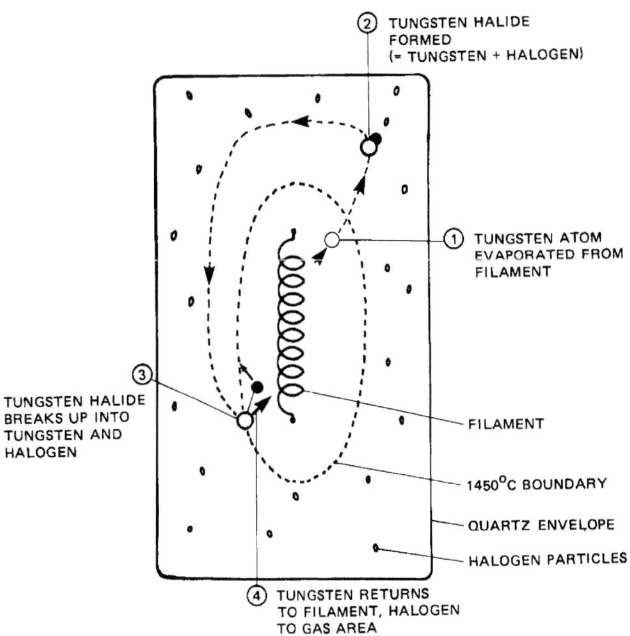


*Fig. 11.9 Regenerative cycle in the tungsten-halogen lamp*

## 8 Sealed-beam light units

**1** In earlier days of motoring, headlamps were made up of separate components – bulbs, glass, reflector, bulbholder, etc. Ensuring that the filament was exactly at the focal point of the reflector was chancy and light intensity fell off quite quickly due to dirt and dust on the reflector surface. Later came the light unit – the front glass and aluminized reflector were combined into a single assembly. Whilst the bulb was of the prefocus type giving much improved precision, dust and moisture would still find a way onto the reflecting surface. This type of lamp is still in wide use today because of relatively low cost compared with a fully sealed lamp.

**2** The sealed-beam lamp shown in Fig. 11.10 has two accurately located filaments but no separate bulb. Lenses are cast into the front glass to produce correct lighting patterns on the road for both main and dip beams. The refracting prisms can give any desired beam configuration because the borosilicate glass is thick (3 to 5 mm) and hence ideal for moulding into prisms. Reflector surfaces in sealed beam units have an evaporated aluminium layer and are protected throughout the lamp life by an inert gas filling. In some designs a pilot lamp window is let into the outerside of the reflector. This allows a pilot side-light bulb to shine through.

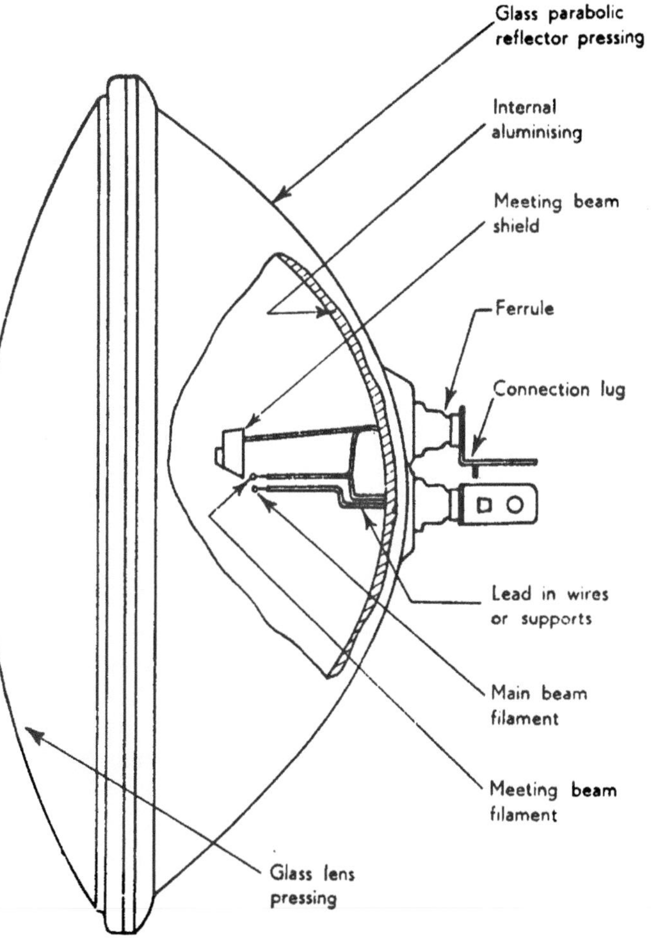


*Fig. 11.10 Internal construction of a sealed beam unit*

3 This unit suffers little from tungsten evaporation because it is spread over a wide area, unlike the conventional bulb. Light output is maintained at greater than 98% of the original figure throughout the estimated five-year life, compared with 58% for a separate light bulb headlamp.

4 For all the technical advance in this design, the sealed beam unit has serious disadvantages which have constrained sales:

*(a) The relative high cost*

*(b) Immediate light failure if the lens is cracked in service*

The requirement in many countries for foreign tourist cars to carry a complete set of spare lamps involves a high cost and space – factors which go against the sealed beam unit.

## 9 Classification of bulbs

1 International agreements exist on the shape, filament, configuration and base fitting of a range of filament bulbs used in automobiles. Bulbs must bear an 'E' or 'e' mark for use for EC countries. The letter E has a number next to it indicating the country where approval was given. A selection of bulbs in common use is shown in Fig. 11.11.

2 Filaments may be either in-line with the bulb axis or at right-angles to it; most bulbs have a single filament and others may have two filaments in one glass envelope. Where two filaments are used in headlamps, one will be located at the reflector focal point to give main beam, the second will be offset from the focal point to give a dipped beam. In other two-filament bulbs, for example the 12 volt 5/21 watt (SBC Index BAY 15d), the 5 watt is used for the red rear lamp and the 21 watt for rear brake light. The glass bulb size of halogen H4 (P43t) types is much smaller than the conventional bulb of similar or smaller wattage.

Note the capless bulb in the example W2x4.6d where wires are brought out from the glass envelope and bent over to form a contact.

## 10 Headlamps

1 **British/American** lamps are circular and may bear a figure 1 or 2 moulded into the glass lens and an arrow to indicate dipped direction. Those with a 1 (or no marking at all) are intended to be checked on the main beam while those with 2 are checked on dip beam. Such lamps have a symmetrical main beam pattern. The asymmetrical pattern required for the dip beam, where in the UK the left-hand side is lit but the right-hand side has reduced intensity, is achieved by displacement of the dip filament away from the reflector focal point and by a band of prisms moulded into the front lens.

2 The dip beam pattern is characterized by having no sharp cut off as in the European headlamp. Glare to oncoming drivers is more pronounced, however.

3 **European** headlamps may be of a variety of shapes including wedge, circular and rectangular. A number 2 moulded into the lens indicates that beam alignment checking is carried out on dip beam. Lens and reflector come as a single unit, while the bulb is fitted as a separate item. The design gives a light cut-off boundary which can be quite pronounced, but with flexibility of shell shapes the illumination pattern can be wide in the horizontal plane. In the UK, cut-off is horizontal to the right and has an upward

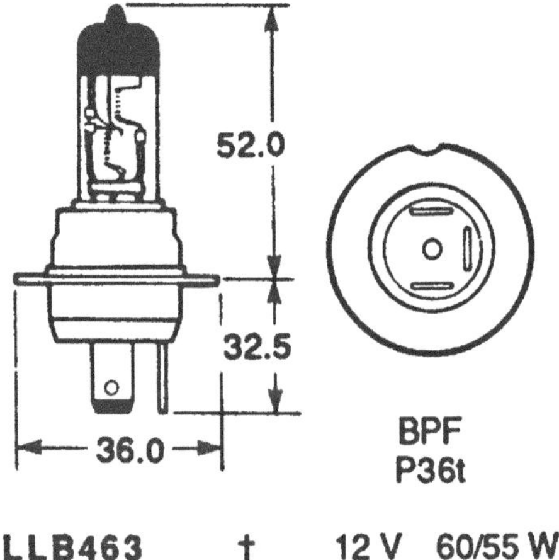


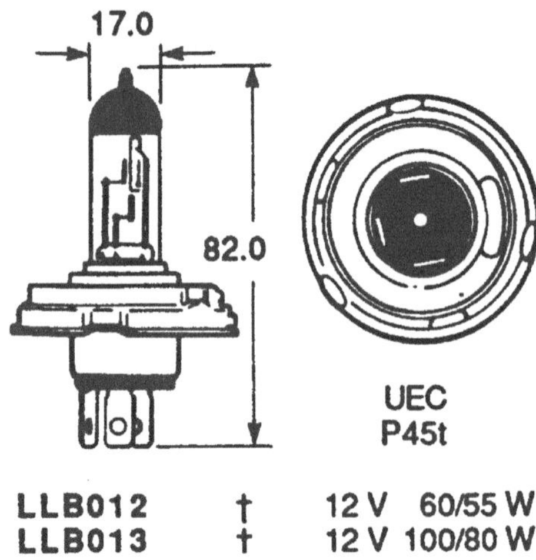


***Fig. 11.11 Bulbs in common use***

LL*Lucas reference numbers*

† *Halogen*

Y *Yellow*

# *Left-hand drive*

‡ *Heavy duty*

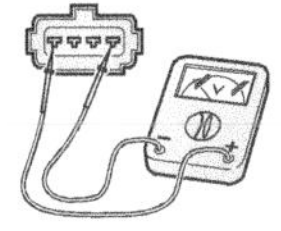

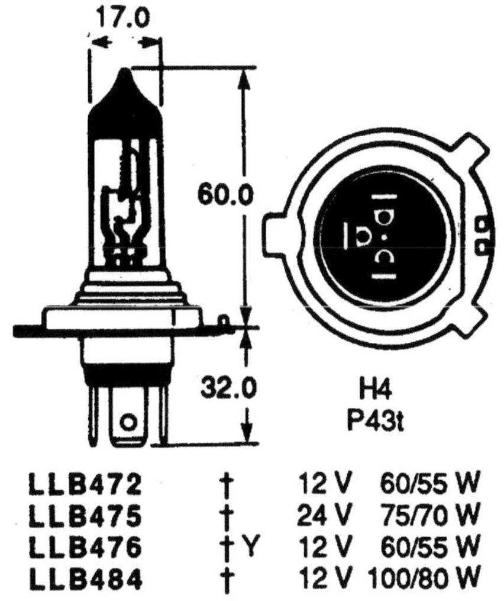


| | | | |
|---|---|---|---|
| LLB472 | † | 12 V | 60/55 W |
| LLB475 | † | 24 V | 75/70 W |
| LLB476 | † Y | 12 V | 60/55 W |
| LLB484 | † | 12 V | 100/80 W |

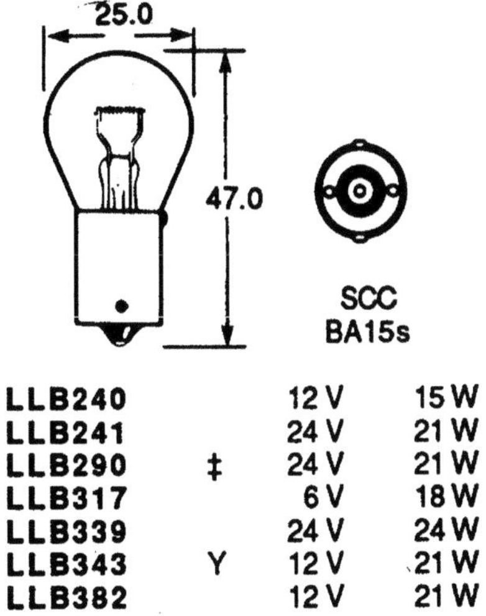


| | | | |
|---|---|---|---|
| LLB240 | | 12 V | 15 W |
| LLB241 | | 24 V | 21 W |
| LLB290 | ‡ | 24 V | 21 W |
| LLB317 | | 6 V | 18 W |
| LLB339 | | 24 V | 24 W |
| LLB343 | Y | 12 V | 21 W |
| LLB382 | | 12 V | 21 W |

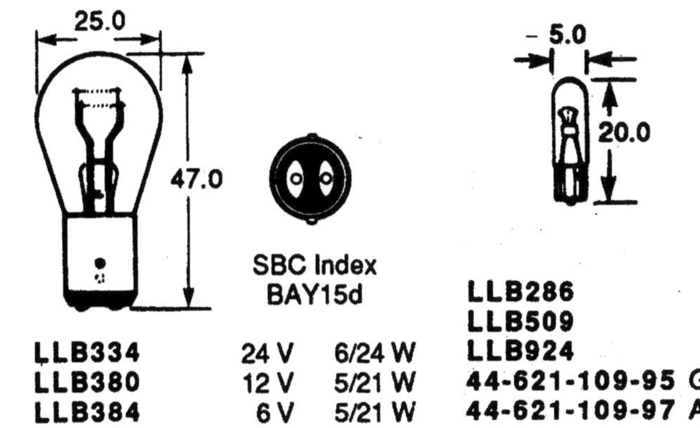


| | | |
|---|---|---|
| LLB334 | 24 V | 6/24 W |
| LLB380 | 12 V | 5/21 W |
| LLB384 | 6 V | 5/21 W |

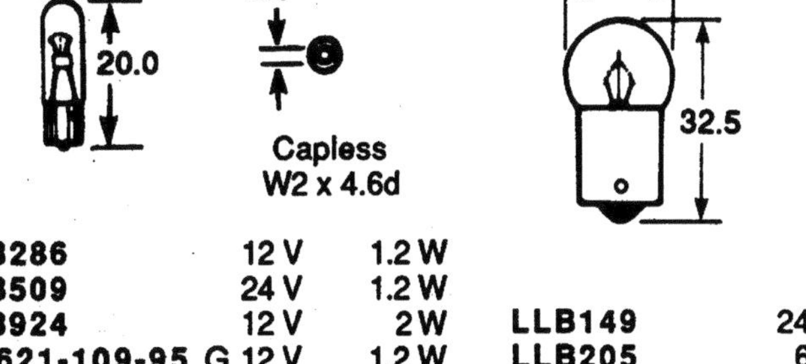


| | | | |
|---|---|---|---|
| LLB286 | | 12 V | 1.2 W |
| LLB509 | | 24 V | 1.2 W |
| LLB924 | | 12 V | 2 W |
| 44-621-109-95 | G | 12 V | 1.2 W |
| 44-621-109-97 | A | 12 V | 1.2 W |

| | | |
|---|---|---|
| LLB149 | 24 V | 5 W |
| LLB205 | 6 V | 5 W |
| LLB207 | 12 V | 5 W |

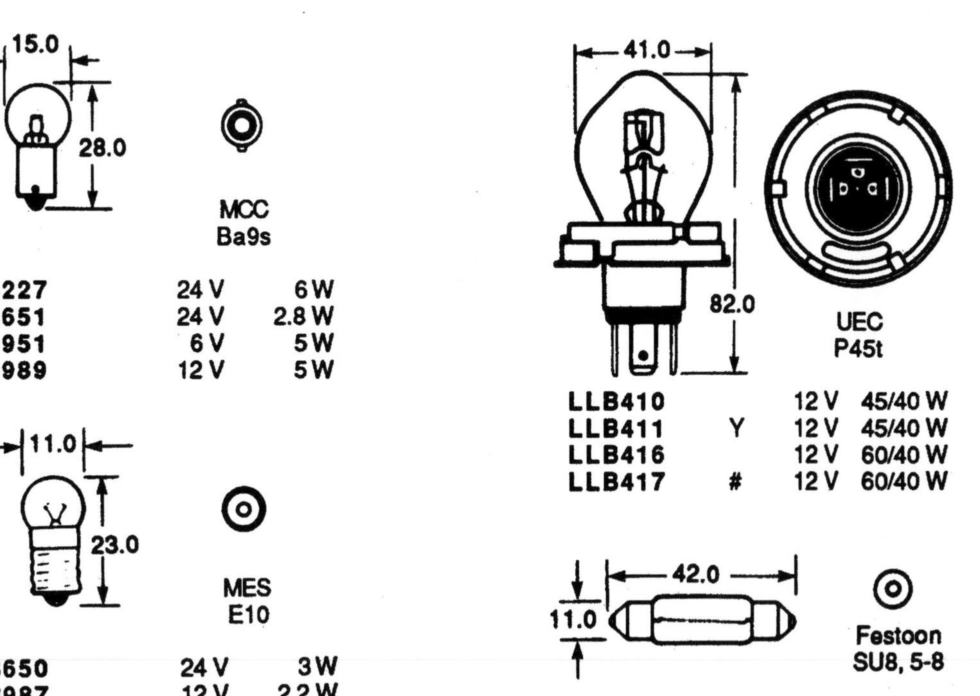


| | | |
|---|---|---|
| LLB227 | 24 V | 6 W |
| LLB651 | 24 V | 2.8 W |
| LLB951 | 6 V | 5 W |
| LLB989 | 12 V | 5 W |

| | | | |
|---|---|---|---|
| LLB410 | | 12 V | 45/40 W |
| LLB411 | Y | 12 V | 45/40 W |
| LLB416 | | 12 V | 60/40 W |
| LLB417 | # | 12 V | 60/40 W |

| | | |
|---|---|---|
| LLB650 | 24 V | 3 W |
| LLB987 | 12 V | 2.2 W |
| LLB990 | 6 V | 2 W |

| | | |
|---|---|---|
| LLB258 | 12 V | 5 W |

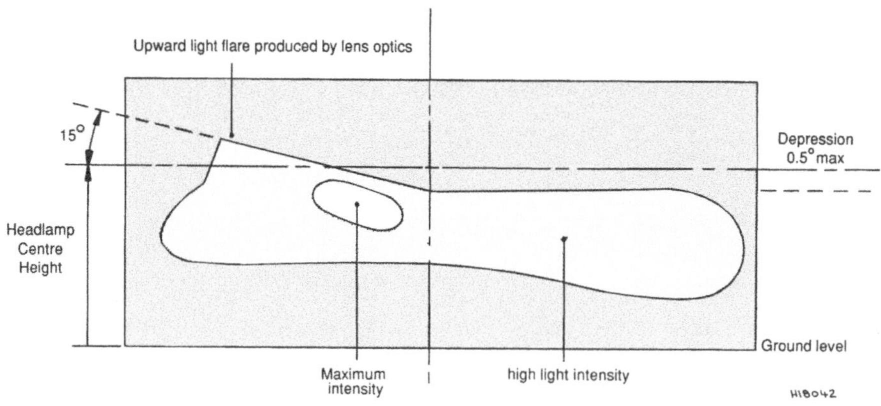


*Fig. 11.12 Correct light pattern for European headlamp on dipped beam (UK standards)*

*Fig. 11.13 Headlamp lens with side flare prisms*

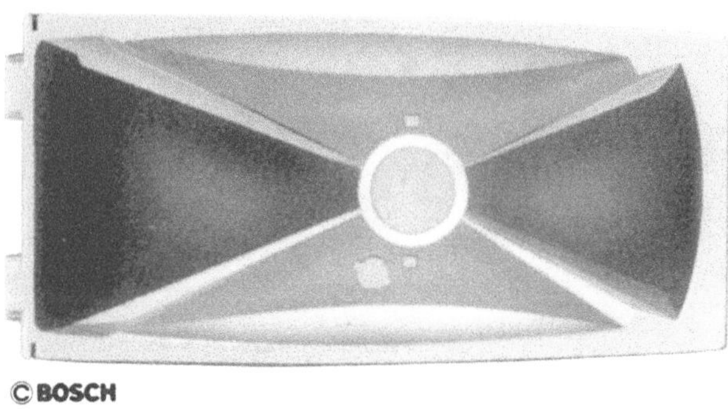


*Fig. 11.14 Homofocular reflector giving low vertical headlamp height*

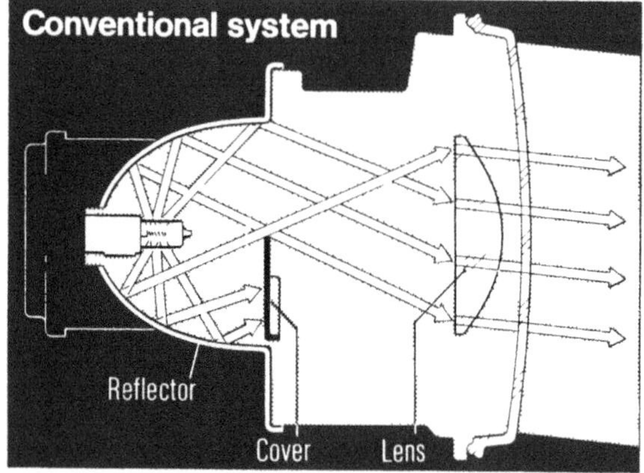


Light distribution

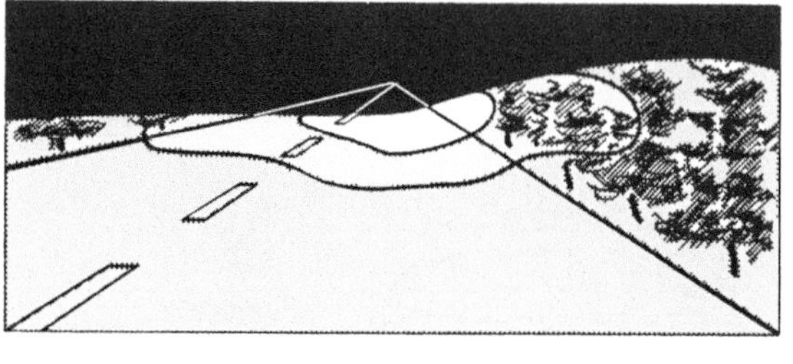

Light distribution with improved foreground illumination

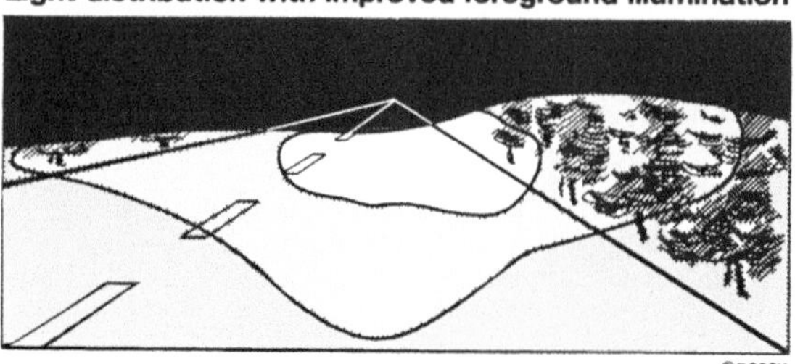


***Fig. 11.15 Polyellipsoid lamp design***
*Bosch press photo*

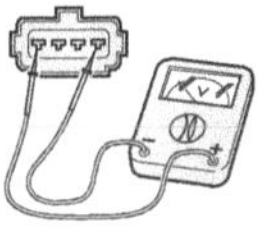

line to the left at an angle of 15° above the horizontal (Fig. 11.12). All European headlamps fitted to UK vehicles must be marked 'E', 'e' or 'BS'.

**4 Lenses** are generally made of glass but manufacturers are also producing a complete plastic unit comprising lens and reflector. The lens itself consists of a series of prism sections and sub lenses which serve to give the main beam a long range light in a fairly concentrated beam shape, yet also give the dip beam a wide band of illumination in front of the car with a side flare for road edge illumination (Fig. 11.13). The design has to be a compromise but excellent results are obtained.

**5 Homofocular** headlamps have a reflector which is divided into different sections. In the homofocular reflector two or more paraboloids with different focal lengths are arranged round the same focal point. The stepped, plastic reflector (Fig. 11.14) results in a low, long range beam, but at the same time providing a large amount of light for diffusion to the sides and front of the vehicle. The central reflector segment which has a short focal length provides light for the close and medium ranges and side areas. Other segments produce the long range illumination with a low beam. With the lower bonnet heights required for low drag factor, this type of lamp meets the need for a lamp of small vertical dimensions.

**6 Polyellipsoid headlamps** are recently developed by Bosch and have a rim aperture of only 60 mm (area 28 sq cm) yet achieve ranges that have previously been attained only by apertures four times as large. The low beam polyellipsoid headlamp is combined with a conventional high beam headlamp. The lower part of the reflector has a different curvature from the upper part and results in a larger light reflecting region (Fig. 11.15).

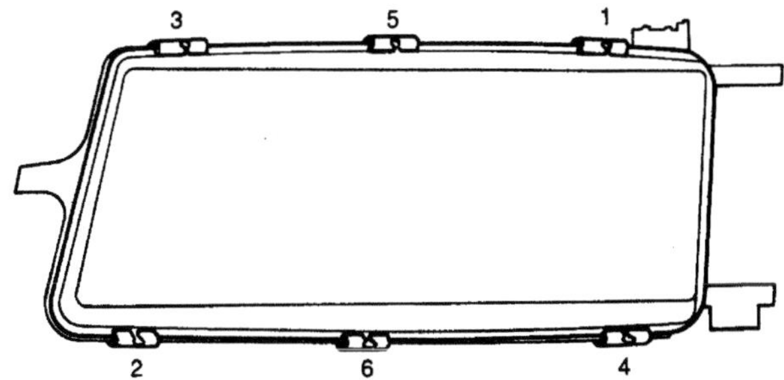


***Fig. 11.16 Lens clips to lamp body in this headlamp design***
*1 to 6 Clips*

**7 Load-levelling headlamps**. Rear seat loading will cause beams to be raised and possibly dazzle drivers of oncoming vehicles. To meet this, manufacturers have developed headlight levelling systems. Also see Section 13 for self-levelling systems. The lamp has also the facility of replacing the front lens by removing six clips (Fig. 11.16). Fig. 11.17 shows the lamp and the levelling motor (f). (b) is the main halogen lamp.

***Fig. 11.17 Load levelling headlamp***

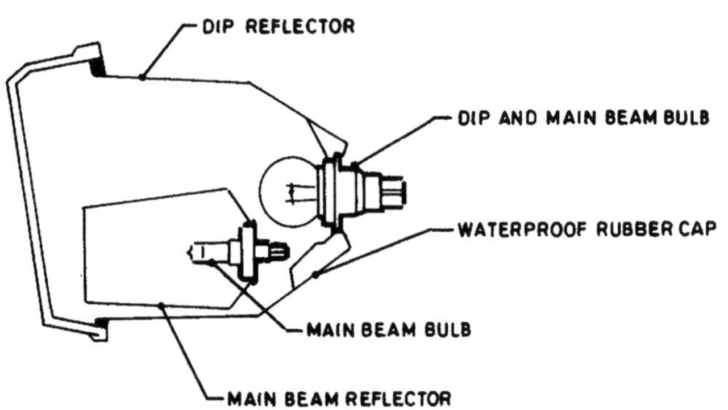


*Fig. 11.18 A double bulb twin reflector headlamp*

**8 Double unit headlamp**. A design by SEV Marchal consists of a headlamp shell which houses two bulbs and two reflectors (Fig. 11.18). The light output for the 7 inch halogen lamp unit is 72 000 candela, which is more than twice the output of a standard headlamp with a conventional bulb. The small reflector unit and the halogen bulb produce the main beam and the back of the reflector serves to cut off the lower half of the rear reflector giving a sharp cut off to the dipped beam.

**9 Dymanic Directional lighting** is now available on production vehicles. An ECU processes information supplied by vehicle speed and the steering angle sensors (see Chapter 14), and swivels the motorised headlamps by upto 15° in each direction, improving the illumination of curves and bends in the road.

## 11 The four-headlamp system

**1** Lamp design to give efficient main and dip beams is, as seen from the previous section, possible but at the cost of some complexity. The use of four headlamps gives uncompromising design for both beams (Fig. 11.19).

*Fig. 11.20 Headlamp beam alignment meter*

*Fig. 11.19 The four headlamp system*

**2** The lamps are mounted either in a line horizontally, or in two pairs one above the other, they may be rather smaller (146 mm diameter) than those used in two headlamp vehicles where the diameter is typically 170 mm.

**3** The inner headlamps each contain only one filament and these two provide the greater part of the main beam. The outer headlamps each have a filament located precisely at the focal point and will give a good dip beam without compromise. In addition the outer lamps have a second filament which is slightly off the focal point and below the dip filament. These are on when main beam is required.

**4** Thus, when main beam is on, the inner lamps are operating together with the lower filaments of the outer lamps. On dip, the outer lamps work alone with the inner lamps switched off.

## 12 Beam setting

**1** Setting of headlamp beam is important so as not to cause dazzle to drivers of oncoming vehicles, but also to achieve an MOT pass for the vehicle. Professional beam alignment equipment gives accuracy, an example being shown in Fig. 11.20.

**2** If a beam alignment meter is not available then it is possible to set the lamps by projecting the beam pattern onto a vertical surface and adjusting the lamps one at a time by the adjuster screws for vertical and horizontal alignment. Most headlamps except British/American are set on dip beam; this is logical since it is the dip beam which may or may not cause dazzle to oncoming drivers. The vertical surface aiming board should be at a distance of about 30 feet from the vehicle and at right-angles to it. Mark out positions where the top centre of the dipped light pattern should be and switch on lights to dipped beam. Cover one lamp and adjust the other lamp. Then reverse the procedure and adjust the second lamp. The distance of the top centre point below lamp level will depend upon the vehicle but will be approximately 5.5 inches. It is advisable to road test a vehicle in the dark after beam setting if the figure for depth below headlamp level is not known.

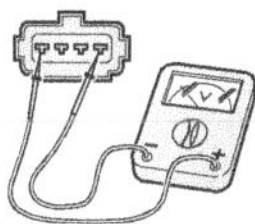

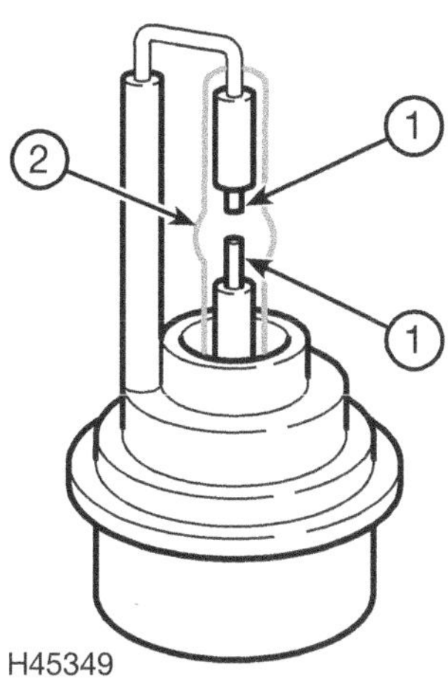


***Fig. 11.21 Gas Discharge (Xenon) headlamp bulb***
*1 Electrodes*
*2 Xenon filled glass tube*

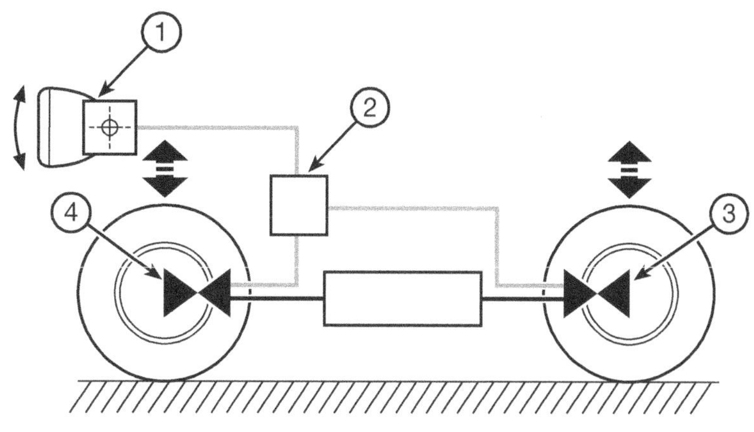


***Fig. 11.22 Headlamp self-levelling system***
*1 Headlight range control motor*
*2 ECU*
*3 Rear suspension height sensor*
*4 Front suspension height sensor*

## 13 Gas discharge (Xenon) headlamps

With gas discharge headlamps, light is generated by an electric arc between two electrodes in a small gas-filled glass tube (Fig. 11.21). There is no filament. The light emitted from the lamp has high levels of green/blue components due to the composition of the gas (Xenon) in the tube.

Although there is a major increase in complexity and cost, the benefits of this system are:

a) *Increased service life (several times that of a normal halogen bulb)*
b) *Due to the design of the lens, reflector and aperture, a much longer and wider beam pattern is produced.*
c) *Output is up to 3 times that of a halogen bulb with no increase in power consumption.*
d) *No requirement for fog lights due to the wide near-field beam.*

A ballast/igniter unit supplies a high-voltage pulse of around 22 000 volts to initiate the electric arc between the bulb's electrodes. After the initial arc, an increased current is supplied for a few seconds until maximum brightness is achieved. Because of this delay gas discharge bulbs are normally only fitted to the dipped beams of the headlamps, a normal halogen bulb is used for the main beam.

To avoid dazzling oncoming motorists with the increased light output, vehicles equipped with gas discharge headlamps must also be fitted with an automatic headlamp levelling system. This systems alters the aim of the headlamps to compensate for any change in the vehicle load. The headlamp range ECU monitors the vehicle loading via sensors fitted to the front and rear suspension, and alters the aim of the headlamps by means of electric motors connected via linkages to the headlamp reflectors (Fig. 11.22).

When working with gas discharge headlamps, several safety aspects must be taken into consideration:

a) *Always disconnect the battery and allow any residual charge in the ballast/igniter to dissipate for a few minutes prior to commencing repairs.*
b) *The gas inside the bulbs is pressurised to in excess of 10 bar. Always wear safety goggles when handling the bulbs.*

# Notes

# Electromagnetic interference 12



## 1 Interference

**1** Interference to radio, television and communication equipment may result from apparatus in which changes or interruption to current flow occur. Motor vehicle equipment includes a number of interference-generating items, in particular the ignition system, starter motor, alternator, rectifiers, switches, wipers, voltage regulators and electric petrol pumps.

**2** In the early days of radio, transmitters worked by high voltage sparks, so it is hardly surprising that the ignition system of an automobile gives rise to radiation – in this case unwanted, and likely to cause interference to nearby television sets, and the vehicle's own receiving equipment, if any. Fig. 12.1 shows the equivalent of an ignition system in which two spark gaps (at the distributor rotor and the plugs) are associated with the coil and HT lead inductances and the stray capacitance of coil, leads and the plugs.

**3** All these components contribute to a form of radio transmitter, generating waves with frequencies ranging from as low as 150 kilohertz (long wave band) through to 600 megahertz, but with maximum effect in the range 40 to 100 megahertz.

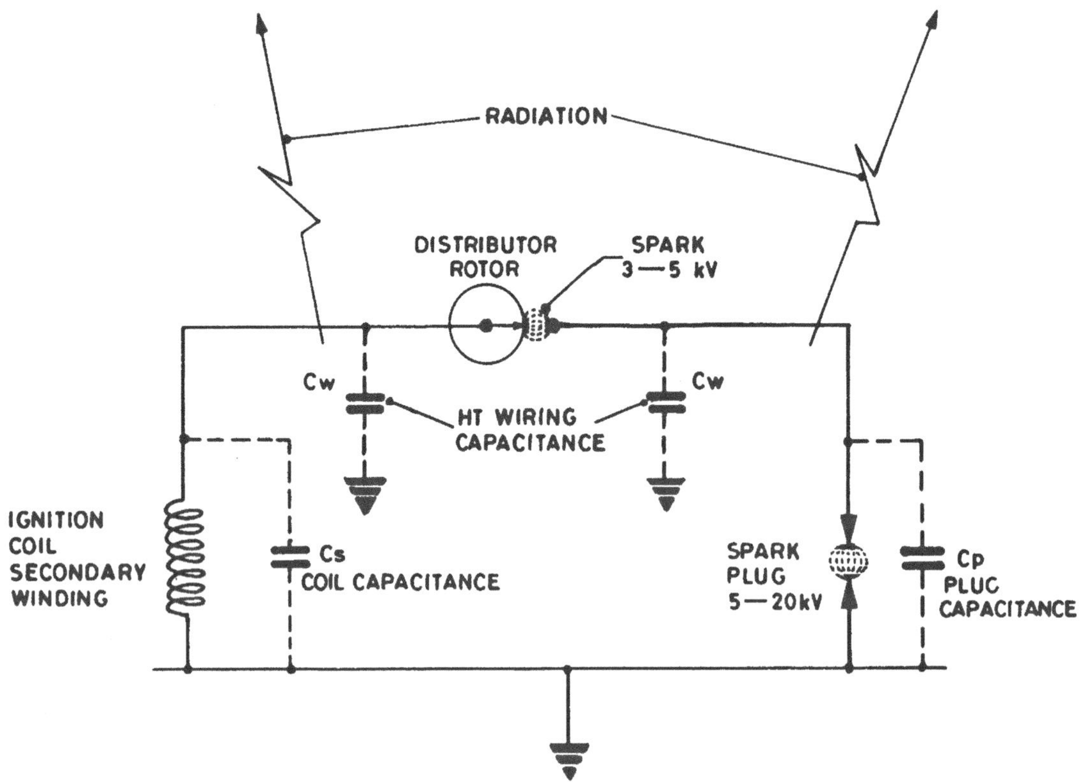


*Fig. 12.1 Equivalent circuit of ignition secondary loop*

**4** The circuit capacitances shown are responsible for most of the interference. When the plug fires, the voltage just before sparking can be several kilovolts: this drops abruptly to a sparking voltage of only a few hundred volts, and the stored energy in the stray capacitances $C_sC_w$ and $C_p$ is discharged in a time period of the order of 1 microsecond.

**5** Radiation from inside an engine compartment is to some extent shielded by the bonnet (hood) and surrounding metalwork, but only if all parts are properly connected (or bonded). If not, metal parts in the radiation path which are wholly or partly insulated can act like aerials which re-radiate interference. This can apply to all sorts of items in a vehicle, such as metal parcel shelves; test bonding with an earthed braid is often the only way of locating the culprit.

**6** Interference can reach in-car radio and other equipment by conduction through cables, and a simple test with radio receivers is to pull out the aerial plug. If the interference disappears or reduces substantially the path is by radiation, but if the noise remains it is reaching the receiver by conduction (Fig. 12.2).

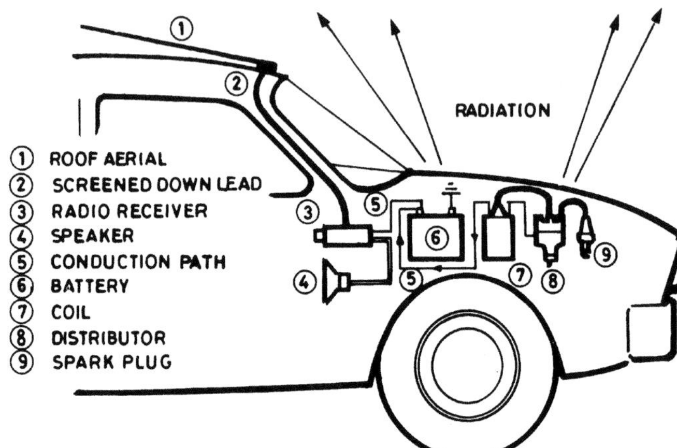


*Fig. 12.2 Radiation and conduction paths of interference*

## 2 Legal suppression requirements

**1** All vehicles manufactured in the UK must comply with regulations relating to the levels of interference. EC regulations are now implemented by all members, together with other European countries.

**2** It is illegal to replace suppression equipment on a vehicle in such a way as to reduce the interference protection to below legal requirements.

**3** Resistive HT cables do not reduce engine performance and should not be replaced with wire HT cabling.

## 3 Radio installation

**1** In the installation of a radio receiver in a vehicle, it is important to check that good earth connections are made,

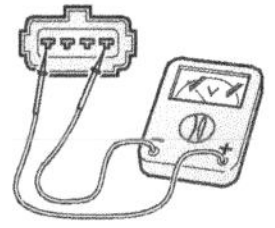

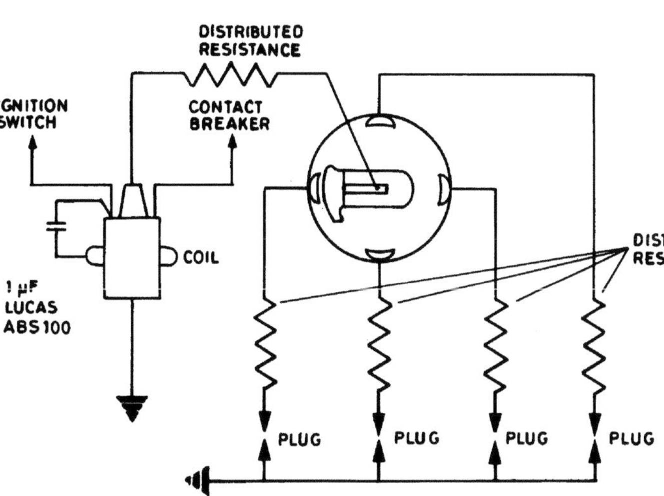


*Fig. 12.3 Resistive cable in each HT lead*

and that wiring is as short as possible. Metal-to-metal contact is vital, and bolting down a receiver or an aerial onto a painted surface will not do. An older vehicle should be checked for corrosion at earth terminations if interference becomes a new problem.

**2** Radio receivers should be given the best possible signal, with the aerial mounted in a good position – having least chance of engine interference pick-up and adequate screening from bodywork. In this respect aerials should be of good quality and windscreen stick-on types avoided. Roof aerials, although requiring extra trouble to fit, are away from the radiation field around the bonnet and are also above the vehicle so as to be able to pick up radio signals from any direction without the car body obstructing the path.

**3** Never use the aerial down-lead braiding as the only earth for the equipment – the power supply should have a good separate earth point.

**4** Receivers are provided with a variable trimmer to match the set to the aerial. Considerable reduction in the signal-to-noise ratio will result if this adjustment is not carried out to the manufacturer's instructions.

**5** Detailed installation information will be given by the radio supplier, and much will depend upon the type of vehicle and desired aerial position. However, the principles of good earthing, shortest earth leads and good aerial position will apply in all cases.

**6** Further notes on installation are to be found in Section 8 of this Chapter, which relates to VHF/FM receivers.

## 4 Suppression methods – ignition

**1** Ignition interference is normally heard as a crackle which varies with engine speed.

**2** Suppressed HT cables are supplied as original equipment by manufacturers and will meet regulations as far as external interference is concerned. Resistive HT cable has a core of graphite-impregnated woven rayon or silk, with a PVC or synthetic rubber insulation.

**3** Such cable comes in two grades, one having a higher resistance per unit length, but plug leads will be arranged to have a resistance of about 10 000 ohms for standard cases (Fig. 12.3). It may be necessary to use higher values in case of bad interference, such as occurs with glass-fibre bodies where no metal screening occurs.

**4** Occasionally vehicles will be found using fixed resistors to each plug, in conjunction with low resistance wire cable. Their performance at VHF is insufficient and they should be replaced by resistive HT cable.

**5** A capacitor of 1 µF (microfarad) connected from the LT supply side of the ignition coil to earth will complete basic ignition interference treatment. The capacitor should be specifically for this job and a good earth made under one of the coil fixing bolts by scraping away any paint. **Never** connect a capacitor on the contact breaker side of the coil, as the points will fail after a short time. The length of wire between the capacitor and its connector should never be altered, since it is critical at higher radio frequencies.

**6** Electronic ignition equipment usually has built-in suppression – see Section 11.

## 5 Suppression methods – line-borne interference (conduction)

**1** Interference from wipers, washers, heater blower, flashers and stop-lamps is frequently taken to the receiver by the vehicle wiring. This should be confirmed by removing the aerial lead, replacing it with a dummy aerial consisting of a polystyrene capacitor of 62 to 82 pF connected to earth at the received input.

**2** With the engine running check for separate noises over the wavebands, switching on the accessories separately. A choke fitted into the receiver supply lead will probably effect a cure (Fig. 12.4). If not, separate suppression of the offending item will be necessary.

**3** Low-priced radio equipment might benefit from the fitting of a 1000 microfarad 16 volt electrolytic capacitor connected from the radio side of the choke down to the radio chassis. **Note:** *polarity is important when using electrolytic capacitors.*

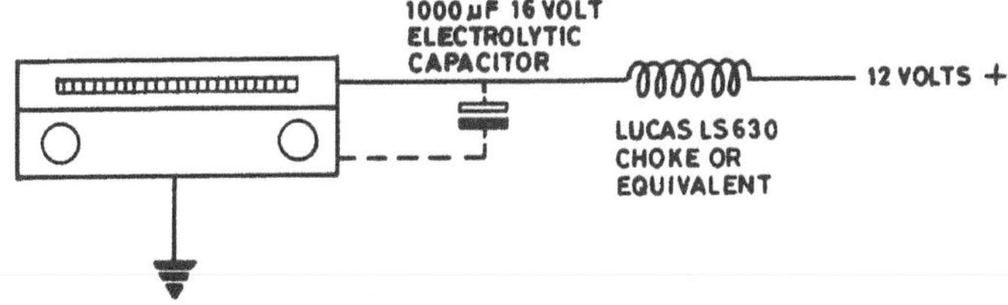


*Fig. 12.4 Line-borne interference suppression*

## 6 Suppression methods – re-radiation

**1** If ignition interference persists after the basic treatment of Section 4, it is possible that a part of the vehicle is picking up radiation and, acting as an aerial, is then re-radiating.

**2** This can be located by systematically going over the vehicle using an earth strap and connecting suspected items to a good earth on the vehicle. Possible re-radiators include:

- Exhaust pipes
- Parcel trays
- Doors or panels
- Engine-to-body
- Front suspension
- Gear lever – especially French and Italian cars
- Steering column – especially French and Italian cars

Once tracked down, permanent bonding down with an earth strap is required.

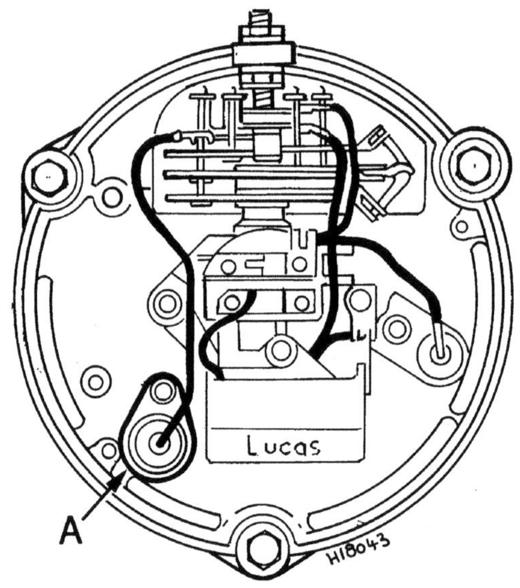


***Fig. 12.5 Suppression of alternator interference***
*A 3 µF capacitor*

## 7 Suppression methods – other equipment

### Alternators and dynamos

Whine varying with engine speed

Connect a 1 µF capacitor from terminal D to earth for a dynamo, or connect a 3 µF capacitor from the main output (thick cable) terminal to earth for an alternator (Fig. 12.5)

### Instrument stabiliser

Connect a 3 A in-line choke in the stabiliser feed (B terminal). If necessary connect a 1 µF capacitor to earth, as shown in Fig. 12.6. Finally try a second 3 A choke in the instrument line

### Voltage regulator

Whine or crackle that cuts in as speed rises, and drops out at low speed or when the lights are switched on (generally not apparent at idling speeds)

Lucas ACR, Delco, Bosch and Femsa alternators; fit a 1µF capacitor between the warning lamp terminal (IND, D +, L or 61) and earth. For dynamo systems fit a 1 µF capacitor between the control box D terminal (the main output lead from the dynamo to the box) and earth (Fig. 12.7). Never connect capacitors from the field terminal to earth

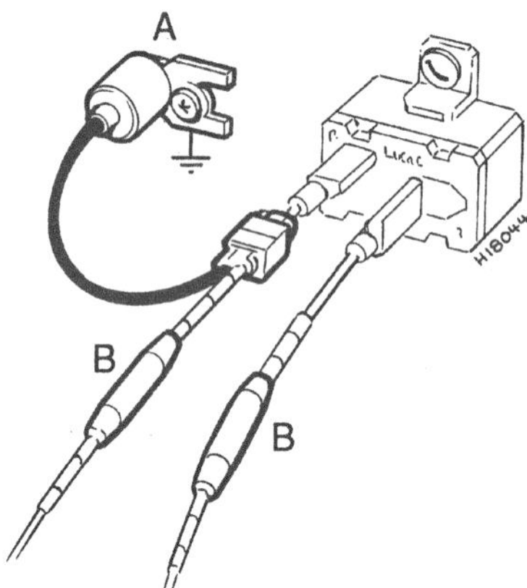


***Fig. 12.6 Suppression of instrument stabiliser interference***
*A 1 µF capacitor*
*B 3 A in-line chokes*

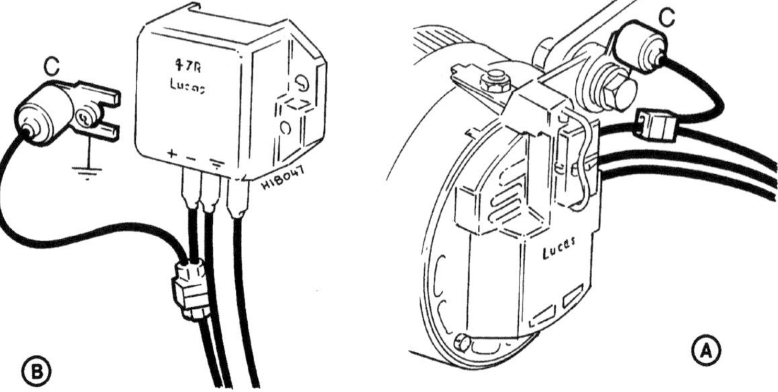


***Fig. 12.7 Suppression of voltage regulator interference***
*A Alternator systems B Dynamo systems C 1µF capacitor*

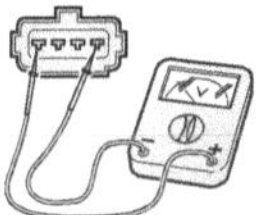

## Wiper motor

Crackling when the motor is switched on (when testing, wet the screen to preserve the blades)

Connect the wiper motor body to earth using a bonding strap. For permanent magnet and wound field motors use a 7 A choke assembly (Fig. 12.8)

## Electronic tachometer

Ignition noise persists after normal suppression

If the noise disappears when the tachometer lead is disconnected suppress the lead by inserting a 3 A in-line choke (Fig. 12.9) at the coil/distributor end

## Horn

A capacitor and choke combination is effective if the horn is connected directly to the 12 V supply. The use of a relay is an alternative remedy, as this will reduce the length of interference-carrying leads (Fig. 12.10)

## Electrostatic noise

Crackles in the receiver output – caused by the build-up of static electricity in non-driven wheels

It is possible to fit spring-loaded contacts between the wheels and the vehicle frame – a dealer will advise on the availability of this method

Crackles in the receiver output, and also electric shocks to people touching the car

Changing a tyre sometimes helps because of tyres' varying electrical resistance. In difficult cases a trailing flex which touches the ground will cure the problem. If this is not acceptable it is worth trying conductive tyre paint on the tyre walls

## Miscellaneous

Including clocks, screenwashers, heater motors, electric fuel pumps, flashers, stop lamps

Try a 1 μF capacitor from feed to earth (or from both wires to earth for heater motors). If necessary, chokes of the appropriate current rating can be added

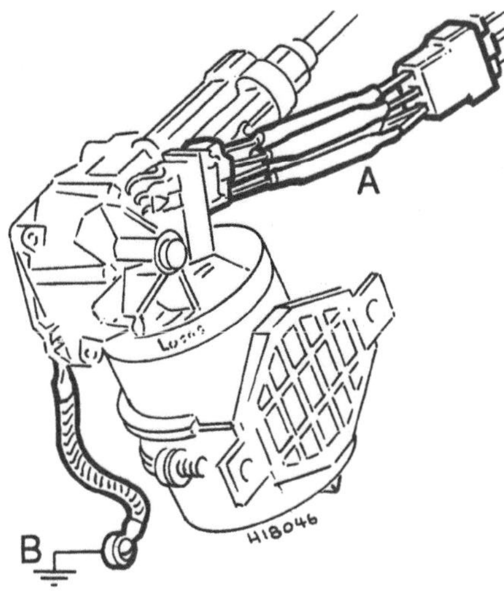


***Fig. 12.8 Suppression of wiper motor xinterference***
*A 7A in line chokes*
*B Earth strap*

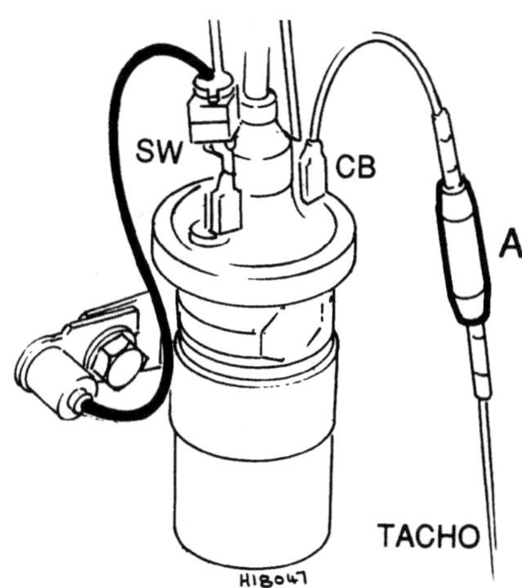


***Fig. 12.9 Suppression of electronic tachometer interference***
*A An in-line choke*

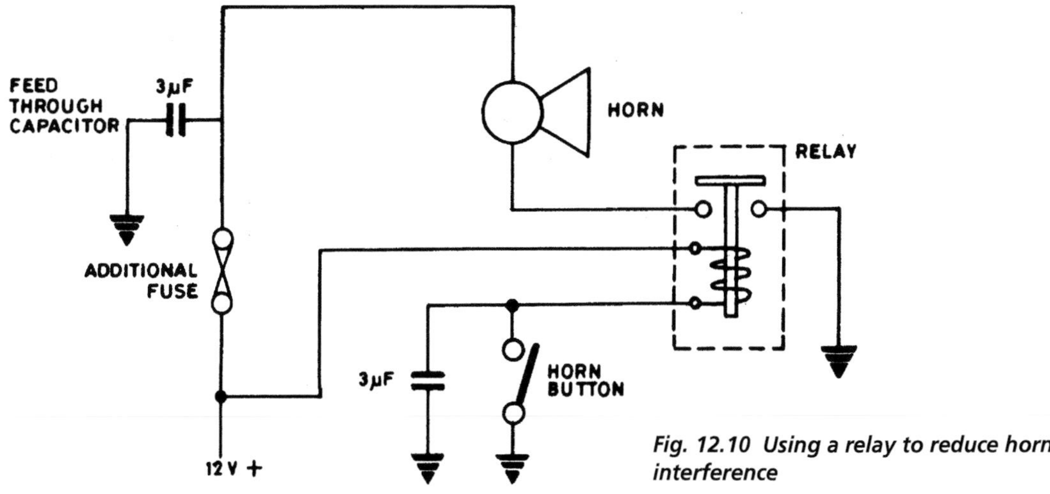


***Fig. 12.10 Using a relay to reduce horn interference***

## 8 VHF/FM broadcasts

**1** Reception of VHF/FM in an automobile is more prone to problems than the medium and long wavebands. Medium/long wave transmitters are capable of covering considerable distances, but VHF transmitters are restricted to line of sight, meaning ranges of 10 to 50 miles, depending upon the terrain, the effects of buildings and the transmitter power.

**2** Because of the limited range it is necessary to retune on a long journey.

**3** Most forms of interference occur in the form of amplitude changes, in that a received radio signal would have superimposed on it an interference impulse tending to make the combined received signal momentarily larger.

**4** VHF transmissions in the UK send information not by variation of the amplitude level – amplitude modulation (AM), but by varying the frequency of transmission by a small fraction in accord with the microphone signal, hence the name frequency modulation (FM).

**5** FM receivers have a limiting device which holds the amplitude of the signal voltage in the set at a constant level so when an unwanted pulse is received it is chopped off by the limiter. It is this single factor which accounts for the success of receivers working on very high frequency (VHF) for they are, in fact, working over a band where ignition interference reaches a peak. However, the protection against interference by the FM receiver limiter depends upon the received signal being above a certain minimum level.

**6** When conditions are poor, interference can arise, and some of the suppression devices described in Section 4 of this Chapter fall off in performance at very high frequencies unless specifically designed for the VHF band. Available suppression devices include reactive HT cable, resistive distributor caps, screened plug caps, screened leads and resistive sparking plugs such as the Champion RN9YC.

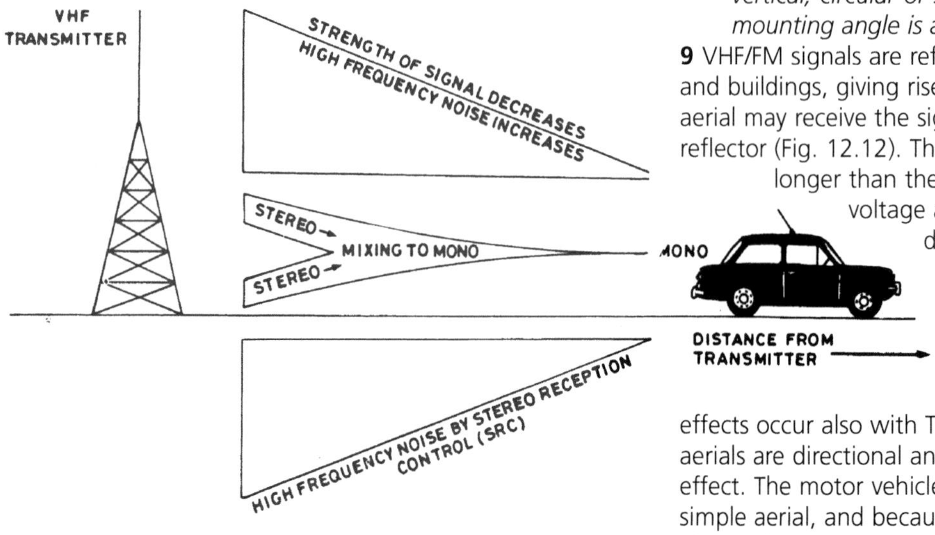

***Fig. 12.11 The action of stereo reception control – SRC***

Fortunately original equipment manufacturers incorporate suppression components in alternators and regulators.

**7** Developments in VHF/FM receiver design include:

(a) ***Muting****, in which incoming signal strength is measured by a circuit which silences the receiver when signal is weakened by hills or buildings. This eliminates the FM noise which is characteristic of signal loss; the system also cuts out FM noise between stations when tuning*

(b) ***Interference absorption circuits*** *which identify unwanted pulses of interference and reject them*

(c) ***Stereo switching*** *– stereo signals need to be about ten times greater in strength than for mono reception. When the received signal in stereo is too weak the set is switched over to mono reception mode automatically, thus eliminating unnecessary noise*

(d) ***Automatic search turning****. Designed for accurate tuning of a programme, the receiver uses a phase-locked loop (PLL) circuit which holds the tuner of a chosen signal. Tuning accurately by manual operation can require attention which is a distraction from driving and this system eliminates the hazard*

(e) ***Stereo reception control (SRC)****. A more refined version of (c), which progressively mixes the stereo channels into mono. It also trims the frequency response to minimise interference and noise, until the signal returns to a level which is sufficient to operate on full stereo again (Fig. 12.11)*

**8** For VHF/FM receiver installation the following points should be observed:

(a) *Earthing of the receiver chassis and the aerial mounting is important. Use a separate earthing wire at the radio, and scrape paint away at the aerial mounting*

(b) *If possible, use a good quality roof aerial to obtain maximum height and distance from interference generating devices on the vehicle*

(c) *Use of a high quality aerial down-lead is important, since losses in cheap cable can be significant*

(d) *The polarisation of FM transmissions may be horizontal, vertical, circular or slanted. Because of this the optimum mounting angle is at 45° to the vehicle roof*

**9** VHF/FM signals are reflected by hard objects, such as hills and buildings, giving rise to the possibility that a vehicle aerial may receive the signal both directly and from the reflector (Fig. 12.12). The length of the reflected path will be longer than the direct path, and the resultant signal voltage at the aerial may rise, fall and even disappear altogether with the vehicle motion. This phenomenon is due to the difference of phase between the two alternating voltage signals, and is characterised by a popping sound. Such reflection effects occur also with TV receivers (ghosting), but their aerials are directional and can be adjusted to minimise the effect. The motor vehicle has the disadvantage of using a simple aerial, and because the vehicle is mobile there is always the likelihood of this effect.

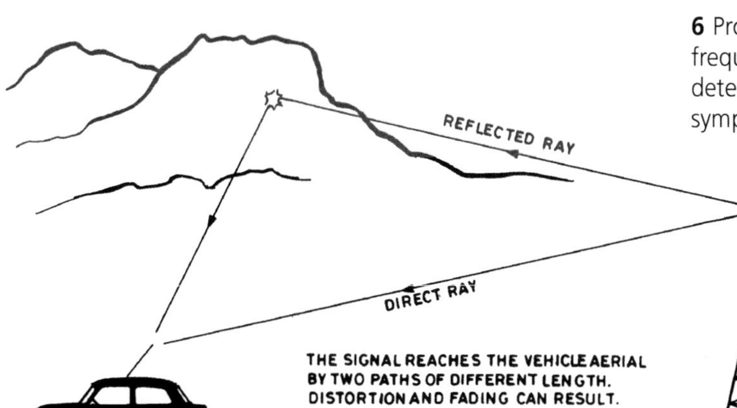


*Fig. 12.12 The effect of reflected signals*

## 9 Citizens' Band radio (CB)

**1** In the UK, CB transmitter/receivers work within the 27 MHz and 934 MHz bands, using the FM mode. At present interest is concentrated on 27 MHz where the design and manufacture of equipment is less difficult. Maximum transmitted power is 4 watts, and 40 channels spaced 10 kHz apart within the range 27.60125 to 27.99125 MHz are available.

**2** Aerials are the key to effective transmission and reception. Regulations limit the aerial length to 1.5 metres, so tuning the aerial is necessary to obtain optimum results. The choice of a CB aerial is dependent on whether it is to be permanently installed or removable, and the performance will hinge on correct tuning and the location point on the vehicle. Common practice is to clip the aerial to the roof gutter or to employ wing mounting where the aerial can be rapidly unscrewed. An alternative is to use the boot (trunk) rim to render the aerial theftproof, but a popular solution is to use the 'magmount' – a type of mounting having a strong magnetic base clamping to the vehicle at any point, usually the roof.

**3** Aerial location determines the signal distribution for both transmission and reception, but it is wise to choose a point away from the engine compartment to minimise interference from vehicle electrical equipment.

**4** The 1.5 metre aerial is subject to considerable wind and acceleration forces. Cheaper units will whip backwards and forwards (Fig. 12.13) and in so doing will alter the relationship with the metal surface of the vehicle with which it forms a ground plane aerial system. The radiation pattern will change correspondingly, giving rise to break up of both incoming and outgoing signals.

**5** Interference problems on the vehicle carrying CB equipment fall into two categories:

*(a) Interference to nearby TV and radio receivers when transmitting*

*(b) Interference to CB set reception due to electrical equipment on the vehicle*

**6** Problems of break-through to TV and radio are not frequent, but can be difficult to solve. Mostly trouble is not detected or reported because the vehicle is moving and the symptoms rapidly disappear at the TV/radio receiver, but when the CB set is used as a base station any trouble with nearby receivers will soon result in a complaint.

**7** It must not be assumed by the CB operator that his equipment is faultless, for much depends upon the design. Harmonics (that is, multiples) of 27 MHz may be transmitted unknowingly and these can fall into other user's bands. Where trouble of this nature occurs, low pass filters in the aerial or supply leads can help, and should be fitted in base station aerials as a matter of course. In stubborn cases it may be necessary to call for assistance from the Licensing Authority, or, if possible, to have the equipment checked by the manufacturers.

**8** Interference received on the CB set from the vehicle equipment is, fortunately, not usually a severe problem. The precautions outlined elsewhere in this Chapter apply, but there are some extra points worth noting. It is common practice to use a slide-mount on CB equipment enabling the set to be easily removed for use as a base station, for example. Care must be taken that the slide mount fittings are properly earthed and that first class connection occurs between the set and slide-mount.

**9** Vehicle manufacturers in the UK are required to provide suppression of electrical equipment to cover 40 to 250 MHz to protect TV and VHF radio bands. Such suppression appears to be adequately effective at 27 MHz, but suppression of individual items such as alternators/dynamos, clocks, stabilisers, flashers, wiper motors, etc, may still be necessary. The suppression capacitors and chokes available from auto-electrical suppliers for entertainment receivers will usually give the required results with CB equipment. Details are to be found in earlier Sections of this Chapter.

## 10 Glass-fibre bodied vehicles

**1** Such vehicles do not have the advantage of a metal box surrounding the engine as is the case, in effect of conventional vehicles. It is usually necessary to line the

***Fig. 12.13 A thin aerial bends, resulting in a distorted radiation pattern***

bonnet, bulkhead and wing valances with metal foil, which could well be the aluminium foil available from builders merchants. Bonding of sheets one to another and the whole down to the chassis is essential.

**2** Wiring harness may have to be wrapped in metal foil which again should be earthed to the vehicle chassis. The aerial base and radio chassis must be taken to the vehicle chassis by heavy metal braid. VHF radio suppression in glass-fibre cars may not be a feasible operation.

**3** In addition to all the above, normal suppression components should be employed, but special attention paid to earth bonding.

## 11 Suppression methods – electronic ignition

**1** Manufacturers of electronic ignition sets build in a certain level of suppression, but this does not relieve the need for suppressing HT leads.

**2** In some cases it is permitted to connect a capacitor on the LT supply side of the ignition coil, but not in every case. Makers' instructions should be carefully followed, otherwise damage to the ignition semiconductors may result.

## 12 Suppression methods – fluorescent tubes

**1** Caravans and public transport vehicles use fluorescent tubes which may give rise to radio and television reception troubles. Both lamp fittings and cables can give rise to interference due to the pulsating nature of the lamp discharge and the presence of harmonics. In addition, the inverter which converts the vehicle voltage to suit the tubes is non-linear and, accordingly, an interference generator.

**2** Location of caravan aerials is important to reduce interference pick-up and obtain maximum signal strength.

**3** Interference may be attenuated by the use of 7 ampere line chokes in the supply lines close to the invertor. Open mesh screening of the tube itself may be necessary in persistent cases (or a length of fine copper wire wound as an open spiral around the tube). In either case the screen should be earthed at one end only and it is important to earth the lamp casing if it is metal.

## 13 Electromagnetic compatibility (EMC)

**1** With the wide increase of electronic equipment in vehicles, interference from external and on-board sources can give rise to serious problems.

**2** External sources of electromagnetic fields include low frequency navigation systems, LW, MW and SW broadcast transmitters, VHF broadcast, amateur mobile transmitters and radar stations.

**3** On-board field sources are the ignition, alternator, switches, solenoids, micro-processors and any circuit where transient conditions exist. Special mention is made of on-board radio transmitters which are commonplace for business.

**4** High field strengths would not be of concern if they did not cause faults on the vehicle.

During tests under conditions of high field strength, faults of a temporary nature have been recorded as follows:

(a) **Engine Management** – Multistriking on ignition<br>Incorrect injector timing

(b) **Instrumentation** – Corruption of digital displays<br>Incorrect speed indication

(c) **Cruise Control** – False throttle operation

(d) **Anti-lock Brakes** – False warning indication<br>Incorrect solenoid operation

(e) **Door Locks** – Locking or unlocking of mechanisms

**5** Certain of these faults could be hazardous and as electronic developments continue in headway control, active suspension and direction displays for example, problems will multiply. Already measures are in-built in designs to minimize the effects of receiving or sending radiation, an example being the shielding by wire mesh of inductive sensors for engine mangement. The subject will undoubtedly become of greater importance and will exist as long as electronic equipment is used on board vehicles.

# Vehicle wiring and test equipment

# 13



## 1 Cable routing and terminations

**1** For convenience of manufacture, wires are gathered together in groups rather than have many single wires in a motor vehicle. The grouping of wires gives a loom which may be formed by taping the wires together or laying them flat side by side in a moulded form, the latter being useful for routeing under carpets. Looms are split into sections which are joined by multi-pin plugs and sockets which are designed to withstand mechanical loading and are usually resistant to water.

**2** Taping or moulding the separate cables (or wires) into the form of a loom gives mechanical strength. This is important in the vehicle since vibration can cause wire fracture if the vibration amplitude is large enough. Cables emerging from the loom will be cut to correct lengths to reach the required point and then will be terminated in some form of connector – a blade or blade socket, eyelet, post connector or self-stripping connector being most frequently found (Figs. 13.1 and 13.2).

**3** Instrument panel wiring is now frequently in the form of a printed circuit board (PCB). The PCB is a sheet of insulating board which has a thin copper foil sheet bonded to both sides. The 'wire routes' are drawn out by photographic

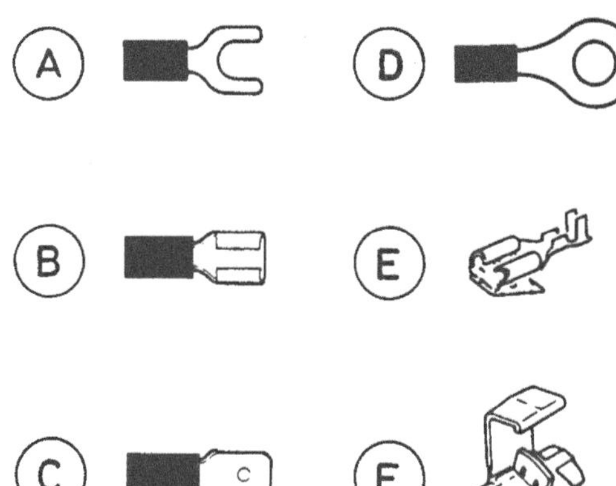


***Fig. 13.1 Typical connectors for auto-electrical equipment***

*A Fork*
*B Lucar female*
*C Lucar male*
*D Eyelet*
*E Lucar piggy back*
*F Self-stripping connector*

**A**

| | DESCRIPTION | OVERALL DIA. |
|---|---|---|
| | SOLDER TYPE | 4·75 mm (0·187″) |
| | CRIMP TYPE, SUITABLE FOR CABLE 14/0·25 mm (14/0·010″) PT AND SPT | 4·75 mm (0·187″) |
| | CRIMP TYPE, SUITABLE FOR CABLE 14/0·30 mm (14/·012″) PT | 4·75 mm (0·187″) |
| | CRIMP TYPE, SUITABLE FOR CABLE 28/0·30 mm (14/·012″) PT | 4·75 mm (0·187″) |
| | CRIMP TYPE, SUITABLE FOR CABLE 44/0·30 mm (44/0·012″) PT | 4·75 mm (0·187″) |
| | SLEEVE TERMINAL $\frac{3}{16}$″ DIA. | |

**B**

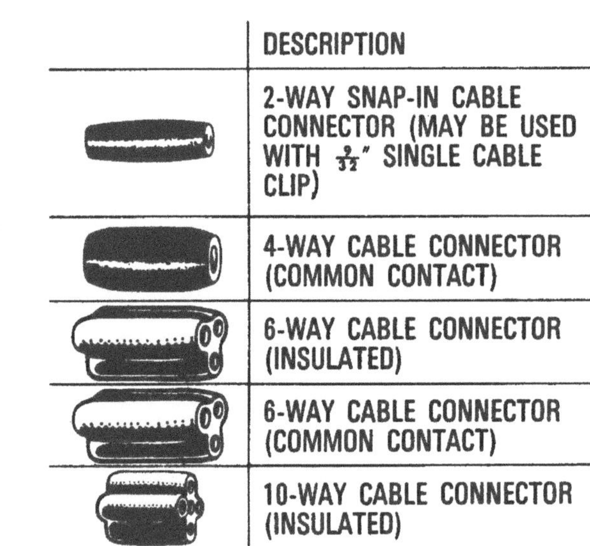

| | DESCRIPTION |
|---|---|
| | 2-WAY SNAP-IN CABLE CONNECTOR (MAY BE USED WITH $\frac{3}{32}$″ SINGLE CABLE CLIP) |
| | 4-WAY CABLE CONNECTOR (COMMON CONTACT) |
| | 6-WAY CABLE CONNECTOR (INSULATED) |
| | 6-WAY CABLE CONNECTOR (COMMON CONTACT) |
| | 10-WAY CABLE CONNECTOR (INSULATED) |

***Fig. 13.2 Snap-in bullet connectors***
*A Male B Female*

means and the unwanted copper stripped away by etching or other means, leaving only the required conducting paths. It is possible to joint points on the back and front of the board by through-pins, which are then soldered. Connectors specially designed to grip and make contact on the board result in a much cheaper method of making the instrument panel connections (Fig. 13.3). Care must be taken to ensure that no current overload occurs on a PCB, because the copper foil quickly blows, like a fuse.

**4** Connections can be troublesome, and it is worth checking the PCB plug and socket if intermittent faults occur. Sometimes capless bulbs are used in the board as indicator lamps, and special attention should be given to ensuring good connections. On modern vehicles it's becoming common place for LEDs to be used for indicator lamps and illumination.

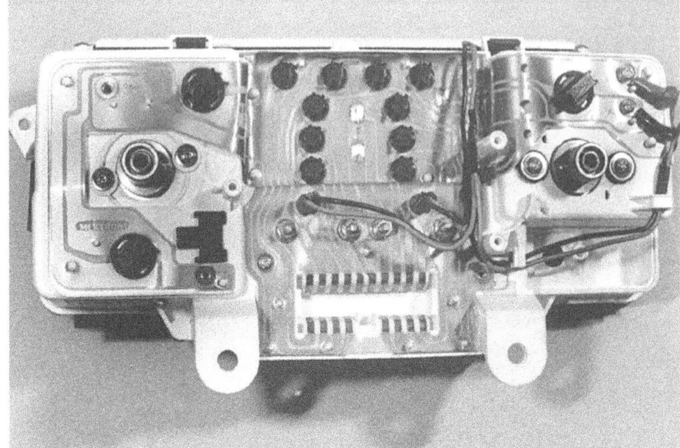

***Fig. 13.3 A typical instrument panel printed circuit board attached to the rear of an instrument cluster***

**5** Should a copper foil strip be damaged and broken, it is possible to bridge a gap with thin tinned fuse wire using the minimum amount of soldering iron heat.

## 2 Cable sizes

**1** It is important that the cross-sectional area of the copper wire is large enough to carry the current without overheating. Additionally the volt-drop in the wire must be low enough to ensure correct operation of the equipment to which it is connected. For all this, on the grounds of cost, the manufacturer will use the minimum size of cable which is consistent with the above requirements.

**2** Rarely is the cable made of one single copper wire, because it would be difficult to bend round corners and, in any case, might fracture with vibration. Cables are made up of strands of copper wire (often tinned) twisted in a slow spiral and then covered with an insulator which is extruded like toothpaste.

**3** Both metric and inch measurements are in use in automobiles, depending upon the country of origin, but the principles of choosing the correct size are the same. The manufacturer will use a cable which is the minimum size to do the job (a thought to bear in mind when adding accessories), the criteria being:

*(a) The volt-drop on full load must not be too great*
*(b) The cable heating must be within specified limits*

**4** In order to carry current to meet condition (a) the copper cross-sectional area must be sufficient; cable heating (b) will also depend upon the cross-sectional area, but additionally the factor of the cable's ability to get rid of the heat is important. A single cable exposed to air can be used to carry

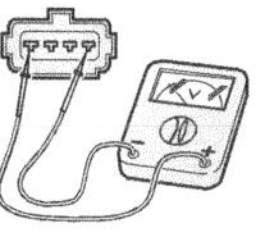

a much higher current than if it were bunched up with other cables as a part of a loom. Cables that carry current for only a short time can be worked at a higher current density, but here the permitted volt-drop is the important consideration.

**5** Wires are graded by denoting the number of strands and the diameter of a single strand; for example, 14/0.01 (inch) has 14 strands, each of which has a diameter of 0.01 inch. In the case of metric cables the same idea is used so 16/0.2 (metric) indicates 16 strands, each of diameter 0.2 mm. Metric dimensions are now in widespread use and will be used here.

## 3 Volt-drop and current ratings

**1** In the accompanying table, it is assumed that the current density is 8.525 amperes per square millimetre ($A/mm^2$) of copper for cables up to 44/0.3 metric and 6.975 $A/mm^2$ for larger sizes.

| Metric cable size | Current (amperes) | Volt-drop rating (volts per meter per ampere) |
|---|---|---|
| 9/0.3 | 5.5 | 0.0271 |
| 14/0.3 | 8.75 | 0.01742 |
| 28/0.3 | 17.5 | 0.00871 |
| 44/0.3 | 25.5 | 0.00554 |
| 65/0.3 | 35.0 | 0.00375 |
| 84/0.3 | 42.0 | 0.00290 |
| 97/0.3 | 50.0 | 0.00251 |
| 120/0.3 | 60.0 | 0.00203 |

The current ratings shown may be reduced to 60% for cables run in the interior of a loom and also in the case of continuously loaded cables of 28/0.3 metric and above.

**2** Common sizes used for automobile circuits are shown here:

| Cable size | Current rating (amps) | Use |
|---|---|---|
| 14/0.3 | 8.75 | General applications: park and tail lamps, flashing indicators, radio/cassettes,etc |
| 28.03 | 17.5 | Headlamps, horns, heated rear windows, etc |
| 65.03 | 35 | Alternators (depending on output) |
| 84.03 | 42 | |
| 97.03 | 50 | |
| 120.03 | 60 | |
| 37.09 | 170 | Starter cable |

## 4 Cable coding

**1** Where cables emerge from a loom they require some form of identification such as colour-coding or numbering. Although the country of vehicle manufacture may have a National Standard, unfortunately no international agreement has yet been reached on colour codes.

**2** In the United Kingdom the British Standard BS-AU7 determines colour-coding of automobile wiring (Fig. 13.4). Lucas use a 7-colour set in which plain colours – purple, green, blue, red, white, brown and green are supplemented by a further group using a base colour with a thin line trace of a different colour, thus:

Black – earth (ground) connections
Green – feeds to auxiliary devices controlled by the ignition switch, eg wipers, flashers, etc
White – base colour for ignition circuits
Red – sidelights (parking lights) and rear lights
Blue with white trace – main beam headlamp
Blue with red trace – dip (meeting) beam headlamp
Purple – auxiliary devices not fed via the ignition switch, eg horn, interior light
Brown – main battery feed

Other colours are used, according to equipment specification, eg light green, pink, slate.

**3** Handbooks are usually printed in black and white only, so the cable colours are identified by a lettering code, such as:

B = Black R = Red
G = Green S = Slate
N = Brown U = Blue
P = Purple W = White

When a cable has a base colour and a second colour spiral trace the code is, for example:

WG = White with green trace

European vehicles using the DIN code will code cables as follows:

BL = Blue (Blau) GR = Grey (Grau)
BR = Brown (Braun) RT = Red (Rot)
GE = Amber (Gelb) SW = Black (Schwarz)
GN = Green (Grun) WS = White (Weiss)

## 5 Wiring diagrams

**1** Automobile wiring diagrams vary considerably in format. Some are concerned with showing electrical connections (Fig. 13.5, Austin Metro), while the diagram for the Volvo 340 (Fig 13.6) shows the relative position of components on the vehicle. This method illustrates groups of cables which would be taped together to form a loom but does allow tracing out the route of a particular cable.

**2** With the advance in wiring complexity, the trend is towards separate diagrams for each sub-section of the wiring system. As an example, the Rover 800 series manuals give separate diagrams for power distribution, interior lamps and central locking, trip computer/vehicle monitoring,

# Chapter 13

| Colour | | Destination |
|---|---|---|
| Main | Tracer | |
| Brown | | Main battery feed |
| Brown | Blue | Control box (compensated voltage control only) to ignition and lighting switch (feed) |
| Brown | Red | Compression ignition starting aid to switch. Main battery feed to double pole ignition switch (a.c. alt. system) |
| Brown | Purple | Alternator regulator feed |
| Brown | Green | Dynamo 'F' to control box 'F.' Alternator field 'F' to control box 'F' |
| Brown | Light Green | Screenwiper motor to switch |
| Brown | White | Ammeter to control box. Ammeter to main alternator terminal |
| Brown | Yellow | Dynamo 'D' to control box 'D' and ignition warning light. Alternator neutral point |
| Brown | Black | Alternator warning light, negative side |
| Brown | Pink | |
| Brown | Slate | |
| Brown | Orange | |
| Blue | | Lighting switch (head) to dipper switch |
| Blue | Brown | |
| Blue | Red | Dipper switch to headlamp dip beam. Headlamp dip beam fuse to right-hand headlamp (when independently fused) |
| Blue | Purple | |
| Blue | Green | |
| Blue | Light Green | Screenwiper motor to switch |
| Blue | White | Dipper switch to headlamp main beam (subsidiary circuit – headlamp flasher relay to headlamp). Headlamp main beam fuse to right-hand headlamp (when independently fused). Headlamp main beam fuse to outboard headlamps (when outboard headlamps independently fused). Dipper switch to main beam warning light |
| Blue | Yellow | Long range driving switch to lamp. |
| Blue | Black | |
| Blue | Pink | Headlamp dip beam fuse to left-hand headlamp (when independently fused) |
| Blue | Slate | Headlamp main beam fuse to left-hand headlamp or inboard headlamps (when independently fused) |

| Colour | | Destination |
|---|---|---|
| Main | Tracer | |
| Blue | Orange | |
| Red | | Side and tail lamp feed |
| Red | Brown | Variable intensity panel lights (when used in addition to normal panel lights) |
| Red | Blue | |
| Red | Purple | Map light switch to map light |
| Red | Green | Lighting switch to side and tail lamp fuse (when fused) |
| Red | Light Green | Screenwiper motor to switch |
| Red | White | Panel light switch to panel lights |
| Red | Yellow | Fog lamp switch to fog lamp |
| Red | Black | Parking switch to left-hand side lamp |
| Red | Pink | |
| Red | Slate | |
| Red | Orange | Parking light switch to right-hand sidelamp |
| Purple | | Accessories fused direct from battery |
| Purple | Brown | Horn fuse to horn relay (when horn is fused separately) |
| Purple | Blue | |
| Purple | Red | Boot light switch to boot light |
| Purple | Green | |
| Purple | Light Green | |
| Purple | White | Interior light to switch (subsidiary circuit – door safety lights to switch) |
| Purple | Yellow | Horn to horn relay |
| Purple | Black | Horn or horn relay to horn push |
| Purple | Pink | |
| Purple | Slate | Aerial lift motor to switch UP |
| Purple | Orange | Aerial lift motor switch DOWN |
| Green | | Accessories fused via ignition switch (subsidiary circuit fuse A4 to hazard switch (terminal 6)) |
| Green | Brown | Reverse lamp to switch |
| Green | Blue | Water temperature gauge to temperature unit |
| Green | Red | Left-hand flasher lamps |
| Green | Purple | Stop lamps to stop lamp switch |
| Green | Light Green | Hazard flasher unit to hazard pilot lamp |
| Green | White | Right-hand flasher lamps |
| Green | Yellow | Heater motor to switch, single speed (or to 'slow' on two-speed motor) |
| Green | Black | Fuel gauge to fuel tank unit or changeover switch |

***Fig. 13.4 British standard wiring code for automobiles***

| Colour | | Destination |
|---|---|---|
| Main | Tracer | |
| Green | Pink | Choke solenoid to choke switch (when fused) |
| Green | Slate | Heater motor to switch (or to fast) (on 2-speed motor) |
| Green | Orange | Low fuel level warning light |
| Light Green | | Instrument voltage stabilizer to instruments |
| Light Green | Brown | Flasher switch to flasher unit 'L' |
| Light Green | Blue | Flasher switch to left-hand flasher warning light |
| Light Green | Red | Fuel tank changeover switch to right-hand tank unit |
| Light Green | Purple | Flasher unit 'F' to flasher warning light |
| Light Green | Green | |
| Light Green | White | |
| Light Green | Yellow | Flasher switch to right-hand flasher warning light |
| Light Green | Black | Screen jet switch to screen jet motor |
| Light Green | Pink | Flasher unit 'L' to emergency switch (simultaneous flashing) |
| Light Green | Slate | Fuel tank changeover switch to left-hand tank unit |
| Light Green | Orange | |
| White | | Ignition control circuit (unfused) (Ignition switch to ballast resistor) |
| White | Brown | Oil pressure switch to warning light or gauge |
| White | Blue | Choke switch to choke solenoid (unfused). Rear heater fuse unit to switch. Electronic ignition TAC ignition unit to resistance. |
| White | Red | Solenoid starter switch to starter push or inhibitor switch |
| White | Purple | Fuel pump No. 1 or right-hand to change-over switch |
| White | Green | Fuel pump No. 2 or left-hand to change-over switch |
| White | Light Green | Screenwiper motor to switch |
| White | Yellow | Starter inhibitor switch to starter push. Ballast resistor to coil. Starter solenoid to coil |
| White | Black | Ignition coil CB to distributor contact breaker. Rear heated window to switch or fuse TAC ignition |
| White | Pink | Radio from ignition switch |
| White | Slate | Tachometer to ignition coil |
| White | Orange | Hazard warning feed (to switch) |
| Yellow | | Overdrive |

| Colour | | Destination |
|---|---|---|
| Main | Tracer | |
| Yellow | Brown | Overdrive |
| Yellow | Blue | Overdrive |
| Yellow | Red | Overdrive |
| Yellow | Purple | Overdrive |
| Yellow | Green | Overdrive |
| Yellow | Light Green | Screenwiper motor to switch |
| Yellow | White | |
| Yellow | Black | |
| Yellow | Pink | |
| Yellow | Slate | |
| Yellow | Orange | |
| Black | | All earth connections |
| Black | Brown | Tachometer generator to tachometer |
| Black | Blue | Tachometer generator to tachometer |
| Black | Red | Electric speedometer |
| Black | Purple | |
| Black | Green | Screenwiper switch to screenwiper (single speed) relay to radiator fan motor |
| Black | Light Green | Vacuum brake switch to warning light and/or buzzer |
| Black | White | Brake fluid level warning light to switch and handbrake switch |
| Black | Yellow | Electric speedometer |
| Black | Pink | |
| Black | Slate | |
| Black | Orange | Radiator fan motor to thermal switch |
| Slate | | Window lift |
| Slate | Brown | Window lift |
| Slate | Blue | Window lift |
| Slate | Red | Window lift |
| Slate | Purple | Window lift |
| Slate | Green | Window lift |
| Slate | Light Green | Window lift |
| Slate | White | Window lift |
| Slate | Yellow | Window lift |
| Slate | Black | Window lift |
| Slate | Pink | Window lift |
| Slate | Orange | Window lift |



***Fig. 13.4 British standard wiring code for automobiles (continued)***

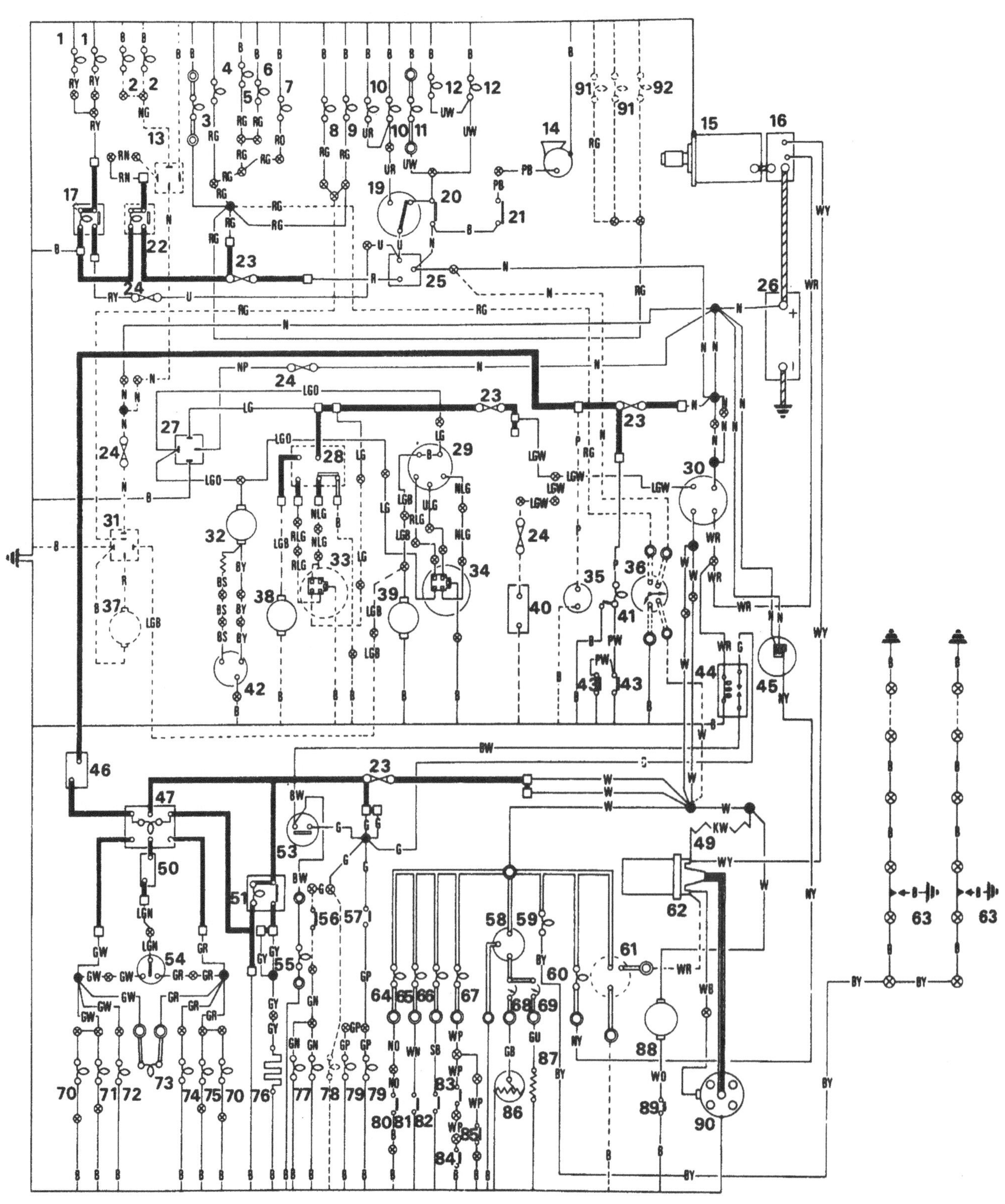

*Fig. 13.5 Wiring diagram for the Austin Metro*

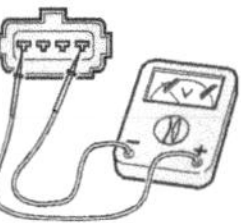

***Key to wiring diagram for the Austin Metro***

*1 Rear fog guard lamps*
*2 Front fog lamps (if fitted)*
*3 Panel illumination lamp*
*4 Cigar lighter illumination lamp*
*5 L.H. tail lamp*
*6 Number-plate lamp*
*7 R.H. tail lamp*
*8 L.H. side lamp*
*9 R.H. side lamp*
*10 Headlamp dipped beams*
*11 Main beam warning light*
*12 Headlamp main beams*
*13 Front fog lamp relay (if fitted)*
*14 Horn*
*15 Starter motor*
*16 Starter motor solenoid*
*17 Rear fog guard lamp switch and warning light*
*19 Headlamp dip switch*
*20 Headlamp flasher switch*
*21 Horn-push*
*22 Front fog lamp switch and warning light (if fitted)*
*23 Fuses*
*24 Line fuses*
*25 Main lighting switch*
*26 Battery*
*27 Auxiliary circuits relay*
*28 Rear screen wash/wipe switch (if fitted)*
*29 Windscreen wash/wipe switch*
*30 Ignition/starter switch*
*31 Headlamp washer relay (if fitted)*
*32 Heater motor*
*33 Rear screen wiper motor (if fitted)*
*34 Windscreen wiper motor*
*35 Cigar lighter*
*36 Clock (digital on HLS models)*
*37 Headlamp washer motor (if fitted)*
*38 Rear screen washer motor (if fitted)*
*39 Windscreen washer motor*
*40 Radio (if fitted)*
*41 Interior lamp and switch*
*42 Heater motor switch*
*43 Door switches*
*44 Brake failure warning lamp relay*
*45 Alternator*
*46 Hazard warning flasher unit*
*47 Hazard switch and warning light*
*49 Ballast resistor cable*
*50 Direction indicator flasher unit*
*51 Heated rear screen switch*
*53 Brake fluid level sensor*
*54 Direction indicator switch*
*55 Brake failure warning light*
*56 Reverse lamp switch*
*57 Stop lamp switch*
*58 Voltage stabilizer*
*59 Brake pad wear warning light*
*60 Ignition warning light*
*61 Tachometer (if fitted)*
*62 Ignition coil*
*63 Brake pad wear sensors*
*64 Choke warning light*
*65 Oil pressure warning light*
*66 Handbrake warning light*
*67 Seat belt warning light*
*68 Fuel gauge*
*69 Water temperature gauge*
*70 Direction indicator repeater lamps*
*71 R.H. front indicator*
*72 R.H. rear indicator*
*73 Indicator warning light*
*74 L.H. rear indicator*
*75 L.H. front indicator*
*76 Heated rear screen*
*77 Reversing lamps*
*78 Gearbox selector panel illumination (Automatics only)*
*79 Stop lamps*
*80 Choke warning light switch*
*81 Oil pressure switch*
*82 Handbrake warning light switch*
*83 Passenger seat switch*
*84 Passenger seat belt switch*
*85 Driver seat belt switch*
*86 Fuel gauge tank unit*
*87 Water temperature transducer*
*88 Radiator cooling fan*
*89 Radiator cooling fan thermostat*
*90 Distributor*
*91 Heater control illumination*
*92 Panel switch illumination*

***Cable colour code***

*B Black*
*G Green*
*K Pink*
*LG Light green*
*N Brown*
*O Orange*
*p Purple*
*R Red*
*S Slate*
*U Blue*
*W White*
*Y Yellow*

***Key to symbols used in wiring diagrams***

*1 When fitted*
*2 Connector*
*3 Instrument printed circuit connector*
*4 Fuse board printed circuit connector*
*5 Sealed joint*
*6 Instrument printed circuit*
*7 Fuse board printed circuit*
*8 Component earthed through fixings*
*9 Component earthed with cable*

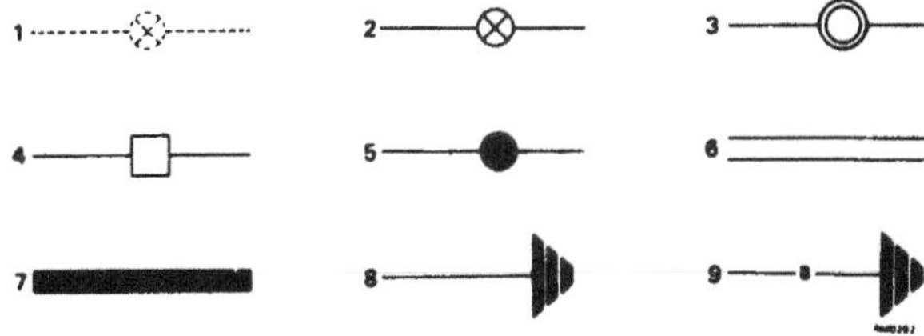

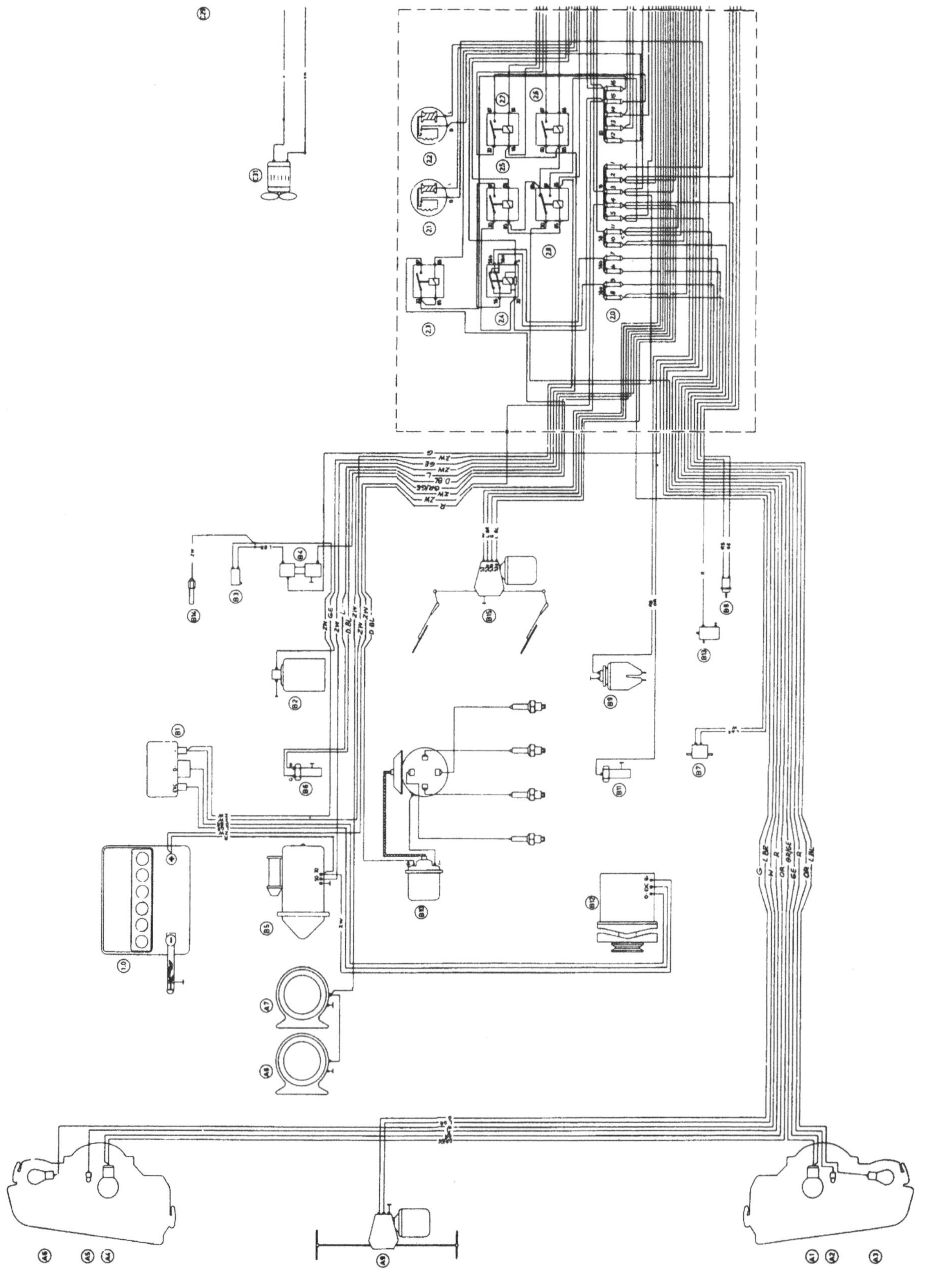

*Fig. 13.6 Wiring diagram for the Volvo 340*

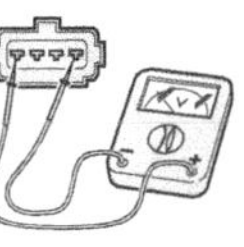

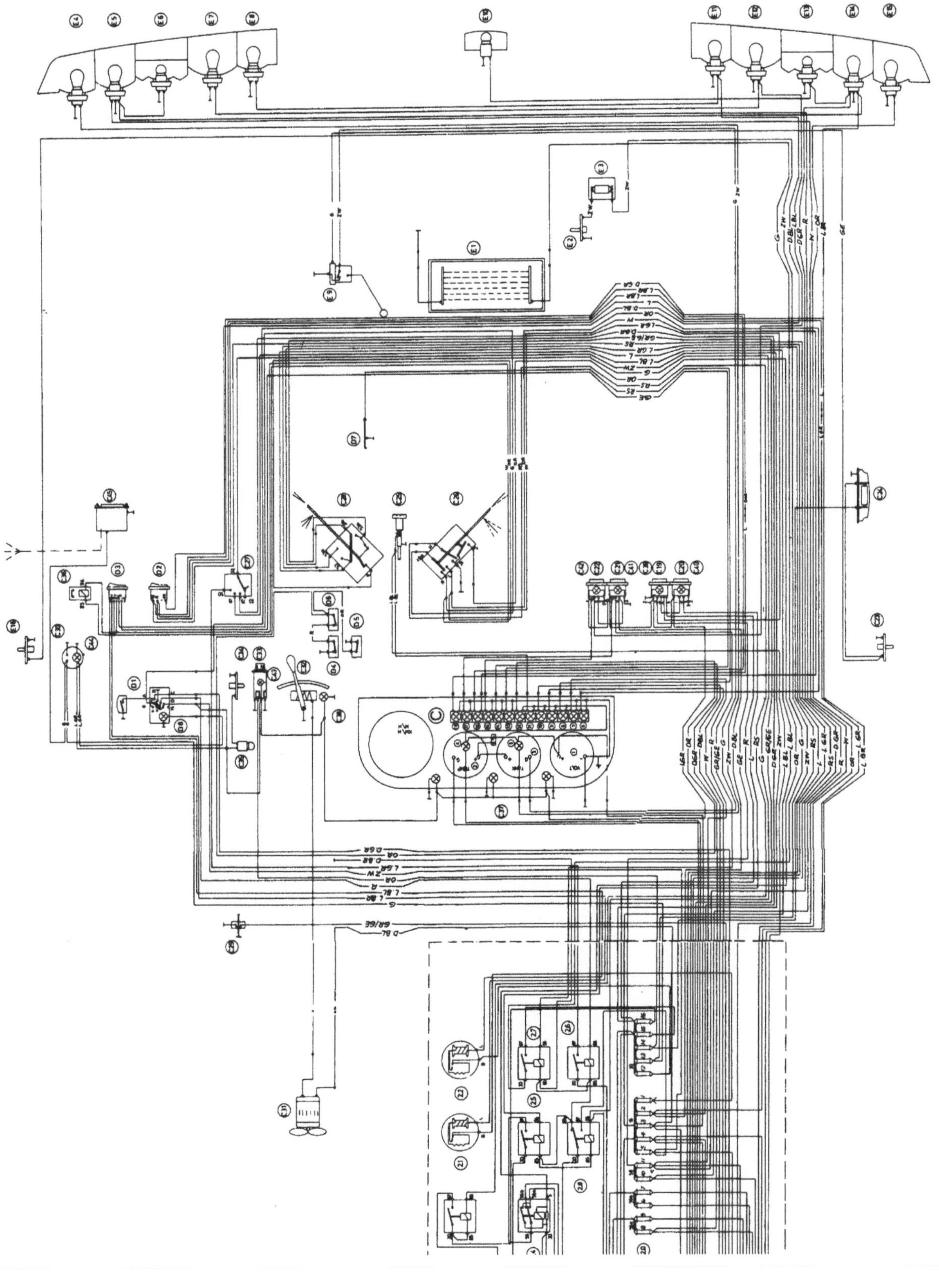

*Fig. 13.6 Wiring diagram for the Volvo 340 (continued)*

# Chapter 13

### *Key to wiring diagram for the Volvo 340*

*A1 Headlamp main beam/dipped beam*
*A2 Parking light*
*A3 Direction indicator*
*A4 Headlamp main beam/dipped beam*
*A5 Parking lights*
*A6 Direction indicator*
*A7 Horn high-tone*
*A8 Horn low-tone*
*A9 Headlamp wiper motor (Nordic)*
*B1 Voltage regulator*
*B2 Water pump*
*B3 Microswitch*
*B4 4-way valve*
*B5 Starter motor*
*B6 Coolant temperature sender/switch*
*B7 Declutching valve*
*B8 Brake light switch*
*B9 Brake fluid level float*
*B10 Ignition coil*
*B11 Oil pressure sender*
*B12 Alternator*
*B13 3-way valve (Sweden)*
*B14 Pilot jet (Sweden)*
*B15 Windscreen wiper motor*
*C1 Voltmeter*
*C2 Temperature gauge*
*C3 Fuel gauge*
*C4 Coolant temperature warning lamp*
*C5 Fuel reserve indicating lamp*
*C6 Direction indicating lamp, left*
*C7 Parking light indicating lamp*
*C8 Handbrake warning lamp*
*C9 Oil pressure warning lamp*
*C10 Brake fluid level warning lamp*
*C11 Choke indicating lamp*
*C12 Seat belt indicating lamp*
*C13 Hazard warning installation indicating lamp*
*C14 Main beam indicating lamp*
*C15 Rear-warning foglamp, indicating lamp*
*C16 Low ratio hold indicating lamp*
*C17 Heated rear window indicating lamp*
*C18 Direction indicating lamp, right*
*C19 Switch for main beam/dipped beam*
*C20 Switch for parking lights*
*C21 Switch for heated rear window*
*C22 Switch for rear-warning foglamp*
*C23 Courtesy light door switch, left*
*C24 Courtesy light, car interior*
*C25 Choke*
*C26 Direction indicator switch*
*C27 Ignition switch*
*C28 Windscreen wiper switch*
*C29 Kickdown switch*
*C30 Clock*
*C31 Blower*
*C32 Blower rheostat*
*C33 Cigar lighter*
*C34 Switch for glove compartment light*
*C35 Lamp for glove compartment*
*C36 Direction indicator*
*C37 Lamp for instrument lighting*
*C38 Lamp for illumination of heater controls*
*C39 Lamp for illumination of main/dipped beam switch*
*C40 Lamp for illumination of parking lights switch*
*C41 Lamp for illumination of heated rear window switch*
*C42 Lamp for illumination of rear warning foglamp switch*
*C43 Lamp for illumination of cigar lighter*
*C44 Lamp for clock illumination (DL)*
*C45 Radio (optional)*
*D1 Selector lever switch*
*D2 Low ratio hold switch*
*D3 Switch for hazard warning installation*
*D4 Seat belt contact, left front*
*D5 Seat belt contact, right front*
*D6 Seat cushion contact, rear seat*
*D7 Handbrake switch*
*D8 Selector scale switch*
*E1 Heated rear window*
*E2 Boot light switch*
*E3 Boot light*
*E4 Direction indicator*
*E5 Tail light/brake light*
*E6 Tail light*
*E7 Rear-warning foglamp*
*E8 Reversing light*
*E9 Float*
*E10 Number plate light*
*E11 Reversing light*
*E12 Rear-warning foglamp*
*E13 Tail light*
*E14 Tail light/brake light*
*E15 Direction indicator*
*E16 Courtesy light door switch, right*
*1.0 Battery*
*2.0 Fusebox*
*2.1 Direction indicator*
*2.2 Hazard warning installation*
*2.3 Horn relay*
*2.4 Main beam/dipped beam relay*
*2.5 Vehicle lighting relay*
*2.6 Interlock (start inhibitor) relay*
*2.7 Heated rear window relay (DL)*
*2.8 Headlamp wash/wipe installation relay (Nordic)*

### *Colour code*

*W White*
*R Red*
*OR Orange*
*RS Pink*
*D BR Dark brown*
*L BR Light brown*
*D BL Dark blue*
*L BL Light blue*
*D GR Dark green*
*L GR Light green*
*GR/GE Green/yellow*
*GE Yellow*
*L Lilac*
*G Grey*
*ZW Black*

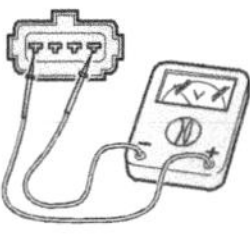

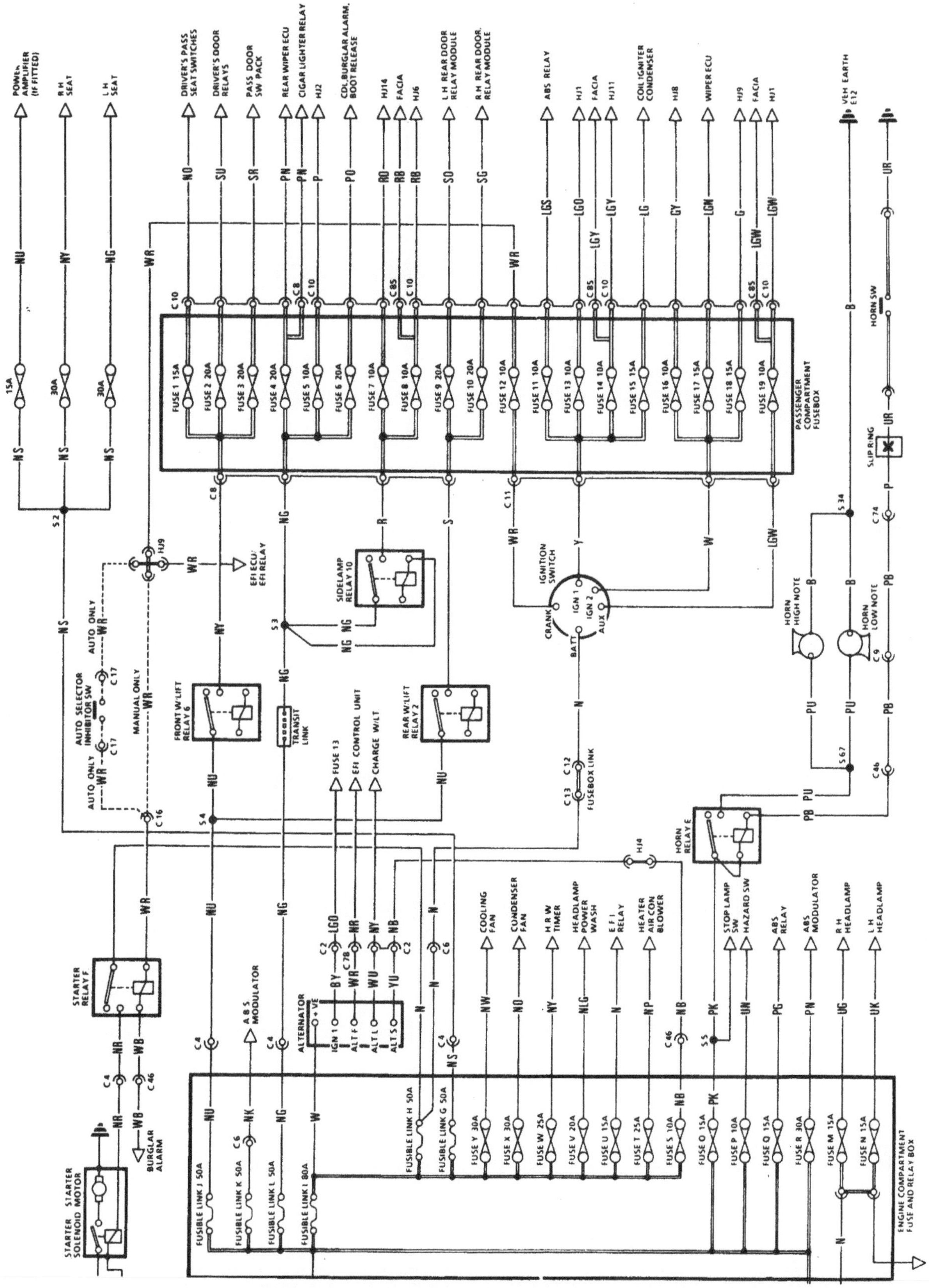

*Fig. 13.7 Power distribution wiring for the Rover 800 Fastback*

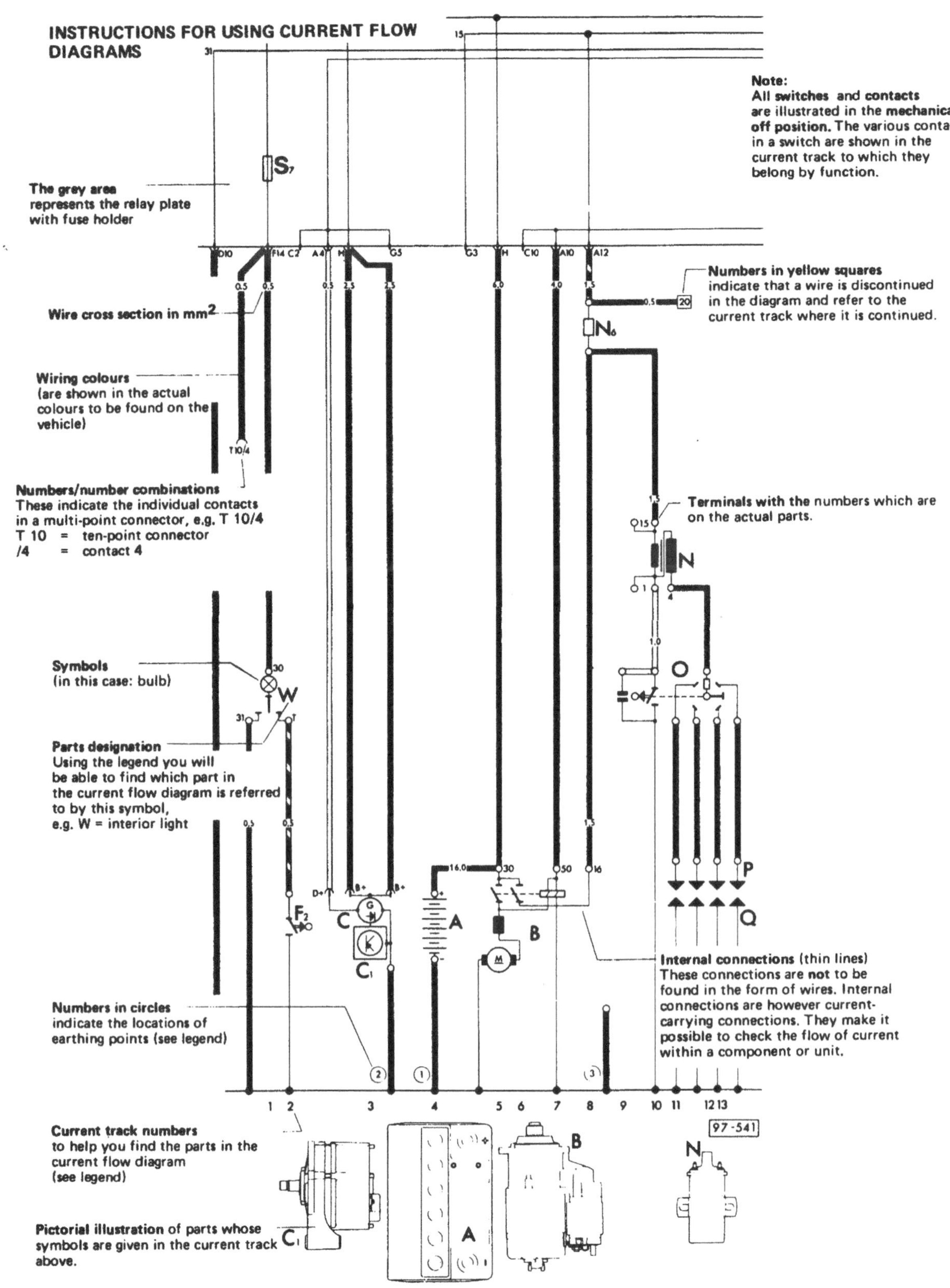


*Fig. 13.8 Instructions for using Volkswagen current flow diagrams*

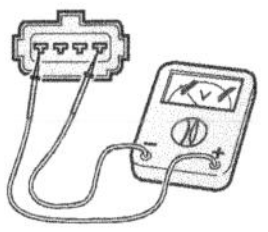

instrument pack, passenger seat electrical controls, lighting and fuelling. Fig. 13.7 shows an extract on the power distribution system in the 2.7 model.

**3** The Volkswagen system is unlike any conventional diagram; their current flow charts show individual circuits of the electrical system of a vehicle divided up into current tracks. All components with their functional connections are shown; components are illustrated by symbols with thin lines indicating internal connections (Figs. 13.8 and 13.9). The current flow chart shown is annotated for instructional purposes and, given a few minutes study, the advantages of the method become apparent. Probably the most advantageous point is the ease of following a wire feed to a component. Also the pictorial illustration at the foot of the current flow diagram assists location of the component on the vehicle.

**4** Symbols for electrical components found in automobiles vary according to the country of origin, but each diagram gives a key or a name near the symbol so usually there is no doubt. Cars of European Continent origin generally employ the German DIN system for symbols, a selection being given in Fig. 13.10.

**5** Terminal marking on equipment and on corresponding circuit diagrams is useful for identification. The DIN system

**Specimen legend**

The same part designations are used in all current flow diagrams.

E.g.: A is always used for the battery or N for the ignition coil

| Designation | | in current track |
|---|---|---|
| A | – Battery | 4 |
| B | – Starter | 5, 6, 7, 8 |
| C | – Alternator | 3 |
| C 1 | – Voltage regulator | 3 |
| F 2 | – Door contact switch | 2 |
| N | – Ignition coil | 10, 11 |
| N 6 | – Series resistance (for coil) | 8 |
| O | – Distributor | 10, 11, 12, 13 |
| P | – Spark plug connector | 11, 12, 13 |
| Q | – Spark plugs | 11, 12, 13 |
| S 7 | – Fuse in fusebox | |
| T 10 | – Connector, ten-point, on instrument panel insert | |
| W | – Interior light | |
| ① | – Earthing strap, battery/body | |
| ② | – Earthing strap, alternator/engine | |
| ③ | – Earthing strap, gearbox/chassis | |

**Explanation** of where a connection is to be found on the vehicle.

**Number of current track** to help you locate the part in the current flow diagram. Current track numbers are not given for fuses, wiring connections and earthing points.

*Fig. 13.8 Instructions for using Volkswagen current flow diagrams (continued)*

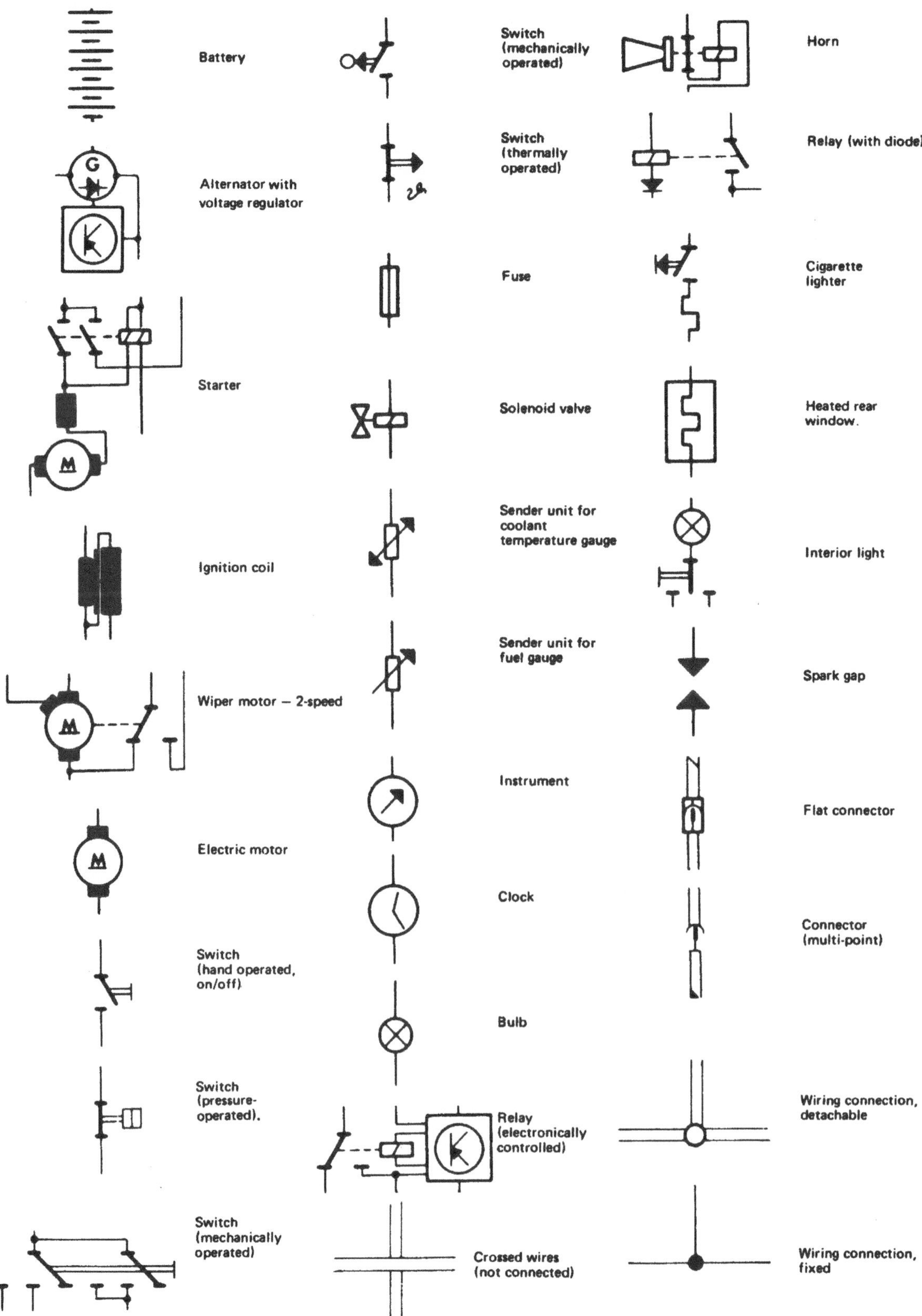


*Fig. 13.9 Symbols used in Volkswagen current flow diagrams*

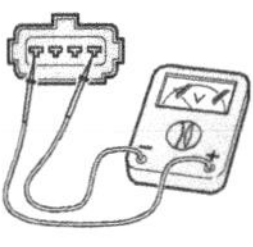

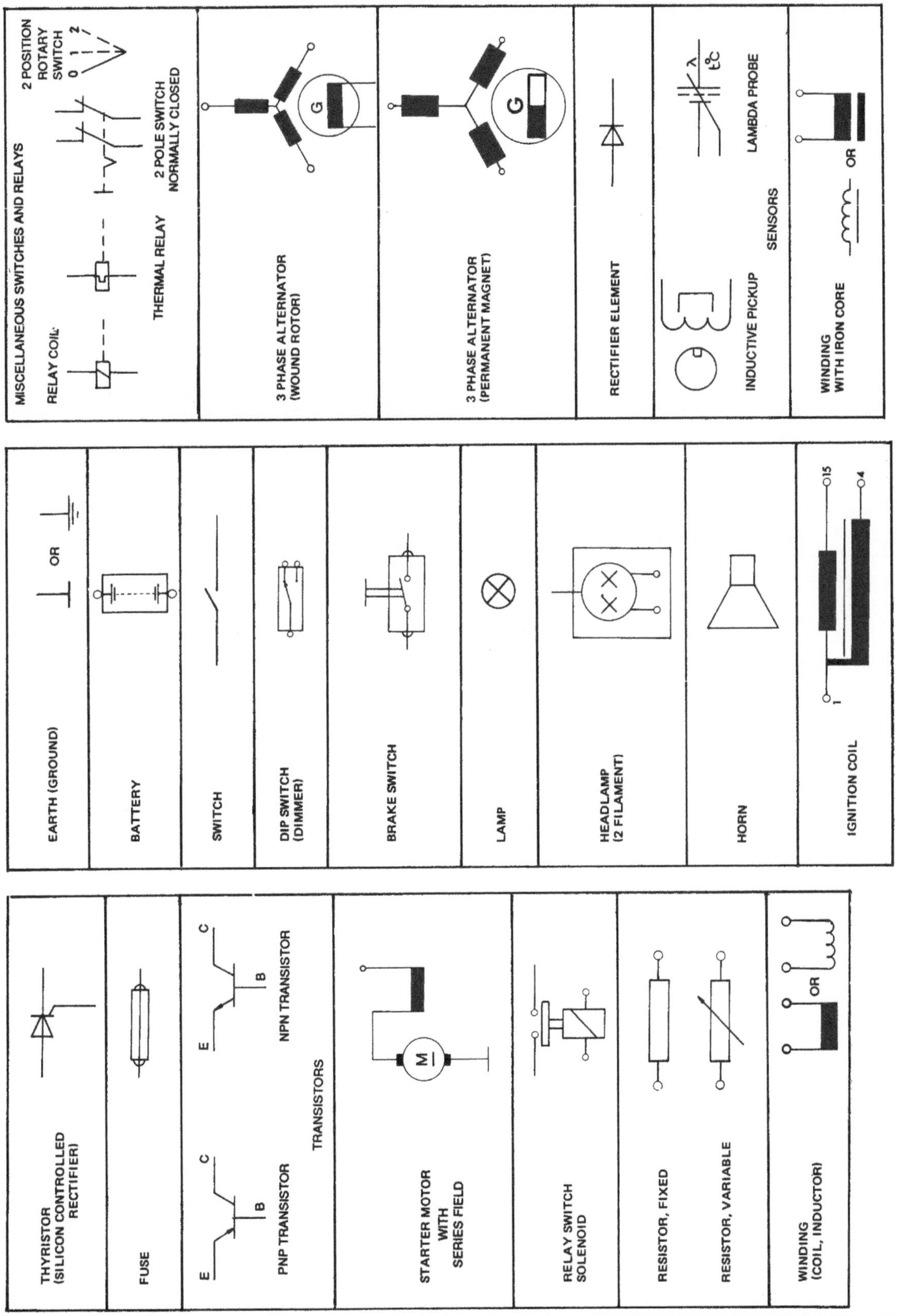

THYRISTOR (SILICON CONTROLLED RECTIFIER)

FUSE

TRANSISTORS

E C B PNP TRANSISTOR

E C B NPN TRANSISTOR

STARTER MOTOR WITH SERIES FIELD

M

RELAY SWITCH SOLENOID

RESISTOR, FIXED

RESISTOR, VARIABLE

WINDING (COIL, INDUCTOR)

OR

EARTH (GROUND)

OR

BATTERY

SWITCH

DIP SWITCH (DIMMER)

BRAKE SWITCH

LAMP

HEADLAMP (2 FILAMENT)

HORN

IGNITION COIL

1 15 4

MISCELLANEOUS SWITCHES AND RELAYS

RELAY COIL

THERMAL RELAY

2 POLE SWITCH NORMALLY CLOSED

2 POSITION ROTARY SWITCH

0 1 2

3 PHASE ALTERNATOR (WOUND ROTOR)

G

3 PHASE ALTERNATOR (PERMANENT MAGNET)

G

RECTIFIER ELEMENT

SENSORS

INDUCTIVE PICKUP

LAMBDA PROBE

λ t°C

WINDING WITH IRON CORE

OR

*Fig. 13.10 DIN circuit symbols*

allots numbers and some letters to terminals of equipment and it pays to remember the more common of them when working on European vehicles. Certain code numbers are most important, so that any terminal marked 30 is live with no switch in the line, and so would be suitable for connection of certain accessories. 31 represents an earth terminal, and 31b is used when an electrical load is operated by a switch in the return path to earth.

**6** The British Standard BS3939 shows recommended symbols and has conformity with the International Electrotechnical Commission, IEC. Manufacturers use certain BS symbols but there is no general use of them.

**7** Below is a selection of code numbers used in vehicles employing DIN standards. For a comprehensive coverage of this subject the reader is referred to the Bosch Technical Instruction booklet *'Graphical Symbols and Circuit Diagrams for Automotive Electrics'.*

| Terminal number | Definition/use |
|---|---|
| 1 | Ignition coil to contact breaker or electronic equivalent |
| 4 | Ignition – HT output to distributor |
| 15 | Feed from ignition switch |
| 16 | Trigger box output to ignition coil and control unit |
| 30 | Battery + |
| 31 | Earth |
| 31b | Return to earth via switch |
| 49 | Flasher unit from ignition switch |
| 50 | Starter solenoid to starter |
| 51 | Alternator output: dc at rectifier |
| 56 | Headlamps |
| 56a | Dip switch to main beam bulb |
| 56b | Dip switch to dip beam bulb |
| 58 | Side marker and tail lamps |
| 61 | Charge warning light |
| 75 | Accessories: radio, cigarette lighter, etc |
| B + | Battery + |
| B – | Battery – |
| D + | Generator + |
| DF | Generator field |

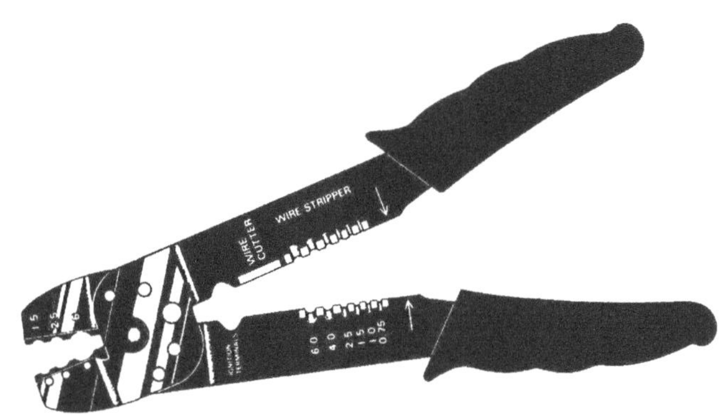


*Fig. 13.11 Crimping tool*

## 6 Connections and connectors

**1** Good, clean connections are vital for trouble-free operation, particularly since certain electrical components will be exposed to weather. The earthing strap/cable from the battery to the body carries all the current used in the motor vehicle. The bolted connection down to the body should be checked for corrosion and even the possibility of paint underneath the earthing terminal tag.

**2** Battery connections can be a source of volt-drop and, when loaded by the starter motor current can go, momentarily, open-circuit giving a sharp 'click' sound from the starter solenoid but no drive – every auto-electrician meets this phenomenon at some time. Lugs and terminal posts should be kept clean, and any white 'fungus' removed. A trace of petroleum jelly on the lugs and posts will be helpful, and even better will be the special anti-corrosion grease now available in car accessory shops.

**3** The heavy cable connection to the lug is sometimes by sweated joint and this can be the source of the break occurring on heavy current demand. This is best checked by putting a voltmeter or bulb onto the solenoid terminal and then moving the cable about at the lug end. Erratic movements of the voltmeter pointer, or the bulb going on or off, indicate a faulty joint.

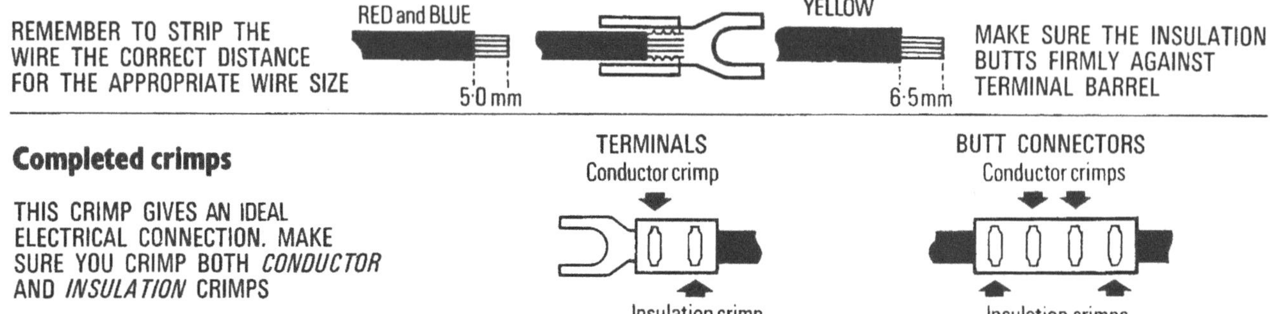


*Fig. 13.12 Crimping hints*

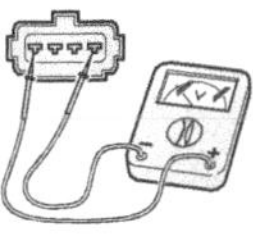

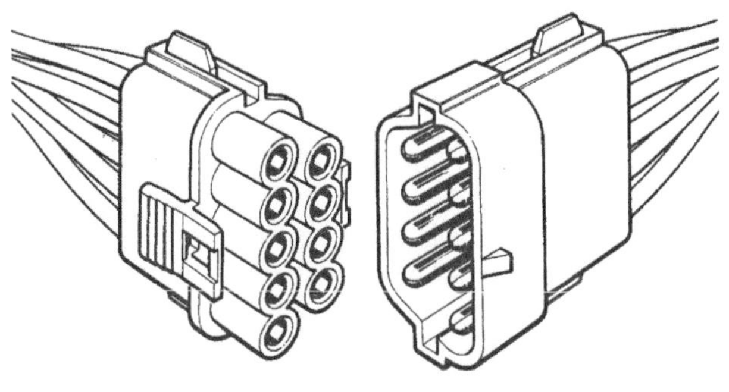

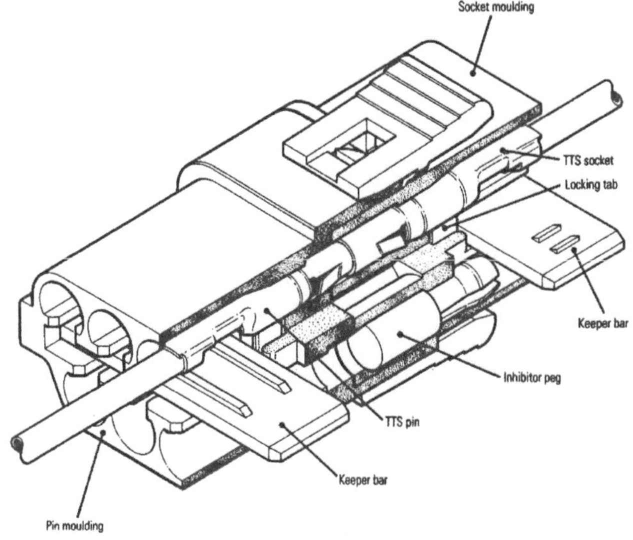


*Fig. 13.13 Total Termination Security (TTS) plug and socket for automobile applications*

**4** Connectors of various types are used for joining parts of a circuit; the safest, but most trouble to make, is a soldered connection. Soldered joints require only that the wire and tags are scraped clean, and only resin flux (not acid flux such as Bakers fluid) is used, because of the danger of subsequent corrosion. The small soldering iron used in electronics is not generally suitable for auto-electrical work, and an iron of 65 to 150 watts rating is recommended.

**5** Crimping of joint requires a tool which is a special form of pliers which crushes the wings of a connecting tag onto the bared wire surface (Figs. 13.11 and 13.12). The electrical connection can be very good, but trouble can arise if the wire and tag are not really clean. Volt-drop due to imperfect crimped joints is always a possibility, and should be checked where circuit malfunction occurs.

**6** Plugs and sockets are used widely in modern automobiles. Most lamp fittings are connected by plugs with blades set in polythene, moulded polypropylene, or nylon. A large range of plugs and sockets are available, some of which are shown in Fig. 13.13. Provision is made to prevent accidental pulling apart of plugs and sockets by a latch and keeper bar. An inhibited plug is one which can be pushed into the socket one way only, this being important where equipment has components with polarity requirement such as transistors and electrolytic capacitors.

**7** General purpose connectors with Lucar crimped blades, male and female, are shown in Fig. 13.14, and these have a current carrying capacity of 17.5A, while the alternator plug (Fig. 13.15) will have terminals of different size to allow for the different current loads of main output and field.

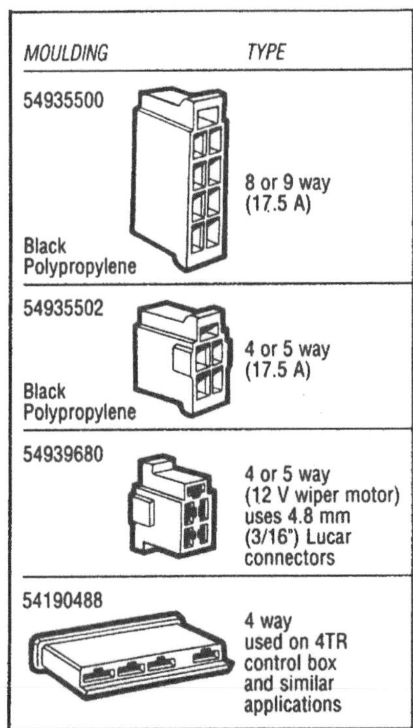

| *MOULDING* | *TYPE* |
|---|---|
| 54935500<br>Black Polypropylene | 8 or 9 way (17.5 A) |
| 54935502<br>Black Polypropylene | 4 or 5 way (17.5 A) |
| 54939680 | 4 or 5 way (12 V wiper motor) uses 4.8 mm (3/16") Lucar connectors |
| 54190488 | 4 way used on 4TR control box and similar applications |

*Fig. 13.14 General purpose connectors*

## 7 Fuses

**1** Many electrical circuits have protective devices so that in the event of a short-circuit, the battery is isolated. The battery is capable of driving a high current into an accidental short-circuit and this may be sufficient to burn the insulation

***European Termination kit*** – comprises cover, moulding, 9.5 mm (3/8") Lucar terminals (x 6.4 mm (1/4") terminal and clip.

Fits – some Lucas, Bosch, Delco, Femsa, Motorola with European Terminations.

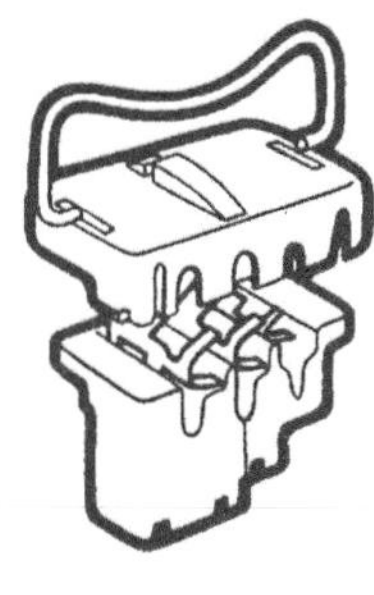

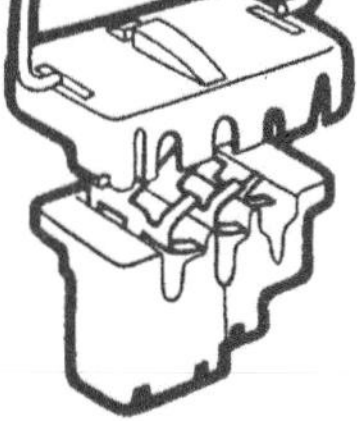

**CYB400**

*Fig. 13.15 Alternator connector kit*

**FUSES (Flat Bladed)**

| *Identification* | *Rating* |
|---|---|
| Purple | 3 |
| Pink | 4 |
| Orange | 5 |
| Brown | 7.5 |
| Red | 10 |
| Blue | 15 |
| Yellow | 20 |
| White | 25 |
| Green | 30 |

**FUSES (glass cartridge)**

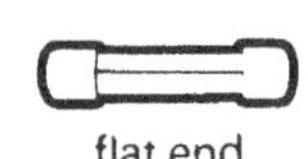


| *Identification* | *Lucas Ratings* |
|---|---|
| Length 25.4mm (1") | |
| *Cone end* | *AMP* |
| Blue | 3 |
| Yellow | 4.5 |
| Nut Brown | 8.0 |
| Red on Green | 10.0 |
| White | 35.0 |
| Length 29.4mm ($1^5/_{32}$") *Flat end* | |
| Red on Blue | 2.0 |
| Red | 5.0 |
| Blue on Green | 8.0 |
| Black on Blue | 10.0 |
| Light Brown | 15.0 |
| Blue on Yellow | 20.0 |
| Pink | 25.0 |
| White | 35.0 |
| Yellow | 50.0 |

**FUSES (ceramic type)**

| *Identification* | *BSS Ratings* |
|---|---|
| Length 25mm | AMP |
| Yellow | 5 |
| White | 8 |
| Red | 16 |
| Blue | 25 |

***Fig. 13.16 Automobile fuses and ratings***

off cables, possibly buckle the battery plates, or cause a fire. The motor vehicle uses the fuse for such protection.

**2** A fuse consists of a cartridge with contacts on either end and a strip of soft metal or length of tinned wire connected between them. When an overload occurs the fuse wire or strip will melt, breaking the circuit.

**3** The fuse may be replaced, but the auto-electrician will need to find and rectify the cause, otherwise the new fuse will also melt.

**4** Four types of fuse are presently in use on vehicles:

*(a) Glass tubular fuses*
*(b) Ceramic base fuses*
*(c) Flat-bladed fuses*
*(d) Fusible links*

It is to be noted that glass fuses are normally rated at their fusing value, but ceramic fuses are rated at the maximum continuous current that they can carry, being half of the fusing value.

**5** Fig. 13.16 illustrates the fuses (a), (b) and (c) and gives codings and current ratings. Fuses shown are usually mounted on fuseboards and located in matching clips, but in-line fuses may be employed, usually for protection of an accessory installed as non-original equipment. An interesting design for an integrated fusebox is shown in Fig. 13.17 in which terminals are crimped directly onto the wiring cables. This reduces the number of resistive joints and the likelihood of unwanted volt-drops.

**6** Fusible links are fitted by many vehicle manufacturers to

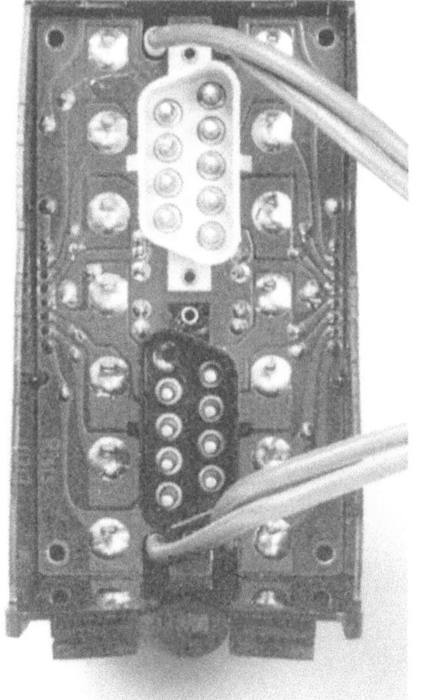

***Fig. 13.17 Integrated fusebox***
*Fuses may be either flat-bladed or glass*

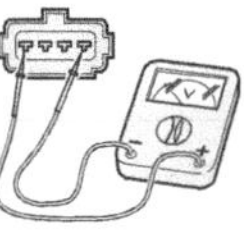

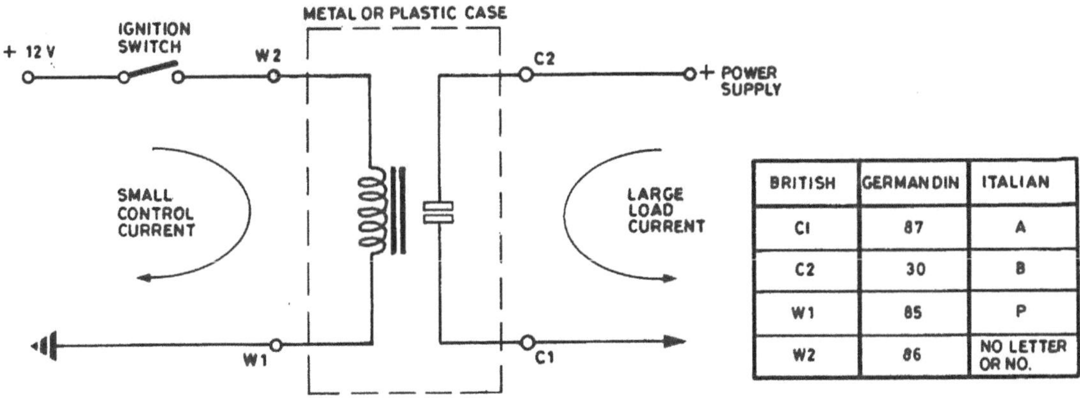


| BRITISH | GERMAN DIN | ITALIAN |
|---|---|---|
| C1 | 87 | A |
| C2 | 30 | B |
| W1 | 85 | P |
| W2 | 86 | NO LETTER OR NO. |

*Fig. 13.18 Connections and markings of relays*

prevent an outbreak of fire in the case of an accident, where wires might be cut or trapped by twisted metal. The link is a highly rated fuse connected in the main supply cable close to the battery and will fail in the event of a massive short-circuit in the wiring system. Some fusible links are easily replaced, but others have to be soldered in.

**7** Little will normally go wrong with fuses, but occasionally they suffer from corrosion of the metal ends which gives rise to poor contact with the fusebox clips. A remedy is to clean them with emery paper or a small wire brush and give them a spray with an electrical cleaning and protective fluid.

**8** Of interest is the thermal breaker which protects lighting circuits and consists of a bi-metal strip and a pair of contacts. Any large abnormal load in the lighting circuit will cause the bi-metal strip to heat and bend, eventually breaking the contacts open. The lighting load is therefore periodically switched on and off; the wiring system is protected, but the driver should have sufficient intermittent lighting to come to a halt safely. A typical unit used in one Vauxhall vehicle will pass 25 amperes, but with a current of 33 amperes should open within 30 to 180 seconds.

## 8 Adding extras

**1** A wide range of electrical accessories is now on sale and care should be taken in ensuring that connections into the vehicle wiring system are appropriate and safe.

**2** The item of equipment will usually come with its own cable, but this cable is often the thinnest that will do the job. It is worth checking on the current taken and to compare the supplied cable with the guide found earlier in this Chapter – if necessary, use a thicker grade.

**3** Wiring-in is dependent upon the type of vehicle, and it must be decided whether the accessory will be connected to the battery supply or be wired through the ignition switch. Wiring to the supply has the danger that the accessory might accidentally be left on when the driver leaves the car, but equally it must be remembered that extra loads on the ignition switch or a lighting switch can cause contact trouble, leading to switch failure. It is a matter of judgement; as examples, heavy current items such as auxiliary lamps, heated rear windows, fog lamps and horns should use a relay.

**4** The relay is an electrically-operated switch (see Chapter 1). The relay coil which closes the contacts magnetically takes a small current for operation, and several manufacturers market such a unit suitable for installation of car electrical extras. Fig. 13.18 shows the basic circuit of the relay, together with terminal markings covering a range of manufacturers, and Fig. 13.19 shows the symbols found on a wiring diagram to represent the relay. Examples of relay applications are given below:

**5** Driving (or auxiliary) lamps are frequently fitted to enhance illumination, and in the UK the law states that these must be

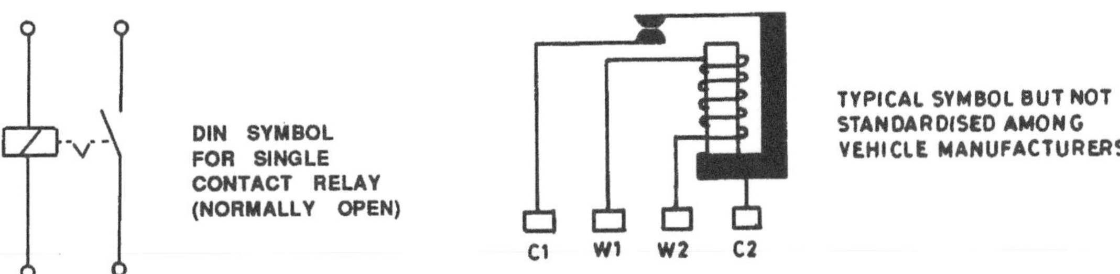


*Fig. 13.19 Relay symbols*

wired so as to extinguish when the headlights are dipped. A relay control is required and, in order to meet the condition above, the feed to the main beam should supply the relay coil (Fig. 13.20).

**6** A heated rear window will take a minimum of 6 amperes and is a case for using a relay. It is preferable to supply the relay from an ignition switch controlled feed to obviate the risk of leaving the heater on (Fig. 13.21).

**7** Wiring in a pair of horns calls for a relay, since the current demand will be high. In the diagram (Fig. 13.22) the horn button is connected in the earth (ground) wire. If the existing horn is fed through a relay, it is possible to substitute the new horns or feed a second relay from the first.

**8** Double connections can be of the plug-in bullet or the self-stripping types. In the case of the convenient self-stripping (Scotchlok) connectors make sure that the right size is chosen. For the Scotchlok type, colour blue is right for most automotive applications, but red is used for thinner cables, and brown or yellow for thicker cables.

**9** Care must be taken not to overload the existing fusebox. Where several accessories are to be added and all must be fused, it is better to use an auxiliary fusebox. This can be fed from a relay which is itself fed from an ignition controlled supply (Fig. 13.23) and also provides more fused circuits supplied direct from the battery.

**10** Fitting extras always involves finding a good earth. This may mean scraping paint back to the bare metal at the point chosen and it is always worthwhile to use a proper terminal. Corrosion can set in at such an earth point, so it is advisable to use a thin smear of anti-corrosion grease of the type recommended for battery terminals.

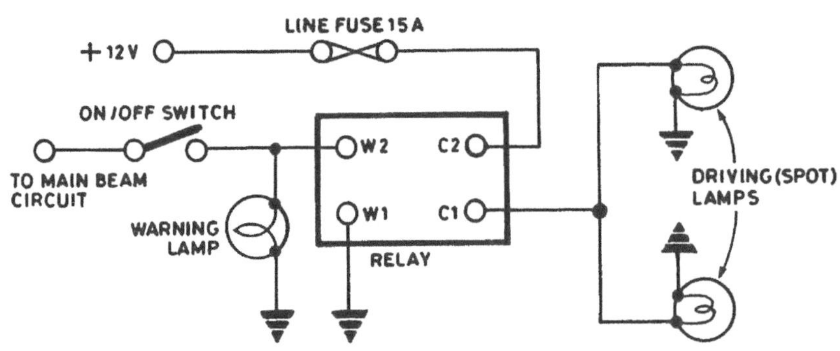


*Fig. 13.20 Wiring in driving lamps using a relay*

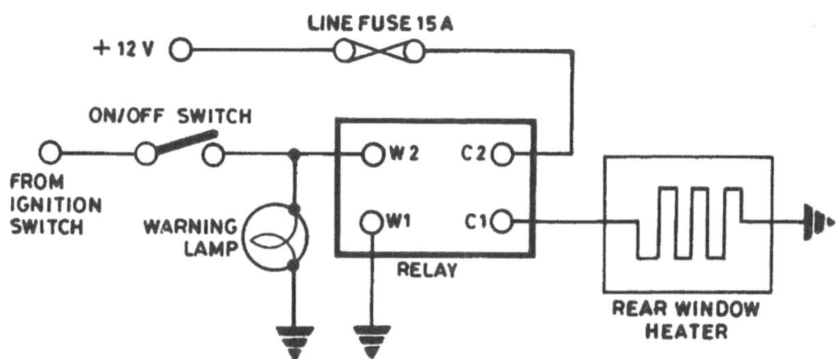


*Fig. 13.21 Circuit for a relay-operated rear window heater*

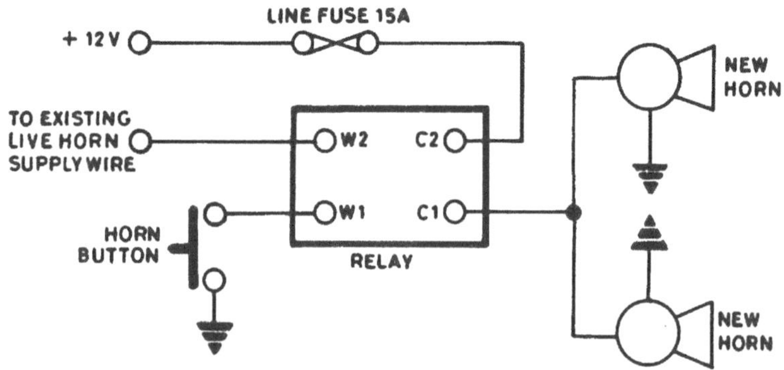


*Fig. 13.22 Circuit for relay-operated horns*

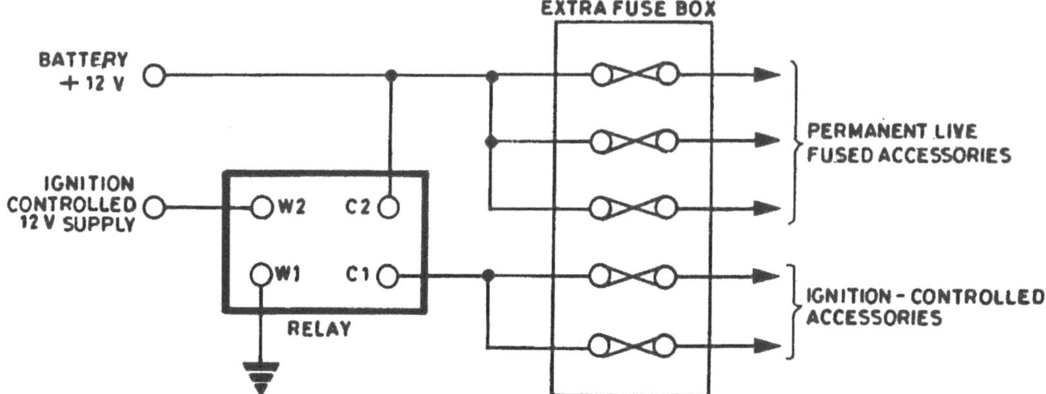


*Fig. 13.23 Auxiliary fusebox connections*

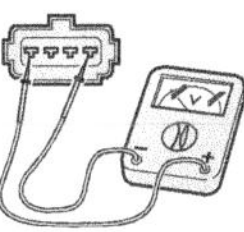

## 9 Electrical tool kit

**1** It is advantageous to keep a set of special tools just for electrical work, since there must be no possibility of oily tools being used anywhere on vehicle circuitry.

**2** Here is a list to meet most needs:

*Pocket knife (for scraping connections clean)*
*Plug spanner with rubber grip for plug tops*
*Electrician's screwdriver set*
*Cross-head screwdriver (chubby and 100 mm)*
*Engineer's combination pliers*
*HT cable pliers (optional)*
*Side-cutting pliers*
*Snipe-nosed pliers*
*Circlip pliers*
*Impact driver*
*Adjustable wire stripper*
*Crimping tool, with box of assorted connectors*
*Sets of Allen keys (Imperial and metric)*
*Ignition spanners*
*Flat file for dressing contact points*
*Feeler gauges (plastic and steel types)*
*Jump leads with heavy crocodile clips*
*Multi-meter (see Section 10)*
*Rubber grommet kit*
*Hydrometer*
*Soldering iron (65 watt minimum, but 150 watt may be needed)*
*De-soldering pump*

## 10 Test instruments and applications

### Multi meters

**1** Universal multimeters are available with ranges specially suited to automobile systems. Ranges for volts, amperes and ohms are normal, but it is rare for meters to be able to measure starter currents directly. In addition, many modern meters incorporate other functions such as dwell, points condition and engine speed (tachometer). Test meters may give readings in digital or analogue form. It is a matter of preference as to which type is chosen, but the digital meter is more accurate and costs no more than the conventional pointer-and-scale analogue meter.

**2** The Draper Automotive Analyser (Fig. 13.24) is a lightweight hand-held electronic digital multimeter with seven functions – DC voltage, DC current, tachometer, resistance (ohms), audible continuity tester, Diode test, and dwell angle. Readers are reminded of the danger of switching ranges on a multi-range meter without first disconnecting the test leads from the circuit. If, for instance, the amperes ranges were switched in accidentally with an external supply still connected to the test clips, then a short circuit would be created and the instrument would be destroyed.

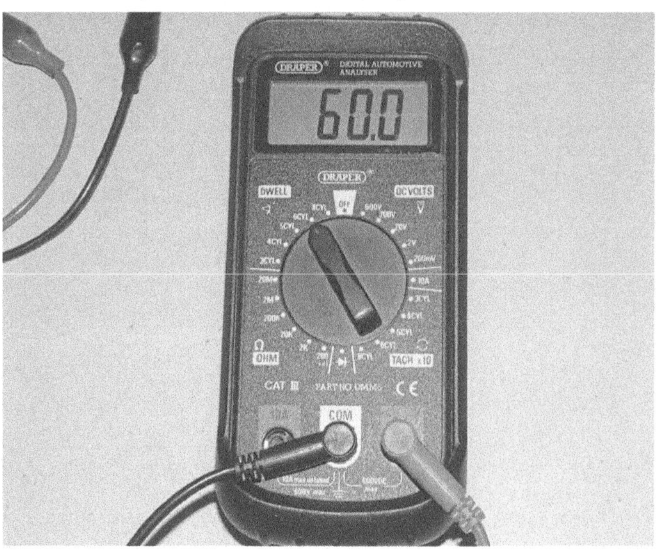


*Fig. 13.24 Draper's Automotive Analyser*

**3** For older vehicles with contact breakers, a useful yet inexpensive meter is shown in Fig. 13.25. This is a voltmeter with an ingenious circuit arrangement so that volts, ohms, dwell, points condition, engine timing and battery condition can be measured. Two of these are worthy of note:

**4** Dwell measurement using this compact instrument is based on the average voltage between the ignition feed line and the distributor as the points open and close. The instrument pointer is not able to follow rapid variations and takes up a position on a scale which is an average of the

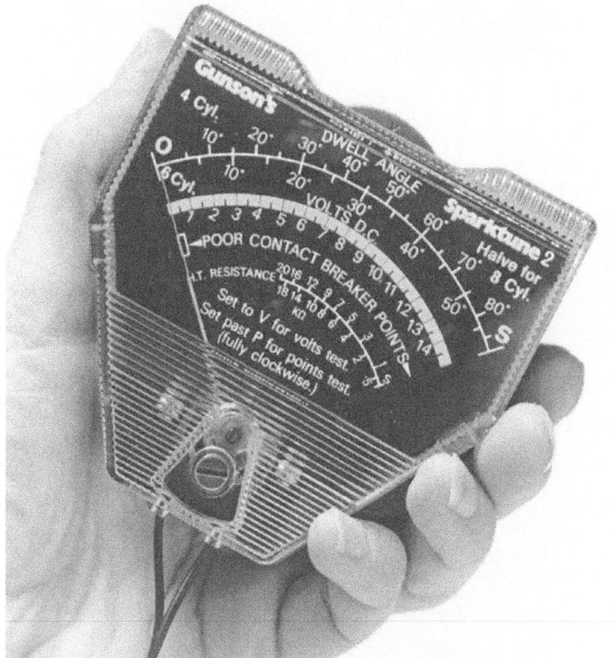


*Fig. 13.25 Sparktune test meter*

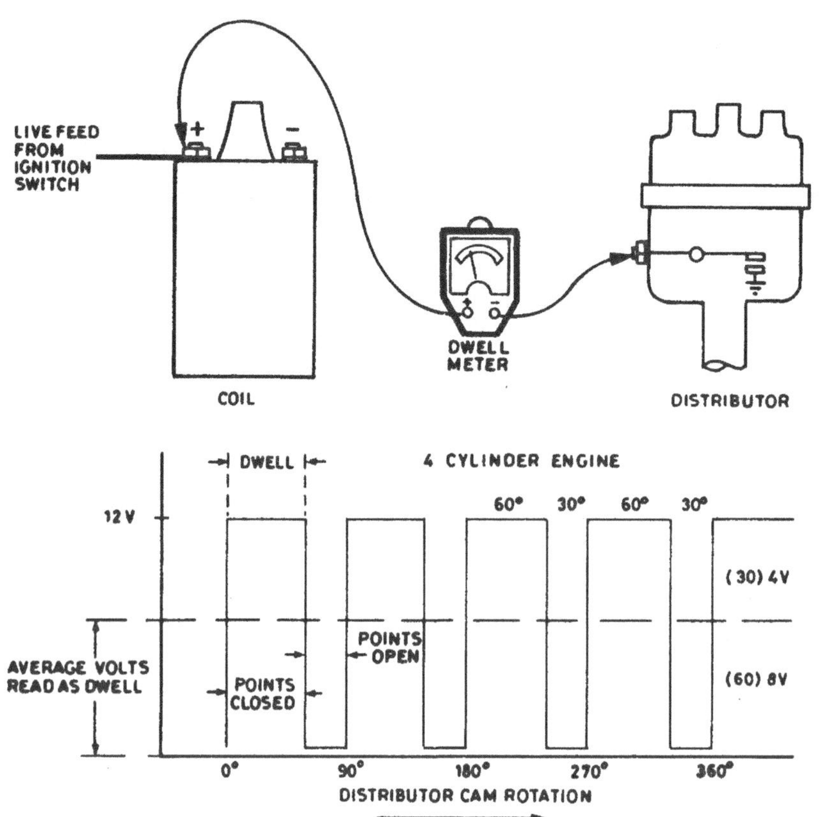


***Fig. 13.26 The use of average voltage to measure dwell***

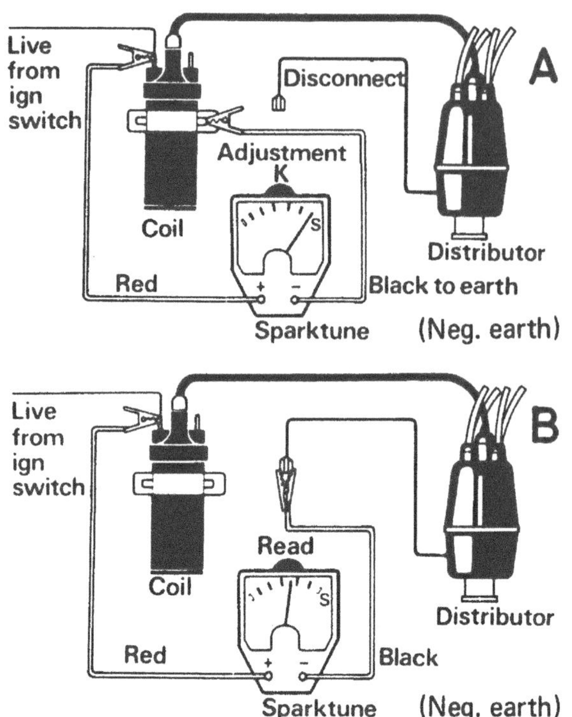


***Fig. 13.27 Using the Sparktune***
*A Setting the meter B Reading the dwell angle*

square pulse of voltage at the input terminals (Fig. 13.26). This scale is calibrated in degrees of dwell angle.

**5** The meter is first adjusted to read full scale whilst connected to the live feed terminal of the coil and earth with the engine turning over on the starter, but not running – the contact breaker lead being disconnected (Fig. 13.27). Next the meter is connected between the live feed terminal of the coil and the contact breaker terminal of the distributor. Note no connection exists between the coil contact breaker terminal and the distributor, so the engine will not fire. The engine is again cranked, and the reading of the meter taken as degrees of dwell.

**6** High resistance may be measured using the properties of a voltmeter, itself having a given resistance so that, for instance, if a resistive HT cable is connected in series with the meter across the vehicle battery, the current through the meter will be lower than without the added cable, and the pointer can be read on an ohms scale.

**7** More sophisticated are the universal meters, some of which employ the latest silicon chip technology. The Gunson Testune referred to above is a good example of such a meter which will serve as a tachometer and measure dwell, amperes, volts, ohms and points condition. The method used for measurement of dwell is such that only a simple connection between contact breaker and earth is necessary. In this case the system is live and the engine running, so before voltage pulses can be measured it is necessary to

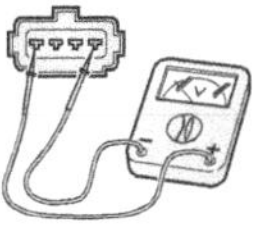

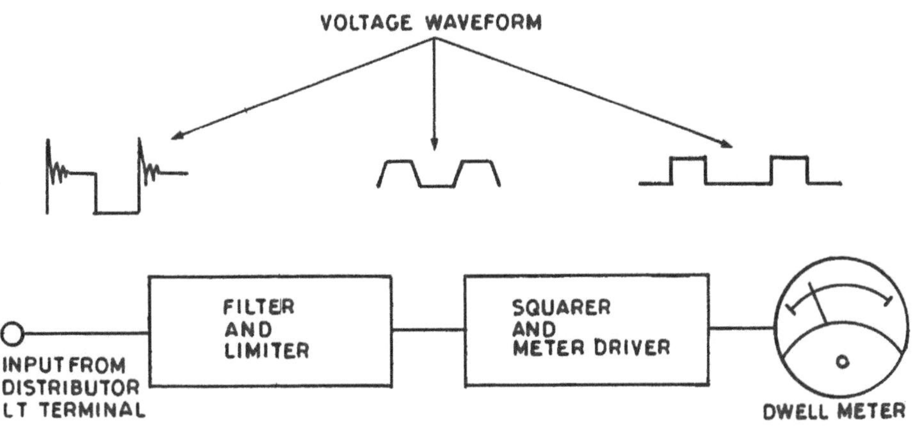


*Fig. 13.28 The silicon chip dwell meter*

remove transient spikes and to clip the height of the waves to a constant amplitude. This process is shown schematically in Fig. 13.28.

**8** A Zener diode is used to maintain a stable voltage and give the waveform a constant amplitude. The Zener diode breaks down and begins to conduct as soon as a particular voltage is reached, ensuring that the design level is not exceeded.

**9** Dwell measurement is really of relevance only to systems using a contact breaker, but despite the complete change to electronic ignition in car designs, many vehicles still in service will be using contact breaker systems for some years to come.

## Stroboscopes

**10** Stroboscopes for ignition timing are high-intensity flashing lamps in which the flashing rate is controlled by an ignition spark. With the engine running, the flashing light can be directed towards the engine timing marks on the crankshaft pulley or the flywheel, and has the effect of freezing the motion so that the marks appear to be stationary. The ignition distributor body can then be slowly moved until the correct alignment of the rotating timing mark and the fixed mark on the engine casting is achieved while the engine is running. Note that there is little point in using this type of instrument to check the ignition timing on late vehicles with full engine management systems. It will be found that the point of ignition constantly varies as the system attempts to create the most efficient combustion conditions in each cylinder. Checking the ignition timing specification can only be done with a fault code reader capable of displaying live data, via the diagnostic socket.

**11** One type of stroboscope is illustrated diagrammatically in Fig. 13.29. A fraction of the No 1 spark plug voltage is passed to the control grid of the xenon or neon tube by the probe lead and a capacitor. The main discharge electrodes of the tube are fed from a capacitor charged up from a high voltage dc supply. When the spark pulse reaches the control grid this is sufficient for the gas in the tube to break down, allowing current to flow through until the capacitor C is discharged. The current flow gives rise to an intense flash of light over a period of only microseconds. Xenon gives a whitish light, and is more intense than the red neon type of lamp, but the advantage is paid for in a higher cost.

**12** Service data for many vehicles gives information for stroboscope timing only and can include the required advance at increasing speeds. It is therefore essential to be able to measure engine speed as well as ignition advance. The Draper digital timing light features an LCD screen

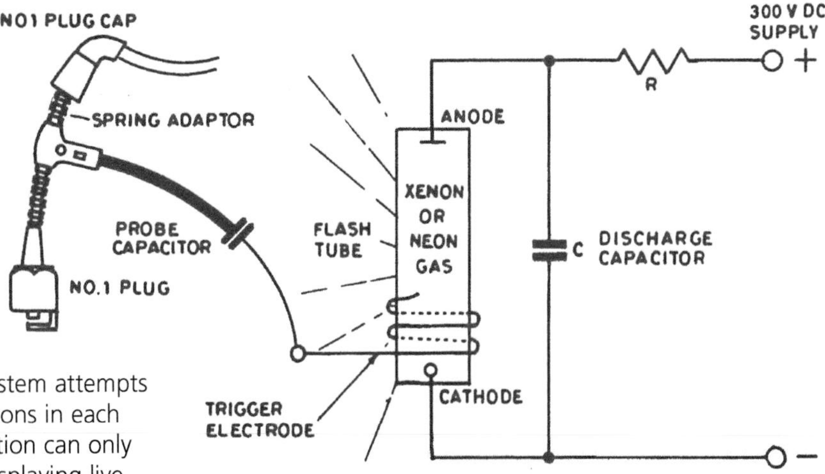


*Fig. 13.29 Operation of a typical stroboscope*

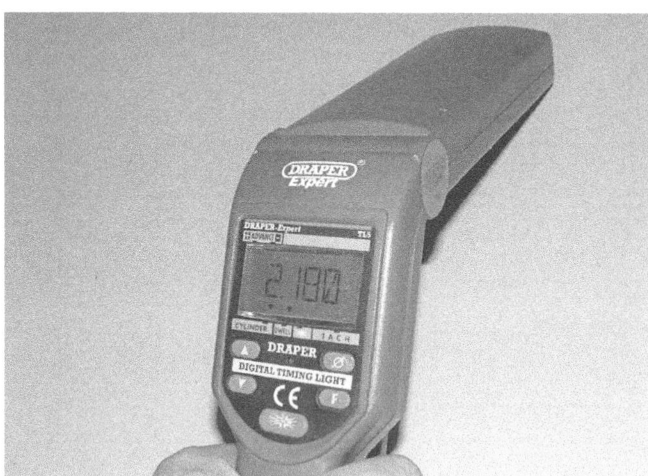


***Fig. 13.30 The Draper digital timing light with LCD screen showing the degrees of ignition advance and the engine speed***

showing not only the degrees of advance, but the engine speed as well (Fig. 13.30).

**13** In the side of the stroboscope pistol is a prism which picks up some of the flashtube light and also the shadow of the vibrating wire. When the tube is flashing at the No 1 plug firing rate, the thumb-wheel is rotated until the vibrating wire comes into synchronisation, as shown by the shadow movement gradually slowing to near standstill. The thumb-wheel has a scale marked in revolutions per minute, and vibration is achieved by pulling the trigger every ten seconds or so; the trigger mechanism plucks the string as with a guitar.

GREAT CARE MUST BE TAKEN WHEN WORKING ON RUNNING ENGINES USING STROBOSCOPES. The visual impression that the fan is stationary has led to many accidents.

## 11 Multiplexing and networks

### Multiplexing

As vehicles become more and more complex, the amount, and weight of vehicle wiring harnesses become a significant factor in their design and construction. In order to reduce the amount of wiring, some later models are being equipped with Multiplex wiring.

Using this system, electrical actuators/motors/controllers are connected to a 'ring' loom of two, or three, wires. One wire supplies the electrical power, whist another is the vehicle ground (earth). The remaining wire is the 'signal' wire.

The central control unit sends a signal to the relevant component to operate. The processor within that component recognises the signal, and connects the component to the power and earth wires. On two wire systems, the signal from the control unit is embedded in the electrical power, in the form of a frequency modulation, or pattern.

### Networks

As the requirements relating to fuel economy, exhaust emissions, driving safety, in-car entertainment and comfort become ever more stringent, intensive communication between the various vehicle ECUs becomes necessary. To avoid the physical connections between these units becoming unmanageable (some ECUs had 121 connector pins), Bosch developed a system whereby all these components communicate via one or two wires. These wires are known as a 'data bus'. Each ECU has an integral transceiver which sends and receives data 'packets' along these wires (Fig. 13.31). As the packet travels along the data bus, each ECU examines the packet and checks whether it needs the data or ignores it. Using this system allows rapid and reliable data transfer between the ECUs/controllers of a network. The first manufacturer to use this system in a production vehicle was VW. They named the system CAN (Controlled Area Network) Data Bus.

#### CAN

This system consists of one or two wires connecting various ECUs within the vehicle. Each ECU is equipped with a transceiver for receiving and transmitting the data 'packets'. The first system had a data bus speed of 62.5 kbit/s (62500 bits per second), but later speeds increased to 500 kbit/s. In areas of high electromagnetic interference and radiation emission (ie. the engine compartment), two wires are used in the network. These wires are known as CAN high and CAN low. When no data is being carried both wires carry a voltage of approximately 2.5 V. When data is being carried the CAN high voltage increases by 1 V, and the CAN low voltage decreases by 1 V (Fig. 13.32). As the data 'packet' is received by an ECU, the transceiver subtracts the CAN low voltage from the CAN high voltage, resulting in a clear data 'packet' voltage of 2.0 V (Fig. 13.33). In order to eliminate electromagnetic interference, radiation etc. these

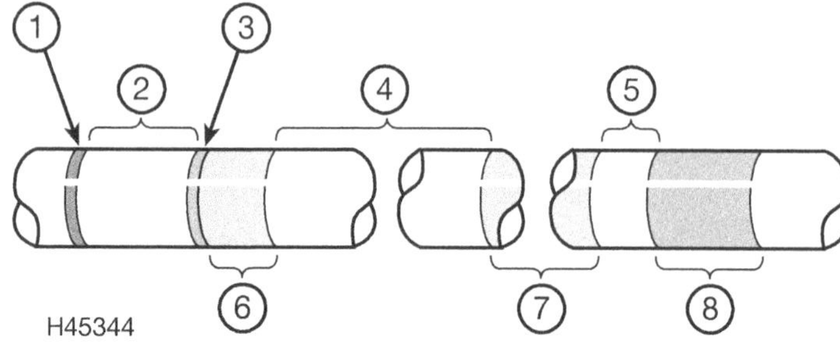


***Fig. 13.31 Data 'packet' - CAN data bus***

*1 Start field (1 bit)*
*2 Status field (11 bits)*
*3 Unused (1 bit)*
*4 Data field (64 bits max.)*
*5 Confirmation field (2 bits)*
*6 Check field (6 bits)*
*7 Safety field (16 bits)*
*8 End field (7 bits)*

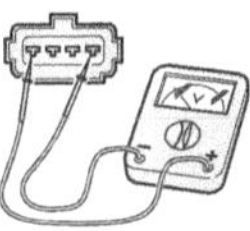

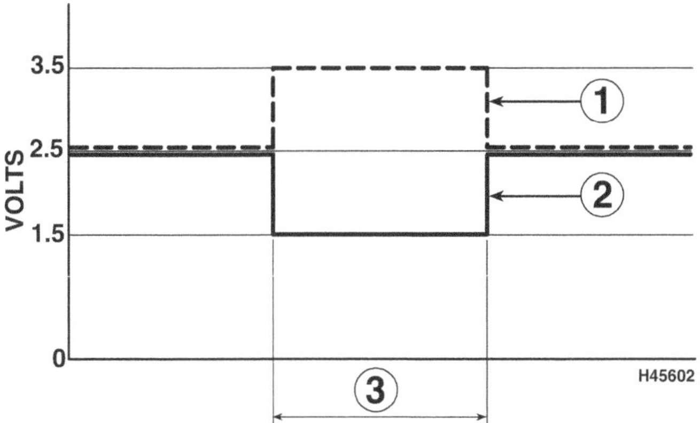


*Fig. 13.32 When there's a data 'packet' to be transmitted, the CAN high voltage increases 1.0 V and the CAN low voltage decreases 1.0 V*

*1 CAN high signal 2 CAN low signal 3 Data 'packet'*

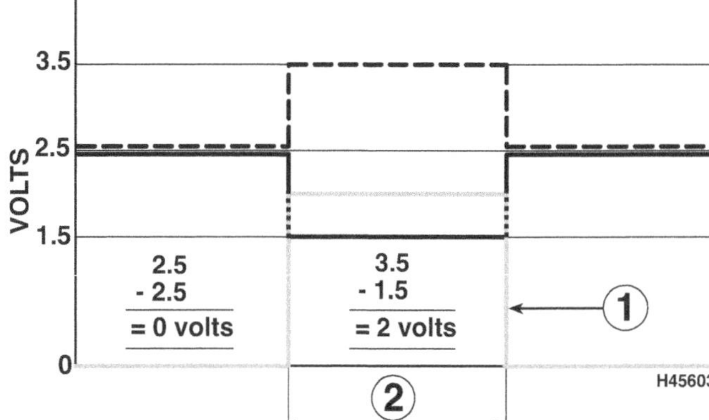


*Fig. 13.33 When the CAN low voltage is deducted from the CAN high voltage, the resulting data 'packet' voltage is 2.0 V*

*1 Resultant data 'packet' voltage 2 Data 'packet'*

two wires are twisted together, so that they both receive exactly the same amount of interference at the same time. As any interference voltage spike is present in both the CAN high and CAN low signal, when the ECU transceiver deducts the CAN low voltage from the CAN high voltage, any spike is eliminated (Fig. 13.34).

**LIN**

Where speed of data transfer and interference is not a concern, some manufacturers use a single wire data transfer system known as LIN (Local Interconnect Network). Here the transfer rate is 1 to 20 kbit/s, and the data packages are carried at battery voltage. Typical usages of this network are air conditioning controls, sun roof, heated windscreens, central locking, etc. The network is organised into one designated master control unit and upto 16 slave units, and works like this: The driver operates the sunroof switch, which places a data 'packet' requesting the sun roof to open, on the LIN. When this 'packet' is received by the master control unit (in this case, the air conditioning control unit), it places a 'packet' commanding the roof to open on the LIN. This 'packet' is recognised by the roof motor control unit which obeys the command. The major benefit of this system is security. Anyone attempting to 'hot-wire' a component of the system (eg. the door locks) would find it almost impossible to manipulate the component without being able to imitate the LIN master control unit signal characteristics including the unique identifier section of the signal 'packet'.

**MOST**

For some systems, the high-speed transmission of large amounts of data is essential. In-car information and entertainment systems are constantly increasing in complexity, and now include satellite navigation, DVD, TV, internet e-mail, digital radio, etc. The previously described

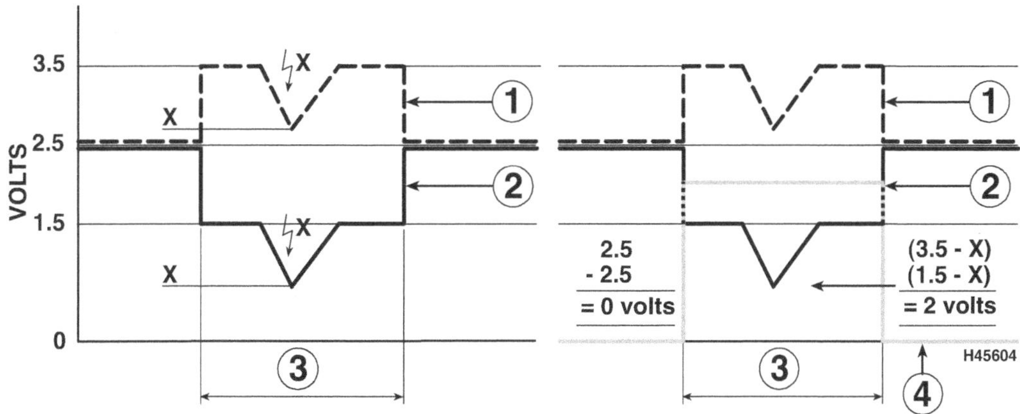


*Fig. 13.34 As any interference spike (or trough) is present in both CAN wires, deducting the CAN low voltage from the CAN high voltage results in a clean 2.0 V signal*

*1 CAN high signal 2 CAN low signal 3 Data 'packet' 4 Resultant signal*

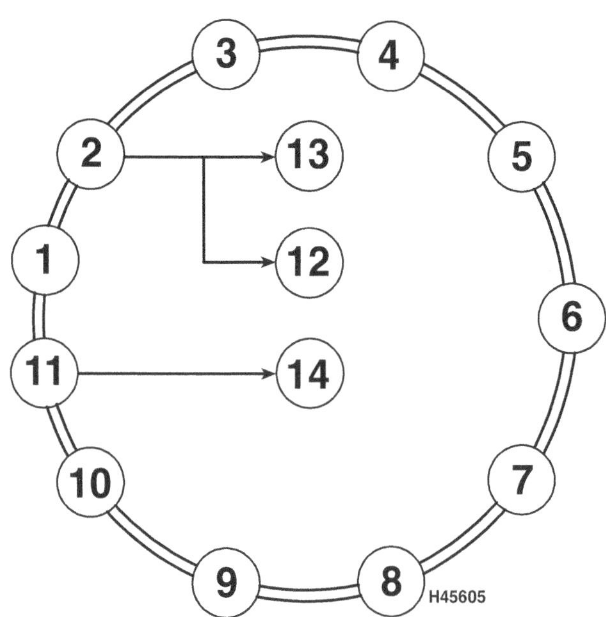


***Fig. 13.35 MOST (Media Oriented System Transport) system layout***

*1 Fibre optic cable*
*2 Information display and operating unit control unit*
*3 CD changer*
*4 Telematics*
*5 TV tuner*
*6 Radio tuner*
*7 Voice control*
*8 Amplifier*
*9 Navigation*
*10 Map reader*
*11 Gateway for diagnostic interface*
*12 Diagnostic connector*

CAN data bus arrangements are not capable of transmitting enough data fast enough for these systems (TV signal with stereo sound requires a transfer rate of approximately 6Mbits/s), so various manufacturers are developing a system called MOST (Media Oriented System Transport). This system using fibre optic cables to connect the various 'infotainment' components in a 'ring' configuration (Fig. 13.35).

Using fibre optics, allows a data transfer rate of upto 21.2 Mbit/s, many times that of the CAN databus. The data are immune to/generate no electromagnetic interference, and are transmitted by means of light wave modulation. Each infotainment component of the network has a control unit equipped with an FOT (Fibre Optical Transmitter) and a transceiver. The FOT consists of a photodiode and a light emitting diode – incoming optical signals are converted by the photodiode into a voltage signal and passed to the transceiver, which relays the data to the infotainment component (eg. the DVD player). In reverse, the transceiver passes a voltage signal to the light emitting diode which converts the voltage signal into a light signal.

The network is organised such that data is relayed by each control unit to the next in the 'ring' in one direction only. Each 'packet' of data incorporates a section that contains the address of the infotainment component that requires it (Fig. 13.36). Consequently, the packet is only accepted by the relevant component – other control units merely relay the 'packet' to the next control unit in the 'ring'.

Due to the different data transfer rates of these networks, it's not possible to join a LIN data bus to a CAN or MOST

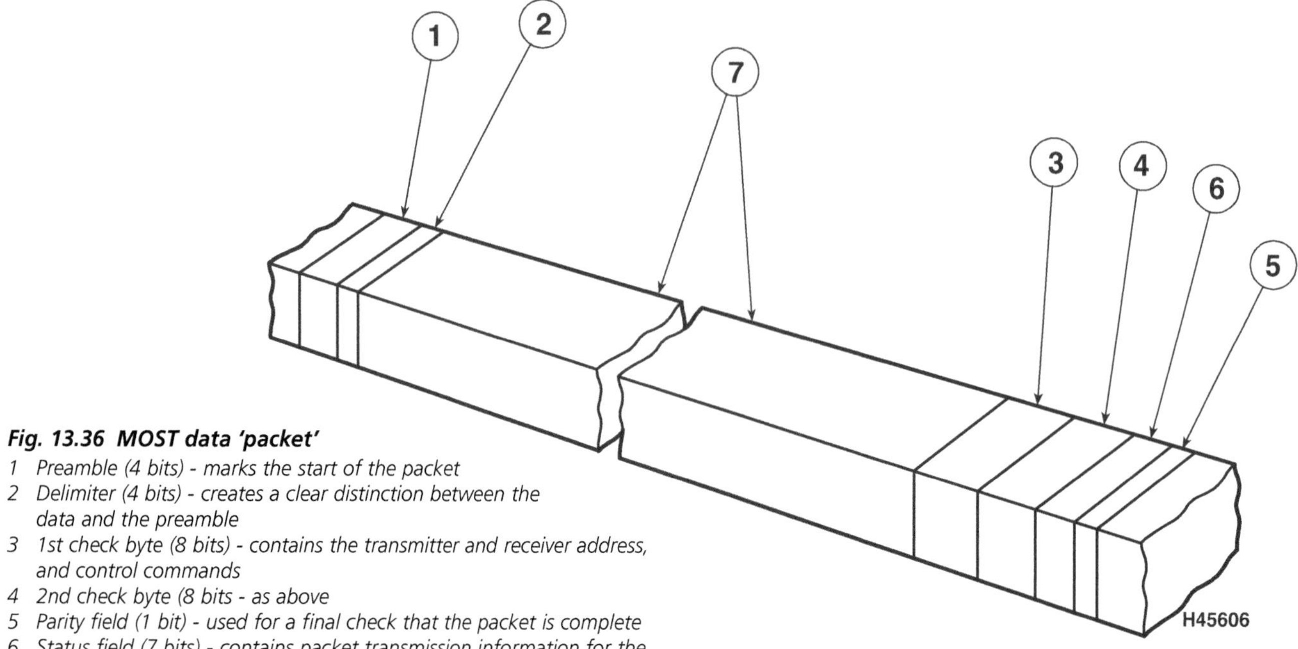


***Fig. 13.36 MOST data 'packet'***

*1 Preamble (4 bits) - marks the start of the packet*
*2 Delimiter (4 bits) - creates a clear distinction between the data and the preamble*
*3 1st check byte (8 bits) - contains the transmitter and receiver address, and control commands*
*4 2nd check byte (8 bits - as above*
*5 Parity field (1 bit) - used for a final check that the packet is complete*
*6 Status field (7 bits) - contains packet transmission information for the receiver*
*7 Data field (480 bits) - the data section of the packet*

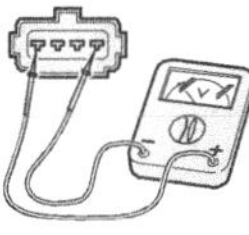

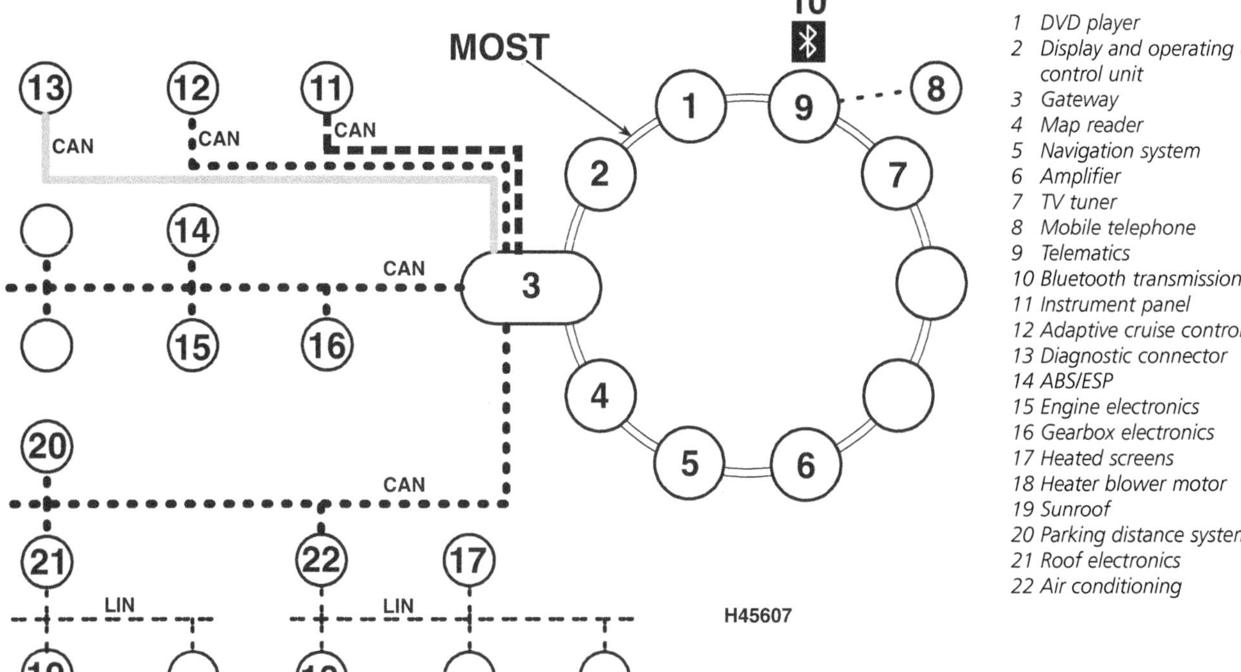


***Fig. 13.37 Typical vehicle network layout***

data bus and pass data along it. However, in order that data can be transferred from one network to another, a device known as a 'Gateway' is used. This device interconnects the different networks, and to use an analogy, works in a similar fashion as a train station. A packet (carriage) on one network (rail) arrives at the gateway (station), the data (passengers) disembark and then embark on another packet (carriage) on another network on the other side of the gateway (station). In this way one fault code reader can interrogate control units and retrieve fault codes across the entire vehicles network.

### Bluetooth

With the ever increasing use of mobile communication and information technology (mobile phones, PDAs, notebooks, etc.), traditional methods of exchanging information (hard-wire, infrared, etc.) are no longer suitable. Each component would have its own transfer protocol, and communication between units could be complex and unreliable. In order to standardise communications between mobile units, Bluetooth™ technology has been developed. A group of over 2000 companies from the fields of telecommunications, data processing, equipment and vehicle manufacturing cooperated and developed a standard for short distance (10 metres) radio signal transmission. This technology is being incorporated into motor vehicle design, and allows mobile devices to integrate with the vehicles networks (Fig. 13.37).

## Fault finding

Obviously from a fault finding perspective, the traditional probing with a multimeter may not reveal the expected results, and may cause damage. Fortunately, vehicles with Multiplex wiring and/or Networks are also equipped with sophisticated self-diagnosis systems, which monitor the integrity of circuits, controllers and components of the vehicle. Fault-finding using an appropriate reader/scanner should be relatively straight-forward and precise. However, as expensive ECUs and components are involved, always interrogate the system for stored faults first, and always examine the relevant wiring diagram before getting the multimeter out and backprobing connectors.

# Notes

# Body electrics and controls

# 14



## 1 Anti-lock braking systems (ABS)

**1** In an emergency, the driver reaction is to apply the brakes with maximum effort. This creates deceleration beyond the grip limit of tyres to the road surface, and the vehicle skids.
**2** When under skid conditions, the driver experiences loss of directional control because turn steering requires a sideways (lateral) force between tyre and road surface – this is not present when skidding. Yawing occurs and the likelihood of an accident is high. In addition, even if the vehicle remained straight, the stopping distance is greater than if the braking force, just short of the skidding point, could have been maintained. A further point concerns cars towing trailers or caravans, and articulated lorries; if skidding occurs, jack-knifing will occur with potentially disastrous results.
**3** ABS (Anti-lock Braking System) prevents skidding by regulation of the braking pressure in individual brake cylinders, giving the following advantages:

*Maximum possible braking is obtained*
*Driving stability is maintained, ie the vehicle can be steered*
*Trailers do not jack-knife*

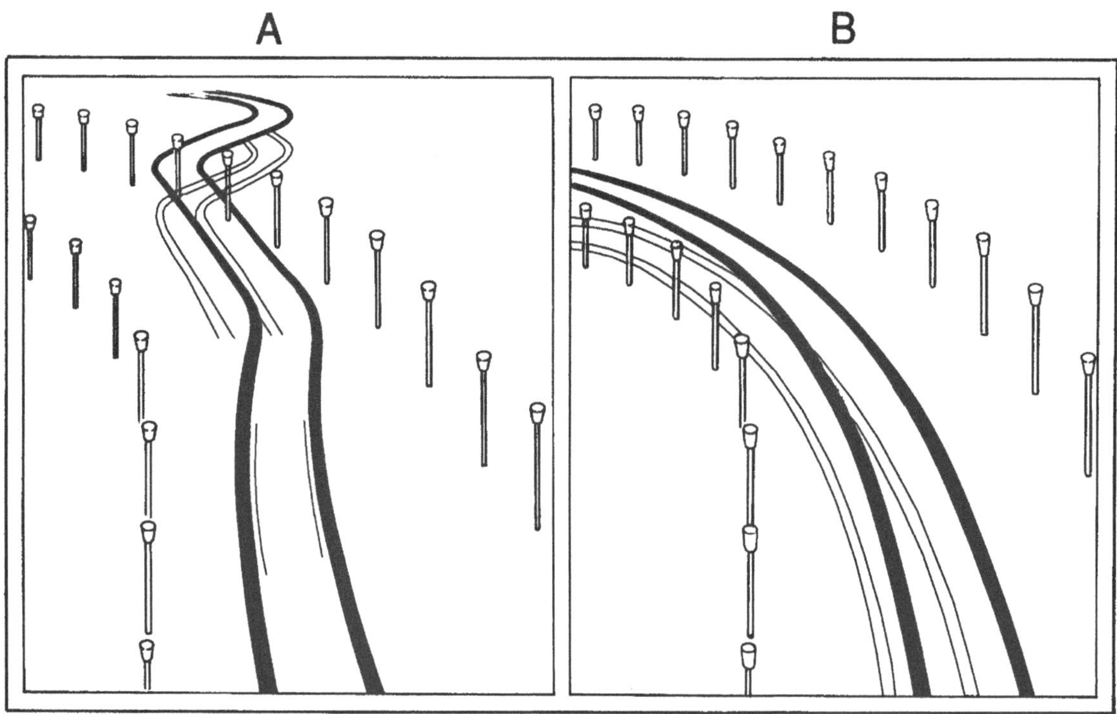


***Fig. 14.1 An advantage of anti-lock braking systems***
*A Without ABS B With ABS*

A graphic comparison between a skidding vehicle and one fitted with ABS is shown in Fig. 14.1, where vehicles were tested under identical conditions.

## Principle of operation for a typical system

**4** Wheel speeds are measured by tooth wheels and magnetic sensors. A continuous train of pulses from each sensor arrives at the electronic control unit (ECU) which then compares the speeds of different wheels. If, during braking, one wheel is on the verge of locking up (ie showing a tendency to skid), the output of its sensor will differ from the sensor signals of the other roadwheels. The ECU reads the difference and sends a signal to the pressure control actuator to reduce the hydraulic brake pressure to the potentially skidding wheel. When the affected wheel speeds up again the brake pressure is reapplied, so a continuous brake pumping action occurs until the ECU reads that deceleration of all the wheels with sensors attached is the same. Fig. 14.2

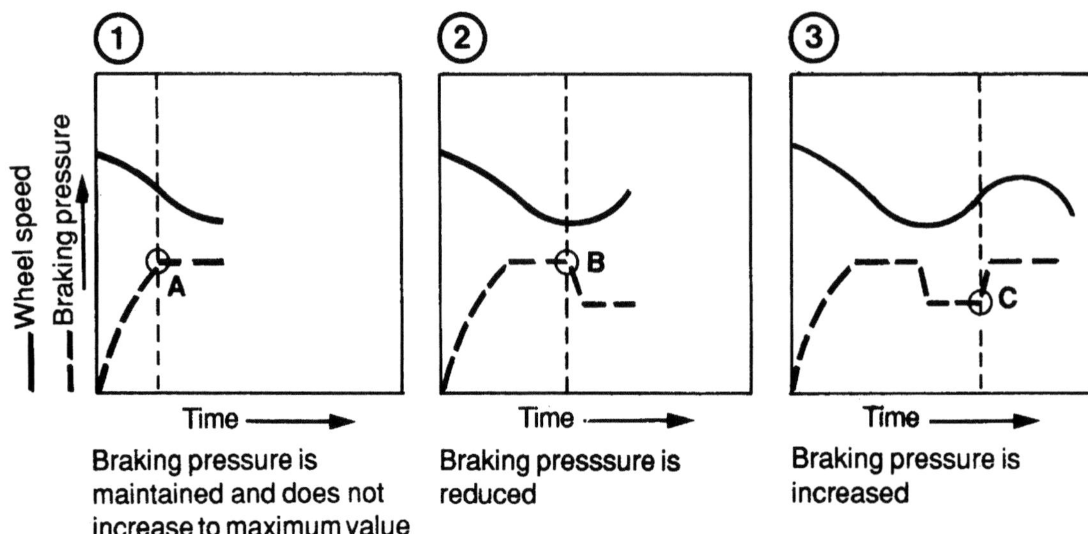


***Fig. 14.2 Wheel speed and braking pressure during ABS-controlled braking***

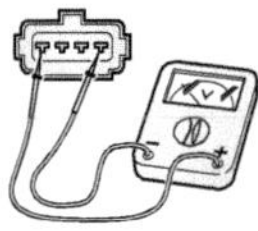



shows the action graphically. In (1) the wheel speed sensor shows a rapid deceleration. The ECU levels out the braking pressure. (2) If the wheel still decelerates the brake pressure is reduced. (3) The wheel accelerates again and, once a limit is reached, the brake pressure is increased again. The cycle is repeated at between 4 and 10 operations per second, the result being that the wheel decelerates as rapidly as possible short of skidding. A dashboard warning lamp lights up during the time that ABS control is in operation.

## Typical ABS components

Fig. 14.3 shows the layout of ABS in a front wheel drive car with speed sensors fitted to each wheel. A tooth-wheel and sensor is shown in Fig. 14.4. The electronic controller is based on large scale integration (LSI) using digital technology. It may be considered as four units using seven integrated circuits:

*(i) Input amplifier for shaping and amplifying the wheel speed sensor signals*

*(ii) Computing unit for carrying out the logic comparisons of wheel speeds, then the arithmetical calculation of wheel slip, acceleration or deceleration, and finally the formation of actuator command signals*

*(iii)A control stage which consists of power devices to drive the solenoid valves via relays in the hydraulic modulator*

*(iv)The monitoring unit is used to sense any incorrect electrical signals. When a fault is detected the monitor switches off the ABS system and informs the driver that ABS is off but normal driver braking control is in operation.*

A second function of the monitoring circuit is to run through a self-check programming of the system when the wheel

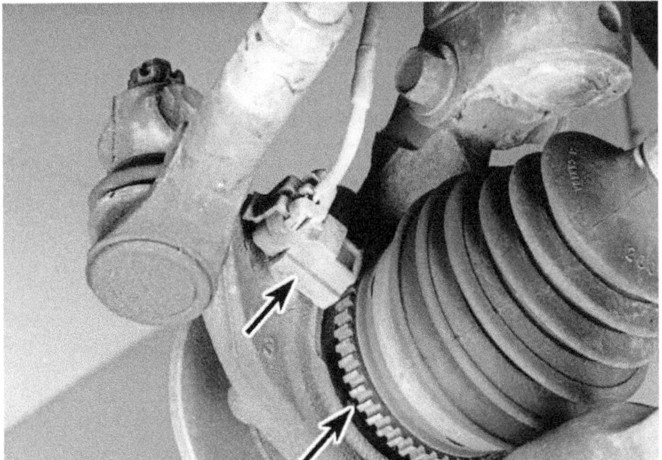

**Fig. 14.4 The toothed signal rotor is pressing onto the end of the outer CV joint (lower arrow) – the wheel speed sensor is mounted on the hub carrier (upper arrow)**

***Fig. 14.3 Typical ABS component layout***

*1 Hydraulic unit*
*2 Wheel speed sensor and toothed signal rotor*
*3 Main relay*
*4 ABS control unit*

speeds are greater than 6 kph. Verification complete, the ABS warning light is switched off.

Thus, in summary:

Signals from the metered wheels pass to the ECU which computes the wheel slip allowable to give optimum braking. Brake fluid pressure is controlled by the ECU using solenoid regulating valves and there is also a system testing programme (Fig. 14.5).

At the start of a journey, the programme is automatically run to check that all parts of the ABS system are working properly. During the journey continuous monitoring takes place and should a fault occur the anti-lock section of the

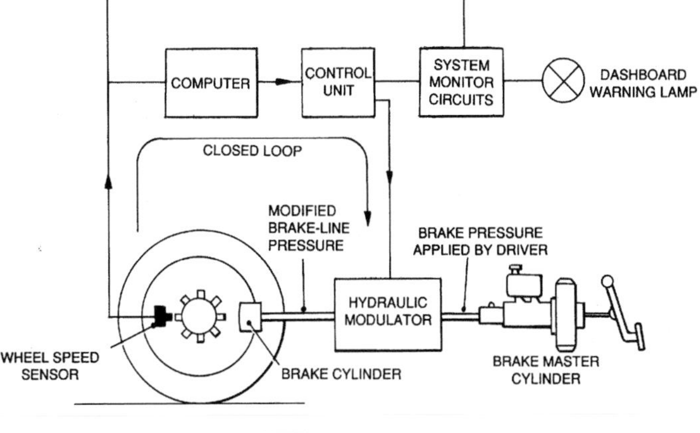


***Fig. 14.5 ABS closed-loop control system***

braking system is closed down and the braking system works as it would without ABS.

The hydraulic modulator is the actuating device which receives ECU signals and carries out brake line pressure variations to maintain, decrease or increase braking force. Brake fluid is supplied to the brake lines by means of solenoid valves, one to each braking circuit. If brake pressure is lowered, surplus brake fluid is passed to an accumulator which stores the fluid under piston spring pressure. It is returned to the brake line by pump if the ECU signals that an increase of pressure is required. In later systems, a pressure pump is also incorporated to rapidly increase the brake fluid pressure when required. This function is also utilised by other systems (ASR/TCS, EBA and ESP) associated with ABS.

## 2 Traction control (ASR or TCS)

**1** Wheel spin occurs when the driver applies, via the transmission, more torque than the driving wheels can transmit to the road surface. This action may be regarded as a mirror image of skidding in that a locking wheel undergoes negative slip and a spinning wheel has positive slip (Fig. 14.6). Traction control reduces the engine torque irrespective of how the driver uses the accelerator pedal.

**2** A traction control (TCS), or anti-slip regulation (ASR) system has been in volume production since 1987 and serves to prevent wheelspin during starting and acceleration, eliminating uncontrolled vehicle swerving. Because of the link between ABS and ASR, manufacturers make dual use of some components for both systems.

### ASR

#### Using throttle valve and brakes

**3** This is one of two versions in which the ABS electronics are extended with an ASR element. The mechanical linkage between the accelerator pedal and throttle valve is replaced by the electronic system in which the pedal position is signalled to the ECU by the position of the wiper arm of a potentiometer. Wheel speed sensors detect any onset of wheelspin. If the drivewheels begin to spin the throttle valve is moved towards the closed position by the ECU. If only one wheel tends to spin, it is braked by the ABS and ASR hydraulics plus the reduction of throttle opening. The effect is of an electronically-controlled differential lock and if necessary both wheels can be braked. This method requires a hydraulic unit addition to ABS.

#### Using throttle valve/ignition/injection

**4** This alternative does not involve the brakes, and the ABS hydraulic system does not require modification. To aid rapid response, the ASR controls the throttle valve through the E-Gas pedal circuit but also retards ignition and cuts off fuel injection; this is said to give vehicle stability improvement. Using these principles an electro-hydraulic differential lock up to 100% may be applied, to improve traction on road surfaces with different friction values on left and right wheels. This combination of ignition and injection control of

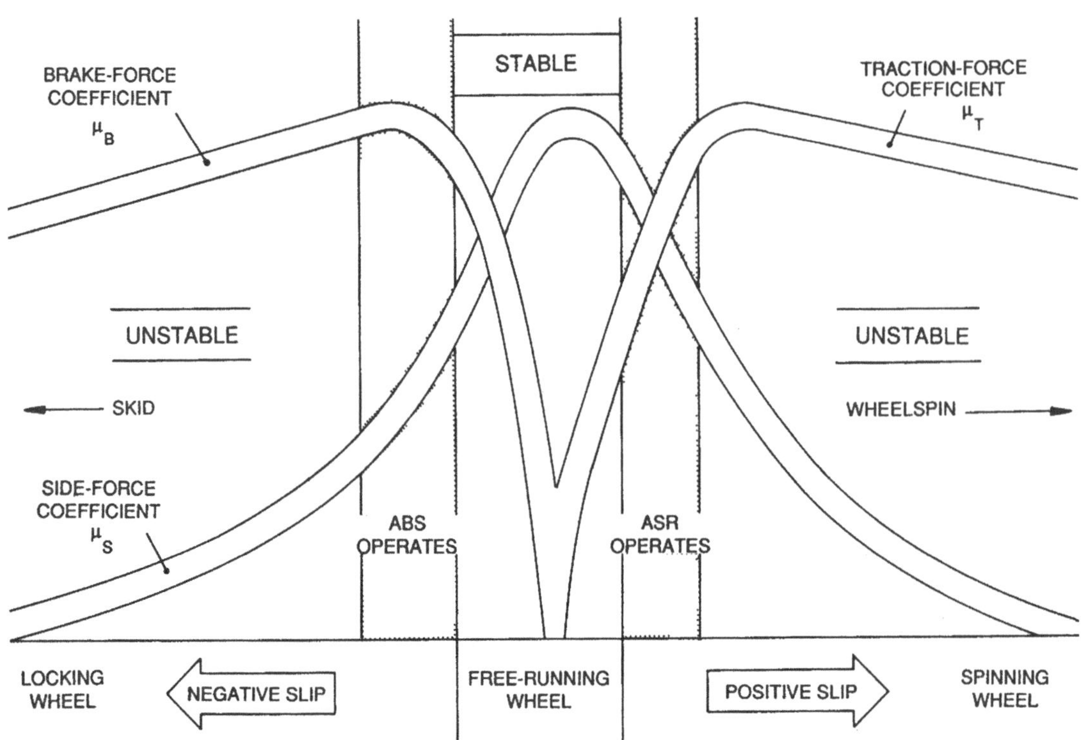


*Fig. 14.6 Relationship between skidding and wheel spin*

ASR with a lock differential is intended for rear-wheel-drive cars. Fig. 14.7 shows a vehicle block layout with the above variations in outline form.

## 3 Vehicle security

**1** It is an unfortunate fact that in the UK alone more than 6000 cars are stolen or broken into every day. Sophisticated alarm systems are now fitted as standard by many car manufacturers, whilst vehicles without alarms can be protected by the fitment of an aftermarket system.

### Factory fitted security systems

**Note:** *The following is a description of a typical alarm system fitted by the vehicle manufacturers. For reasons of security specific details of the alarm system construction and theory are neither given nor available.*

**2** Ultrasonic or microwave movement sensors monitor the vehicle's interior, whilst the system utilises some of the vehicles central locking components to provide monitoring of the doors, hatchback etc. There are no separate switches specifically for the alarm system. The door/tailgate/fuel filler flap locks themselves are 'deadlocked', meaning that when set, there is no mechanical connection between the lock assembly and the operating handles, lock buttons etc. This denies the would-be thief of the possibility of gaining entry by manipulating the handles, lock buttons etc. In order to protect the locks from direct attack, lock shields are fitted between the lock assemblies and the door/tailgate/boot outer skin. Shock sensors are used which are able to detect any movement of the vehicle (attempted attack, door

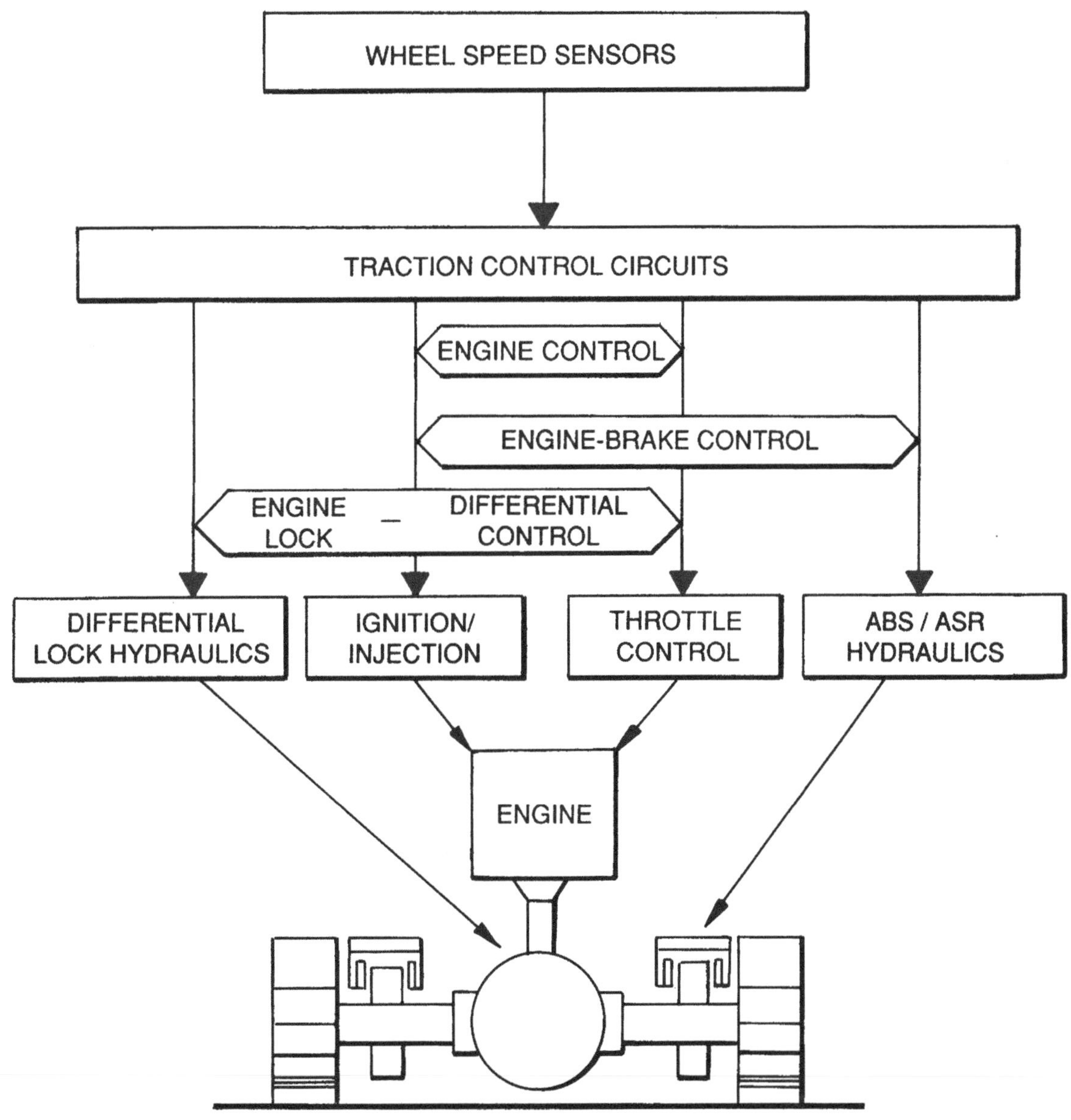


*Fig. 14.7 Schematic layout of traction control system (anti-slip regulation – ASR)*

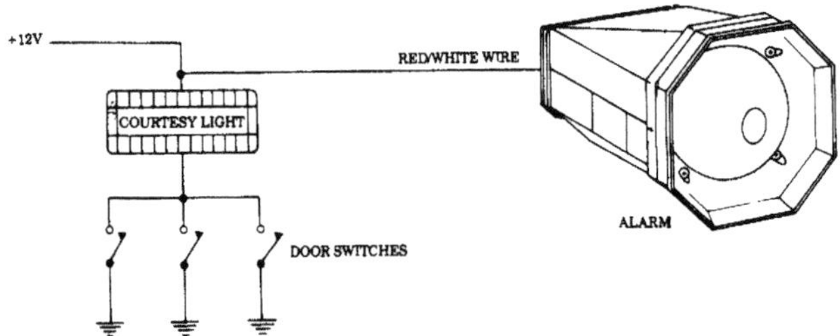


*Fig. 14.8 Microprocessor detects battery supply volt-drop when the doors are opened*

opening, tilting, etc.). All these systems are activated by locking the vehicle via the door locks, or more commonly, by remote control. The ignition key with an integral transponder transmits a coded signal to a receiver located on/in the vehicle. If the code transmitted matches that expected by the vehicles alarm ECU, the vehicles alarm system is deactivated, and the vehicle unlocks. To further enhance security, matching codes are chosen at random every time the vehicle is locked. These systems are often integrated into the vehicles engine management system to provide an almost infallible engine immobiliser facility. Once entry to the vehicle is granted, a receiver integral with the ignition switch, must receive a coded signal from the transponder in the ignition key before the vehicle can be started. The level of sophistication is now such that thieves often no longer attempt to break into and steal luxury cars, instead they resort to stealing the keys or hijacking the vehicle. On some vehicles, even this may not prove successful as a vehicle tracking system can be fitted, which by using GPS technology, allows the position of the vehicle to be pin-pointed to within a few meters. Once triggered, the vehicles alarm system will sound a loud piercing noise from a siren fitted to the vehicle, and operate the hazard warning lights. Some systems will also alert the owner via mobile phone or pager.

## Aftermarket security systems

**Note:** *The following is a description of a typical aftermarket alarm system, normally retro-fitted to older vehicles.*

**3** Security systems are now widely used as an aftermarket kit, and are sophisticated in design to combat the car thief.

*Fig. 14.9 Tilt sensor detects jacking up or ramp loading*

**4** Alarm equipment can be simple, covering door or boot opening only, or can be comprehensive according to how much the car owner wants to spend; here we shall look at the features of a complete system of which, if required, only part may be fitted.

**5** Common to all systems is a siren which is triggered by one or more sensors. The siren will emit a piercing note of about 120 decibels and is controlled by a microprocessor specifically designed for security work.

## Door entry

**6** Nearly half of all car theft is effected by entry through the doors. Opening of doors can be detected by pin switches which work on the same principle as a courtesy light switch; where a courtesy light switch is fitted, all that is needed is a connection to the supply wire. Operation of the courtesy light will lower the system voltage sufficiently to trigger the microprocessor alarm (Fig. 14.8).

## Forcible entry

**7** Pin switches may be fitted to bonnets, bootlids and doors to protect against non-forcible entry but if force is used then a shock sensor accelerator will operate the alarm. This is an in-built component of the microprocessor system and has adjustable sensitivity. Shock sensors used to be on a pendulum design but recent types now use a piezo crystal with a weight (mass) attached in two planes at right angles. Shock will cause the inertia of the masses to exert a force on the piezo crystal. Piezo crystals can be of quartz, Rochelle salt, or barium titanate and possess the property that, when a force is applied between one pair or opposite faces, an electric charge appears between the adjacent opposite faces. Rochelle salt was mainly used for record player pick-ups, quartz for oscillators and underwater sound transducers, barium titanate for accelerometers.

## Tilt sensor

**8** If the thief tries to take off wheels or trailer the vehicle away, then a tilt sensor will detect jacking or running up a ramp (Fig. 14.9). This sensor takes the form of a roller ball in a chamber which takes the vehicle attitude at parking as standard and alarms at any change.

## Engine immobilisation

**9** This facility may be used to disconnect the ignition system when the alarm is triggered. ignition is automatically switched on again when the alarm resets, but recently manufacturers have preferred to use the facility to cut the starter solenoid (starter kill) or the electric fuel pump supply.

## Battery backup

**8** The thief will try to stop the alarm by disconnection of the battery (Fig. 14.10), but a backup system of nickel-cadmium batteries in the alarm housing will counter this. The batteries have sufficient power for 25 minutes alarm operation and are automatically kept charged by the vehicle charging system.

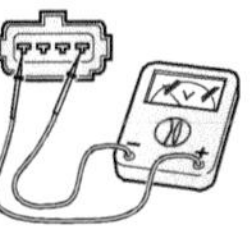



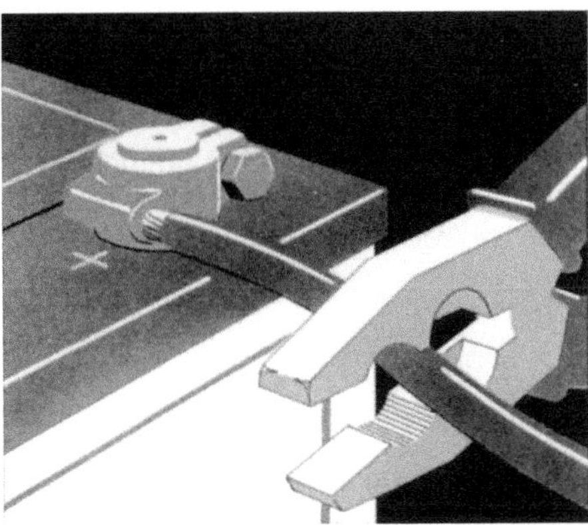

*Fig. 14.10 Some alarms have nicad battery backup to counter this approach*

## Ultrasonic interior flooding

**9** An ultrasonic wave generator comes as a small unit for fitting at a convenient location in the passenger compartment. The waves reflect from all surfaces resulting in a flooding of the interior with a stationary wave pattern.

Entry or disturbance can upset the pattern and will trigger the alarm. A new development is to flood the car interior with microwaves instead of ultrasonics. The advantages are that the system may be used with soft tops or no top at all, or with a window down. One model (Fig. 14.11) has a series of flashing light-emitting diodes (LED) which serve to warn a potential thief that the vehicle is armed. The LEDs do not otherwise contribute to the system.

## Electric fan sensing override

**10** Some vehicles have an engine cooling fan which runs after the ignition is switched off. The microprocessor is connected to the fan supply lead and shuts down the voltage sensing facility until the fan has stopped, when this facility is restored.

## Personal security button

**11** One system has an interior 'panic' button setting off the alarm to attract attention, summon help or deter an attacker.

*Fig. 14.11 Ultrasonic scanner and receiver*

It is possible to use a remote key to trigger the car alarm if the owner is outside the vehicle.

## Electric window lift interface

**12** If the vehicle has electrically-operated windows, an alarm system may have the facility of closing all windows automatically when the remote control arms the alarm system.

## Accessory protection

**13** By connecting valuable accessories, eg stereo equipment, electrically to the control unit, any attempt to remove the accessory will result in the alarm sounding.

## Arming and disarming the alarm

**14** Some systems may be armed by a coded key pad (Fig. 14.12) which allows 60 seconds exit and 10 seconds entry times for the driver before the alarm triggers. Remote arming/disarming may be by a short range (7 to 8 m) coded transmitter or, by use of a more sensitive receiver with a short aerial mounted on board the vehicle near a window, the operation range may be extended to approximately fifty metres according to the location (Fig. 14.13). Remote control transmitters work at frequencies of 173 and 418 MHz as authorized by the DTI.

*Fig. 14.12 Coded key pad to arm/disarm the alarm*

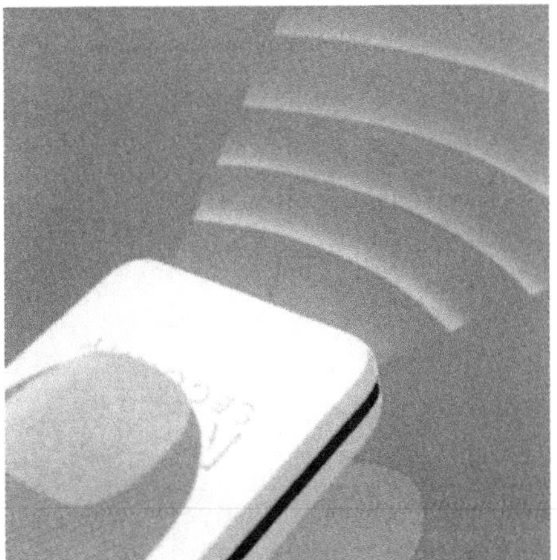

*Fig. 14.13 Remote alarm transmitter*

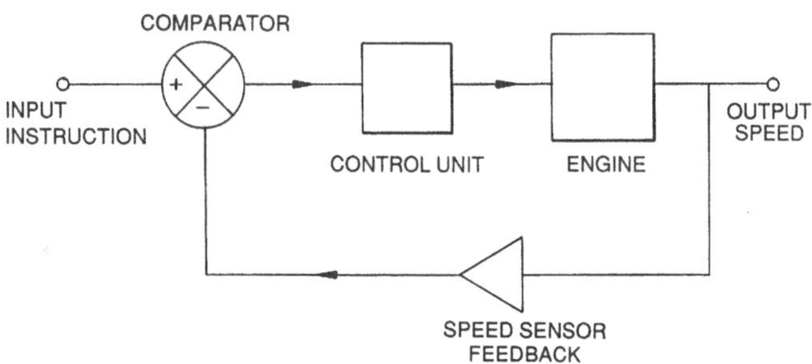


*Fig. 14.14 Cruise control system*

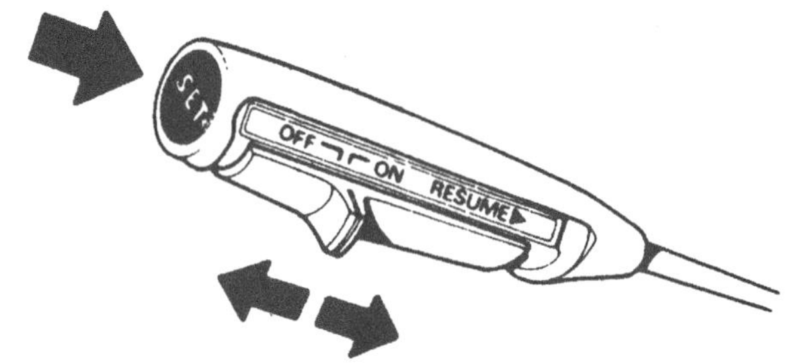


*Fig. 14.15 Cruise control switch*

### Alarm triggering

**15** The alarm, once triggered, will sound the siren, flash the lights and immobilise the vehicle for a period of 60 seconds and reset in the armed condition after a further 5 seconds.

## 4 Cruise control

**1** Useful in travelling long distances where it is tiring to maintain a steady speed, cruise control has been popular in the USA for some years and is now becoming available in Europe. The control takes over from the driver to maintain a constant speed irrespective of wind resistance or gradient. A closed loop control system maintains constant speed by comparing the output speed with that required by the input instruction (Fig. 14.14). When the comparator detects a difference between the required speed (instruction) and the actual speed, a difference signal is fed to the control unit which alters the throttle by means of an actuator, or on later vehicles by the engine management ECU altering the position of the throttle valve.

**2** A switch on the brake pedal ensures the instant disconnection of the control system, and some versions have a clutch pedal switch to prevent engine race if gear changing is necessary. The cruise control switch is often stalk-mounted (Fig. 14.15) and usually has provision for setting the speed and switching on the control system, switching off the control system and finally resume or reactivate. The vehicle is accelerated by the driver to the desired speed while holding the 'set' button. The button is released to allow the control system to take over and is usually operational only above a set speed around 30 mph (50 kph). If the system has been disabled by brake or clutch switch, switching the stalk switch to 'resume' will restore the original condition.

**3** The control unit is frequently digital but analogue systems are available. The setting of desired speed is stored in memory and the processed signal from the speed sensor is compared with the stored instruction. The difference is calculated and if necessary operates an actuator.

**4** The actuator is frequently an electro-pneumatic solenoid-operated device which uses the inlet manifold vacuum to pull a diaphragm which in turn is linked to the throttle (Fig. 14.16). A solenoid is switched on and off to open and close the vacuum to maintain the throttle at the required position. A more expensive and superior solution is to use a separate vacuum pump driven by the vehicle electrical supply.

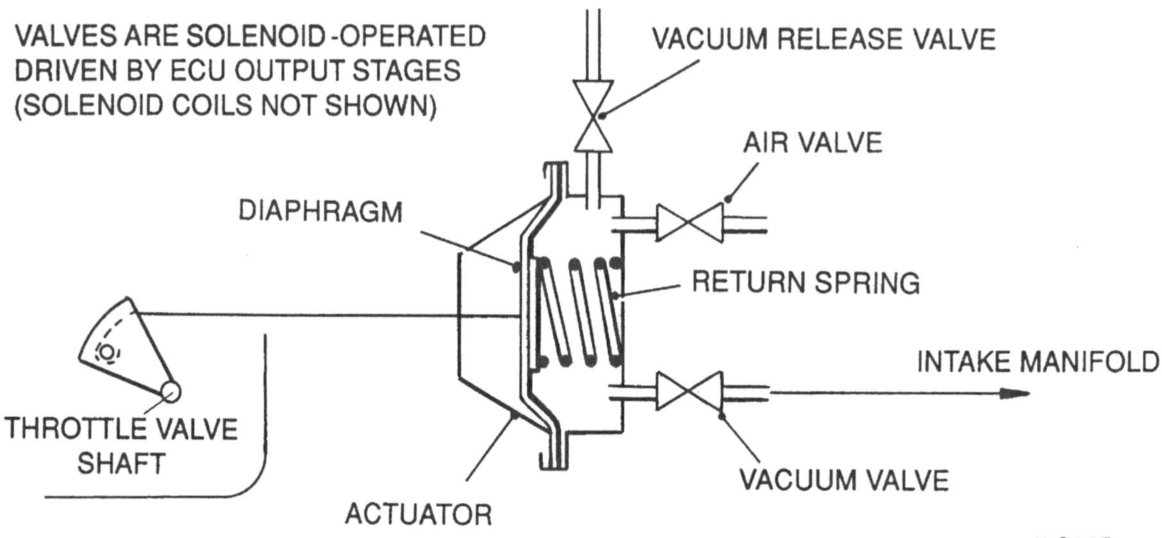


*Fig. 14.16 Cruise control actuator*

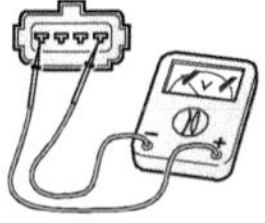

## 5 Tyre pressure monitoring system

**1** A system which detects low pressure in each tyre has been developed by various vehicle manufacturers. The benefits of such a system are:

*1) Increased driving safety – 85% of tyre blowouts are caused by low pressure overheating the tyre.*

*2) Elimination of regular tyre pressure checks – pressures only need correcting when indicated.*

*3) Increased tyre life – 0.3 bar pressure deficit can result in a 25% reduction of tyre life.*

*4) Decrease in fuel consumption due to correct tyre pressures.*

**2** The tyre pressure is monitored by a sensor fitted to the tyre valve. The sensor records the tyre pressure constantly and transmits this information, at regular intervals, by radio (normally 433 MHz) to a receiver antenna mounted in behind the liner of each wheel arch (Fig. 14.17a). Should the tyre pressure differ from that expected by the systems ECU, the driver is alerted by a warning symbol in the instrument cluster.

**3** The pressure sensor fitted to the tyre valve is also able to monitor the temperature, so that the system is able to compensate for pressure change due to temperature change. The sensor is sophisticated enough to be able to differentiate between a slow loss, and sudden loss of pressure – the driver is warned accordingly. The power source for the sensor is provided by a long-life lithium battery integral with the sensor (Fig. 14.17b). Thanks to the energy management characteristics of the sensor, battery life is quoted as more than 5 years.

## 6 Automatic Proximity Control (APC)

**1** This system works in conjunction with the vehicle's cruise control system to maintain a set time gap between the itself and the vehicle in front. Similar to the system used by bats, the APC uses millimetre-band radar waves to determine the distance to the vehicle ahead.

Designed for use primarily on motorways, or straight main roads when the cruise control system is operational, the driver sets the desired speed or desired time gap between him/herself and any vehicle in front. The system will maintain the desired speed, until it encounters a vehicle ahead in the same lane (maximum range 150 m). The system will then gently apply the brakes (upto 30% of maximum braking power) and/or reduce engine output to maintain the desired time gap. If the vehicle ahead speeds up or changes lane, the system will increase the vehicle speed upto the preset desired level.

**2** The system comprises of the following main components:

*1)* ***Steering column electronics control unit****. Monitors the steering angle (see Section 12), and the driver controls (set speed, time gap, etc.).*

***Fig. 14.17a Tyre pressure monitoring system***

*1 Tyre pressure sensor and valve*
*2 Receiver antenna behind the wheel arch liner*
*3 Electronic control unit (ECU)*

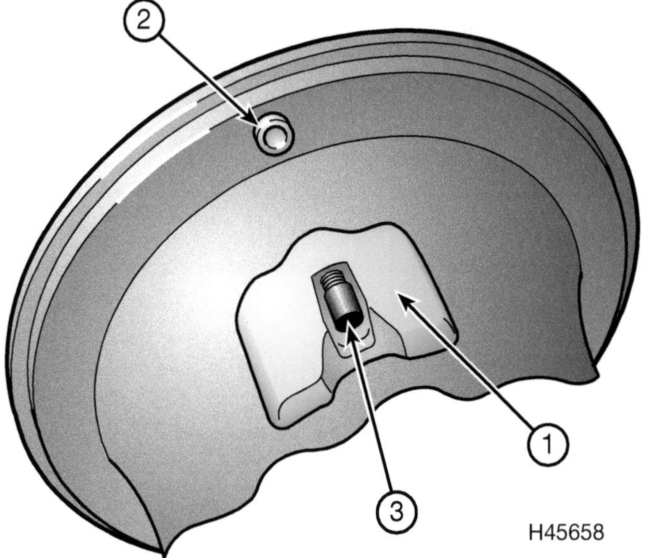


***Fig. 14.17b Tyre pressure sensor***

*1 Tyre pressure sensor with integral transmitter, battery, and temperature sensor*
*2 Metal pressure valve*
*3 Retaining bolt*

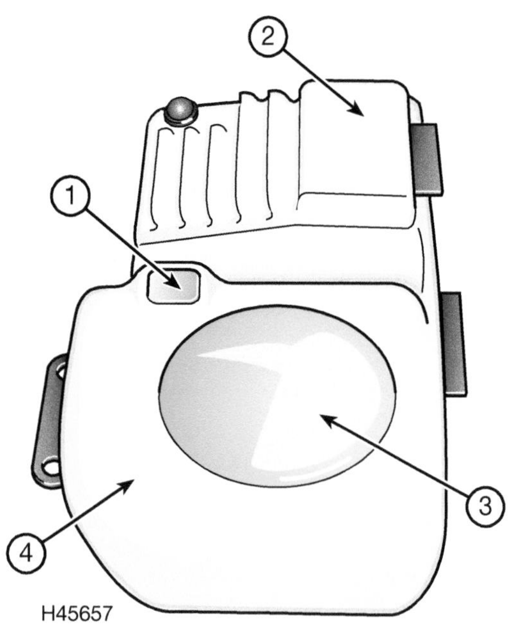


*Fig. 14.18a* ***Proximity control sender***

*1 Alignment lens*
*2 ECU*
*3 Radar lens*
*4 Radar waves transmitter/receiver*

2) ***Instrument panel display unit**. Informs the driver of the system status, provides audible and visual alerts when driver action is needed.*
3) ***Proximity control sender**. Fitted behind the front bumper, this unit sends and receives the radar signals, and evaluates the results (Fig. 14.18a). The unit is responsible for distance/speed control, activation of the engine management ECU signals, brake servo ECU signal, instrument panel display, and self-diagnosis function.*
4) ***Brake servo control unit**. Receives signals from the proximity control sender, then activates and monitors the electronic components of the electronic brake servo.*
5) ***Electronic brake servo**. Upon receiving the appropriate signals from it's ECU, the servo can apply the brakes upto 30% of the vehicles maximum braking power (Fig. 14.18b). If braking in excess of this level is required (eg. the vehicle ahead comes to a sudden stop), the driver is alerted to apply the brakes.*
6) *In addition to the above items, the system is networked via a CAN databus (see Chapter 13, Section 11) to the ABS and ESP systems of the vehicle. Therefore the information gathered by these systems (eg. vehicle speed, yaw rate, lateral acceleration, etc.) is also available to the APC system.*

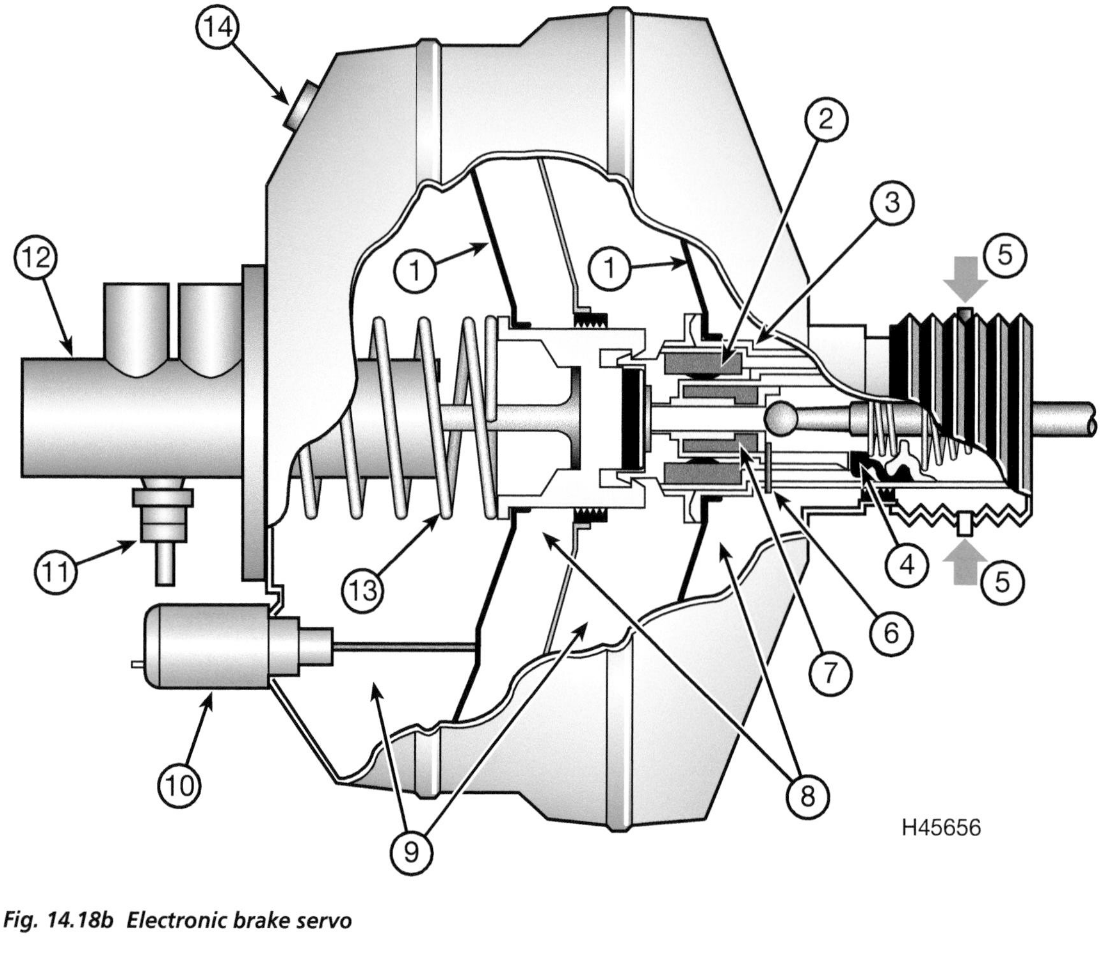

*1 Membrane disc*
*2 Proportional magnet*
*3 Valve body*
*4 Disc seal*
*5 Atmosphere*
*6 Release switch*
*7 Magnet armature*
*8 Working chamber*
*9 Vacuum chamber*
*10 Membrane position sensor*
*11 Brake fluid pressure sensor*
*12 Master cylinder*
*13 Membrane spring*
*14 Vacuum connection*

H45656

*Fig. 14.18b* ***Electronic brake servo***

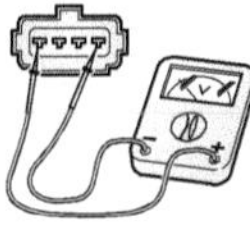

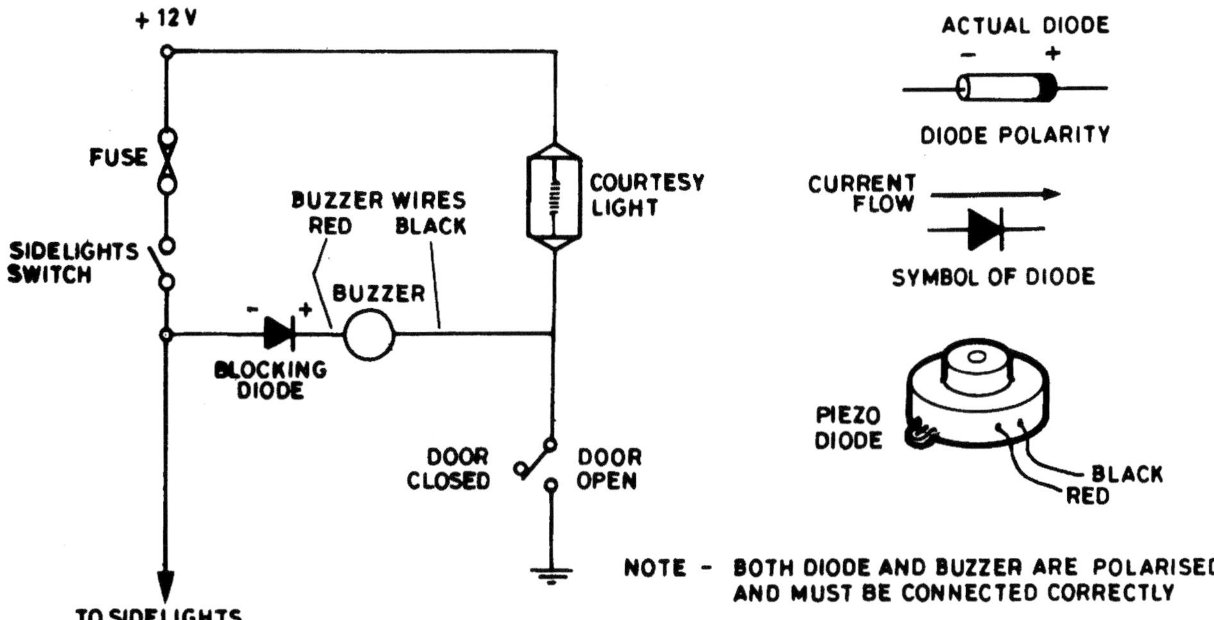


*Fig. 14.19 'Side-lights on' audible warning circuit*

## 7 Warning devices

**1** Many warning circuits use an audible buzzer in the passenger compartment. The buzzer is available in a convenient form in the Piezo buzzer, with blocking diodes. This buzzer will operate within the range 6 to 24 volts, and may be obtained from electronic component stores; the diode is of the silicon p-n junction type and the range IN4000 is suitable. In conjunction with the door courtesy switch (usually located in the door post between the hinges), the diode and buzzer will warn of several possible situations.

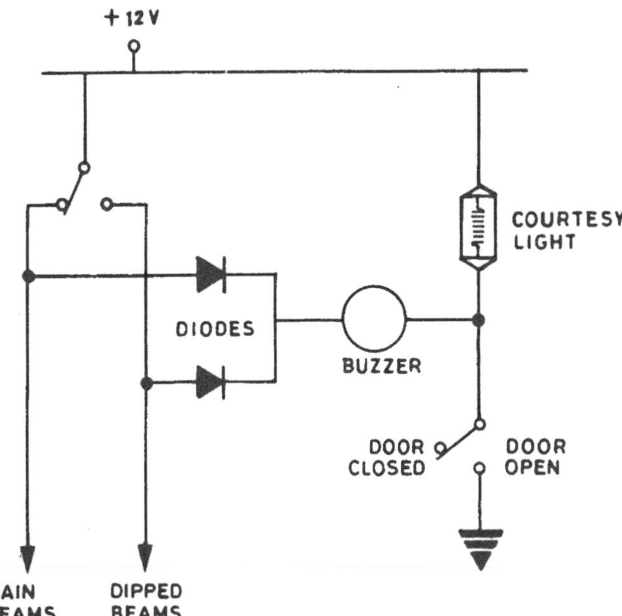


*Fig. 14.20 'Headlights on' audible warning circuit*

**2** Fig. 14.19 shows the principle of working in which a warning will be given if the side-lights (parking lights) are left on. As the driver opens the door, the courtesy light switch closes and connects the diode and buzzer to earth (ground). If the side light circuit is live, ie the lights are on, then the buzzer will sound. Note the purpose of the diode which passes current in one direction only; if it were not used then current would leak through the courtesy light, the buzzer and the side-lights.

**3** An adaption of this idea to warn when headlights are left switched on is given in Fig. 14.20. A single buzzer may be used, but two blocking diodes are required. Another application, such as an audible warning of the indicators working, uses the same components, but they are connected across the feeds to the left and right flashers and earth. In this case, the door courtesy switch is not used.

## 8 Airbags and seat-belt pre-tensioners

**1** Head-on crashes cause the occupants to be thrown forward giving rise to injuries of head, neck and chest. Two solutions for avoidance of serious injury have been developed, one being a rapidly inflated airbag for driver and front seat

Airbag folded in the steering wheel.

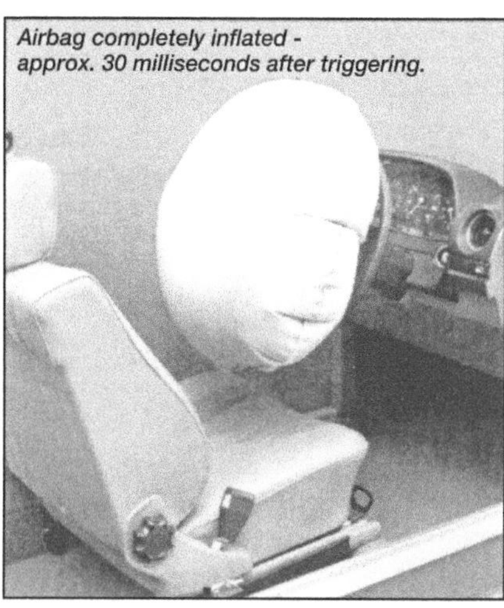
Airbag completely inflated - approx. 30 milliseconds after triggering.

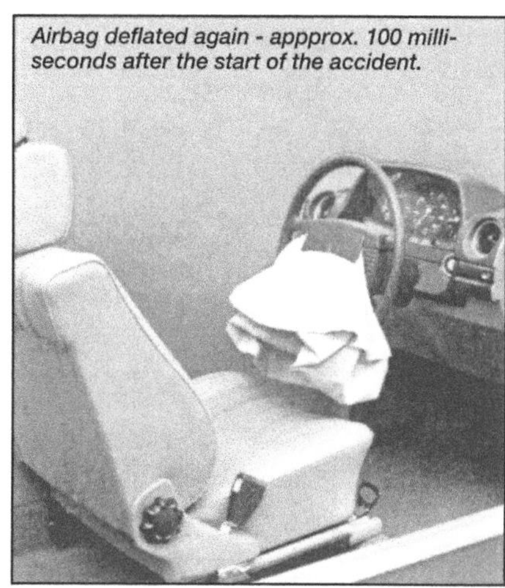
Airbag deflated again - appprox. 100 milli-seconds after the start of the accident.

©BOSCH

***Fig. 14.21 Airbag safety protection against head-on collisions***

passenger (Fig. 14.21). Seat-belt pre-tensioners are used in conjunction with the airbag system. Note that in order to reduce serious injuries sustained due to side impacts, airbags may also be incorporated into the sides of the front seats, and into the headlining above the side windows (curtain airbags). Although the location is different, the principle of operation is similar to that of the driver's and front passenger's air bag.

**2** The driver's airbag is located in the steering wheel and is triggered by a deceleration equivalent to an 18 kph frontal collision with a solid object. When the deceleration is signalled, the triggering device sends an electrical firing pulse to a firing pellet located in a gas generator. The propellant detonates within a few thousandths of a second and inflates the airbag. This is fast enough to prevent the driver from striking the steering column or windscreen.

**3** To give rapid seat belt tightening the same triggering process obtains, but here the propellant drives a turbine wheel (Fig. 14.22). The wheel rotation causes the belt roll-up shaft to turn rapidly until the belt is taut against the user's body.

**4** A power standby is necessary in case the battery is destroyed on impact. A permanently charged capacitor will then discharge into the electronic control equipment long enough to carry out the airbag or belt tightening operation. A voltage converter is also provided which ensures a sufficient voltage is available for the triggering device if the battery voltage drops to 4 V. System checking is carried out every time the ignition is switched on. A lamp lights and stays on for a few seconds while a test cycle is run. If the system is satisfactory, the lamp extinguishes.

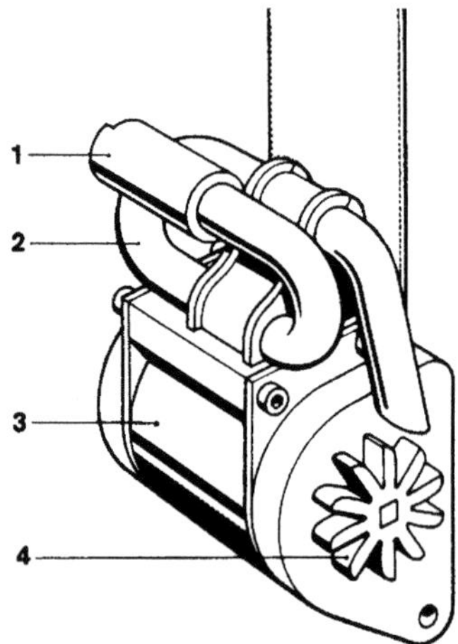


***Fig. 14.22 Electrically-operated seat belt pre-tensioner triggered by impact accelerometer (crash sensor)***

*1 Housing with propellant capsule, thrust chamber and piston*
*2 Tube*
*3 Roll-up shaft*
*4 Impeller wheel of the turbine*

*The propellant in the capsule is detonated by means of an electrical pulse. The high pressure created in this manner forces the plunger through the tube which is filled with fluid. This causes a sealing membrane to tear at the other end of the tube. The fluid, a mixture of water and glycerin, is forced at high speed on the blades of the turbine by the nozzle-shaped end of the tube. The rotation of the turbine turns the shaft of the roll-up mechanism backward thus tightening the seat belt*

## Operation

**5** The accelerometer consists of a spring-mass device (Fig. 14.23). When an impact occurs the mass bends the flat

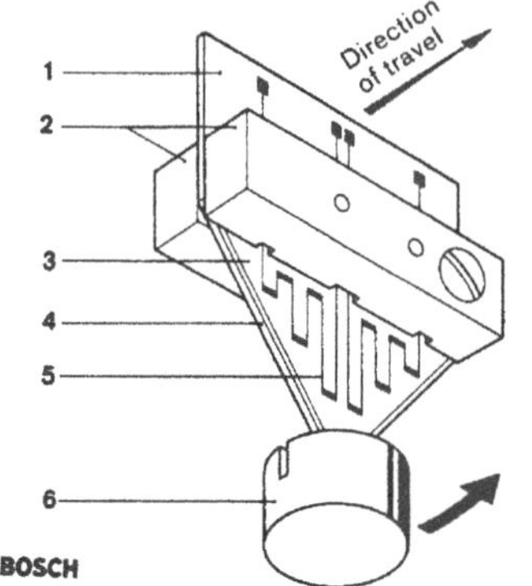


*1 Contacts*
*2 Mount*
*3 Insulation*
*4 Spring*
*5 Strain gauge*
*6 Weight*

***Fig. 14.23 Impact accelerometer (crash sensor)***

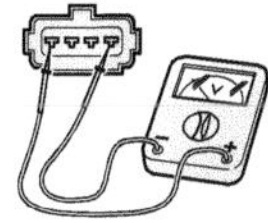

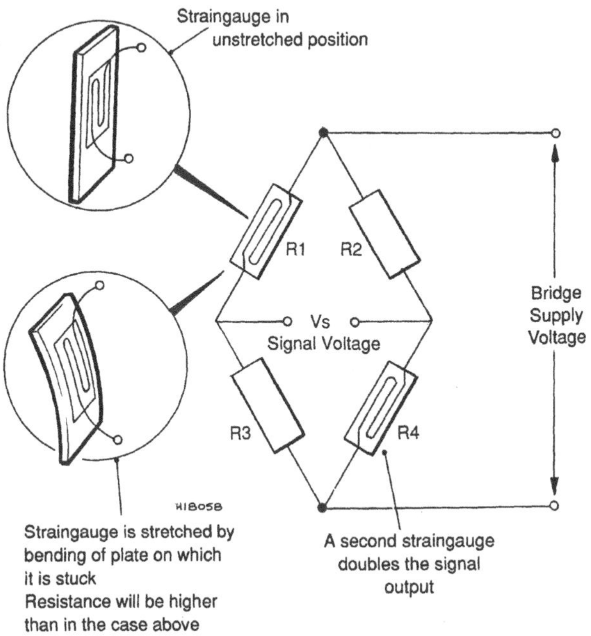

*Fig. 14.24 Strain gauges in Wheatstone Bridge circuit*

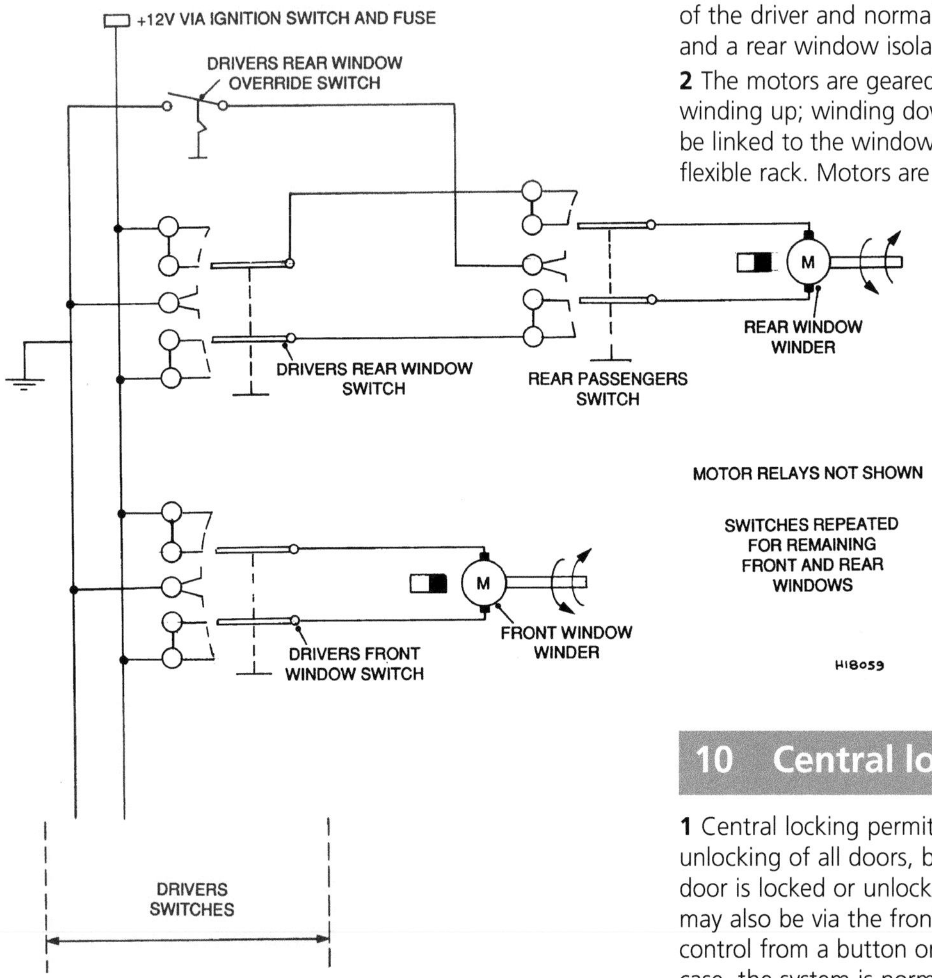

*Fig. 14.25 Electric window winder switching*

spring on which two resistors are mounted. Two other resistors are mounted on a non-moving surface. These four resistors are connected in a Wheatstone Bridge arrangement. Two resistors act as strain gauges since they are mounted on the flat spring. When the spring bends on impact, the strain gauges will stretch, change in resistance, and unbalance the bridge (Fig. 14.24). The bridge output voltage will be directly proportional to deceleration. A subtraction circuit then subtracts a 4g acceleration value corresponding to accelerations encountered in normal driving. This prevents accidental triggering. The passenger wearing a seat belt will need to be held tightly in place before moving forward and so the onset triggering is set 'earlier' than for the airbag, namely at 15 kph impact against a solid object. The electronic controller consists of two integrated circuits for control and monitoring.

## 9 Electric window winders

**1** Provision is made for windows to be wound up and down by permanent-magnet 12 volt dc motors at all four windows in a four-door car. The main switch panel is within easy reach of the driver and normally consists of four window switches and a rear window isolator switch (Fig. 14.25).

**2** The motors are geared down to supply sufficient torque for winding up; winding down being less demanding. Drives can be linked to the window winding mechanism directly or via a flexible rack. Motors are usually relay operated and require two relays per motor to achieve reverse rotation. Thermal cut-outs are used to prevent overloading if, for example, the drive switch is held on after the window has reached its limit of travel. Modern systems also incorporate an auto wind-back facility, which operates should the window glass encounter an obstruction as it closes (e.g. a child's arm). If the current required to close the window exceeds a pre-set limit before the window reaches the fully closed position, the motor electronics immediately begin to open the window.

## 10 Central locking

**1** Central locking permits the simultaneous locking and unlocking of all doors, boot or tailgate, when the driver's door is locked or unlocked. In some arrangements control may also be via the front passenger's door lock, or by remote control from a button on the ignition key or key fob. In this case, the system is normally integrated with the vehicles security system – see Section 3 of this Chapter. Manual

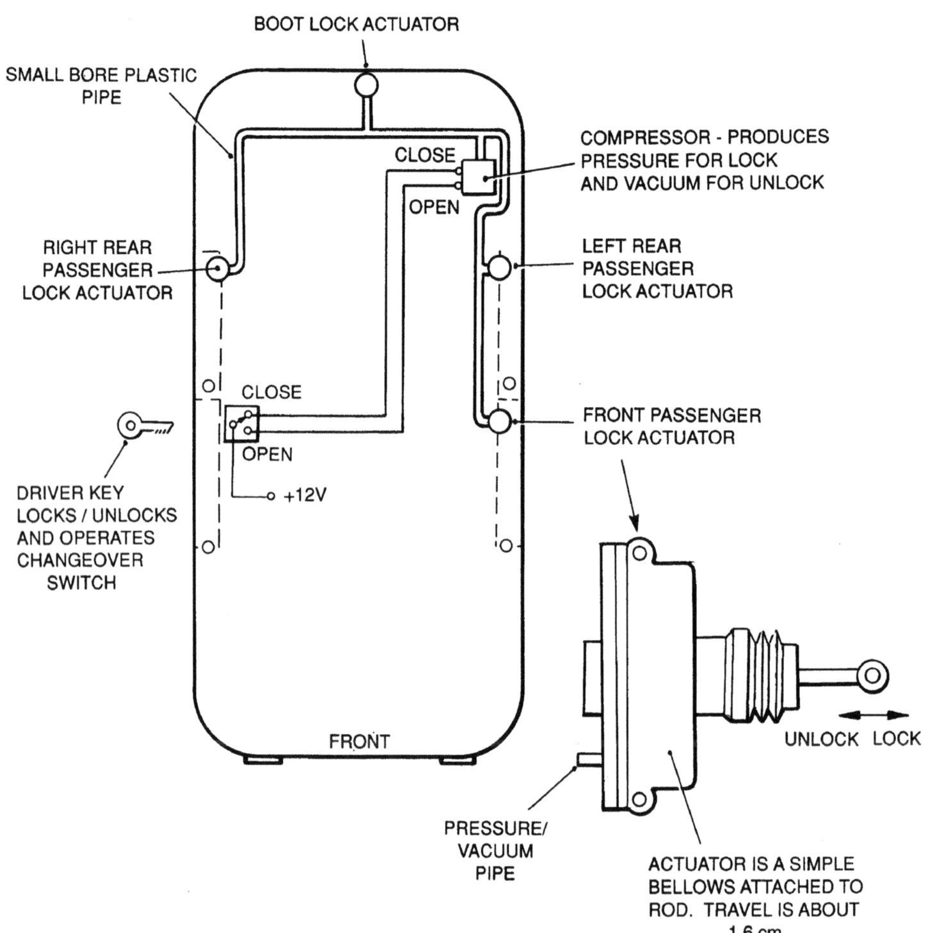


***Fig. 14.26 Electro-pneumatic central locking (simplified)***

operation of door locks from inside the car must over-ride the central locking system for safety considerations.

**2** The majority of manufacturers fit permanent magnet motors for actuating the door locks, but notably Mercedes-Benz, Audi and Volkswagen have used pneumatic linear actuators driven by a pump usually located in the car boot.

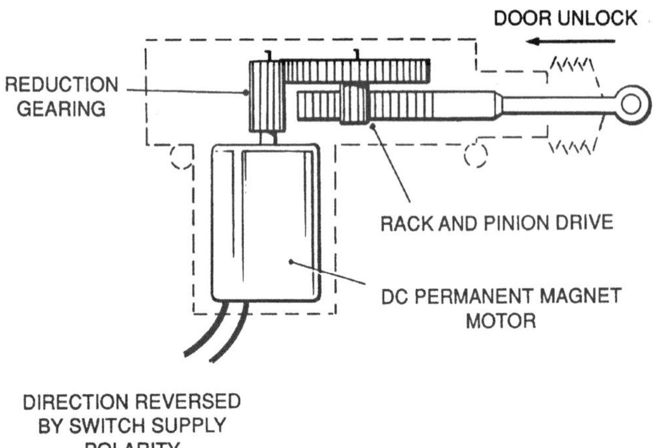


***Fig. 14.27 Door lock actuator***

Both methods have advantages; the electric motor actuator operates quickly (about 2 seconds) while the pneumatic actuator is quiet but takes 6 seconds.

**3** A simple electro-pneumatic circuit is shown in Fig. 14.26. The driver's key opens or closes the lock and also operates a change-over switch. This energises the pump to produce either pressure or suction to operate the door lock. What is missing from this diagram is some means of switching off the pump once door locking is completed. In practice, a timed supply voltage will switch off the 12 volts, and change over contacts for the next instruction; for this a controller is used. The controller may have two different actuation times depending on whether it controls a pneumatic system (long period) or electric motor (short period).

**4** Electric actuators are 12 volt permanent magnet motors which are reversed by changing over the polarity of the supply to the two motor wires. The exception is the Ford door lock motor which rotates always in the same direction, but by means of a crank wheel the motion is first in one direction and then the other. Switching off by a micro switch is carried out at the end of each stroke.

**5** The design of the reversible electric motor is shown in Fig. 14.27. Gearing down gives sufficient torque to actuate

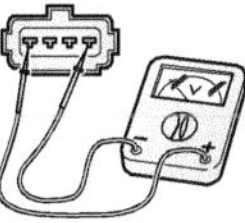

lock mechanisms and linear motion is obtained by use of a plastic rack driven by brass gears. Rods connect the actuator shaft to the locks (Fig. 14.28).

## 11 Parking assistance

**1** When parking a vehicle, it can often be difficult to judge exactly how close the vehicle behind or in front is. In order to assist the driver, many vehicle manufacturers offer a parking distance sensing system as a standard fitment or an optional accessory for the vehicles. It's also possible to purchase and fit several aftermarket systems, designed for DIY fitment.

**2** The systems all work on the well established ultrasound technology, and have several sensors fitted to the rear (and sometimes the front also), of the vehicle. Normally these sensors are recessed into the bumper cover(s). The sensors send and receive ultrasonic waves, which bounce off obstacles. The time delay between sending and receiving the ultrasonic signal is proportional to the distance from the sensor to the obstacle (Fig. 14.29).

**3** The driver is informed of the distance to the obstacle by an audible signal and sometimes a visual display as well. The sound is emitted by a buzzer or loudspeaker. A typical audible signal will increase in frequency as the vehicle approaches the obstacle, and eventually a continuous tone as contact becomes imminent (e.g. within 25 cm). The visual display can take the form of an LED display, normally above

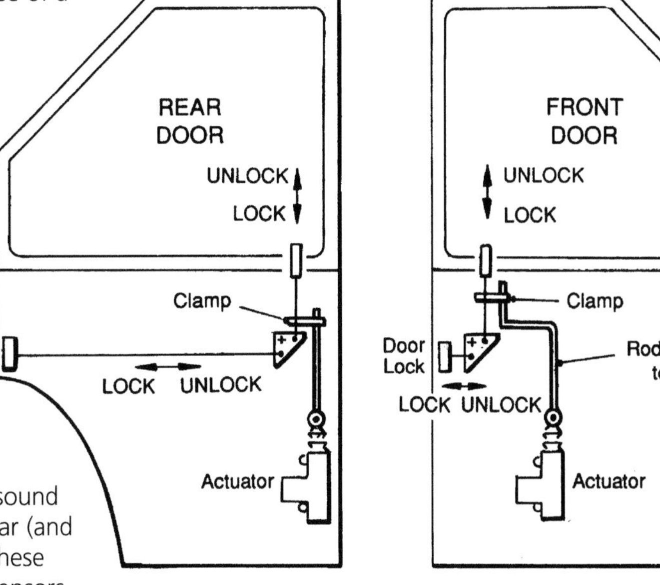


***Fig. 14.28 Actuators attached to door lock linkage***
*Actuator locations shown are typical, other positions are possible*

the rear windscreen, built into the rear view mirror, or an LCD display which indicates the actual distance to the obstacle.

**4** On some vehicles, a miniature camera is located at the rear of the vehicle to show any potential obstacles behind the vehicle. The scene behind is displayed on a screen on the facia, or shown as part of the rear view mirror, and is activated by selecting reverse gear.

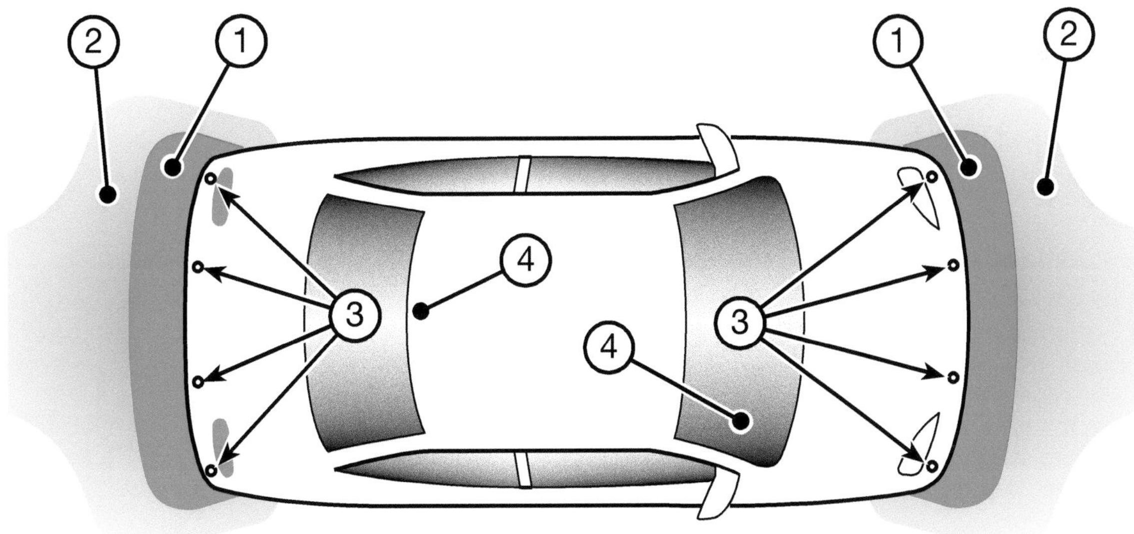


***Fig. 14.29 Parking assistance system***

*1 Continuous signal area* *2 Intermittent signal area* *3 Ultrasonic sensors* *4 Visual warning display units*

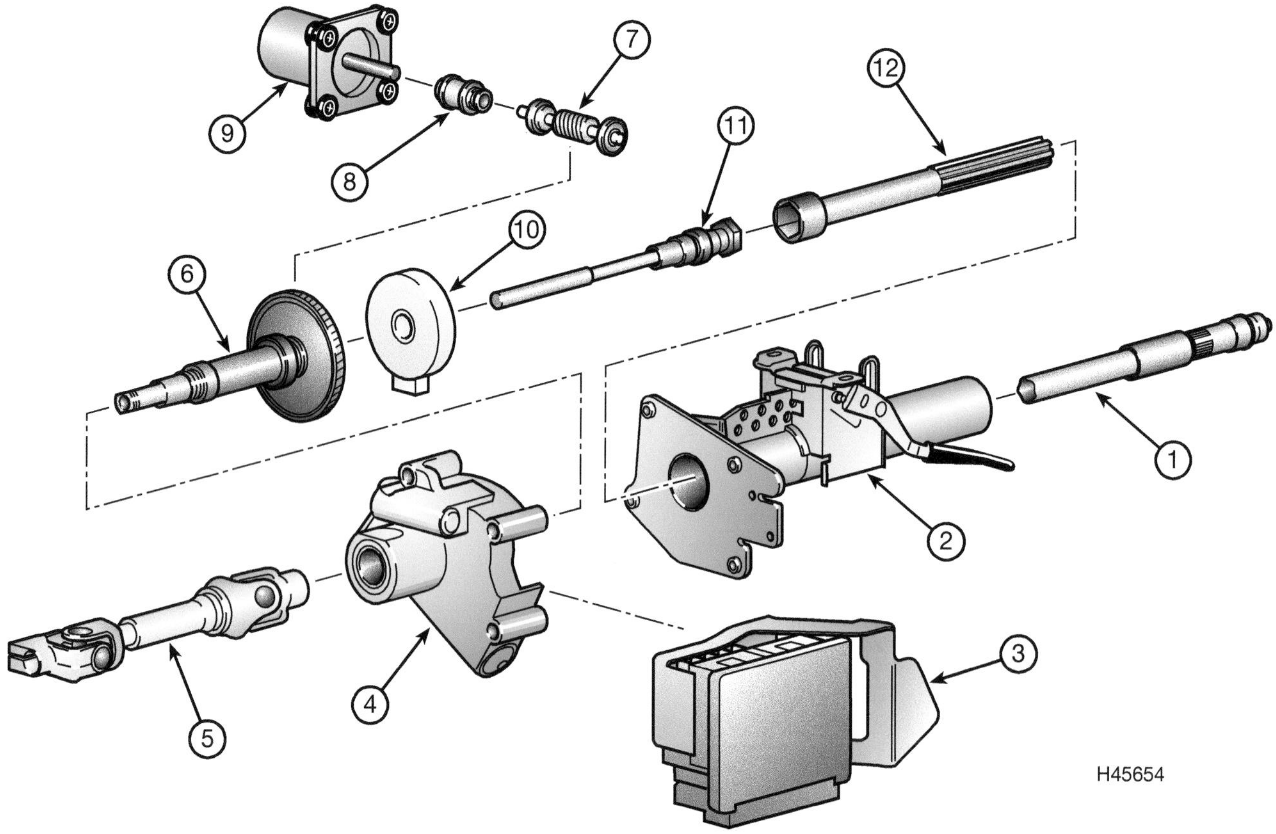

*Fig. 14.30a Electro-mechanical power assisted steering system*

1 Steering column shaft
2 Column tube with height adjustment
3 Electronic control unit (ECU)
4 Steering gear housing
5 Column lower shaft with universal joints
6 Drive gear
7 Worm gear
8 Coupling
9 Electric motor
10 Combined steering angle and moment sensor
11 Torsion bar
12 Intermediate shaft

## 12 Electro-mechanical and Electrically powered hydraulic steering

### Electro-mechanical power assisted steering

**1** In order to decrease fuel consumption, and therefore reduce exhaust emissions, instead of the steering system being assisted by an hydraulic system powered by an engine driven pump, this system employs an electric motor mounted on the column to assist the driver. The amount of power assistance is speed dependent, whilst still giving road-feedback to the driver.

**2** The system consists of a conventional steering wheel attached to a tempered steel torsion bar. The lower end of the torsion bar is attached to the lower section of the column shaft, and the universal joint. However, the torsion bar is designed to twist slightly as the driver applies steering effort. At the upper end of the torsion bar is fitted a combined steering position sensor and a steering moment sensor. The position sensor monitors the steering wheel lock and position of the steering, whilst the moment sensor monitors the rotation angle of the torsion bar in relation to the lower column shaft, ie. the amount of torque applied by the driver (Fig. 14.30a and 14.30b). If the calculated torque

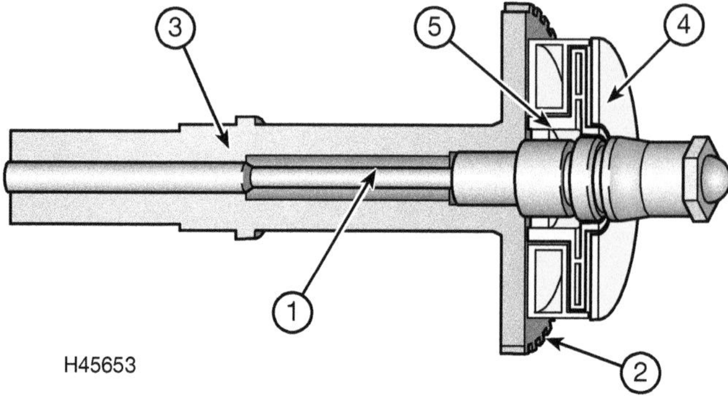


*Fig. 14.30b Combined steering angle and moment sensor*

1 Torsion bar
2 Drive gear
3 Intermediate shaft
4 Steering moment sensor
5 Steering angle sensor

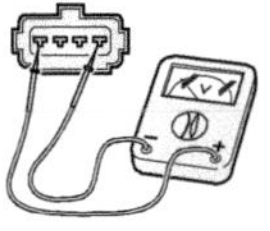

exceeds a value of 0.01 Nm, the control unit assumes steering assistance is required. As the driver continues to turn the steering wheel, the torsion bar twists further. This is signalled to the ECU which commands the electric motor to provide more assistance.

**3** If the driver reduces the amount of torque applied, the twist in the torsion bar is reduced. This is signalled by the moment sensor and the ECU commands the motor to reduce the amount of assistance. Should the driver release the steering wheel whilst cornering, the twist in the torsion bar is relieved, and the motor is turned off. If then vehicle is still not travelling in a straight line (monitored by the steering position sensor), the electric motor is started again and the steering is turned to the straight ahead position.

**4** Actual assistance is provided by an electric motor mounted on the column assembly. A worm gear on the motor shaft meshes with a gear on the column shaft, giving a ratio of approximately 22:1. The motor is mounted on rubber bushes so that no vibration is transmitted to the steering column, and therefore the steering wheel. The motors has a maximum power consumption of approximately 700 W, although unlike conventional power steering, when the vehicle is travelling is a straight line, no power is consumed. The entire assembly is considered to be non-serviceable, and no dismantling should be attempted. The ECU is equipped with a sophisticated self-diagnosis function and can be interrogated via the vehicle's diagnostic connector using a fault code reader.

## Electrically powered hydraulic steering

**5** In a conventional hydraulic power assisted steering system, the hydraulic power is supplied by an engine driven pump. The pump is normally driven by the auxiliary belt from the crankshaft. With this arrangement, the pump is constantly providing hydraulic power, whether it is needed or not. With an electrically powered hydraulic steering (EPHS) system, the power assistance is still provided by pressurised hydraulic oil, but the pump providing that pressure is driven by an electric motor (Fig. 14.31). Assistance is only provided when needed.

**6** The motor is integral with the pump, ECU and fluid reservoir. A power steering sensor is fitted to the pinion housing of the steering rack to monitor the steering angle, and the steering angle rate-of-change. This information is signalled to the ECU, along with the vehicle/engine speed (supplied by the engine management ECU) which then determines how much steering assistance is required. Consequently, when little or no assistance is required (cruising on the motorway), the motor/pump is almost inactive, and when maximum assistance is required (parking),

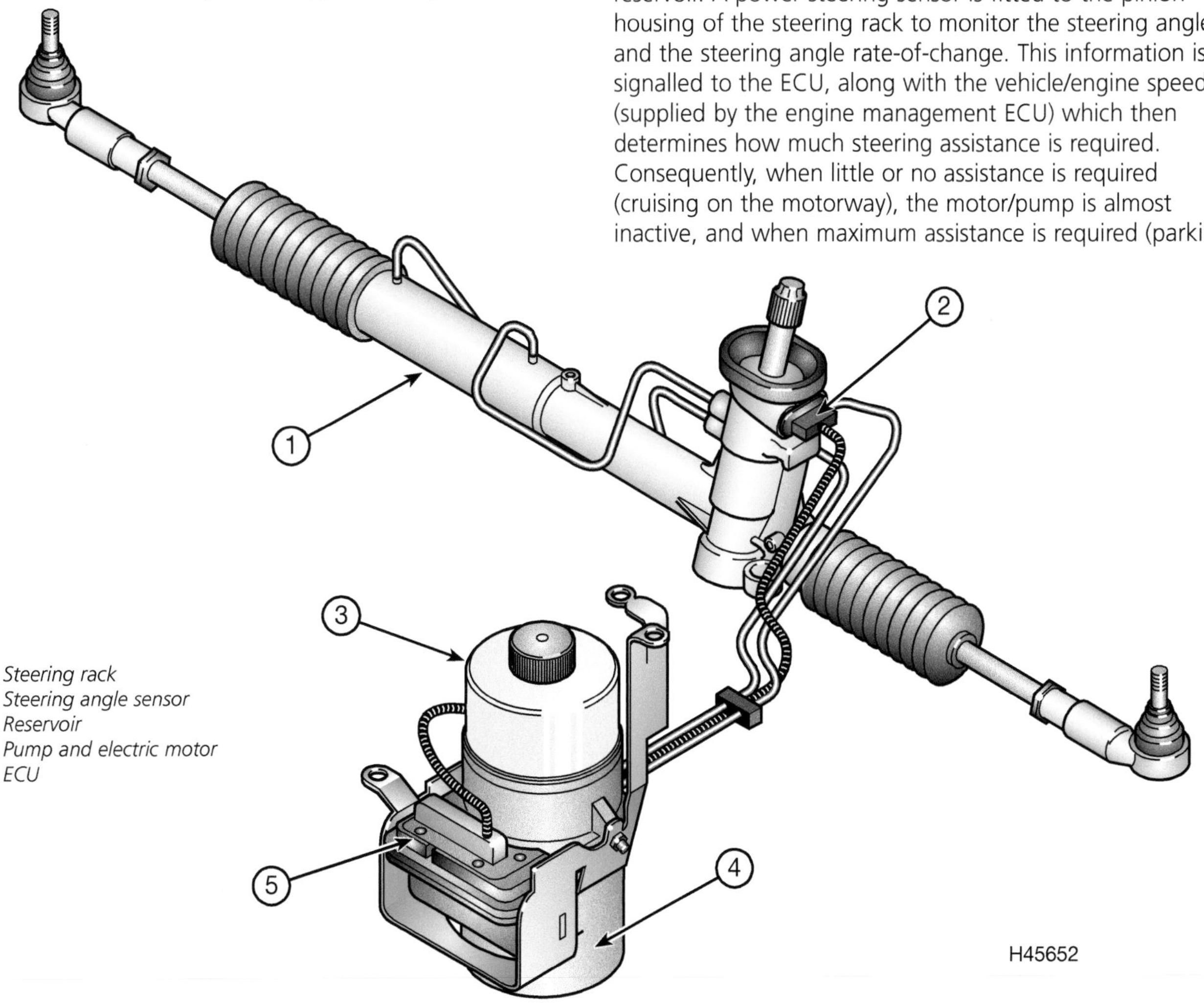

1 *Steering rack*
2 *Steering angle sensor*
3 *Reservoir*
4 *Pump and electric motor*
5 *ECU*

H45652

***Fig. 14.31 EPHS – Electrically powered hydraulic steering***

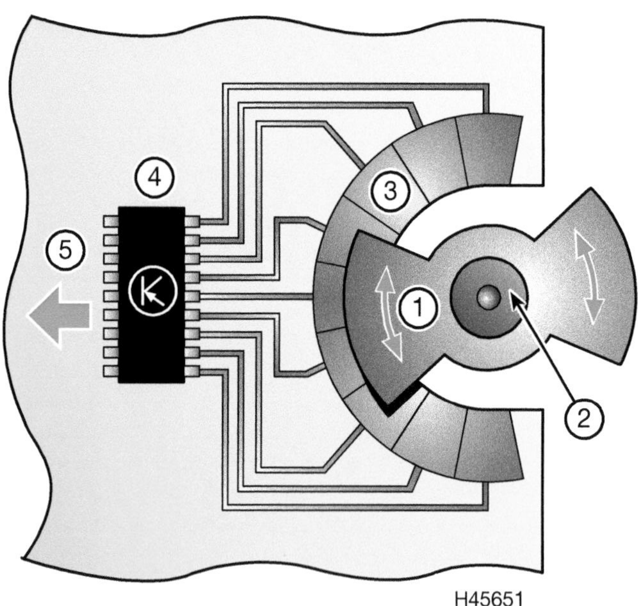


*Fig. 14.32 Steering angle capacitive sensor*

*1 Rotor*
*2 Input shaft*
*3 Capacitor electrodes*
*4 Sensor electronics*
*5 To the ECU*

the pump/motor provide maximum hydraulic pressure. This can result in energy savings of as much as 85% compared to conventional power assisted steering.

**7** Several different designs of sensors are used to monitor the steering angle and rate-of-change, the first example is a capacitive sensor, where a metal rotor is mounted on the steering input shaft and rotates between nine plate-type capacitors (Fig. 14.32). As the rotor moves it distorts the capacitance of the plate-type capacitors, this distortion is signalled to the ECU which calculates the steering angle and rate-of-change.

**8** Another example of steering sensor is the Hall type (Fig. 14.33). A rotor consisting of 60 magnets is mounted on the steering input shaft, and an sensor consisting of a printed circuit board with a semiconductor layer, Hall integrated circuit (IC) and magnetically soft conductor is mounted in a fixed position adjacent to the rotor. As the rotor moves the adjacent south and north pole oriented magnets cause a voltage to rise and fall in the Hall IC of the sensor. As the ECU has a stored value for the straight-ahead position, it can calculate the steering angle by counting the voltage peaks and troughs. To obtain the steering angle rate-of-change, the ECU monitors the frequency of the voltage peaks and troughs.

**9** In order to determine exactly how much power assistance the steering requires, and when, the ECU references a stored map in its memory (Fig. 14.34). The ECU is equipped with a self-diagnosis facility, which can be accessed by a fault code reader via the vehicle's diagnostic connector.

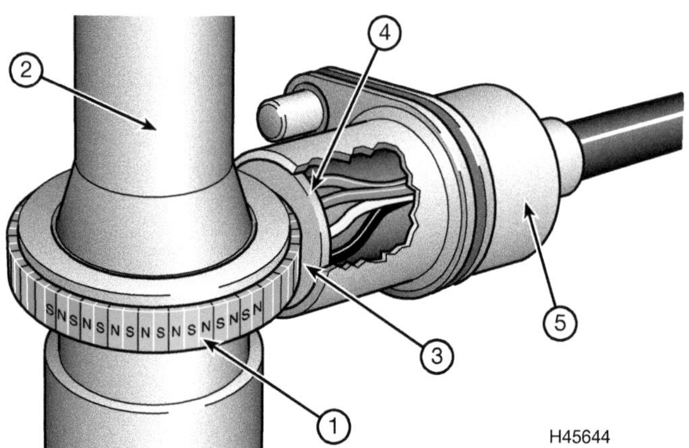


*Fig. 14.33 Steering angle Hall sensor*

*1 Rotor with 60 magnets*
*2 Input shaft*
*3 Air gap*
*4 PCB with semi-conductor, soft conductor and Hall IC*
*5 Sensor housing*

## 13 Electronic Stability Program (ESP)

**1** ESP is a further development of ABS (see Section 1). It's designed to assist the driver in demanding driving situations, to compensate for any over-reaction by the driver, and to prevent the loss of vehicle stability. It does this by slowing the appropriate wheel(s) as the vehicles corners, and in some cases by reducing engine output at the same time. The principle is illustrated in Fig. 14.35a to Fig. 14.35d·

**2** The system utilises the same brake components, solenoid valves, wheel speed sensors, brake pressure sensors as the ABS system, but requires a few more sensors as well. A

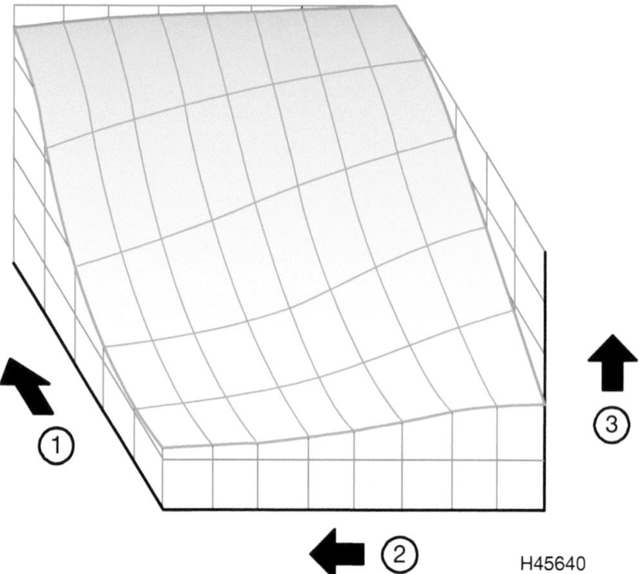


*Fig. 14.34 ECU reference map*
*1 Steering angle rate 2 Vehicle speed 3 Volume flow*

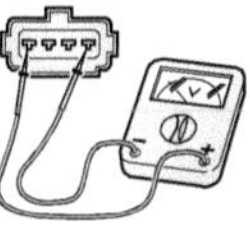

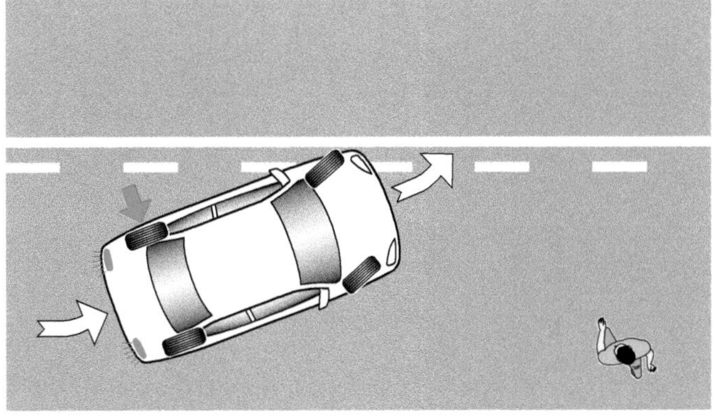


*Fig. 14.35a If the driver attempts to avoid an obstacle in the road and swerves, the ESP system recognises when the vehicle is about to lose stability, and calculates the necessary measures to enhance stability. In this case the system applies brake pressure to the left-rear wheel (arrowed) . . .*

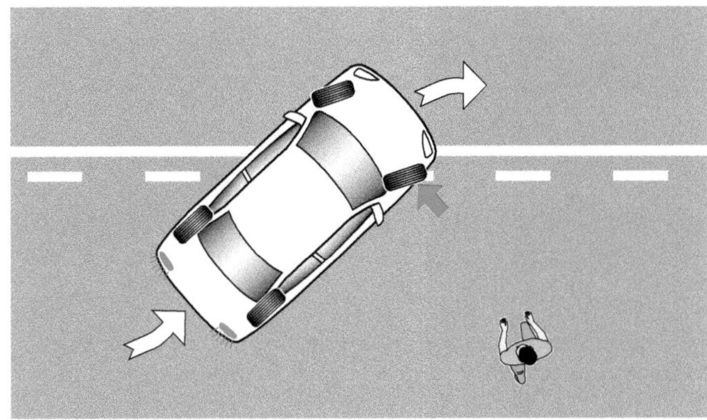


*Fig. 14.35b . . . as the vehicle is now swerving to the left, the drivers steers into the oversteer to the right. The ESP system assists by braking the front-right wheel (arrowed) . . .*

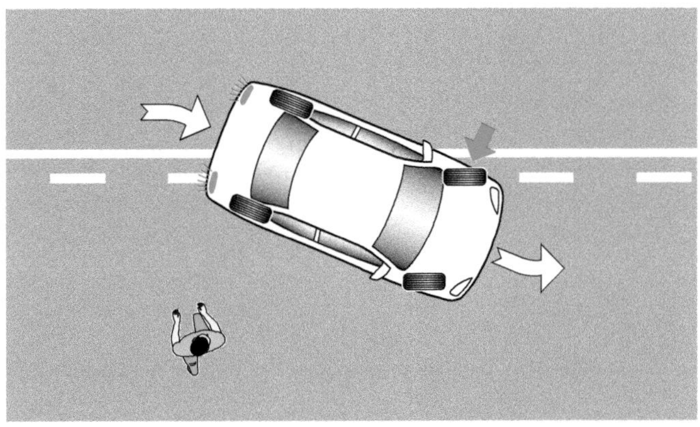


*Fig. 14.35c . . . as the vehicles rotates around a vertical axis, to prevent the rear of the vehicle from breaking away, the front-left wheel (arrowed) is braked . . .*

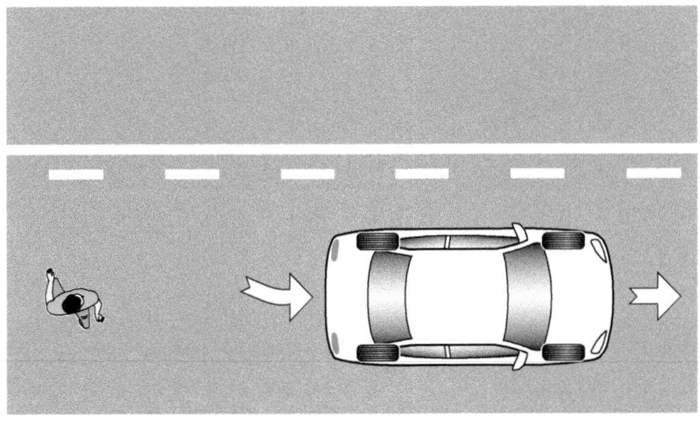


*Fig. 14.35d . . . once the vehicle is back to a stable condition, the ESP resumes inactivity*

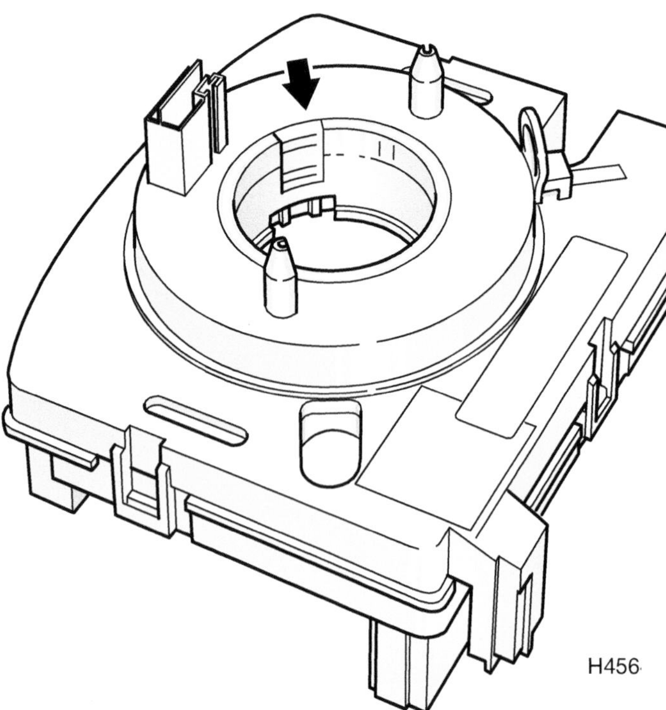


***Fig. 14.36 Steering angle sensor with integral airbag contact assembly (arrowed)***

steering angle sensor (Fig 14.36) is fitted to the steering column between the steering wheel and the column switch gear. Often the airbag contact assembly is integral with the sensor housing.

Other sensors necessary are a Yaw rate sensor, lateral acceleration sensor, and on some vehicles, a longitudinal acceleration sensor. Yaw is the turning force which tries to rotate a vehicle around a vertical axis as it corners. Lateral acceleration is the rate at which the vehicle tries to move sideways as it corners, and longitudinal acceleration is the rate at which the vehicle accelerates forward or backwards.

**3** The steering angle sensor can be an optical device using a light source, an encoding disc, four optical sensors and a full turn counter (Fig. 14.37). The encoding disc comprises of two rings, one with regular incremental holes and one with irregular hole spacing. The two rings pass either side of the light source as the steering angle changes, and the photodiodes are positioned with the rings between them and the light source. As light strikes the photodiodes a voltage is produced. The ESP ECU compares the two voltages outputs from the optical sensors and calculates how far the rings have revolved.

**4** The lateral acceleration sensor must be located as closely as possible to the vehicles centre of gravity to ensure an accurate 'picture' of the lateral forces acting on the vehicle. In simplistic terms, the typical lateral acceleration sensor comprises of a permanent magnet mounted on a flexible, sprung arm, with a Hall sensor rigidity mounted adjacent to it (Fig. 14.38). Any lateral force causes the arm to deflect and the magnet to move in relation to the sensor, which produces a positive or negative voltage in proportion to the magnitude of the force. Often the lateral acceleration sensor is combined in one unit with the Yaw rate sensor.

**5** A typical Yaw rate sensor works on the Coriolis force principle. The Coriolis force is a force which acts upon any moving body in an independently rotating system. The effect is named after the French physicist Gaspard de Coriolis (1792-1843), who first analyzed the phenomenon mathematically. For example, if you fired a cannon ball from

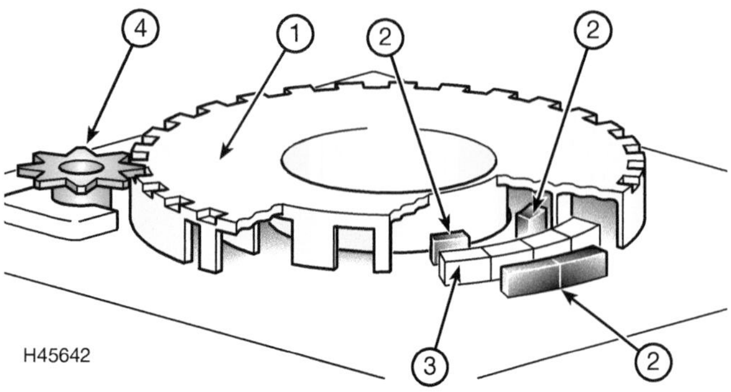

***Fig. 14.37 Inside the a typical steering angle sensor***

*1 Encoding Disc*
*2 Optical sensors (photodiodes)*
*3 Light source*
*4 Full revolution counter*

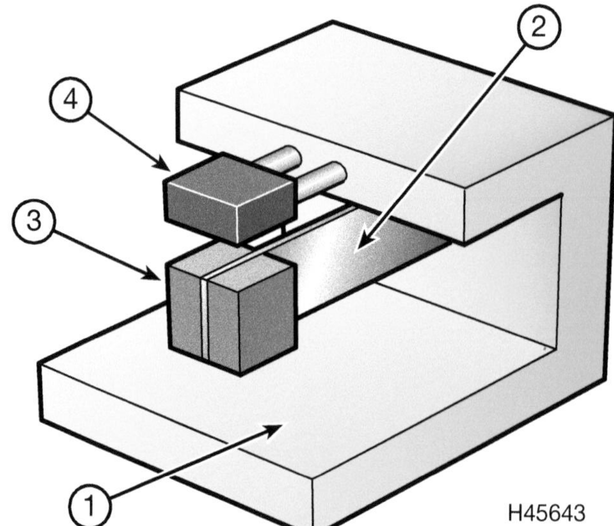


***Fig. 14.38 Simplified diagram of a typical lateral acceleration sensor***

*1 Frame*
*2 Sprung arm*
*3 Permanent magnet*
*4 Hall sensor*

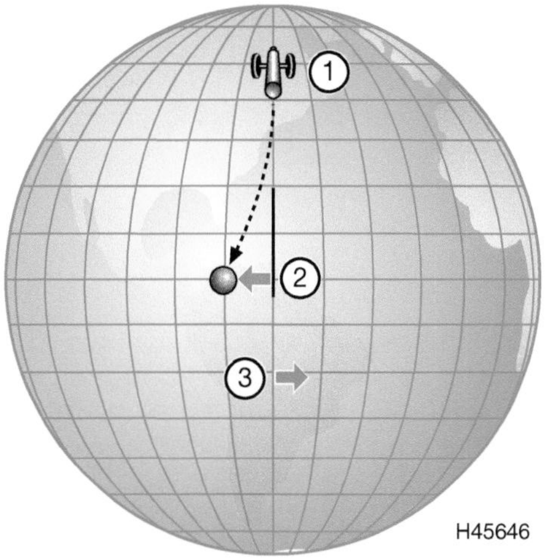

**Fig 14.39 Coriolis force principle**

1 Cannon
2 Coriolis force
3 Direction of earth rotation

the northern hemisphere directly along the earths lines of longitude, to an observer rotating with the earth, the ball would not appear to travel in a straight line – the ball would accelerate against the earth's rotation (Fig. 14.39).

Using this principle, in our typical sensor a magnetic field with north an south poles are mounted either side of a mass with a printed circuit board attached, mounted in a frame (Fig. 14.40). When an AC voltage is applied to the conductors on the PCB, the mass oscillates. When an angular force is applied (Yaw), the mass no longer oscillates in a straight line (compared to the frame and magnets) due to its inertia (Coriolis force). Because this change happens in an magnetic field, the electrical behaviour of the conductors on the PCB changes. This change is measured by the sensors evaluation electronics, which sends a signal to the ESP ECU in proportion to the Yaw rate.

The above sensors are by no means the only designs of sensors used, but generally speaking the principles explained apply to the majority.

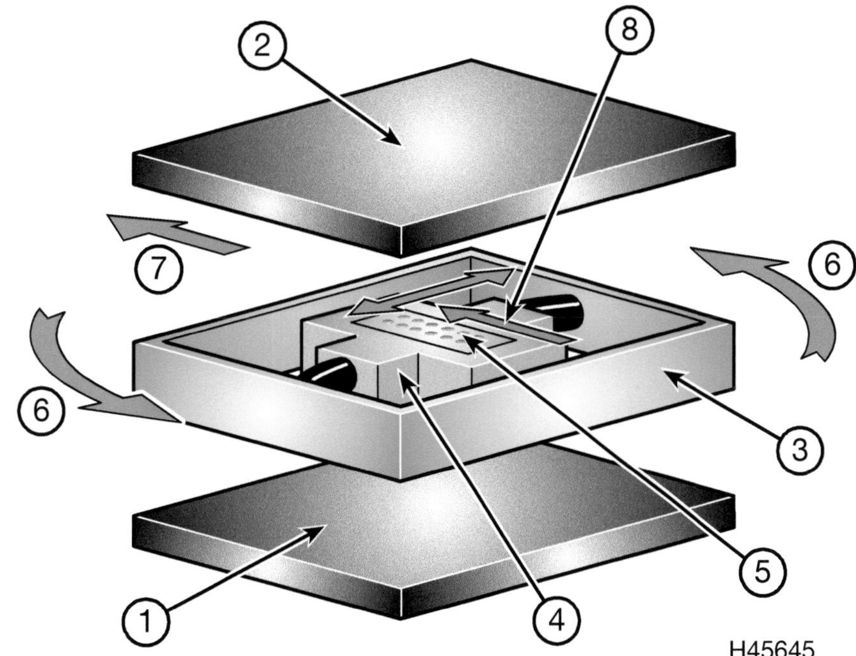


1 South pole
2 North pole
3 Frame
4 Vibrating mass
5 PCB
6 Yaw rate and direction
7 Direction of travel
8 Coriolis force

**Fig. 14.40 A typical Yaw rate sensor using Coriolis force**

# Notes

# Troubleshooting 15



## 1 Introduction to test equipment

The goal of any electrical diagnosis is to determine where the fault which prevents the current from flowing through the circuit as originally designed is located.

As manufacturers load up modern vehicles with electrical devices, the potential for problems increases dramatically. Due to the complexity of these electrical systems and the high cost of many replacement parts, a hit-and-miss approach to troubleshooting is unsatisfactory. An organized and logical approach to diagnosis is essential to repair these electrical circuits in a prompt and cost-effective manner.

Since electricity is invisible, specialized test equipment is necessary to trace circuits and check components. An accurate method of measuring electrical flow is essential if the problem is to be found without unnecessary parts replacement and wasted time.

### Jump wires

Jump wires are mainly used to find open circuits (no continuity) and excessive resistance by bypassing a portion of an existing circuit. They can also be used for testing components off the vehicle. They may be purchased already assembled, or home-made.

Jump wires may be equipped with various types of

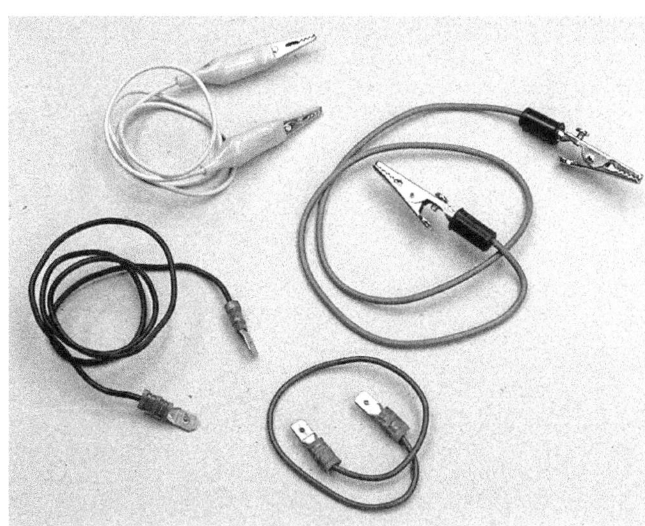

*Fig. 15.1 Jump wires*

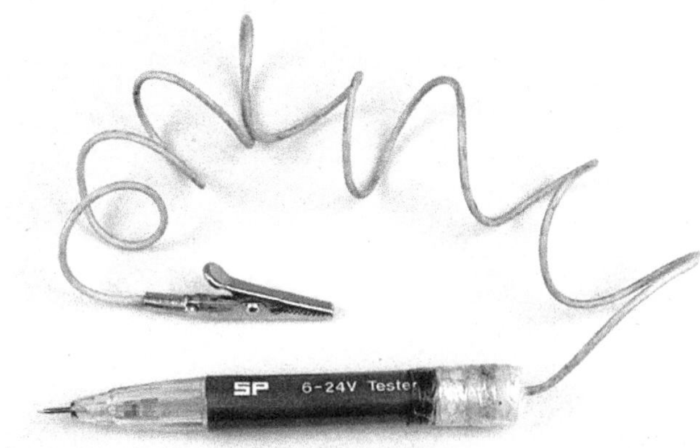


*Fig. 15.2 A typical test light*

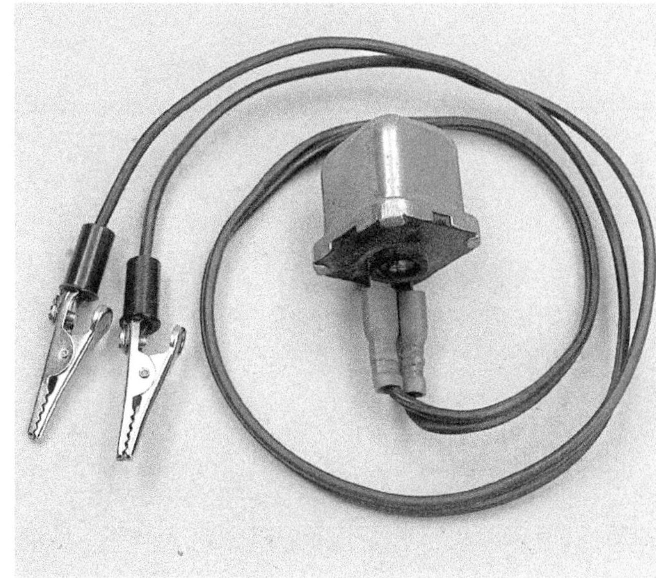

*Fig. 15.3 A typical test buzzer*

terminals for different uses. Those used to carry current from the battery to a component should have an in-line fuse installed to avoid an overload, and should also have insulated boots over the terminals to prevent accidental earthing.

***Warning: Never use jump wires made of cable that is thinner (of lighter gauge) than the wiring in the circuit you are testing. Always use a fuse with the same (or lower) rating as the circuit had originally.***

## Test lights

Test lights are used to check for voltage in a circuit while power is connected to the circuit. Test lights are among the least expensive testing devices available and should be included in every tool box. They may be purchased already assembled, or made at home.

Test lights come in several styles, but all have three parts in common; a light bulb, a test probe and a wire with an earth connector. Six, 12, or 24 volt systems may be tested by changing the bulb to the appropriate voltage.

Although accurate voltage measurements aren't possible with a test light, large differences may be detected by the relative brightness of the glowing bulb.

**Note:** *Before using a test light for diagnosis, check it by connecting it to the battery to check the bulb lights brightly.*

## Test buzzers

Test buzzers work the same way as test lights; however, they offer the advantage of remote operation. For example, one person working alone may test the brake light circuit by stepping on the brake pedal and listening for the sound of the buzzer connected to the brake light bulb socket.

A test buzzer may be fabricated at home with jump wires and a buzzer.

Test buzzers are used in the same manner described for test lights. Additionally, they may be used to find shorts to earth.

## Continuity testers

Continuity testers (also known as self-powered test lights) are used to check for open or short circuits. They consist of a light bulb, battery pack and two wires combined into one unit.

Continuity testers must only be used on non-powered circuits; vehicle battery voltage would burn out the low-voltage tester bulb.

***Caution: Never use a self-powered continuity tester on circuits that contain solid state electronic components, since damage to these components may occur.***

## Test meters

Refer to Chapter 13.

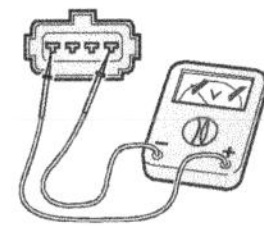

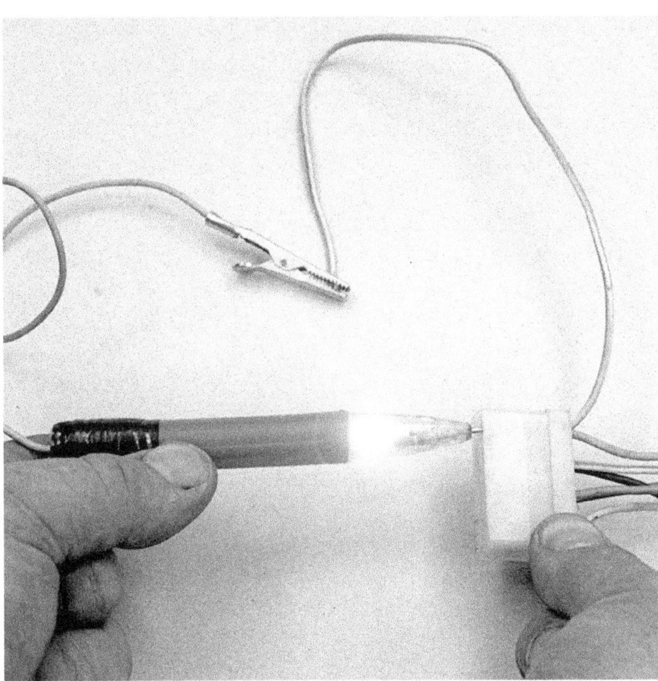

***Fig. 15.4 A continuity tester being used to check a wire and connector plug***

## 2 Troubleshooting strategies

Before you begin troubleshooting a circuit, it is imperative that you formulate a plan of action. Check for simple problems first, such as blown fuses, corroded or loose connections, burned out bulbs or broken, frayed, chafed or burned wires – these are also the most common problems.

Operate the problem circuit in all modes. Determine what components, if any, in the circuit still work. Is it a complete or partial failure? What other circuits are affected? When does it occur? Is the problem intermittent or does it happen all the time?

Be sure to check the operation of all other electrical components on the vehicle. Sometimes what seems to be a problem affecting only one component is also causing (or being caused by) a problem in another circuit. If necessary, make notes of all the affected components and the specific symptoms.

This will help you figure out the problem after you've looked at the wiring diagrams and had a chance to think about it. Think carefully about all the electrical components which have been disturbed or worked on recently. These are prime suspects.

Check that the circuit you are working on is not part of a network (obtain a wiring diagram). Network problems must be investigated with a fault code reader first.

### Problems affecting a single component

If a single component of a circuit is affected, start to test at that component and work back towards the fuse. Use a logical process of elimination to narrow down the problem. For example, if you find that only one light is inoperative, you have eliminated the fuse, switch and main wiring harness as potential sources of the problem.

Here are four conditions that cause single component failures and how to check for them:

**The component is not receiving current**. With the circuit switched on, test for voltage at the component. If there's no voltage, continue to test for voltage in the circuit, working backward towards the fuse. When you reach a point where there is voltage, you know the problem lies between that point and your last test point.

**The component is not earthed properly**. This condition can be tested two ways:

1 *With power to the component, you can test for a voltage drop between the component and earth. The drop should be less than 0.2 to 0.3 volt.*

2 *With power removed from the component, you can check for resistance between the component and earth. The reading should be zero (or very close to zero) ohms.*

**The component itself is faulty**. For components designed to operate on full battery voltage, check the operation using a fused jump wire, as described below. For components that operate on less than battery voltage, measure the resistance or check for a voltage drop.

**The wiring is faulty**. This can be checked two ways:

1 *With no power to the circuit, check continuity.*

2 *With power to the circuit, check for a voltage drop in the wiring.*

### Problems affecting multiple components

If the fault affects multiple components, start to test at the point where the circuit gets its power (usually the fuse board or fusible link). Check the fuses, circuit breakers and/or fusible links. If the circuit protection devices are blown, look for a short circuit; if they are intact, look for an open circuit (no continuity) or wires from different circuits contacting each other.

Obtain the wiring diagrams for the specific vehicle you are working on whenever possible.

Read about the various types of circuits and learn how to tell which type you are working on.

Familiarize yourself with the current flow in the circuit by tracing the path in the wiring diagram (see Chapter 13). Determine where the circuit receives current, what the circuit protection is, what switches and/or relays control current flow and how the components operate.

Identify each component in the wiring diagram for the circuit you are testing and find the components on the vehicle.

Sometimes, multiple components can be affected by two wires from different circuits contacting each other. Take, for example, two simple circuits, each having one light bulb and a switch. If the wires between each switch and each bulb come into contact with each other, closing either one of the switches will light both bulbs, but one or both bulbs will light more dimly than normal. Closing the other switch will alter the relative brightness of the two bulbs.

In complicated circuits, there may be many symptoms affecting several components, all related to such a problem.

### Intermittent problems

The most difficult type of electrical problem to diagnose is an intermittent one. Intermittent opens or shorts are usually caused by something rubbing or a component that changes resistance when it heats up or cools down. Corroded and loose connections are also frequently the cause of such problems.

Note when the problem occurs and try to discover how to duplicate the problem during diagnosis. For example, if it only happens when you're going around a corner or over a rough level crossing, wiggling the wiring harness may duplicate the problem.

If it only happens after the engine is completely warmed up, heating the suspected faulty parts with an electric hair dryer may duplicate the problem. If the problem only occurs during wet weather conditions, a water misting bottle may help you duplicate the problem.

Once you can duplicate the problem, follow the test procedures applicable, based on the symptoms.

## 3 Using test equipment

Before you can go chasing electrical gremlins, you have to know how to use test equipment. In this Section we will explain how to use the various testers introduced previously.

**Note:** *Most testers come with instructions. If they differ from the general procedures described here, follow the specific instructions provided by the manufacturer of the tester.*

***Caution: Never connect solid state circuits to battery voltage and never test them with any device other than a digital multimeter.***

### Checking for a bad earth

Connect the jump wire between the component case (or earth terminal) and a clean bare metal spot on the vehicle chassis. If a circuit works properly with the jump wire in place, but doesn't work when the jump wire is removed, the earth circuit has an open (or high resistance) which needs repair – check for loose connections, corrosion, and a broken component earth strap.

### Checking a component which operates on battery voltage

Earth the component with a jump wire as described above and connect a fused jump wire from the positive battery terminal to the positive terminal on the component being tested. If it now works normally, remove the earth jump wire. If the device stops working, the earth connection is definitely faulty, but the other side of the circuit may also be bad.

If the device continues working with the earth jump wire removed, look for an open in the positive side of the circuit. If the device won't work, even with both jump wires in place, the component is faulty.

### Checking for voltage

To use a test light (or buzzer), connect the tester's earth wire to a clean, bare metal earth which is connected to the vehicle chassis. With the circuit switched on, insert the probe into the terminal or socket to be checked. If necessary, the probe can be pushed through the insulation to make contact with the wire. If the bulb lights, voltage is present, meaning the part of the circuit between the test light and the battery is okay.

After testing is complete, tape over any wires punctured by the probe. Test lights are not sensitive to polarity and can be connected with the probe and the earth wire connected to positive or negative.

To use a test meter, set the voltmeter scale selector switch to the appropriate range (this normally should be higher than battery voltage) and check to see if the test leads are connected to the correct terminals on the tester. The negative lead is black and the positive lead is red.

When measuring the voltage in a portion of a circuit, the voltmeter must be connected in parallel with the portion of the circuit to be measured. To avoid damage to the meter, always connect the negative lead to the negative side of the circuit and connect the positive lead to the positive side of the circuit.

### Checking for continuity

Continuity may be checked with a number of devices. If the circuit has power to it, a voltmeter, test light or test buzzer may be used as described above. If the circuit is not powered, an ohmmeter or self-powered continuity tester should be used.

***Caution: Do not attempt to use a self-powered continuity tester or ohmmeter on a powered circuit. The test device will be damaged.***

To use a continuity tester, first isolate the circuit by disconnecting the battery or removing the fuse or circuit breaker. Select two points along the circuit through which there should be continuity. Connect one lead of the tester to each point. If there is continuity, the tester will light.

**Note:** *The procedure for checking continuity with an ohmmeter is similar to the procedure using a continuity tester. If there is continuity, the ohmmeter will read close to zero ohms (no or very low resistance).*

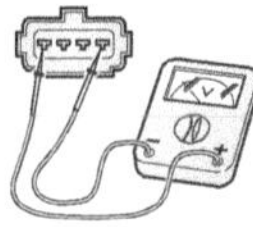



## Checking resistance

Resistance is checked with an ohmmeter. Turn the scale selector switch to the proper ohms range for the device you will be measuring. Make sure the wires are connected to the proper plugs on the meter and turn the meter on.

Check that the meter reads 'infinity' before testing is begun, then touch the test probes together to ensure the meter goes to zero. Connect one test lead to the positive terminal of the device being tested and connect the other lead to the negative terminal or housing.

After testing, switch the ohmmeter off to conserve the batteries.

## Tracing short circuits

Shorts to earth are most easily found with a test buzzer. If you discover the short is not at a component (meaning it is somewhere in the wiring harness), inspect the exposed portions of the wiring harness for obvious evidence of a short (burned wire insulation, chafing, etc).

**Note:** *A test light or voltmeter may be substituted for the buzzer. However, an assistant will be needed to watch the light or meter while you disconnect components and wiggle the wiring harness.*

**1** Remove the blown fuse, leaving the battery connected.

**2** Attach the crocodile clips of the test buzzer to the fuse terminals.

**3** Turn on all the switches that are in the circuit you are troubleshooting.

**4** If the circuit is still shorted to earth, the buzzer will sound.

**5** Working your way backwards, disconnect each terminal in the circuit until the buzzer stops sounding. Also wiggle the wiring harness from side-to-side in areas where it's exposed.

**6** When the buzzer stops, carefully check the portion of the circuit you just disconnected (or the part of the wiring harness you were wiggling) for a short. If disconnecting a switch, relay or harness connector caused the buzzer to stop sounding, the short is either there or somewhere between there and the component.

**7** Repair or replace components or wiring as needed.

## Checking voltage drop

This test checks for voltage being lost along a wire, or through a connection or switch while current is flowing (also see Chapter 9, Section 12).

**Note:** *When no current is flowing, there can be no voltage drop.*

**1** Connect the positive lead of a voltmeter to the end of the wire (or to the side of the connection or switch) which is closer to the battery.

**2** Connect the negative lead of the voltmeter to the other end of the wire (or the other side of the connection or switch).

**3** Select the voltmeter range just above battery voltage.

**4** Switch on the circuit.

**5** The voltmeter will show the difference in voltage between the two points. A difference (or drop) of more than about 0.2 to 0.3 volt indicates a problem (except when the voltmeter is connected across a load, in which case a substantial voltage drop is normal).

**6** Clean and repair the connections as needed or replace any faulty components.

## Checking current flow

**Note:** *Ammeters are always connected in series with the circuit being tested (except units with inductive pickups).*

**1** To connect an ammeter into a circuit, unplug a fuse or connector and attach the test leads to the exposed terminals. Remember, the ammeter must always be hooked up in series with the circuit.

**2** Switch on the circuit and read the amperage shown on the meter. If it shows a negative reading, reverse the test lead connections. No reading at all indicates an open (incomplete) circuit.

**3** The reading should be less than (but not substantially less than) the circuit's fuse rating. If the reading is substantially less than the fuse rating, there's excessive resistance somewhere in the circuit. If the reading is higher than the fuse rating, there's a short to earth.

## Checking for battery drain

This test will indicate whether there's a constant drain in the vehicle's electrical system that can cause the battery to discharge.

**1** Make sure no accessories are turned on. If the vehicle has an underbonnet light, verify it's working properly, then disconnect it.

**2** Detach the cable from the battery earth terminal and attach one lead of a test light to the cable end. Touch the other lead to the battery earth terminal. The test light should not glow.

**3** If the light glows, it indicates a constant drain which could cause a discharged battery.

**Note:** *On vehicles equipped with components which normally cause an ignition-off battery drain, it's normal for the test light to glow dimly. If you suspect the drain is excessive, hook up an ammeter in place of the test light. The reading should not exceed 0.5 amps.*

**4** The prime suspects for current drain problems are lights (underbonnet, glove box, boot, etc) that don't shut off properly. If the drain isn't caused by a light, remove the fuses one at a time until the cause of the drain is located. When you pull the fuse for the circuit that is draining the battery, the test light will go out.

**5** If the drain is still undetermined, the problem is likely a shorted starter solenoid or a short in the wiring to the solenoid. Inspect the wiring and connections. If no short is found, disconnect the wires from the solenoid until the light goes out.

### Testing relays

**Note:** *Chapter 1, Section 15 covers the general operating principles of relays and the terminology of their parts. The information that follows does not apply to polarity-reversing relays, which are used in some power accessory circuits.*

**Note:** *Some circuits on some newer vehicles use solid-state (electronic) relays. This procedure applies only to electro-mechanical (non-electronic) relays. Electronic relays must be tested by a dealer or auto-electrician.*

**1** We recommend using the correct wiring diagram for your vehicle to determine the proper hook-ups for the relay you're testing. However, if wiring diagrams are not available, you may be able to determine the test hook-ups from the information that follows.

**2** On most relays with four terminals, two of the four terminals are for the relay's control circuit (they connect to the relay's coil). The other two are for the relay's power circuit (they connect to the armature contact and the fixed contact).

**3** If you have wiring diagrams for the vehicle, you can figure out which terminals hook up to which parts of the relay (see Chapter 13 for information on wiring diagrams). Often, relay terminals are marked as an aid.

**4** As a general rule, the two thicker gauge wires connected to the relay are for the power circuit; the two thinner gauge wires are for the control circuit.

**5** Remove the relay from the vehicle and check for continuity between the relay's power circuit terminals. There should be no continuity.

**6** Connect a fused jump wire between one of the two control circuit terminals and the positive battery terminal. Connect another jump wire between the other control circuit terminal and earth. When the connections are made, the relay should click. On some relays, polarity may be critical, so, if the relay doesn't click, try swapping the jump wires on the control circuit terminals.

**7** With the jump wires connected, check for continuity between the power circuit terminals. Now there should be continuity.

**8** If the relay fails any of the above tests, replace it.

**9** If the relay has three terminals, it's a good idea to check the vehicle's wiring diagram to determine which terminals connect to which of the relay's components. Most three-terminal relays are either case earthed or externally-earthed.

**10** On a case-earthed relay, one side of the relay's control circuit earths through the relay case, eliminating the need for the fourth terminal. This type of relay requires the case to be securely connected to a good chassis earth. Check this type of relay the same way you would a four-terminal relay, noting that one of the control circuit's terminals is actually the relay case.

**11** On an externally-earthed relay, one of the relay's terminals is connected to a positive power source. We'll call this the battery power terminal. Inside the relay, the battery power terminal is connected to one side of both the relay's power and control circuits. Another terminal is connected to the other side of the control circuit; the circuit is completed through a switch to earth. The third terminal is connected to the other side of the power circuit; it's earthed at the component controlled by the relay. This type of three-terminal relay is sometimes a plug-in type with no connection between the case and earth.

**12** To check an externally-earthed relay, remove it from the vehicle and check for continuity between the relay's battery power terminal and its power circuit terminal. There should be no continuity.

**13** Hook up a fused jump wire between the battery power terminal and the positive battery terminal. Connect another jump wire between the relay's control circuit terminal and earth. The relay should click.

**14** With the jump wires in place, connect a test light between the relay's power circuit terminal and earth. The test light should light. If the relay fails any of these tests, replace it.

## 4 Starter motors

Most of the time, starting system problems aren't caused by the starter motor. They're caused by malfunctions elsewhere in the starting system, such as a discharged or defective battery, a bad battery cable connection or a weak or non-functional starter solenoid.

Refer to Chapter 4, Section 14, for basic troubleshooting. Listed below are additional procedures to help you identify the cause(s).

### The starter rotates, but the engine doesn't

**1** Remove the starter, check the overrunning clutch and bench test the starter to make sure the drive mechanism extends fully for proper engagement with the flywheel ring gear. If it doesn't, disassemble the starter to locate the problem.

**2** Check the flywheel ring gear for bent areas, missing teeth and other damage. With the ignition turned off, rotate the flywheel so you can check the entire ring gear.

### The starter is noisy

**1** If the solenoid is making a chattering noise, first check the battery (see Chapter 5). If the battery's OK, check the cables and connections and perform the voltage drop and current draw tests described below. If you have not located the problem, check the solenoid (see the procedure below).

**2** If you hear a grinding, crashing metallic sound when you turn the key to Start, check for loose starter mounting bolts. If they're tight, remove the starter and inspect the teeth on the starter pinion gear and flywheel ring gear. Look for missing or damaged teeth.

**3** If the starter sounds fine when you first turn the key to

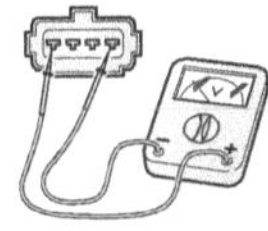

Start, but then stops rotating the engine and emits a zinging sound, the problem is probably a defective starter drive that's not staying engaged with the ring gear. Replace or overhaul the starter.

**4** If the starter makes a high-pitched whine or clanging sound while it's rotating the engine, the clearance between the pinion gear and flywheel ring gear is probably incorrect. To check it:

(a) *Disconnect the battery earth terminal, then remove the flywheel cover and pull the starter drive out to mesh it with the ring gear.*

(b) *Check the clearance between the gears. Generally, the pinion teeth should engage the flywheel teeth about 3/4 of the way down from the top of each tooth. Check the clearance at several locations around the circumference of the flywheel. This will help you identify if the flywheel is bent or has runout.*

**5** If the starter makes a high-pitched whine after the engine starts, as the key is being released, the return spring in the starter is weak or the pinion gear-to-ring gear clearance is too small. Check the clearance as described above. If it's OK, replace the return spring.

## The starter rotates slowly

**1** Check the battery (see Chapter 5).

**2** If the battery is okay, verify all connections (at the battery, the starter solenoid and motor) are clean, corrosion-free and tight. Make sure the cables aren't frayed or damaged.

**3** Check to see if the battery cables are the same gauge as original equipment. Many inexpensive aftermarket cables use a smaller gauge wire encased in thick insulation. They look as big in diameter as the original equipment cable, but their smaller diameter wire can't handle the amperage load. During the summer, when cranking loads are lighter, these cables may work OK. But when winter arrives, they often can't carry enough current and the starter rotates slowly. If you doubt any of the cables, check for a voltage drop (see the procedure below).

**4** Check the voltage drops at the battery terminals, starter solenoid and starter connections (see the procedure below).

**5** Check that the starter is bolted securely to the engine so it earths properly. Also check the pinion gear and flywheel ring gear for evidence of a mechanical bind (deformed gear teeth or other damage).

**6** Check for a short to earth.

**7** Perform a current draw test (see below).

**8** If the current draw is excessive, and there are no excessive voltage drops in the starter circuit, either the starter is defective or there is a mechanical bind in the engine. With the ignition turned to off, rotate the engine through two revolutions by hand. If it rotates smoothly and easily, replace the starter.

## The starter does not rotate at all

**1** Turn on the headlights and turn the key to Start. Have an assistant observe the headlights. If the headlights do not dim when you turn the key, check for an open in the starting system, as described below. If the headlights dim, continue with this procedure.

**2** Perform tests 1 to 8 for The starter rotates slowly.

## Testing for an open in the starter circuit

***Warning: The starter may operate during the following tests, so make sure the vehicle is not in gear and stay away from components that move during engine operation.***

**Note:** *The battery must be in good condition and fully charged for the following tests.*

**1** Check the starter solenoid (see below).

**2** If the solenoid check reveals no voltage at the control circuit wire, check the neutral start switch, if fitted (see below). If the switch tests OK, the open is in the ignition switch or in the wiring between the fuse and the control circuit terminal on the solenoid.

**3** If the solenoid check reveals the solenoid is operating normally, have an assistant hold the ignition key in the Start position. Check for voltage along the cable running to the starter, beginning at the battery. When you reach a point where you find no voltage, the open lies between that point and your last test point.

## Checking for voltage drops

***Warning: The starter may operate during the following test, so make sure the vehicle is not in gear and stay away from components that move during engine operation.***

**Note:** *Section 3 contains additional information on checking for voltage drops.*

**1** In the starting system, the most common places for voltage drops to occur are at the cable connections at the battery, solenoid and starter, and along the cables.

**2** Disable the ignition system. On most vehicles, you can simply pull the coil high tension lead from the distributor cap and connect a jump wire between the terminal on the end of the wire and earth.

**3** Have an assistant turn the key to Start while you check for a drop at each of these locations. There should be no more than a 0.1 volt drop at any connection or along any one-foot length of cable. There should be no more than a 0.5 volt drop between the battery and the starter.

## Testing the starter solenoid

***Warning: The starter may operate during the following tests, so make sure the vehicle is not in gear and stay away from components that move during engine operation.***

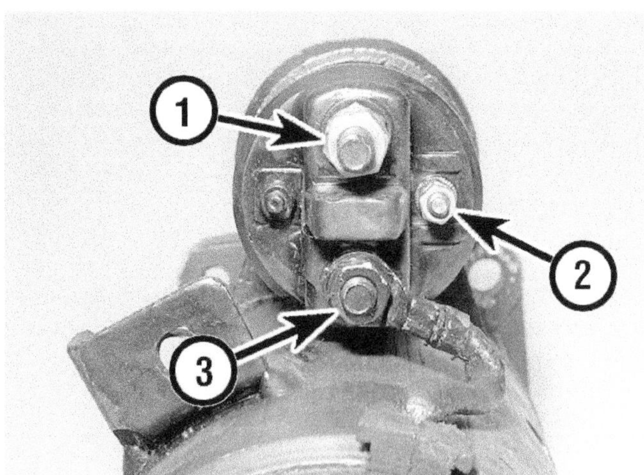


*Fig. 15.5 The terminals on a typical on-starter solenoid*
1 *Battery cable terminal*
2 *Control circuit terminal*
3 *Starter motor connection*

*Fig. 15.6 The terminals on a typical remote-mounted starter solenoid*
1 *Cable connection (battery side)*
2 *Cable connection (starter side)*
3 *Control circuit terminal*
4 *Ignition bypass terminal*

**Note:** *The battery must be fully charged and in good condition for the following tests.*

**1** Disable the ignition system. On most vehicles, you can simply pull the coil high tension lead from the distributor cap and connect a jump wire between the terminal on the end of the wire and earth.

**2** Have an assistant turn the ignition key to Start while you listen for a click at the solenoid. If there's a solid click, proceed to Step 6 or 7, as appropriate. If the click is weak or the solenoid chatters, proceed to Step 4.

**3** If there's no click, remove the control circuit wire (the small wire) from the solenoid terminal. Check for corrosion, looseness or other causes of a bad connection.

**Note:** *Some solenoids have two small wire connections. One is for the solenoid's control circuit; the other bypasses an ignition resistor during starting. The one for the solenoid control circuit is often marked S. If you're not sure which connection is which, check the wiring diagram for the vehicle.*

**4** Connect a jump wire between the battery positive terminal and the solenoid's control circuit connection. A solid click indicates normal solenoid operation. If there's no click, or if the click is weak or the solenoid chatters, check for a loose solenoid, corrosion at the solenoid base or other causes of a bad solenoid earth. If the solenoid is tight and earthed properly, and it still doesn't click, replace the solenoid.

**5** While an assistant turns the key to Start, check for voltage at the control circuit wire with a voltmeter. If there's no voltage at the wire, there's an open in the circuit to the solenoid (see Testing for an open in the starting circuit above). Reconnect the control circuit wire.

**6** On vehicles with on-starter solenoids, have an assistant turn the key to Start while you check for a voltage drop between the battery cable terminal and the starter motor strap. The voltage drop should not exceed 0.2 volts. If it does, replace the solenoid.

**7** On vehicles with remote solenoids, have an assistant turn the key to Start while you check for a voltage drop across the two cable connections on the solenoid (connect the positive voltmeter probe on the battery side). The voltage drop should not exceed 0.2 volts. If it does, remove the cables, clean the connections and retest. If it's still over 0.2 volts, replace the solenoid.

**8** On vehicles with remote solenoids, remove the control circuit wire and connect an ohmmeter between the solenoid's control circuit terminal and earth bracket. The ohmmeter reading should not exceed 5 ohms. If the resistance is higher, replace the solenoid.

## Testing the neutral start switch

**1** A quick check for the neutral start switch is to place your foot firmly on the brake and hold the ignition key to Start while you move the gear selector through all its positions. If the starter operates in positions other than Park and Neutral, the neutral start switch is damaged or out of adjustment.

**2** To check the switch, remove its electrical connector and hook up a jump wire between the terminal of the connector that receives battery voltage and the terminal that leads to the starter solenoid. If the starter now operates normally, adjust or replace the switch.

**Note:** *Neutral start switch designs vary, and many incorporate the reversing light switch. To check the switch, you may need to obtain the wiring diagrams for the vehicle. Also, check any specific procedures in the Haynes Service and Repair Manual written for your vehicle.*

## Testing starter current draw

This test will tell you how much current is being drawn by the starter motor, cables and solenoid. It requires use of an inductive pick-up ammeter.

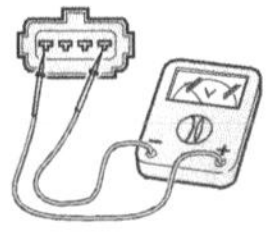

*Fig. 15.7 Testing starter current draw with an inductive ammeter*

***Caution: Never operate the starter for more than 15 seconds at a time without pausing to allow it to cool down for at least two minutes. Overheating caused by excessive operation will seriously damage the starter motor.***

**1** Check that the battery is fully charged and in good condition. If it's not, this test will not be accurate.

**2** Disable the ignition system. On most vehicles, you can simply pull the coil high tension lead from the distributor cap, connect a jump wire to it and connect the other end of the jump to a good earth on the engine.

**3** In accordance with the manufacturer's instructions, hook up an inductive pick-up ammeter to the positive or negative battery cable.

**4** Have an assistant in the vehicle operate the starter for about ten seconds. Observe the ammeter scale. The reading shouldn't exceed 110 amps for a four-cylinder engine, 200 amps for a six-cylinder or small V8, and 250 amps for a large V8.

## 5 Alternators and dynamos

**Note:** *Steps 1–3 of this procedure also apply to dynamo systems.*

**1** If a malfunction occurs in the charging system, do not automatically assume the alternator is causing the problem. Refer to Chapter 3, Section 19, and also check the following items:

*(a) Make sure the alternator mounting bolts are tight.*

*(b) Check the fusible link (if equipped) or main fuse located between the starter solenoid and alternator. If it is burned, determine the cause, repair the circuit and replace the link or fuse. (The vehicle will not start and/or the accessories will not work if the fusible link or main fuse is blown.) Sometimes a fusible link or main fuse may look good, but still be bad. If in doubt, remove it and check for continuity.*

*(c) Start the engine and check the alternator for abnormal noises (a shrieking or squealing sound indicates a bad bearing or slipping drive belt).*

*(d) Disconnect the battery cables (earth first). Inspect the battery posts and the cable clamps for corrosion. Clean them thoroughly, if necessary. Reconnect the cables (earth last).*

*(e) With the ignition off, connect a test light between the battery earth post and the disconnected earth cable clamp. If the test light does not come on, reattach the clamp. If the test light comes on, there is a short in the electrical system of the vehicle. The short must be repaired before the charging system can be checked. Note: On vehicles equipped components which normally cause an ignition-off battery drain, it's normal for the test light to glow dimly. If the light is bright, disconnect the alternator wiring harness. If the light goes out, there's a problem in the alternator. If the light stays on, pull each fuse until the light goes out (this will tell you which component is shorted).*

**2** Start the engine, increase engine speed to approximately 2000 rev/min and check the battery voltage. It should now be approximately 14 to 15 volts.

**3** Turn on the headlights. The voltage should drop, and then come back up, if the charging system is working properly.

**4** If the voltage reading is more than approximately 15 volts, check the regulator earth connection (vehicles with remotely-mounted regulators). If the earth is OK, the problem lies in the regulator, the alternator or the wiring between them. If the vehicle has an internal regulator, replace the alternator. If the vehicle has a remotely-mounted regulator, remove the electrical connector from the regulator and repeat Step 2. If the voltage drops with the regulator disconnected, replace the regulator. If the voltage is still high, there's a short in the wiring between the alternator and regulator or there's a short in the rotor or stator within the alternator. Check the wiring. If the wiring is OK, replace the alternator.

**5** If the voltage is less than 13 volts, an undercharging condition is present. If the vehicle is equipped with an indicator light, turn the ignition on and see if the light illuminates. If it does, proceed to the next Step. If it doesn't, check the direction indicator light circuit (see Section 7). In some vehicles, a faulty circuit could cause the alternator to malfunction.

**6** If the indicator light circuit is OK, check for a bad earth at the voltage regulator. If the earth is OK, the problem lies in the alternator, regulator or the wiring between them. If the vehicle has an internal regulator, replace the alternator. If the vehicle has a remotely-mounted regulator, check the wiring. If necessary, disconnect the battery earth terminal and check for continuity, using the vehicle's wiring diagram for reference. If the wiring is OK, you'll have to determine whether the problem lies in the alternator or regulator.

**7** A good way to determine whether an undercharging problem is caused by the alternator or regulator is with a full-field test. Basically, the full-field test bypasses the regulator to send full battery voltage to the alternator's field (the rotor). Caution: Full-fielding sends high voltage through the vehicle's electrical system, which can damage components, particularly electronic components. Carefully monitor the charging system voltage during full-fielding to be sure it doesn't exceed 16 volts. Also, do not operate a full-fielded alternator for an extended period of time. Operate it only long enough to take the voltage reading. If the charging voltage is normal when the alternator is 'full-fielded,' you know the alternator is OK. If the voltage is still low, the problem is in the alternator. It's best to obtain wiring diagrams for the vehicle to determine the best way to send battery voltage to the field. However, the following gives some general guidelines which may help you in determining how to full-field the alternator:

*(a) On older Delco alternators with remotely-mounted regulators, disconnect the electrical connector from the regulator and connect a jump wire between the BATT and F terminals of the connector.*

*(b) On Ford Motorcraft alternators with remotely-mounted regulators, disconnect the electrical connector from the regulator and connect a jump wire between the A and F terminals of the connector.*

*(c) On Chrysler alternators with remotely-mounted electronic voltage regulators, disconnect the regulator connector and connect a jump wire between the green wire terminal of the connector and earth.*

Make the connections with the ignition turned off, then repeat Step 2, above. The voltage reading should be high (about 15 to 16 volts). If it's not, the alternator is faulty. If it is, the regulator is probably bad.

## 6 Direction indicators and hazard flashers

The most common problems in the indicators and hazard light circuits are burned out bulbs, blown fuses, defective flasher units and corroded or loose connections. The first step in diagnosing a failure is to visually check the lights. Operate the indicator or hazard lights and walk around the vehicle, checking to see which lights are not working. Once you've identified the problem, check all the possible causes in the following list.

If the symptom persists after checking all the possible causes, check the switch and wiring, as discussed in the procedure following the symptom list.

**Note:** *On some vehicles, the turn signal switch and hazard light switch are wired separately, but the wiring between the switches and lights is shared. This makes checking the wiring between the switch and the signal lights simple. For example, if the indicators do not work on one or both sides, but do work when the hazard lights are turned on, you know much of the wiring is good.*

### One indicator on one side doesn't work

**1** Check the bulb.

**2** Check for a corroded, worn or damaged bulb socket.

**3** Check for a bad earth. Use a jump wire between the earth side of the bulb and a good chassis earth.

**4** Beginning at the non-functioning light and working backward through the circuit, check for a short or no continuity (see Section 3).

### Hazard lights or indicators light but don't flash

**1** Replace the flasher unit. **Note:** *On some vehicles the flasher unit and hazard flasher unit are one and the same - sometimes built into the hazard switch.*

### Indicators don't light in either direction

**1** Check for a blown fuse.

**2** Check the bulbs.

**3** Check for corroded, worn or damaged bulb sockets.

**4** Check for a bad earth. Use a jump wire between the earth side of the bulbs and a good chassis earth.

**5** Replace the flasher unit.

**6** Check the turn signal switch (see below).

**7** Check for a short or no continuity (see Section 3).

### Front and rear lights on one side don't work

**1** Check the bulbs.

**2** Check for corroded, worn or damaged bulb sockets.

**3** Check for bad earths. Use jump wires between the earth sides of the bulbs and a good chassis earth.

**4** Check the turn signal switch (see below).

### Flasher rate too fast or too slow

**1** Make sure the correct flasher unit is installed.

**2** Make sure the correct bulbs are installed. **Note:** *If LED bulbs have been fitted to replace conventional bulbs, a suitable resistor may have to be fitted in series with the bulbs to simulate the original electrical load.*

**3** If the rate is too fast, check for an overcharging condition. If the rate is too slow, check for a weak battery or an undercharging condition.

### Indicator light(s) on dashboard don't flash, only glow

**1** Check the lights with the circuit turned on.

**2** If the lights are also glowing steadily, replace the flasher.

**3** If the lights are not on, check the light bulb.

**4** Check for a corroded, worn or damaged bulb socket.

**5** Check for a bad earth. Use a jump wire between the earth side of the non-functioning light(s) and a good chassis earth.

**6** Beginning at the non-functioning light(s) and working backward through the circuit, check for an open (no continuity, see Section 3).

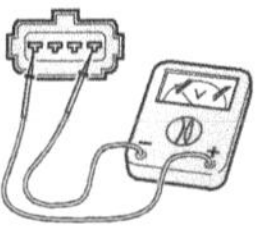



### Indicators work but hazard lights don't

**1** Replace the hazard flasher.

**2** Check for a faulty hazard flasher switch.

## 7 Brake lights

### One brake light does not work, but others do

**1** Check the bulb.

**2** Check the bulb socket for corrosion, damage and worn terminals.

**3** Check for a bad earth connection by hooking up a jump wire between the earth terminal of the non-functioning light and a good chassis earth. If the light now works, repair the faulty earth connection.

**4** Beginning at the non-functioning light and working backward through the circuit, check for a short or no continuity (see Section 3).

### No brake lights work

**1** Check the fuse and check for corrosion at the fuse terminals.

**2** Check the brake light switch (see below).

**3** Check for a bad earth at the brake light bulbs, burned out bulbs and corroded or loose connections.

### Brake light bulbs burn out quickly

**1** Check for an overcharging condition, or excessive vibration.

## 8 Horns

**1** If the horn is inoperative, check the fuse.

**Note:** *Some vehicles must have the ignition switch on for the horn to work.*

**2** If the horn sounds weak, have an assistant operate the horn button while you listen at the front of the vehicle. Note whether the vehicle has multiple horns and determine if they are all working (touching each horn while it's operating and feeling for a vibration is an easy way to do this).

**3** If a horn is weak or inoperative, check for a faulty earth at the horn (relay-type systems) and check for full battery voltage going to the horn (do this with a voltmeter).

**4** If the horn tone is still poor, check for an adjustment screw and adjust for best tone.

### Relay-type circuits

**5** When the horn button is depressed, the relay's control circuit is connected to earth, which causes the horn relay to connect the horn(s) to the battery.

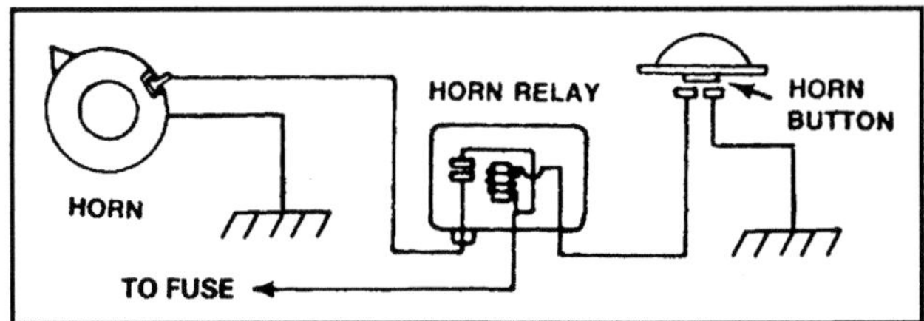


*Fig. 15.8 A typical relay horn circuit*

**6** The horn won't stop. Disconnect the horn(s), then check for a stuck horn button by disconnecting the button and re-connecting the horn(s). If the horn is now silent, replace the horn button. If the horn is still blowing, disconnect the wire that goes to the horn button at the relay. If that doesn't shut it off, replace the relay. If disconnecting the wire shuts off the horn, check the horn button wire for a short to earth.

**7** The horn doesn't work. Check the fuse. If it's OK, check for voltage at the terminal on each horn when the horn button is depressed. If there's voltage at each terminal, check for a bad earth at the horn(s). If the earth is good, replace the horn(s).

**8** If there's no voltage at the horn(s), check the relay (see the relay check procedure in Section 3). Note that most horn relays are either the four-terminal or externally earthed three-terminal type.

**9** If the relay is OK, check for voltage to the relay's power and control circuits. If either of the circuits is not getting voltage, inspect the wiring between the relay and the fuse.

**10** If both relay circuits are receiving voltage, depress the horn button and check the wire that goes from the relay to the horn button for continuity to earth. If there's no continuity, check the wire for an open. If there's no open in the wire, replace the horn button.

**11** If there's continuity to earth through the horn button, check for an open or short in the wire that goes from the relay to the horn(s).

### Non-relay type circuits

**12** On non-relay type horn circuits, voltage is connected directly from the fuse to the horn. The circuit is earthed through the horn button.

**13** The horn won't stop. Disconnect the horn, disconnect the horn button, then reconnect the horn. If the horn is now silent, replace the horn button. If the horn is still sounding, check for a short to earth in the wire going from the horn to the horn button.

**14** The horn doesn't work. If the general troubleshooting checks listed above don't find

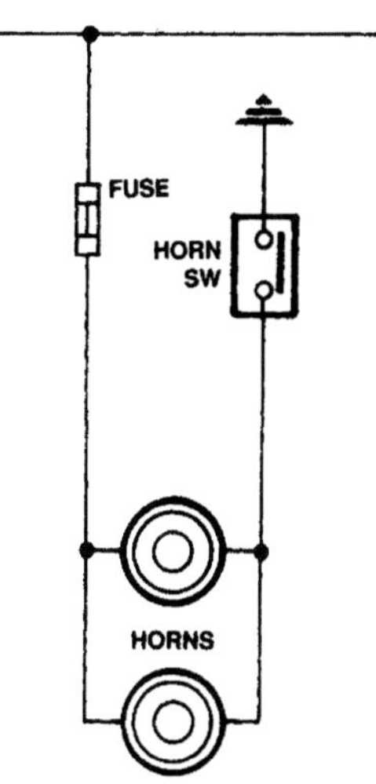


*Fig. 15.9 A typical non-relay horn circuit*

the problem, disconnect the horn and run power directly to the horn from the battery with fused jump wires. If the horn doesn't work then, replace it.

**15** If the horn works with jump wires, check the wire that runs from the fuse to the horn for voltage at the horn. If there's no voltage, there's a short or open between the fuse and the horn.

**16** If there's voltage at the horn, depress the horn button and check for continuity between earth and the wire running from the horn to the horn button, with the wire disconnected from the horn. If there's no continuity, check the wire for an open. If the wire's OK, replace the horn button.

## 9 Electric windows

### No windows work

**Note:** *Always examine the appropriate wiring diagram for your vehicle before attempting any trouble shooting procedures. Vehicles with networked window systems (see Chapter 13), must be interrogated with a fault code reader first.*

**1** If the power windows don't work at all, check the fuse or circuit breaker.

**2** If only the rear windows are inoperative, or if the windows only operate from the master control switch, check the rear window lockout switch for continuity in the unlocked position. Replace it if it doesn't have continuity.

**3** Check the wiring between the switches and fuse board for continuity. Repair the wiring, if necessary.

### One window doesn't work

**4** If only one window is inoperative from the master control switch, try the other control switch at the window. Note: This doesn't apply to the driver's door window.

**5** If the same window works from one switch, but not the other, check the switch for continuity.

**6** If the switch tests OK, check for a short or open in the wiring between the affected switch and the window motor.

**7** If one window is inoperative from both switches, remove the trim panel from the affected door and check for voltage at the motor while the switch is operated. For information on removing the trim panel, check the *Haynes Service and Repair Manual* for your particular vehicle.

**8** If voltage is reaching the motor, disconnect the glass from the regulator. Move the window up and down by hand while checking for binding and damage. Also check for binding and damage to the regulator. If the regulator is not damaged and the window moves up and down smoothly, replace the motor. If there's binding or damage, lubricate, repair or replace parts, as necessary.

**9** If voltage isn't reaching the motor, check the wiring in the circuit for continuity between the switches and motors. You'll need to obtain the wiring diagram for the vehicle. Some window circuits are equipped with relays. If equipped, check that the relays are earthed properly and receiving voltage from the switches. Also check that each relay sends voltage to the motor when the switch is turned on. If it doesn't, replace the relay.

**10** Test the windows after you are done to confirm proper repairs.

## 10 Heated rear windows

**1** Check the fuse and replace it, if necessary.

**2** With the ignition on (engine off), switch on the heated rear window with the driver's door open. The interior light should dim considerably.

**3** If the light dims when the demister is switched on, check the rear window for damaged grid lines (see below).

**4** If the light doesn't dim, check for a bad connection at the window grid. If the connections are OK, trace the circuit and check continuity of the switch and of the wiring from the fuse to the switch/relay and from the relay to the rear window. Repair or replace as necessary.

**5** If the circuits and switch have continuity, replace the relay.

**6** The demister should stay on for about 10 minutes before the timer relay switches it off (check your owner's manual). If the demister won't stay on for the specified time, replace the relay.

### Checking and repairing the rear window heater grid

**Note:** *The following procedure applies only to grids attached to the surface of the window. Some vehicles have the grid inside the glass. On these vehicles, you must replace the window to repair a faulty grid.*

**7** Visually inspect the edges of the rear window grid for missing or broken wires or bad connections.

**8** Start the engine and turn the demister switch on. Allow several minutes for the glass to warm up.

**9** Verify operation by holding your hand against the glass in the grid area to feel for warmth or by watching the ice or mist (you can mist the glass by breathing on it) disappear from the window. If the glass only warms up in certain areas, the grid may have open segments.

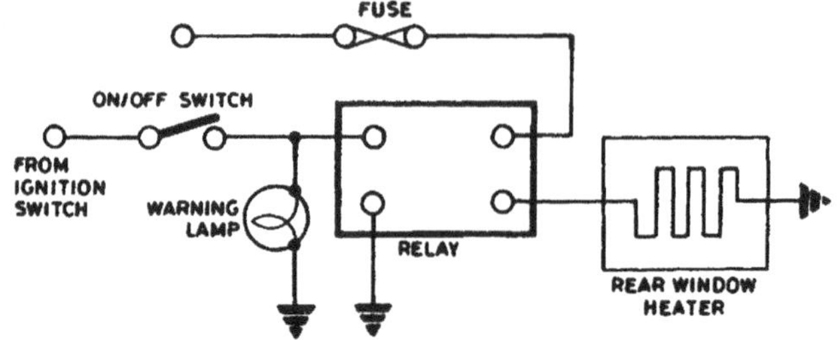


*Fig. 15.10 A typical heated rear window circuit*

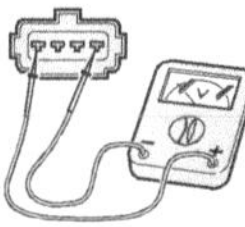

**10** The specific grid lines that are open may be determined by noting which ones don't demist.

**11** Locate the open spot in the grid line by looking for a small gap in the line. If the gap is invisible, use a test light to find it. Starting at the positive side of the grid, touch the test light to the grid line at various points along the line. When you reach a point where the test light no longer lights, the gap lies between that point and your last test point.

**12** Mark the damaged spot with a crayon or tape on the outside of the glass. The grid lines may be repaired with a special kit available from dealers and auto accessory shops. Follow the instructions provided in the kit. Note: Large breaks in the grid require window replacement.

## 11 Windscreen washers

**1** Check the washer fluid level. If it's OK, turn on the washer pump with the ignition switch on, but the engine off. Listen for the sound of the pump operating, you should hear a whirring sound.

**2** If you can hear the pump operating but no fluid is being expelled from the washer nozzles, trace the hoses and lines between the pump and nozzles to be sure there's none kinked, damaged or disconnected.

**3** If the hoses and lines are OK, disconnect a hose as close to a nozzle as possible and operate the washer again. If a strong stream of fluid is expelled from the end of the hose, the nozzle is probably clogged. Often, nozzles can be unclogged by inserting a pin or paper clip into the hole in the end. If this doesn't unclog the nozzle, replace it.

**4** If there's no fluid being expelled from the hose, trace it back to the pump and disconnect it there. Operate the washer again. If a strong stream of fluid is expelled from the pump, there's a clog in the line between the pump and nozzle(s). If no fluid is expelled from the pump, but you can hear it operating, replace it.

**5** If there's no sound coming from the pump when it's turned on, have an assistant operate the washer button (ignition on) while you check for voltage and earth at the pump. If there's voltage and a good earth, but the pump doesn't work, replace the pump.

**6** If voltage isn't getting to the pump, check the switch and wiring for continuity and repair as necessary.

## 12 Windscreen wipers

Refer also to Chapter 10.

### The wipers work slowly

**1** Make sure the battery is in good condition and has a strong charge.

**2** Remove the wiper motor and operate the wiper arms by hand. Check for binding linkage and pivots. Lubricate or repair the linkage or pivots, as necessary.

### The wipers don't work at all

**3** Check the fuse or circuit breaker.

**4** If the fuse or circuit breaker is OK, connect a jump wire between the wiper motor and earth, then retest. If the motor works now, repair the earth connection.

**5** If the wipers still don't work, turn on the wipers and check for voltage at the motor. If there's voltage at the motor, remove the motor and check it off the vehicle with fused jump wires from the battery. If the motor now works, check for binding linkage (see Step 2 above). If the motor still doesn't work, replace it.

**6** If there's no voltage at the motor, check for voltage at the switch. If there's no voltage at the switch, check the wiring between the switch and the fuse for continuity. If there's voltage at the switch, check the wiring between the switch and motor for continuity.

***Caution: If the vehicle you are working on has intermittent wipe, use a digital ohmmeter for continuity checks – other devices may damage the solid state circuitry in the control module.***

**7** If the wiring is OK, obtain a wiring diagram for the circuit and use it to check the continuity of the switch. Replace the switch, if necessary.

### The wipers only work at one speed

**8** Check the continuity of the wires between the switch and motor. If the wires are OK, replace the switch.

### The intermittent wipe is inoperative

**9** Check the continuity of all the wiring between the switch and motor. If the wiring is OK, replace the interval module (governor).

### The wipers do not park

**10** Check for voltage at the wiper motor when the wiper switch is off but the ignition is on. If voltage is present, the limit switch in the motor is malfunctioning. Replace the wiper motor. If no voltage is present, trace and repair the limit switch wiring between the fuse board and wiper motor.

### The wipers only stop when the ignition is turned off

**11** Disconnect the wiring from the wiper control switch. If the wipers stop, replace the switch. If the wipers keep running, there's a defective limit switch in the motor. Replace the motor.

### The wipers won't park below the bonnet line (if applicable)

**12** Check for mechanical obstructions in the wiper linkage or on the vehicle's body which would prevent the wipers from retracting.

**13** If there are no obstructions, check the wiring between the switch and motor for continuity. If the wiring is OK, replace the wiper motor.

# Index

## F



## G



## H



## I



## J



## K



## L



## M

# Index